POLICE
IN AMERICA

REPORT OF SELECT
COMMITTEE ON POLICE
AND MINUTES OF EVIDENCE

Gt. Brit. Parliament. House of Commons.

Select Committee on Police

ARNO PRESS & THE NEW YORK TIMES
NEW YORK,   1971

192504

Reprint Edition 1971 by Arno Press Inc.

LC# 77-156284
ISBN 0-405-03395-8

Police In America
ISBN for complete set: 0-405-03360-5
See last pages of this volume for titles.

Manufactured in the United States of America

FIRST REPORT

FROM THE

SELECT COMMITTEE

ON

P O L I C E;

WITH THE

MINUTES OF EVIDENCE,

Ordered, by The House of Commons, *to be Printed,*
10 *June* 1853.

REPORTS FROM COMMITTEES:

1852-53.

THIRTY-TWO VOLUMES:—CONTENTS OF THE

TWENTY-NINTH VOLUME.

N. B.—*THE* Figures *at the* beginning of the line, *correspond with the* N° *at the* foot *of each* Report; *and the* Figures *at the* end of the line, *refer to the* MS. Paging *of the Volumes arranged for The House of Commons.*

POLICE:

Martis, 26° *die Aprilis,* 1853.

Ordered, THAT a Select Committee be appointed to consider the Expediency of adopting a more Uniform System of Police in England and Wales, and Scotland.

Jovis, 5° *die Maii,* 1853.

Committee nominated of,—

Mr. Rice.	Mr. Rich.
Mr. Sotheron.	Mr. Moody.
The Lord Advocate.	Mr. Mackie.
Mr. Walpole.	Mr. Brand.
Mr. Fitzroy.	Mr. Charles Howárd.
Mr. Burroughes.	Sir James Anderson.
Lord Lovaine.	Mr. Philipps.
Sir John Trollope.	

Ordered, THAT the Committee have power to send for Persons, Papers, and Records.

Ordered, THAT Five be the Quorum of the Committee.

Jovis, 9° *die Junii,* 1853.

Ordered, THAT the Committee have power to report the Minutes of Evidence taken before them, from time to time, to The House.

FIRST REPORT.

THE SELECT COMMITTEE appointed to consider the Expediency of adopting a more Uniform System of Police in England and Wales, and Scotland, and who were empowered to Report the MINUTES OF EVIDENCE taken before them from time to time :——

HAVE considered the matters to them referred, and have agreed to report the Minutes of Evidence taken before them to The House.

10 *June* 1853.

LIST OF WITNESSES.

MINUTES OF EVIDENCE.

Jovis, 26° die Maii, 1853.

MEMBERS PRESENT.

Mr. Rice.	Mr. Sotheron.
Mr. Walpole.	Mr. Fitzroy.
Mr. Burroughes.	Sir John Trollope.
Mr. Mackie.	Sir James Anderson.
Mr. Rich.	Mr. Phillips.

EDWARD ROYDS RICE, Esq., IN THE CHAIR.

Captain *William Charles Harris,* called in; and Examined.

1. *Chairman.*] YOU command the constabulary in Hampshire?—I do.

2. For how many years have you done so?—For 10 years.

3. Was not Hampshire the first county which adopted the police?—No; three counties adopted the police previous to Hampshire, but only by a month or so.

4. In how many other counties has the police been adopted?—In 22 counties in England and Wales.

5. Have you seen the Parliamentary Return which has been made every year of the counties which have adopted the police?—I have.

6. Is that return correct?—I do not consider it so.

7. Can you furnish a corrected return?—Yes; I have a return of the counties in which the Act has been adopted; it has been adopted for the whole of 22 counties in England and Wales, in parts of seven others; but in 22 counties the old parochial system still continues.

8. Does that return differ materially from the Parliamentary Return?—I am not prepared to say.

9. Perhaps you will put that return in?—I can vouch for the correctness of this return.

Captain
W. C. Harris.

26 May 1853.

[*The Witness delivered in the following Return:*]

RETURN of the several Counties that have adopted the Provisions of the Constabulary Act

For the whole County:

Bedford.	Salop.
Cambridge.	Southampton.
Durham.	Stafford.
Essex.	Suffolk.
Gloster.	Surrey.
Hertford.	Wilts.
Lancaster.	Worcester.
Leicester.	Cardigan.
Norfolk.	Carmarthen.
Northampton.	Denbigh.
Nottingham.	Montgomery.

In Parts only:

Cumberland.	Warwick.
Dorset.	Westmoreland.
Rutland.	York.
Sussex.	

Captain
W. C. Harris.

26 May 1853.

The following Counties continue the system of Parochial Constables:

Berks.	Northumberland.
Bucks.	Oxford.
Chester.	Somerset.
Cornwall.	Anglesey.
Derby.	Brecon.
Devon.	Carnarvon.
Hereford.	Glamorgan.
Huntingdon.	Merioneth.
Kent.	Radnor.
Lincoln.	Flint.
Monmouth.	Pembroke.

10. Can you generally say that the adoption of the police under the Act has proved efficacious in Hampshire?—In my opinion it has; serious offences are rare, and in most cases followed by detection; petty depredations are prevented, vagrancy checked, and beerhouses controlled.

11. Can you refer to any documents to prove that crime has decreased in Hampshire since the police force has been established?—Yes, by reference to the criminal returns of the force under my command (1851), it will be seen that since the year 1847, the year in which a register of offences was first commenced in Hampshire, the offences against property, as likewise the value of property lost, and the crime undetected, have all gradually decreased.

12. Perhaps you can state to the Committee generally the purport of those returns?—These returns I commenced keeping in 1847; in that year the number of felonies committed in our county were 709; the total amount of property lost was 1,338 *l.* 13 *s.* 4 *d.*; the number of prisoners committed for trial was 334; the number of offences undetected was 388; and the per-centage of undetected crime on the number of offences committed was 54. I will now take the last year, 1851. In that year the number of felonies committed was 609; the total amount of property lost was 476 *l.* 15 *s.* 1⅛ *d.*; the number of persons committed for trial was 316; the number of offences undetected was 281; the per-centage of undetected crime on the number of offences committed was 46.

13. Can you give the Committee a statement of the condition of the county before the establishment of the police force?—No, I cannot.

14. Mr. *Rich.*] How long was the first year you have mentioned subsequent to the appointment of the police?—The police was established in December 1839; the first year in which this register of crime was kept was 1847.

15. *Chairman.*] Do you know, of your own knowledge, whether similar returns are kept in other counties?—I should imagine they are kept, but I do not think they are printed.

16. They are printed with you?—They are printed with us.

17. For the use of the magistrates?—Yes, for the use of the magistrates.

18. Will you put in that return?—

[The Witness delivered in the following Return :]

SUMMARY of the Number of FELONIES affecting Property that have been Committed during the undermentioned Years, within the Jurisdiction of the *Hants* Constabulary; showing the First Amount of Loss, and the Amount Recovered, the Number of Persons Committed for Trial, and the Number of Undetected Offences.

Year.	Number of Felonies.	AMOUNT OF LOSS.			Number of Persons Committed for Trial.	Number of Offences Undetected.	Per-Centage of Undetected Crime on the Number of Offences Committed.
		First Loss.	Amount Recovered.	Total Loss.			
		£. *s.* *d.*	£. *s.* *d.*	£. *s.* *d.*			
1847	709	1,880 5 3	541 11 11	1,338 13 4	334	388	54
1848	687	*3,405 9 9	†523 19 1	*2,933 10 8	374	329	47
1849	678	869 1 – ½	316 – 8½	553 – 4	369	348	51
1850	615	777 13 5½	261 19 3½	515 14 2	350	290	47
1851	609	723 9 10	246 14 8½	476 15 1½	316	281	46

* 2,141 *l.* of this amount was timber stolen from the New Forest.
† 52 *l.* of this amount was stolen in Berkshire.

Captain
W. C. Harris.

26 May 1853.

19. Can you form any comparison with reference to the proportion of the detection of crime in Hampshire, as compared with that in other places where there is what is considered an efficient police force?—Yes, if I compare the state of crime in Hampshire with that of the metropolitan police district, considered to be the most efficient force in Great Britain, I find, whether in respect to the prevention or the detection of crime, we are not behind the metropolis; whilst the number of men in London is as $3\frac{1}{2}$ to 1. Take the metropolitan police district, they have one offence to 214 inhabitants; in Hampshire we have one to 438 inhabitants. In the metropolis there is one prisoner convicted to every $4\frac{30}{100}$ths offences, in Hampshire we have one prisoner convicted for every $2\frac{58}{100}$ths. In the metropolitan police district there is one constable to 457 inhabitants; in Hampshire one constable to 1,571 inhabitants. I should say, that this calculation is based on the census of 1851. As London, however, might be considered the focus of crime, and Hampshire simply a rural district, I have drawn a comparison between the metropolis and Gosport, rather a disorderly place, from the large number of licensed public-houses there.

20. What is the police force at Gosport?—Gosport is a part of the county, and we have five men stationed there. There are 85 public-houses; 35 beer-houses licensed to consume on the premises, and three licensed to consume off the premises; making a total of 123 houses of public entertainment in that town alone, the population of which, according to the last census, amounted to 16,908. This is my reason for selecting Gosport to compare with the metropolis. As I mentioned before, in London there is one offence to 214 inhabitants; in Gosport one to 286 inhabitants. In the metropolis there is one prisoner convicted for every $4\frac{30}{100}$ths offences; in Gosport one for every $2\frac{58}{100}$ths offences. In London there is one constable to every 457 inhabitants; in Gosport one constable to every 3,381 inhabitants; or seven times the number in London to what we have in Gosport.

21. Mr. *Rich.*] Have you any comparison between Hampshire and any county in which the police does not exist?—No; I do not think there is any possibility of making a comparison where there is no police.

22. *Chairman.*] Do you conceive that it would be conducive to the efficiency of a county constabulary if the several forces were united with it?—Most decidedly.

23. Mr. *Fitzroy.*] What principal boroughs are there in Hampshire?—There are several boroughs in Hampshire; but Portsmouth and Southampton are the most important.

24. *Chairman.*] You would call them first-class boroughs?—Yes; there are likewise the boroughs of Winchester, Andover, Newport, Basingstoke, Romsey, and Lymington.

25. In which of those boroughs has the police force been consolidated with the county police?—Andover for some years, and Lymington recently.

26. Sir *J. Trollope.*] Can you separate the payment for those boroughs which have been consolidated with the county?—In the case both of Andover and Lymington there is merely an arrangement made by which 65 *l.* per man is paid to the county, which is the average cost of the whole of the constables.

27. Do the separate charges for the performance of extra duties fall upon the county?—The only extra charge made to the borough of Andover is for the conveyance of prisoners. In Andover they have a separate court of quarter sessions, and their gaol not admitting of separate confinement, their prisoners are committed to Winchester, to which place they are conveyed by the county constabulary. The charge of conveyance is made according to the table of fees.

28. Do you charge that to the borough?—We charge the borough with the conveyance of the prisoners; that is the only additional charge to the 65 *l.* per man.

29. In fact, the county is borne harmless from those extra charges by the allowances from the boroughs?—By the allowance of 65 *l.* a man, and in that superannuation is included.

30. *Chairman.*] Do you think the expense of the constabulary in the county and boroughs together, would be materially increased by the union of the boroughs with the county?—No; if the whole were consolidated into one force the expense to each would be lessened.

31. Do you think it would be increased to both ?—I think the whole expense per man would be decreased.

32. Sir *J. Trollope.*] In the case of boroughs there are a great number of officers to a few men. If the principle of amalgamation were adopted, a separate superintendent could be allocated, who should be responsible to some inspector for the county ?—The borough of Andover, for instance, has a sergeant and four men allotted exclusively to do duty within the borough, and that sergeant and four men are all under the direction of the superintendent of the Andover division.

33. Does the 65 *l.* per man cover the increased pay which you would give to the higher ranks of the constabulary ?—It does.

34. Mr. *Rich.*] You have stated that you think it would be conducive to an efficient police, if the police of the boroughs were incorporated in the police of the county ; will you state the inconveniences which now result from those boroughs not being incorporated ?—The want of co-operation between boroughs and counties is a great evil ; if the forces were consolidated fewer men would be needed. The boroughs are generally the central points from whence criminals issue into the surrounding districts to commit offences, and to which they return with their plunder ; the town force having no interest in the prevention or detection of offences committed in the county, parties are allowed to pass un-questioned.

35. Mr. *Fitzroy.*] Can you tell the Committee in which of the boroughs in Hampshire there is a police force separate from the county ?—Portsmouth, Southampton, Winchester, Newport, and Basingstoke.

36. Mr. *Rich.*] You say you find there is a want of co-operation in the police force ?—Yes, there is a want of co-operation ; there is no denying that a jealousy exists between the two forces, but not in my opinion to such an extent on the part of the county as the boroughs, the county constabulary being the larger force of the two. Our men are always willing to afford assistance to the borough police. I will mention a case of the want of co-operation which recently occurred : one of the superintendents of the Hants constabulary was proceeding on duty from the Southampton terminus in plain clothes, when he saw in the train a desperate character, who a year and a half previously had effected his escape by violence from two of the constables of our force ; the superintendent immediately seized him, and brought him out of the train ; the superintendent sent to the borough station to borrow a pair of handcuffs to secure his prisoner ; the loan of these was refused ; " they had none to spare ;" and the only mode of securing the prisoner was by his leaving him in charge of the railway officials, and proceeding into the town to call upon one of the borough police to aid and assist in the Queen's name, and thus he obtained the handcuffs.

37. Are your superintendents in communication with the superintendents of the borough police ?—Not in constant communication.

38. In the event of the occurrence of a crime, do your superintendents imme-diately communicate the fact of that crime having been committed to the super-intendents of the various boroughs ?—Certainly they do, if it is a matter of importance ; they would not perhaps mention a petty depredation.

39. Inversely, do the superintendents of the boroughs communicate with your superintendents ?—Very rarely.

40. Mr. *Phillips.*] In the case of a borough like Andover, where you have five men, do you change them ?—They are constantly changed.

41. *Chairman.*] You stated that Lymington had lately joined the county ; can you state any facts illustrating the benefits of the arrangement ?—Only this ; last week there was a fair at Lymington ; as many as 11 of the swell mob of London came there for the purpose of committing depredations. The super-intendent of the New Forest division, who was there on duty, immediately recognised the party. He told some of them that they had better go, that they were not wanted there. They replied, " We did not know that the borough was under your jurisdiction, we were not aware that the borough had joined the county." The superintendent replied that they had just come in, and that they had better go. Most of them took his advice and left, but three remained, who were apprehended, and after being dealt with under the Vagrant Act for being there for an unlawful purpose, were committed for trial for a felony.

42. Is

Captain
W. C. Harris.

26 May 1853.

42. Is the borough of Romsey consolidated with the county ?—No.

43. Can you give the Committee any information with regard to the state of crime in the borough of Romsey ?—Yes, I have returns.

44. Mr. *Fitzroy*.] Is there a municipality in Romsey ?—Yes; but they have no separate Court of Quarter Sessions; there is a mayor and magistrates separate from the county. I beg to put in these two returns, showing the state of crime in the Romsey division, extending to 50,980 acres, and 11,426 inhabitants; and the borough of Romsey, the acreage of which is 380, and the population 1,919. I mention 1850 because it is the only year in which I have been able to obtain a return. There were 16 offenders committed in the county, and eight in the borough. The value of the property lost in the county was 6 *l*. 11 *s*., in the borough it was 10 *l*. 3 *s*. The number of prisoners committed for trial in the county was 14, and in the borough there were two, both of which were detected by the county constabulary, one by the superintendent of the Wilts, and the other by the superintendent of the Hants constabulary. The number of offences undetected in the county was three, and in the borough it was six. There were eight offences committed, and the only two detected were by the county constabulary.

[*The Witness delivered in the following Returns :*]

RETURN of the Number of FELONIES affecting PROPERTY that have been Committed in the *Romsey* Division; the First Amount of Loss, the Amount Recovered, the Number of Persons Committed for Trial, and the Number of UNDETECTED Cases, between the 1st January and 31st December 1850.

DESCRIPTION of FELONY.			Number of Felonies.	AMOUNT OF LOSS.			Number of Prisoners Committed for Trial.	Number of Offences Undetected.
				First Loss.	Amount Recovered.	TOTAL LOSS.		
				£. s. d.	£. s. d.	£. s. d.		
Burglary - - - -			1	3 11 –	3 1 –	– 10 –	2	—
Breaking into a dwelling-house -			1	2 – –	2 – –	–	1	—
„ „ Building, &c. -			2	– 15 –	– 3 –	– 12 –	1	1
Sheep stealing - - - -			2	2 1 –	–	2 1 –	–	2
Simple larceny - - -			1	– 2 –	– 2 –	–	1	—
Larcenies.	In a Dwelling House.	Common.						
		Goods, &c. exposed for sale -	3	– 18 –	– 17 –	– 1 –	3	—
		Tools, lead, glass, from unfinished houses -	1	– – 6	– – 6	–	1	—
		Poultry, &c., exposed in an outhouse -	2	– 14 6	– 14 6	–	2	—
		By servants - -	1	3 – –	–	3 – –	1	—
		* By doors being left open - - -	1	– 1 6	– 1 6	—	—	—
	From the Person.	Picking pockets -	1	2 9 –	2 2 –	– 7 –	2	—
			16	15 12 6	9 1 6	6 11 –	14	3

* Prisoner apprehended, but the Owner declined to prosecute.

Population - - - - - - 11,426.

Acreage - - - - - - - 50,980.

RETURN of the Number of Offences against Property that have come to the knowledge of the *Hants* Constabulary, as having been committed within the Borough of *Romsey* during the Year 1850.

Upon whom Committed.	Description of Property Lost.	AMOUNT OF LOSS.			Committed for Trial.	Undetected.	REMARKS.
		First Loss.	Amount Recovered.	Total Loss.			
		£. s. d.	£. s. d.	£. s. d.			
Eliza Roberts, inn-keeper.	7 fowls	– 10 –	– . –	– 10 –	– . –	1	
Arthur Cooper, carpenter.	2 tame rabbits	– 3 –		– 3 –	– . –	1	
William B. Crockford, draper.	– – 30 yards plaid silk, and a quantity of ribbon.	5 – –		5 – –	– . –	1	
George Sharp, timber merchant.	– – 5 fowls and 2 tame rabbits.	– 10 –		– 10 –	– . –	1	
Moses Pepper, draper	– – A quantity of ribbon.	. – Value unknown			– . –	1	
William Pointer, inn-keeper.	A silver watch	4 – –	. –	4 – –	– . –	1	
Chas. J. Robinson, bootmaker.	A pair of boots	– 10 6	– 10 6	– . –	1	– . –	– – Detected by superintendent of the Hants constabulary, seven years' transportation.
George Moore, dealer	A dog cart	1 10 –	1 10 –	– . –	1	– . –	– – Detected by superintendent of the Wilts constabulary, 6 months' hard labour.
		12 3 6	2 – 6	10 3 –	2	6	

Population   -   -   - 1,919   Acreage   -   -   - 380

45. Mr. *Fitzroy.*] Have the magistrates and authorities of the boroughs which have coalesced with the county any voice at all in the appointment, or promotion, or dismissal of the constables?—None whatever; not in the borough of Andover.

46. Or in Lymington?—Or in Lymington. They are all county constables. The chief constable of the county appoints them, and he has the general disposition and government of them.

47. Have you ever considered any plan for compulsorily joining the boroughs with the counties with reference to the appointment of the officers?—I have considered such a plan in my own mind.

48. Would you contemplate in such a plan giving the borough magistrates any voice at all in the election or dismissal of the officers?—Not unless the borough contained a population of 100,000.

49. Do you think it would very much facilitate the arrangement if you were to give them any voice at all in the appointment of the officers?—No, I do not consider that it would facilitate the arrangement. My impression is that such boroughs as Southampton and Portsmouth ought to be considered in the light of separate divisions of the county. We have 14 divisions in Hampshire; Portsmouth and Southampton would therefore be two additional divisions.

50. Sir *J. Trollope.*] What petty sessional divisions?—We have 14 petty sessional divisions in Hampshire, and I should consider Southampton and Portsmouth as two more.

51. Have you at all considered, in case of consolidation, whether the county magistrates should have the appointment of the constables, or of the chief constable solely?—Solely the chief constable.

52. If the borough police were consolidated with the county police, would you still consider it advisable to continue the appointment in the same form as at present?—I do not consider that the service can be carried on satisfactorily if the chief constable has not the appointment of the men, for the performance of whose duty he is responsible.

53. Mr. *Fitzroy.*] Would you consider that the rate raised in Southampton and Portsmouth should be expended solely upon the men employed within those boroughs, or would you spread the rate over the whole of the county, and make those towns contribute their quota?—I should say that a fresh valuation of all property

Captain
W. C. Harris.

26 May 1853.

property in boroughs and counties should be made; and that all should contribute equally to one general rate.

54. *Chairman.*] With regard to Southampton and Portsmouth, would you give the magistrates the power of choosing their own chief constable?—Not in such small boroughs as those named.

55. Only in boroughs above 100,000 inhabitants?—Yes; such as Liverpool, Birmingham, Manchester, Leeds, and Bristol; I think those are the only five boroughs in England with a population of 100,000.

56. How would you propose to deal with those large boroughs?—I should consider them as separate counties.

57. Mr. *Fitzroy.*] Would you give a separate force to those boroughs, or change the men from different parts of the county into them?—With regard to the five boroughs named, I should treat them as separate counties.

58. What is the total number of your police force in Hampshire at present?—One hundred and seventy-six.

59. What is the number of parishes?—I am not prepared to say off-hand.

60. Do you know what the police rate in Hampshire is in the pound?—Twopence halfpenny.

61. Am I right in thinking that you intend, supposing such an arrangement to be made, to have a force located in Portsmouth and Southampton, which should be a distinct force from the rest of the county, specially devoted to that service, although under your command?—I am merely giving an opinion; my impression is that a borough containing less than 100,000 inhabitants ought to be considered a part of the county in which that borough is situated, so that you may have the opportunity of changing the men from the county into the borough, and from one borough to another, so that the men may not become locally connected.

62. Do you think, after consolidation in point of expenditure, that the rate generally in the county would be lightened or increased?—My impression is that the Government would derive so much benefit from the consolidation, that they ought to contribute a proportion of the expense.

63. I ask you simply as a matter of pounds, shillings, and pence, whether you think the result of such an arrangement would be to lighten the rate, or increase it?—The greater the number of men, the more it must lighten the rate; the staff is thrown over a larger surface, and therefore the individual cost of the constables must be diminished.

64. Sir *J. Trollope.*] You would save some of the higher classes of appointments if you consolidated the boroughs with the county, you would save having a higher class of officers over each separate borough as at present?—You would be obliged to have a police superintendent at Portsmouth and at Southampton.

65. How many superintendents have you?—Fourteen.

66. What is your next grade?—Sergeants.

67. How many sergeants have you?—Fifteen; I should say that there is one chief clerk who ranks as a superintendent.

68. He is entirely confined to office work?—Exclusively.

69. In the cost of these operations in the counties, have you any table of fees for extra duties performed by the constables, such as attending the assizes or quarter sessions sometimes out of their own district; for instance, when they have to take prisoners to other counties, or attend other courts of jurisdiction?—We have no scale of allowances.

70. Is that left to the magistrates, or to the judges of assize?—To the chief constable; I allow the men what I conceive will cover their bare expenses.

71. Supposing some of your men are taken to another county with prisoners for trial, and have to attend to give evidence against them, are they allowed to make out a bill *ad libitum*?—I stop their pay whilst they are absent on the duties of another county, and they receive their allowances as ordinary witnesses.

72. How are those allowances regulated?—In the county to which they go, for mileage and attendance; I stop their pay as long as they are in the service of another county.

73. What is your stoppage per head, per man, for the superannuation fund?—Two and a half per cent.

74. Mr. *Fitzroy.*] After how many years are the men entitled to superannuation?—Not till they are 60 years of age.

Captain
W. C. Harris.
—————
26 May 1853.

75. What is the amount of the police force now in Southampton?—I am speaking from recollection; but I think it is 28 or 30. Not more than 30.

76. Is that an efficient force?—I should imagine not. The subject of an increase of 10 men to the force was only brought before the Council last week.

77. Mr. *Rich*.] With regard to the aggregate expense to the whole county, in case the police were put under one authority, do you imagine in the county of Hampshire, by adding to the present expenses of the county the expenses incurred by all those boroughs which are independent of the county, that it would exceed the expenses which would be incurred by the amalgamation of the new police in the county and in the boroughs included under one head?—No, my impression is that it would not be so much.

78. You said that you would shift the constabulary?—Yes.

79. Do you attach much importance to that?—Very great importance. I would not allow a constable to remain for a day after it had come to my knowledge that he was locally connected. If it was reported to me that a police constable had got into low company, I should shift him immediately.

79*. In bringing those other boroughs, which are now independent of you, under your authority, you would be able to exercise the same power of shifting the constables in these boroughs?—Yes.

80. Do you consider that mischief arises to the boroughs from the constables not being shifted?—Yes; it is impossible that a man can do his duty if he is locally connected. If police constables become acquainted with beershop keepers, for instance, it is impossible they can do their duty. If I see any indication of intimacy of that kind, I remove the constable to another part of the county, perhaps 40 or 50 miles away.

82. Are there any counties bordering on Hampshire without a constabulary police force?—Berkshire and West Sussex have no police force, and Dorsetshire is without one. Wiltshire has a police force.

83. Do you observe whether there is any difference between the parts contiguous to those counties which have not a police force, as to the commission and non-detection of crimes, compared with those which have it?—I recollect previous to the establishment of the constabulary in Surrey, that occasional depredations were committed on our borders. I attribute that, however, in a great measure to offenders not knowing the line of demarcation.

84. Do you remark any difference between the parts of Hampshire bordering on Wiltshire, where they have a police force, and the other parts contiguous to counties which have not a police force?—I think any person going from Hampshire into Dorsetshire might know when they were without the county, by the swarms of gipsies which they see encamped.

85. Do you find any inconvenience in Hampshire from having those bad neighbours?—Occasionally we do. I recollect, in the north of the county, there was a party came from Reading, and committed a burglary in Hampshire, in the parish of Heckfield. They were immediately followed up by the superintendent of the Odiham division, and were all brought to justice, and I believe seven transported. They had committed burglaries all round Reading, without a single case of detection.

86. *Chairman*.] I think you have stated that the amount of expenditure was 2 ½ d. in the pound?—Yes.

87. What amount do you carry to the credit of the county for the services performed, on the other hand?—I have here the treasurer's account of our county for the last year, and I find the total amount carried to the credit of the police rate was 2,537 l. 18 s. 11 d.

88. What was that for?—From the Government, for the conveyance of prisoners, 332 l. 18 s. 2 d.; from the general county rate for the same purpose, 700 l. 7 s. 6 d.; inspecting weights and measures, 550 l. 14 s. 6 d. There are several other items, such as the sale of cast horses, the attendance of the constables at the sessions and assizes, &c. The total amount is 2,537 l. 18 s. 11 d.

[*The Witness delivered in the following Paper*:]

RECEIPTS:	£.	s.	d.
From Government, for conveying of prisoners - - - - -	332	18	2
From general rate - - ditto - ditto - - - - - -	700	7	6
From - ditto - inspecting weights and measures - - - -	550	14	6
From - ditto - for medical attendance on prisoners - - -	9	18	–
From the borough of Andover, for services of constables - - -	251	1	8
From the sale of cast horses - - - - - - - -	90	2	6
For service of process - - - - - - - - -	206	10	11
From stoppages from constables absent on leave - - - - -	22	7	3
From - ditto - ditto - for medical attendance - - -	36	19	4
From constables, for lodgings provided at stations - - - -	126	6	3
From Government, for attendance of constables at sessions and assizes -	191	15	1
From the Customs, for conveyance of smugglers - - - - -	9	19	5
From sale of old harness - - - - - - - - -	4	18	–
From other sources - - - - - - - - - -	4	–	4
£.	2,537	18	11

Captain
W. C. Harris.

26 May 1853.

There are several other items; such as the sale of cast horses, the attendance of the constables at the sessions and assizes, &c. &c.; the total amount is 2,537*l.* 18*s.* 11*d.*

89. Sir *J. Trollope.*] Has not there been a saving under another head in Hampshire since the establishment of the police; I apprehend, before the establishment of the rural police, you had high constables or chief constables, who were paid officers?—No; the high constables are not paid officers in Hampshire; in some counties they are.

90. Had they no chief constables or high constables who were paid out of the county rate?—Not in Hampshire.

91. Mr. *Phillips.*] I think you said you shifted the constables from Andover in order to avoid the evil of local connexion?—Yes.

92. Do not you think you incur in some degree the risk of want of local knowledge from such a practice?—No.

93. Sir *J. Trollope.*] You do not move them all at once, I presume?—No, we only move one man at a time; we seldom move a superintendent.

94. Have you any difficulty in finding residences for the men?—Where the county has not built or provided stations, the men take private lodgings.

95. Has the county of Hampshire built any stations for the accommodation of the police?—Yes.

96. What number?—Several divisional stations have been built; in divisions where there is no station the property of the county, stations are rented.

97. Where there are stations with buildings attached to them, have the constables lodgings found by the county?—They pay for them.

98. Then when there is a change of men there is always a residence for them?—Where there is a station built.

99. Are those men provided for in other houses?—The men provide their own lodgings, and pay generally about 2 *s.* a week.

100. Mr. *Fitzroy.*] What do the men pay to the county for lodgings?—The same amount.

101. What is their weekly pay?—Our constables are in four classes, at 15*s.*, 17 *s.*, 19 *s.*, and a guinea a week.

102. Sir *J. Trollope.*] If the county do not find the lodgings, do they hire them, and stop the cost out of the pay of the men?—No.

103. What is the system which is adopted?—The men find their own lodgings; but if there is a county building, then we stop the amount from their pay at the rate of 2 *s.* a week; I see the amount stopped for lodgings last year was 126 *l.* 6 *s.* 3 *d.*

104. Have the whole of the lodgings which are found by the county been built out of the county rate?—Latterly we have invested the superannuation fund of the constabulary in building stations; we have upwards of 4,000 *l.* in the superannuation fund.

105. Then the rent of those lodgings furnishes the fund; is that so?—The county pays the interest of the money invested, and we stop a certain amount for lodgings from the pay of the constables; but only 2 *s.* a week.

106. Is it intended by degrees to find lodgings for the whole force?—No, I do not consider it possible. The only thing I contemplate is the building of

Captain
W. C. Harris.

16 May 1853.

divisional stations for the superintendents; the constables in Hampshire are scattered through the villages, not concentrated in stations, as in some counties.

107. You would build stations only at the head-quarters of the division?—Only at the head-quarters of the division.

108. *Chairman.*] You have stated the amount carried to the credit of the county; can you state any other items of deduction relative to which you can form an estimate?—By giving notice to the coroners, the expense of the coroners inquests has been reduced 313 *l.* 10 *s.* 2 *d.*

109. I understand, from another source, that there was a report from a select committee on county expenditure; have you got that report?—I have.

110. Mr. *Fitzroy.*] When you speak of the expense of the coroners, do you mean that the police have given notice of deaths, have summoned the jury, and so on?—Yes; in place of the parish constables giving notice of any sudden death, the county constabulary (having previously made some inquiries) give notice to the coroner.

111. Have you had any representations as to that duty not being efficiently performed by the constabulary?—No; I have had representations made by the coroners of the satisfactory manner in which the evidence has been brought before them, and the trouble they have consequently been saved.

112. Has it at all checked the number of inquests held?—I do not think it has materially; it has lessened the expense.

113. Mr. *Burroughes.*] What sum do you save by the police giving those notices?—£.313. 10 *s.* 2 *d.*

114. Do you inspect the weights and measures?—We do.

115. *Chairman.*] Will you state who were the members of the committee on county expenditure?—Melville Portal, Esq., M.P., was the chairman; the Right Honourable the Speaker, the Right Honourable Lord Henry Cholmondeley, Sir William Heathcoate, Bart., Henry C. Compton, Esq., M.P., Henry Beaumont Coles, Esq., M.P., John Simeon, Esq., M.P., John Bonham Carter, Esq., M.P., William Hans Sloane Stanley, Esq., William Crawley Yonge, Esq., F. Jervoise Ellis Jervoise, Esq., John Willis Fleming, Esq., Edward Hulse, Esq., George Haynes Jones, M. D., Henry Joyce Mulcock, Esq., Rev. John Thomas Maine. If you will allow me, I will read a portion of the report. " Your Committee have not been able to ascertain the amount that was yearly paid by parishes to their constables prior to the establishment of this force; but it is calculated that not less than 1,500 *l.* per annum must have been expended in this respect, which is now altogether saved to the ratepayers. But besides these sums, which before the establishment of the constabulary were payments actually out of pocket, it must be remembered that considerable saving is indirectly effected to the public by means of this force. The value of the constables' lost time (before the establishment of the county constabulary), for which he was never adequately remunerated, must not be left out of the calculations in estimating the advantage of a paid police. It may also be observed that, coincident with the employment of police constables as assistant relieving officers in unions, there has been a very great decrease in vagrancy, and that without any additional cost to the unions; a considerable credit ought therefore, in their opinion, to be taken in favour of the constabulary under all these heads, as well as under that of saving to the public by the diminution of business at petty sessions, by the recovery and protection of property, by the absence of the necessity for associations for the prosecution of offenders, and by non-payments to special constables; and, although it is impossible to estimate with any accuracy the amount of indirect expense thus avoided by the county, yet when it is recollected that a saving of only 1 *d.* per acre would amount to a sum of 4,154 *l.*, it may be safely asserted that the actual additional cost to the ratepayers is very trifling in comparison with the advantages which accrue to them from the maintenance of the police force. In illustration of the expenses in which the county may be involved when unprotected by the police, they would refer to the burden thrown upon the rates by a short period of rioting in 1830, which appears, by Table No. 1, to have amounted to 9,235 *l.* 15 *s.* 3 *d.*, a sum exceeding the cost of paying the police force for a whole year, and to which must be added the amount of the damage and destruction of property at that time."

116. Mr. *Fitzroy.*] What is the average area which each of your constables have to watch and superintend?—The area of the county, including the boroughs of Andover and Lymington is 1,006,210 acres, and we have 176 men to that acreage.

Captain
W. C. Harris.

26 May 1853.

117. *Chairman.*] Supposing the Rural Police Act were made compulsory, and the counties and boroughs were consolidated, have you made any calculation as to what number of men would be required in England and Wales?—The police force of England and Wales (exclusive of the Metropolitan and City Police) amounted in 1851 to 7,381, and were supported at a cost to the rate-payers of 445,084 *l.* 0 *s.* 10 *d.*

118. Mr. *Mackie.*] Does that include Wales?—It does. If a force were raised upon the basis of acreage and population, taking in the rural districts, 4,000 acres, and a population of 1,200 to each constable (in boroughs a population of 1,000 to each constable, except under an Order in Council), it would give a force (based upon the census of 1841) of 12,307 men for England and Wales. It might be necessary, for instance, to have more than one constable to 1,000 inhabitants in such boroughs as Liverpool and Manchester.

119. Sir *J. Trollope.*] That is something greater than you have in Hampshire?—Yes; it would give us a larger number of men.

120. Your proportion being 1,571 inhabitants, your police is about one to 4,000 acres?—It is more than 4,000 acres to each constable.

121. *Chairman.*] Do you take one constable to 1,000 inhabitants as the maximum for the force?—Yes; except under an Order in Council, when it might be necessary, as in Liverpool and Birmingham, to have a greater number of men to the population.

122. Your calculation is made upon two maximums; 1,200 in counties, and 1,000 in boroughs to each constable?—Yes, with a small reserve force in each county in addition; that would amount (exclusive of the chief constables of counties) to 12,307 men. The cost of this force would amount to 773,799 *l.* 5 *s.* 2 *d.*

123. Mr. *Mackie.*] Is not that considerably more than it is at present?—The present charge is only for 7,381.

[*The Witness delivered in the following Returns:*]

SUMMARY of the Number of CONSTABLES proposed to be appointed in each County.

COUNTY, &c.	Acreage.	Population.	Number of Constables proposed to be stationed in each.						Existing Force.
			Chief Clerks.	Super-intendents	In-spectors.	Serjeants.	Con-stables.	TOTAL.	
Bedford - - - - -	297,632	107,936	1	4	1	5	83	94	60
Berks - - - - -	473,920	161,147	1	6	1	13	138	159	51
Bucks - - - - -	463,820	155,983	1	6	- -	9	121	137	18
Cambridge - - - -	536,313	164,459	1	8	- -	13	139	161	144
Chester - - - -	649,050	395,660	1	11	- -	16	257	285	84
Cornwall - - - -	849,200	338,697	1	12	- -	14	236	263	36
Cumberland - - - -	969,490	178,038	1	13	1	17	198	230	28
Derby - - - - -	663,180	272,217	1	10	1	14	200	226	43
Devon - - - - -	1,636,450	533,460	1	22	3	33	456	515	150
Dorset - - - - -	627,220	175,043	1	8	- -	16	161	186	54
Durham - - - - -	679,530	324,284	1	9	2	14	222	248	209
Essex - - - - -	925,260	304,988	1	13	1	20	239	274	229
Gloucester - - - -	780,600	309,087	1	11	1	16	225	254	271
Bristol (City) - - -	9,870	122,296	1	2	4	9	118	134	252
Hereford - - - -	543,800	113,878	1	7	1	9	112	130	17
Hertford - - - -	374,380	146,720	1	5	- -	8	108	122	80
Huntingdon - - - -	241,690	58,549	1	2	1	4	53	61	5
Kent - - - - -	911,490	423,717	1	13	5	28	307	354	104
Lancaster - - - -	1,105,890	1,137,584	1	18	4	26	636	685	688
Liverpool (Borough) - -	5,300	286,487	1	2	5	9	283	300	800
Manchester (ditto) -	6,070	242,983	1	2	5	9	239	256	445
Leicester - - - -	511,340	215,867	1	8	2	12	168	191	114
Lincoln - - - -	1,663,850	362,602	1	20	3	30	351	405	54
Monmouth - - - -	324,310	134,355	1	4	- -	6	95	106	21
Norfolk - - - - -	1,292,300	412,664	1	20	3	31	361	416	279
Northampton - - - -	646,810	199,228	1	9	1	15	165	191	77

(continued)

COUNTY, &c.	Acreage.	Population.	Number of Constables proposed to be stationed in each.						Existing Force.
			Chief Clerks.	Super-intendents	In-spectors.	Serjeants.	Con-stables.	Total.	
Northumberland - - -	1,165,430	250,278	1	16	2	21	260	300	110
Nottingham - - -	525,800	249,910	1	8	3	14	191	217	153
Oxford - - -	467,230	161,643	1	7	-	10	130	148	44
Rutland - - -	97,500	21,302	-	1	-	3	19	23	1
Salop - - -	864,360	239,048	1	11	2	18	214	246	83
Somerset - - -	1,028,090	435,982	1	15	1	21	325	363	108
Southampton - - -	1,018,550	355,004	1	16	4	23	302	346	266
Stafford - - -	736,290	510,504	1	10	2	16	303	332	303
Suffolk - - -	918,760	315,073	1	13	1	19	251	285	209
Surrey - - -	385,580	118,867	1	5	-	7	120	133	86
Sussex - - -	907,920	299,753	1	14	3	19	254	291	140
Warwick - - -	549,150	218,793	1	8	2	12	174	197	78
Birmingham (Town) -	18,780	182,922	1	2	4	9	179	195	327
Westmoreland - - -	485,990	56,454	1	6	1	9	82	99	7
Wilts - - -	868,060	258,733	1	12	1	16	212	242	213
Worcester - - -	459,710	233,336	1	7	1	13	169	191	121
York (East Riding) - -	711,360	194,936	1	10	2	15	184	212	154
York (North Riding) - -	1,282,870	204,122	1	18	1	22	232	274	8
York (West Riding) - -	1,653,830	1,040,368	1	23	2	32	633	691	328
Leeds (Town) - -	21,450	152,054		2	5	9	149	165	145
TOTAL of England - -	31,355,475	12,777,011	44	419	82	704	10,054	11,333	7,213
TOTAL of Wales - - -	4,752,000	911,603	12	48	-	60	854	974	168
	36,107,475	13,688,614	56	497	82	764	10,908	12,307	7,381

RETURN showing the EXPENSE of carrying out the foregoing Proposition.

RANK, &c.	Rate of Pay.	Number.						
	£.		£.	s.	d.	£.	s.	d.
Chief Constables, 1st Class, at per annum -	700	19	13,300	-	-			
Ditto - ditto - 2d ditto at ditto -	600	19	11,400	-	-			
Ditto - ditto - 3d ditto at ditto -	500	19	9,500	-	-			
						34,200	-	-
Chief Clerks, at per annum - - -	100	56	-	-	-	5,600	-	-
Superintendents, 1st Class, at per annum -	110	166	18,260	-	-			
Ditto - - 2d ditto at ditto -	100	166	16,600	-	-			
Ditto - - 3d ditto at ditto -	90	165	14,850	-	-			
						49,710	-	-
Inspectors, 1st Class, at per annum - -	75	28	2,100	-	-			
Ditto - 2d ditto at ditto - -	70	27	1,890	-	-			
Ditto - 3d ditto at ditto - -	65	27	1,755	-	-			
						5,745	-	-
Serjeants, 1st Class, at per week - -	25/	255	16,575	-	-			
Ditto - 2d ditto at ditto - -	23/	255	15,912	-	-			
Ditto - 3d ditto at ditto - -	23/	254	15,189	4	-			
						47,676	4	-
Constables, 1st Class, at per week - -	20/	3,636	189,072	-	-			
Ditto - 2d ditto at ditto - -	18/	3,636	170,164	16	-			
Ditto - 3d ditto at ditto - -	16/	3,636	151,257	12	-			
						510,494	8	-
Average yearly amount of clothing - -						50,028	13	2
Divisional expenses and contingencies (say 10 per cent. on the pay and clothing) -						70,345	-	-
		12,304			£.	773,799	5	2
Average expense of each constable - -					£.	62	17	5

124. Mr. *Sotheron.*] That is 65 *l.* per man?—No; 773,779*l.* would give only 62*l.* 17*s.* 5*d.* per man, on account of the larger number of men.

125. Sir *J. Trollope.*] Then the constabulary would be cheaper consolidated in the way you propose?—It would cost 62*l.* 17*s.* 5*d.*

126. That would be less than it now costs in the county of Hampshire?—By about 3*l.* per man.

127. *Chairman.*] That you think is the amount of saving by consolidation?—Yes.

128. Sir *J. Trollope.*] Does the 773,779*l.* include the horses and the remounts?—The remount of 500 horses.

129. What is the total number of horses you propose to have?—Five hundred.

130. *Chairman.*] Notwithstanding your calculation being 773,779 *l.*, do not you think that consolidation, and the facilities it would give for the detection of crime, would lead ultimately to a still further saving?—Yes, it might; I think myself there would be a decrease in the expense of prosecutions.

131. Mr. *Rich.*] You state the gross saving upon the whole plan; I apprehend there are also incidental expenses into which you do not now enter?—Yes.

132. *Chairman.*] After having saved the sum of money you have stated, if this number of men is necessary now, do you not think, with the decrease of crime, that a less number of men would be ultimately sufficient?—No; I do not myself think that you can do with a less number of men, because the population is increasing.

133. Mr. *Sotheron.*] How do you make out that 62*l.* 17*s.* 5*d.* per man is the probable cost of the constables if they were established throughout the whole of the kingdom?—I have put down the actual number that would be required of every rank, and I have calculated according to a rate of pay which is in this return, and 62*l.* 17*s.* 5*d.* is the total amount that it would come to

134. I understood you to give as a reason, that you would obtain a larger number of men at a lower rate of pay than according to the present proportion?—No; I think the difference will arise in this way, that the staff at head quarters will be thrown over a larger surface.

135. Therefore what may be called the staff charges, or the charges of the superior offices, will not be increased in proportion to the number of men?—No.

136. Consequently, per head, the rate would be smaller than it is at present?—Yes.

137. Mr. *Rich.*] Your estimate of the expense per man is based upon your experience?—Yes.

138. Sir *J. Anderson.*] Would not the expense vary in different counties; would it be necessary to have a uniform rate of pay all over the country?—I should say one uniform rate of pay would be desirable throughout the whole of England.

139. *Chairman.*] Would any part of this additional outlay, in your opinion, giving a very large accession of force, and better organized, be repaid to the Government by any saving in other departments?—Yes; in all maritime counties where the force is now established, the men are armed with deputations from the Customs for the protection of the public revenue; if the force were thus augmented, a reduction in the number of men employed in the coast guard would be warranted.

140. Do the counties receive anything for those services so performed from the Customs?—Nothing whatever; I find by a Return recently presented to Parliament, that the number of men in the coast guard amounts to 5,770, of which 810 are employed afloat; the annual cost of this force, according to the same Return, amounts to 460,963 *l.* 19 *s.* 5 *d.* Of this number 3,232 are stationed in England and Wales. If 1,000 of this number were retained to do duty in boats, 2,232 would be available for duty elsewhere, and might be drafted on on board our steam guard ships (the coast guard being already drilled to great gun exercise). The value of the services thus obtained may be shown to amount to more than 158,000 *l.* a year.

141. Can you state, of your own knowledge, the number of coast guard in Hampshire?—On the Hampshire coast there are four inspecting commanders, 25 officers, 34 chief boatmen, and 273 men; total, 336; the cost of this force is about 23,930 *l.* a year.

142. You say that your men have been employed under deputations. Have seizures been made by your men as well as by the coast guard?—I cannot say what number of seizures have been made by the coast guard; I have applied

officially to the Controller general of the coast guard for information on this subject, but have received no reply; I have not, however, heard of a single seizure having been made.

143. Have your men made any seizures?—Yes, two; the parties were fined 100 l. each.

144. Sir *J. Trollope.*] Does the constable get any benefit from those seizures? —He does.

145. Is a portion of the reward given to him?—A small portion; one moiety of the reward, but it does not amount to much.

146. Do you pay the men, or do they take it from the Customs?—One moiety is paid by the Collector of Customs to the constable, and the other to the Superannuation Fund.

147. Mr. *Fitzroy.*] Have you heard any objections on the part of the ratepayers, to the constables being employed in aid of the coast guard?—Not the slightest.

148. Mr. *Burroughes.*] Do you continue their pay during the time they are so employed?—Yes, they receive their pay.

149. Sir *J. Trollope.*] Do you take the constables out of their district to perform this duty?—No, we have 50 men stationed along the coast within two or three miles; if the men happen to fall in with a smuggler (now they have received deputations), they stop him.

150. Mr. *Rich.*] You mean that they form an inner circle behind the coast guard?—Yes.

151. Mr. *Phillips.*] Do you apprehend any interference with the discipline of your men from their being employed in aid of the coast guard, which might bring them into connexion with smugglers?—No, I do not think they are likely to become connected with smugglers.

152. You do not apprehend any interference with the disciplince of the force from their being so employed?—Not the slightest.

153. Mr. *Rich.*] In places where such deputations are not given, after the smuggler has passed the coast guard, he considers himself safe?—Yes.

154. Now he is liable to be taken by the police?—Yes; the whole of our men, in every part of the county, have deputations.

155. Sir *J. Trollope.*] It is not confined to the 50 men on the coast?—No.

156. Mr. *Rich.*] In the event of the coast guard being called off for any active pursuit of offenders anywhere, your police would be competent to act for a time as coast guard?—Yes.

157. *Chairman.*] Do you think if the police were employed in the maritime counties in place of the coast guard, that you might save the expense of the coast guard entirely?—I think if you were to retain 1,000 men to do duty in boats, that the police could do the whole of the other duty.

158. Do you think the 12,000 men you have calculated upon would be sufficient to do that duty?—Quite.

159. In that case, as there would be a great saving to the Government, you think that the Government ought to contribute something?—The Government would save close upon 160,000 l. a year.

160. Mr. *Fitzroy.*] Do you contemplate the duty being performed in the same manner as it is performed by the coast guard; that your men are to keep incessant watch, day and night, on the coast?—If the number of men I contemplate were appointed, we should have almost sufficient to watch the coast in the same manner as the coast guard do at present; retaining 1,000 men of the coast guard to do duty in boats.

161. Had you contemplated this duty when you fixed the number at 12,364? —No, I had not.

162. Mr. *Rich.*] You have viewed them more as auxiliaries to the coast guard? —Yes; in the event of the coast guard being withdrawn.

163. Sir *J. Trollope.*] The coast guard have to act in concentrated bodies; have you the power of concentrating your men in large numbers?—Yes.

164. In the same way in which the coast guard is now assembled?—Yes.

165. You do it now for the preservation of the peace?—Yes.

166. *Chairman.*] Do you consider that any benefit would arise from training the police to the use of arms?—Most certainly; from the very superior intelligence of the constabulary, their height, youth, and athletic pursuits, they are

peculiarly

peculiarly adapted to act as light troops; they might be trained to the use of arms, but yet not carry them, except under an Order in Council.

167. Sir *J. Trollope.*] Are not your men drilled at present?—Yes; I withdraw one or two from each division of the county at a time, for the purpose of drill. I have found so short a time is necessary to make them efficient soldiers, that their absence from their beats is hardly felt.

168. To the use of arms?—No, only to sword exercise.

169. As regards the constables being a charge upon the ratepayers of the county, do you not apprehend it would be taking them beyond their duty if they had the entire protection of the revenue of the country as coast-guard officers?—At the present moment they assist the coast guard, but if they had the entire protection of the revenue of the country, the Government should contribute towards the support of the force.

170. Would it not be an injustice to the ratepayers of Hampshire?—Decidedly, if the Government did not contribute.

171. You do not contemplate that they should undertake this duty without a contribution on the part of the Government, as an Imperial measure?—I am of opinion that the Government ought to provide the excess of expenditure beyond the amount produced by a rate of $1\frac{1}{4}d.$ in the pound, levied equally on counties and boroughs. A rate of $1\frac{1}{4}d.$ in the pound would produce 445,737 *l.*, so that the Government would have to provide 328,062 *l.*

172. How is that to be provided for?—From the Consolidated Fund.

173. Mr. *Rich.*] Do you practically find that the present performance of their duty, as auxiliaries to the coast guard, interferes with the performance of their routine duty as police of the county?—Not in the least; the patrols do not watch for smugglers.

174. That being the case, there would not be any strong claim for paying for the duty which is now done, which does not appear to be a duty required by the county?—I think the constabulary have a claim upon the Government.

175. Mr. *Fitzroy.*] Is it compulsory upon the constabulary to act in this manner, to assist in the apprehension of smugglers in the way in which they do now?—No; the Customs made an application to the magistrates at quarter sessions to allow the men to be associated with the coast guard.

176. In fact, it is a private arrangement between the magistrates and the Customs?—Between the Customs and the court of quarter sessions; the magistrates consented to the appointment.

177. Upon what ground do you claim anything from the Government on account of services which are merely the result of a voluntary arrangement?—We do not claim anything whatever; I am only speaking in the event of the force being made general.

178. I understood you to say you had some claim upon the Government on account of those services?—We perform the duty, and are not paid for it.

179. Mr. *Rich.*] How many counties have received such deputations?—I imagine all the maritime counties.

180. How long is it since you received yours?—In February 1852.

181. Do your men like the duty?—Yes; they do not object to it in the slightest degree.

182. Mr. *Fitzroy.*] Is it within your knowledge that such an arrangement exists in other counties?—In Essex I know it does, and I believe in all the maritime counties.

183. Sir *J. Trollope.*] I wish to call your attention to one particular class of duty performed by the constabulary, and to know how far it has been available in the suppression of vagrancy; in your county you have a district in which both vagrancy and petty offences against property were very prevalent; I speak of the New Forest District; I wish to know whether the establishment of the police force has totally put an end to the encampment of gipsies, and encroachments upon the property in that district?—We have very few gipsies now in the county; I am not prepared with a return.

184. Do they venture to come within your jurisdiction?—No, except at fairs.

185. In addition to gipsies, there are many other persons who go about living in carts and so on?—Yes.

186. Do you permit them to be in the lanes and commons?—No, certainly not; we impound their cattle, and move them upon all occasions.

Captain
W. C. Harris.

25 May 1853.

187. Have petty offences decreased since the establishment of the police, such as stealing wood, breaking fences, and those minor offences which come before the petty sessions?—To a great ext

188. Have you any table to show that?—There is a difficulty in proving the fact; I have been informed by large occupiers of land, that in sheep alone they have saved their police rate; whilst others have said that dead fences would cover the amount of theirs. I recollect a gentleman residing near Winchester (Mr. Bailey, of Worthy), assuring me that he had annually to replace a dead fence previous to the establishment of the police, but that now it was never touched.

189. You have alluded to a higher class of crime; has that decreased since the establishment of the police?—Very materially.

190. Have you any returns to indicate whether the property of the farmers has been more protected from incendiarism since the establishment of the rural police?—I have no such returns.

191. Has not that been a prevailing crime in Hampshire?—We have had no case of incendiarism for some time.

192. For some years do you mean?—I do not like to speak to any particular period; two or three years.

193. Is it on the decrease?—I cannot call to mind a single case for the last two or three years.

194. *Chairman.*] You stated that there were but few gipsies and vagrants in Hampshire; are they much more numerous in the lanes of the adjoining counties over the border?—Very much more numerous.

195. Where there is no police?—Yes.

196. Mr. *Sotheron.*] Have you made arrangements that your constables shall take charge of vagrants who apply to the union workhouses?—Our constables are appointed in many unions assistant relieving officers for vagrants, and they perform that duty without any charge whatever upon the union.

197. Do they take charge of all vagrants upon their first coming into a town, and march them out the following morning?—No.

198. Will you describe what course they take?—The vagrant, instead of applying to the relieving officer of the district, applies to the superintendent of police, or whoever is appointed assistant relieving officer, for a ticket of admission to the union, and the officer exercises his discretion whether he thinks the applicant is a fit subject for relief.

199. *Chairman.*] Was that in consequence of a recommendation from the Poor Law Commissioners?—Yes.

200. Sir *J. Trollope.*] Are those vagrants searched?—They are seldom searched.

201. Was not that one of the instructions from the Poor Law Commissioners?—It was merely a suggestion thrown out.

202. Mr. *Sotheron.*] The vagrants having been housed in the union-house for the night, do you take charge of them the following morning?—No.

203. Your officers are not in the habit of marching them out of the town?—If the officer was to march them out of the town he would only convey them into his own district; it would be useless, unless he could march them to the borders of the county where there was no constabulary.

204. Do your constables in any way prevent those persons who pass the night in the union-house from going back to receive any money which they might have deposited with any person in the town?—No.

205. Practically do you think that the employment of your constables has tended to decrease vagrancy?—Very considerably indeed.

206. Could you give any return showing the decrease?—No, I have no return upon that subject.

207. Mr. *Fitzroy.*] Has sheep stealing been a very prevalent crime in Hampshire?—Formerly it was a very prevailing crime; the number of cases in 1851 was only 30.

208. Mr. *Sotheron.*] Although you may not have this return with regard to vagrancy, it would be very easy to obtain it, would it not; and can you furnish a return of the number of vagrants relieved in the workhouses in the county of Hampshire the year before your constables were appointed, and the last year, for instance?—Yes, I will furnish the return.

209. Mr.

Captain
W. C. Harris.
———
26 May 1853.

209. Mr. *Rich.*] Is the police force popular in the county?—Very; at least I do not know anything to the contrary; we have no petitions for a decrease of the force, but we have many petitions presented to the court of quarter sessions for an increase.

210. Is the feeling of the masses of the people favourable or unfavourable towards the police?—I know nothing to the contrary of the feeling being favourable.

211. Have you had any remonstrances from the ratepayers as to the expense?—I cannot call to mind having heard of any.

212. You stated that you would recommend that the constables should be drilled to the use of arms?—Yes.

213. Do you consider that that would be an additional means for the preservation of the peace of the county?—I consider that it would not only tend to the preservation of the peace of the county, but it would form a great element of national defence, if the men were drilled to the use of arms. The men are young, energetic, and active, and patrolling for seven hours every night of their lives, are in splendid condition for marching.

214. Do you think that it would tend to make the force itself more popular, and that the men would feel additional self respect?—I think it would myself.

215. Do you think that there would be any germ of unpopularity in the idea of constables being armed?—I do not indeed.

216. You are not afraid that accustoming them to the use of arms would raise a feeling of jealousy on the part of the population of the county?—No.

217. *Chairman.*] Do you contemplate using them as a military body for police purposes?—I merely suggest that the men should be drilled to the use of arms, but not carry them except on the occasion of a threatened invasion, or when some serious disturbance of the public peace has taken place, or is apprehended, when an Order in Council might be given.

218. You mean that they should be armed only on such occasions as a military force would be employed?—Yes.

219. Mr. *Rich.*] For the suppression of riots, for instance?—Yes.

220. Sir *J. Trollope.*] Are the constables allowed any cutlasses?—The whole body is drilled to the use of the sword.

221. Is the night patrol armed?—Some few constables are supplied with cutlasses, whose beats are so situated, that in the opinion of two justices of the county it is necessary for their personal protection in the performance of their duty.

222. Are they armed when they assist the coast guard?—No.

223. *Chairman.*] Do they never carry arms except under an order from two magistrates?—Except on any sudden emergency, when I have issued orders for the men to be armed; when I report the same, and the reasons for such order, to the Secretary of State, and any two justices of the peace, as soon afterwards as is practicable.

224. Mr. *Fitzroy.*] Are the constables drilled to the use of the cutlass?—Yes, to the use of the sword.

225. Mr. *Rich.*] Are many of the constables old soldiers?—No; I have an objection to old soldiers.

226. You prefer young men?—I do not like to take men who have been soldiers, even after three or four years' service; they are invariably addicted to drinking.

227. Have any of your men suffered injuries from collisions?—Yes; one man was overpowered and wounded.

228. Have you any further suggestion to make as to the development of the police force?—I have not made any statement with regard to the amount that might be saved in the cost of prosecutions by the establishment of an efficient police. The cost of prosecutions at the Assizes and Sessions (paid by the Government) amounted in 1850 to 217,324 *l.* 17 *s.* From this sum, with an efficient constabulary, may fairly be deducted at least one-third (the diminished cost of prosecutions consequent upon the decrease of crime); this will give a saving of 72,441 *l.* 12 *s.* 4 *d.* In this calculation I have not taken into account the amount now expended in the punishment of offenders; viz., in the maintenance of delinquents in gaols, in transports, and in the penal colonies. And here I may mention that a decrease in the number of committals would tend to solve the difficulty attending the disposal of transports. I would wish to call the

*Captain
W. C. Harris.*

16 May 1853.

attention of the Committee to one important fact; that by the adoption of some such measure as that I have proposed, the country would have at its disposal a force which, ordinarily employed in the suppression of crime, would, in case of invasion, be equal to 13 regiments; the pay alone of which, as a part of the standing army, would amount annually to 351,777 *l.* 6 *s.* 11 *d.*; whilst the total cost would be little short of 500,000 *l.* a year.

229. Mr. *Phillips.*] There is no definite age at which they cease to be policemen; you judge by their health, do you not?—Yes; but I never take a man above 30.

230. What is the age of your oldest man in the police?—We have men as old as 50, who came into the force when it was first established.

231. Mr. *Rich.*] I see in your letter to Lord Malmesbury you state that you contemplate forming the police into something like a military organisation?— Yes, I propose to ingraft the discipline of the Irish constabulary upon the system of doing duty in this country.

232. Do you still adhere to that opinion?—Yes, I consider it would be extremely advantageous for the country.

233. Sir *J. Anderson.*] How do you account for the jealousy which you have stated exists between the borough and county police, so that they do not co-operate well?—I have no mode of accounting for it.

234. Would a general system applicable to all those boroughs having under 100,000 inhabitants, work well in those towns?—I certainly think it would. I cannot conceive any reason why it should not work well.

235. If there were a county police instead of borough police?—It would be a general police.

236. Mr. *Mackie.*] You are of opinion that if a national police were established, jealousy would cease?—It is my opinion, that if there was a national force there would be no jealousy whatever.

237. You have stated that the policemen find a difficulty in tracing a culprit from the county to the towns; do you mean, find any difficulty in following a criminal from Hampshire to Berkshire, or any of the other adjoining counties? —If he goes into Berkshire, we have no force to assist in tracing offenders.

238. In fact the police, in a national point of view, is most inefficient in that respect?—Yes, most certainly.

239. At present it is merely a county police, and however active the policemen are within your county, when you come to follow a criminal without the county, you find that you have no power?—We have no person to go to for information but the parish constable.

240. Mr. *Sotheron.*] Supposing an offender should go into a county which has an existing police, do you find that the fact of that police existing affords a facility of following him up?—We have always found the greatest assistance from the police in every county in England which is upon the same footing as ourselves.

241. Mr. *Rich.*] Have you turned your attention to the establishment of electric telegraphs in the counties?—No; but it has struck me that in the event of a general police being established, we should derive great benefit from having detective police constables at the terminus of every railway, to observe all persons departing from great towns and returning; and we might avail ourselves of the electric telegraph to report to these termini any depredations which were committed.

242. If the electric telegraph were in communication with all the police-stations in Hampshire, do you not apprehend that you would be more likely to detect and deter crime?—It might be useful; indeed it could not fail to be useful.

Sir *William Heathcote*, Bart.; Examined.

*Sir W. Heathcote,
Bart.*

243. *Chairman.*] You are the late Member for Hampshire and the late Chairman of the Quarter Sessions, are you not?—Yes.

244. Has your attention been frequently directed to the working of the police system?—To a considerable extent.

245. Perhaps you will state to the Committee your opinion of the result, in a moral point of view, of the appointment of the police as to the detection of offences and the prevention of crime?—I think it has been very successful with us. The point in which it is most successful, namely, the diminished amount of

undetected

Sir W Heathcote,
Bart.

26 May 1853.

undetected crime, is one which cannot be tested by numbers, because there is no return of those offences, in respect of which no person was committed for trial before the establishment of the police, but it is a matter of common notoriety that there is much less of undetected crime than there was before. With respect to the criminals who have been brought to justice, Captain Harris has given you returns showing the comparisons; and with reference to them, I have examined two periods of five years: five years immediately before the establishment of the force in our county, and five years immediately before I ceased to be Chairman of the Quarter Sessions; and I find that the proportion of convictions has risen from 64 to 69 per cent. of the whole number committed for trial, while the expense of prosecutions has become lower per head, and this last result has followed notwithstanding that the prosecutions have become in one respect more expensive, from its being the habit at the Sessions to allow briefs to counsel more liberally, both in the number and in the amounts of the fees. The cases are got up with more care and intelligence, which will account for the larger proportion of convictions, and there are fewer unnecessary witnesses, which will account for the diminished expense.

246. Will you state your opinion of the result of the appointment of the police in an economical point of view?—It is difficult to test the amount of the economical advantage, which consists very much in the saving of the immense waste which takes place from successful depredation; but it is to be remarked that this advantage falls to the share of the poorer classes especially, because they, in proportion to their property, are greater sufferers from depredation, in a district without police, than their wealthier neighbours. Farmers and other men of property have servants on their premises, and gentlemen of large possessions have usually an efficient police in their gamekeepers; but labourers, whose whole families may be out at work, are obliged, in a district where there are none but parish constables, to leave their cottages practically unprotected. It often happened to me, before the establishment of the police, to take measures for tracking the offenders, when any of my poor neighbours were robbed; but I do not recollect that it ever occurred to me to think of the parish constable as a person likely to throw light on the subject; my own keepers could do what was required much better.

247. Do you think the value of property has increased in the neighbourhoods where a well regulated police has been established?—I have no means of judging whether there is any difference in the market value; but if I were myself buying a property, I would give much more for it in a county which had a police force than in one which had not.

248. Perhaps I need hardly ask whether, in your opinion, the parochial constables are efficient for the protection of property and the prevention of crime? —I am sure that they are not, and cannot be expected to be so, except at a ruinous loss to themselves. They are men whose time is fully occupied. The position of parochial constables would appear to be this, that they must either be inert, or in proportion to their activity they must be expensive. If they do nothing there are no allowances to be made to them; but if you have occasion to employ them in cases of real intricacy, they must be paid more than you would give to a policeman: you must pay them at a higher rate per day; you can only escape from their being expensive by not employing them at all.

249. Do you think the parochial constables are to be depended upon for the good regulation of beerhouses and public-houses?—No; they are under the influences of neighbourhood; it is not fair to call upon them to perform the duty; without there being an actual collusion, they will be slow to interfere with their neighbours.

250. Do you think they are to be relied upon for what is more important, the suppression of vagrancy?—I should think not; it is not their business to patrol and fall in with vagrants. I apprehend it is quite out of their way.

251. You are aware as to the arrangement that is made in Hampshire, by the constabulary being assistant relieving officers?—I have not considered the effects of that at all; I am not able to give any opinion upon it.

252. Do you think the parish constables could be rendered more efficient, or made really efficient by the appointment of superintendent constables in each division?—No, except at a very great expense; you cannot withdraw them from their usual occupations except at a grievous hardship, unless you remunerate them sufficiently for their time in proportion to their activity. The mere

Sir W. Heathcote,
Bart.

16 May 1853.

putting of a superintendent of police amongst them would no more make them efficient constables, than the residence of a drill sergeant among them would make them soldiers. It is only by constant practice and great expense to the county, and a grievous hardship to the men, that you would make them good police constables.

253. You stated that in your opinion you thought it was desirable for the poorer classes of society that there should be a rural police?—Yes; there are several aspects in which it is so. If a depredation is committed, the police constables are able to engage in the search at once, without reference to the wealth or poverty of the person injured; but if there are only parish constables, such reference is necessary. Perhaps a very long and laborious search may be required; if that be successful, no doubt an allowance for the expense and time may be made, under a magistrate's certificate, at the trial in the Court of Quarter Sessions, or Assizes; but if the search is unsuccessful and there is no committal, there can be no allowance, and the cost will fall on the person who has employed the parish constable. It can only be a rich man who can venture in an intricate case to employ a constable of that sort. I have alluded in a former answer to one kind of depredation to which, in the absence of efficient police, the poor are especially exposed, namely, housebreaking in the day time. That offence has been greatly diminished in Hampshire since the establishment of the police. If we had the means of reckoning up the cases in which the perpetrators used to escape detection altogether, the difference between the two periods of five years which I mentioned before would be enormous; and even in the cases brought to trial there is a diminution of 14 per cent. in the latter period, although in this scarcely any have escaped detection.

254. Do you think in the absence of a well regulated police system, that justice is denied to the poor man, by his not having the means to employ a constable?—It falls more heavily upon the poor man than upon the wealthy farmer or gentleman, both with reference to prevention and to redress.

255. Are you prepared to state whether a uniform system of police would be desirable?—I am less able to tell you than a person who is actually employed like Captain Harris. It is obvious that a facility of communication between the different forces would be an advantage in the apprehension of offenders, for the small jurisdictions in the midst of the county police afford places of safe retreat for bad characters.

256. Mr. *Rich.*] You stated that cottagers would derive a great benefit from the establishment of police; has not the property of farmers in Hampshire derived great benefit from the establishment of police?—I apprehend they have, particularly in sheep; I very rarely hear of sheep-stealing now, whereas we used to hear of it very frequently.

257. Is there any diminution in the destruction of the fences?—I have not turned my attention much to that subject, but I have not heard complaints of it.

258. You stated, did you not, that a great benefit would arise from the destruction of the subordinate jurisdiction of the boroughs as to the police; do you think that a similar benefit would accrue from having a compulsory Act for the establishment of police in those counties which have it not?—That would be still more important than the other consideration.

259. Could you point out to the Committee any way in which that could be made acceptable to the other counties?—I should think that the course of inquiry upon which the Committee are now engaged will make it acceptable to persons who have not been called to consider the facts of the case. This inquiry will make known the advantages which certain counties have derived from the establishment of the police.

260. Could you state from your own knowledge whether those parts of Hampshire which are contiguous to counties which have not the police, are or are not less subject to depredations than those adjoining counties which have the police?—I am not able to tell the Committee of my own knowledge, as I live rather in the centre of the county; but I know, from the reports which I have from time to time received from Captain Harris, in the course of business, that on the borders of Sussex and of Surrey, before they established a police, we were exposed to a lawlessness not to be found elsewhere, and were in consequence obliged to keep a strength of police there which was beyond our average.

261. In fact the objections which apply to the smaller jurisdictions within the

the county, extend to the non-establishment of police without the county?—

They are very much greater; the only difficulty with the boroughs is, that their police, even if doing its duty under their own jurisdiction, does not appear to work very cordially with ours. In the other case there is an entire lawlessness.

262. Are you acquainted with the working of the police with regard to their assisting the coast guard in the manner which has been stated by Captain Harris?—Not at all.

263. Sir *J. Trollope*.] Have you found any inconvenience from there being a separate jurisdiction existing in the boroughs as contradistinguished from the counties?—Certainly, I am sure that there is less efficiency in a small police than there is in one which is organised on a larger scale.

264. Have you found any inconvenience from the want of concurrent jurisdiction generally?—No; on the contrary, it occurs just as much in some boroughs where the county magistrates have a concurrent jurisdiction for the purposes of committal for crime.

265. In the case of the larger boroughs having separate jurisdiction, is there any jealousy of action?—I have understood that there is; it has not come under my own observation; there may be difficulties from some little jealousies.

266. Are you aware of the amount of the police rate in the pound in Hants?—I do not recollect exactly; it is about 2½ d.

267. During the time that you were chairman of the court of quarter sessions, had you any remonstrances upon the subject of the county expenses in consequence of the establishment of the police?—I will tell the Committee the circumstances attending its original establishment; the question was referred to a committee consisting of one magistrate from every division, who conferred with his brethren. In each division the magistrates conferred and voted upon it, and all the divisions agreed to it; some unanimously, and some by a great majority; the committee so deputed came to the same conclusion, and it was finally adopted at the quarter sessions without a division. Afterwards one or two magistrates, who although they had not decided, were not entirely satisfied with the arrangements, were desirous of abolishing or reducing the force; but it never in fact came to a question, because the concurrence of five magistrates in the manner prescribed by the Act could never be obtained. With respect to representations, we have had several; but they have generally been not complaints of the amount of the force, or of the amount of the expense, as being too great, but complaints that of the existing force the petitioners did not get a sufficient share in their own districts, and sometimes even applications for an increase in the force. About two years ago, one of the magistrates thought some of the expenses incurred had been excessive, and called the attention of the quarter sessions to them; but after debate they were approved by a large majority, 34 to 4. Practically it may be said that the county has been unanimous from the beginning in the establishment and maintenance of the police force.

268. Mr. *Phillips*.] From your experience of the court of quarter sessions, and being a person well conversant with the condition of Hampshire, you are decidedly of opinion that the vast mass of the cases in which the police have been useful have been cases of small ratepayers, and small holders of property, far beyond the proportion which would naturally exist between gentlemen's houses and smaller houses; still setting that out of the calculation, you think that the largest number of cases in which the police have been a benefit, have been those of the poor?—I have not sifted the cases so as to be able to say how many belonged to the very poorest class. Probably a large number were those of little shopkeepers, and others a little above the cottagers.

269. Far beyond that of a higher grade?—Certainly; and the point to which I particularly desire to call attention is, that in a county where there is no police, a poor man is not only exposed to more depredation, but is exposed to the risk of much greater expense in obtaining redress than where there is such a force.

William Hans Sloane Stanley, Esq., called in; and Examined.

270. *Chairman*.] YOU are a Magistrate for Hampshire, are you not?—Yes.
271. Have you turned your attention to the effect which has been produced by the police force in the county since its establishment?—I have.

272. Will you state your opinion upon the subject, with respect to the

W. H. S. Stanley, Esq.

26 May 1853.

boroughs in Hampshire?—I can speak particularly to the borough of Romsey, near to which I reside. I consider the police there, under the control of the corporation, to be quite inefficient; it consists merely of two men for day work and night work, and I think that is not at all efficient, being neither detective, nor does it prevent crime being committed; it has no supervision over the beerhouses, which are kept open, I may say, for nights and nights together without being closed.

273. Is that the case at all in the districts in which the county police exists? —No; I believe there a rigid supervision is exercised over all the public-houses and beershops The consequence of this want of supervision in the town of Romsey is, that the rogues, thieves, and vagabonds are driven from the rural districts into the borough of Romsey.

274. You mean that Romsey is a sort of Alsatia?—Quite so.

275. Sir *J. Trollope*.] You have a town police?—Yes; under the control of the watch committee of the corporation.

276. How many men are there?—Two, for both day and night work; so that if a man is ill, there is really but one.

277. What is the population of Romsey?—About 1,900.

278. *Chairman*.] Does any material inconvenience arise from the want of co-operation between the county and borough police in Hampshire, in your opinion?—I think so.

279. Will you state why you think so?—I think if Captain Harris, as the chief constable, had the power of control over the constables of the borough of Romsey, that the borough of Romsey would be in a different position from what it is now.

280. Do you know anything with regard to the borough of Andover?—I can state with regard to the borough of Andover, that since Captain Harris has had the control of it within the last two or three years, they have had three maiden quarter sessions, there being no prisoners for trial at all.

281. Mr. *Fitzroy*.] Can you tell the Committee anything of the condition of Hampshire as to crime before the introduction of the police?—The parish constables were very inefficient in the discharge of their duties; it could be hardly expected that they would be otherwise. A great number of them were labourers that were selected, and they had their own work to look after, and their own occupations, and any time that was devoted to constabulary purposes was so much loss to them unless they did detect a culprit, and then certain allowances were made.

282. Can you furnish any statistics as to crime in Hampshire before the introduction of the police, as compared with the state of things since that introduction?—No, I cannot do that; I had been only in the commission of the peace for a few years previous to the introduction of the police.

283. *Chairman*.] Do you think that the number of undetected offences has greatly decreased?—It has greatly decreased of late; about three per cent. in the last year, compared with the preceding year.

284. Mr. *Phillips*.] You stated, did you not, that there were two policemen in Romsey; do you know what they are paid? £.120 a year; about 60 *l*. a year each; they are locally connected with the place, and therefore are ineffective.

285. Mr. *Rich*.] The whole of the town of Romsey is not under the management of the borough?—Romsey consists of two districts, Romsey Infra and Romsey Extra; and it is only Romsey Infra that is within the borough. In the same town we have two distinct polices. Attempts have been made by some persons in the town of Romsey to consolidate the two forces, but the corporation do not like to give up their petty privileges, and combine with the county force; besides which (I believe it is not the case in Romsey alone, but in many boroughs) the brewers have great power; they possess the public-houses and supply the beerhouses, and they have great power with the corporation in preventing the amalgamation of the forces.

286. In the same way they would prevent any rigid enforcement as to the closing of the beerhouses at earlier hours?—It would be against their interest to do so.

287. If the police were under the control of the county, they would possess greater power, which the brewers would find it difficult to resist?—Yes.

288. *Chairman*.] Is the police force generally popular with the ratepayers of Hampshire?—I think it is; every amount of taxation is onerous to the ratepayers, however small it may be.

289. The

W. H. S. Stanley,
Esq.
———
26 May 1853.

289. The expense is a direct tax?—Yes.

290. Do not you think that the indirect savings are very great?—The indirect savings are great. I think the police rate is about 2¼ d. upon the old valuation. We are just entering upon a new valuation; and I think it will not come to more than 2¼ d., as we have increased the basis of the valuation.

291. Are you at all prepared to state what the expense was previous to the establishment of the police?—I cannot do that.

292. Can you give the Committee any notion of the cost of the parochial constabulary?—I think you might state the round numbers from 1,500 l. to 1,600 l. a year.

293. Sir *J. Trollope.*] Was there not a plan which was very prevalent, of having a private rate to pay the constabulary in the villages?—I do not know that there was such a plan in the county of Hants.

294. No instance of that kind has come to your knowledge?—There were associations for the prosecution of offenders, which are now saved, to which the farmers used to contribute.

295. Are those associations entirely given up?—I have heard of none lately.

296. *Chairman.*] Do you know of your own knowledge that they did exist before?—I know that they did exist before, and that is a saving.

297. Mr. *Fitzroy.*] Can you suggest to the Committee any improvements upon the present system, either in the decrease of expense, or the better arrangement of the force?—I think our force ought to be increased.

298. So far as the system is concerned, can you suggest any improvements or alterations?—Not in our own force; I think it is admirably conducted under Captain Harris.

299. Mr. *Mackie.*] Would you approve of a national police?—Yes, I should, decidedly so; I think that what is good for one county, would be good for all the counties in England.

300. Mr. *Fitzroy.*] By a national police, do you mean a force on the same principle, paid for in the same manner as that which you have at present?—When it comes to be a national force, it ought to be under the control of the Government, and the Government ought to contribute a portion of the expense.

301. What control do you propose to give to the Government?—I think that there ought to be some central control, like that which the Poor Law Commissioners at present have; the whole force should work systematically throughout the whole of the country. Of course the officers would be appointed by the Government.

302. Do you recommend that the appointment of the chief constable should rest with the Government, instead of the magistrates?—I have not considered that point.

303. Mr. *Rich.*] Is it your opinion that the compulsory enforcement of a system of police, similar to that which exists in Hampshire, would be generally beneficial?—I think so.

304. Do the counties which have it not prejudicially affect those which have it?—I think so.

305. Mr. *Phillips.*] Have you ever heard any complaints of petty and vexatious interference by the police in matters which it would be wiser for them to leave alone?—No, I never have; I always find the policemen ready to assist in every possible way, both in the detection and prevention of crime.

306. Mr. *Fitzroy.*] Do the constabulary take any part as to the preservation of game?—None.

307. Are they allowed to assist if their services are required?—If their services are called for, they would be allowed to assist, I have no doubt.

308. Mr. *Rich.*] With a view to the protection of life more than of game:—With a view to the preservation of the life of the gamekeepers.

309. Mr. *Mackie.*] Night-poaching is now a crime by statute law; do your constables consider it a part of their duty to assist in repressing a crime of that kind by apprehending night-poachers?—Certainly; if they see a man with a gun go into a wood at night, they will pursue him.

310. Then to a certain extent, they are employed in the preservation of game?—I mean they are not placed at the cover's side.

311. Mr. *Fitzroy.*] They have no directions to abstain from apprehending a

W. H. S. Stanley,
Esq.

26 May 1853.

person whom they see prepared to commit an offence against the game laws?
—No.

312. Sir *J. Anderson.*] Do you know how much the rate in the borough of Andover is in the pound?—I do not.

313. Mr. *Rich.*] On the whole, is there a kindly feeling entertained in Andover towards the police?—Yes, amongst the respectable classes of all ranks.

314. Do you know what the rate in the borough of Romsey is?—No; I have not been able to ascertain that. I do not know what it is in the pound.

315. Mr. *Phillips.*] What is the average of the county rate in Hampshire?—I can tell the Committee that by the return, but I cannot tell off-hand.

316. Sir *J. Anderson.*] Do not you think that it would diminish the efficiency of the police if the Government had the appointment of the superintendents or the head constables; would not that be considered an interference?—It would by the counties generally, especially if the Government were not to contribute to the expense. The magistrates in quarter sessions only appoint now the chief constable, and the chief constable makes all the other appointments in the police force (the magistrates do not interfere at all), and he is held responsible for the appointments. I think if the whole expense was to fall upon the Consolidated Fund, that the Government ought to have the appointment of all the officers.

317. Mr. *Rich.*] Has the nomination by the chief constable only worked thoroughly well in your county?—Yes.

318. Sir *J. Trollope.*] Has the appointment of the subordinates by the chief constable been satisfactory to the magistrates?—Very much so. I never heard a single complaint.

319. Mr. *Rich.*] Does the chief constable hold his appointment from year to year?—No, he is a permanent officer.

320. You mean permanent so long as he gives satisfaction?—Yes.

321. Sir *J. Trollope.*] In your opinion, has the present system worked well?—Very well.

322. Mr. *Phillips.*] Is there any anxiety on the part of the population to get employed in the police?—Yes, amongst the young men.

323. Amongst what class?—Farmer's and tradesmen's sons.

324. Sir *J. Trollope.*] Are the police taken from the labouring classes?—No, generally a degree higher than that.

325. What are the qualifications that they must possess?—They must be able to read and write, and they must have a certificate of good character from a clergyman and their neighbours.

326. Mr. *Fitzroy.*] Are the wages of policemen much higher than those given to agricultural labourers?—Yes, they are higher.

327. What is the rate of agricultural labourers' wages now in Hampshire?—It is 9 *s.* now; it has been raised 1 *s.* lately.

328. Sir *J. Trollope.*] The ordinary constables have 15 *s.* ?—Yes; I believe there are some slight stoppages to the Superannuation Fund.

329. Is there any stoppage for clothing?—I am not aware. Captain Harris could give the Committee better information upon that subject than I can.

330. Mr. *Phillips.*] Are the majority of the men in the Hampshire police Hampshire men, or are they men from different counties?—I believe the majority of them are Hampshire men.

331. Mr. *Burroughes.*] Can you tell the Committee how the expenditure is controlled; do the accounts go direct to the sessions, or what control is there over the expenditure?—The expenditure is brought before the court of quarter sessions regularly every quarter, and the accounts are audited by the finance committee.

332. Is there a general finance committee?—Yes.

333. Not a committee appointed specially to supervise the police accounts?—No.

334. Mr. *Phillips.*] The magistrates occasionally get applications from young men to be recommended as policemen, do they not?—Yes; and if a magistrate knows a young man to be a respectable person, he recommends him to Captain Harris.

Fielder King, Esq., called in ; and Examined.

F. King, Esq.

16 May 1853.

335. *Chairman.*] WHERE do you reside ?—At Buriton, near Petersfield, in Hampshire.

336. Are you a large occupier of land ?—I farm 2,500 acres in the counties of Hants and Sussex.

337. Do you think, as a large occupier of land, that you have derived much benefit in regard to the protection of your property from the establishment of the police in Hampshire ?—I derive much benefit from the establishment of the police in Hampshire in the protection of my property, and also in the better regulation of our villages and beershops.

338. In what species of property did you suffer losses most, previously to the establishment of the police ?—Sheep particularly.

339. Can you state to the Committee the number of sheep you lost before the establishment of the police, compared to the numbers which you have lost since ?—Since the establishment of the police I have lost none; before that my average used to be seven, or eight, or nine in a year.

340. Mr. *Phillips.*] How many years is it since you have lost any sheep ?— I think it is 10 years; some years I lost 10 or 12, but I think the average was about seven or eight.

341. *Chairman.*] In what other species of property did you suffer loss; did your fences suffer ?—In the fences, poultry, turnips, and so on ; farmers' property is liable to depredation from exposure.

342. Before the establishment of the police, was your loss great in the species of property which you have named ?—The heavy loss was particularly in sheep.

343. Have your losses in agricultural property decreased since the establishment of the police ?—Very materially.

344. In fact, do you think you save your rate ?—Yes, I think I save double my rate, if I take every kind of property into consideration.

345. Sir *J. Trollope.*] You speak of Hampshire only, I presume ?—I speak of Hampshire only.

346. You say that you occupy land in Sussex as well as in Hampshire ?— I do.

347. I believe there is no police in the western division ?—No, but the rate-payers of the parish are so convinced of the advantage of a police force, that they have established a private watchman for some years.

348. Are you as well protected by that system as you would be by the rural police under the Act of Parliament ?—No.

349. Do you consider that you still continue to lose property in Sussex to a greater extent than in Hampshire ?—Since we have established our private policeman, losses have diminished.

350. What is the area which that private policeman watches ?—Only one parish.

351. What is the extent of that parish in acres ?—I think about 3,000 acres.

352. Is that man on duty in the daytime only ?—Day and night, but then he is his own master ; there is no one to control him.

353. There is no regulation as to what duty he shall perform ?—No.

354. Is that a faulty system ?—Yes.

355. Is he responsible to any one ?— No.

356. Does anybody know when he goes out at night ?—No.

357. Mr. *Phillips.*] How many persons contribute to that private policeman ? —The whole of the ratepayers, by a voluntary rate.

358. What is your proportion ?—Mine is a small farm of about 300 acres ; 120 acres of this farm are in the adjoining parish, which has no constable. I think my rate would be about 3 *l.*

359. Do you know the difference between the voluntary rate in Sussex and the compulsory rate in Hampshire ?—No, I have made no comparison.

360. *Chairman.*] Besides this 3 *l.*, have you all the expenses to pay of the local constabulary ?—We save nothing, but we are so convinced of the advantage of a police force, that we have established a private policeman.

361. Mr. *Rich.*] Would you not willingly see that man displaced by the general police force for the county ?—Certainly.

362. Sir *J. Trollope.*] Is that the general feeling in the parish ?—Yes, as far as my knowledge extends.

F. King, Esq.

26 May 1853.

363. Mr. *Fitzroy*.] Have any other parishes adopted the same system?—Medhurst, I think, has. There are some small parishes which have not any police.

364. Have any representations been made by the ratepayers in West Sussex in favour of establishing a constabulary in that part of the county?—I am not aware of any.

365. Mr. *Phillips*.] At how much is your farm in Hampshire rated for the purpose of the county rate?—I am rated at about 1,000 *l.* a year, I think.

366. And how much for the Sussex property?—About 200 *l.* a year.

367. Mr. *Rich*.] Is your property in Sussex near Hampshire?—It is within three or four miles of the border.

368. To a certain extent, I presume, it has received benefit from its contiguity to a county that is under the police system?—We receive a benefit in this way, that the vagrants all go over from Hampshire into Sussex.

369. *Chairman*.] Can you speak, from your own knowledge, of the great decrease in vagrancy in Hampshire since the establishment of the police?—In Hampshire, particularly in my own neighbourhood, there has been a very great decrease; indeed we have no vagrants encamping in the lanes or in the commons in the county; but immediately over the borders, when you get into Sussex, we have a great number.

370. Sir *J. Trollope*.] Have those persons which encamp in Sussex carts, and horses and donkeys?—Yes.

371. Do they commit depredations?—Yes, in the way of breaking the fences and stealing the turnips.

372. Do they turn their cattle into the fields, or rob the haystacks at night?—Yes.

373. Mr. *Fitzroy*.] Did you suffer much from sheep stealing on your Sussex farm before you established a private watchman?—At that time I had no farm in Sussex.

374. *Chairman*.] Have you lost sheep within the last 10 years in Sussex?—I have.

375. Mr. *Fitzroy*.] From your knowledge of West Sussex, is sheep stealing a prevalent crime in that division of the county?—I do not think it is in my immediate neighbourhood.

376. What were the losses which you feared in your farm in Sussex which induced you and your neighbours to establish this system of a private watchman?—The depredations upon the fences, and the loss of turnips and poultry.

377. Is not it a thinly populated neighbourhood?—Not in Sussex.

378. Near what town are you?—The nearest town is Midhurst.

379. At Midhurst they have a voluntary system of police, the same as you have in your parish?—They have.

380. Is there in any part of Western Sussex what is called the parish constable system?—I think all the parishes have it.

381. Is that under any superintendence?—No, not of the police.

382. Mr. *Rich*.] Have you any incendiary fires in Hampshire?—We have had none for several years past.

383. Do you recollect Hampshire at the time of the burnings?—Yes, I do; we had two or three incendiary fires at that time, but we have not had any since.

384. Nor in Sussex?—Nor in Sussex.

385. Mr. *Phillips*.] You do not know exactly what you pay for this voluntary rate in Sussex?—No.

386. You said that you paid about 3 *l.*—About 3 *l.*

387. Sir *J. Trollope*.] How long has that voluntary rate existed?—I think for the last seven or eight years.

388. Does the whole of the parish pay *pari passu*?—Yes, according to the rate.

389. Have you any opponents to the voluntary rate?—No.

390. Are there some who pay and some who do not pay?—Perhaps a beer-shop-keeper is rather opposed to a rate of this kind.

391. Mr. *Fitzroy*.] Has the question of the rural constabulary ever been mooted in the western division of Sussex?—Yes.

392. When did that take place?—Some few years ago, but the Lord Lieutenant was very much opposed to the establishment of police.

393. Is

F. King, Esq.

26 May 1853.

393. Is he still opposed to it ?—I do not know.

394. Do you think, but for a feeling of deference which was paid to the wishes of the Lord Lieutenant, that the rural police would have been established before now in western Sussex ?—I really think it would.

395. Mr. *Rich.*] Would the establishment of police be popular with the farmers ?—Yes, in my own neighbourhood ; I have asked the question of a great many of my neighbours, if they wished to see the police done away with, and their opinion is, that the police is of the greatest possible benefit.

396. From knowing the opinions of those persons in Sussex, with whom you are acquainted, do you think the establishment of a police in Sussex, similar to that in Hampshire, would be popular ?—I am quite sure that that is the feeling of my own parish.

397. *Chairman.*] You say the police is popular with the occupiers of land ; is that growing feeling the result of experience ?—I think so, decidedly.

398. Sir *J. Trollope.*] Has any step been taken to ascertain the feeling of the people in Sussex, beyond that of the Lord Lieutenant ?—I am not aware.

399. Did not the magistracy decide not to introduce the Act ?—I cannot answer that question.

400. *Chairman.*] Has the parish in Hampshire in which you reside become more orderly ?—Certainly, particularly on the Sunday.

401. Mr. *Walpole.*] In Sussex, since you have had a watchman who is paid by the voluntary rate, which you have mentioned, has any difference taken place in the parish with reference to plundering or with reference to the beershops ? —I am not prepared to answer that question, being only occasionally there.

402. *Chairman.*] In Hampshire, where you do reside, you say you have observed a great difference as to the public-houses and beerhouses being better regulated ?—I speak for my own parish. I see a great improvement in the parish on the Sunday ; if our constable is away on duty, we see a change in the order of the village.

403. Mr. *Fitzroy.*] Has the person whom you have appointed and paid by the voluntary rate in your parish, any power to inspect public-houses or enter beershops ?—Yes, he does inspect the beershops and public-houses.

404. How has he the power to do so ?—He is sworn in as a parish constable.

405. Sir *J. Trollope.*] Do you clothe him as a policeman ?—We do not.

406. *Chairman.*] Have you heard of any cases of burglaries or highway robberies in Hampshire recently ?—Not in my own division.

407. Were there cases to your knowledge before the establishment of the police ?—Yes, there were.

408. Do you reside on the borders of the county ?—Yes.

409. Do you hear of any offences of that sort being committed ?—Two or three years ago we had several cases of burglary in the adjoining county.

410. Mr. *Rich.*] Were those cases of night burglary ?—Yes.

411. Have you had instances in Sussex of cottages being plundered during the absence of the labourers in the day, whilst they have been working in the field ?—Not latterly.

412. In neither Hampshire nor Sussex ?—No ; it used to be of frequent occurrence in both counties, particularly in the summer months.

413. Previously to the establishment of the police ?—Yes.

414. Sir *J. Trollope.*] Are the farm houses in that part of Sussex and Hampshire isolated, and scattered singly about the country ?—Not so much so as in the parish in which I reside.

415. Before the introduction of the police, were you annoyed by vagrants when all the servants were away, by their alarming the females in the house and obtaining alms from fear rather than from charity ?—Constantly.

416. Has that nearly subsided ?—I do not recollect a case for some time past.

417. Was it of frequent occurrence formerly ?—Yes.

418. Mr. *Phillips.*] In round numbers, your farm in Sussex is about a third of the value of your farm in Hampshire ?—About that.

419. Mr. *Rich.*] You pay double for your bad watching in Sussex that you pay for your good watching in Hampshire ?—Yes.

420. *Chairman.*] Do you pay more for your watchmen in Sussex, in proportion to your rate, than you do in Hampshire for your police ?—Yes, much more.

Mr. *Henry Thompson*, called in; and Examined.

Mr. H. Thompson.

26 May 1853.

421. *Chairman.*] YOU are the Mayor of Andover?—I am.

422. Have you ever held that office prior to the present period?—I have, in 1843–44.

423. Previously to the establishment of the police?—Yes.

424. In Hampshire?—In Andover, in Hampshire.

425. It was established in 1841, in the county, was it not?—I think it was, or thereabouts.

426. Is the police of Andover consolidated with the county?—It is.

427. When did that consolidation take place?—In the year 1846.

428. Can you describe the state of the town of Andover as to crime previously to the establishment of the police?—I can give you some description as to the state of the town when I first held office; I found that there was a great amount of petty theft, very few cases of which were detected; that a great portion of the poorer population was very much demoralized; they had little or no idea of moral responsibility; the controul of the town, therefore, was in a very inefficient state; the means for detecting offences and keeping the peace were quite inefficient.

429. In consequence of that state of things, did you advocate the establishment of the police, and the consolidation with the county?—I did, strongly; as soon as my term of office was over, I had been led to notice the good effects of the system of police adopted by the county; and having seen the sad state of things in our own town, I was anxious that the benefits derived in the county should be participated in by us, and I used every endeavour with my fellow townsmen to induce them to adopt the measure.

430. Did you succeed in your endeavour?—I did at last.

431. Was there much opposition?—Opposition arose from many of the respectable inhabitants having a jealous feeling of the rights of the borough being interfered with, and a great dread of the amount of expense.

432. Do you think that that feeling still exists?—I do not think it is quite obliterated; but I am satisfied that the very persons who objected to the police at that time, if by any possibility the establishment of the police could be rescinded, would oppose the measure entirely. The gentlemen who voted in the town council against the police at the time of its establishment would now support its being maintained.

433. You think experience has made them converts?—Yes.

434. Before that time you had had no police at all?—We had a beadle and a paid constable; but they were very inefficient indeed, and there was no one to control them.

435. Mr. *Walpole.*] What force have you in Andover now?—Four constables and a sergeant, and the addition of a superintendent, Andover being the local depôt for the county.

436. *Chairman.*] In point of expense, is your expense greater now than it was before the consolidation of the borough with the county?—No doubt; but then the benefit is concomitant.

437. Do you think the benefits are equal to the additional expense?—More than equal.

438. Mr. *Fitzroy.*] Is there any arrangement made as to the proportion you are to pay?—We pay 65 *l.* per man; it is a charge of 360 *l.* a year upon us.

439. Do you pay that out of the borough rate?—Out of the borough rate.

440. *Chairman.*] Are there any complaints on the part of the ratepayers as to that borough rate?—They were very jealous as to its being imposed upon them at first; but I think no ratepayer would vote for the police being abolished; no respectable man would wish to see the police done away with.

441. Mr. *Walpole.*] Has the question been brought before the town council? —No.

442. As a matter of fact, the question never has been mooted?—No.

443. Sir *J. Anderson.*] What is the rate in the borough per pound?—Sixpence in the pound for the year is the amount of cost of police.

444. Mr. *Phillips.*] Do you know what the actual expense of the police of Andover was before the adoption of the present system?—About 75 *l.* was paid

to

Mr. *H. Thompson.*

26 May 1853.

to the constables; and there were other charges which did not come under the amount paid to the constable.

445. *Chairman* (to Captain *Harris*).] Do you know what it is in other boroughs?—No, I do not.

446. Do you know what it is in Lymington?—I do not. (*Witness.*) The cost of the police is mixed up with other payments, but when it is deducted the police charge has been 6 *d.* in the pound. I think the better way would be to say that, whereas it might have cost 100 *l.* a year formerly, it now costs 350 *l.*

447. Sir *J. Trollope.*] Was the former police good for anything?—Not one farthing. I am bound to say that I think we save money.

448. *Chairman.*] Do you think the property saved is equal to the additional 250 *l.*?—I am satisfied that, in comfort to the inhabitants and the property saved, it far exceeds the difference of the amount paid to the police.

449. Can you give the Committee an idea of the number of offences committed prior to and since the establishment of the police?—I have here a statement of the number of cases convicted before the magistrates in petty sessions, and committals for trial.

450. When did you adopt the police?—In 1846.

[*The Witness delivered in the same, which is as follows :*]

CASES Convicted before Magistrates in Petty Sessions, and Committals for Trial :

1843	-	-	-	-	-	- 48	1848	-	-	-	- 33
1844	-	-	-	-	-	- 78	1849	-	-	-	- 62
1845	-	-	-	-	-	- 67	1850	-	-	-	- 41
1846 {5 months' old constables 23 / 7 months' police - - 18}						41	1851	-	-	-	- 41
							1852	-	-	-	- 14
1847	-	-	-	-	-	- 65	1853	-	-	- half-year	16

Witness.] The Committee will observe, that there is a relative increase and decrease after the adoption of the police, for this reason; they found the cases out, and they have been decreasing regularly ever since.

451. Mr. *Fitzroy.*] Can you give the Committee any reason for the extraordinary diminution in the last year, as compared to any other year?—Although the police has had a good effect in the town, I find that last year was a cheap year, and a cheap year is a year in which we have less crime.

452. Was last year cheaper than the present year?—Yes.

453. Mr. *Walpole.*] Was last year a year of full employment?—Yes.

454. That return would not lead the Committee to suppose that the decrease in crime is entirely in consequence of the establishment of the police?—No, certainly not; it has relatively had a good effect.

455. *Chairman.*] That return does not give the number of cases brought before the magistrates and dismissed?—No, there are very few discharged. The numbers that escaped prior to the establishment of the police were very enormous.

456. Mr. *Phillips.*] At what time were the railway works carried on in Andover?—I think 1849.

457. Will you give the number of cases in 1849?—Sixty-two; in 1848 it was 33, in 1850 it was 41, and in 1849 it was 62.

458. Sir *J. Trollope.*] The railway works ceased in that year?—I think they did.

459. And then they were resumed in a few months?—Yes.

460. *Chairman.*] Has the business at your sessions declined?—We have had five maiden sessions, and only one committal to assizes; that was a post-office robbery; we have now one prisoner for trial at the sessions, and only one at the assizes; but we have had five consecutive sessions without a prisoner. There is another return which I should like to place before the Committee, which is a return of the cost of crime from the year 1841 to 1852; the expenses of sessions, prosecutions, maintenance of prisoners at Andover, conveying prisoners to Winchester, maintenance of prisoners at Winchester; in 1841 it was 251 *l.* 6 *s.* 6 *d.*; in 1842, 114 *l.* 6 *s.* 1 *d.*; in 1843, 164 *l.* 2 *s.* 3 *d.*; in 1844, 210 *l.* 1 *s.* 1 *d.*; in 1845, 209 *l.* 6 *s.* 11 *d.*; and in 1846 it was 132 *l.* 0 *s.* 4 *d.*; then the new police came into operation, and you will observe that immediately

Mr. *H. Thompson.*
————
26 May 1853.

the cost increased. In 1847 it was 211 *l.* 2 *s.*; in 1848, 213 *l.* 16 *s.*; in 1849, 297 *l.* 1 *s.* 1 *d.*; in 1850, 172 *l.* 19 *s.* 6 *d.*; in 1851, 123 *l.* 11 *s.* 1 *d.*; and in 1852, it was 112 *l.* 8 *s.* 5 *d.*

[*The Witness delivered in the following Statement:*]

	1841.			1842.			1843.			1844.			1845.			1846.		
	£.	s.	d.	£.	s.	d.	£.	s.	d.	£.	s.	d.	£.	s.	d.	£.	s.	d.
Expenses of Sessions -	18	14	7	17	2	1	37	10	6	25	2	6	19	19	6	23	19	6
Prosecutions - -	84	17	4	17	10	–	23	18	–	79	13	–	44	1	8	37	18	–
Maintenance of Prisoners at Andover - -	17	15	10	20	6	6	17	10	–	27	5	9	33	8	10	9	16	1
Conveying Prisoners to Winchester - -	6	7	–	9	9	–	5	15	–	10	7	–	15	11	6	8	9	–
Maintenance of Prisoners at Winchester - -	123	11	9	49	18	6	79	8	9	67	12	10	94	5	5	51	17	9
£.	251	6	6	114	6	1	164	2	3	210	1	1	209	6	11	132	–	4

	1847.			1848.			1849.			1850.			1851.			1852.		
	£.	s.	d.	£.	s.	d.	£.	s.	d.	£.	s.	d.	£.	s.	d.	£.	s.	d.
Expenses of Sessions -	17	5	10	33	12	4	22	19	–	23	5	5	28	4	7	12	19	10
Prosecutions - -	56	3	1	44	16	–	47	8	–	12	12	6	18	5	4	17	4	5
Maintenance of Prisoners at Andover - -	16	10	4	15	7	7	56	2	5	15	3	11	15	3	–	12	12	4
Conveying Prisoners to Winchester - -	6	18	11	25	2	9	35	13	9	13	–	6	11	6	11	7	17	8
Maintenance of Prisoners at Winchester - -	114	3	10	94	17	4	134	17	11	108	17	2	50	11	3	61	9	7
£.	211	2	–	313	16	–	297	1	1	172	19	6	123	11	1	112	3	5

461. That return corresponds with the return which you gave before, showing that immediately after the establishment of the police the expenses for a period increased, and then rapidly decreased to the present time?—Yes, they have regularly decreased.

462. Mr. *Mackie.*] What is the population of Andover?—Five thousand.

463. Mr. *Rich.*] Have the bad characters left the town?—Yes; they are kept in control, and they go elsewhere, those that have not been convicted; we have had some heavy prosecutions; we have got rid of several bad characters who had always evaded justice.

464. Now they have quitted the town?—Yes.

465. Mr. *Burroughes.*] Some of them were transported, I suppose?—Yes.

466. *Chairman.*] Are you an occupier of land?—To a small extent.

467. Do you consider that as many depredations have been committed on your property recently as before the establishment of the police?—I am a merchant, and I felt it more in that respect than in my farming proceedings; I used to leave small matters about upon the premises in the hope of saving the loss of larger ones: we had no means of controlling and detecting them; it was impossible, unless I had kept a watch.

468. Sir *J. Anderson.*] Is this 6 *d.* in the pound upon the gross rental of the borough?—Not upon the gross rental, I think it is upon two-thirds of the house property.

469. Is not that more than the rating in the county?—I do not know exactly; the rating upon land is generally to the full amount; the rating upon house property is generally two-thirds, I believe.

470. Mr. *Rich.*] Would not the rate be lower than 6 *d.* in the county?—Yes, considerably lower than in boroughs.

471. Sir *J. Anderson.*] Do you think the difference in the rate is the reason why the boroughs object to the amalgamation of the police?—I do not know that that reason operated in our own case; the objection was more from a jealousy of the rights of the town being interfered with than a dislike to join with the county; now they have felt the good effect of it, the whole of that feeling has worn

worn off; ro really respectable inhabitant of the town would wish to see the division again.

Mr. H. Thompson.

26 May 1853.

472. Mr. *Walpole.*] From what source are those accounts taken?—From the book of the treasurer of the borough.

473. *Chairman.*] You said that you had great losses in your property; have those losses ceased?—Yes; directly I find I have any loss, I give notice to the police, and it is generally corrected immediately. We have no small offences comparatively to what we had; the state of the town is now agreeable and pleasant, whereas formerly it was very disreputable.

474. Mr. *Phillips.*] Do you ever hear any complaints of vexatious interference or over zeal on the part of the police?—On the contrary, I have found very great attention whenever I have required the police to attend to anything.

475. Are not the men shifted constantly?—Yes, they are; and I think it is an excellent plan in a town with such a population as ours, or they would get into habits and connections which would render it very undesirable that they should remain. I think one of the great points in the effectiveness of the police is that they are changed.

476. Sir *J. Trollope.*] Within your borough do the police execute all processes, and serve summonses?—Yes.

477. Do they attend upon the petty sessions?—Yes.

478. Mr. *Fitzroy.*] Do they serve the notices for coroners' inquests?—Yes.

479. Sir *J. Trollope.*] Have you any saving to set against the expenses of the police beyond the pay of the persons whose services you formerly had?—The abovenamed expenses must be saved in reality.

480. Have you made a per contra account, to show what the gain or what the loss is?—No, I have not.

481. Do you think it is anything considerable?—I can hardly answer that question.

482. Have you any officers called town serjeants or town mace-men?—We have; they are wearing out.

483. You permit them to die off?—Yes.

484. You do not intend to fill up the vacancies?—We have not done so.

485. Then there will be a further saving to set off against the expense of the police?—Yes.

486. *Chairman.*] You think there has been a great saving of property?—I should say double the expense. If any one were to say to the people of Andover, "Will you pay double for the police, or will you do without it," I think they would say they would pay double; I would.

487. Mr. *Fitzroy.*] Is there a great difference in the public-houses and beer-shops?—Very much so. If a complaint is made (which is seldom), a caution not to renew the offence has had the desired effect.

488. Do you believe, from the inspection which goes on, that a complaint would be made by the police if there were any irregularity on the part of beer-shop keepers or publicans?—I am satisfied of that; we had one or two complaints in the country, and a caution has acted efficiently.

489. Mr. *Phillips.*] Is there a coroner at Andover?—Yes.

490. Is he the local coroner?—The town-clerk holds the office of coroner.

491. Mr. *Fitzroy.*] Have you any lodging-houses licensed under the Act?—We have not.

492. You have none registered under the Common Lodging-house Act?—There are two or three lodging-houses, and we inspect them.

493. Under the regulations of the Lodging-house Act?—We have not brought the Lodging-house Act into force; in short, it is not necessary for Andover.

494. Sir *J. Trollope.*] Have not you a tramps' lodging-house at Andover?—No; to a great extent the tramping has ceased.

495. That class of people do not come to Andover?—Not by any means so much as formerly.

496. Mr. *Fitzroy.*] Do the police inspect the lodging-houses?—Yes.

497. Mr. *Rich.*] To what do you attribute the cessation of tramping?—I think they find there is a better control in the town; that the town is kept in better order, and they do not find it answer their purpose to come there.

498. Can you give the Committee a debtor and creditor statement of the cost and of the saving with regard to the police which has been established?—I do not think I could exactly do that; the cost of the police is so much mixed

Mr. *H. Thompson.*

26 May 1853.

up with one thing and another, that it would not be a fair account. I would rather state it from having watched the thing myself, from having lived all my life in the town of Andover, and been somewhat observant.

499. With regard to the 6 *d.* in the pound, is that upon a rating of two-thirds of the value?—The greater part of the property in the town is house property, which is rated upon two-thirds of the value.

500. In comparison with the 2 ¼ *d.* in the county, it is not so high?—Certainly it is not so high.

John Reynolds Beddome, Esq., M. D.; Examined.

J. R. Beddome,
Esq., M.D.

501. *Chairman.*] Do you reside in Romsey?—Yes; I have resided there upwards of 40 years.

502. Do you hold any official situation in Romsey?—I am one of the two senior aldermen; I have held the office of mayor four times, and I am permanent justice of the peace.

503. Is there a separate jurisdiction in Romsey?—We have no sessions at present; we had under the old Municipal Act. We petitioned not to have any sessions, because it would involve a great additional expense.

504. What is the condition of the police at Romsey?—For the purposes of the prevention and detection of crime, it is anything but satisfactory. In the year 1845, at the request of many of the most respectable ratepayers of the town, I brought the subject before the town council; but it was summarily rejected, upon the plea that no application had been made from the ratepayers, and the matter then remained quiescent for some years. Being aware of the importance of the subject, I have continually urged some of the most respectable inhabitants to memorialise the town council. Last year, when I was in the office of mayor, a memorial was sent to me, headed by Lord Palmerston, who is resident amongst us, and signed by the vicar and many of the respectable inhabitants of the town, requesting the town council to amalgamate the borough police force with the county. Another counter memorial was at the same time put into my hands, which I also brought before the town council, signed by a party of the smaller ratepayers, and by nine beerhouse-keepers, and two or three publicans. One of the beerhouse-keepers, to my knowledge, has said, that if the county police was in the town, he should be had up every day of his life. I brought these memorials before the town council, and myself urged the council to amalgamate with the county. A great deal of discussion took place upon the subject. The present mayor of Romsey moved a resolution, that it was neither expedient nor desirable to amalgamate the borough force with the county, and that resolution was carried by a majority of five. But the agitation of the question did a great deal of good, for the watch committee, under the recommendation of the town council, determined to do away with all the old police force, and to have one day constable, and one night constable; and they paid our efficient chief constable, Captain Harris, the compliment of saying, that they should like to have two men whom he had educated as policemen; and accordingly we had two, one of whom resigned his place in the county force, in order to come into the borough, and the other I believe was requested to resign. I think there was something of that kind, and those are the only two officers we have now.

505. Do you find them efficient for the protection of the property in the borough?—Not at all; the protection of property in the borough is most unsatisfactory; we have but one officer by day, and one by night. Whenever either of those officers is ill, which happened to the day constable for several weeks this last year, we have no protection, and but one man to do day and night duty. If either of our officers takes a prisoner to Winchester, the town is left the whole day; or if a coroner's inquest is to be summoned, he is away the whole of the day, and the town is left. The protection of the town with those two officers is, in my opinion, most unsatisfactory; it is so considered by the respectable inhabitants. I have nothing to allege against the men themselves, but the system appears to be wrong. Those men are always the same; they get acquaintances in the town; and there has not been a single instance for six years of a beershop-keeper being summoned before the magistrates, though many of those houses are most irregular; one of them is a common brothel; and I was urged last year, when mayor, to take every step I could to put it down, but I could get nobody to inform. I desired our own constables to

inform,

J. R. Beddome,
Esq., M. D.

26 May 1853.

inform, but they said they could not. Nothing has been done, and the house is open to this time. It was said to me only a few days since, without the parties knowing that I was to appear before this Committee, " If, sir, you had carried the measure about the county police, and had only put down that house, it would have been a blessing to the place." One of our publicans in October came up for his licence, but as we had very good information that the house was an irregular one, and that he had been repeatedly fined or warned, we refused to give him his licence; he bade us defiance, and he said he would immediately get a beerhouse licence, which he did. He is the only beerhouse-keeper who has been summoned before me for the last six years. He was summoned last Thursday; and it was proved that the constable had demanded admittance at 11 o'clock at night, and he hesitated so long in giving him admittance, that there was no doubt, and it has since been proved, that a person escaped at the back door. The mayor fined him 20 s. On Monday morning I said to one of the neighbours, " How is that man going on?" and he said, " Worse than ever, sir; you did not fine him half enough; the house is quite as irregular as it has ever been."

506. Mr. *Fitzroy*.] You spoke of discharging all your former police; of what did they consist?—The old police was formed under the paving commissioners; there was a clause in the Paving Act allowing us to watch and light the town, but it was worse at night than anything that has occurred since. There were four watchmen who, as far as my recollection goes, were appointed, not for their efficiency, but for their being willing to watch for 1 s. 6 d. a night. They were men who had been hard at work all day. I myself, being professionally out in the night, have seen them asleep under the gateways: they were of no use. About 17 years since, I had seen so much of the evil resulting from the unprotected state of the town, that I went myself to the parish vestry, to urge upon the vestry to appoint a town beadle. There appeared to be a good deal of difficulty in it, but it was agreed that the parish should pay a man 7 s. 6 d. a week to get rid of the vagrants, and the pavement commissioners should give him 7 s. 6 d. to be also the inspector of the pavement, and I was to swear him in so as to make him a day officer; but he turned out such an intemperate man, that he was of no use whatever. I think it has been remarked by Mr. Stanley, in his evidence, that the thieves congregate in our borough. That is very much the case; they are driven out of the rural districts and reside in the borough, and then sally out at night.

507. What do you pay to your two constables?—The one is paid 18 s., I think, and the other 16 s., a week.

508. Out of what fund are those men paid?—From the borough rate; there is 30 l. a quarter for the payment of those men and a few incidental expenses.

509. Who has the appointment of the men?—The watch committee.

510. If representations are made to the watch committee of the inefficiency of those men, will they take steps to remove them, or require them to do their duty?—The difficulty has been, that the watch committee say you must prove it; there is no evidence of their inefficiency, and the difficulty with us has been the opposition to the county police, and the unwillingness on the part of certain persons to find anything against our police, for fear we should get the county police amalgamated with ours. A large proportion of the respectable inhabitants now are in favour of the amalgamation between the borough and the county police.

511. Supposing the police to be as inefficient as you represent, is it not in the power of the respectable inhabitants to inform the watch committee of their inefficiency?—It is in their power; I have informed the watch committee, and they have said, " You are only able to give information from current opinion." I am not satisfied with our watch committee. The mayor of the town is *ex officio* the chairman of the watch committee, but the whole time I was mayor, I was not called to one single committee meeting.

512. Are there any brewers in Romsey?—Yes.

513. Are they members of the watch committee?—One of the brewers is the managing secretary.

514. Does he appoint the police?—My own idea is, that the secretary is the acting man; for when I complained to him that I, as mayor, had not been summoned to a single meeting of the watch committee, his reply was, " Why, really, we are so unaccustomed to have a chairman, that I did not think of it."

J. R. Beddome.
Esq., M. D.

26 May 1853.

515. In fact, it would be against the interest of the gentleman who manages the watch committee if any information were laid against the beerhouses?—I do not know whether he supplies the beerhouses or not; I have heard that he does; but it has been stated that our police are unwilling to inform against the beerhouses for fear of offending the watch committee.

516. Therefore, for all useful purposes, the borough of Romsey is totally devoid of police?—It is devoid of an efficient police.

517. *Chairman* (to Captain *Harris*).] What number of policemen would be required at Romsey if the borough were incorporated with the county?—Three at the most.

518. The expense, if they were incorporated, would not be more than a third in addition to the present expense?—Certainly not.—(*Witness.*) Our police costs about 120*l.* a year; then there is the average of nine guineas a year for taking prisoners to Winchester, and three guineas a year for serving summonses; the two latter would be saved if we had the county police. I should state that the borough of Romsey is only one-third of the town; two-thirds are out of the boundary of the borough; and in that part of the town which is not in our jurisdiction there is a most efficient station of the county constabulary, and an active, energetic superintendent and officers.

519. Is it your opinion that the establishment of police would be more efficient for the prevention of crime in Romsey if it were united with the county constabulary?—Most decidedly.

520. Do you think that with a cost of one-third more the saving of property would be more than a compensation?—Yes.

521. Mr. *Phillips.*] Do you know how much the police rate in the pound would be?—I do not know how much our rates are in the pound, they vary so much; our borough rate is uniform.

522. How much is that?—£.30 a quarter; that is, for the police; we do not employ the borough rate in lighting at all; it is only in watching. My argument with the town council was that our police was totally inefficient, and, as an individual, I would rather pay twice what I did, to have an efficient force. The state of our police is a serious injury to the trade of the town; ladies of rank in the neighbourhood have told me that they are unwilling to come in and deal in the town, and have almost determined to abandon Romsey to its fate, because our police is so bad; they are infested with beggars.

523. Do you think Romsey is infested with vagrants to a great extent?—Very much. Attempts have been made within the last month to build a new town hall, and applications were made to the gentry to assist, but they said it could not be expected that they would assist the town of Romsey when it was so notoriously defective in its police arrangements. I think it is essential for us to have the county force.

Veneris, 27° die Maii, 1853.

MEMBERS PRESENT.

Mr. Rice.	Sir John Trollope.
Mr. Mackie.	Mr. Burroughes.
Sir James Anderson.	Lord Lovaine.
Mr. Sotheron.	Mr. Howard.
Mr. Rich.	Mr. Phillips.
Mr. Walpole.	

EDWARD ROYDS RICE, Esq., IN THE CHAIR.

Mr. *Andrew Robert Fennick*, called in; and Examined.

Mr. A. R. Fennick.

27 May 1853.

524. *Chairman.*] WHERE do you reside?—At Netherton, in Northumberland.

525. Are you a large occupier of land?—I am; I may also state that I am a visiting magistrate of Northumberland.

526. Will you state to the Committee what the nature of your police is?—We
have

have a riding police, the persons in which are allowed 100 *l.* a year, and out of that they are obliged to keep a horse.

Mr. *A. B. Fenwick.*

27 May 1853.

527. What number have you in the county?—Twelve.

528. Do they extend over the whole county?—They extend over the whole county.

529. What area has each of those men to superintend?—There is one man to each petty sessional division; there are 12 petty sessional divisions in Northumberland.

530. Is that under the Parish Constables' Act?—Yes.

531. Mr. *Phillips.*] Have you lock-up houses?—Yes.

532. *Chairman.*] Do you find your police force efficient in Northumberland? —Very much so; we have no complaints; they have no fees.

533. Do you mean that they have no fees for the apprehension of offenders?— They have no more than the common expenses, and we scarcely allow them to keep the lock-up house.

534. Is the lock-up house under the direction of another constable?—It is, generally.

535. Under the same Act?—Yes; we have not had a single complaint about the men from the farmers, or people in towns, or anybody, so far. I think it would be an improvement if there were one superintendent over the 12.

536. Are you aware that that is proposed in a Bill which is now before Parliament?—No, I am not aware; I should also recommend that they should report occasionally.

537. Sir *J. Trollope.*] Do your men make any reports at present?—They report once a month at the petty sessions what has taken place during that time; they are mostly old policemen taken from the different police forces.

538. Mr. *Howard.*] Do you find any jealousy existing between your police and the police in large towns?—Not the slightest; we have had no complaint whatever.

539. Sir *J. Trollope.*] Do your men find their own horses?—They find everything; they are allowed no uniform.

540. Mr. *Sotheron.*] What has been the result with regard to the diminution in offences?—I was not aware that I was to be called, and therefore I am not prepared to answer that question. I can only state, that I was in the prison at Morpeth the other day, where the prisoners generally average about 100, and there were only 60 or 70.

541. *Chairman.*] Is the number of prisoners less than it was?—Indeed I never knew it so low.

542. Mr. *Sotheron.*] Is it your impression, and that of your brother magistrates, that since the establishment of this police force, of which you are speaking, the offences have been more detected, and the number of offenders is diminished? —I only speak for myself; but I think the offences are more detected.

543. Mr. *Phillips.*] Are these men appointed in quarter session?—About three years ago, since the vote of the whole of the magistrates, this situation was advertised, and then there were arrangements made to give one man to each petty sessional division, one to Morpeth, one to Alnwick, and one to Belford, and so on; the men were all examined by the magistrates who attended locally to those places.

544. Do they receive their appointment from the court of quarter sessions?— Yes.

545. How are they selected?—There were about 20 or 30 men came; of course each petty sessional division recommended one person, and they were all selected by a very large meeting. I must say that I do not know a single exception to their acting remarkably well: most of the men were recommended from the police at Newcastle, and other different places.

546. Mr. *Sotheron.*] What authority do they exercise over the other constables, if they exercise any?—You can scarcely say that they do exercise any; they are sent to give notice to the parish constables that they are to attend; we had some disturbance last year where I live; we summoned them all, and they were sworn in as special constables; but we think the parish constables are a very inefficient body of men.

547. Have those constables any men under them?—None.

Mr. *A. R. Fennick.*

27 May 1853.

548. In case more force is wanted than one constable, to whom have they the power of applying for assistance?—They would first apply to the parish constables, and then they would apply to the magistrates to swear in special constables.

549. For the ordinary purpose of looking after offenders, have they any assistance whatever?—None whatever, without there is any serious case, and then they can apply to the magistrate in another division, and if there is a clever intelligent person, that person is sent; in an important case we send two or three to look after it. There was a large fire took place not long ago, and the person who resides in one of the petty sessional divisions was sent 30 miles off.

550. What is the nature of their duty; is it the ordinary duty of common constables?—Their duties are to attend in the morning and go round the district, as much as possible, to see if there is anybody at any particular point.

551. *Chairman.*] What is the extent of a district?—Some of the districts are about 20 or 30 miles.

552. Do you mean 20 or 30 miles across?—Twenty miles one way and 15 another; there is a district close to me that is not more than five or six miles one way and three or four in another; in that district there is more to do, from the works which are there.

553. Mr. *Sotheron.*] Is it part of their duty to serve summonses?—Of all kinds.

554. Do they serve all the warrants and all the summonses which are issued by the magistrates in their respective places?—Very generally.

555. Therefore they perform the whole of the duty of constables?—Some of the parish constables and other constables sworn in are more active than others, and they get a little business to do.

556. Sir *J. Trollope.*] Is there any high constable or chief constable?—No; they are all upon a level.

557. Had you any chief constable before this force was established?—No.

558. By whom are the precepts served?—By the high constable.

559. Then you had a chief constable?—We had a party to serve the precepts.

560. Was he paid by salary or by fees?—By a very small salary or fee.

561. Was not that some expense to the county?—I do not know I am sure; I should think it was very small; the parish constables only serve once in their lifetime, in one neighbourhood, and they are very unwilling to serve.

562. Mr. *Phillips.*] Have any vacancies occurred in your force?—I think there was one.

563. Was the man discharged?—I do not recollect now.

564. Mr. *Sotheron.*] Is it part of the duty of these constables to take charge of the prisoners, to remove them either from the place of examination to the gaol, or from one gaol to another?—Certainly.

565. They do the whole of that duty?—Sometimes, and other duty too. There is one thing I should mention to the Committee, that our men are not allowed to do anything with game; that was particularly laid down at the time of their appointment.

566. Do you mean by their not being allowed to do anything with game, that they have nothing to do with the apprehending or taking before a magistrate a person who had committed an offence under the Game Laws?—Certainly; it was supposed at the time that gentlemen might get them out to assist the keepers, and it was specially provided that they were not to do it. If they see a man committing a breach of the peace, it is their duty to apprehend him, but it was particularly taken care of, at the time they were appointed, that they were not to do anything in the preservation of game.

567. Mr. *Mackie.*] Did you say that there were only 12 policemen for the whole of the county of Northumberland?—Twelve riding policemen.

568. How many others?—I do not know; the Board of Health in the different towns have the appointment of the police.

569. You only speak of the county police?—Yes; the other men are paid by the towns; and then there are parish constables still; every township in Northumberland has a parish constable.

570. Mr.

Mr. *A. R. Fennick.*

27 May 1853.

570. Mr. *Sotheron.*] So far as a paid constabulary is concerned for the county of Northumberland, you have only these 12 men?—We have only one attached to each petty session division.

571. *Chairman.*] Are you aware that the magistrates of the county of Northumberland have applied sometimes to the police authorities at Newcastle for assistance?—I am almost certain they have on one or two occasions; they applied at the election last year at Hexham.

Sir *Robert Sheffield*, Bart., called in; and Examined.

Sir R. Sheffield, Bart.

572. Sir *J. Trollope.*] You reside in the county of Lincoln?—I do.

573. Are you the Chairman of the Court of Quarter Sessions of the parts of Lindsey at Kirton?—Yes.

574-5. Have you been long in that office?—I have been chairman at Kirton in the parts of Lindsey many years, about 25.

576. What is the acreage of the parts of Lindsey?—A million acres or thereabouts; but perhaps you will allow me to state, first of all, the mode in which the business of the court of quarter sessions is conducted in the parts of Lindsey, and if I state that shortly to the Committee, it will enable them better to understand what the magistrates have done with regard to the police in the parts of Lindsey; the parts of Lindsey is divided into two subdivisions for quarter sessions, the Kirton subdivision taking the western side, and the Louth and Spilsby subdivision the eastern side; Kirton is made the original quarter sessions, which are carried on by adjournment alternately at Louth and Spilsby; they have each a chairman and a deputy-chairman, the same clerk of the peace, one county rate in common, and the accounts are alternately inspected on one side and the other, and occasionally, though rarely, the magistrates find it necessary to hold a general meeting of all the magistrates for Lindsey. When the Act of Parliament of 1839, which we call the Rural Police Bill, was passed, we had a general meeting at Lincoln to discuss the propriety of adopting the provisions of that Act, and then it was agreed by the magistracy that there was no necessity for it at that time, and we did not act under it at all.

577. *Chairman.*] Was that decision unanimous?—It was not unanimous, I think it was not carried by a large majority.

578. Sir *J. Trollope.*] You were chairman of that meeting?—Yes; and the Lord-lieutenant attended, although he did not take any part; he was pleased to express himself satisfied with the decision of the magistrates. Another Act was passed in 1842, to regulate the payment of parish constables, which gave the power to the magistrates in quarter sessions, on the requisition of five magistrates, to build lock-up houses; and when that is done, requires them to appoint superintendent constables, having the management of certain districts; that Act of Parliament was put in force, first of all, on the Spilsby side; the magistrates of the Kirton bench soon followed the example, and did the same thing at Gainsborough; and they eventually decided to have one at all the petty sessions of Lindsey, 13 in number, the parishes placed under the superintendent being made nearly commensurate with the petty sessional district. The superintendents were appointed, and were put under regulations, of which I have a copy here; each superintendent has a salary of 120*l.* a year; they have a small light cart, found by the county; they find a horse themselves, and keep it themselves; they have to visit all the parishes in their districts every fortnight, and attend and report to the petty sessions held every fortnight throughout the division; to take persons to gaol when not on other duties; and to assist, advise or direct all the parish constables in the different districts. This plan, as I said before, has been gradually adopted now throughout the whole of Lindsey; and the expenses for the year ended 5th January last is 1,860 *l.*, of which I have a return here showing the expenses of each of the lock-up stations.

[*The Witness delivered in the same, which is as follows:*]

Sir R. Sheffield,
Bart.

27 May 1853.

LINCOLNSHIRE—LINDSEY.

AN ACCOUNT of the CHARGES and EXPENSES of LOCK-UP HOUSES and SUPERINTENDING CONSTABLES, in the Parts of *Lindsey*, for the Year ending January Sessions 1853.

LOCK-UP or DISTRICT.	APRIL SESSIONS, 1852.			JULY SESSIONS, 1852.			OCTOBER SESSIONS, 1852.			JANUARY SESSIONS, 1853.			TOTAL for the Year.
	Salary.	Extras.	Total.	Salary.	Extras.	Total.	Salary.	Extras.	Total.	Salary.	Extras.	Total.	
	£ s. d.	£ s. d.	£ s. d.	£ s. d.	£ s. d.	£ s. d.	£ s. d.	£ s. d.	£ s. d.	£ s. d.	£ s. d.	£ s. d.	£ s. d.
Alford	30 - -	9 16 9	39 16 9	30 - -	5 3 -	35 3 -	30 - -	16 5 11	46 5 11	30 - -	15 10 9	45 10 9	166 16 5
Barton	30 - -	6 13 8	36 13 8	30 - -	8 19 -	38 19 -	30 - -	4 10 5	34 10 5	30 - -	9 2 10	39 2 10	149 5 11
Brigg	30 - -	9 10 9	39 10 9	30 - -	9 12 11	39 12 11	30 - -	7 19 6	37 19 6	30 - -	5 18 6	35 18 6	152 3 8
Burgh	30 - -	7 17 7	37 17 7	30 - -	8 12 7	38 12 7	30 - -	4 5 -	34 5 -	30 - -	10 3 3	40 3 3	150 18 5
Epworth	30 - -	8 - 10	38 - 10	30 - -	7 6 7	37 6 7	30 - -	1 6 6	31 6 6	30 - -	17 18 8	47 18 8	154 12 2
Gainsbro'	35 - -	13 14 8	48 14 8	35 - -	2 8 4	37 8 4	30 - -	17 9 2	47 9 2	30 - -	5 4 2	35 4 2	168 15 11
Grimsby	30 - -	16 3 6	46 3 6	30 - -	6 5 10	36 5 10	30 - -	6 2 10	36 2 10	30 - -	4 12 9	34 12 9	153 4 11
Horncastle	30 - -	9 17 2	39 17 2	30 - -	13 14 2	43 14 2	30 - -	12 13 11	42 13 11	30 - -	8 9 9	38 9 9	164 15 -
Market Rasen	30 - -	18 3 9	48 3 9	30 - -	9 2 8	39 2 8	30 - -	11 16 3	41 16 3	30 - -	9 13 9	39 13 9	168 16 5
Lincoln	30 - -	5 8 9	35 8 9	30 - -	6 8 11	36 8 11	30 - -	4 19 -	34 19 -	30 - -	8 7 4	38 7 4	145 4 -
Burton	30 - -	4 14 7	34 14 7	30 - -	6 6 4	36 6 4	30 - -	8 17 1	38 17 1	30 - -	7 - 1	37 - 1	146 18 -
Stather													
Wragby	30 - -	3 12 3	33 12 3	30 - -	2 17 4	32 17 4	30 - -	6 16 4	36 16 4	30 - -	4 14 11	34 14 11	138 - 10
												£.	1,860 4 8

Sir R. Sheffield, Bart.

27 May 1853.

579. Sir *J. Trollope*.] Have you made any calculation of the comparative expenses between that system and the system under the General Rural Police Act of 1839 ?—I have read of the expenses, and seen the expenses reported in other counties. I should think the expenses of this system is not above one-fourth of the expense of the rural police; I take that as the highest. Then in 1850, there was another Act of Parliament passed to amend the Act of 1842, and which repeals the 23d section of that Act, which requires a superintendent to be appointed with the control of certain parishes wherever a lock-up is built, and instead of that section, directs that the superintendent shall be appointed to the special sessional district, and also that whenever a lock-up is built, a paid constable shall be appointed, which makes this difference, as we understand the Act of Parliament; whereas by the first Act of Parliament, which confines the magistrate to appointing one superintendent with the control of parishes where a lock-up is built, a district of parishes being allotted to that superintendent as nearly as possible commensurate in area with the special sessional district, the expense is defined and limited; we know the extent of the expenses. The second Act of Parliament, by repealing the 23d section of the first Act, and directing superintendents to be appointed to special session districts, and adding that, whenever a lock-up is built, a paid constable is to be appointed, has the effect of giving a power to magistrates to build a lock-up in any place they think proper, with a paid constable besides the superintendent; and this has opened the door to an undefined and unlimited expenditure, and under this power the magistrates on the Louth side have built a lock-up, costing 600 *l*., and appointed a constable at 60 *l*. a year. In consequence of this alteration, the magistrates considered that it would be expedient to have a general meeting, and another general meeting took place of the magistrates for the parts of Lindsey, at Lincoln, in July 1851. A committee was appointed to have the management of the police of Lindsey formed of four of the magistrates on one side and four on the other, and this was done in order to secure an equal expenditure in the two divisions, and that the same mode should be adopted by the one and the other. The magistrates then agreed that they would not build more than one lock-up house in the same district without having a report first of all upon it from the police committee; that committee meets at Lincoln at the assizes in the spring and in the summer. The rules for the guidance of the superintendents which had been in force were afterwards confirmed by that committee, and are the rules and regulations under which they now act. With this alteration in the Act of Parliament, if the law remain unaltered, the probability will be that lock-up houses and paid constables will be established at a few other places in the parts of Lindsey, and that will run the expense up from 1,800 *l*. to 2,500 *l*. or thereabouts. I think if, under this last Act of Parliament, lock-up houses are built at two or three places on a smaller scale, with constables' houses, it will run the expense up to 2,500 *l*. With regard to the commission of crime since this alteration, I have not any accurate information, but judging from a little paper which I have in my pocket, showing the county-rate for the last 20 years, I should say there is not much difference in the crime; the money paid for prosecution by the Government amounts to much the same for the last six years. I have observed, at several of the last sessions, that many of the prosecutions have been for trifling offences; perhaps they are looked up better than they were.

580. *Chairman*.] Do you think the amount of undetected crime is less?—Yes; I have not any accurate data to go by, I only judge of that by the offences being trifling which have been tried at the quarter sessions of late years.

581. This return, which you have put in, was for 13 divisions?—Thirteen divisions. Louth has not got one; Louth has a police of its own; there has not been a county superintendent appointed for it.

582. The cost for the lock-up houses alone was 1,860 *l*. 4 *s*. 8 *d*. per annum, and you think the cost of the system under the new Act would amount to about 2,500 *l*.? —I think it would; I have here a paper which shows the area of the districts in acres, and the population of those different districts which the superintendents look after.

[*The Witness delivered in the following statement*:]

Sir R. Sheffield,
Bart.

27 May 1853.

LINCOLNSHIRE LINDSEY.

A RETURN from the Parts of *Lindsey*, in the County of Lincoln, in which SUPERINTENDENT CONSTABLES have been appointed, under the Acts 5 & 6 Vict., c. 109, and 13 & 14 Vict., c. 20, stating whether as Superintendents of Lock-ups solely, or as Superintendents of Parish Constables, or as acting in both capacities, with the Pay and Allowances of each Superintendent Constable, and the Area and Population of the Petty Sessional Division to which he is appointed, together with the Total Expense incurred in the said Parts, for the Year ending January 1853.

Petty Sessional Division.	Whether Superintendent of Lock-up solely, or of Parish Constables, or both.	Pay and Allowances of each Superintendent Constable.	Area of District, in Acres.	Population.
Alford - - -	Both - - -	- - Annual salary of 120*l.*, including the purchase and keep of a horse; 1 *s.* on serving each summons; 10 *s.* a day for attending as a witness at assizes or quarter sessions.	58,670	11,752
Barton - - -	Both - - -	The like - - -	45,000	10,065
Brigg - - -	Both - - -	The like - - -	72,370	12,405
Burton Stather -	Both - - -	The like - - -	80,970	12,734
Epworth - -	Both - - -	The like - - -	50,590	13,111
Gainsburgh -	Both - - -	The like - - -	55,710	15,839
Grimsby - -	Both - - -	The like - - -	66,450	12,713
Horncastle -	Both - - -	The like - - -	98,850	21,140
Lincoln - - -	- - Superintendent of parish constables.	- - The like, with an allowance of 10 *l.* per annum for house-rent.	98,160	14,520
Market Rasen - -	Both - - -	- - Annual salary of 120 *l.*, including the purchase and keep of a horse; 1 *s.* on serving each summons; 10 *s.* a day for attending as a witness at assizes or quarter sessions.	57,230	9,206
Spilsby - - -	Both - - -	The like - - -	116,860	22,710
Wragby - - -	- - Superintendent of parish constables.	- - The like, with an allowance of 10 *l.* per annum for house-rent.	58,900	7,388
Binbroke, in the Market Rasen district.	- - Constable in charge of lock-up.	60 *l.* per annum.	—	—

Note.—The Population Returns of 1851 not being yet published, the population is given from the Census of 1841; if 10 per cent. is added to these figures, it is supposed a fair approximation to the population of 1851 will be attained.

TOTAL EXPENSE.

The Total Expense incurred by the Parts of Lindsey, for lock-up houses and superintendent constables, for the year ending January 1853, was 1,860 *l.* 4 *s.* 8 *d.*

Clerk of the Peace's Office, Spilsby,
14 May 1853. }   *John H. Hollway,*
Clerk of the Peace for the Parts of Lindsey.

583. Can you state from that return the largest amount of population in any division in any district, under one superintendent constable?—The largest is Spilsby, which is 116,860 acres; the parishes vary very much.

584. Sir *J. Trollope.*] Is not Spilsby a thinly populated district?—Yes, it must be; there are 22,710 population.

585. *Chairman.*] Is that under one superintending constable?—That is under one superintending constable.

586. I presume he is a mounted officer?—Yes, he is a mounted officer; they each of them have a horse and cart.

587. Does the return of 1,800 *l.*, which you have put in, include the expense of the horses?—Yes; they keep their own horses.

588. Do not you find the carts very useful?—Yes.

589. And they make the constables much more efficient?—Yes; when constables.

stables take parties who are reluctant to walk, the carts save the county some expense.

590. Sir *J. Trollope.*] Are the carts fitted up with proper security for the conveyance of prisoners?—Yes.

591. Is the conveyance of prisoners included in that expenditure?—When the superintending constable is not engaged in any other duty, he takes all the prisoners from the petty sessions which he attends off to gaol without any assistance whatever, or any expense to the county.

592. Have you ever had any escapes?—I do not recollect any; we had a determined sort of man taken last autumn; he was sent to gaol afterwards for a breach of the peace; he ran away from the petty sessions; as soon as the chief constable had bridled his horse he mounted and went after him, and being on horseback, he soon retook him.

593. Mr. *Phillips.*] What does a cart cost?—I should think about 20 *l.* There was one complaint made last winter in the neighbourhood of Caistor, of there being a good many depredations committed there; there were a good many sheep stolen, and the complaint was that the offenders were not apprehended quickly enough, or not looked after sufficiently. I do not know whose fault it was, whether it was the superintendent in that district or not; special constables were appointed for a time, and it was put down again. Caistor is one of the places where a lock-up will be made, and an additional constable appointed, if we go on upon this present plan. All I can say further about it is, that the advantages which already seem to arise from the plan are, that in the towns and places where the superintendents are stationed there is much more orderly behaviour than there was before; the beerhouses, alehouses, and vagrants' common lodging-houses, are better looked after; the peaceable and well-disposed inhabitants are protected and the bad characters are kept in check; indeed I can speak from my own knowledge with reference to Winterton, where many of the principal inhabitants have expressed their great satisfaction upon the appointment of the superintendent, and the different order of things since that has taken place. At one time in last year there was a complaint made of a great many depredations on the river Trent; some parties in boats committed depredations on each side of the river, to a large extent, upon the farmers. By putting the superintendents of the adjoining districts into communication with each other, three men of these parties were taken, and that put an end to it. I am only speaking as far as the system seems to have been serviceable to us. Our men were employed at Lincoln on the occasion of the large meetings which we had about two years ago, when there were about 7,000 people in the castle-yard, and the only police force were the superintending constables, with special constables under them. Last year there was a contested election, and that went off very well under the same police. After all it can only be said to be an experiment, but it is an experiment which we are desirous of carrying out to see whether it will answer. I do not pretend to say that it would be efficient in populous districts, but ours are only agricultural districts; and we are in great hopes that the system will be efficient if time be given for it to be carried out.

594. Sir *J. Trollope.*] Can you give the Committee any account of the comparative saving you have made upon the other system, under the 5 & 6 Vict. c. 109, as regards the salaries and payments to the chief constables?—We have made some saving in that respect by doing away with the chief constables. The only duty which the chief constables are legally entitled to be paid for is collecting the county rate.

595. *Chairman.*] To what did the whole cost amount under the old system of chief constables?—The chief constables, when I was first chairman, were paid by fees from parishes, which was totally illegal; that cost 1,500 *l.* a year; afterwards, when the new poor law came into operation, the auditors would not allow those accounts, and then the magistrates were obliged to pay them legally, and they paid them under the Act of Parliament for collecting the county rate; that amounted to 1,000 *l.* a year.

596. Mr. *Mackie.*] It was reduced from 1,500 *l.* to 1,000 *l.*?—When the parishes paid it was 1,500 *l.*, and as soon as the magistrates paid it it was reduced to 1,000 *l.*

597. Sir *J. Trollope.*] You saved that 1,000 *l.* subsequently?—We saved 500 *l.* per annum subsequently, and shall save the rest as vacancies occur. We do not want them now, because the superintending police supply their places.

Sir R. Sheffield,
Bart.

27 May 1853.

598. In fact you are gradually increasing the credit to the county ?—As far as 500 l. goes.

599. Are you aware that by the Act of Parliament the poor-law boards are only authorised to collect the rates where there is absolutely no chief constable at all; where both have died, or been removed. ?—I think it is so.

600. If both die you cannot fill up the vacancies?—Not for the purpose of collecting the county rate.

601. Then you have a considerable sum to set off against this system of constabulary ?—Yes, and an increasing sum.

602. On the whole, is the system satisfactory to the district ?—I have heard no complaints against it ; I can only mention the complaints from Caistor and Barton, which I have before stated.

603. Have you not a superintending constable at Barton ?—Yes.

604. And you are about to place one also at Caistor?—An application has been made for a lock-up and paid constable there.

605. Did you consider, when that is done, that the whole of the arrangements under this Act of Parliament will be complete, as far as you consider them necessary ?—With two or three others, or a few additions.

606. And you think the whole expense will not exceed 2,500 l. ?—That iwll cover the whole of the expense, as far as I can judge.

607. As regards the discipline of these superintending constables, have you any regulations beyond the reports to the petty sessions once a fortnight ?—The regulations are contained in the paper which I have handed in to the Committee.

608. Do you find that a sufficient supervision is exercised over the men?—There is no head constable.

609. Do you consider that a defect in the system ?—Yes; I think it might be desirable that there should be one still; I cannot speak with confidence about it; ours are all men of a certain age; good selected men, between 30 and 45; and I do not know whether they would work better under supervision than they do at present.

610. On the whole, are you satisfied with the system as it is ?—Very well, so far as we have gone; we do not know what the result of the experiment will be with regard to crime; we expected it would increase at first, but we were in hopes it would diminish afterwards; certainly the country looks to the superintendents very much as protectors; they send to them directly if any offence is committed.

611. Chairman.] You think the feeling of the neighbourhood is in favour of the system ?—From what I can judge I think it is; I think the ratepayers are anxious not to have any more expense put upon them.

612. You have stated that the magistrates resolved not to adopt the Rural Police Act, the 3d & 4th Victoria ; was that chiefly on the ground of expense ?—Yes, chiefly on the ground of expense.

613. Are your prisoners which are conveyed to gaol, all conveyed by these superintending constables?—No; they have directions to take the prisoners to gaol whenever they are not on any other duty.

614. When the superintending constables are on duty, are the prisoners conveyed to gaol by the parochial constables ?—Yes.

615. Can you state to the Committee what the expense of conveying prisoners to gaol by the parochial constables is in your division of the county ?—No; not the total annual sum.

616. Sir J. Trollope.] Have you a table of fees ?—Yes.

617. Chairman.] What is the amount paid to the parish constables?—The superintending constables have not any pay for these services at all ; it is included in their salary, and the whole of the costs for the conveyance of prisoners to gaol that we incur in the county is paid to the parish constables.

618. Can you state at all what is paid to the parochial constables in proceedings before justices?—No, I cannot do that; but there is a scale of allowances.

619. Can you state at all what is the expense paid to parish constables for serving summonses and warrants, which they do sometimes, I presume ?—Yes; they serve some of the summonses and warrants, but I am not prepared to state the cost; it is all regulated by a scale.

620. Do your parochial constables attend the assizes and sessions?—They attend only when required as witnesses.

621. Are they paid for it ?—Yes, according to the scale.

622. Are

Sir R. Sheffield, Bart.

27 May 1853.

622. Are you prepared to state what the cost of those parochial constables is for attending on those occasions?—No; there is a table of allowances.

623. Do your paid policemen summon the coroner's juries?—No, I think not.

624. You are not prepared to say what the payment of the parochial constables is under any one item whatever?—No, not as a whole annually; they are paid by the scale.

625. Then all the amount that is paid to the parochial constables for the purposes which I have mentioned to you, must be added to the expense of the 2,500 *l.* a year, whatever it may be?—Certainly.

626. Mr. *Sotheron*.] In other words, the 2,500 *l.* is paid in the county of Lincoln, in addition to the amount which was previously paid for the constabulary work?—No, it would save a part of it; the carts and horses which I have mentioned take a great many prisoners to gaol, for which service the parish constables would have been paid.

627. Sir *J. Trollope*.] Are the superintending constables allowed to receive anything?—Only 1 *s.* for serving summonses.

628. *Chairman*.] You give no reward to any paid constable for apprehending a felon?—No.

629. How is he paid for his attendance at the sessions?—He is paid 10 *s.* a day, let him be employed in as many or as few prosecutions as he may.

630. Do you mean to say that your constables are paid 10 *s.* a day for their attendance at the sessions?—The superintending constable has 10 *s.* as a witness.

631. Mr. *Sotheron*.] In addition to his ordinary salary?—Yes.

632. Mr. *Mackie*.] Is that included in the 2,500 *l.* a year?—No.

633. Where does that come from?—That will come in the expenses of the prosecution in which he is concerned, and is eventually paid by the Treasury.

634. Sir *J. Trollope*.] It is only for quarter sessions; is there anything allowed for petty sessions?—No.

635. Mr. *Mackie*.] Supposing a serious riot were to take place in the county of Lincoln, do you consider that your police force is sufficient to check it in the commencement?—We have not had any serious riot occur.

636. Have you had any riot?—No; it is a rural population.

637. Mr. *Phillips*.] Are your superintending constables appointed inspectors of weights and measures?—No; we have a separate inspector of weights and measures. I have a little memorandum in my pocket of the county rate for the parts of Lindsey for the last 20 years, though, perhaps, it is not exactly applicable to this inquiry. I first took this account down at the different annual inspections which were made into the county rate. I have taken down for every year, for the last 20 years, what the expense of the county rate has been. I began in 1833. In 1833, it was 16,616 *l.*; then it was thought heavy, and a finance committee was appointed to inspect the books. The next year it was reduced to 13,678 *l.* The reason of the first year being so high was that there were a great many county bridges repaired. In 1852 it was 16,229 *l.*, and deducting 3,987 *l.* received from the Treasury for prosecutions, &c., it leaves the county rate only 12,242 *l.*, including the expense of police and lock-ups.

638. Sir *J. Trollope*.] Therefore it is very nearly the same; it is less than 20 years ago?—If you make allowances for the expenses under the new Acts of Parliament for the establishment of police, and the inspection of weights and measures, you may put down about 3,000 *l.* less. If I take 3,330 *l.* from the 16,200 *l.* I bring it down less than it was 20 years before; but altogether our county rate is pretty much the same.

639. Do you know what the county rate is in the pound?—A farthing in the pound raises between 1,400 *l.* and 1,500 *l.*; I think the whole of the county rate is 2 *d.* in the pound.

640. If you had the Rural Police Act, the 3d & 4th Victoria, put into execution, it would more than double the county-rate, would it not?—It would, take it under the most favourable circumstances, taking the amount at 65 *l.* per man; we have a population of about 200,000, and if you take one to every 1,000 inhabitants it will increase our expenses to 13,000 *l.* for police.

641. Mr. *Howard*.] What effect has been produced upon vagrants by the appointment of superintending constables?—It has reduced the number of vagrants, but they are still numerous; there are one or two places where the vagrants are numerous; I do not attribute that to the want of police, so much as I do to there not being a vagrant ward at all the poor-law unions; it

is optional with the ratepayers whether they will have it or not; there is a disinclination to have a vagrant ward at one place I know, and the consequence is, that they are obliged to give some out-relief, although that is made as low as it can be made.

642. Sir *J. Trollope.*] Some of your union houses have not vagrant wards?—No.

643. Do you think that tends to encourage vagrancy in the district?—I have told them so over and over again.

644. Mr. *Howard.*] Do your police examine the lodging-houses?—They do; under the Act of Parliament they are paid for it separately by the parishes; I do not know the amount.

645. Mr. *Phillips.*] Have you any superannuation fund or retiring allowance for these men?—No.

646. Do you anticipate any difficulty in dealing with them when they become old and infirm?—We have not contemplated that.

647. Mr. *Sotheron.*] Has not every parish in this district at least one parish constable?—I think they have all two, and some more.

648. For all the services performed by those constables payment is made from the parish funds and not from the county, except only the allowances which they receive when they bring prisoners before the magistrates?—They are paid according to a scale; the losing party pays in many cases where a conviction takes place.

649. Have you any means of giving any information to the Committee as to the amount of money which is paid by the parishes in your district to their parish constables, either at this time or at any past time?—No.

650. *Chairman.*] Is not the amount to be received by the constables in cases of non-conviction generally settled by the parties with the constable out of court?—Yes; where a conviction does take place, then the expenses are included in the judgment.

651. Mr. *Sotheron.*] In making a comparison of the expense of your constabulary force, such as you describe it to be, with the expense of the paid police in the counties, in which it is established under the Act of 1839, ought you not to make a considerable allowance for sums not paid out of the county rate, but by the parishes to their parish constables?—I am not sufficiently acquainted with the rural police to answer that question.

652. But in truth the 2,500*l.*, which you say will be the expense of your system when completed, is a sum in addition to, and exclusive of, whatever may be paid by the parishes to the parish constables?—Except as to taking prisoners to gaol.

653. *Chairman.*] Are all your officers appointed by the magistrates?—Yes, in quarter sessions.

654. Are the persons now holding the appointment of parochial constables generally small tradesmen, or industrious persons?—Yes; we have a number to select out of; we make some inquiries when we appoint them, and we take them in rotation, as far as we can.

655. Is it not an inconvenience to those persons to hold the office of constable?—Yes.

656. Is not their time money to them?—Yes.

657. Is not holding the office of parochial constable a money charge upon them?—Yes, certainly it is a loss to them; they are pretty well paid for their services, according to the scale of allowances.

658. Are they paid from other sources than those which you have described?—From no other sources.

659. Lord *Lovaine.*] Is not the parish constable open to local influences of every description?—Yes.

660. Mr. *Sotheron.*] With regard to the supervision of these constables, I think you said that there was no chief above them?—No; we have made a regulation now that we are to have a report once a year to the quarter sessions, from the magistrates of petty sessions, upon the conduct and behaviour of the superintendents.

661. Have you any other source to which you can look, except that which you have now mentioned, to enforce the attendance and attention on the part of these men to their duties?—No; we have always given notice that we desire to hear any complaints against them at quarter sessions.

662. Supposing one became lax in the discharge of his duty, and did not turn
out

Sir R. Sheffield, Bart.

27 May 1853.

out sharp in the performance of his duty, what could the magistrates do?—Nothing beyond the regulation we have made, calling upon the magistrates to report upon their exact behaviour for the last year. We have made a regulation now that the magistrates in petty sessions should send a return once a year to the quarter sessions of the behaviour, during the preceding year, of the superintending constable in that respect, whether he has been active and alert in the discharge of his duties.

663. Have not you said that you thought that it would be an improvement if you had a chief constable to keep control over the others?—I have a little doubt about it; I cannot come to a decided opinion upon the subject; these men are all chosen men, of between 30 and 45 years of age; they are well-conducted active men, and I doubt whether they would be better at that age under superintendence.

664. Although these men, while they are young men, just chosen, and up to their duty, may require no control, do not you think 10 years hence, for instance, it would be a desirable thing that there should be some person to keep them up to their work?—Probably it would be best to have one appointed as superintendent; I have no doubt of the description of men that we do employ being all picked men.

665. Chairman.] Is it any part of the parish constables' duty to patrol either by day or night, for the purpose either of preventing or detecting crime?—No direction has been given of that sort.

666. Lord Lovaine.] Legally, I apprehend such directions could hardly be given?—No, I think not.

667. Chairman.] Have you anything further to state to the Committee?—I may observe that we have built all these lock-up houses with the sanction of the Secretary of State.

668. How do you pay for the lock-up houses?—They have been paid for out of the county-rate.

669. Have you borrowed money at all for the purpose?—No.

670. Sir J. Trollope.] What has been the cost for each of the lock-up houses, on the average?—They vary; the general run of them have been built with a magistrates' room; they cost 1,200 l. in that case, some less, without that accommodation.

671. For the petty sessional divisions?—Yes.

672. Chairman.] The average is about 1,000 l. for each division?—Yes, as near as I recollect.

673. Mr. Sotheron.] Is the cost of the lock-up houses included in the sum you have given the Committee as the expense of the police force?—No; I have mentioned that in accounting for the county-rate.

Captain *William Charles Harris*, called in; and further Examined.

Captain W. C. Harris.

674. Chairman.] I THINK you stated, after your examination yesterday, that you wished to add something to your evidence, as to the efficiency of the county constabulary over the superintending constables, in following in pursuit of criminals?—I wish merely to mention one case which occurred in Hampshire, illustrating the advantages of a county constabulary over that of superintending constables. A poor man's house in the parish of Sherfield English was broken into during the absence of the family at church; the circumstance was reported to the superintendent of the Romsey division, who proceeded at daylight the next morning to examine the premises; and having found the tracks of several individuals, he made inquiries, and ascertained that four men and two women had been in the neighbourhood the day before. From inquiries, he was led to believe that they had taken the Salisbury road, and he tracked them through White-parish and Whaddon into Salisbury. From further inquiries he found that a party answering the description had slept in Salisbury the night previous, and were gone on the road to Wilton. Beyond Wilton he overtook the party, and, pulling up his horse, he waited until they came to a wall, when he drove alongside of them, and turning his horse's head sharp into the wall, directed the constable who was with him to jump out before, whilst he got out behind, thus enclosing the party between the cart and the wall. The party showed fight, but he knocked two of them down, and throwing their sticks over the wall, he handcuffed the four men, and made them and the women get into his cart, and thus

Captain
W. C. Harris.

27 May 1853.

conveyed the whole back to Salisbury. All the stolen property was found in the possession of the persons apprehe... . I merely mention this fact to show that whether a poor or a rich man is robbed, the county constabulary proceed at once to do their duty; whereas a superintending constable would have to stop to inquire who was to pay him his expenses. So it is with the borough police; they have no means of recovering their expenses if they are unsuccessful in pursuit; and thus many a zealous officer, who is anxious to discharge his duty, is deterred, by risk of losing his money, unless the prosecutor or person robbed is sufficiently wealthy to guarantee him his expenses.

675. You mean that the difficulty in following in pursuit in this case was from its being a poor man's house that had been robbed?—Yes; in the case I speak of, the man would not have been able to furnish the superintending or parish constable with the means of following in pursuit.

Captain *John B. B. M'Hardy*, R.N., called in; and Examined.

Captain J. B. B.
M'Hardy, R.N.

676. *Chairman.*] ARE you Chief Constable of the county of Essex?—Yes.

677. How long have you been chief constable of the county of Essex?—Thirteen and a half years chief constable of Essex; I had been eight years inspecting commander of the Coast Guard in different parts of England previously to becoming the chief constable of Essex, which I deemed my apprenticeship, qualifying me for the chief constableship.

678. Will you state to the Committee the number of your force, its classification and grades?—Two hundred and two men, including myself and the deputy; 14 superintendents in three classes, 20 inspectors, and constables in three classes.

679. Do you consider that number calculated to insure efficiency?—I consider that it is calculated to insure the greatest amount of efficiency practicable under existing arrangements.

680. What do you mean by existing arrangements?—I mean that we have not a sufficient co-operation between the existing police forces, nor between the controlling authorities, and that better arrangements in this respect would be a great benefit, and would tend to a saving of expense.

681. Do you mean between the authorities in boroughs?—Yes; and imposing additional duties upon the police it would tend still more to lessen the gross expense, and thus would justify an increase in the numbers.

682. What do you consider, as a chief constable, to be the principal objects of the police force?—The prevention of crime, the detection of offenders, and the preservation of the public peace.

683. Have you directed your attention to the existing system of constabulary throughout Great Britain?—I have, ever since my connexion with the constabulary, making my leading object the producing of the required qualities at the least expense, expense being the instrument solely used by its opposers to render it unpopular; but I never knew a ratepayer in my experience who could state what the expense to him individually was.

684. Lord *Lovaine.*] Do you mean under the old system?—Under the present system; I never knew a person in any class of society who could tell me what he paid for the police.

685. *Chairman.*] What is your opinion of the fitness of the present system for the objects you have described?—I consider the present system requires a greater union of action, not only between the boroughs, but also between the counties; not only a greater union of action between the boroughs and the counties in which the boroughs are situated, but a greater union between the counties themselves.

686. Have any of the counties adjoining Essex adopted the police force?—On the establishment of our force none of the adjoining counties had adopted the Act, but the effect of an efficient constabulary in Essex obliged the adjoining counties, with the exception of Kent, that is, Suffolk, Hertfordshire and Cambridgeshire, most reluctantly to follow our example.

687. Are you aware of the causes which led to the adoption of the police in Cambridgeshire?—I believe it was not only from their being overrun with vagrants, but also the extraordinary number of fires, which I think have almost entirely ceased since the adoption of the police there. Kent not having been supplied with a constabulary, filled Essex with vagrants; they moved across from Kent by Grays in such numbers that there was a regular track. This circumstance led the Board of Guardians to give way to my struggle for years by
allowing

allowing the police of the county to be appointed assistant relieving officers for casuals.

Captain J. B. B.
M'Hardy, R. N.

27 May 1853.

688. Was not that system adopted in consequence of the recommendation of Mr. Buller, at the time he was President of the Poor Law Board?—It was. I had recommended it for years myself, and they did it then reluctantly, and only partially. It effected a difference in one union in Essex, namely Chelmsford, in the first year of 5,000 and odd.

689. Do you mean vagrants?—Yes; the first year of the adoption of the police as assistant relieving officers for casuals made that difference.

690. Can you state the numbers relieved before, and the numbers afterwards, which will show the difference?—I can show it for one half year; the half year in 1849, while the police did the duty, there were 79 relieved, and in the half year previously 2,605; falling from 2,605 to 79.

691. Lord *Lovaine.*] Was not there a circular issued by Mr. Buller, enabling the Boards of Guardians to judge of the conditions of the vagrants, and not to relieve if they did not think them fit subjects for relief?—I have read that minute carefully, but I do not find that it armed the Boards with any authority which they did not possess before.

692. Did not Mr. Buller's circular recommend the enforcement of the authority which they possessed?—They had not the means of enforcing it without resorting to the police; if they had attempted to do so, and had refused those parties relief, who were mostly thieves and depredators, they would have met with great difficulty; the vagrants attempted it with us, and we had a great deal of difficulty in the commencement. It was a delicate duty, and required to be discharged with great caution, and very discreetly. Had one person died from want of relief, we should have been placed in a very uncomfortable position.

693. *Chairman.*] Do not you think the numbers were reduced from another reason; that the vagrants have a great objection to come at all into contact with the police?—The check was from a variety of causes; we have a regular form, and every vagrant is regularly entered, and almost his description taken, before he has relief given to him; and that prevents his return, particularly if he has committed any offence; therefore he does not come a second time.

694. Lord *Lovaine.*] Do you search the vagrants?—We discharge that part of the duty with delicacy; we are authorised to do so, but we thought the less offensively the police discharged the duty the better.

695. Sir *J. Trollope.*] Were not the vagrants subjected to some processes in the union houses, which were more disagreeable to them than anything you did to them?—I am not capable of judging; I should not have supposed so.

696. Did not they go through other processes in the union houses; were they not washed when they were admitted into the unions?—I have not the least idea.

697. *Chairman.*] Did not those processes apply to the 5,000?—Not that I am aware of.

698. Do not you suppose that they were subjected to all those regulations?—No.

699. Sir *J. Trollope.*] You do not know what occurred within the walls of the union?—No.

700. Do you attribute the diminution of vagrancy to the police regulations?—Entirely.

701. Were not other things which took place within the walls of the union as likely to diminish the number of vagrants as anything you could do to them, in the way of inspection?—Not knowing what applications were used in the union houses, I cannot say.

702. You say that you only searched them delicately; do you mean that you did not search them in all cases?—No; I attribute the diminution, principally, to their objection to coming in contact with the police. I do not believe there are 100 deserving characters worthy of relief out of the whole number, and with the examination they undergo, they see the possibility of being detected, or traced, if they have been guilty of some offence. These are imaginary causes; all I can speak of is the effect; the causes would be a mere matter of speculation.

703. Lord *Lovaine.*] You are not aware of any difference of treatment in the workhouse subsequently to your undertaking the charge of the vagrants?—No; if I were to give an opinion, I should say that I believe there is no change.

704. Sir *J. Trollope.*] Were the duties of your police who were appointed

assistant relieving officers, merely to examine those persons who applied for relief at the unions?—That was an additional duty, and it also rendered them more efficient in discharge of their police duties.

705. They do not stop vagrants who do not beg or demand relief?—No.

706. Their duties only relate to those who want to get into the union house?—I had tried stopping them, and had about 1,000 committed in three years; but it produced no effect, except to increase the magistrate's clerk's fees, and increasing the expense in gaol, and as it was an unsuccessful attempt, I thought it desirable to try something else.

707. *Chairman.*] What is the nearest union to Tilbury, when they cross from Kent?—Orsett; then they go down to Billericay, and then to Chelmsford; that was the principal route for vagrants.

708. I am speaking of the first union at which they would be relieved?—Orsett.

709. Can you state, previously to the appointment of the police as assistant relieving officers, what numbers were relieved at that union in one year coming from Kent?—In half a year the decrease on the total number was 1,678.

710. What was the gross number of vagrants relieved at Orsett previously to the police acting as relieving officers?—One thousand six hundred and ninety-four in the preceding year.

711. What was the number after the appointment of the police?—Sixteen.

712. Then the difference between 1,694 and 16 was thrown back upon the county of Kent, were there was no police?—That was my object; that was what I endeavoured to do.

713. You said that the counties of Cambridge, Herts and Suffolk, which are adjoining counties to Essex, had adopted the police?—Yes, they have adopted the police.

714. On the same system as yours?—The police of Cambridgeshire is exactly on the same system; each of the others is different.

715. Mr. *Mackie.*] At what dates were the police adopted in Essex and the adjoining counties?—In Essex, in February 1840; Suffolk followed, and Hertfordshire next.

716. In what year was the police adopted in Suffolk?—I am not positive; and lastly, Cambridgeshire about a year and half ago. I believe all those three counties were induced to adopt it from necessity, not voluntarily.

717. *Chairman.*] What was the necessity in Cambridgeshire?—The great number of fires and robberies; we rendered every assistance that we could. Our police bordering on Cambridgeshire, were continually acting in Cambridgeshire; and I believe that gradually reconciled the parties to having a police, from the services which they saw performed in their own county.

718. Did your police act in Cambridgeshire under any requisition from the magistrates?—I directed them to do so. Many of the magistrates on the borders of our county are magistrates for the adjoining counties. I felt it my duty, when these things occurred, to follow them up, as far as I could in self defence, because the bordering counties not having a police is a great disadvantage to our own county; they harbour robbers who commit depredations in our county, and then run out of it, and once out of the county the offender has every chance of escape, in consequence of our imperfect system of police. As a proof of that, I may mention that a farmer on the borders of the county told me that he was obliged to drive his sheep into Essex to feed them at night, previously to their having a police in Suffolk.

719. What is his name?—Mr. Viall.

720. Mr. *Burroughes.*] Were any police employed from the metropolis, or any other place in Cambridgeshire, previous to their adopting the constabulary?—I do not know. I think sending policemen to places where they have no local knowledge is very little benefit.

721. *Chairman.*] Is there a satisfactory system of mutual co-operation between the police in different counties and boroughs?—There certainly is not.

722. Do you think it is possible by any means to enforce a system of mutual co-operation?—I think if the spirit of the Act of Parliament under which we are acting at this moment were strictly carried out, it would be effected. There are certain sections in the Act of Parliament under which the county constabularies are established, which permit the boroughs to unite with the counties, but they are very jealous of doing so. I took very great pains to effect the object, but always failed.

The

The want of combination is chiefly known in the boroughs, where they are incapable of keeping the peace themselves, and then they are glad to take our services.

723. Lord *Lovaine*.] Is there a great jealousy existing between the police of boroughs and the police of counties?—On both sides.

724. *Chairman*.] Do you think it would be remedied if the adoption of the police were made compulsory?—I think it would; the intention of the Act of Parliament was to leave it discretional; the Act of Parliament under which we are acting not only permits the boroughs to unite with the counties, but enables the magistrates, if they think proper, to appoint one chief constable for two or three adjoining counties, which, if carried out, would tend to lessen the existing jealousy.

725. Supposing, by any system of legislation, boroughs under a population of 100,000, which now have a police of their own, were still left, in a certain degree, independent as to the management of their police, can you suggest any means by which co-operation might be insured under those circumstances between the county police and the police of those boroughs?—I think if sections 14 and 15 of the Act 3 & 4 Vict., cap. 88, were made imperative instead of discretional, the object you refer to would be effected; and, with reference to remedying the want of union between the counties, I think that would be done if the intention of section 4 of the Act 2 & 3 Vict., cap. 93, were carried out.

726. What is the marginal note of that section?—"One or more chief constables of the county to be appointed, who may serve for more than one county." I would make that section compulsory which is now discretional; I would propose, as a remedy for want of union between the counties, that England be divided into four districts; that there should be a general constabulary, and a chief officer as director, appointed and paid by Government for each district, with a responsible director-general; that would be carrying out the spirit of this 4th section, which is left discretional with the magistrates; if I may go so far, I may say that I deem it an evil appointing two chief constables for one county; where counties are formed into two divisions for Parliamentary purposes, it is discretional with the magistrates to have two chief constables instead of one, and I think it is productive of much evil because it increases the evil which arises from the want of union.

727. Mr. *Burroughes*.] I believe that is done in very few instances?—Suffolk has two chief constables, and Cambridgeshire has a separate one for the Isle of Ely; they are both small forces.

728. *Chairman*.] In speaking of four divisions, do you include Wales and Scotland?—No; I would have one for Wales, and two for Scotland.

729. And only two for England?—Four for England; north, south, east and west; Wales one, and Scotland two.

730. In proposing the appointment of these inspectors, am I to understand that you are not in favour of centralization in London?—Decidedly I am not in favour of entire centralization. I think, for numerous reasons, it would be anything but advisable; you would lose the great advantage of local supervision; for every police constable has several superintendents, particularly with the smaller ratepayers, who are ready to point out any irregularity.

731. Do you know of any instance of adjoining counties having been consolidated for police purposes?—No.

732. Is there any prospect of such a provision being carried out?—Certainly not, when counties avail themselves of the opportunity of dividing, as Cambridge and Suffolk have done.

733. You have mentioned the number of policemen in your force; are you enabled to train recruits thoroughly before entrusting them with the responsibility of their duties?—No, from the constant demand for constables.

734. By whom is that demand made?—By the public; it is an increasing demand; I generally pass them from the head-quarter station, where I reside myself, through those stations which are occupied by superintendents, which enables me to remove constables, to meet the demand, who do not so much need the eye of the superintendent.

735. From your experience, do you think that the police has become popular in Essex with the ratepayers?—Yes; those persons who were most opposed to it, and who took great pains to obstruct its progress, even after its introduction, are now its strongest supporters; and in some instances, when I am under the necessity of removing a constable from their immediate locality, they write to say that they cannot leave home comfortably unless I replace the constable.

Captain J. B. B.
M'Hardy, R. N.

27 May 1853.

736. Do you think that a separation of the police forces leads to unnecessary expense?—Certainly.

737. Why do you think so?—From requiring a greater number of staff officers; the boroughs suffer most, in consequence of there being no prospect of advancement. When I am applied to to supply boroughs with recruits, or parties to fill up vacancies, my men give that as one of their principal reasons for objecting to go, even with the increased pay, and also there being no superannuation fund in most of the boroughs.

738. Have you any station houses, or strong rooms built?—We have station houses and strong rooms in every division of the county; there are three not quite complete; we have two in some divisions.

739. What do they generally cost?—They vary from 1,000 l. to 2,000 l. The head-quarter station, where I reside, cost 4,000 l. and odd.

740. Does that include barracks for the men at the stations?—Yes; and I have been enabled to prove that they produce a greater interest than the capital invested, and paid for by the county.

741. Do you mean to say that there is a profit carried to the credit of the county?—Yes, equal to the interest paid by the county on the money borrowed, to be repaid in 20 years, thereby showing that the county derive advantages from becoming security for the property. I do not believe it to be possible to organise a creditable constabulary without stations, and that was the principal difficulty I had in organising the Essex constabulary, from the general belief that it was involving the county in a large expense.

742. Take the most expensive of the stations, the one at which you reside, which cost 4,000 l.; I wish to ascertain from what sources the payments are made by which you pay the interest upon the cost of those buildings?—I have it here; but the most expensive station does not always produce the most revenue; it depends upon local circumstances; if you will permit me, I will give you the total sum invested in the stations, which is 18,325 l., borrowed in instalments; the rent during the last eight years upon those stations has amounted to 3,347 l. 9 s. 3 d.; the cash received from Government for prisoners remanded amounts to 3,871 l. 19 s. 6 d., making a total of 7,219 l. 8 s. 9 d.; whilst the interest paid during that period was 4,846 l. 2 s. 6 d.

743. Lord *Lovaine*.] That item would hardly enter into the consideration, because the Government would equally have paid if the prisoners had been remanded to prisons?—The Government have been relieved, by the erection of the stations, of 2,179 l. 4 s. 4 d. in mileage for conveying prisoners remanded to prison and back again before the magistrates during the last eight years; that is, the mileage would have been charged upon the Government in the specification for conveying remanded prisoners to gaol and back again before the remanding magistrates; therefore the Government is benefited to that amount by the erection of stations.

744. What I mean is, that you can hardly charge that in your account to the credit of the police stations, inasmuch as the same amount would have been paid by the Government for the confinement of those people in prisons?—No, it would not, because for the prisoners that are remanded there is no charge made in the gaol to the Government; one of the great advantages of the station is, that our physical force is improved by economizing the time of our men, without increasing them numerically. I would rather have 20 policemen less with stations, than 20 policemen more without the stations.

745. I am talking of it as a matter of money; you claim for the credit of the police certain sums which the Government pay for remanded prisoners?—I should not claim it under any other circumstances without the stations.

746. It would have gone into the county's pocket if these prisoners had been remanded into the county gaols instead of the police stations?—No, you would not only lose the money, but you would lose the time of the constables in travelling backwards and forwards over the county.

747. Would not it have been charged to the subsistence of the prisoners?—The subsistence of the prisoners is a different thing; this is for safe keeping; the subsistence is a trifling charge of a shilling for the 24 hours; it used to be 2 s. 6 d. when the old parish constables were established; I looked at all these expenses for the purpose of making a balance-sheet to meet the gross expense of the stations.

748. Those sums are paid for the safe custody of the prisoners in your stations?—Yes.

749. *Chairman*.]

Captain J. B. B.
M. Hardy, R. N.

27 May 1853.

749. *Chairman.*] How many boroughs in Essex have separate police forces?—Four; Maldon, Harwich, Saffron Walden, and Colchester.

750. Are any of those boroughs consolidated with the county?—No, none.

751. How are the police in the boroughs appointed?—They are appointed, I believe, by the watch committee; but I have nothing to do with the boroughs, and have very little information about them; the watch committees are generally composed of individuals who are interested on different sides, and in different parties.

752. Mr. *Burroughes.*] Do not you think one reason why there is, what has been generally stated with reference to the boroughs, a jealousy and an indisposition to place themselves under a consolidated constabulary, is losing the appointments in the police?—They object to losing the appointments in the police; their police are very inefficient in many cases; I could read letters to the Committee attributing the safe keeping of the peace at Colchester and Harwich, at the time of the elections, entirely to the county police; I consider the certainty of having the police of the county as a reserve upon which to fall back in times of difficulty is one of the reasons why the boroughs have not joined with us; if they had not had our force at their disposal in times of difficulty, I think they would have joined with us.

753. *Chairman.*] Do you know the description and the number of police officers which there are in the boroughs in your county?—Colchester has 11 and Harwich has four.

754. Do you know Colchester well?—Yes.

755. Supposing Colchester were consolidated with the county, what number would be sufficient, in your opinion?—I should say 15 would be sufficient, from the union of action giving them the benefit of the county police in times of difficulty. When they last required me to come and keep the peace they wished me to come with 60, and I told them I would not come with less than 100.

756. Do you think that the ends of public justice are frustrated by the existence of separate jurisdictions?—Yes.

757. In what way?—From the want of co-operation more particularly; our constables have no authority in the boroughs, whilst the borough constables have authority in our county; showing how advisable it is that the county constables should have authority in the boroughs, if it be necessary that the borough constables should have authority in the county.

758. Are any of the boroughs in Essex known as the resort of offenders?—The boroughs are always the places of rendezvous for the principal offenders, and they require a large force in the neighbourhood, and therefore cause the county to pay for protecting the boroughs.

759. Has your constabulary force been requested to act at any time, in any borough within your county, for the preservation of the peace, or on any other emergency?—Yes.

760. When was that?—Principally at the last election; the authorities attributed the keeping of the peace and the legal termination of the elections to the assistance of the county constabulary.

761. What number of men did you send?—I took one hundred and twenty to Colchester, and I did not find that I had one man too much. My object is always to have a sufficient force to prevent parties being tempted to a breach of the peace.

762. Had the men extra pay from the borough?—They were paid merely their expenses of going; the county paid them their usual weekly pay, but as this was a special service, and the men were put to expense, they were paid 2 s. a day, and 1 s. a night, to cover their expenses.

763. What are the constables paid for attending quarter sessions? Two shillings a day and 1 s. a night. My object is to guard against the police officers profiting in any way by crime; one of the greatest evils which can exist in a system of constabulary is to permit any member of it to have an interest in crime; my object is to confine his interests solely to the prevention of crime.

764. Then you think, if at any place, in any police force, the system is to give a reward for catching a thief, that is objectionable?—Decidedly, because it is an encouragement to the men to have an interest in crime; my rule ever has been never to give a reward; excepting a man risks his life, under no circumstances do I give a reward.

765. Do not you think, under the old system, the parochial constables must have had an interest in the increase of crime?—That is the principal evil of the

parochial constable system ; there are many other evils, but that is particularly the evil of any system which does not remove an interest in crime ; I think a great recommendation of the county constabulary is, that the poor man is protected, and the same interest is taken to follow up any injury he may receive as in the case of the rich man ; whereas, in the other system, unless the party can produce the funds the parochial officer will not follow up the case, and it cannot be expected that he should at his own expense.

766. In anticipation of any disturbance in the boroughs, what system has generally been adopted for the prevention of those disturbances ?—Generally they have sworn in special constables ; they have written to me since we have had the county police ; the special constables are little more than useless, and that was my reason for giving the boroughs the assistance of the county constabulary ; I think the special constables are useless on such occasions for many reasons.

767. Do you know any cases in which they have been found so ?—I never swore them in but once, and that was to prevent their tending to disorder during the Chartist meetings. I thought it advisable to swear those men in, because then I had them under my immediate supervision.

768. Have you ever tried the system of parochial constables, under superintending constables ?—I have, under much greater advantages than under the Act of Parliament by which the superintending constables were appointed ; upon my appointment to my present office, I pointed out to the magistrates that it would be very desirable to ascertain whether parochial constables could be rendered effective if they were properly paid, because it was said that the only difficulty in procuring the article was money. Upon the amended Act passing, which provided that the parochial constabulary were to be paid according to the opinion of the court of quarter sessions, I recommended the magistrates of Essex to establish a very liberal scale of fees indeed, which they did. Perhaps the Committee
Vide Appendix.
will allow me to put in this Report—(*the Witness delivered in " Report of the Chief Constable to the Magistrates of the County of Essex, in Quarter Sessions assembled, April 5th,* 1842."*)* Under that Act of Parliament, with great pains and with the assistance of the parochial officers, clergy, and gentry, I supplied for Essex 600 local constables, of the best material that could be found, but the difficulty being to induce a superior class of persons to act as local constables, the office having got into disrepute, I induced several of the leading yeomen to become local constables. There are advantages in establishing the parochial constable system under the name of local constables, under our Act, which do not exist under the Parochial Act ; the difference is, that under our Act no parochial officer could submit a list of constables to the magistrates in special session, which is done by the chief constable. Practically, there is no difference, except in the party submitting the list ; but the advantage of the system under our Act over the other is, that there is a central power in the chief constable, and the superintendents are amenable to that chief constable ; whereas under the other Act they are all appointed by the same authority, and consequently there is no centre ; and even if the proposed Act were passed for appointing a chief constable, that chief constable, in counties, would be without any power ; he would not have the appointment of the subordinates and superintendents ; it is totally impossible that that can act well ; I took the liberty of recommending to Mr. Deedes the appointment of the chief constable under our Act, as more likely to produce a sound state of things, by the union of the two Acts of Parliament, although I do not think this is at all practicable.

769. Have you any constables at the head-quarters to fill up vacancies ?—We cannot afford it. I move the constables so as to bring the inferior constables under my eye and superintendence ; the men distributed are the better men, and the men in whom I have most confidence.

770. You say the boroughs are unwilling to adopt your police ; do you think they rely upon the assistance of the military in cases of disturbance ?—Particularly, which I think is a dangerous thing to trust to, more particularly from the military acting only in a body, and the constabularly acting disjointedly, that is singly, or two or three together, as well as in a body.

771. Are the police in Essex trained to arms ?—No, I would not do so, for fear of rendering the force unpopular.

772. Are the police required to assist the coast guard in the prevention of smuggling ?—I endeavoured to get them armed with the necessary powers, under the 33d section of the Custom House Act. I did not succeed until I put in evidence

that

that we fell in with waggons laden with contraband goods; subsequently 200 policemen were armed with the power, and with the result I had anticipated. As I told the Board of Customs, on their having that power, we should never see a contraband article. One of my objects for urging it particularly was, that the Government was paying 9,000 *l.* for 127 men upon the coast of Essex, and if the county of Essex could give them a force of 200 men without cost, they might ultimately have a claim for a part of the expenses of the constabulary.

Captain *J. B. B. M'Hardy,* R. N.

27 May 1853.

773. I want to know, generally speaking, the result of the experiment which you tried of having local constables under superintendents?—We had 15 superintendents to give the experiment a fair trial, because I was anxious for my own credit's sake to produce the greatest protection at the least expense. I told the magistrates that the prospects of success would be much improved if they would give 20 inspectors to assist the superintendents in carrying on their duty.

774. Did the magistrates do so?—They did; I wished to give it a fair trial; and therefore we had a large body of officers.

775. Did the experiment fail?—It did; the magistrates were satisfied that every thing had been done, and they augmented the rural police force.

776. They gave up the appointment of local constables?—They were never afterwards sworn in; but I should have felt it imperative upon me to have complied with the Act of Parliament had not the Parish Constables Act subsequently passed.

777. What other supplementary duties do your police perform in Essex beyond the maintenance of the peace?—The inspection of weights and measures; that was a duty which was unsatisfactorily performed at much expense, and, on my representation to the magistrates, they transferred the duty to the police; that has produced an annual saving of 562 *l.* 10 *s.* during the last eight years, which is one of the items I take credit for as a set-off against the gross expense of the county constabulary.

778. Have they performed any other duties?—Yes; besides the relief of vagrants, and assisting the revenue officers, they act as inspectors of nuisances and common lodging-houses, under some of the local Boards of Health.

779. Mr. *Burroughes.*] Did you adopt the inspection of weights and measures by the police from the commencement?—No; on the introduction of the police the system was new, and I thought we had better supersede those local employments gradually; there are many duties which the police might do exclusively of those which they perform in Essex, and which, I hope, they will be permitted to do in addition.

780. *Chairman.*] You mention those additional duties?—I am satisfied, from my experience, that the police might collect all the rates and taxes, and from the extension just now of the post-office establishment, that all the letter carrying might be conducted by the police in patrolling; and by passing them from the different parishes, you might almost have a post-office in every parish; those duties would then be performed by trusty characters, and it is very difficult in the country to get such characters to perform the duty of moving the letters about and delivering them.

781. Are there any other duties which you would suggest should be performed by the police beyond what you have named?—I have turned my attention to the subject a good deal, and I have considered that the police might undertake the inspection of the highways; I was anxious to take the turnpikes, but there was a feeling against the turnpikes; in my opinion, nothing more is wanting to make the Highway Act perfect than that suggestion being put in motion; I think the police being employed as road surveyors would render the present Act perfect, and remove the present difficulty upon that subject, by an extension of the Highway Act, and the consequent abolition of the turnpike gates, with all their attendant expenses.

782. Do you think it would be possible to employ them as road surveyors?—I do.

783. Mr. *Rich.*] Do you think that would afford them additional means of detecting vagrants?—Yes; my idea is, that the more you can employ a local policeman the more efficient he is; all the persons upon the roads, if you had an efficient system, might be special constables, to act with what I may call the more intelligent constables; every member of the police force must be not only a man of high physical power, but he ought also to have great mental qualities and mental qualifications. I do not mean to expect that a special constable would have those

Captain J. B. B
M'Hardy, R.N.

27 May 1853.

qualities, but he would be able to act in conjunction with and under the guidance of the intelligent constables. I also think if a national constabulary were established it might be made the nucleus of a very valuable defensive force. I would take care to keep all those arrangements under the local authorities. I do not think it practicable to carry this out without keeping the constabulary establishment strictly local, excepting in so far as would be necessary to secure complete efficiency and uniformity of system.

784. *Chairman.*] Do you think a night patrol is necessary for the prevention of crime?—I think prevention of crime cannot be effected without a night patrol, and without this all other establishments are merely detectives, who have an interest in offences being committed rather than prevented.

785. Are you able to carry out a night patrol with the force you have at present?—We are, but not in so perfect a manner as if we had more men.

786. Is your force employed at all in any way, directly or indirectly, for the preservation of game?—By law they have no power, and however great an advantage might be derived by our exercising a power with which we are not armed, I never permit it, and therefore the police never exercise any authority with which they are not armed; even in bringing offenders to justice I never countenance any act but what the law justifies, however favourable the result might be.

787. Mr. *Rich.*] In the event of a riot, or a collision between gamekeepers and poachers, would not the police interfere?—That is a case where parties have assembled for an illegal purpose. I merely confine my observations to the fact, that the law arms us with no powers for the protection of game. If parties assemble for a breach of the peace, then it becomes the duty of the peace officer to exercise his authority.

788. *Chairman.*] Do you think the escape of criminals is facilitated by the uncertainty of detection?—Yes; because thieves calculate, like smugglers, upon the chances of escape before they commit the offence, and inasmuch as a smuggler is prevented by an efficient protection of the public revenue, so is a thief by the existence of an efficient police.

789. Do you think the appointment of a general and efficient system of police would tend to shorten the criminal career of offenders?—Yes, I think it would undoubtedly have this effect; because detection would more certainly and speedily follow the offence. I would notice here that the criminal returns do not supply a satisfactory index to the actual state of crime, inasmuch as they only show the number of persons apprehended, and consequently the establishment of a national constabulary would cause an apparent increase; and this would be only temporary.

790. Is the escape of criminals facilitated under magistrates' warrants, from the inconvenience of having the warrants backed?—I believe it is, to some extent, but most of our magistrates are also magistrates for the adjoining county, and they were induced to become so from being aware of the inconvenience and of the delay arising from the necessity of backing warrants.

791. Are you of opinion that the establishment of a national constabulary on a more uniform system is practicable, and would be nationally beneficial?—I think it would be the greatest blessing that could be conferred upon the country. I do not say so hastily, for I have given it my closest attention; I am satisfied there is no other means to be adopted. From the inquiry I have made of the superintendents, appointed under the Parochial Constables Act, I have never heard anything favourable of it; my opinion was asked prior to its being established, and I unhesitatingly said it would be the most inefficient and the most expensive mode that could be adopted; but as it was popular, I thought the opinion of the public should be respected.

792. I think you have said that you would give no rewards to constables for detecting offences?—No, nor for attending at fires; it is against my rule to give a reward under any circumstances, except where a man risks his life.

793. You think such a course objectionable?—It operates objectionably in every sense of the word. I think the predominant evil in the different police establishments is giving the members of the establishment an interest in crime; it is the thing most to be guarded against in every arrangement.

794. Lord *Loraine.*] Do you mean to say that you do not allow your constables to accept any reward which may be offered for capturing an offender?—By the regulations they can receive no reward without my permission. Now and then, but

Captain *J. B. B. M‘Hardy, R. N.*

27 May 1853.

but very rarely, parties do offer small rewards. One of the great difficulties I find in our constabulary system is caused by the defect in our criminal code of having no public prosecutor; we find a great difficulty from this defect, because few people will prosecute if they can avoid it.

795. Have you found that there is any great diminution in the cases of ordinary violence and petty assaults?—There has been a very great reduction in most of those cases. The establishment of a permanent and perfect police force in Essex has been a great check to sheep-stealing; in two divisions out of 14 in the county of Essex 140 sheep were stolen the year previously to the establishment of the police; that number has never been taken in the whole county subsequently.

796. Do you think that any modification of your system could be adapted to the wild districts of counties which are thinly inhabited, where the distances are too large for the men to travel over except on horseback, and the districts too thinly inhabited for much crime to go on in them, but in which there might be places for the concealment of stolen goods, and so on?—The principle upon which policemen are distributed over a county is, that the county is separated into divisions; the divisions into detachments, and those detachments are subdivided into guards or beats; in dividing them, it requires a local knowledge; a place thinly inhabited would not have anything like the number of men that there would be in a place thickly inhabited; those places would be inspected during the day, to guard against the practices which your Lordship refers to. A horse patrol is most inefficient in the detection of crime; the very noise of a horse's feet upon the road will disturb a depredator, and he will conceal himself; it is a beacon for him to avoid, and I would never recommend the introduction of a horse patrol, except for supervision.

797. My question was put with reference to the county I represent, which is Northumberland; that is now under the Superintending Constables Act; it is a district in which for 15 miles together you will hardly find a cottage, but, nevertheless, upon the farmers a considerable amount of depredation in the way of sheep-stealing has gone on hitherto; I wish to ascertain whether, with any modification of your system, you could meet the necessities of such a situation without incurring a very great expense?—If it was under my supervision, I should erect a building in the centre of it, and let one or two men who occupied the centre traverse the district in opposite directions; they would surround the spots referred to by your Lordship, each man going half way round the circle; they would cover it both ways by one or two men coming from the centre to both sides; if they went their rounds at 10 o'clock at night and two o'clock in the morning, that would insure their passing over the ground; those are local arrangements that must be left to the parties.

798. You will observe, that in Northumberland the distances are so enormous, that it is impossible for the men to patrol them unless on horseback?—The only thing which I should suggest would be, that a party should be located as near the centre of the place as possible; I do not suppose it is more than 15 miles.

799. Suppose it is a district of 50 miles?—The only way to protect that is to occupy it by different parties; thieves do not occupy it; they would possibly be in the parts thickly inhabited, and by watching the resort for depredators you would prevent the commission of offences.

800. Are you of opinion that there is any use in swearing in common constables in counties where there is a rural police?—No. I have had experience many years as inspecting commander of the coast guard, and what I saw in that capacity led me to believe that I was preparing to fill the office which I now hold; on the coast the common constables could not be sworn as assistants, and I have never seen an instance of special constables being of any avail.

801. Are not the common constables still retained in some counties, though they are not allowed to act?—Yes; the ordinary parish constables are still appointed in all counties, and cause considerable expense by performing petty duties which might be easily and much better performed by the police.

802. Is there any additional protection to the public from the existence of common constables?—I have no hesitation in saying no; I say it without prejudice.

803. With regard to the boroughs, is there any possibility of amalgamating the forces without taking away altogether the power of the inhabitants to appoint their own police?—I do not speak hastily upon the subject, for I have fully considered it; I am satisfied, whilst you leave the appointment of constables in the

Captain *J. B. B.*
M'Hardy, R. N.
———
27 May 1853.

local authorities in boroughs, you never can render the force efficient; there are clauses in Act 3 & 4 Vict., c. 88. which make provision for your doing so. I always have said to our magistrates, should the boroughs wish to unite their force with the county, I trust you will never consent, except upon their placing themselves in the same position as that in which the magistrates of the county have placed themselves; that is, by leaving the subordinate appointments to the chief constable.

804. Mr. *Rich*.] Would you object to giving the authorities in the boroughs a voice in the election of the chief constable for the county?—That is a thing upon which I am unprepared to give an opinion. I should consider that the large proportion which the magistrates bear to the authorities of the boroughs would guard against the evils which I inwardly apprehend.

805. Might not an objection justly exist on the part of the boroughs if they had no voice in the management of the police, and if it were entirely absorbed by the county, and if the boroughs had a concurrent voice in the election of the chief constable with the magistrates, that jealousy might be done away with?—That is a subject for your consideration; if there were an equal number of controlling parties in the boroughs and an equal number of county magistrates, I should think it was very injurious, but if the magistrates had a safeguard by having a predominant number I should think it worthy of consideration.

806. Have you many fires in Essex?—No, we have but few compared with what we had.

807. When you were appointed there were more than there are at present?—Much more.

808. In what part of Essex do the fires occur?—The recent fires have been about Hallingbury, not far from Bishop's Stortford. I find great reluctance on the part of the insurance offices to take any steps, to detect incendiaries.

809. You think there should be a public prosecutor?—I think a public prosecutor is indispensably necessary, for the purpose of carrying out our criminal code; nothing calls more for interference and immediate remedy than the expenses attending the conducting of prosecutions.

810. Mr. *Phillips*.] What is the total expense of the police in Essex?—The total expense was 16,000 *l.* in the year 1852.

811. Do you know what that is in the pound in Essex?—A penny rate raises 6,125 *l.* 9 *s.*; therefore it is a little more than 2 ¼ *d.* I wish you to understand that we have a great set-off.

812. Sir *J. Trollope*.] What is the total amount of the set-off, from allowances from Government, and other sources?—I will put in this return of the heads under which the different savings and earnings are effected; they amount to 15,805 *l.* 13 *s.* 9 *d.* In a report, dated October 1850, I used these words: "And I am satisfied that this court will readily acknowledge, although there may be in the minds of a few a difference of opinion on some of the items now submitted, that the Essex constabulary does not actually cost the county one-third of its apparent expense."—(*The Witness delivered in "Report of the Chief Constable to the Magistrates of the County of Essex, in Quarter Sessions assembled, 15th October* 1850.")

Vide Appendix.

813. Mr. *Howard*.] Do you think there is anything peculiar in the habits of the people of Essex, with reference to smuggling, which renders a larger force necessary than in any other counties?—I do not think the revenue force in Essex is equal to that in Sussex and Kent, as to the distance occupied. I think there is a difficulty in connecting the Essex coast, from its irregularity; where there is a straight coast you are enabled to link the patrols together, but you cannot link the patrols where the coast is intersected by rivers, as in Essex.

814. May not the result of that be the introduction of lawless habits among the people?—I do not know.

815. Mr. *Rich*.] Do you think the establishment of electric telegraphs would tend to the efficiency of the police force?—If you ultimately carried the electric telegraph to all the different superintendents' stations, you might, of course, communicate an offence of importance to them, and then, by carrying it to the head quarters of the chief constable, you may telegraph to those points; you would be able to circulate information by that means; the information would get before the depredator. Those are points of detail to be left to subsequent arrangement.

816. Is the feeling of the majority of the people of Essex kindly or not.
towards

towards the police, in your opinion?—Particularly so; there was a great feeling at first against it, but I think that has quite subsided.

817. Lord *Lovaine*.] When you spoke of your police becoming surveyors of roads, I presume you only intended that they should report upon the state of the roads in the districts which they patrol?—I intend that they should see the duties carried out, because in the discharge of their other duties they must be upon the roads; they could give it proper supervision, and they could have the advantage of all the constables under their superintendence in explaining where water-courses are stopped, or where there has been any breach of the Highway Act. An individual acting for that purpose, except a member of the police force, would not have that assistance and co-operation; that is the principal reason why I recommend the members of the police doing it.

818. Sir *J. Anderson*.] Do you know what the police rate is in the borough of Colchester, for instance?—I do not; I think it is worth mentioning, that at Maldon, at the last election, from the want of proper peace officers, there were a number of boxers brought from London to protect one party, whilst the gipsies protected the other; I mention that to show the want of peace officers.

819. Mr. *Burroughes*.] Is there not a police force at Maldon?—One man; they wrote to me to nominate a man I could recommend, but our men would not accept borough employment.

Maurice Swabey, Esq., called in; and Examined.

820. *Chairman*.] ARE you a Magistrate for Buckinghamshire?—Yes.

821. And also for Surrey and Middlesex?—Yes.

822. Were you formerly a police magistrate?—I was for 11 years.

823. Where do you reside now?—Langley Marish, in Buckinghamshire.

824. What is the system of police in Buckinghamshire?—There are 10 superintending constables, and no system at all; they do exactly as they please; there are magistrates in different parts of the county with different views; there is no one system.

825. Is the whole of the county under superintending constables?—Yes, 10 in number.

826. How many divisions are there?—For police purposes, 10 divisions.

827. For magisterial purposes, how many are there?—A great many more; in many hundreds there are petty sessions held legitimately, according to acknowledged divisions, of hundreds and half hundreds, and in others they are held as a matter of convenience, and not properly held, according to my opinion.

828. You mean that the county has been divided, for police purposes, into 10 divisions?—Only 10 divisions.

829. Is there a superintendent for each of those divisions?—Yes.

830. Are they mounted police?—They have a horse and cart.

831. Do you know what they are paid?—I think they are paid about 90*l.* a year.

832. Have they to keep their horse and cart?—I think they are allowed for that; I am not quite certain.

833. Are the parochial constables entirely under their direction?—Yes; but in almost every parish there is a man paid two or three or four or five pounds a year; other men are sworn in, but they never do anything.

834. You mean that every parish has a paid constable besides the superintending constable?—Yes, a great many parishes; the larger ones chiefly.

835. Is that paid constable paid for the whole of his time, or only for a part of his time?—He is paid a sort of a retaining fee; he is to be at the call of any of the inhabitants who want him. We do not see these men for months and months at the magistrates' meetings, and I do not consider them of any use adequate to the money they receive.

836. From your experience as a police magistrate and as a magistrate for a great many years in Buckinghamshire, do you think that the parochial constables are of any use?—Not the slightest; we could do quite as well without them.

837. Do you think they are to be depended upon for the control of public-houses, or beershops?—Not in the slightest degree.

838. Do you think vagrancy has been much checked by the appointment of those superintending constables?—I think it has had that effect in some degree, and very much more where they have sworn in the superintending constables is

M. Swabey, Esq.

27 May 1853.

assistant relieving officers for that purpose; the vagrants are afraid of going near them, and that certainly has had a good effect; it lessens the number of vagrants' applications at the union houses.

839. Was not that done under the recommendation of the Poor Law Board?—Yes; and it has had a very good effect.

840. Has the adoption of the rural police ever been proposed in Buckinghamshire?—It was proposed about 10 or 12 years ago by Sir William Young, who was one of the members for Buckinghamshire, and myself; we took a great deal of pains, and the expense seemed to be the objection; we were in a decided minority at the sessions.

841. Do you think it was opposed on the ground of expense alone?—Expense was the principal ground of opposition; there might have been a little admixture of politics, but I think I may say generally it was on the ground of expense it was rejected; that was the avowed ground.

842. Do you think it would be desirable to have a more general system of police in Buckinghamshire?—I think so.

843. Do you suffer from your contiguity to places which have a police force, to which the Metropolitan police extends?—Yes; there is the borough of Windsor, which is in Berkshire; and there is Uxbridge; the vagrants get driven out from Uxbridge into Buckinghamshire, and we have no means of coping with them; the borough of Windsor sends hundreds into our county; the river Thames merely divides the two counties; it is a great expense to the county, independently of police matters, in the numbers we have to relieve; at Windsor they point our union house out to them, and they say there is a union house where they will relieve you; they never relieve anybody in Windsor; they can see our union house, and their own happens to be further distant, in the part of the county called Old Windsor.

844. From your experience as a police magistrate, do you think that vagrancy is a great source of crime?—I have no doubt about it; they begin by being vagrants, and they end by becoming thieves.

845. Are not the majority of vagrants thieves?—I cannot say that; I have experience enough to say that I think, very probably, they are. In my opinion, the want of a public prosecutor is a very great denial of justice: I am aware that there is an objection to increase new appointments, but the subject occurred to me when I was speaking to one of the Honourable Members for Lancaster this morning, and his view was, that the appointment should not be given to the Government of the day, but should rest with the Judges in the Court of Queen's Bench, which I approve of.

846. As far as your experiences goes, the system of superintendence does not render the parochial constables more efficient?—I think not; I think we are not much better off, having the superintendents, than we were without them; there is a want of co-operation; there is a jealousy among many of those people; there is no avowed head. I think the system has hardly had a fair trial as it is carried on in Buckinghamshire.

847. Mr. *Rich.*] You have said that the vagrants are driven out of Windsor and Uxbridge into Buckinghamshire; that the magistrates rejected the proposition for having a police force in the county, on account of their fear of the expenses; do you think subsequent experience has modified that opinion on the part of the magistrates?—I think on the part of a great number of individuals it has; I have my doubts whether the sessions would listen to it; they would use this argument: "We have gone to a considerable expense since that time by having paid superintendents, and we have established a system, we have a system that we had not then;" that would be the answer that would be urged against the more expensive system.

848. Do you think, on the whole, the resistance to the adoption of a police force would be less strong now than it was 10 years ago?—I am fearful it would be resisted; there are a great number of causes which would operate upon the minds of individuals.

849. Do you hear complaints from parties of small depredations on their property?—No, I do not. The farmers are very careless and very negligent about their property. There is one thing I will take the liberty of mentioning with reference to farmers; the farmers do not care about fires; they are no losers, for they get the best market price for their corn; and instead of old and bad barns, they

M. Swabey, Esq.

27 May 1853.

they have new ones built at the expense of the insurance offices. The insurance offices have been extremely liberal, and have given the farmers the best price for their corn, even though the corn might not have been sold at that price; the farmers do not look much after fires.

850. Are fires frequent?—In the northern part, about Newport Pagnell and Olney, I have had conversations with the magistrates, and they complain very much of the want of co-operation.

851. Mr. *Howard.*] Is there a chief constable amongst those superintending constables?—No, there is not; that is one thing of which I complain.

852. Sir *J. Trollope.*] Is there a lock-up built in each district?—There may be in as many as eight out of ten.

853. Is it proposed to have one in each district?—They propose doing so. I need not tell the Honourable Members of the Committee, many of whom are country gentlemen, the local feelings in one division unless they have as much public money laid out upon them as another. The case is seldom met upon its own merits. There are a hundred reasons why we do not advance under the present system.

854. You have stated that the quarter sessions would not entertain any project for altering it?—I fear not. I do not think it will be brought forward, from what I see at present.

855. What is the feeling amongst the ratepayers of Buckinghamshire; are they satisfied with the present protection to their property, or do they desire it to be more extended?—I do not hear any complaints.

856. Their property is protected as much as they require?—Yes, it should seem so.

857. Do you think, under the system in Buckinghamshire, detection follows crime, or the contrary?—I hardly know how to answer that question; a great many crimes are not detected, but that is not the fault of the police; there is a great unwillingness to prosecute.

858. Do you find that is general?—I think it is general throughout the whole country, that people would rather suffer the loss than be at the trouble of going to the county town.

859. At your sessions and assizes, are not your prosecutors' expenses allowed? —Yes, the same as they are in other counties; but there are many expenses that they do not cover.

860. Mr. *Phillips.*] You say that you are a magistrate of Surrey and Middlesex; have you any local acquaintance with those counties?—Very little; I have a small property in Surrey.

861. They have a police in Surrey, have they not?—Yes.

862. Can you speak to the comparative state of a county with a police, and of yours without a police?—No; I should be more able to compare Oxfordshire with Buckinghamshire; I am not intimately acquainted with Oxfordshire; they have constables in Thame, who drive the vagrants into Buckinghamshire.

863. *Chairman.*] You think, generally speaking, the counties where there is a police drive the vagrants into the surrounding districts which have no police?— Very much so; it is part of their instructions to get rid of them.

864. Sir *J. Trollope.*] Do you wish that the Rural Police Act should be introduced in its entire force in the county of Bucks?—It would be my wish.

865. Do you think it would tend to the benefit and protection of personal property?—I think it would knock up a great number of separate systems.

866. Is it not under one system now, the 5th & 6th of Victoria, cap. 109?— It is extremely disjointed; we seem to change every six months.

867. Have you any municipal towns within the county of Bucks which have a town police, for instance, Amersham or Aylesbury?—Wycombe has a small police, so has Buckingham, being borough towns; Aylesbury an inadequate one.

Jovis, 2° die Junii, 1853.

MEMBERS PRESENT.

Mr. Rice.
Sir John Trollope.
Lord Lovaine.
Mr. Mackie.

Mr. Burroughes.
Sir James Anderson.
Mr. Moody.

EDWARD ROYDS RICE, Esq., in the Chair.

James Parker, Esq., called in ; and Examined.

J. Parker, Esq.

8 June 1853.

868. *Chairman.*] WHERE do you reside?—At Great Baddow, in Essex; I carry on business as a Solicitor in Chelmsford and in London.

869. Was your father clerk of the peace for the county of Essex?—Yes.

870. For how many years did he hold that office?—He was about 25 years clerk of the peace for the county of Essex.

871. Were you associated with him during any part of that period?—I was, for 20 years.

872. Were you the clerk of indictments?—I was clerk of indictments in the years 1846 and 1847.

873. In the execution of the offices which you have described, have you received effective assistance from the police in Essex?—I have received great assistance from the police.

874. Will you state to the Committee in what way you have received assistance?—When I first took office, I found the greatest delay in preparing bills of indictment, from the witnesses not being forthcoming, and from the depositions being imperfect; it was impossible for me to prepare the bills of indictment without seeing the witnesses. I applied to the chief constable, to allow the police to assist me; they invariably collected all the witnesses together, and gave me their names, and made a sort of analysis of their evidence, so as to enable me to prepare the indictments at future sessions with far greater facility; and so much so that generally in one day the whole of the bills were prepared, and the grand jury discharged; they having been formerly, generally speaking, two days.

875. Have you had considerable experience in the conduct of prosecutions?—I have had very great; and in the conduct of those prosecutions, through the chief constable and his officers, I have been enabled to get further information for the completion of the evidence; the depositions themselves frequently being so very imperfect that crime, in many cases, could not be established against the prisoners without further evidence.

876. Therefore you think you have derived great advantage from the police in the collection of evidence?—Very great.

877. Has that been the means of saving expense to the county?—It has been the means of saving expense, as the police were enabled, by their knowledge of men and localities, to obtain evidence with far greater facility than I could possibly have done, and saved the expense of my professional journies.

878. Have the police effected a saving in any other respects?—A saving has been effected in their being inspectors of weights and measures, and the duties of that office they have performed to the entire satisfaction of the county at large. The importance of that office I need not describe to the Committee; I believe the poor have saved a vast sum of money by the weights and measures being kept in proper order.

879. Do you think those duties have been more efficiently performed than they were by the persons who performed them before?—Yes.

880. Were the inspectors of weights and measures generally local constables?—They were not always local constables; the duties are far more efficiently performed now; the e is a greater detection, at least there was at first, in false

weights

J. Parker, Esq.

8 June 1852.

weights and measures, and a saving of expense, because the superintendents of police, who have been appointed the inspectors of weights and measures, are enabled, with their carts and horses, with great facility to travel the county; and to examine from time to time the weights and measures in the different parts of the county.

881. Do you think there has been a greater certainty of detection of offences by the police as compared with the parochial constables?—Certainly; the one gives his whole time and has his whole attention occupied in the duties of his office; whereas the old parish constables were frequently shopkeepers in the parish, and for the most part they were very ignorant men; in addition to which many of the parish constables made a kind of living of it.

882. In what way?—They kept the different cases with which they had to do to the very last part of the sessions; and increased the expense from the witnesses being kept longer than they ought to have been.

883. Do you think that criminals ever escaped through the neglect or ignorance of the parochial constables?—Not only through the neglect and ignorance of the parochial constables, but also through other means, in the shape of bribes, interest, affection or regard for perhaps some of the criminals, and if not for the criminals, for some of their friends.

884. From local connexions?—Precisely so.

885. Are there any other services in which the police, as established in Essex, are more efficient than the parish constables?—I think as relieving officers they have caused a great saving to the county.

886. Do you mean as relieving officers for the vagrants?—As relieving officers for the vagrants, I think there has been a considerable saving to the county; also, we are not troubled with those vagrants which we were before troubled with. They went about from union-house to union-house; but since the police have been appointed to that office we have not had nearly so many vagrants as we had before.

887. Do you think the establishment of the police has caused a decrease of crime in Essex?—I think so, certainly.

888. Do you think that petty depredations in Essex have been decreased by the establishment of the police?—I think they have been decreased; I think the police force has prevented a great deal of crime; and, through the unity of action, and the way in which crime is communicated from one policeman to another, there is far greater certainty of detection; but the system is not so perfect as it might be made by the Legislature.

889. Do you think the establishment of the police has increased the value of property at all to the occupiers, and, consequently, to the owners?—I do; as in proportion as crime has diminished and security insured, property has increased in value.

890. Have you the management of any properties in Essex?—Yes, of large estates.

891. Do you also act as the agent of other persons?—Yes.

892. Do you know whether those persons for whom you act as agent approve of the appointment of the police?—I should say, certainly, in all cases; I do not know of any disapproval.

893. Has there been any public expression of opinion on the part of the magistrates on the subject of the appointment of the police?—Yes; just after the July Session of 1840 there was an expression, on the part of the grand jury, of their extreme approbation of the manner in which the police had conducted all matters when they had appeared before them.

894. Do you know what that was?—I have not got it.

895. Do you speak of the fact of your own knowledge?—Certainly; in 1850 there was some talk, in consequence of the reduced price in corn, that there ought to be a proportionate deduction from the amount of the stipend given to the different officers; and there was, at the general court of quarter sessions, an expression of opinion.

896. Sir J. Trollope.] When was that?—In October 1850: "That the Essex constabulary is highly valuable, and is essentially necessary to the protection of the public property and the proper administration of public justice."

897. Was that passed by the magistrates unanimously?—It was unanimously. It is made an order of the court and entered upon the records.

898. Chairman.] Do you think that the parish constables could be depended

upon for investigating cases with. any reward?—Decidedly not. I think in cases where the prosecutor was not tolerably well off, and was unable to pay them, very little investigation took place, as the parish constable could not afford to give up his time.

899. Was the police force unpopular at its first appointment?—It was.

900. Do you think that feeling has decreased?—Entirely so. The general feeling I know is, that there are not a sufficient number of policemen.

901. Do you think the county expenditure has been lessened or increased by the establishment of the police?—I do not suppose the county expenditure as regards the police has been lessened. I consider their services are more than equivalent to the expenses incurred, and there are considerable sets off to these expenses.

902. Do you think the local constables are of any use in cases of public disturbance?—No, I never found them of the slightest use.

903. Had you any machine breaking in Essex, in 1830?—There were some few instances.

904. Machine breaking was not general in Essex, was it;—There was a slight disturbance in the Tendring district.

905. Sir *J. Trollope*.] You had not the advantage of the police at that time? —We had not the police, but the coast guard assisted.

906. *Chairman*.] Do you think crime has increased from criminals calculating upon the chance of escape?—I do not think they calculate upon escape now as they did before. I think they did generally calculate upon the chance of escape in the little petty crimes.

907. Do they calculate upon the chance of escape into other counties where there is no police?—No doubt; we keep a vast number out of the county by having a police.

908. Supposing a uniform system of police were established in the different counties of England generally, do you think the chance of escape would be much decreased?—Decidedly; if there was unity of action between the counties in the same way that there is unity of action between the different parishes throughout the Essex. If each county had uniformity of action in the same way that every parish in the county has, I think the chance of escape would be less.

909. If it appeared in evidence before the Police Commissioners, that the undetected career of thieves and rogues on the average was six years, do you think that would be very much decreased by the establishment of a uniform police force?—I think, after a year or so, they would find it impossible to escape detection.

910. If there were a uniform system of police throughout the kingdom, and the career of thieves was decreased, do you or not think that the expense of the police in each county might be decreased?—No doubt about it.

911. Sir *J. Trollope*.] What was the year in which you ceased to assist your father as clerk of the peace for the county of Essex?—He died in 1847.

912. You have stated that the police have assisted you in preparing indictments, and that the depositions upon which they were founded very frequently came before you imperfect, and that you were obliged to get up further evidence through the police; was it the practice to get up evidence when the parties who were charged were not present to hear it?—No.

913. Did you take further evidence in the way of depositions in cases upon which the persons committed for trial were not present?—If I was acting as solicitor for the prosecutor, and I found that the depositions did not substantiate the charge, I should take further evidence. As clerk of indictments, I have frequently found that the depositions were insufficient to substantiate the case.

914. Did you think it your duty to take further evidence when the party who was under charge was not present to hear what that evidence was?—I did not take further evidence in his absence, and never upon oath.

915. Was that evidence made use of upon the trial?—Certainly.

916. Still it was not included in the return to the court?—Precisely.

917. Is not that an irregular proceeding as clerk of indictments?—The prosecutor or the prisoner could have a copy of the depositions; if I found that the depositions did not make out the case clearly, as clerk of indictments I obtained further information to enable me to prepare the indictment, and without which I could not have done it.

J. Parker, Esq.

2 June 1853.

918. Did you include them in the depositions handed up to the court?—I did not; they were merely for my own information.

919. Did the imperfection in the depositions which you have spoken of arise from the magistrate's clerk taking them down imperfectly or irregularly?—No; the recorded depositions might be quite sufficient to establish a *primâ facie* case, but not sufficient to support a case before a jury.

920. You have stated that the parish constables had an interest in prosecution; have the police no interest in prosecutions?—Not the slightest.

921. Are they not allowed expenses for attending quarter sessions and assizes? —A very slight sum, I could not tell exactly what that is.

922. Are they not allowed a daily sum?—I am not aware of it; I believe they are allowed expenses out of pocket.

923. But they are allowed their expenses, are they not?—Yes; expenses out of pocket.

924. Have you any records from your office to give this Committee, showing the amount of increase or decrease of criminal offences in Essex?—No.

925. Lord *Lovaine.*] Can there well be a worse system of police than one which gives the police officer, whoever it is, a decided interest in crime?— Decidedly not; I think it goes to the root of destroying his usefulness, and the good of his office.

926. Does not the parish constable exist in a great measure by fees which he receives for apprehending criminals, and attending prosecutions?—He is paid a slight salary in many parishes.

927. Is not the great amount of the emoluments of the parish constable calculated with regard to the crime which is likely to prevail in his parish?— Precisely.

928. Have you ever known cases in which a parish constable has refused to serve a summons or a warrant from personal fear?—I have not; I do not call any such instance to my recollection.

929. Are there not a great number of commons and wild districts in Essex?— No, we are very cultivated; there is a wild district in my own parish, but crime there has very much diminished. In my own case, I think so much of the police, I have a house close to my own garden, which I had let for 15 *l.* a year; but I was glad to take a constable at 5 *l.* for protection.

930. Sir *J. Trollope.*] Is that one of the rural police?—Yes.

931. Do you act as a magistrate for Essex?—No.

932. Lord *Lovaine.*] Do you believe that the present inspectors of weights and measures are open to local influence at all? I mean, whether the inspectors of weights and measures are occasionally inclined to overlook fraudulent weights and measures?—I believe in no case; I think every case is brought forward.

933. Do you believe there was any collusion at all under the old system?— Certainly; both from their own acquaintances and connexions, which the police are utterly independent of; they have a duty to perform, and they think of nothing but that, and they have performed it with extreme satisfaction in Essex.

934. Sir *J. Trollope.*] You are not aware of any instance of their having overlooked cases of fraudulent weights?—No.

935. *Chairman.*] Have you had any individual charges brought against the police?—I never recollect any.

936. Sir *J. Trollope.*] I think you have stated that at one time there was an impression that the salary of the police ought to be reduced, owing to the diminished cost of the necessaries of life; was it effected or not?—It was not carried; that resolution which I have referred to was made an order of the court of quarter sessions.

937. Was October 1850 the time when that attempt was made?—Yes.

938. Upon the whole have you reason to believe that the ratepayers of the county are satisfied to bear the expense, considering the benefits they are supposed to receive from the system?—I am quite certain they are.

939. You are satisfied that there is no feeling against the great cost of the police?—Certainly.

940. Are you aware of the total cost of the police for the county of Essex?— I am not.

941. Is it about 10,000 *l.*?—I could not say.

H 4

J. *Parker*, Esq.

2 June 1853.

942. You do not know what amount of rate in the pound is required to pay for the police for the county of Essex?—I do not.

943. Do you know what proportion it bears to the county expense as regards the county rate?—No; I have never heard anything but satisfaction of the police, and very much so of the chief constable.

944. *Chairman*.] You are not prepared to say that there is no difference of opinion upon the subject?—I never heard any.

945. Sir *J. Trollope*.] Do you generally reside in the county?—Entirely.

946. Do you come backwards and forwards to your office in London?—Yes; my chief business lies in Essex.

947. Does not your business take you a good deal in the daytime away from the county?—No, I am generally in the country.

948. Have you the means of knowing the feelings of the country?—Yes.

949. Are you engaged in any professional business in the county?—Yes, principally.

950. Lord *Lovaine*.] Your business in London is only a branch business? —Yes.

Mr. *Robert Baker*, called in; and Examined.

Mr. R. *Baker*.

951. *Chairman*.] WHERE do you reside?—At Writtle, near Chelmsford, in Essex.

952. Are you a land agent?—I am a farmer and land agent; I have been all my life in general country business.

953. Are you a large occupier of land?—I have occupied upon an average about 600 or 700 acres for the last 10 years. I used to occupy more.

954. Do you act as a land agent?—Yes. I have had the general management of Writtle parish matters, which is one of the largest parishes in the county.

955. What is the size of that parish?—I think the number of acres is upwards of 8,000 acres, between 8,000 and 9,000 acres; I was assistant overseer for several years; I have been churchwarden for same period.

956. Is your occupation in the parish of Writtle?—Yes, principally; I had also the management of Boreham parish, in Essex. I have been more or less in parish office for 35 years without cessation.

957. Have you, as an occupier of land, received benefits from the establishment of police?—Yes.

958. In what respect?—Depredation is not so frequent as it used to be; in fact, our village was rather notorious for the amount of depredations committed in it; we very rarely could say that we had not some one belonging to our village in the county gaol; now I do not believe we have had for several years a person there; in fact, I now hardly hear of a theft in the parish within the last two or three years; so far as my own property has been concerned, I do not think I have had a prosecution before the bench for the last ten years, which I attribute entirely to the presence of the police. The loose part of the community about us find that they are so closely watched, it is not worth their while to go out, and there is such difficulty in getting home with stolen property that they do not venture out; I think that is the chief benefit.

959. You think property has been much benefited?—I think property has been very much benefited.

960. Do you think it has had a good moral effect upon the character of the population?—Very great; our parish, before the establishment of police, was a most dissolute parish; there was scarcely a night passed but there were some petty offences, such as throwing gates off the hinges; I believe for some years the coping-stones of the bridges were thrown off wantonly by persons, but now we never hear of anything of the kind.

961. Therefore your opinion is, that the offences against persons and property have both decreased?—Very much so. I was averse to the police in the first instance; I took a decided objection to it; in fact, I headed an opposition against it, but I have become so thoroughly convinced of its utility that I have done all I could to support it. It was supposed that it was something in the character of espionage upon us. I do not think it was so well arranged or so well understood; there was a prejudice against the principle of it by English people; I believe that

prejudice

prejudice, even with the labourers themselves, has subsided; I think all the best of the labourers approve of the police as well as the farmers.

962. Is it your opinion that the poor man's property is peculiarly protected by the police?—Undoubtedly it is; his property was always subject to depredations; the allotment gardens were frequently pilfered; persons used to cultivate allotment gardens, both private and public gardens, and they were mostly pilfered, but we never hear anything of it now.

963. Do you think, from your experience, that the increased expenses of the police have been more than repaid by the advantage which you have derived from it?—I am quite certain of it; I do not think the increased expense is near as much as is imagined; I know, practically, it is not; when I came to dissect matters, which I did for my own information, I found it was very little more than, I think, as two to five, of our constable expenses; the general expenses were about three-fourths of the whole of the present expenditure; I know, from having paid the bills for many years, that the sum we used to pay to our parish constables was about 30 l. per quarter. There are four divisions in the parish, and the police expenditure was about 40 l. to 45 l. a quarter. I find, having been assistant overseer, after the police force was established, the county rates we then paid were about 80 l. a quarter; that was about the proportion they stood us in.

964. Now, as the occupier of land, and as agent for other property, are you of opinion that the value of land has been increased to the occupier, and consequently to the owner, by the establishment of the police in Essex?—Whatever would give protection to property must give an increased value to property. I have no hesitation in saying that the value of property is increased; as a farmer, I would sooner take a farm, all other things being equal, where a good police force has been established, than I would where there was not one; previously we were liable to sheep-stealing and horse-stealing, when I commenced farming.

965. Do you mean to say, if you were about taking a farm in Essex, that you would give some trifling addition in rent if you knew there was a good police force, more than you would if there was not a police force?—Yes; I am more satisfied with things as they are than I was before the police was established.

966. Mr. *Burroughes*.] You are equally well satisfied that your opinion, with regard to the establishment of the constabulary, was wrong in the first instance? — Yes; there were a great many prejudices; farmers look at expenditure, and never at the principles of a thing.

967. Sir *J. Trollope*.] You stated that you have been 35 years as a parish officer in various capacities?—Yes.

968. Have you not encouraged education by schools, and other means?—Yes; the whole tone of society has been improved; I think the introduction of the new poor law has had an astonishing effect.

969. Do you attribute the moral improvement in your parish to other causes besides the establishment of the police?—Not entirely to the police.

670. You attribute it to the measures of improvement, besides the measures of restraint?—Yes.

971. There has been a general improvement from other causes besides the establishment of police?—Undoubtedly.

972. You have mentioned schools and the new poor law; can you attribute the improvement to any other sources?—I think there is a better system of farming pursued; more labour is taken up, and there are not so many dependent upon the poor rates. Under the old poor law there was a large number of idlers that depended upon the poor rates; they would rather remain in idleness than work.

973. Are you a poor law guardian for the parish?—I am.

974. Have you been so since the introduction of the new poor law?—Not all the time continuously.

975. Is the labour of the idlers absorbed?—It is; a very large proportion of our labour has been withdrawn, not as emigrants, but to fill up gaps which emigrants have made; they get up to the metropolis.

976. Has the population decreased in your parish?—No, I think not.

977. Have you seen the Census of 1851?—Yes; we have an increase upon that.

978. You have stated that the constabulary under the old system cost you 30 l. per quarter for your parish?—No; the constables' bills averaged about 30 l.

979. Was that a charge upon the parish or upon the individuals?—Upon the parish.

I

980. In

Mr. *R. Baker.*

2 June 1853.

980. In what way did that arise?—Entirely upon the poor rates.

981. In what way did that arise?—From the occasional attendance of the constables before the bench of magistrates; to show the difficulty we had in the management of the parish at that time, I have known sometimes 40 applications made in a week from the idlers and dissolute part of the population out of employment.

982. Were your constables paid by salaries or by fees?—By salary and fees; they were paid for all their attendances.

983. The difference of cost, therefore, between that system and the present is 10 *l.* per quarter?—I am only speaking vaguely as to what the cost immediately is; at the time I paid it as assistant overseer I know the sum we paid to the police commonly was about 40 odd pounds, and the old constables have been 30 odd pounds per quarter.

984. Do you know the amount in the pound you have paid towards the police force in your own parish?—Two-pence farthing.

985. Has it always been the same since the institution of police?—It has not much varied.

986. Do you know what your county rate for other purposes amounts to?—I cannot say exactly; at the time when I paid the county rate it was about doubled by the police rate; each payment was about twice 40 *l.*, or 80 *l.*

987. Is the county rate in Essex about 4 *d.* in the pound?—I do not know; at that time, I should think seven years ago, perhaps it might be longer than that, when I was assistant overseer, it was about 80 *l.*; I only know from the sums I used to enter.

988. Your contribution to the county rate was double what the contribution for the same quarter was for the police?—I should hesitate speaking positively upon that point; whether originally it was 40 *l.*, or 80 *l.* including the police rate, I am not able to say now; one would be as much as the other; when we paid the police rate it was incorporated in the county rate.

989. Do you think the 4½ *d.* would include the police, or is it without the police?—I think the 4½ *d.* would include the police; I could have ascertained these points, but I did not know it would be necessary.

990. Have you lost any sheep lately in your district from thieves?—Not one.

991. Have you heard of such cases?—Not one.

992. Is sheep-stealing a prevailing crime in Essex?—We used frequently to lose sheep; I have lost several myself; to give some idea of the extent to which that went on: I was member of a society for the prevention of crime and for the apprehension of offenders; I frequently have received money from that society, before the police was established, towards my expense for prosecution; since the police has been established I have not had a single prosecution, nor an application from the society for any rate, which shows that crime has decreased.

993. Do you know of any cases of horse-stealing since the establishment of police?—Very few; I heard of nothing lately; I have not heard of one in our district for several years being lost.

994. The other species of farmers' property which is subject to depredation is the poultry; do they take your poultry still?—I have never lost any but in one instance.

995. Was that since the establishment of police?—Yes; that was from one of our own servants.

996. Was the person taken?—Not at the time, but it turned out afterwards who it was, after finding him out in some other crime; we did not suspect him in the first instance.

997. Lord *Lovaine.*] How long is it since the police was established in Essex?—I think, from my recollection, 12 or 14 years. I cannot speak positively to that point.

998. You mentioned that an improvement had taken place in the moral character of the inhabitants; was there a marked improvement immediately after the establishment of the police?—A very marked improvement. I do not think there was a more dissolute class in any parish in Essex, and I do not think that there is a more orderly class than they are now.

999. My question was directed more as to the immediate consequences of the establishment of the police?—Of course it was gradual; it was not apparent at once, but I know we have been gradually improving.

1000. Do you think that the main instrument in this improvement was the police?—I do. I think, as I stated in the first instance, those who are badly

inclined

inclined are afraid to move at night, because if they are not detected in anything, or if they are found out after certain hours, it creates a suspicion towards them, and they are looked to afterwards.

1001. Do not the police prevent the spread of crime?—They prevent the spread of crime; it is thoroughly known with our labourers, if there is a suspicion that there is anything going on wrong, we can get the assistance of the police. They are quite aware that they are looked after closely. In fact I had a notification of a depredation taking place in my cornfields last year; we knew of it, and at my suggestion Captain McHardy had the field watched for me. The thief got intelligence of it, and he told me when I accused him of it, that he saw the shining hat over the hedge, and he knew that they were looking after him.

1002. Was that system of watching ever practised with the old constables?— Never; the difficulty with the old constable was that he was generally a person in the parish who was mixed up with relatives and acquaintances; and it was quite notorious, if a supposed transgressor or person was detected, not one-half of those cases went before the Bench; the constables, from either pecuniary motives or from some motive, managing to make up matters, as it was termed; matters were compromised. That I have known in several instances; and in two or three, particularly, the parish took it up, after the constable had, not refused to do so, but had failed to do so.

1003. You have been asked a question as to the increase in the value of property: I put it to you, as a farmer, would you take a farm, supposing all things equal, with the addition of a police rate paid for an efficient police, in preference to one at the same rent where there was no police?—I would greatly in preference; I think that the benefit I directly derive from the police force having been established, is more than equivalent to the sum I pay; I would pay it as an insurance to have the same protection to my property as I receive at present.

Mr. *William Hamilton*, called in; and Examined.

1004. *Chairman.*] WHERE do you reside?—At Wendover, Bucks.

1005. What are you?—Superintending constable.

1006. What is the system of police in Buckinghamshire?—Parish constables under superintending constables.

1007. In each division?—Yes, recently; they had only nine, until the last quarter sessions; now they have appointed one for each petty sessional division.

1008. How long have you been superintending constable?—Eighteen months.

1009. Have served in any other police force?—Yes; in the Irish constabulary, the Lancashire county constabulary, and the Essex county constabulary.

1010. For how long?—Sixteen years altogether.

1011. Do you consider that the system of superintending constables, with parish constables, is an efficient system of police?—I do not.

1012. Have you had much experience of it?—I had 18 months; and nine years in the Essex constabulary under Captain M'Hardy.

1013. In Essex there was a different system, was not there?—Yes; that is a very efficient force.

1014. Do you think, from your experience, that a police force, consisting of superintending constables, with the aid of parish constables, is not an efficient police?—Nothing at all like it.

1015. Why do you think so?—In the first place, there is no chance of detection; you do not receive information often for two days, and perhaps you reside 10 miles from the place where the robbery has occurred; and the property is not traced; the parish constable happens to be out for a considerable time, and sometimes constables are very careless in giving information.

1016. Have you had any experience with respect to police in boroughs and towns?—Some slight experience; not very much.

1017. Have you ever been in the borough police?—No; but I have gone into the adjoining boroughs.

1018. In what way have you gone into adjoining boroughs?—When I was in Haybridge, in Essex, I was sent into the borough of Maldon.

1019. Were you sent into Maldon by your superior officer?—No; frequently duty called me there.

Mr. W. Hamilton.

2 June 1853.

1020. What was the result of your experience in boroughs?—I very seldom found them work in co-operation; there is generally a jealousy between the county and town forces.

1021. Notwithstanding that jealousy they are willing to avail themselves of your services?—Generally so.

1022. Are there any other boroughs into which you have ever been as a police officer?—I am inspector of weights and measures for the borough of Aylesbury; there is a sergeant and two men, appointed under the Lighting and Watching Act, stationed in the town there.

1023. But the borough of Aylesbury is not under the system of police in Buckinghamshire generally?—No; they find their own police; it has nothing to do with the county, and there we do not find them very often co-operate.

1024. If they have a separate police in Aylesbury, do not their own officers inspect their weights and measures?—No.

1025. You, as one of the superintending constables of the county, do that duty?—Yes.

1026. Have you formed any opinion as to the manner of the appointment and control of the police in Buckinghamshire; do you think that is efficient?—No, I do not think it is.

1027. Why not?—They are generally under the control of the tradesmen, such as grocers and drapers, and such persons as form the town council.

1028. I am speaking as to the county police?—They are only parish constables, with the exception of the superintending constables. I have got 70 parish constables, but no paid policemen.

1029. How many parishes are there in your district?—I had 30, but since this last alteration I have had about 15; the district has been divided.

1030. Do you receive any effectual assistance from the parish constables?—Very little.

1031. Are they ever unwilling to obey your directions?—I have had one or two fined for neglect of duty. In fact, there is a case in another division, not in my own, in which a parish constable was called out in the night, and he refused to act, because it was not in his parish. A gamekeeper went to another constable in the parish, and he said his wife was ill, and he refused to get up. A sheep was stolen in the place, and in consequence of the neglect of duty the parties got off. One stated as his reason that it was not in his parish where the offence was committed, and the other stated that his wife was ill; and so neither of them acted.

1032. In those cases in which the offenders escaped justice in consequence of the neglect of the parish constables, do you think if there had been an efficient police force, as there is in Essex, that they would have been detected and taken?—No doubt they would, at once.

1033. Are you aware of any boroughs in which the police officers are permitted to pursue their own trade and calling?—When I served in Lancashire they were allowed, in Liverpool, to follow their own occupations.

1034. Is not that the case in Buckinghamshire?—No, not in Buckinghamshire at the present time; they canvass at the elections at Wycombe.

1035. Sir J. Trollope.] Do you mean the superintending constables?—No; the borough police.

1036. Lord Lovaine.] What do you mean by their canvassing at elections at Wycombe?—They go round to the different voters.

1037. To ask for votes?—Yes.

1038. Chairman.] Do you believe that, under those circumstances, the police officers can perform their duties faithfully and impartially?—I think not.

1039. Why not?—They are under the control of the aldermen and town council; they have too many masters; it is not like having one regular head.

1040. You have stated that both in Essex, and as a superintending constable in Buckinghamshire, you have had occasion often to go into the boroughs?—Yes.

1041. Have you, upon those occasions, found the officers in those places willing to co-operate with you in effecting your object?—Sometimes; on some occasions I have found a little jealousy amongst them.

1042. Has the chance of the escape of a prisoner been increased, in consequence of that want of co-operation?—I think so.

1043. Do you know any instance of that sort?—Not particularly, but it is my opinion.

1044. Have

Mr. *W. Hamilton.*

8 June 1853.

1044. Have you ever considered the parochial constabulary, as compared with the county police?—I have.

1045. What is your opinion of their usefulness and efficiency?—I think it is a very inefficient force; I consider the county force far superior and less expensive, according to the efficiency of its members.

1046. From your experience in the county of Buckingham, do you think the parochial constables have been rendered more efficient and better police officers from having superintending constables?—They are certainly better than they have been, but now they are very deficient.

1047. In what respect are they better?—Because they are guided by the superintending constables; in cases of robbery they co-operate with them. There was no one formerly to control them, and they took no notice of trifling offences; the first question they asked was, who was to pay them.

1048. Are the constables tradesmen?—Generally so; tailors, shoemakers, grocers, and so on.

1049. Do you think that a person exercising a trade or calling can efficiently discharge the duties of a constable?—I have no doubt that they cannot. I have frequently had opportunities of knowing that, in respect of disorderly conduct at public-houses. When I have called upon them with respect to those houses, they have said that they would be willing to get information about the conduct of the house if I did not call them as witnesses; they did not wish to offend their customers, and so they did not wish to be called as witnesses in the case.

1050. If you had reason to think that a house was disorderly, have you been unable to act from finding them very unwilling to give information?—I have had several cases; I have got constables reprimanded for neglect of duty.

1051. How many are appointed in your district?—I had 70; I have now about 30.

1052. That is about two to each parish?—Some have six; it is according to the size of the parish.

1053. Do you know what has been paid to them at all?—Not positively; I should say about 15 l. a year each parish, taking one with another; some parishes pay as much as 40 l. a year.

1054. How much do you mean to say that the expense of the parochial constabulary is to the parishes?—There are 30 parishes; Aston Clinton pays as much as 35 l. or 40 l.; in Great Missenden parish they pay one of the constables 10 l. (who is the fixed constable), and there are five or six others; Risborough amounts to about 35 l.

1055. Sir *J. Trollope.*] Are those parishes within your district?—They are.

1056. Are your superintending constables mounted?—Yes; we have a horse and cart.

1057. Are you obliged to find your own horse?—We find the horse, and the county finds the cart and harness.

1058. What is your salary?—£. 80., and 35 l. is allowed for keeping the horse, and the cart and harness in repair; I have half the fees paid for stamping weights and measures, and half the fines which are paid for convictions for false weights and measures.

1059. What do your total receipts amount to?—I should say from 130 l. to 140 l. a year.

1060. Are you allowed anything for serving summonses, or for any other duties?—We do not serve summonses, nor execute warrants of apprehension.

1061. When you attend assizes or quarter sessions, or petty sessions for prosecutions, have you any allowances?—Six shillings a day, without any regard to the number of cases.

1062. You are paid for a day if you have half a dozen cases; you do not charge for them separately?—We get paid from the Government, and we give an account to the county of what we receive in each case, and they allow us 6 s. a day.

1063. Does that cover all the expenses of the horse and cart whilst you are from home?—That is the whole of the allowance which they make.

1064. You have been so recently appointed, that probably the county of Buckingham has hardly got into working order, under the 5th & 6th of Victoria, chapter 109?—I think it is impossible for them to get into order under that system; in fact, if you get a parish constable that is good for anything, the parochial authorities grumble about his expenses, and they want to throw him off the next time; they say, " His bill is so expensive, and we will appoint another who will do it for less money."

1065. Were you one of the first superintending constables appointed?— I was.

1066. When was the whole county re-organised and divided?—At the last quarter sessions, in April last.

1067. About two months since?—Yes.

1068. Do you think a system perfect which has been working two months?— I do not consider it could be perfect.

1069. Is that because you have been bred under another system in Essex? —Yes.

1070. Do you consider the Essex police more efficient?—I consider there is not a more efficient police in England at the present day.

1071. In how many police forces have you served?—I have served in Lancashire, and I have had great experience in the adjoining districts to Essex.

1072. Do you consider the Essex police better than the Herts police?—I do.

1073. In what respect?—If an officer in Essex is good for nothing he must perform his duty; there are so many checks upon him he has no opportunity of skulking; but in the adjoining districts they do their duty as they like.

1074. In Essex they keep a man whether he is good for anything or not?— No; they make him do his duty, or else discharge him; one man is a check upon another.

1075. Mr. *Burroughes.*] Are you the only mounted constable?—Each superintendent has a horse; we are each appointed an inspector of weights and measures, and high constable; the superintending constables convey in all practicable cases, all prisoners to gaol who are committed at the petty sessions.

1076. There are nine altogether mounted, are there not?—Fifteen.

1077. Sir *J. Trollope.*] Are you thinking of giving up your situation?—I am not dissatisfied with it.

1078. Are you aware that a subsequent Act of Parliament, the 15 & 16 Vict., c. 20, has been passed, by which additional constables may be appointed to undertake the duties in your absence?—Yes.

1079. And to take charge of the lock-up?—We have no lock-up except at a few places.

1080. Are not they contemplated in all the divisions?—I believe they are.

1081. Have you any at all?—I have a lock-up, but it is only a temporary cage.

1082. Was it built for the purpose?—No.

1083 Is it inefficient?—Very inefficient; there is no accommodation for the superintending officer to live in.

1084. There is no house?—No.

1085. Are none of the superintending officers found residences?—No.

1086. Is it not contemplated to build efficient lock-ups with proper residences? The lock-ups and the residences they have built are only qualified for a constable to reside in, and not for a superintending constable.

1087. Have you a resident constable?—Where they have an appointed lock-up they have a housekeeper.

1088. Have the authorities appointed resident constables under the last Act? —In some places they have, and at quarter sessions they are going to appoint four or five more.

1089. Have you no lock-up?—No; I am near Aylesbury Gaol; I have only 10 miles, the furthest journey, to convey my prisoners.

1090. Is it not required that a constable should be in charge of the lock-up during your absence?—Yes; I always apprise the parish constable of my absence; I have no paid officer.

1091. You put the parish constable in charge while you are out; is that the plan?—That is the plan.

1092. *Chairman.*] Do you think that motives of private interest sometimes interfere with the performance of their duty?—I do.

1093. Have you met with any direct obstruction from the want of confidence on their part?—I have; once when I went in search of a stolen sheep I put confidence in a parish constable, and I found out afterwards that the man I supposed

to

to be the thief was his brother-in-law; and I found out in the morning that the suspected person was acquainted with the case before I went to search his house.

Mr. W. Hamilton.

2 June 1853.

1094. Do you think, looking at the different systems of police in the adjoining counties, that they can work well together; for instance, where there is this system which you have in Buckinghamshire, and, in the adjoining counties, a system similar to that which there is in Essex?—They cannot work together.

1095. Have you ever had an opportunity of seeing the use of special constables in cases of disturbance?—I have; during the time I was on duty in Lancashire in elections, and I found them of very little use.

1096. You know that they have police in Lancashire?—Yes; I have been on duty there.

1097. Was that before the appointment of the Lancashire police?—This was the police force; we found that we got but little assistance from the special constables; it is a difficult matter to prevent them getting drunk, and they are therefore more injury than good.

1098. Do you mean that in Blackburn they did swear in a certain number of special constables?—Yes.

1099. And they were of very little use?—Yes.

1100. Lord *Lovaine.*] Can you conceive of any plan by which the parish constables can be made effective under the present law?—I cannot.

1101. The parishes which you have named pay, as you say, an average annual amount to their constables of 450 *l.*—I should say about that.

1102. Supposing you divided that by the cost of a rural constable, you will find that that comes within a few shillings of what eight efficient rural constables would cost. Would those eight be sufficient to look after a district?—I should prefer four regular paid constables to the 70 parish constables I have got; and certainly eight efficient rural constables would be far preferable to the present force.

1103. What do you give to the keepers of lock-up houses?—They generally get 5 *s.* a day allowed; if it is a parish constable he charges 3 *s.* 6 *d.*

1104. Have you any lock-up houses which are in the charge of the man dwelling in the house?—There is one at Chesham, another at Wycombe, and one at Slough.

1105. What do you pay him?—He had 5 *s.* a day, but I think he has now 20 *l.* a year.

1106. Do you think that, in rural towns and boroughs, the police ought to be independent of the rural constabulary?—No; I should think they would work together better under one head. I have known several cases in borough towns, in which they have been afraid to offend some of their inspectors, as they call them; that is, the tradesmen in the town. If they saw them committing an offence they would not mention it. In many cases they would say, " We must not offend them."

1107. The appointment is a matter of partiality and favour in the borough, is it not?—Exactly so.

1108. Mr. *Mackie.*] Who appoints the constables in the county of Buckinghamshire?—There is a list of qualified persons agreed to at a vestry, and published according to the Act, and laid before the magistrates in petty session, who make the appointments annually; but I have a list sent to me, and if I object to any one I get him discharged; I pick one out of the list. There is a list sent of all the persons qualified to serve as constables, and it is submitted to me, and if any constable is in the list that I object to, I strike him off the list.

1109. Have you the power of dismissal?—Yes, with the confirmation of the magistrates; the magistrates do not generally object to anything of that sort.

1110. Were those constables, at the place to which you have referred, who refused to leave their beds to pursue a criminal, dismissed?—That was not in my division; they were fined.

1111. How many have been dismissed?—I had two men dismissed for neglect of duty.

1112. *Chairman.*] By the magistrates?—Yes.

1113. What you mean to say is, that a list is submitted to you, and you have an opportunity of correcting that list?—We hold office as high constables; and all those lists are submitted to us, and the magistrates ask us what remarks we have to make; and the appointments are generally made according to our advice or recommendation.

Mr. *George Marris*, called in; and Examined.

Mr. G. Marris.

2 June 1853.

1114. *Chairman.*] WHERE do you reside?—At Caistor, in Lincolnshire.

1115. What is your occupation?—I am a solicitor.

1116. Have you held any office which has particularly directed your attention to the subject of offences committed in that district?—I am clerk and treasurer of a large association for the prosecution of felons; and offences against property have come under my notice, of course.

1117. During the last winter, has the neighbourhood of Caistor been much infested with bad characters, and has there been much depredation?—Very much indeed.

1118. What has been the character of those depredations generally?—We have had every species of offence against property: burglary, sheep-stealing, breaking into granaries and outhouses, and stealing from all those places. I should think offences against the property of the members of the association has averaged one a week; and taking into account the offences against the property of those persons who are not members, I might venture to say together they have averaged nearly two a week.

1119. Have the cottages of the poor people been broken into?—Many attempts have been made upon the cottages of the poor; and when they have killed a pig, in many instances they have been obliged to sit up all night to prevent its being stolen from them.

1120. To what do you attribute that prevalence of crime in your district?—We have no one to prevent it; we have nothing but parish constables.

1121. Have you no lock-up house?—None.

1122. Have you represented this want of protection to the magistrates?—I did, in a memorial very numerously and respectably signed.

1123. What was the result of that memorial?—It was referred from the Kirton sessions to the police committee at the Lincoln assizes.

1124. What did the police committee do?—The police committee then came to a certain resolution; but I may mention that, in the first instance, crime was so extensive, that a detective policeman was had down from town.

1125. By order of the police committee?—No; Lord Yarborough and some of his friends and tenants had a policeman at their own expense.

1126. As a private watchman?—Yes.

1127. Did the police committee do nothing for you?—Hitherto they have not. The magistrates at Brigg, when I went before them, at my request and at the request of others appointed the same policeman for three months.

1128. What was the name of the policeman?—Henry Matthews.

1129. When you had Matthews did he do you any good?—While he was in disguise he did not do us any good; he could not get into the secret haunts of the parties; the area was too large. As a detective he did not do much good. When he was appointed publicly, and his office became known, it had a sensible influence upon crime.

1130. Is Matthews still with you?—No.

1131. Why did he go away?—The magistrates refused to continue him. He was appointed under the Act of Parliament only as a special constable for three months, and when the time was about expiring I applied to the petty session for a renewal of the appointment.

1132. Did they renew it?—No.

1133. Why not?—They said the expense was too heavy.

1134. What was the expense?—Thirty shillings a week or 18 l. a quarter.

1135. In consequence of that expense, the magistrates refused to reappoint Matthews?—So the magistrates told me.

1136. From what source did that money come?—From the county at large.

1137. He was merely appointed from time to time?—He was appointed once only.

1138. Mr. *Burroughes.*] Was he paid from the county rate?—Yes.

1139. *Chairman.*] When Matthews went away did the depredations again commence?—The following day after that they began.

1140. How far are you from the nearest police establishment?—Nine miles.

1141. You have a superintending constable, I presume?—There is one in the division of Yarborough.

1142. How far is that from you?—He is nine miles off.

1143. What

Mr. G. Morris.

2 June 1853.

1143. What is the extent of his district?—Speaking in round numbers, I should say about 25 miles long by 15 or 18 miles broad.

1144. How many parishes are there in the district?—I could not say.

1145. Do you think it is possible for any one man to protect such a district with the assistance of parochial constables?—I think not; I am sure of it.

1146. Do the robberies in your neighbourhood come to your knowledge?—Yes, generally; and certainly if upon members of my society.

1147. Do you offer handsome rewards?—Yes.

1148. Have you paid rewards?—Occasionally; they are only paid on conviction for the crime, that is, where the parties are prosecuted and found guilty.

1149. In pursuing an offender against the property of one of the members of your association, supposing you pursued him unsuccessfully, how are the expenses paid?—Out of the funds of the society.

1150. That is paid out of your funds, and not out of the county rate?—Yes.

1151. Mr. *Burroughes*.] I understood you to say that you paid the reward only upon conviction; but you pay the expenses, I understood you to say, of prosecutions, and all the other circumstances attending the apprehension of non-offenders, from your funds, although conviction does not take place?—There may be a few expenses if there is no conviction.

1152. Do you know the amount per annum?—No.

1153. *Chairman*.] Do you think the establishment of railways has increased the facilities for crime?—No doubt it enables parties to come and land at small railway stations to reconnoitre the country, and to commit depredations, and they are off again before they can be at all noticed.

1154. Have you any protection beyond parish constables?—None, save the police nine miles off.

1155. Have not they other duties to attend to?—They are very respectable men, as a body; but the more respectable they are the more inefficient they are.

1156. Is that because they have other duties to perform?—Yes.

1157. Is not the time of the class of persons appointed as parish constables valuable to themselves in their own business?—Yes, very.

1158. Is not their time money to them?—Of course it is.

1159. If they are put to the inconvenience of acting as parish constables, is not that a loss to them individually?—Certainly.

1160. Therefore acting as parish constables is money lost to a large and useful class of persons?—Yes; and not only so, but they do not like the duties of the office.

1161. Mr. *Mackie*.] What do you pay the constables?—I do not know what pay they get at all; they perhaps are paid so much a day from the parish rates.

1162. Sir *J. Trollope*.] You have stated that when all these crimes took place in your neighbourhood in the course of last winter you made an application to the magistrates for a superintending constable, or for some police assistance?—I did.

1163. Did you do that in the form according to the Act of Parliament; I think you said that you sent in a memorial?—I made an application, I think it is under the 1 & 2 Will. 4, c. 41, for a special constable, and my application was granted by the magistrates in petty sessions by appointing Matthews.

1164. By bringing down a detective from London?—By appointing the man who was then down from London.

1165. You have stated that you sent in a memorial for some other purposes?—I sent in a memorial to the Kirton sessions for a lock-up and policeman, and it was referred there to the police committee at Lincoln assizes; and it turned out that we ought to have had the recommendation of five magistrates.

1166. Is not that the law?—It is.

1167. Have you looked at the statute?—That particular section did not catch my eye.

1168. That Act is the 5 & 6 Vict. c. 109; you probably have since referred to that Act?—I have.

1169. If you had set it in motion legally, have you any reason to apprehend that the magistrates would have refused you?—I do not know.

1170. Have you never had a direct answer from the magistrates, that if the application were made in conformity with the Act, they would attend to it?—I have not had a direct answer; there has been a resolution come to by the police committee in the grand jury-room at Lincoln.

1171. Have you a copy of that?—I have.

1172. Perhaps you will be good enough to state what it is?—" Lincolnshire:

Lindsey. Resolution passed at a meeting of the committee held at the Grand Jury-room, Castle of Lincoln, 1st March 1853. The committee took into consideration the application made at the last Kirton sessions for a second lock-up house in the wapentake of Yarborough, to be erected at Caistor, and which application was, according to the rule in such cases, referred to this committee; and thereupon it is resolved,—That this committee sees no objection to the erection of a lock-up house at Caistor, provided the building, and the expenses of the constable to have charge of it, be kept strictly within the limits of the Act of Parliament; and that such constable be not, in fact, constituted a superintending constable, with a district of parishes assigned to him, there being already a superintending constable having jurisdiction over the whole wapentake.'

1173. Then the magistrates did not refuse you the assistance you applied for? —They neither refused it nor agreed to give it. It is a mere passive resolution that they see no objection, provided this, and provided that.

1174. Did they not refuse your application because you applied for the appointment of a stranger?—Certainly not.

1175. Have you any reason to suppose, if your application is made in the proper form, that it will be refused to you?—I do not know; I think if the subject is kept alive it will be granted; if it is not kept alive the application will be refused.

1176. *Chairman.*] May the Committee understand that the refusal only was to re-appoint the London constable?—No; expense was the objection.

1177. Sir *J. Trollope.*] That would depend upon the local bench at Brigg?— Yes, the refusal.

1178. Are you within the petty sessional division of Brigg?—Yes.

1179. What is the population of Caistor?—It is between 2,000 and 3,000.

1180. Have you any petty sessions held there?—None.

1181. Is all the business of the hundred transacted at Brigg?—For Caistor it is.

1182. That is a distance of nine miles?—Yes.

1183. You have stated that there is an association for the prosecution of felons. Were they at any expense in protecting the country by additional means when these robberies took place last winter?—No, not the society; some of the members were.

1184. They paid something out of their own pockets for additional protection? —Yes.

1185. To what purpose are the funds of this association devoted?—Advertising for the apprehension of offenders and prosecuting them, and then when I get the county allowance I give credit to the society to that amount.

1186. Do you take any other steps besides advertising?—Occasionally some person who has lost property may send his men, or go himself in pursuit, and communication is made by post to the distant police by me, as clerk.

1187. Do you know anything of a system of aiding one another in the pursuit of felons?—No.

1188. Do you meet annually?—Once a year, to settle; when the members of the association dine together.

1189. Out of the funds of the association?—No, they contribute; there is a certain allowance out of the funds of the association, but it is not enough for the dinner; and they pay themselves the rest.

1190. Are not a great portion of the funds devoted to entertainment?—I think there is nothing, but to ensure the landlord remuneration for a large provision ; the absentees pay a little, that is all.

1191. You think that a police force would be a much more effectual mode of protecting property than anything you could do by your association?—Judging from such little experience as I had in the case of Matthews, I think it would.

1192. What did he do?—He prevented crime entirely.

1193. Did he catch anybody?—There were no crimes committed during his appointment.

1194. You have stated that there was one crime a week with respect to members of the association, and two with respect to non-members?—Before he came.

1195. Did he find out none of those cases after he came?—There were none committed whilst he was there.

1196. Did he find out any of the cases of sheep-stealing which had been previously committed?—No.

1197. Had any horse been stolen in the neighbourhood?—No.

1198. What

Mr. *G. Marris.*

2 June 1853.

1198. What were the crimes which were committed?—Sheep-stealing, burglary, breaking into granaries and outhouses, stealing bacon, and so on.

1199. Were none of those offenders taken?—There was one conviction for sheep-stealing at the Spilsby sessions, and only one.

1200. Do you think, if you had a superintending constable stationed at Caistor, in the same mode as in other divisions of the county, it would be sufficient for the preservation of property?—It would be a preventive to crime, and improve our condition.

1201. Should you be satisfied with that force for the preservation of property, without carrying the Police Act into effect?—I do not profess to give an opinion upon the Police Act throughout the kingdom.

1202. Lord *Lovaine.*] What is the average subscription of your members to your association?—It comes to about 7 s. a year for each member.

1203. Are you of opinion, from the state of crime in your district, that the payment of a county rate of 2 ½ d. in the pound would be deemed a very heavy burden?—I really think, looking at the losses which people sustain, that it would not.

1204. Sir *J. Trollope.*] Were the persons who committed those crimes last winter chiefly people of the locality, or were you invaded by people from a distance?—Only one conviction took place, I think, this last twelvemonth, and that was a person in the neighbourhood. I have no means of judging who they were who committed the other offences.

Mr. *Alfred Hughes*, called in; and Examined.

Mr. *A. Hughes.*

1205. *Chairman.*] WHERE do you reside?—In the City of Bath.

1206. Are you the head of the police in Bath?—I am chief of the police in the city and borough of Bath.

1207. How many men have you?—Eighty-two.

1208. How are they appointed?—They are appointed by the watch committee of the city.

1209. You have a code of regulations, I suppose?—Yes.

1210. By whom were they drawn up?—Some of them have been drawn up by myself, by the previous chief of the police, and some by the watch committee.

1211. Has your force ever been found inadequate to the maintenance of the public peace?—No, not since I have been there.

1212. Has the military force ever been called in, in cases of disturbance? —No.

1213. Do the members of your force ever receive any reward or fee?—Not without the sanction of the watch committee. When gratuities are reported to the watch committee, they sometimes allow half the gratuity to the men, and the other half to be applied to the sick fund.

1214. When the watch committee reward an officer, do they do that with your concurrence, and from information which they receive from you?—I never knew any case of the watch committee rewarding an officer; I have known them allow him compensation for injuries, when he has been injured in the execution of his duty.

1215. In case they are not performing special services, where are those earnings carried to?—They are carried to the borough fund by the cash-in-hand book, and shown by me every week as cash in hand, and that amount is deducted from the weekly bill.

1216. Have you any regulations as to rendering assistance to other police forces?—No; when officers from other places apply to the inspectors under me, they generally give assistance.

1217. Where from, do you mean?—Let them come from anywhere else; when they come to Bath we generally give them assistance.

1218. What are the adjoining police forces to Bath?—There is no police in the county of Somerset; if a constable were to come from anywhere else to Bath, and say, "I want a man, so and so;" we should send a man with him, to show him, if possible, where he was.

1219. Therefore if a criminal is supposed to be in Bath, and a police officer comes in pursuit of him, you give him all the assistance in your power?—Yes.

1220. Do you think that your present force is sufficient?—Yes, for the city.

1221. Have you served in any other police force ?—Yes, I was for 12 years in the Metropolitan police, and I have served as superintendent in the Surrey constabulary.

1222. Has crime decreased in Bath ?—Materially.

1223. Can you state any fact in illustration of that ?—I have two reports of the Bath Quarter-sessions, and I was likewise in court when the recorder delivered this charge to the grand jury at the July sessions, 1852. He stated that his experience of crime in Bath extended over a period of 20 years, and he had known the calendar at the Quarter-sessions amount to between 50 and 100. Since I have been in Bath I do not think the calendar has exceeded 30 ; it has generally been about 18 and 22 each Quarter-sessions; I have been there a year and a half, and I am certain there has been only one burglary effected, and that only to the amount of 14 *l.* The recorder likewise said that he attributed the difference to the establishment of an effective police. I have also another report.

1224. What is that ?—To the same effect, as regards crime in Bath. The recorder then stated that the present calendar exhibited a smaller number of prisoners than usual, and the nature of the offences was of a very trifling character.

1225. When was that ?—In April 1852.

1226. Under whose control are your police ?—Under the control of the magistrates and the watch committee.

1227. By whom were you appointed ?—By the watch committee.

1228. Have they the power of dismissing you ?—Yes, and the magistrates also ; the watch committee or two magistrates.

1229. Sir *J. Trollope.*] Is the watch committee composed of magistrates ? —The watch committee is composed of magistrates, tradesmen, and professional men, such as surgeons and solicitors.

1230. Are they all members of the Town Council ?—Yes.

1231. The watch committee is composed of the magistrates and the Town Council ?—Yes, they are members of the Town Council.

1232. *Chairman.*] Do you find any inconvenience from being under those two jurisdictions ?—I do not myself, but the officers under me do.

1233. Can an officer under you be dismissed by the watch committee, if they choose ?—Yes.

1234. Without giving any reasons ?—That is one of their regulations, but I never knew it enforced.

1235. They can do that without the consent of the magistrates, can they not ? —Yes.

1236. And without the consent of the Secretary of State ?—Yes.

1237. Without the consent, in fact, of any superior authority ?—Yes.

1238. Mr. *Burroughes.*] Is the appointment under those conditions ?—Yes.

1239. How are your officers paid in Bath for pursuing offenders in the county ?—If they succeed they are paid in the ordinary way their expenses, included in the magistrate's certificate. If they do not succeed, and they are not acting under the order of a justice, which occasionally occurs, there is no means whatever of paying them. There is no provision for special service. That is provided in the county, under the head of " special service ;" and likewise in the Metropolis, under the head of " extraordinary expenses."

1240. Have officers of the same rank various rates of pay ?—Various rates of pay.

1241. Is that from the period of service ?—No ; I cannot account for it. It was upon the re-organization of the force previous to my going to Bath.

1242. Supposing an officer is appointed at a certain rate of pay, have the watch committee arbitrary power of increasing his pay ?—Yes, subject to the approval of the council.

1243. Without the approval of the magistrates ?—Yes.

1244. Sir *J. Trollope.*] Has your force ever been called upon to act beyond the jurisdiction of the city ?—Yes.

1245. In the county of Somerset ?—Yes, I receive precepts from the county justices of Somerset to send a sufficient force to Lansdowne fair and races, which last four days, two days the races and two days the fair, each year; and that requires a force of about 40 men and officers to preserve order there.

1246. Is that day and night ?—No, from morning till night.

1247. Is there any night duty ?—At night they call in the parish constables.

1248. Have you a separate charge upon the county for that duty ?—No, I have

no

no charge upon the county; the race committee generally pay the expenses of the officers during the time they are doing duty there.

1249. Should you see any difficulty in acting with the rural police if it were established in the county of Somerset?—Not if the whole force were amalgamated with the county.

1250. Otherwise you think there would be difficulty?—Yes.

1251. Is it your opinion that if a county police were established in the county of Somerset it would be advisable to amalgamate them with the city of Bath? —Yes.

1252. And to amalgamate all the other cities and boroughs as well, to insure uniformity of action?—Yes, because police officers, generally speaking, are jealous of each other. If a police officer applies to another place for assistance, each officer generally endeavours to get the offender for himself.

1253. Does not that feeling act as a stimulant to exertions on both parties?— It does; but sometimes it has a contrary effect.

1254. Lord *Lovaine*.] Did not you once serve in Northumberland?—Yes.

1255. Were not you there in the position of superintending constable?—Yes.

1256. In your opinion, is it possible to bring that system into effective operation? —No, I do not think it could ever be brought into effective operation, especially in that county.

1257. Why do you say in that county especially?—Because I may have experienced more inconvenience there than perhaps the generality of men in my position; in that county there is a very strong antipathy to what they call south countrymen, and as I am a south countryman, that may account for my having experienced more inconvenience from them than perhaps others would.

1258. Was that prejudice testified by the refusal of the constables to obey you? —I found them so corrupt there that I was obliged to have nothing at all to do with them, and act entirely on my own hands. I found that some of them had been convicted of felony, and others were continually drinking in company with the most notorious thieves and poachers, and they had likewise relatives who were so, and licensed dealers in game.

1259. You are speaking principally of the towns, are you not?—I am speaking principally of the towns; after I had been there a little while I would not have anything at all to do with them, and I acted generally on my own account. If I was obliged to use them at all I never let them know what I wanted them for; I brought them right to the spot, without letting them know what I was going about.

1260. Do you know enough of the county to say whether the same thing prevails to the same extent in the wild districts of Northumberland?—I believe it prevailed all over that county.

1261. It would appear from what you have stated, that the rivalry of the constables of the different police forces is extremely likely to conduce to the escape of a prisoner?—Yes, sometimes, and sometimes it will operate the other way, and stimulate the men to exertion. I could show many instances in which a jealousy exists between one officer and another. During the time I was in the metropolitan force I took a man down to King's Heath, about 10 miles from Birmingham; for the superintendent of the county force had been previously in London for him, and had been an hour too late at Cold Bath Fields when he was discharged; he came to me at Paddington, and said, "If you can get him, do so." I got him, and took him down to King's Heath, and as soon as I took him into the police station, the superintendent shook his head, and said, "That is not the man." I said, "Not the man? that is the man you told me to take; how do you know he is not the man?" He said, "I have known him from his childhood, he was bred and born near me." I said, "If you will undertake to say that he is not the man, I will not detain him any longer;" upon which he put his hand in the desk, and gave the man a shilling, to get some bread and cheese, at a public-house next door. The man went there, and while the man was getting his refreshment, I noticed that the superintendent was particularly uneasy, and occasionally going to the window, and looking out; he left me, and not returning soon, I went out, and walked up the road towards Birmingham, and there I met the superintendent bringing the man back. If that man had taken to the fields, instead of keeping on the road, he would have escaped, and I should have been minus my expenses; and he was the right man after all.

1262. Mr. *Burroughes*.] Had you taken him as a prisoner?—Yes; the super-

Mr. A. Hughes.

2 June 1853.

intendent vouched for his not being the man, and on that statement I released him.

1263. Lord *Lovaine*.] And then he apprehended the man himself? —Yes.

1264. Sir *J. Trollope*.] Was there a reward at issue? —No.

1265. Mr. *Burroughes*.] The Committee are to understand that you did not go away, that you met the superintendent, and then he had taken the man prisoner?—He had brought the man back; the man had gone from the public-house; he expected that I should return by the next train, and then he would take him himself, but in the mean while the man might have escaped; when I met him he was bringing him back.

1266. As his prisoner?—As his prisoner.

1267. Lord *Lovaine*.] You have served in the Surrey county police, have you not?—Yes.

1268. Had not you a wild district allotted to you?—Yes; but it was nothing in comparison with the North.

1269. Had you a district very notorious at one time for burglaries and depredations of every description?—Yes, I had; the first few months I was there I had a great deal more trouble than during the latter part of the time.

1270. If I recollect rightly you apprehended some persons there whom no parish constables would have dared to seize?—There were many.

1271. Did they not threaten to murder one of the police constables afterwards? —Yes.

1272. Do you find that the method of the appointment and payment of the police of the borough of Bath militates against its efficiency?—I do; I find that the borough system is more conflicting than the metropolitan or the county system.

1273. Do you think it would be a good thing to give jurisdiction over the city police to some authority who would also have under his government the police of the surrounding counties?—I do; I consider that that would be the best measure that ever was introduced.

1274. Is there much crime in the county of Somerset?—Yes, a great deal; I was in court at the Somerset assizes last August, when Mr. Baron Platt made some very strong comments on the calendar of the county; he said they had murder most prominently, and manslaughter; they had brutal assaults, and almost every other crime, indicating the absence of education and the prevalence of drunkenness, unbridled lust, and revenge; I was in court, and heard him say that. I was in court again at the assizes, in March 1853, when Mr. Justice Erle also observed, that, from the number and nature of the crimes in the calendar, the jury would have a grave and serious charge to perform. Again, Mr. Miles, the chairman of the court of quarter sessions of the county of Somerset, at the same time that the recorder of Bath was congratulating the city on the decrease of crime, said, at the county sessions, that there appeared in the circumstances of the present time great reason to hope that crime would diminish, but he found, from some cause or other, it was evidently increasing.

1275. Do you know anything of the Gloucester police?—I do not.

1276. You do not know the state of crime in that county?—I do not; to show that the co-operative system is necessary, about a fortnight ago one of my inspectors wanted to go into the country, as he had some information. He said he had information that was sufficient for a remand, if not for a committal, and in consequence of having been myself engaged on county business, and having had to wait perhaps 10 or 12 months to be reimbursed my actual expenses, we now never interfere in county matters, except by order of a Justice. This case he wanted to go about was a case where a stable was broken into at Somerton, Somerset, and two valuable cart stallions were hamstrung and cut to pieces. Since then this Bill has come out, offering a reward of 100 *l.*, signed by 100 different farmers and yeomen. If a police force had been established in the county, I have no hesitation in saying that this offence could have been brought home; and so it would have been if I had allowed the inspector to go into the county and investigate the case.

1277. In your own force it appears that you have no power to dismiss? —No.

1278. And no power in fact to punish?—I fine for trifling offences, but at the same time that I do fine I give the men the option of going before the watch committee if they think proper.

1279. Has

Mr *A. Hughes.*

2 June 1853.

1279. Has the watch committee the whole power of the administration and government of the police?—The Act of Parliament vests rather more power in the magistrates than in the watch committee.

1280. As regards yourself, you have no other power than slightly fining the men under your orders; but the whole of the punishment and the whole of the administration is entrusted to the watch committee?—Yes.

1281. Does not that watch committee consist of tradesmen in the town?—Yes.

1282. Do they attend the watch committee regularly?—There is generally a full committee.

1283. Do they attend to your representations?—Generally; but the evils which we experience are not perhaps in their power to remedy.

1284. At all events, you think it is not the proper body to govern the police of either the county or city?—I consider that if we were placed under a committee of magistrates we should not experience the evils which we now do from being amenable to two bodies; in fact, we are subject to three, being obliged to obey the precepts of the county justices as well.

1285. I suppose you would prefer being under one body, or even one individual?—One body, or one individual.

1286. Do you give it as your decided opinion that it is impracticable to carry on the superintending constable system with the help of parish constables?—I am certain it never can be efficient, because under the superintending constable system the superintending constable has a large area of ground, and he has to depend mainly upon the efficiency of the parish constables, and the duties which they have to perform are so contrary to their interests, that you would never get them to do it. I know from what I have observed in the counties of Somerset and Northumberland that they are completely useless.

1287. What does the police rate amount to in the pound?—The watch rate is 4 *d.* in the pound.

1288. Do you think that rate is paid without reluctance?—It is paid reluctantly by some; but I think the generality are satisfied with it.

1289. Are you sufficiently acquainted with the feeling of the trading classes of the county of Somerset to give an opinion as to their willingness to pay an additional rate of 2 *d.* in the pound for the purpose of protection?—I am not. I know that many of the county magistrates are aware of the necessity for a police force in the county of Somerset, and they are likewise aware of the evils which exist in the county. The supervision in the city is almost useless where there is no system beyond it in the environs; I know by the public-houses in Bath; we have a very strict supervision over them; yet before one o'clock in the day on the Sunday, drunken people are coming into the city from the outside. I have seen no less than eight individuals from Bath admitted into a public-house on a Sunday morning, during divine service, about a mile out of Bath. I mentioned it to one of the most active of the county magistrates; he said he knew it was so, but that he could not get any one to take it up.

1290. Then the evils of the absence of police in the surrounding counties are felt in the towns, very largely?—Yes; more perhaps than outside itself as regards the public-houses; they go from the town, where they cannot get drink; you may see the roads like a fair on a Sunday morning.

1291. Is it not the fact that thieves and depredators of every description very often reside in a town and leave it for the purpose of committing depredations and burglaries outside?—Yes; Isaacs, the captain of the Frimley gang, located himself, the whole of the time that the officers were after him, at Frome; he was taken at Frome, and from the inquiries I have made since I find he was daily in company along with those three men, Maggs, Hurd, and Sparrow, who were tried for the Frome murder. I have no hesitation in saying that he was organising another gang for the county of Somerset.

1292. Sir *J. Trollope.*] Have not those men all been apprehended?—There is one or two of them left.

1293. Are not the men whose names you have mentioned all convicted?—Yes; Hurd is out again. To show that the parish constabulary and the county parish constables are not of the slightest use, two parish constables followed one of the Frome gang named Whimpey. A burglary had been committed in Frome in a draper's shop; a roll of cloth was part of the stolen property; they followed this man on a Sunday evening going towards Bath; they passed him on the road;

he

Mr. A. Hughes.

2 June 1853.

he was then carrying the stolen property under his arm; and although he was by himself, they passed him and came into Bath and asked me to get him for them, and they had lost sight of him. I took an inspector out with me; we walked about the town for half-an-hour, and we apprehended him and went back to the public-house where he had been, where we got the property. I may observe that he had his hand in a sling; he was tried and convicted.

1294. *Chairman.*] Was he disabled?—I believe he had got his hand severely cut in breaking through the fanlight of the door.

1295. The two parish constables refused to take this disabled man?—They said he was such a desperate fellow; and that he had been previously convicted of felony. There was another case occurred about three months ago. A parish constable made an application to the Bath police; he had a man given in charge for stealing pork; he took the man to a public-house, and the man, by some means or other, made off; he missed the man, and when he came back he found the pork was gone too; he had lost the property as well. At the last assizes for the county of Somerset, a man of the name of Thare was apprehended by one of the inspectors under me in Bath; he was tried and convicted of a burglary in the vicinity of Burnham. He had property in his possession which he had taken in five burglaries. When he was taken I should say that he had 150 keys that would open any place. Ten robberies and burglaries were traced to him, and that man had made arrangements with the Government emigration agent to sail to Australia; he was to have left the very day after he was apprehended. That man would have escaped had it not been for the Bath police. We have frequent cases in the county of Somerset of apprehensions, by the assistance of the Bath police, and other towns, and by the magistrates' precepts in the county, Somerset being without a county constabulary.

1296. Do you think, in a county where the rural constabulary exists, the presence of separate jurisdictions in the towns, having separate police forces of their own, is not a very serious evil?—It is; if the boroughs were amalgamated with the counties, and the chief constables of such counties were amenable to a commissioner, I think it would remedy all the evils, because it must ensure co-operation.

1297. Would not a great diminution take place in the amount of the police force, both in counties and towns, if there were one uniform system of police?—Not in the towns; you must bear in mind that a system of duty which is applicable to the towns is not applicable in a rural district; the town forces must always be up on a different system from the rural police force. Since I have been in Bath I have, as nearly as I possibly could, adopted the metropolitan principle, and by so doing I have effected a saving of about 500 *l.* a year; but a constabulary system of duty the same as the rural police could not work well in a large town; it would be a moral impossibility.

1298. My question was directed to the possibility of diminishing the numbers, and, therefore, the cost of the rural police and of the city police, by putting a certain number of counties and towns under the same chief constable?—Yes, the cost would be decreased.

1299. Sir *J. Trollope.*] Would not you derive another advantage from having the power of removing the men from the town to the county, and *vice versâ*, so as not to permit the men to form local connexions?—That is an evil in the present system; a man is, perhaps, a native of the city, and he applies for employment; if it were left to the will of the chief constable I would not allow it, but the watch committee have not sanctioned my refusing.

1300. Do you prefer strangers?—Yes.

1301. Are your men in the police force in the city of Bath chiefly natives or strangers?—There are some strangers; I do not take more natives than I am obliged.

1302. You feel the local connexion to be an evil in those who are above you, and those who are below you?—Yes.

1303. Would it not be a great advantage to the service, if you could shift the men about to more distant places, where they have no local connexions?—Yes.

1304. Do you do that as far as you can within the limits of the city?—They are frequently changed, but that is of very little effect, because the locality is not wide enough.

1305. Lord *Lovain.*] Do you think the rural police system, as it is established in Surrey and Essex, is as perfect as the limited cost will permit?—I do; I consider

sider

sider the Surrey constabulary is as perfect as a rural police can be; but the rural police must always be, in my opinion, a separate system of duty from that in a town.

1306. But that would not prevent the two forces being put under the command of the same person?—Decidedly not; you would always require a larger number of police in a town.

1307. Sir *J. Trollope.*] There would be no difficulty in apportioning both the men and the cost, if amalgamation took place?—None whatever.

1308. Mr. *Mackie.*] Am I to understand you to say, that a uniform system of police, such as an amalgamated force, would be a great improvement upon the present system?—Most decidedly; none of the evils could exist then which exist now; it would be a very good thing for the police officers and for the public, especially for the public, because it would ensure co-operation; now if one chief of police writes to another, requesting special inquiry into a robbery, I have no doubt it is afforded, but it is not unless it is particularly requested; they are generally engaged in investigating offences committed in their own localities.

1309. Do the 82 men under your charge perform night and day duty?—Yes.

1310. The same men?—Yes; that is to say, they are on night duty for so long, and then on day duty, and so changing about.

1311. Lord *Lovaine.*] In the county of Northumberland, could a police force be established in your opinion without a very heavy expense, considering the extraordinary character of the district?—Yes; I consider that a very good and efficient police might be established in the county of Northumberland at almost the same cost as the parish constables. You cannot imagine the cost to the county of the parish constables, nor the frauds which are practised by them upon the county.

1312. *Chairman.*] It is difficult to ascertain?—You cannot ascertain it; I know I was at an inn at the last assizes, and an offender was tried whom the parish constable had previously wanted; this parish constable, finding that the man was about to be tried, went and made a declaration that he had been engaged for 30 or 40 nights after this man. After he came back to the inn I heard him myself say that he had not been over the threshold of the door; and in that case he drew a sum of nearly 10 *l.*; it was all momentary; he never thought of it before.

1313. You do not think that the existence of great tracts of country, where there are hardly any fields, and yet peculiarly exposed to the depredations of sheep and horse stealers, is necessarily any objection to the establishment of a rural police?—No, I do not; because where the district is wide, and there are not many inhabitants, you have nothing to do but to put fewer men. The more the population, of course, the more the force must be.

1314. I suppose that, in your opinion, the amalgamation of such a district as that which borders the Tyne from Newcastle to Tynemouth, would be a matter of interest and importance to all those places?—Yes.

1315. Are not the police forces of all those places very inefficient?—Particularly so. Bath is universally admitted to be the best borough police force in England.

1316. With reference to Tynemouth, Shields, and Newcastle, is there not a very inefficient police force in those places?—Yes, in my opinion. I think on inquiry you will find that in particular boroughs they are very corrupt as regards police matters. I knew one place, not far from Bath, where the parish constables actually fine the prisoners without their going before a magistrate; I mean only for drunkenness.

1317. Sir *J. Trollope.*] Do you refer to the rural police?—The superintending constable used to levy a fine when the prisoners came out of the cell without taking them before a magistrate; they do not do so now.

1318. When they were placed there for custody or safe keeping?—Yes. The present superintending constable there has told me that he has been offered the same thing by them; he has immediately said, "I cannot do anything of this kind." They have said, "Come, take it. We never used to go before the magistrates; we used to pay so and so." I do not think the salary of that party is above 30 *s.* a week, and by fees and emoluments his salary amounts to nearly 200 *l.* a year; I am sure it amounts to 170 *l.*

1319. Lord *Lovaine.*] The receipt of those fees does not make the constables particularly anxious to inspect the beerhouses?—No.

1320. Sir *J. Trollope.*] Do you think that system is in operation still?—I do not think it is, as regards the fining of the prisoners; but the fees must be considerable for 30 *s.* a week to be increased to 170 *l.* a year.

1321. Have you ever known any cases of the police under your orders taking money to hush up offences?—Never. I do not remember a case of bribery against a police constable in the whole 16 years I have been in the police. I cannot call one case to my mind.

1322. Sir *J. Anderson.*] Is it your opinion, if the watch committee were to vest in you the power of appointing and discharging the men, it would not go far to remedy the difficulty of which you speak?—I consider the borough force, by being amenable to two bodies, has a very conflicting effect: in fact, it puts the men in jeopardy, and likewise renders them very insecure, because if they do right they are called to account, and if they do wrong they are liable to punishment.

1323. If you had the entire appointment and dismissal of the men would not that go far to remedy the objections of which you have spoken of the men being under local control; are you aware that that is the case in Scotland?—I am not aware of the practice in Scotland.

1324. In the case of the amalgamation of the borough and county police, could not you secure co-operation if you had the men entirely under your control?—If it was the same as the county, where the chief constables are under the control of a body of magistrates, that would place the boroughs upon the same footing as the county constabulary, and the whole would be amenable to the police committee.

1324.* Lord *Lovaine.*] When you served in the Surrey constabulary, did you ever meet with any obstruction from the magistrates?—I never met with any obstructions from the magistrates in Surrey, or in Northumberland, or in Bath.

George Warry, Esq., called in ; and Examined.

1325. *Chairman.*] ARE you a Magistrate for Somerset?—Yes, I have been a Magistrate for some years.

1326. For how many?—More than 20.

1327. What is your system of police in Somerset?—We have no system of police; we have only the appointment of constables under the Parish Constables Act.

1328. Have you not adopted the system of superintending constables?—No.

1329. You have no police except the old parish constables?—No.

1330. From your experience have you found them efficient as a police force?—Certainly not.

1331. Will you state in what respects?—They are unqualified for the performance of their duties as ministers of the law, and also as conservators of the peace. They are persons who are very loath at all times to set themselves in motion for the prevention of crime and for the detection of thefts which have been committed, and they are altogether certainly very inefficient.

1332. Holding that opinion, do you desire to obtain a better system of police? —I have taken a very great interest in the question, from the very commencement of the inquiry into the police of the country. At the time when the constabulary commission was issued in 1837, inquiries were directed under the constabulary commissioners. I took a great interest in it; a string of questions was sent to the Bridgewater Board of Guardians, over which I presided, and individually, as a magistrate, I forwarded my opinion, which they did me the honour to notice in the Appendix to their Report.

1333. Did you ever endeavour to obtain the adoption of the Superintending Constables Act?—Yes; I attempted, when the Police Act, 3 and 4 Vict., passed, to persuade the county of Somerset to adopt it.

1334. Failing in that, did you ever attempt to get the appointment of superintending constables?—Yes; I co-operated with Mr. Langton, one of the Members for Bristol; I did all I could to get some amendment of the system.

1335. You have referred to the parochial system; do you think there is an interest in the increase of crime given to those officers by paying them for the apprehension of offenders?—I cannot say that I have positive proof from any instance of the kind; it must necessarily lead to it: it is the only way in which a parish constable can get paid. If a crime is committed, and followed up by commitment, he gets paid for his services. If he interests himself to prevent the commission of that crime, he gets no pay.

1336. Mr. *Moody.*] Was not the attempt of Mr. Langton, the Member for Bristol, to which you have alluded, the partial introduction of the measure with

with reference to the neighbourhood of Bath and Bristol?—I rather think it was for that division; the crime of that division more particularly urged him to the attempt.

O. Werry, Esq.

2 June 1853.

1337. And not extending over the whole county?—No; I co-operated with him because I was inclined to think, if we could make a move in any direction, it would be an improvement on the present system.

1338. *Chairman.*] Have you found difficulty in offenders being brought to justice under the parochial constable system?—I have found difficulty in detecting the perpetrators of offences; after the offender has been pointed out and marked as being the person, I do not think there is any difficulty in laying hold of him; but there is great difficulty in following up offences and in detecting them.

1339. You mean to say there is great difficulty in the pursuit of criminals?— Yes, certainly, if a person has been robbed. A grazier in my neighbourhood, about two years ago, lost as many as eight sheep; those sheep were stolen and driven all across the county through Bristol into Gloucesterhire; as soon as he got into Gloucestershire he was within the operation of the Police Act. The policeman then on duty, seeing this man with the sheep, entered into conversation with him, and from conversation he was led to suspect there was something wrong in his statements. Finding that he had stated that which was not true, he took him into custody, searched him, and found a letter with an address leading to the locality near me in Somersetshire. He made further inquiry, came down, and found out the grazier who had lost those sheep. The man was discovered, prosecuted, and convicted, and the property restored to the owner.

1340. You mean to say that the pursuit of the offender in this case in the county of Somerset, was ineffectual?—There was no pursuit at all.

1341. Then the prisoner would have escaped altogether if there had not been a police force in the county of Gloucester?—I think so, certainly.

1342. Have you formed any idea of what the expenses of the parish constables are?—I took occasion the other day to ask the clerk of our union at Bridgewater, the expenses that had been paid for the Bridgewater division for the year ending Lady-day 1852.

1343. What is the number of parishes in the division?—Forty parishes in the union, 37 in the division; the population is about 33,000; the expenses paid under the present system of parish constables in 1852 was about 168*l.* 10*s.*; the expenses of the constables were 65*l.* 5*s.* 9*d.*; attending proceedings before magistrates in the preceding year, it was 82*l.* 11*s.* 10*d.*, and the expenses of the constables, 90*l.*, before the justices.

1344. In speaking of proceedings before magistrates, do you mean cases where convictions took place?—No; there are certain expenses paid to the justices clerks for the orders and appointment of constables: various expenses are paid out of the same fund.

1345. Are you chairman of the Bridgewater Board of Guardians?—I was chairman at the formation of the union for the first two years; I have been three years chairman again since that; now I am vice-chairman.

1346. As chairman of that Board of Guardians, can you give any information to the Committee as to the necessity or the utility of the police in the suppression of vagrancy and tramping?—I think it would be very desirable; a police force is the most effectual way of repressing vagrancy altogether.

1347. Does vagrancy abound in that district?—I think so. A case occurred not long since to a neighbour of mine who happened to be with me: he had left his house; we were watched out of his premises, and a vagrant, a very clever fellow, in conjunction with two others, went to his house, and having got hold of our names he obtained 5*s.* or half a sovereign, I do not know which, from the lady of the house, on a false statement; I forget exactly what it was. Those three vagrants went on imposing upon various parties. When the gentleman came home he found, of course, that his wife had been imposed upon, and he being a man with more energy than his neighbours, followed those men from his house, tracing them to Glastonbury; from Glastonbury to Somerton; from Somerton to Langport, where we got near them. His horse was very tired; and whilst he was stopping to give it some food, his servant, more eager than discreet, with the constable whom they had taken at Glastonbury to assist them, went on a little outside the town of Langport; they came upon these three men, and very rashly laid hold of one of them and the other two escaped; they took the third into custody, and in coming over the bridge he managed to throw his papers into Langport river. The man was brought before me afterwards. I have no doubt he was one of the party ; but the person who went to the house and imposed upon the lady escaped ; there was no means of connecting him with the person we had in custody, consequently all three escaped. All that resulted from it was, that the gentleman had to pay, in my presence, a considerable sum of money for the expenses he was put to in prosecuting the case.

1348. In your experience is there a great deal of expense incurred from the depredations of tramps and vagabonds ?—I am a great sufferer myself.

1349. Are you aware of the magistrates being put to expense by the want of police ?—I remember an instance which I stated to the constabulary commissioners. A case of arson, of very strong suspicion, was brought before me, and it was necessary to remand the prisoner, thinking that clearer evidence might be supplied by further inquiries ; it was not so, and I was obliged to discharge the man ; certain expenses were incurred which were paid by myself and others out of our own pockets.

1350. In the case of a robbery being committed on your property, you, having the means, could employ parochial constables in order to pursue the offenders at your own expense ?—It would be at my own expense.

1351. A poor man with no means would not have the same facility to employ constables ?—Certainly not ; that, I think, is the hardship.

1352. If there were a paid constabulary, the poor man would be on the same footing as to the recovery of his property as the rich man ?—Undoubtedly. I should feel satisfied in contributing to his relief.

1353. Sir *J. Trollope*.] Do you take any means to check vagrancy at your Poor-law union ?—We do.

1354. Do you put in force the regulations of the Poor-law Commissioners ?—We have few vagrants to what we had.

1355. Do you attribute the decrease to the mode in which you deal with the vagrants who apply for relief at the union-house ?—I cannot say ; there are very few applications in that way.

1356. Are you as much infested with them in the county ?—I think there are as many about the county.

1357. Has not vagrancy decreased since there has been better employment throughout the country ?—There are a great number now.

1358. Has not the number of vagrants decreased throughout the country ?—No, I think not in our district ; I think we have as many as we always had.

1359. Mr. *Moody*.] Is not the number of applications by vagrants at the union-house a strong indication as to whether vagrancy is increasing or decreasing ?—No ; I think the professional vagrant rather abstains from applying at the union-house. I think they do a better business by confining their operations to families.

1360. Do you find that those who go into the union-house object to working, after their night's rest, in the morning ?—My attention has not been called to that subject ; we have so few applicants in that way. On my last visiting the workhouse the master informed me that the vagrants' beds were seldom occupied.

1361. Do you know the population of the Bridgewater division ?—I think it is more than 30,000.

1362. Sir *J. Trollope*.] Have you considered the advisability of incurring the expense of the police in Somerset ?—I have no hesitation in saying that the advantages would be quite commensurate with the expense.

1363. *Chairman*.] Supposing the expense incurred were $2\frac{1}{2}d$. in the pound, do you think the advantages to be derived from the police would be equivalent to that expense ?—Certainly $2\frac{1}{2}d$. in the pound in our county would produce upwards of 20,000*l*.

1364. Do you think that the value of land to the occupier, and consequently to the owner, would be increased by the establishment of a well regulated police ?—I think it would ; I confess, individually speaking, that I should consider my own property more valuable, and my woods more valuable, by being freed from the depredations which I suffer from the high road passing through them, and the damage I sustain in the plantations by the sapling trees being cut, and wood of various kinds being cut for the supply of things which these men make, such as clothes-pins and other things, and for fuel.

1365. Sir *J. Trollope*.] As a proprietor of woods subjected to these depredations, if this loss is so great, would it not be worth your while to have an individual

G. *Warry*, Esq.

2 June 1853.

-vidual watchman over your own property, such as a woodman?—It would not pay me to do it.

1366. Would it pay you to have the county police?—My contribution to the county police would be far less than the expense of a private watchman. I will give the Committee an instance which occurred not long since. A party of tramps and gipsies, with a great number of horses, came and pitched their tent very near my wood; the keeper was going through the wood, and he fell in with a fellow who had cut a lot of young oak saplings, which he carried across to the place where the tent was pitched; the man, being single-handed, could not go and take this person away from the party; he came home; it was evening. I went to the parish constable, and we proceeded to the place where the parties were encamped; when we got there every single male person in the party was gone. Some of these oak saplings were thrown over the hedge, and others were upon the fire half burnt; and of course all the party went off.

1367. Did not you deal with them as tramps and vagrants?—No.

1368. You might have done so by law?—I must have been the prosecutor, and it would not have been satisfactory to me. I knew the name of the party, for I took the name on the cart; and if there had been any police in the neighbourhood I could have given notice in which direction they had gone. I have often been subject to the same thing. It adds to the expenses of property, and I think by mutual insurance we should be able to defend each other.

1369. Lord *Lovaine*.] If you had had a private watchman, and he had followed these parties, would not your property have been left unprotected?—Yes.

1370. Mr. *Burroughes*.] I presume it would have been a very heavy expense to have sent a parish constable to Gloucester after the eight sheep to which you have referred, but if you had had a police force they never would have got so far?—No; I think that we in Somersetshire ought to be able to requite Gloucestershire with like service.

1371. Mr. *Moody*.] It would appear from your evidence as though there were no attempts at detection in Somersetshire?—Really there is not a great deal of attempt at detection.

1372. Was the farmer who had lost the eight sheep so apathetic that he did not attempt to follow them?—He had no means of knowing which way to go; he must have gone to the neighbouring towns and published handbills, and that is a very inefficient way of detecting crime; he had no one to tell his loss to whose services would have been at his command, without aggravating his loss.

Mr. *Thomas Heagren Redin*, called in; and Examined.

Mr. T. H. *Redin*.

1373. *Chairman*.] WHERE do you reside?—At Carlisle.

1374. What are you now?—The governor of the county gaol.

1375. Had you previously served in the Liverpool police force?—I served 5½ years in the Essex county constabulary, and 4½ years in the Liverpool borough police force.

1376. What situation did you hold in the Liverpool borough police force?—I was chief superintendent of the north division.

1377. Why did you leave that situation?—On my promotion as governor of the county gaol, at Carlisle.

1378. Were you the head of the force at Liverpool?—I was the second; the chief constable, or commissioner, is the head of the force; there are two divisional superintendents, each with 500 men under their charge.

1379. Have you directed your attention to the different systems of police now existing throughout Great Britain?—I have.

1380. What are they?—At the time I was connected with the Liverpool police force, we prepared a great mass of statistics, with reference to the police force generally, there being a hostile feeling existing between the magistracy and the watch committee, the superintendent had the statistics prepared for some years, in the event of anything transpiring; and I was employed by the commissioner to procure that information, showing a comparison between the county constabulary and the borough police, and the working of the two systems. I of course formed my opinion mainly from the working of the Essex constabulary. I have also observed the working of another county constabulary.

1381. In what other county?—In Lancashire, which is extremely good.

1382. Therefore you have a specimen of two counties, one in a purely agricultural county, and the other a large manufacturing county?—Yes. The Essex

Mr. *T. H. Redin.*

2 June 1853.

system worked extremely well; at the commencement there was vast opposition to the force, but it gradually subsided.

1383. Does the Lancashire system work well?—It does as a rural police, very well; still there is a want of co-operation between the Liverpool borough force, and the Lancashire men. A system of jealousy exists for which I see no remedy, except putting the two forces under the chief constable; I would put all the borough establishments under the same authority as the county; I would take the county, for instance, and amalgamate the county constabulary with the borough forces.

1384. Might not there be a jealousy in Liverpool in placing the head of the constabulary in the county?—There would be on the part of the watch committee, but not on the part of the magistracy.

1385. Supposing the system were adopted of placing two or three adjoining counties, classing the larger counties as boroughs, under one head, would not that remove any jealousy on the part of the boroughs?—I do not think it would remove the jealousy of the municipal bodies.

1386. Would not they be placed upon one equal footing with the counties?— Not if you delegated the power to the magistrates, in lieu of the chief constable.

1387. If you placed the borough of Liverpool under the direction of the chief constable for Lancashire, do not you think that would remove the jealousy? —I think the two forces would work harmoniously and well together.

1388. Do you think there would be no jealousy on the part of the magistracy? —It might exist for a short period, but it would soon subside; they would work as one family.

1389. Sir *J. Trollope.*] Would not the family be too large?—I think not.

1390. What is the number of county police?—Upwards of 500.

1391. What is the number of police in Liverpool?—It was 900, but it has been reduced to 800.

1392. Could that large body be worked as well under one head?—It would work well under one head.

1393. Would not there be a difficulty in passing the accounts of so large a body?—Not at all.

1394. Do you think it practicable to work a city of any size with the county —I do.

1395. Do you propose to extend it beyond the limits of the counties, and put two or three counties together?—Lancashire would be an exception to the rule, there being Liverpool with the force I have mentioned, Manchester having 400, and there is a police force at Bolton and Preston.

1396. Would you, as a rule, put two or three counties together?—I would.

1397. What would be the total force you would have in counties and boroughs? —I think from about 1,700 to 1,800.

1398. You would not exceed 2,000?—I think not; Preston has not more than 23.

1399. Manchester has 400?—Yes.

1400. And Liverpool 900?—It is reduced now to 800.

1401. And 500 in the county?—Yes.

1402. Making 1,800?—Yes.

1403. Would that be too large a body to work together?—I think not.

1404. Have you ever been in the metropolitan force?—I was stationed at Dunmow, and I have been occasionally ordered to come into London to act.

1405. Having acted with the metropolitan police force, you see no difficulty in working the force on a more extended scale in the county?—Not the slightest.

1406. *Chairman.*] Do you believe that the establishment of county police forces has been attended with beneficial results?—I am quite satisfied of it.

1407. Will you state some of the objects thereby effected?—In the north Hinckford division of the county of Essex, the police was established in 1840, and in the article of sheep alone the farmers in that division in 1839 lost 99; some farmers refused to give me any information. I have the means of ascertaining that they had lost some 8 or 10, but for 99 I have an honest return. The first year the police force was established their loss amounted to five, and two parties were transported for sheep-stealing; I have every reason to believe that they stole the five, as they were all stolen in a small area. In the following year the loss was one or two. Burglary was not known after the establishment of the police; the vagrants vanished by magic, and we had scarcely any in the county. The Rev. Mr. Gooch, a very active magistrate near Topesfield, gave me a certificate

on

Mr. T. H. Redin.

2 June 1853.

on leaving Essex; and he stated in the certificate that "what had been the rule was then the exception," (with respect to crime). Those are the very words he made use of.

1408. Sir *J. Trollope.*] What office did you hold in the Essex police?—I was a superintendent of the first class.

1409. Have you any rural police in the county of Cumberland?—We have four men stationed in the Derwent division; one at Keswick, two at Cockermouth, and one at Maryport.

1410. *Chairman.*] Is there any chief constable?—There is one at Cockermouth, a superintendent in charge of the three. They are efficient as far as they go; but it is too wide a district.

1411. Are they sufficient for a night patrol?—No.

1412. Sir *J. Trollope.*] Of course the Keswick policeman has no communication with the others?—No.

1413. Is the superintendent at Cockermouth?—Yes.

1414. What is the distance from Keswick to Cockermouth?—I am not aware; it is a considerable distance.

1415. Is there any police at Whitehaven?—There is one, which is supported by the Town and Harbour trustees.

1416. There is no rural police?—There is no rural police. The eastern parts of Cumberland and the borders of Northumberland are infested with vagrants; robberies are rife, and the farmers frequently turn out in a gang and attempt to secure the depredators; but before they can be secured they have gone to the borders of Scotland, and vanished from Cumberland.

1417. Can you give the Committee the number of prisoners in the gaol, to show the state of crime?—With reference to the state of crime in the county, the numbers are low; that is particularly the case as regards the natives; three-fourths of our prisoners, as the statistics will show, both for felonies, larcenies, as well as misdemeanours of a milder description, are strangers.

1418. Have you not a mixed population in the city of Carlisle itself?—We have.

1419. Are there not a considerable number of Irish and Scotch?—There are.

1420. Being on the borders you have idle characters from all the counties?—We have very few Scotch prisoners; our prisoners are principally Irish, or persons born of Irish parents, resident in Cumberland. In the average of the last seven years, the committals for trial have been very light. In 1846 it was 144; in the last year it was 138; but that is no criterion, I am sure more crime was committed.

1421. Do you mean to say that it remains undetected?—It remains undetected purely from the want of some channel to apply to.

1422. Is it not the fact, that the condition of the people in the county of Cumberland is remarkably good as regards wages?—The agricultural labourers board in the farm houses; they are hired for a term, and they get from 6 *l.* to 7 *l.* and 10 *l.*, according to their capability. The married men's wages average about 8 *s.* or 9 *s.* a week, at present I believe 9 *s.* to be about the average. The number of vagrants that slept in Carlisle in the year ending November 1852, which number was registered, and every information procured by the police, was 45,718; for the present quarter, ending the other night, the numbers amounted to 10,236; that is wholly independent of those who pass through Carlisle during the day-time; those are the parties that actually slept in Carlisle.

1423. Mr. *Moody.*] Of what class were those vagrants generally?—Itinerant thieves.

1424. Sir *J. Trollope.*] The whole of them?—I asked the superintendent, and he said they were itinerant thieves principally; three-fourths of my prisoners are of that class.

1425. What is the state of the police force in the city of Carlisle?—It is established under the Municipal Corporation Act, paid for from the corporation funds.

1426. What is the number of the police?—Twenty-two.

1427. Is it well managed?—Yes.

1428. Are the lodging-houses in the city of Carlisle placed under the Lodging-house Act?—Yes; this is a return from the police officers of the lodging-houses; the vagrants will not apply to a union; the professional thief never applies for a ticket at the poor-house; he prefers the low lodging-house.

[*The Witness delivered in the following Return:*]

LODGING-HOUSE RETURNS, from 23d November 1851 to the 20th November 1852.

DATE.	Males of full Age.	Females of full Age.	Males from 8 to 21 Years.	Females from 8 to 21 Years.	Males under 8 Years.	Females under 8 Years.	TOTAL.
1st quarter -	7,917	2,811	154	231	356	240	11,709
2d ,, -	7,506	2,667	121	102	268	165	10,849
3d ,,	8,944	2,924	142	125	175	153	12,463
4th ,,	8,027	2,314	33	76	100	147	10,697
TOTAL - -	32,394	10,716	4.	534	919	705	45,718

For the present quarter - - - - -	10,236

1429. Have you many of such low lodging-houses in Carlisle ?—I am not prepared to state the number, but there are a great number.

1430. Have many of those low lodging-houses been abandoned since more stringent regulations have passed ?—No; they have generally managed to get their license.

1431. Do you consider those low lodging-houses to be receptacles for stolen goods ?—Unquestionably they are receptacles for stolen goods ; according to the term made use of by the thieves they act as a "fence ;" if the thief does not know of any other method, he manages to dispose of his property through the keepers of those houses.

1432. Were not some portion of this vast number of vagrants Irish, who were driven by the state of their own country into England or Scotland ?—I think so.

1433. Is it fair to class the whole of them as thieves ?—I am confirmed in that opinion by the superintendent of police. I have a great many in my custody; we have about 600 prisoners in the year committed to gaol.

1434. Is Carlisle Gaol the only gaol in the county ?—There is none other.

1435. What has been your daily average of prisoners for the last few years? —In 1851 it was 101, last year 94, and the present year 88.

1436. The numbers have been on the decrease ?—Our recommittals have decreased, but we have the same class of persons constantly coming into the gaol.

1437. Mr. *Moody.*] Supposing these vagrants to live as thieves, you detect a very small portion of the felonies that are committed ?—Yes; especially in the neighbourhood of Bewcastle, on the borders of Scotland.

1438. Sir *J. Trollope.*] Seeing the position of Carlisle, which is the gate into Scotland, is it not inevitable that you must have a great number of vagrants passing to and from England and Scotland ?—I think so, as a matter of course.

1439. Are not many of those persons coming from Glasgow, to seek work in England, at the large manufacturing places ?—They are wanderers upon the face of the earth ; that was the expression of the superintendent.

1440. Are the same parties in the habit of passing to and fro ?—Very probably; it is a neighbourhood where many live in the fields ; and those men steal where they can.

1441. *Chairman.*] Do not you think that parochial constables are perfectly inefficient for the purpose of remedying this evil ?—Quite so, from the fact that I very seldom receive a prisoner from a parochial constable, in any form or shape.

1442. Do you think they are capable of performing their duty ?—I think it is utterly impossible, from their local connexion, and their own interest ; they are generally small tradesmen, such as tailors and shoemakers.

1443. Are they unwilling to accept the office of constable, generally ?—I cannot give any opinion upon that point ; we find it to be the case.

1444. Did you give any rewards in Liverpool ?—The watch committee, upon the representation of the Commissioner, if a man exerted himself, would give him 10 s. or a pound.

1445. Did

1445. Did they do that without the assent of the superintendent of police?— No.

1446. Does the system of paying constables by fees and allowances become oppressive to the sufferers from offences, particularly as regards the lower classes? —I conceive, under the present system, the poor man receives no protection at all; if he is robbed, he must put up with the loss; but where there is a policeman he is equally protected with the rich.

1447. Were the public-houses and beer-houses well controlled in Liverpool?— Not in a satisfactory manner; far from it.

1448. Are those places generally the chief resort of thieves in the town?— They are; there are some 18 or 20 houses in Liverpool which are notorious as the resort of thieves.

1449. You have spoken of the inefficiency of the parochial constables; have you had any means of calculating the expense of parochial constables in any districts?—I made the attempt to analyze it, but I found it impossible to arrive at the exact amount paid. I arrive at it in this manner, that a meeting, assembled to oppose the police, went away satisfied that the expense was not greater than that incurred by the parish constables.

1450. *Chairman.*] Where was that?—At North Hinckford, in Essex.

1451. Considering the question of efficiency, do you believe that the direct and indirect expense of a parochial constabulary is equal to, or greater than, the cost of a well-organized police force?—I think the inhabitants at large would save the expense of a police from the absence of vagrants; the toll they levy is enormous.

1452. You are aware of the Act by which there is the middle system of appointing constables for each division of a county; are you of opinion that parochial constables can be rendered efficient, or more efficient than they are at present, by the appointment of superintending constables?—Knowing the material with which you have to deal, I think not; I have never seen the working of the superintending constable system; I have heard of it, but it is not satisfactory, because a parochial constable will not co-operate; there is always some interest clashing against the proper discharge of their duties.

1453. You state that uniting counties with towns would not be productive of jealousies?—I cannot see any jealousy which could arise; the pay would be the same, and the promotion would go on the same.

1454. Sir *J. Trollope.*] If it could be shown to the boroughs that they would save something by it, would not they be inclined to adopt it, in your opinion?—I think they would.

1455. Do not you think, practically, the expense of superintendence would be saved?—The expense of the staff would be reduced.

1456. You think that would induce the boroughs to consent to amalgamation, without jealousy of feeling?—Yes.

1457. *Chairman.*] Could it be done without increasing the expense to the county?—I think it could; you would merely take the cost and divide it amongst the respective boroughs and counties.

1458. Do you think that the boroughs depend upon the assistance and aid of the military when the police force is found to be inefficient?—At the time I was at Liverpool, in 1848, we anticipated a serious outbreak with the Chartists; the men in the police force were all drilled to the use of the cutlass; a certain number of constables of the rural police were mounted and armed in the outskirts; we had 100 picked men trained to the use of the carbine; we depended upon our own force; the military came into Liverpool, but they took no part in the arrangements.

1459. Sir *J. Trollope.*] Had you any mounted police?—No.

1460. *Chairman.*] Do you know anything of the police in Blackburn?—No.

1461. Have you experienced or observed any inconvenience or delay in the discharge of police duties from the restriction of the constable's power within certain limits?—That is particularly the case when a man knows that he is not a constable beyond a certain limit.

1462. Supposing the large boroughs, such as Liverpool, Leeds, and Birmingham, with a population of more than 100,000, were placed in the situation of separate counties or districts, do you think there would be any advantage in adding certain districts round those boroughs to their districts, irrespective of absorbing them in the whole county?—We found in Liverpool this fact, that the thieves seldom committed a serious robbery in the borough.

Mr. T. H. Redin.

2 June 1853.

1463. Assuming that those boroughs were considered as separate counties, with a chief constable at their head, with an independent police force the same as a county, would it be desirable to add any district round those boroughs to those boroughs?—I say in Liverpool we found it to be the fact that burglaries were rarely committed; they were committed in the outskirts, at a distance of two or three or four miles; if our men had had liberty to patrol as far as that, I think the thieves would have been defeated, and they would remain at home rather than go eight or ten miles for nothing.

1464. Have you had any experience as to the beneficial results of transferring local duties to the county constabulary?—The Essex constabulary were the first that performed the duties of inspectors of weights and measures; it effected a very great saving on the whole; it used to be a sum of 600 l. An expense was saved to the county by transferring the duty to the county constabuiary, and it is the opinion of the county generally that the superintendents have discharged that duty very satisfactorily; they have discharged it satisfactorily in this way, that a shopkeeper never knows when the superintendent is coming into his shop. The parish constable used to acquaint all his neighbours: "The inspector of weights and measures is coming, and you must look out." The superintendent of police can walk in at any time and detect the fraudulent dealer. Also with reference to sanitary matters, all the duties in connection with the Board of Health are far better discharged by the police, in Liverpool, than by the inspector of nuisances, as he is termed; the whole of those duties are performed by the police much better than the limited staff which they keep.

1465. Under whose direction is the police in the borough of Liverpool?—Entirely under the watch committee, from the head to the lowest constable.

1466. Have the watch committee the power of dismissing?—They have.

1467. And also the power of appointing constables?—Yes.

1468. Mr. *Burroughes.*] Is the watch committee a portion of the town council?—They are members of the town council. The watch committee consists of 25 members selected from the town council.

1469. Is it an annual appointment?—It is; the election takes place on the 9th of November.

1470. *Chairman.*] Did any inconvenience arise from that?—Constant interference.

1471. What was the nature of that interference?—We have had several cases of positive interference, and three or four conspicuous ones, in members of the watch committee. We had one case where an officer was active in apprehending a number of boys for breaking the collegiate windows; it was a paltry affair in itself, but he chanced to arrest two sons of an elector in the ward. As soon as the father discovered that, he posted off to the member of the watch committee of his ward, and requested that he would interfere and get the constable removed from his beat. I thought it was such an outrageous interference that I declined to listen to him. I said, "It is a preposterous interference; the man has done his duty properly, and I shall continue him on his beat." That gave great offence, and that member of the watch committee never spoke again to me while I remained in Liverpool.

1472. Has there been any interference with the police in the borough of Liverpool in consequence of their inspection and control of the public-houses and beer-houses?—Yes; we found a very significant fact, that the houses belonging to the members of the watch committee who were publicans, brewers, and spirit merchants, were seldom reported.

1473. Do you mean to say that any members of the watch committee were publicans?—In 1845 there were several members of the watch committee who were brewers and spirit merchants; that is the leaven that does so much mischief. In the year 1846 the chairman of the watch committee was a brewer.

1474. Sir *J. Trollope.*] And the owner of public-houses?—A vast number. In 1848 there were several brewers and spirit merchants on the watch committee. In 1849 the deputy chairman was a brewer. In 1850, on the nomination of the watch committee, a considerable discussion took place in the town council as to the impropriety of having brewers and publicans on the committee; the magistrates had given some hint that they objected to the body; it resulted in only one or two being appointed. I am not prepared to say the number. In 1851 and 1852 the number was increased again; this year there is only one brewer, the owner of several public-houses. In the year 1847 a publican, who had an

information

Mr. T. H. Redin.

2 June 1853.

information laid against him by one of the police constables, came to the station attended by a member of the watch committee of the ward in which his house was situated, for whose election this publican was chairman of the committee, and impudently threatened to take the policeman's coat off his back if he dared to interfere.

1475. Was that a member of the watch committee?—No; he had beaten up his friend to come to the station and endeavour to interfere; many other matters occurred.

1476. *Chairman.*] You are of opinion that it would be better that the police should be placed under some more independent power?—Yes. I really do not think that the men can conscientiously discharge their duty under many circumstances.

1477. Sir *J. Trollope.*] Do you mean under the present system?—Exactly. If he saw the most flagrant case, if it belonged to a member of the watch committee, he would be a marked man if he reported. If once a prejudice is raised in a committee it is difficult to overcome it.

1478. You think it would be an improvement if the police were under the magistracy, with no control on the part of the watch committee?—Yes; the fact of the watch committee being an elected body, and depending upon popularity, must lessen their independence.

1479. You mean that the policemen might be severely handled by the watch committee from the representations of the constituents of that body?—Exactly. It is nothing more or less than dread and intimidation. The watch committee would listen to a case which the magistrates would scout.

1480. Can you suggest what you think would be the best mode of acting with such cases; under what authority would you place the police?—I think there is no better power than the magistrates, who are a permanent and responsible body; which is not the case with the town council.

1481. Lord *Lovaine.*] Do you think even the magistrates would be a fit body to appoint the police?—I think not; I think the head of the police is the best judge of the qualities of the men he would accept in the service; I have known most improper men appointed in the Liverpool police force.

1482. Mr. *Burroughes.*] Do you know any instance in any county where the appointment is not vested in the chief constable?—I believe it is vested in the chief constable by the Rural Police Act.

1483. Sir *J. Trollope.*] Do you think the police in Liverpool were appointed from corrupt motives?—I have reason to believe they have been appointed from political motives.

1484. Are the police in Liverpool chosen by the whole body of the watch committee, or by a sub-committee under them?—By the whole body; the sub-committee sit daily, and their proceedings are submitted to the whole body each Saturday before the final appointments take place.

1485. Have the superintendents any voice in the matter?—For the last two years they were allowed to come before him from a list; he submitted his list of approved candidates, supposing there were four vacancies; they had virtually the selection after all, because he was bound to send more candidates than there were vacancies.

1486. By that check improper men could not gain admission?—It was felt to be an improvement, but not a sufficient check.

1487. Lord *Lovaine.*] The persons appointed would be those whom the superintendent had sent up as candidates?—No doubt, but still he felt the pressure from without.

1488. Sir *J. Trollope.*] Did they come before you in the first instance?—No; I never saw them till they had their uniform on, and reported themselves as being appointed.

1489. Have you had occasion to report those men as unfit for duty?—Yes.

1490. Did the watch committee attend to your representations?—They used to fine them sometimes. I have frequently reported men as being incompetent for the duty, and the watch committee have asked me in what particular manner the man was incompetent. I would say, "The man has not common intelligence," or, "He is not an active man." And they would say, "Give him a further trial; the man is anxious to get his living;" and by that means we were encumbered with men who were perfectly useless.

1491. What

Mr. *T. H. Redin.*

2 June 1853.

1491. What was the cost of the police force to the borough?—About 40,000 *l.*; they are paid out of the corporation funds, and by a small rate, the eighth of a farthing only.

1492. Were your men employed in assisting the civil power in the collection of the Customs dues at Liverpool?—The whole of the north docks were under my charge; we had 200 men there, and they were allowed, with the sanction of the Customs, to arrest any person passing through the gates with contraband goods, for which they received a reward.

1493. Had that any effect upon the discipline of the men?—I think they looked more after smuggling than after theft.

1494. Do you think the reward was a stimulant to that species of duty?—Yes; if I had my will, I would never give rewards in such cases.

1495. You saw no objection to their performing that duty if they had not had that stimulant?—No.

1496. You think rewards have rather a demoralizing effect upon the police? —Yes.

1497. Mr. *Burroughes.*] Do not you think the Government ought to pay something for that protection to the revenue, and that the expense ought not to fall entirely upon the ratepayers?—Of course; they are a protection to property as well. A man may be taken up for smuggling goods; if the police see a man rather more bulky than usual, and they are induced to search him, it may prove that he has stolen cotton about him.

1498. Sir *J. Trollope.*] Was it not the duty of the police also to look after the shipping and the goods, and to protect property generally?—Yes.

1499. Did they ever go on board the ships?—Only at tide-time, to see that each vessel had its proper watch, which was in conformity with the bye-laws of the borough. The docks were all closed, and the constables were stationed as sentinels at the gates.

1500. Is there not a dock police at Liverpool?—They were amalgamated with the town force in 1836, with good effect. Previously to that time they used to act as two distinct forces; one would act directly hostile to the other.

1501. Lord *Lovaine.*] Do you believe it possible to establish the rural police in the mining districts of Cumberland?—I do. The mere fact of constables patrolling would act as checks, and vagrants would not come into the county.

1502. Is there not a good deal of crime at Alston and the mining district of Cumberland, in poaching and otherwise?—Yes.

1503. Are there not desperate characters in that district, who commit crimes in broad daylight, setting the law at defiance?—Yes.

1504. Do you believe those parties would be checked by the establishment of a rural police?—The uncertainty of the movements of the rural policeman is the terror to thieves.

1505. Could you collect a body of policemen to oppose the armed gangs which go about in broad daylight in that district, on the spur of the moment?—A policeman would not properly discharge his duty if he were not acquainted with the residences of the suspicious characters; he ought not to allow a gang to be so organized that he could not get assistance.

1506. You think mining occupation is not a bar to the establishment of police? —I think not.

1507. You say that you have never known the magistrates interfere in the conduct of the police?—No; I have never heard the magistrates interfere with the conduct of the policemen.

1508. Have the magistrates ever dismissed men for misconduct?—Mr. Rushton dismissed several of my men.

1509. Have the magistrates ever threatened them with dismissal?—Never to intimidate them.

1510. With reference to the rural constabulary, are you aware whether they have ever met with undue interference on the part of the county magistrates?—I never heard of it.

1511. Sir *J. Trollope.*] When you were in the Essex rural police, did you entirely dispense with the services of the parish constables?—I only remember one instance, in a village where I was stationed: I requested a constable to take charge of a prisoner; that constable was a decent respectable man.

1512. They were not altogether dispensed with by the magistrates?—They were appointed by the vestry.

1513. Were

Mr. T. H. Redin.

2 June 1853.

1513. Were they entrusted with no duties whatever?—No.

1514. Did they never attend at the sessions or assizes?—No.

1515. Were the entire expenses of their services saved to the county?—Yes.

1516. Then the appointment of constables was a mere formality, and not attended with any advantage?—I only on one occasion required the assistance of a parish constable, in which he had a case at the sessions.

1517. Is it your opinion that, under a perfect organization of a rural police force, it would be possible entirely to dispense with parish constables?—Yes.

1518. In fact, the law requiring their appointment might be repealed?—Yes, because their duties might be discharged by the police.

1519. If they were in sufficient numbers?—Yes, such as serving precepts and minor matters.

1520. The law contemplates not more than one policeman to every thousand inhabitants. Are you of opinion that the maximum number would be sufficient to discharge all the duties of the parochial constables as well as those of police?—I think it would.

1521. Lord *Lovaine*.] Is there any utility, in your opinion, to be derived from continuing the law as it now stands, that there must be a parish constable for every parish?—I cannot see the slightest utility in it, except in counties where there is no police. They would be a nuisance if they were appointed in conjunction with the police.

Veneris, 3° die Junii, 1853.

MEMBERS PRESENT.

Mr. Rice.	Sir John Trollope.
Mr. Burroughes.	Mr. Mackie.
Mr. Fitzroy.	Sir James Anderson.
Mr. Charles Howard.	Lord Lovaine.
Mr. Rich.	

EDWARD ROYDS RICE, Esq., IN THE CHAIR.

Mr. *Thomas Heagren Redin,* called in; and further Examined.

Mr. T. H. Redin.

3 June 1853.

1522. *Chairman*.] WILL you state your opinion as to the comparative expense of prosecutions under the rural police, and under the old system of parish constables?—The expense of prosecutions averages in Cumberland 18 *l.* each, and in Essex it is a few shillings under 8 *l.*

1523. Are there any local circumstances which would increase the expense in Cumberland?—I think it is to be attributed entirely to the heavy expense of the parish constables in the pursuit and securing of prisoners; their bills are very heavy in Cumberland.

1524. Sir *J. Trollope*.] Do you mean for sessions and assizes together?—Yes.

1525. Cannot you separate them?—No, I cannot.

1526. Lord *Lovaine*.] You have stated that the remuneration of police constables at Liverpool is under the Watching and Lighting Act; to whom, in your opinion, ought the remuneration to be given?—I think to the head of the police.

1527. Do you think the police should be irremovable except at his pleasure?—The magistrates have the power under certain Acts to remove the men for misconduct; under ordinary circumstances the appointments and dismissals ought to be in the hands of the chief constable.

1528. You think the management of the police should be concentrated as far as possible in the hands of the head of the police?—Most decidedly; that is my opinion.

Captain *John Woodford*, called in ; and Examined.

1529. *Chairman.*] WHERE do you reside ?—At Preston, in Lancashire.

1530. You are the chief constable ?—I am chief constable of Lancashire.

1531. Can you state what is the number of your force, and its classification ?—We have, exclusive of supernumeraries, 546 ; and we have 13 supernumeraries.

1532. Do you know what proportion the number of your police bears to the population ?—The proportion of men to the population varies in the different districts ; each petty sessional division of the county of Lancaster is in itself a police district.

1533. Do they pay their expenses separately ?—They pay their expenses separately ; their accounts are kept separately.

1534. What is the reason for that ?—It originated upon the attempt to abolish the police in 1842 ; upon the failure of the proposition to abolish the police a resolution was come to to separate the county into districts, under the provisions of the Act of the 3 & 4 Vict., c. 88.

1535. Was the objection to the police that the expenses were greater in proportion to the wants of the different divisions ?—Precisely so. The rural districts considered, if they were called upon to pay an equal rate, they were supporting the police of the populous districts.

1536. Do you think that is just ?—I think it is just that each district should be called upon to bear its own expenses, and no more ; I could not devise a better plan to give general satisfaction.

1537. Do you think that objection would apply to a county purely agricultural ? —I should imagine not.

1538. Mr. *Fitzroy.*] Are the appointments, and promotion, and the general discipline of the men carried on in the same way as if the rate were paid equally over the whole county ?—Precisely so ; the men are as completely under my direction as if it was one single district, and removable from one place to another.

1539. Do you mean that they are removable from one police force to another ? —If I find a man does not work well in one district I place him in another.

1540. *Chairman.*] Have not you the power, in any one of those manufacturing districts, in the case of an outbreak, to remove any number of men that you think proper into that district ?—Yes.

1541. What boroughs have you in your county ?—The boroughs in Lancashire are Lancaster, Preston, Blackburn, Bolton, Oldham, Ashton-under-Lyne, Manchester, Salford, Liverpool, Warrington, and Wigan.

1542. How many of those boroughs have a police of their own, and how many have not ?—All of them have police forces of their own.

1543. Has Blackburn a police ?—Yes, since it separated from the county it has a force of its own.

1544. When was that ?—Last year.

1545. Have you ever been called in to assist the police in any of those boroughs ? —In several of those boroughs, in cases of disturbance.

1546. Which of them ?—In Preston.

1547. When ?—At the last general election in 1852, and at former elections.

1548. How many men did you send to Preston at the election ?—I think about 40 or 50.

1549. Into what other borough have you been called ?—To Bolton ; we sent but a few men there. We have also sent men to Wigan and Warrington.

1550. Mr. *Fitzroy.*] Was that also at the time of a contested election ?—Yes.

1551. Are those the only occasions on which the county police has been asked for by the magistrates of the boroughs ?—Not the only cases in which we have been asked, but the only cases in which we have acted ; we have been asked to go in to suppress ordinary disturbances in a borough.

1552. Have you had many applications of this description ?—We had one from Wigan immediately following the last general election.

1553. Consequent upon that election ?—Consequent upon that election ; a disturbance took place the day after the declaration of the poll. We could not afford them help, and they were obliged to call for the aid of the troops, as our hands at the time were completely full at Bury and elsewhere.

1554. Have

1554. Have you had repeated applications from the magistrates of the different Capt. J. Woodford. boroughs to assist them with a detachment of your men on any other occasion than contested elections, or riots growing out of contested elections?—No.

1555. *Chairman.*] Was there a disturbance at Blackburn?—There was a disturbance at Blackburn at the last election.

1556. Were you applied to for assistance then?—We were.

1557. Did you give it?—We did not give it.

1558. Why did you not?—Because Blackburn is not in our charge.

1559. Had you not acted in places which were equally not in your charge?—Wigan was not in our charge; Blackburn had been, but they left us.

1560. What did they do at Blackburn?—They appointed special constables.

1561. Mr. *Fitzroy.*] Has Wigan any police of its own?—Wigan has a police force of 10 men.

1562. *Chairman.*] Were the military called out in the borough of Blackburn?—The military were called out.

1563. Mr. *Fitzroy.*] Will you explain why you had no objection to furnish men in the case of Wigan when you had an objection in the case of Blackburn, where they had a separate police force neither under their control?—I felt myself in a difficulty, Blackburn having relinquished our connexion; I therefore laid the case before the constabulary committee, and the committee, upon consideration, came to the conclusion that it was not expedient to take the men from the duties for which they were paid, to preserve order in the town of Blackburn, which contributes nothing towards their support.

1564. The same circumstances seem to have occurred with respect to Wigan; why was the decision different in one case from the other?—I never appealed to the committee in any other case.

1565. Did you deal with it on your own responsibility?—Yes.

1566. Are the Committee to understand that the only reason why you refused to grant the application of Blackburn was because you thought they had better have remained under your control; in fact, it was by way of signifying to them your displeasure?—I think they would have acted more wisely to have remained under our charge, and perhaps it was thought desirable that they should be allowed to feel their weakness.

1567. Lord *Lovaine.*] In other words, you thought that, having refused to pay their proper share towards the general police rate of the county, they were not entitled to any assistance?—I considered, that having so refused, they were no longer entitled to any assistance.

1568. *Chairman.*] Are the Committee to understand that there was this difference between Wigan and Blackburn, that Wigan never had been consolidated with the county?—Never.

1569. And Blackburn had?—Yes.

1570. Mr. *Fitzroy.*] What is the number of the police force in Blackburn?—Thirteen; when we had charge of the town it was 22.

1571. Sir *J. Trollope.*] What is the population of Blackburn?—Forty-six thousand five hundred and thirty-eight.

1572. Are 13 policemen adequate to preserve the peace and discharge the ordinary constabulary duties, in a general way?—I have already mentioned to the Committee that I had 22 in the town, and I did not consider that number more than sufficient, aided as it might have been by any necessary augmentations in cases of emergency.

1573. Mr. *Fitzroy.*] Has the police force been increased since the last election, or has there been any proposal for increasing it?—Since this Committee has been appointed, they have, I believe, added six to their number.

1574. On the occasion when you were called in to aid in suppressing the riots were the county constabulary paid by the borough authorities?—Their extra expenses were defrayed, and their expenses in being conveyed from place to place; there was the ordinary allowance given to the constables to defray the expenses to which they were put.

1575. Was it stated, when the application was made to you for this additional police force at Wigan, that they would be called upon to pay?—They were fully aware that they would be called upon to pay.

1576. Was the same offer made in the case of Blackburn?—The same offer was not made; I do not bear the thing perfectly in mind, but I think the impression in Blackburn was, that the constabulary of the county would be received as special constables, and the expense borne by the county at large, and not by the borough; I think also that that was one reason which actuated the committee in refusing assistance.

1577. Mr. *Howard.*] Were not the county police lately called upon to act at Clitheroe ?—Yes, at the last election; a few days since.

1578. What is the number of their police ?—They are in charge of the county; it was my duty to go in there and preserve order.

1579. Lord *Lovaine.*] How many men did you take to Clitheroe ?—Two hundred men.

1580. Mr. *Fitzroy.*] Was that number adequate for the preservation of the peace ?—Quite.

1581. Sir *J. Trollope.*] Was order kept at Clitheroe last week ?—Perfectly.

1582. Was there any disturbance or annoyance to any person ?—No; there was not even a pane of glass broken.

1583. Mr. *Fitzroy.*] Was there a demand for the county constabulary at the last election at Oldham ?—Not at the last election; at the general election a demand was made.

1584. Was it acceded to ?—It was not acceded to, for this reason, that they refused to bear the expenses; the borough declined to bear the expenses.

1585. Was the assistance of the police refused on that ground only ?—It was, I believe, refused on that ground only.

1586. Sir *J. Trollope.*] There was scarcely a contested election in Lancashire at which there were not serious disturbances, was there ?—There were none at Bury.

1587. Did you send men there ?—Yes. Bury is in our charge, and therefore entitled to our services. Neither did any disturbance take place at Wigan while we were in charge of the town.

1588. Would there have been a disturbance if you had not sent a force into Bury ?—A most serious disturbance, without any question.

1589. You think that the presence of your force prevented it ?—Yes, most certainly.

1590. Have you considered the question with reference to the county of Lancaster, whether it would be desirable to amalgamate the police force placed under your control both in the counties and boroughs ?—I think there is some peculiarity regarding Liverpool which would require consideration.

1591. Are you aware of the number of men now employed in Liverpool ?—Yes; they have 886.

1592. Do you consider that Liverpool has so large a force that you could not deal with it in conjunction with the county police ?—I do not say that.

1593. Do you consider that you could arrange matters so as to superintend the whole of the county ?—I think any one man could manage the police of Lancashire with better effect, as a whole, than divided as it now is.

1594. Including the whole of the boroughs ?—If it became necessary to place it under one man it could be done, and I have no doubt well done.

1595. Would it be desirable to leave out such boroughs as Liverpool and Manchester ?—I think it would be desirable to treat Liverpool and Manchester as districts by themselves, and treat the county as another, and rule under one head.

1596. You think that you can find sufficient force to preserve peace in the boroughs and in the county ?—Yes, without the aid of a single soldier, except under most unusual circumstances.

1597. *Chairman.*] You mean according to the 3 & 4 Victoria, placing different counties under one head, and making Liverpool one of them ?—Yes; I think Liverpool would necessarily be separate, because the expenses are defrayed out of the borough funds, and not out of the rate.

1598. Mr. *Fitzroy.*] Have you any reason to imagine that the police force of Liverpool is insufficient ?—No; I think generally it is a sufficient establishment, even for extraordinary emergencies.

1599. You think the number sufficient ?—Yes.

1600. Has it latterly been reduced ?—It had been reduced, but recently has been increased 80 men.

1601. Sir *J. Trollope.*] What was the original force ?—I cannot remember.

1602. Was it much larger than the present force ?—I do not think it was much larger.

1603. Do-

1603. Do you consider that the force, as now managed, for the protection of the peace and property in Manchester and Liverpool, is sufficient without calling in the aid of the rural police?—Liverpool has never looked to us for any help except in 1848, and then we aided them only by sending some additional force to the outskirts, ready to help in case of need.

1604. Have you ever given any assistance to Manchester?—Never, except in a similar way.

1605. Mr. *Fitzroy*.] You stated, did you not, that you have never been called upon to give assistance to any of those boroughs except in the case of contested elections, or in the case of a riot growing out of a contested election?—I beg to correct myself. In 1842 there was a general insurrection, as it may be termed, and then we were called in to the borough of Preston, but not until after the borough police force had been found to be altogether defective, nor until after the troops had been called upon to act, and had fired, and killed and wounded several men.

1606. Where there is a separate police force in the boroughs, have you found any difficulty or hindrance in the administration of justice, in consequence of that separate and distinct force?—We have found a disinclination to co-operate with us in the detection of offenders; assistance has not been given with cordiality, and rarely with effect.

1607. Do you think that there is any feeling in those boroughs against the amalgamation of the borough police with the county constabulary?—I think there was a very much stronger feeling against it than exists at present, but I think there is a growing feeling in some of the smaller boroughs to come over to the county.

1608. Do you think that the fact of the repeated occasions in which they have called in the assistance of your force, and in which such assistance has been given to them, has induced them to alter their minds on the question?—I think that would probably be one reason; I think, moreover, they find now that the expense is not so great as was anticipated.

1609. Lord *Lovaine*.] Supposing the boroughs were to come over to the county police, would the present force of the boroughs be sufficient?—No, decidedly not. In some of the smaller boroughs, if they were to come over to the county, there would be, or there ought to be, a very considerable increase in the numbers.

1610. Evidence has been given before the Committee that the manner in which the police of Liverpool and those other boroughs are appointed is a serious impediment to the proper performance of their duties; are you of that opinion?—Most decidedly; I think no more prejudicial system to the working of a good establishment of police can exist than for the management of the men to be vested in a fluctuating body, such as watch committees or town councils.

1611. You are of opinion, are you not, that in the case of such amalgamation of the forces it would be absolutely necessary for the head of the police to do that which the Watching and Lighting Act vests in the hands of the watch committee?—The power should be vested in some competent person, some individual, either some officer appointed by the magistrates, or by the Government if they choose to take the matter in hand.

1612. You are of opinion that a committee of the magistrates themselves would hardly be a safe body to whom to trust the appointment?—I think it is desirable that the chief man should have the appointment, being held accountable for the men he may appoint.

1613. Would the arrangement of the county into petty sessional divisions answer where there are a great number of large towns?—I think it answers well in Lancashire.

1614. But the large towns are not included?—We could include them all with good effect; some towns of considerable magnitude are already included.

1615. When you speak of large towns, do you mean Liverpool and Manchester?—We could include the large towns, such as Liverpool and Manchester, in those petty sessional arrangements, but my answer to the last question referred particularly to the other boroughs or towns.

1616. Do the magistrates in those petty sessional divisions fix the number of men to be employed, or is that arranged in quarter sessions?—It was done thus: in the first instance, in 1842 an attempt was made to abolish the police; that failed, and then a resolution was come to by the magistrates dividing the county into districts, and the magistrates of each district were called upon to fix the

Capt. J. Woodford.

3 June 1853.

Capt. J. Woodford.

3 June 1853.

number of men for their respective districts; upon those returns being sent in to the quarter sessions, they were generally adopted, upon which a reduction of the establishment took place from 502, which was the original establishment, to 355, upon the 1st of August 1842.

1617. Is it your opinion that those petty sessional divisions were fairly represented by the numbers which they assessed themselves?—No; as a clear proof of that, we have been augmented from time to time, on account of the growing wants of the districts, up to 546, which exceeds our original number by 44.

1618. Does not it appear to you that great injustice might be done to one part of the county, by reason of one or other of the petty sessional divisions refusing to appoint a sufficient number?—We have not found it so; I think the magistrates generally have appointed very sufficiently; now they rarely appoint additional men, except upon the strong representations of the ratepayers that more protection is required.

1619. Would not the amalgamation of the boroughs and the county necessitate an additional expense?—I do not think it would upon the county.

1620. Would it enable you to do with fewer men in the rural part of the county?—The immediate effect would be to increase the men in the boroughs; I think it would enable us in the course of time to reduce our numbers in the county, because as the boroughs are now managed they are the nurseries of crime, and we have to keep a larger force in the immediate neighbourhoods of those boroughs, in order to protect ourselves from their thieves.

1621. Mr. *Fitzroy*.] Was the attempt to reduce the police made before the insurrection?—On the 1st of August the reduction took place; the insurrection commenced on the 9th, and we felt ourselves completely crippled.

1622. *Chairman*.] Is Ashton-under-Lyne one of your divisions?—Ashton-under-Lyne is a division so called; we name our divisions from the principal boroughs, or from the names of the hundreds; but the town of Ashton-under-Lyne is a borough having a police force of its own, 14 in number.

1623. Is there not a great variety of different police systems in Ashton-under-Lyne?—There is the county constabulary in the out townships, and the police establishment in the borough.

1624. Have they the county constabulary?—Not in the borough itself, in the petty sessional division.

1625. Have they also the borough police?—They have the borough police.

1626. Has Stayleybridge a police force?—Stayleybridge is partly in Cheshire and partly in Lancashire; it does not come under the operation of the Act; that town is entirely under a local Act.

1627. In those three immediate districts you have three different systems of police?—Yes.

1628. You have got in that immediate neighbourhood the police of Cheshire, the county constabulary; in Ashton-under-Lyne you have got your rural police, and you have also got a police force in the immediate neighbourhood of Stayleybridge, under a local Act?—Yes.

1629. What do you think is the effect of the different systems in that district? —I think it is impossible they can act with effect or cordiality, or benefit to the public; there is no unity of action, nor can there be with so many diverse systems

1630. Mr. *Fitzroy*.] Do you consider the objection entertained on the part of the boroughs to join in the county constabulary arises chiefly from the fear of increased expense, or principally from the fear of losing patronage?—I think the main fear is the loss of patronage by certain members of the town councils; other members of the town councils would be perfectly content to put themselves under the county, but they are resisted by some who are more influential or more talkative.

1631. Do you think it would be desirable to devise a plan by which a portion of that patronage might be preserved to the borough authorities, if the appointment and control of the police were vested in the chief constable?—I think the divided authority would be very hazardous; I should myself be sorry to share it.

1632. You think it is an essential part of the scheme for amalgamation, that the nomination and promotion of the men should rest, as it does now in the rural constabulary, with the chief constable?—I think so, especially in order that the men may not be under local influence, which they sometimes are.

1633. *Chairman*.] Have the railways also in the district a separate police?—Yes.

1634. Therefore

1634. Therefore there could be five or six separate police forces in the district? *Capt. J. Woodford.*
—Yes.

1635. Lord *Lovaine*.] Would it be possible to amalgamate the railway police *3 June 1853.*
with the rural police?—I see no difficulty in it.

1636. Mr. *Fitzroy*.] Have you any means of knowing generally the state of the
police within those boroughs where you have no control?—I believe it to be very
defective in the small boroughs.

1637. Have you any means of ascertaining whether beer-shops and public-
houses in those boroughs are worse regulated than those more immediately under
the control of your officers?—I have not the means of ascertaining, and I am not
prepared to state at this time, but that they are under a worse supervision I have
no doubt.

1638. Can you state that positively as a fact?—I believe the fact is that they
are not under proper supervision; I think it is hardly possible that they could be,
because it is well known that in town councils brewers and licensed victuallers
have become members, and those men must have an influence over the constables
whom they appoint; it is a necessary consequence.

1639. Are frequent reports made to you of the bad order of the beer-shops and
public-houses within your own district?—We have frequent reports; publicans
are frequently brought before the magistrates for misconduct, upon the reports of
the police of the county, and those publicans are invariably punished, so far as
my recollection goes.

1640. You have no means of judging of the comparative numbers reported by
the borough police, and those reported by your men?—No, not at all; I receive
no information from the boroughs.

1641. Mr. *Rich*.] Have any of the boroughs been transferred from the local
authority to your authority?—Not any.

1642. Has any effort been made to transfer them?—No decided effort has ever
been made; two boroughs have removed from us.

1643. What were the circumstances under which that took place?—They have
obtained charters of incorporation, and have established police forces of their
own.

1644. Mr. *Mackie*.] Is the police force popular in the county of Lancaster?—
I think it is becoming popular, for this reason, that applications are frequently
made for an increase of police in various districts by the ratepayers.

1645. It was not popular on its first establishment?—Not at all; there was a
strong prejudice against it, but I think that has nearly died away.

1646. Has crime decreased in consequence of the establishment of the police?
—No question of it.

1647. Is the decrease of crime one of the great causes of the force becoming
more popular in the county?—I think it is, and the confidence people feel; they
feel more safe, more secure; there are districts where it is well known that doors
are left unbolted, and clothes are left out now without fear, which could not
have been done in former days.

1648. *Chairman*.] You have mentioned that you have seven different systems
of police in Lancashire, near Ashton-under-Lyne; do you know Mr. Hall, the
clerk to the magistrates there?—Yes.

1649. Has he ever expressed any opinion to you that there was great difficulty
in managing the business in consequence of those different systems?—He has
never so stated to me.

1650. It is your opinion that there is great difficulty?—I should say so; I
should say there must be difficulty.

1651. Mr. *Fitzroy*.] What is the rate of pay in your force?—It varies.

1652. Will you give the Committee the different grades?—A scale of pay
was established at the January sessions 1847, which has been in existence ever
since; the chief constable receives per annum 500 *l.*

1653. Lord *Lovaine*.] Including all allowances?—No; his travelling expenses
are defrayed; that is, actual expenses out of pocket.

1654. Mr. *Fitzroy*.] Has the chief constable received any increase of pay?—
No; that is what I received in the first instance; there has been no variation in
my pay; an assistant was appointed at 200 *l.* upon this scale, after three years'
service he will receive 250 *l.*, and after a further service of four years 300 *l.*, and
that is the maximum.

1655. Lord *Lovaine.*] What class of person is your assistant chief constable?—He has served as a lieutenant-colonel under General Evans.

1656. Does he fill your place in case of your absence?—Yes.

1657. Has he all your power on such occasions?—Yes, during my absence.

1658. Mr. *Fitzroy.*] What are his duties when you are present?—To visit the various districts, to inspect closely the books and proceedings, and to examine and report upon the interior economy of the divisions. The superintendents upon appointment, or promotion from an inferior rank, receive 100 *l.* a year; after a service of three years in that rank, they receive 130 *l.*; after a further service of four years, making upon the whole seven in that rank, without reference to previous service, they obtain 15(*l.* and that is the maximum.

1659. Have you a superannuation fund?—We have. We have two clerks; the chief clerk is paid as a superintendent: the next in rank are the inspectors; they have a daily pay, upon appointment, or promotion of 4 *s.*; after a service of three years they receive 4 *s.* 6 *d.*; and after a further service of four years, 5 *s.* The sergeants are the next in rank; the sergeant receives 3 *s.* on first appointment and promotion; after a service of three years he receives 3 *s.* 3 *d.*; and after a further service of four years, 3 *s.* 6 *d.* The sergeants are also admissible to a class which we call the class of merit; that is, the men who distinguish themselves are permitted to wear a badge, and upon this badge being granted to them they have a further additional pay of 2 *d.* per diem. Constables of the first class receive 2 *s.* 7 *d.* per diem; after a service of three years, 2 *s.* 8 *d.*; and after a further service of four years, 2 *s.* 9 *d.* They are also eligible to the class of merit upon the same rate of pay, 2 *d.* per diem. The two other classes are the second-class constables, at 2 *s.* 5 *d.* a day; and the third class at 2 *s.* 4 *d.*, and they receive no more until they become first class; their service does not tell till they are first-class constables.

[The Witness delivered in the following Paper :]

COUNTY OF LANCASTER CONSTABULARY FORCE.

SCALE OF PAY.

RANK.	On Appointment or Promotion.			After Service of Three Years.			After further Service of Four Years.			Class of Merit.		
	£.	s.	d.	£.	s.	d.	£.	s.	d.	£.	s.	d.
Chief Constable - per annum	500	—	—	—			—			—		
Assistant Chief Constable - ditto -	200	—	—	250	—	—	300	—	—	—		
Superintendent - - ditto -	100	—	—	130	—	—	150	—	—	—		
Chief Clerk - - ditto -	100	—	—	130	—	—	150	—	—	—		
Inspector - - per diem	—	4	—	—	4	6	—	5	—	—		
Assistant Clerk - ditto -	—	4	—	—	4	6	—	5	—	—		
Sergeant - - ditto -	—	3	—	—	3	3	—	3	6	—	—	2
Constable, 1st Class - ditto -	—	2	7	—	2	8	—	2	9	—	—	2
Ditto - 2d Class - ditto -	—	2	5	·	·	·	·	·	—	—	—	2
Ditto - 3d Class - ditto -	—	2	4	·	·	·	·	·	—	—	—	2

1660. Is that a higher rate of pay than is generally given in boroughs?—I think in boroughs it is larger generally; our highest rate of pay does not come up to the ordinary rate of pay of a borough constable.

1661. What deduction is made from their pay for the superannuation fund?—Two per cent.

1662. Lord *Lovaine.*] In what state are the lock-up houses in your district?—We have a very considerable number of stations; we have some which have been built, and others which are hired; we have ten which have been built at a cost of 8,575 *l.* odd; they have 26 cells for the safe custody of prisoners: we also rent 99 station-houses, having in them 150 cells for prisoners.

1663. Do

1663. Do those buildings comprise good lodging-rooms for the constables?— Yes, and for the superintendents and other officers.

1664. Are they a species of barracks?—Yes.

1665. Are all your men lodged?—No; some find and pay for their own lodgings.

1666. Are all the men quartered in barracks?—No.

1667. Would it be an advantage if they were to be so quartered?—We have found it so advantageous that we have adopted the practice as far as we can; at all the principal stations there are men so quartered, and at all places where prisoners are kept in custody.

1668. Do the men pay for their lodgings?—Yes.

1669. Mr. *Rich.*] Are your men subjected to any drill on joining the force?—A very slight portion of drill; we are not in a condition to give them as much as we should otherwise do, in consequence of not having a sufficient reserve, and again, not having charge of the town where the head-quarters are stationed. We have therefore no means of instructing the men so well as I could wish before they are sent out to divisions.

1670. If you had a larger force and better means should you subject the men to drill?—Decidedly; they ought to be able to move in compact bodies. I should not recommend that they should be drilled as soldiers.

1671. Would you drill them to the use of arms?—To the use of the sword only; I would not place fire-arms in their hands at all.

1672. *Chairman.*] Have your men cutlasses?—Yes; to be used only in cases of emergency.

1673. From the peculiar character of your population, where you are more likely to have popular outbreaks, is it not more necessary to have the men armed than in other counties?—I think it is not necessary in the agricultural districts, but in Lancashire it is desirable, so far as I have stated.

1674. *Chairman.*] What other duties besides the maintenance of the public peace do your men perform?—Partially the inspection of weights and measures, but not entirely.

1675. How is that?—Because those inspectorships fall to us as they become vacant.

1676. Invariably, when the office becomes vacant, has it been transferred to your force?—Not invariably. There is one instance in which it has not been so, and another in which a constable was removed from our force to put him in that situation.

1677. Does not that arise from there being a different number of managements in certain divisions?—Yes; it is the recommendation of the general court of quarter sessions that these appointments should be held by the constabulary.

1678. Lord *Lovaine.*] Do you agree in that opinion?—It is my opinion that it would be beneficial to the public.

1679. Mr. *Fitzroy.*] Do you mean as a saving of expense, or in the way in which the duties are performed?—As a saving of the poor man's pocket; I do not mean a saving of expense to the public always; I mean that it would save the poor man from fraud; and I am of opinion that the duties generally would be more efficiently discharged.

1680. Do you think that the duties are better performed by the police?—Some of the existing inspectors do their duties admirably.

1681. *Chairman.*] Do you perform any other supplemental duties?—Partially we are inspectors of lodging-houses.

1682. Mr. *Fitzroy.*] Has the Lodging-house Act been adopted in Lancashire? —Yes.

1683. In which of the towns of Lancashire is that Act in operation?—I cannot enumerate them, but I fancy pretty generally.

1684. Is it in operation at Preston?—Yes.

1685. Is it in operation in Bury?—Not under our charge; nor in Preston under our charge.

1686. Is it at Preston in the charge of the corporation?—I think it is; it is not a matter to which I have turned my attention.

1687. Do the police give notice to the coroners upon deaths taking place?— Yes, in all cases.

1688. Is that duty in your district universally performed by the police, for which no extra charge is made to the county in consequence?—Yes, without charge.

1689. Lord *Lovaine*.] Therefore it is a saving of the salaries of the parish constables?—It is a saving of the salaries of parish constables.

1690. *Chairman*.] What is the nearest district of Yorkshire to you?—Todmorden, Clitheroe, and Colne are Lancashire towns upon the border.

1691. Have your police ever been employed in Yorkshire?—They have occasionally gone into Yorkshire, and the cases that they have observed or acted upon have been adjudicated upon in Lancashire.

1692. Before the magistrates?—Yes.

1693. Of course for the benefit of the clerk of the magistrates?—That led to some very sharp observations upon the part of the inhabitants of that part of Todmorden which is in Yorkshire; it was more than insinuated that those Lancashire constables went into Yorkshire for the purpose of getting cases for the clerk of the magistrates; and it was also insinuated that they did so for their own benefit; so soon as this came to my knowledge I thought it my duty to put a stop to a matter of that kind, and I directed that they should not in any case, except in the absolute pursuit of thieves, act at all in Yorkshire; the consequence has been, that disorders which were heretofore noticed by the county constabulary of Lancashire are now left unnoticed, owing to the want of a proper police establishment in Yorkshire; reports have been made to me showing how many cases have occurred within a very recent period, which would otherwise have been noticed by our men, if I had not checked them, as I felt it my duty to do.

1694. Was an application made from any individuals in Yorkshire for your men to go into Yorkshire; what was the cause of their going over the borders?—Because they noticed the disorders; they observed them under their own eye; they could not fail to see them; it is but across an imaginary line; and they went into Yorkshire to suppress those disorders.

1695. What was the nature of the disorders?—Cases of drunkenness and fighting in public-houses; cases of public-houses being kept open at unseasonable hours, or cases of vagrancy; in another case it was a pugilistic fight; I thought, and think still, that it was the business of the Yorkshire people to keep order in their own county.

1696. Did your men go into Yorkshire by your orders?—No; as soon as it became known to me, and that these insinuations were cast upon them, I thought proper to stop it.

1697. Was there a police force at that time in Yorkshire?—I believe they had only parish constables.

1698. Had they no superintending constables?—I do not know of any superintending constable at Todmorden, or within eight or ten miles.

1699. Do you think there is great disorder and rioting in Yorkshire, immediately over the borders of Lancashire?—Yes.

1700. Have you witnessed it?—My constables have reported it to me; I have not with my own eyes seen it.

1701. Mr. *Howard*.] What is the system in Yorkshire?—Superintending constables with parish constables under their directions.

1702. Lord *Lovaine*.] A suggestion has been made that it would be possible to recruit for the army through the means of the police; do you think such a suggestion could be carried out?—I have hardly given the subject a thought; we collect the men together for the militia very rapidly and simply.

1703. It has also been suggested that the police should superintend the highways and turnpikes; do you think that could be carried out?—I think it would be attended with very considerable advantage if every turnpike-gate keeper was a constable.

1704. *Chairman*.] Under the chief constable of the county?—Yes; and bound to report to him.

1705. Sir *J. Trollope*.] Would not the adoption of police as turnpike-gate keepers take away the system of letting the turnpikes as they are let now?—Yes; I would let the Government take them in hand.

1706. Mr. *Fitzroy*.] What do you mean by saying that the police get the men together for the militia?—We serve their notices upon them individually.

1707. When they are enlisted?—We fill in the notices in some cases, in which the clerks of the lieutenancy refuse, because they are not paid for it; they have thrown a good deal of trouble upon us; the notices were sent to us at so late an hour that we had men up all night to get them ready.

1708. Sir *J. Trollope*.] Do the police induce volunteers to join the militia?—
They

They did in the first instance; a reward of 5 s. was offered by Act of Parliament. Capt. J. Woodford.

3 June 1853.

1709. Were the men permitted to take that 5 s. per head?—I should have been very sorry to have deprived them of it, as I thought no means should be left untried to obtain volunteers.

1710. Have you allowed them to receive it?—I never interfere with a reward which is given to the men by the Government.

1711. Was the reward of 5 s. to get recruits for the militia acted upon?—In some few districts; it was not generally acted upon; I think it was only in two or three districts.

1712. Do you discourage your men receiving rewards?—I take no steps to discourage it on procuring recruits for the militia.

1713. Have you received any instructions to do so from the police committee? —No.

1714. Do you not think that the police would be very valuable assistants in obtaining persons to volunteer in the militia, from their mixing so much with the poor?—I think they might be made to do so. Perhaps there might be some feelings of jealousy go forth if they were made to recruit for the army; for the militia I think it might be done with good effect.

1715. Lord *Lovaine.*] You consider it is not impossible for the police to recruit for the army?—It is not impossible for the police to recruit for the army; I think it a little foreign to their present duties, and not unlikely to induce bad habits.

1716. Mr. *Fitzroy.*] As they are entitled to receive 5 s. for the men they induce to volunteer for the militia, is it not the case that they have used all the exertions they can for the sake of that reward?—I do not think they have exerted themselves much; they might be made to do so.

1717. Sir *J. Trollope.*] You have stated that you discourage your men receiving rewards from Government; do you allow them to receive rewards from any other sources; in cases of felony, for instance?—There have been cases in which rewards have been offered by parties, which reward has been backed by the offer of a reward from Government; in such cases, where the men have been successful in convicting, I have looked upon it as a Government reward, and the whole has been divided amongst the parties who have been instrumental in bringing the offenders to justice; but I approve of none, and I discourage as much as possible the giving of rewards by private persons, being fearful that the constables might be disposed to pay too much attention to the property of those persons who would give money, rather than turn their attention to the property of those who are unable to give. I consider it would have an evil effect if they were allowed to receive rewards indiscriminately.

1718. Would it not encourage the police to get up prosecutions?—I am satisfied it would.

1719. You never permit the men to receive rewards without your knowledge and concurrence for services rendered?—Some two or three cases have come to my knowledge in which the men have received rewards without my sanction, and I have discharged them.

1720. Have you any difficulty in obtaining recruits for the police?—Latterly the men have been more slack in coming forward than they were in former days. We have no great number of vacancies; we have only 12 just now, which is not a material number in a body like ours. I must say, for the last six or seven months, I have not had so good a choice of men as I had formerly, but then there are various causes to account for that.

The Rev. *John Holmes*, called in; and Examined.

The Rev.
John Holmes.

1721. *Chairman.*] ARE you a Magistrate for Norfolk?—I am.

1722. Have you a police force in Norfolk?—Yes; it has been established since the year 1840.

1723. Have you a police committee in Norfolk?—Yes.

1724. Were you the chairman of the police committee?—Ever since the original establishment of the police force I have been on the police committee, and the chairman since 1845. I am not quite sure as to the period, but I think it was 1845 when I became chairman of the police committee.

1725. What is the gross expense of the police in Norfolk?—The amount raised in the county amounts to 1 $\frac{5}{8}$ d. in the pound, which is equal to 9,698 *l.*

The Rev.
John Holmes.

3 June 1853.

1726. Is the whole of that expended, or is there a balance?—There is a very small balance; it is nearly expended.

1727. What are the other general expenses of the county?—I am speaking of the year 1852; the general expenses of the county were 1 ½ d. in the pound, which amounted to 11,084 l.

1728. What was the amount of the rate raised altogether?—About 21,000 l., including the police rate and the county rate.

1729. Do you think the ratepayers generally are acquainted with the amount of rate which they contribute to the police force?—I think not generally; I think the better informed are; many more are now informed than they were at the original establishment of the police force, from this circumstance, that within a few years it has been ordered by the magistrates that a book shall be made public, with a very detailed account of the police expenses in all its forms, both as to the general expenses and the police expenses; a copy of the expenses is sent to every board of guardians in the county, and all those ratepayers who feel any interest in it, all the large occupiers, have the means of seeing this book, and I have no doubt that in consequence they are better informed upon the subject.

1730. From your knowledge as a magistrate, do you think the ratepayers dislike the force?—I think they have been converted from the original feeling which existed amongst them; I have very little doubt the feeling was against the police; there were one or two largely signed memorials from the ratepayers, but I think that feeling has very much subsided.

1731. Mr. *Fitzroy*.] What is the amount of your force?—The present amount of the force is 132 policemen, 1 inspector, 13 superintendents, one of whom is the deputy chief constable, and the chief constable himself.

1732. Lord *Lovaine*.] Is that force sufficient?—I do not think it will be right for me to say; there has been a committee sitting to consider the condition of the police, on a report which has been made by our present chief constable regarding the police; we have taken into consideration a farther increase of the force.

1733. Sir *J. Trollope*.] Is that increase recommended by the present chief constable, Captain Black?—Yes.

1734. Does not he recommend another item of expense, in building lock-ups and residences for the police?—Certainly.

1735. Lodging-houses for superintendents, and lock-ups to a considerable extent?—Lock-ups, which are to comprehend lodgings for the superintendents.

1736. Do you recollect the number of men Captain Black recommends to be added to your force?—Two additional superintendents, six additional inspectors, 23 additional policemen, and three, under the name of sergeants, to be used as detectives in the three principal towns in Norfolk.

1737. In fact, Captain Black recommends the addition of 34 men of different grades?—Yes.

1738. Have you entered into a calculation of the additional expense to be incurred; the buildings which he recommends?—Yes.

1739. What is the amount of it?—We think, having considered the subject tolerably accurately, it will be something like 9,000 l. I think the amount of money we propose to suggest to the quarter sessions, to allow an expenditure in order to be quite sure that we may cover the whole, is as much as 10,000 l., to be borrowed and paid in a certain number of years, and not to be raised in a year; he recommends about 18 stations.

1740. Mr. *Burroughes*.] Does not the chief constable contemplate considerable annual savings in consequence of these new arrangements which he is about to make?—Very large savings indeed, and I confess I am much of the same opinion; by the adoption of the plan proposed, by building lock-ups, and the further adoption of the plan of having county horses and carts, a very large saving will be effected to the county.

1741. Does not Captain Black contemplate charging rent for all the stations?—Certainly.

1742. *Chairman*.] Will the rent pay a sufficient interest for the money borrowed?—Certainly not a sufficient interest for the money borrowed for building the lock-ups.

1743. Sir *J. Trollope*.] As you seem to speak favourably of this recommendation, as being necessary to make the force thoroughly effective in the county of Norfolk, have you calculated what the annual expense to the ratepayers, in
addition

The Rev.
John Holmes.

3 June 1853.

addition to the 1 $\frac{5}{16}$ d., will be?—Taking into consideration the savings which will be made, as we suppose, we have reason to conclude, from the use of horses and carts in conveying prisoners, and other objects they may be used for, and the other things which are suggested, such as appointing the superintendents inspectors of weights and measures, we consider the whole of the additional force may be obtained for a sum within three-sixteenths of a penny in the pound additional to that which is now raised in the pound.

1744. Do you think 1 $\frac{1}{4}$ d. would cover the police rate?—It would more than cover it.

1745. Including the buildings?—I am imagining the buildings to be already made; I mean only including the maintenance of the police after those buildings have been erected and paid for.

1746. Supposing the buildings cost 10,000 l., will there not be an additional charge for that money?—Till it is paid.

1747. And also a certain amount of principal to be repaid in each year?—Yes.

1748. Chairman.] Will not some of those buildings pay rent?—They will all pay rent : I think the calculation of the net rent that will be received for those buildings, after the necessary deductions shall have been made for meeting the necessary expenses belonging to the county, such as warming, lighting, cleaning, and so on, I calculate a net revenue will be derived of 160 l. a year.

1749. Lord Lovaine.] Will not the 160 l. a year be added to the amount of the savings which you contemplate making?—Yes; that forms a part of what I call savings.

1750. Therefore, in round numbers, you will have to pay about 600 l. a year additional for interest and sinking fund for the 10,000 l. borrowed?—I do not know what it will be, not having made the calculation.

1751. Sir J. Trollope.] What is the estimate of the expense of each separate lock-up, with the buildings attached to it?—There are two classes; the inferior classes would be 400 l., the superior 600 l.; and there is one central lock-up, which is a station of a larger description, which it is proposed to put in the neighbourhood of Norwich, and which will cost 1,000 l.

1752. Does that include stabling for the mounted police?—Yes.

1753. Are any of those lock-ups intended to be built in petty sessional divisions for magisterial purposes as well?—There is no magistrates' room with them whatever.

1754. They are to be built entirely for the use of the police?—Yes.

1755. Chairman.] You have stated that this expenditure, whatever it is, is so published that all the ratepayers have an opportunity of knowing what it is?—Undoubtedly.

1756. Was not there a time when this expenditure was very unpopular?—At the first establishment of the police it was unpopular.

1757. Do you think experience has made it more popular?—Certainly.

1758. Do you think that feeling has increased to a great extent?—To a considerable extent.

1759. What will be the expense to an occupier of property of a net rental of 100 l. a year?—Supposing the rate to be raised to that which I have now said, namely, to 1 $\frac{1}{2}$ d., it will be 12 s. 6 d. on 100 l.

1760. Then an occupier of 200 l. a year would have to pay 25 s. a year?—Yes; that is, on the net rating, not the gross.

1761. Do you think it would be the opinion generally of occupiers of land to the amount of 200 l., that that 25 s. a year would be more than repaid by the security of property?—I have had an opportunity repeatedly of speaking to the more enlightened and better informed of the ratepayers, who were ignorant of what they had to pay, who simply looked at the sum of money spent in gross, amounting then to 10,000 l. or 11,000 l. a year; when I had explained to them exactly the sum of money they would have to pay upon 100 l. they were satisfied to pay it for the benefit which they would receive, setting aside all moral considerations; merely in a pecuniary point of view, the answer has been that they thought the money extremely well spent.

1762. You think, in an economical point of view, it is the opinion of the ratepayers, as well as of yourself, that the establishment of police has been of great advantage to the county?—I have no doubt it is the general feeling; if I have a right to express an opinion, judging from the sentiments expressed by individuals I have talked to, I have never found a person dissenting from that opinion.

1763. When you speak of 12 s. 6 d. upon 100 l., which the occupier would have to pay, have you or not taken into consideration what the cost of the old system was?—No.

1764. Do you think the cost of the old system bore any proportion to the present system?—I have never calculated it; I have no doubt it is a great deal more.

1765. Mr. *Burroughes.*] Perhaps you may be able to give an instance of the operation of the old system, which arose in some districts where there was no protection to property?—It has happened to me individually, when I have had coals stolen from a barge, to put a warrant into the hands of the parish constable to execute; that parish constable has been actually afraid of going amongst the people to serve the warrant, and it has been obliged to go into a different district, where the constables are established under the Watch and Ward Act; they dare not meddle at all.

1766. Lord *Lovaine.*] Are any of the large towns included in the rural police force?—The only towns which are exempted are Norwich, Yarmouth, Thetford, and Lynn; I think, excepting those four places, all the other towns in Norfolk are included in the police.

Henry Dover, Esq., called in; and Examined.

1767. *Chairman.*] ARE you the Chairman of the Quarter Sessions in Norfolk? —Yes, I have been Chairman of the Quarter Sessions for 22 years.

1768. When was the police established in Norfolk?—In 1840.

1769. Can you state generally your opinion as to the advantages or disadvantages which the county derives from the police force?—I can, quite decidedly. At first, I doubted about the policy of establishing a police force; after considering it, I thought that it deserved a fair trial. I watched it as much as I could, and I compared it as much as I could with the old system, and I have no doubt that the county has derived advantage in every way from it.

1770. Are the Committee to understand that you were opposed to its adoption? —When I first heard of it I felt disposed against it. Upon considering that it deserved a fair trial, I watched it; and ever since its establishment I think great advantage has been derived from the change.

1771. What is the result of your experience, having watched the working of the police system?—That it is a great improvement upon the old system, and capable of more improvement; I think the area which our police have to go over is more than they can do justice to. I think, with the extension which the Committee have heard proposed, we shall be able to do the system of police at an expense altogether of from 1 $\frac{1}{2}$ d. to 2 d. in the pound.

1772. For buildings and all?—Yes.

1773. Upon considering the question, were you at all able to ascertain what the expense of the county was under the old system?—It varied so very much; I have not a doubt as to the mere question of vagrancy, for instance, a very large proportion, I should say certainly more than half the expense of the present system has been saved to the county.

1774. From the dishonest practices of the vagrants?—Yes; which fell chiefly upon the poor; I had more than once gipsies and other vagrants brought before me by the police shortly after their establishment, and they said at once, " Let us go this time; we did not know there was such a force; we will go to Cambridgeshire or to Lincolnshire;" and, as far as I know, they kept their word.

1775. Do you consider that vagrancy is a great source of crime?—Certainly.

1776. Is it not your opinion, that under the old system of parochial constables, pursuit could be only made after offenders by persons capable of paying them? —Certainly.

1777. The poor man, being incapable of paying them, had not the same protection as the rich man?—He could not start the constable at all in a doubtful case; if it was a clear case the constable would get his expenses at sessions or at assizes, but in a doubtful case there was not much care taken about it; there was nobody to pay, and the consequence was, that a great deal of unpleasant duty was thrown upon the magistrates, the chief constable, or upon active farmers; but the most hopeless resort was the old parish constable, in five cases out of six.

1778. It

H. Dover, Esq.
———
3 June 1853.

1778. It was stated by an experienced magistrate for Hampshire, that if a robbery were committed, the parish constable was the last person almost that he should think of applying to; that he should as soon think of sending for an old woman; do you agree with that opinion?—I can go to that extent; the parish constable was generally appointed from some local interest, and was very frequently the most unfit man in the parish; perhaps I may state that I have seen a good deal of the criminal justice; I was at the Bar 11 years before I became the chairman of quarter sessions, and I have had a good deal of criminal practice; therefore I have been able to look at crime almost in all ways.

1779. You have stated that when the police was first proposed in Norfolk you had great doubts as to its adoption being desirable; do you think that those doubts were shared by other proprietors?—Yes, of all ranks.

1780. Do you think that that feeling has been diminished by experience?—Very much indeed; I should say, if I represented it by figures, two-thirds; if you took the whole county, you would find two-thirds in favour of the system.

1781. Do you think, in consequence of the establishment of a well-regulated police in the county of Norfolk, that the value of land has been increased to the occupier to some extent?—Yes; I think this will be found to be the case from witnesses who live on the borders of the county, or in other counties, that they would give a higher rent for the land with the police in the county than in neighbouring counties where there was no such establishment. There is one part of the farmer's property of very considerable importance which is very much exposed, namely, his sheep, and they constantly move them from one place to another; they move them from where they will not be looked after to where they will be; and the great benefit is this, that immediately any property is lost in a county which has rural police, the police is gone to at once, and there is fresh pursuit; that is not the case where there is only the old constable; everything, in cases of sheep-stealing, depends upon fresh pursuit.

1782. Mr. *Burroughes.*] Of course you can state, from your experience as chairman of quarter sessions, the mode of conducting prosecutions; has not there been a saving of expense from unnecessary witnesses not being brought up?—Yes; the police are better witnesses, and they know better how to get up the cases; you have not the same number of witnesses called, and you have better witnesses; the police very commonly carry a case from beginning to end.

1783. In your opinion, is there a saving of time as well as of expense?—Indeed I think so.

1784. Have you had any opportunity of considering the benefit which might be derived from amalgamating the police of the towns with the police of the county?—Only generally; I have had no opportunity to send for papers. I have considered that subject; unless you mean a very large town, where they could have a chief constable as good as we could in the county; in all the small boroughs the greatest advantage on both sides would be derived from such an amalgamation.

1785. Mr. *Howard.*] Did not the parish constables receive fees on prosecutions?—The parish constables would not move very commonly without they received money in hand. The police is bound to move, but the parish constable was his own master; you could hardly say that he was responsible to the magistrates; he would not move in a doubtful case unless he was paid for it.

1786. Was not there a great addition thereby to the county rate?—There was a good deal of money spent, and I think badly spent.

1787. Mr. *Mackie.*] Do you think that it would be beneficial to have one uniform system of police, taking in more counties than one in your neighbourhood?—Ours is a very large acreage, and I do not think it would. I think the county of Norfolk is quite as much as one chief constable can manage, as chief constable.

1788. My question refers generally to a system of police embracing England and Wales?—That is a subject I have never considered; I should not like to give a rash answer off-hand.

1789. *Chairman.*] Do not you think that a uniform system, creating unity of action between adjoining counties in the pursuit of offenders, would give greater facilities in the detection of crime?—So far as I know, were the force *ejusdem generis*, they would be all eager and anxious to help one another. There is some little difficulty where there are other parties to deal with, but never with police constables.

1790. Mr. *Mackie.*] Is there any county adjoining Norfolk where they have not

H. Dover, Esq.

3 June 1853.

not a police ?—No; I had a great correspondence with a friend of mine in Cambridgeshire; they resisted it a long while, and were very much opposed to it; but they gave in at last, for they found that all our rogues went to them.

1791. Before they adopted a system of police I presume you found great inconvenience?—Certainly; you could not follow anything up, everybody was against you; you had nobody to communicate with; and directly offenders got across the borders you could find nobody to tell you anything.

John Wybergh, Junior, Esq., called in; and Examined.

J. Wybergh, jun., Esq.

1792. *Chairman.*] ARE you Clerk to the Magistrates at Liverpool?—I am.

1793. What is your system of police at Liverpool?—The police are appointed by the watch committee of the town council of the borough, and they are under their regulation and management.

1794. What is the number of police in Liverpool?—I believe there are about 880 this year, which is an increase of 80.

1795. What is the population of Liverpool?—Three hundred and seventy-four thousand four hundred and one.

1796. Do you know what the expense of the police force is?—About 40,000*l.* a year.

1797. Do you know how much that is in the pound upon the rating?—There is the power to levy a watch rate in Liverpool, but I believe of late years that rate has never been collected. The expense of the police is borne out of the borough fund.

1798. You state that the police are appointed by the watch committee?—Entirely.

1799. Have you a chief constable?—There is a head constable, who is also appointed by the watch committee.

1800. Does the head constable appoint his subordinates, or does the watch committee appoint them?—The watch committee have the appointment; I suppose they delegate some of their power to him, but to what extent I do not know; very likely in the selection of the candidates for office.

1801. Who has the power of dismissing the men?—The watch committee.

1802. Does the power of dismissal rest entirely with the watch committee?—The magistrates exercise a concurrent jurisdiction in dismissing the police for misconduct before them, but the watch committee have the power of dismissing any constable, irrespective of complaints, if they choose to exercise it.

1803. You have said that the magistrates have the power of dismissing the constables for offences by complaints before them?—Yes.

1804. Have the watch committee also that power?—Yes.

1805. Is that power arbitrarily exercised, without giving any reasons?—They may exercise an arbitrary power of dismissal under a clause in the Municipal Act.

1806. Do you consider it an inconvenience that the police of the borough of Liverpool should be under two jurisdictions?—I think the evil of divided authority is very great.

1807. Have you experienced evil from it?—We have.

1808. What evils have you experienced?—It has given rise to several disputes between the council and the magistrates, in reference to the police.

1809. In consequence of what?—In consequence of the state of the law. There is a clause in the Municipal Act which confers upon the town council, or upon the watch committee of the town council, this power over the police concurrently with the magistrates.

1810. Are the duties of the police generally to superintend public-houses and beer-shops, to see if there is anything going on wrong?—Yes; and the preservation of order generally.

1811. Are any of the watch committee the owners of beer-shops and public-houses?—I believe there are members of the watch committee who are owners of public-houses, and largely interested in them. I do not think there are so many persons connected with those trades on the watch committee as there were formerly. A few years ago the chairman of the watch committee was the owner of public-houses to a great extent in Liverpool.

1812. Do you think inconvenience has arisen from those interests on the watch committee?—

committee ?—I think so. I think it is the tendency of the system that the police officers will not lay informations; they will be indisposed to prosecute offenders against the licensing laws where the houses to be informed against belong to members of the town council, or members of the watch committee.

J. Wybergh, jun., Esq.

3 June 1853.

1813. Without asking you whether the members of the watch committee would dismiss constables who inspected the public-houses, do you believe this to be the case, that the constables so employed would not do their duty, from fear of giving offence to certain members of the watch committee ?—I think that is the tendency of the present system.

1814. Supposing, from your knowledge, as magistrates' clerk at Liverpool, of the offences committed in the neighbourhood, under a uniform and more general system of police, Liverpool was formed into a separate district like a county, do you think there would be convenience in adding any of the districts round Liverpool to that district ?—No; I think Liverpool is a town of so much importance, and has such a large population, that it would be very much more simple to confine the district to Liverpool only, and let the county provide for its own wants.

1815. Do you think, supposing Liverpool was a separate district, that the county of Lancaster and Liverpool might be placed together under one head or chief constable ?—I think they might, but he would have a very large force to command in that case. I think it will be more efficient to have two chief constables, one for the county and one for the borough.

1816. Lord *Lovaine.*] Evidence has been given before this Committee that certain local jealousies exist between county and borough police forces; are you of opinion that there is any feeling of that nature between the county and the borough police forces of Lancashire ?—I am myself not cognizant of any such feeling; I think it is likely to be the case, but I have not observed anything of it in Liverpool.

1817. Has not the metropolitan police district been extended to 13 miles round the outskirts of London ?—Yes; and I think it would be a great improvement if that system were extended to the whole country.

1818. Sir *J. Anderson.*] Is there not a separate police system at Birkenhead ? —Yes.*

1819. Do they co-operate with the Liverpool police ?—Yes, when the occasion may require it. The Birkenhead police are under the Town Commissioners of Birkenhead, and chiefly under their management.

Major *George F. White*, called in; and Examined.

1820. *Chairman.*] YOU are Chief Constable of Durham ?—I am.

Major G. F. White.

1821. What is the strength of your force ?—One hundred and seventeen of all ranks, including myself.

1822. What is the population of Durham ?—The population of the county in the rural districts under my jurisdiction is about 320,000.

1823. What proportion does each constable bear to the population ?—Two thousand seven hundred and fifty persons to each constable.

1824. Do you conceive that force to be sufficient ?—I do not, for all purposes.

1825. In what way is the force insufficient ?—As far as the prevention of very serious crimes is concerned the force is perhaps sufficient, but not for general police purposes.

1826. Is the force sufficient for an efficient night patrol ?—It is not so efficient as I should wish, for want of numbers, each constable's beat averaging nearly nine square miles.

1827. Is it not desirable that there should be a night patrol ?—Quite so; particularly in a county like Durham; I have established it partially, and with advantage.

1828. Are

---

* The fines and penalties on police informations are paid by the clerk to the magistrates into the borough. After deducting all the expenses of the magistrates' office, including the salary of the stipendiary magistrate and the salaries of the clerks to the magistrates, it leaves a clear balance in favour of the corporation of upwards of 3,500 *l.* per annum. In any alteration of the law it is suggested that the magistrates should have the power of paying their own expenses out of the fees for business done by the clerks, and hand the balance over to the borough fund, or any other fund which may be chargeable with the maintenance of the police.

Major G. F. White.

3 June 1853.

1828. Are you capable of stating what the feeling with regard to the police force is in Durham; is it popular or unpopular?—I make every effort to inquire into that; I ride about the county, and I make inquiries from those people who do not know who I am, and who will therefore give an unbiased opinion, and I think the force is popular with the county; I never hear a different opinion expressed.

1829. Has there been any attempt in the county of Durham, from its expense, to abolish the police force since it has been established?—Never since I have been there; I have been there four years and a half, and there has never been a petition against the force; nor since the first five years, to my knowledge; but they were frequent at one time, at the early establishment of the force.

1830. Have you experienced any inconvenience from the want of a uniform system in the adjoining counties?—I have, constantly; we cannot communicate readily with them when a thief escapes beyond the border of our own county; we immediately lose all trace of him for a time; it is a matter of chance if we get further information.

1831. You mean to say that the pursuit of criminals is much more difficult in consequence of the want of a uniform system in the adjoining counties?—Very much so indeed, and we fear to encounter the expense, where the probability of success is so remote.

1832. What boroughs are there in Durham which have a police force?—Sunderland, Gateshead, South Shields, Hartlepool, and Stockton-on-Tees.

1833. Are they incorporated with the county?—Stockton-on-Tees has been for two years consolidated with the county force, and with great advantage and satisfaction to the place.

1834. Have they a corporation at Stockton-on-Tees?—Yes.

1835. Are they satisfied with the result of that incorporation?—Yes; during the last two years I have never heard the slightest complaint; I think I must have heard of it if there had been a complaint.

1836. Do you make any use of the parochial constables?—None whatever; they are almost obsolete in our county.

1837. Are they still appointed?—They are still appointed, but it appears to me to be a useless expense incurred.

1838. Have you had any experience of the use of special constables in cases of disturbance?—We have occasionally sworn them in more for the sake of appearance than anything else, when a combination of workmen has been going on, and perhaps it has a good effect to see a certain number of those men take the side of the law. So far it has had a good effect, but as for any amount of physical assistance we have received from them on those occasions, I think it was very little.

1839. You have sworn them in as a demonstration?—Yes; rather as a demonstration.

1840. Do you perform the duty of the inspection of weights and measures in your county?—We have inspected the weights and measures for four years now, and with great saving and advantage to the public, directly and indirectly.

1841. Is not that general in all the counties where there is a police force?—No; I think there are some that do not do it.

1842. Do you know any counties where they do not?—I am sure there are several. I do not think the police inspect the weights and measures in Norfolk or Suffolk.

1843. Do you think a uniform system of police would be as beneficial to the boroughs as to the counties?—I think the advantages would be reciprocal, particularly in the small boroughs.

1844. Are there any farmers' associations in your county for the prosecution of felons?—They are diminishing every year; there are a few still existing.

1845. Do you know how many there were when the force was first established?—No; I have not a correct account of it; there were many existing before; they were numerous then. It appears to me a useless expense now, and I think they will die away. If an adequate police force existed, I conceive that beyond the payment of his police-rate, no inhabitant should be called on to pay anything further towards bringing offenders to justice. The rate, if regarded as an insurance against crime affecting life and property, would be paid cheerfully to any moderate amount.

1846. Do you think that the establishment of the electric telegraph would be useful?—I have often thought it would be, if the expense could be lessened.

1847. Would

1847. Would the expense be very great?—At present it is more than 2*d.* a mile for a short message; we have occasionally used it.

Major *G. F. White.*

3 June 1853.

1848. You have to go to the places where it is established?—Yes.

1849. Would it be useful if the electric telegraph were established in the different divisions in your county?—Yes, to the chief places; I can only judge of the expense by what it costs where it now exists.

1850. Your opinion is that it would be very useful, but very expensive?—At present; but I think, if it were more generally made, a contract might be entered into which would lessen the expense, so as to make it available.

1851. Do you think, if any contract could be made to establish a general communication by electric telegraph between the police stations, it would be an expense which would be repaid by its advantages?—I think that is quite practicable.

1852. Lord *Lovaine.*] What is the state of the Gateshead and the South Shields police; is it sufficient?—I have heard no expression of dissatisfaction from those who appoint them.

1853. Was not there a robbery committed lately at Ravensworth, in which there was a little difficulty in obtaining evidence between the Gateshead police and your own?—Nothing to remark; there was a little difficulty, as there always is in those cases; there was some little jealousy, but not more than we usually have when the rural police go into a borough in search of information. I cannot say that it exists on the part of the heads of the departments.

1854. Do you think that is a difficulty which constantly occurs?—I think it is a constant thing.

1855. Have you ever employed your men in boroughs as assistants to keep the peace?—We have occasionally been asked to render assistance. At the last Durham election a force of 20 or 25 men were asked for, and with the permission of the magistrates I granted it. A previous election had taken place two or three months before, and there was a severe riot in the town, which very nearly led to a disputed election. At the election which followed we gave assistance with this number of rural police, and the greatest quiet prevailed throughout the town. I was thanked by the borough magistrates for the assistance which we had rendered.

1856. Do the habits of miners, and the power which they have of withdrawing their persons from the grasp of justice, interfere much with the efficiency of the police?—It certainly increases the difficulty of detection.

1857. Would a larger number of police be required in consequence?—I think so, in proportion; to work the thing efficiently, and to give it a fair chance with a mining population, we ought to have a larger force in our county than in a totally rural district.

1858. Do you think the proportion of one man to 1,000 inhabitants would be sufficient?—I think it would be ample; and in this event, various other duties, such as inspectors of nuisances, or of common lodging-houses, or of roads and highways, might with advantage be undertaken by the police, so as to more than counterbalance the expense.

1859. Is not the mining population generally a quiet population?—Except during strikes and combinations, which are frequent; almost every year.

1860. Is not some of your district a very wild country?—The westward.

1861. Do you find any difficulty in maintaining order?—No; there we have very few police; crime is more rare in those districts.

1862. The facility of concealment, therefore, does not increase the difficulty of maintaining the rural police in a wild district?—No; I think we are generally successful in the wild districts. A new comer is soon known to the policeman into whose beat he comes, whereas he would be lost sight of in the dense population of a pit district.

1863. Do you think it is essential for the general advantage of the county that there should be an amalgamation of the police in the borough with the rural constables?—Having tried the experiment with Stockton-on-Tees, I do not see why it should not answer for all moderately-sized boroughs; such places as Liverpool and Manchester might form exceptions.

1864. And even the larger boroughs, if this jealousy exists?—I think the benefit would be mutual; moreover, I feel certain, from my own knowledge and experience, and from the experience of others, greater than my own, that any

Major *G. F. White.*

3 June 1853.

system of police will be defective unless made uniform; each county under one head, and the whole under some proper control or inspection.

1865. Mr. *Howard.*] Is there much vagrancy in Durham?—It has very much decreased during the last five years, and more especially since the rural police have partially acted as assistants to the relieving officers.

1866. Therefore the applicants for relief must be subject to the inspection of the police?—The applicants must pass the ordeal of the inspection of the police officer, whom they avoid, for fear they should be recognized as amongst their list of suspected characters.

1867. Lord *Lovaine.*] What is the police rate in Durham?—$1\frac{1}{8}$ d. in the pound; a 2¼ d. rate would give a fair force.

1868. Have you any police stations?—We have a great many of one sort or another.

1869. Have they been built at the public expense?—Yes, chiefly so; we are now progressing with the stations; the larger ones combine justice rooms with the police accommodation.

1870. Have you quarters for the men in the police stations?—One or more in all of them.

1871. Do they serve as barracks?—Yes; the greatest amount we have in any one station is five.

1872. Do the men pay rent for those lodgings?—They do pay rent; it is almost a self-paying arrangement; it is merely the interest of the money so expended. In speaking of the preservation of the peace of the district, I may mention that there are frequent riots, and now they are often suppressed by the police without calling in the military, which used formerly to be a matter of more frequent occurrence.

1873. *Chairman.*] Do not you think it is much more desirable to call in the police than the military for the suppression of riots?—Yes; the timely presence of the police will generally render the military unnecessary.

1874. Is it not frequently the fact that the police, in the suppression of a riot, go into the crowd and endeavour to persuade the men to desist from their proceedings? —Yes; and I have known a superintendent of our force go into a crowd of upwards of 1,000 men, a great number of those men being armed with picks, and some with guns, and merely from the fact of his being dressed as a policeman, and seeing that there was another force of policemen at hand, captured the ringleaders, for whose apprehension he held a warrant, and the crowd have been too terrified or astonished to offer any opposition.

1875. Would not a policeman, if he only used his truncheon, always have one arm at liberty with which to hold a man?—Exactly.

1876. Is it not the fact, if a soldier is employed with a musket in his hand, that both his hands are engaged for that purpose, and he has no means of securing the prisoner?—Yes; and the musket may be used fatally, as probably it would.

1877. Lord *Lovaine.*] Do you arm your men in cases of riots?—With cutlasses; but they have never had occasion to draw them.

1878. Do you continue that practice?—Yes, occasionally, with the permission of the magistrates.

1879. Is that with the view of awing the mob?—Yes; the mob knowing that the men are armed has an effect, without obliging the men to use their arms. We have never had any instance of a fatal accident, although we have had repeated rencontres with the mob.

1880. Have you not some very desperate characters in that county, upon the borders?—Yes.

1881. Mr. *Burroughes.*] Do not you consider that the local knowledge that the police have of the different persons concerned in those riots renders a police force more effective in preserving peace than a military force would be?—The police generally find out those who are the ringleaders.

1882. You have mentioned an instance of one of your superintendents going into a mob and apprehending the ringleaders: do not you consider the local knowledge which he had of those parties was of considerable assistance to him, whereas a soldier would have no local knowledge?—Without that local knowledge, the superintendent could not have done what I stated; the mob perceived that they were watched, and confidence in themselves was shaken.

Mr.

Captain *Henry Fowler Mackay*, called in ; and Examined.

Captain
H. F. Mackay.

3 June 1853.

1883. *Chairman.*] ARE you Chief Constable of Sussex ?—Of East Sussex.

1884. What is your force ?—Fifty-two, all hands.

1885. What is the population ?—About 140,000, exclusive of the boroughs.

1886. Was the force always of the same amount ?—They commenced with 18 and 3 superintendents.

1887. What proportion would 18 have borne to the population ?—I think the population was then about 127,000 ; it was about 1 to 6,000.

1888. What proportion does your present number bear to the population ?—One to 2,600 and odd.

1889. Then your maximum of police force is one man to 2,600 ?—Yes.

1890. Do you think that force is sufficient ?—No.

1891. Have you represented that to the magistrates ?—I have.

1892. Lord *Lovaine.*] Do they show any indisposition to increase the number ?—They show an indisposition on account of the expense.

1893. What is your rate in the pound ?—The last rate was 2 *d.*, which produced 4,425 *l.*

1894. *Chairman.*] Do you mean that the force of one man to 2,600 of the population of your county has cost 2 *d.* in the pound ?—Yes, because we employ besides local constables, and it includes payments for buildings.

1895. For what purpose do you employ the local constables ?—They are employed occasionally during the hop-picking season, and for night watching.

1896. Do you know what they cost ?—About 220 *l.* a year.

1897. What are your buildings ?—The buildings are lock-up houses ; there was one built this year ; we have four.

1898. Do you contemplate building any more ?—One more this year.

1899. How many divisions have you ?—Eleven petty sessional divisions and three police divisions ; in the course of the year I should propose more lock-ups to be built, for I consider a station is as good as a police officer.

1900. Do you think the time will come when your force will become more efficient ?—I should hope so.

1901. Lord *Lovaine.*] Have you any expectation of obtaining an increase of men ?—None whatever at present.

1902. Can you give any reason why you are so far behind other counties ?—We originally had a 3 *d.* rate, that was reduced to 1½ *d.* ; now we have got a 2 *d.* rate. A 3 *d.* rate would make us more efficient ; there was an increase three years ago of 10 constables, the actual increase of expense was about 200 *l.* a year ; there was a saving in other items which I contemplated at the same time.

1903. Is there more crime than there ought to be, in your opinion ?—Crime decreased last year ; the larcenies were 299, and the year before 442.

1904. *Chairman.*] Is Brighton in your division ?—It is in my division of the county.

1905. What is the police force at Brighton ?—Sixty men.

1906. Under what authority is that force ?—Under the chief officer.

1907. By whom is that chief officer appointed ?—By the commissioners ; Brighton is not a borough.

1908. Are they commissioners of pavement ?—Town commissioners, under a local Act.

1909. Is there any difficulty with respect to co-operation between your force and the Brighton force ?—Not with the heads ; I think there is a feeling of jealousy amongst the men frequently ; the head officers are willing to give us every assistance, and we are ready to assist them.

1910. Has it ever happened to you to have given them assistance ?—Very frequently.

1911. In what way ?—In apprehending people in my division ; on information sent from them we co-operate.

1912. Have you ever sent your men, at their request, in consequence of any local disturbance ?—No ; I have had occasion to apply for assistance, which they could not afford.

1913. Under what circumstances ?—A disturbance took place at Lewes, and the metropolitan police came down.

1914. Was that owing to the hop-picking ?—It was an excitement on the 5th

Captain
H. F. Mackay.

3 June 1853.

of November; there was a disturbance at Lewes on the 5th of November; there was a conversation about applying to Brighton, and some of the magistrates said they could not send us sufficient assistance.

1915. Did you get any assistance from London?—Eighty men came down.

1916. Did those 80 men answer the purpose?—For that night.

1917. Could you have done without them?—We could not, certainly.

1918. When they went away, did you find the want of them?—Yes, for nearly three weeks we had disturbances.

1919. Do you think those disturbances would not have taken place if you had had a sufficient force?—Yes.

1920. Lord *Lovaine.*] Could you have checked those disturbances if you had had a force on a more perfect footing?—I could; I had only 40 men in the whole county.

1921. Mr. *Mackie.*] You have mentioned that crime has decreased, in consequence of the establishment of the police; is it your opinion that as crime has decreased, property has increased in value?—I consider a police force is like an insurance of property, and thus indirectly rendered more valuable.

Mr. *John Wayte*, called in; and Examined.

Mr. *J. Wayte.*

1922. *Chairman.*] WHERE do you reside?—At Calne, in Wiltshire.

1922*. Has your attention been directed to the state of the police from any office you have held?—Yes; for many years, at least from the year 1817, I have given my services gratuitously to the suppression of vagrancy; it was my fancy. I have given up a great deal of time and money to it. I had not money to pay officers, therefore I have made use of the governor of the poorhouse. It runs to a considerable expense.

1923. During the time you were mayor of Calne, did the police render you much service?—Yes; in reducing the number of vagrants from 4,749, that frequented the town, in the year 1819, to less than 400; and although the numbers were so reduced not one destitute person was refused relief.

1924. Had you a Mendicity Society, and by whom was the relief given to the vagrants?—When the thousands visited our town they were relieved by the master of the workhouse; when reduced to less than 400 yearly they were relieved by the policemen, who also enabled us to detect those vagrants that were getting money from the overseers by false passes.

1925. Has the vigilance of the police lessened the number of the lodging-houses that were frequented by the thieves and beggars in your town?—Yes; there were three, but now only one.

1926. What was the number relieved at the adjoining union of Chippenham, for the first nine months of the year 1847, and at Calne, for the same period in that year?—The master of the Chippenham Union informed me that he had relieved 1,530. The number relieved by the policemen at Calne, for the same period, was under 240.

1927. How do you account for this great difference?—By the vagrants being more strictly examined by the policemen in our district, who have more time to do so, and the dislike they have to policemen. The master of the Chippenham Union told me that one man had called on him from Bristol, stating that he was going to Cheltenham, but in a few weeks he returned again for relief, and when questioned he acknowledged that he had been wandering about the neighbourhood of Melksham, Devizes, Pewsey and Marlborough, and had been relieved at each union. If this vagrant had been taken by a policeman to the railroad for Cheltenham this imposition would have been prevented.

1928. Do you think the police may be made more efficient if employed in the suppression of vagrancy?—I quite believe that with the aid of the constabulary force this kingdom may be freed from vagrants, and thousands of thieves now raised by vagrants prevented, at a saving of tens of thousands of pounds yearly. I am of Mr. Patrick Colquhoun's opinion, that the sending vagrants to their parishes is the best and cheapest mode of providing for them. I would, with all due submission, recommend all destitute persons to be so disposed of.

Mr.

Mr. *John Dunne*, called in ; and Examined.

1929. *Chairman.*] ARE you the Chief Officer of the Police Force at Norwich?
—I am.

1930. How long have you held that office?—Two years the 29th of next August.

1931. Had you previously served as a superintending constable?—Yes, in the Bearstead division of the county of Kent.

1932. For what period did you serve in that capacity?—Thirteen months.

1933. Why did you leave it?—In consequence of getting the appointment at Norwich, which was superior.

1934. When you went to Norwich you went with testimonials from the magistrates in Kent, where you had acted?—Yes.

1935. Had you served in a police force before you were in Kent?—Yes. I joined the Manchester police in 1840, and there served for one year under Sir Charles Shaw; I served seven years as constable and inspector in the Essex County Constabulary, under Captain M'Hardy; I served two years as inspector of the Bath Police, under Mr Oakley; I served 13 months as superintendent in Kent, from which I succeeded to my present position at Norwich.

1936. You had been in a borough police twice before your present appointment; seven years in a rural constabulary, and 13 months as superintending constable?—Yes.

1937. You are now the chief of the police at Norwich?—Yes.

1938. Will you state your opinion of those different systems of police in which you have served; take the borough police first; do you think the borough police is generally efficient?—No, I consider it inefficient; it is impracticable to establish an efficient police in any borough town, in accordance with the present divided system of organization and government; want of uniformity and cordial co-operation and communication in the pursuit, apprehension, and conviction of offenders tends to render it most inefficient.

1939. Do you think the borough police, in which you are serving, is inefficient?—It is not in such a satisfactory state of efficiency as I should like to see it.

1940. For what reasons?—When I was appointed to the office of chief of the police of the city of Norwich, I found existing there two distinct bodies of police; one was termed the day police, and the other the night watch; the day police consisted of 27 men, six supernumeraries, six inspectors, and one chief officer; the night watch consisted of an equal number; I found that in the day police the inspectors and constables received nearly the same pay; the inspector received 16 s. and the constable 14 s.; they were permitted to receive fees and allowances for all special duties which they performed, which were considered sufficient to make up for any deficiency that existed as regarded their pay; the most ordinary duty which they were called upon to perform by any inhabitant they were paid for; and a similar system was connected with the night watch; those men were not at all supervised during the night; they checked themselves by a clock, an old system, which I believe existed in connexion with the constables in London previous to the establishment of the metropolitan police; in the course of inquiry I ascertained that it was possible for one man to attend to the clocks of three or four; the mode of ascertaining whether a man had attended to his clock was by the superintendent going round the city every morning and examining the face of the clock, which revolved; there was a peg which moved on the dial, which, on examination, showed whether the man had pulled at the time laid down in the regulations for him to do so. I found that nearly all the men were in trade and business in the city, and they generally used to attend to it every day. It was the opinion of many of the respectable inhabitants that receiving fees by the watchmen and policemen was an indirect incentive to the commission of crime. If a policeman or watchman apprehended any party he received a fee for it, and was allowed to retain that fee and appropriate it to his own uses. Viewing it, then, as a whole, I considered it to be in a most inefficient and defective state; I stated so to the watch committee, to whose authority I am subject, and also to the magistrates, and explained everything in connexion with both forces, particularly alluding to the want of co-operation and communication existing between both bodies, especially as they were allowed to receive fees. If one of the night watchmen saw any

Mr. *J. Dunne.*

3 June 1853.

Mr. J. Dunne.

3 June 1853.

suspected parties during the night, and observed anything which he ought to have communicated to the day policeman, so as to give the public the advantages of the services of an efficient police, he would attempt to do that duty himself, for the purpose of getting the fee, thereby frequently frustrating the ends of justice; so it was *vice versâ* with the police force as regards the watchmen.

1941. Has that system been altered?—Yes; I drew up a report in reference thereto, which was adopted.

1942. Does that report contain more in detail the objections which you have now stated?—Yes.

1943. Was the system altered in consequence of that report?—Yes; both the bodies were amalgamated and established, similar in detail to the Essex constabulary and the metropolitan police force.

1944. Do you think the force is more efficient?—I do; serious crime has greatly decreased; pursuit, apprehension, and conviction of offenders facilitated; life and property better protected: the system insures the performance of the duties; the respectable inhabitants have expressed themselves gratified with the change; considerable savings are effected; my report, however, has not been fully carried out, particularly as regards the appointment and promotion of the men, and other circumstances, which render the force still defective.

1945. Mr. *Fitzroy.*] Have the numbers been increased?—No; the consolidated force is equal in numbers (80) to the two bodies previously existing.

1946. What is the population of Norwich?—Between 70,000 and 80,000.

1947. *Chairman.*] Do you know what the cost of the old force was?—About 3,687*l.* 16*s.* 8*d.* per annum; the new about the same.

1948. Lord *Lovaine.*] What is the rating in the pound?—About 2*d.* police rate.

1949. Mr. *Fitzroy.*] Will you point out in what respects the police forces in boroughs are deficient?—I consider that the police force of a borough being placed under the divided control of the magistrates and the watch committee, tends to render effectual action almost impossible. In many instances the watch committee lay down instructions, and give orders which the magistrates countermand. One of the magistrates in Norwich, recently, ordered a policeman to perform a certain duty, and while in the performance of that duty another magistrate came up and found fault with him, and spoke to him in the street in such a way that the man resigned. Every borough has some system or other peculiar to itself; there is no uniformity, no co-operation, no communication, no effectual action; thereby the ends of justice are frequently defeated; they are generally defective in numerical strength, unequal to any emergency, and rely too much upon military aid; local interests and influences are brought to bear.

1950. *Chairman.*] Do you think the rural police in Essex is efficient? I do; I consider it the most efficient rural police force in England. The establishment of station-houses and police districts in connexion with that force have been attended with most advantageous results, and to meet the gross expense, a variety of duties have been engrafted on the force, which, whilst adding materially to its efficiency, has considerably reduced the net expense, which example has been followed in Hampshire and other counties.

1951. What is your opinion of the efficiency of the superintending constable system?—I consider the system inefficient; it is quite impossible to ever become effective.

1952. What difficulty did you find in carrying out your duties there?—I found that the men from whom the rural constables were chosen, under Act 5th & 6th of Victoria, were men generally disinclined to serve as constables; they never voluntarily or cheerfully accepted their office. In the general performance of the duties they are called upon to exercise there appears to be a reluctance on their part to do their duties, particularly in consideration of their being brought into collision with the parties from whom they obtain their livelihood. They are generally chosen from tailors, blacksmiths, agricultural labourers, and men who keep little shops in the parish in which they may reside. I found that it was quite impossible to carry out any system so as to ensure the performance of the duties appertaining to a police force.

1953. Did you find any difficulty in pursuing offenders?—I did; I often found great obstruction in the pursuit and apprehension of offenders, which often entirely frustrated their detection, and defeated the ends of justice.

1954. Have you any means of stating to the Committee what the expenses of the

the superintending constables were in the county of Kent?—The expense of the superintending constable system I consider to be far greater than any person is able to show by statistics which can be obtained, inasmuch as the performance of the duties by the constables is generally paid for, indirectly, by individuals and by the overseers of the parishes; there are no accounts kept, and this makes it almost impossible to conceive the extreme expense incurred by the system; the superintending constables' salaries amounted to 85 l. a year, and 25 l. a year as an allowance for horse, cart, and re-mount; then for the performance of special services there was a quarterly contingent account made, which was taken before the constabulary committee to be approved by them; in many instances charges were disallowed on examination by the constabulary committee; subsequently the salaries were increased to 150 l. per annum, with other allowances.

1955. Were those charges independent of the fees paid by order of the magistrates to the local constables?—Entirely.

1956. Have you the means of stating what those fees were in your division?—The expense for the performance of any occasional duty required under a written order of a justice was at the rate of 2 s. 6 d. a day, and 3 s. a night; and all other fees and allowances were paid in accordance with a table laid down, and approved by court of quarter sessions.

1957. Had the magistrates any power of ordering a watch?—Yes; on the application of the superintending constables, or other person, on his apprehension that any offence was likely to be committed, the magistrates had the power to order as many constables as they thought necessary to remain on duty, both day and night, as long as they deemed proper, at that rate of payment.

1958. Do you know at all what the expense in your division was of a watch, under orders of magistrates?—I tried what the effect might be of calling out the constables on one occassion; the neighbourhood was infested with a great number of vagrants and reputed thieves, and I considered that the calling out of the constables might have the effect of watching those parties, who were continually prowling about, and be thereby attended with the prevention and detection of crime; I made an application to a magistrate, and on his order I placed a great many constables on duty, but in the working out of the system I found it to be most defective; if I gave any orders to the constables to watch certain parties or to supervise beershops or public-houses, I found that they deceived me and rarely performed the duties necessary to enable me to discharge my duty with any advantage to the county. The expense of 10 constables on duty for one month under this system would be 77 l.

1959. Mr. *Fitzroy*.] Under what Act was power given to magistrates to order parish constables to watch?—The 5th and 6th Victoria, c. 109, and 13th and 14th Victoria, c. 20.

1960. Does it give the magistrates power to call out constables to watch, in case of apprehended danger?—Yes; it was exercised to a great extent. The indirect expense thereby incurred was very large. There was no return made of it; and it is impossible to conceive the excessive amount caused by this and other circumstances in connexion with the superintending constable system.

1961. Is that expense paid out of the county rate?—Out of the poor rates; an order is made out by the magistrates' clerk, signed by the magistrates, and paid by the overseer of the parish.

1962. So far as your knowledge of that system goes, do you think that one great drawback to its well working is the want of a chief constable at the head of the whole of the superintending constables?—Certainly not; I consider that a chief constable at the head of the superintending constables would not at all improve the system. I cannot see how it can be improved by having a chief superintending constable. He could not possibly establish an efficient system of supervision. The superintending constables are subject to no control, except to the court of quarter sessions. I have known instances of the superintending constable acting in such a manner as could not be allowed in a police force, where there was any system, so as to insure the legal and due discharge of his duty.

1963. Would it not probably be the case that the appointment of a chief constable would introduce more system into the working of that plan?—I do not think it is practicable, particularly for the want of having a proper class of men as local constables, such as the superintending constables could derive assistance from.

1964. Lord *Lovaine*.] You mean that it is impossible to make a parish constable an efficient officer ?—It is impracticable to do so.

1965. *Chairman*.] Do you mean that in your opinion a superintending constable could not make the parish constables efficient police officers ?—I do ; it is quite impossible.

1966. If the superintending constable under whose immediate direction they were could not improve them as police officers, do you think that one chief constable over the whole would make any difference in their efficiency as police officers ?—None whatever.

1967. Mr. *Fitzroy*.] How long were you employed in the police in Kent ?—Thirteen months.

1968. From your knowledge of the system, you would pronounce it to be a totally inefficient system for the purposes of police ?—Quite so. I think it is attended with great evils. There is a system in Kent—I am not aware of its being carried out in any other county—under the 3d and 4th William the 4th, chapter 90, the vestry has the power of appointing paid watchmen, who act as police officers for the parish for which they are appointed. In 12 parishes in the division of Bearstead the provisions of this Act were carried into effect, and for those 12 parishes there were no parish constables appointed under 5th and 6th and 13th and 14th of Victoria ; the men appointed under that Act were quite independent of my control ; they were not under my jurisdiction in any way ; the consequence was, that if I wanted any assistance for the supervision of beerhouses or public-houses, or the performance of any other duty, I had no person to assist me, for those men generally acted against me instead of giving any cordial co-operation.

1969. *Chairman*.] Was the appointment of those persons made in consequence of a direct recommendation of the magistrates from the bench ?—They were appointed upon the recommendation of a majority of the vestry in consequence of the feeling which prevails in that county among the middle classes in favour of an efficient police force, and finding the parish constables so inefficient, the vestry, under this Act, appointed those policemen.

1970. Mr. *Fitzroy*.] How long did they continue ?—They were there during the whole of my service. The Act provides that if it is once adopted it cannot be discontinued for a period of three years. The men were under no efficient control ; the inspectors who supervised them were selected by the vestry, such as farmers and shopkeepers, who knew but little of the duties.

1971. Were not those duties more efficiently performed by those paid watchmen than by the parish constables who were not paid ?—In some respects they were ; still there was a want of supervision and a want of uniformity in the system which rendered them ineffective. They felt independent ; they were under no control ; and if applied to for assistance they would not generally render it. They were in no way subject to my control. I made an application to the magistrates at the Bearstead petty sessions on account of the want of assistance and co-operation on the part of those men.

1972. Were not those men under the control of a superintendent ?—No.

1973. Had the superintending constables nothing to do with their appointment ?—Nothing, directly or indirectly.

1974. Lord *Lovaine*.] Did you ever make a calculation of the expense incurred for parish constables in the division over which you presided ?—I did.

1975. What did you make it come to ?—Taking the expenses as a whole, direct and indirect, connected with the superintending constabulary system and police, from 1,000 *l*. to 1,300 *l*. a year.

1976. How many constables had you under you ?—I had 35.

1977. With how many rural policemen could you have effectually watched and guarded the district ?—Judging from the extent of the division, and comparing its area with divisions of counties where police forces are established, if I had had 20 good active men, one inspector, and two serjeants, I could have carried out an efficient system in that division, providing the force was general.

1978. Taking the average cost of a rural policeman to be about 60 *l*., which would amount to 1,200 *l*., upon your calculation of 1,300 *l*. the county would be a clear gainer of 100 *l*. ?—I feel confident it would.

1979. Are you of opinion that it is impossible to make the superintending constable system act efficiently ?—I am.

1980. And you deem it to be quite inefficient ?—Quite so.

1981. *Chairman*.] Do you know the whole extent of the divisions in Kent under

under the superintending constables?—The largest division in the county of Kent is Wingham, which consists of 56 parishes.

1982. Do you know how many superintending constables they have for that division?—Only one.

1983. Do you think it possible that one man can superintend such a district? —It is not possible to do it efficiently; even in my division, which was composed of 32 parishes, I was very frequently obliged to go out with three horses a day, in the performance of my duties; when I returned home from one part of the division, I would find waiting for me some communication from another part of it, to the effect that I was required; that there had been a serious robbery, or something requiring my attention, and the magistrates had sent me an order to go immediately; I have never, in one instance, met with effective co-operation or assistance from the local constables; they would not subject themselves to any control.

1984. Could you pursue criminals with the assistance of the local constables? Certainly not; with regard to the supervision of beerhouses and public-houses, I have frequently arranged to make a visit at an appointed time for the purpose of visiting some house, and the parish constable has gone and told the publican or the beerhouse-keeper that the superintendent was coming at such a time. They are so much mixed up with local connexions in their general business that it is impossible for them to act independently; it is imposing upon them duties which they cannot perform consistently with their own interests, viewing it as a money question.

1985. Do you know that it is the fact that no police constable can get into a public-house unless he is called upon by the publican?—I know that is a regulation of the police.

1986. Do you think that parish constables would generally consider it an invidious duty to have to enter public-houses for the purpose of control if they were called upon?—I have known many instances in which they have skulked out of the way to avoid it.

1987. Lord *Lovaine*.] You have stated that under the method of appointing the police in the boroughs, it is hardly possible to make the force efficient? —Yes.

1988. Is it your opinion that it would be an advantage to those boroughs that they should be amalgamated, as far as regards the police, with the counties?—I do certainly think that it would tend to render them more efficient. I think consolidating the borough police with the county forces would be attended with the most beneficial results.

1989. Would you give the appointment of the men to the head officer of the police, whoever he might be, or to any body or committee, either magistrates or town council?—I think it is absolutely necessary that the chief officer of the district should have the entire control of the force.

1990. In the same manner as in the rural constabulary?—Yes.

1991. Mr. *Fitzroy*.] By whom were you appointed at Norwich?—By the watch committee.

1992. Does the watch committee appoint the whole of the other constables?— Yes.

1993. Have the magistrates the power to dismiss or suspend the men?—They have; the control is divided between the watch committee and the magistrates; the watch committee and the magistrates frequently differ as to the merits of cases in connexion with the police which may be brought before them. I have known instances occur in which the magistrates have suspended a policeman, and recommended his dismissal, and when before the watch committee, the watch committee reinstated him. When that same officer again appeared before the magistrates to give evidence in court, one of the magistrates who suspended him stated on the bench that he would not believe the man upon his oath, and if he saw the man in a court of justice he should think it his duty to stand up and state that he thought the man was not worthy of belief on his oath. I reported that to the watch committee; but, notwithstanding, the man was retained in the service.

1994. Is there any complaint on the part of the inhabitants of Norwich that a sufficient supervision is not exercised over the beerhouses?—Yes.

1995. Is there a complaint that information is not laid by the police when the publicans are known to transgress the law?—Yes.

1996. Is that attributable to the manner in which they are appointed?—I believe so, in some measure.

1997. Lord *Lovaine*.] How many brewers are members of the watch committee?—Three; the late chairman of the watch committee was a brewer; there are in Norwich 670 beerhouses and public-houses.

1998. Mr. *Fitzroy*.] When did you get that return?—Last Monday. There is one fact in connexion with these houses which is, I think, peculiar to Norwich; of this number, 344 took a spirit license, 107 a wine license, and 219 are little better than beerhouses, inasmuch as they receive the magistrates' license to sell beer, but they have no spirit license, nor wine license; after receiving a beer license they save about 3 *l.* by not taking out a spirit license from the Excise.

1999. Do not you know that they do not take out a spirit license from the Excise?—They pay 3 *l.* 6 *s.* 0 ¾ *d.* to the Excise for the spirit license, and 1 *l.* 2 *s.* 0 ½ *d.* for the magistrates' beer license.

2000. Lord *Lovaine*.] Are the Committee to understand that these 670 beerhouses, alehouses, and wine-shops are all under the control of one individual?—No; there are eight owners of houses, exclusive of free houses.

2001. Under the control of the brewers there are 670 houses, exclusive of free houses, and those houses where spirituous liquors of one sort or another are sold are all under the control of eight individuals?—Yes, exclusive of free houses, which are about 120.

2002. Mr. *Burroughes*.] When you speak of control, do you mean ownership? —Yes; and with respect to the control exercised by the police, I have caused informations to be laid against some of them for disorderly conduct; I have had the parties summoned, the offence has been proved by the police officers, and the party has been called upon to assign his answer to the charge; he has pleaded guilty, and notwithstanding, the case has been dismissed. One was a case of a man keeping a disorderly house on Sunday morning during the hours of Divine Service.

2003. Mr. *Fitzroy*.] Do you mean that he opened his house?—Yes, and I felt it my duty to bring the case before the magistrates.

2004. Do you mean that an information had been laid before a bench of magistrates?—Yes, and the party summoned.

2005. Had you received any instructions from the watch committee with respect to the public-houses?—The watch committee told me not to summon any public-house-keeper or beerhouse-keeper without first submitting the report for their approval, and to receive their orders and instructions thereon.

2006. The information being laid; before whom was it laid?—Before the magistrates.

2007. You say that the information has been laid before the magistrates, the case has been heard, the man has pleaded guilty, and then the information has been dismissed?—In two instances.

2008. Were any of those magistrates who heard the information members of the watch committee?—They were.

2009. *Chairman*.] Of how many members does the watch committee consist altogether?—Eighteen.

2010. Mr. *Fitzroy*.] Were any of the magistrates who heard the information, to which you have referred, brewers, connected with the public-houses in the town?—I cannot say.

2011. Had those informations which were laid before the magistrates been first submitted to the watch committee, and had you received their directions upon the subject?—No; there were so many complaints from respectable inhabitants and the clergy, of the state of the public-houses, that to remove the responsibility from myself and to see what the magistrates would do, I laid those informations upon my own responsibility, and the result is what I have told you.

2012. Are the Committee to understand from the statements you have made, that the influence exercised by these members of the watch committee who are connected with the publicans, over the other members of the watch committee, is sufficient to insure a decision such as will be convenient to the members of the watch committee who are connected with the public-houses?—I am unable to say so.

2013. Do you mean to say that these two cases in which informations were dismissed, although the parties pleaded guilty, are an example of the influence which the watch committee have over the conduct of the magistrates?—I cannot

say

say that those two cases were dismissed by the magistrates in consequence of the influence of the watch committee. I do not know the cause; there are only two of many cases I could refer to, to show the difficulties experienced by the police in the performance of their duties under the present system.

2014. Do you mean to say that there is generally a total want of interference with the regulation of the public-houses?—It is very difficult to efficiently supervise them.

2015. Is it your impression that it is the wish of the magistrates that the public-houses and beershops should not be interfered with?—Judging from the difficulty of carrying out strictly an information, it appears so.

2016. Mr. *Burroughes.*] Has there been any application for a stipendiary magistrate at Norwich?—I am not aware; I believe it is the feeling of the inhabitants generally that it would be a very great advantage to the city to have a stipendiary magistrate. I was told that some of the leading gentlemen in the city have got up a petition to the effect that a stipendiary magistrate is necessary for the advantage of the city, and the protection of the public.

2017. Mr. *Fitzroy.*] But as a stipendiary magistrate would have nothing to do with the dismissal or the appointment of the police, would the evil to which you have referred, namely, the want of proper regulations of the public-houses and beershops, be remedied at all by the appointment of a stipendiary magistrate?—No, I consider it would not; assuming the police to remain under the same control and jurisdiction; but if an information was brought, the party would be punished as he deserved, and justice impartially administered.

2018. Lord *Lovaine.*] Which, in your opinion, is not the case now?—In my opinion it is not.

2019. Mr. *Fitzroy.*] Are any directions issued to yourself to prevent the police interfering with these public-houses?—None, excepting what I have stated.

2020. It is your impression that such a course is understood on the part of the watch committee?—It is my impression, as Inspector Peck informed me that an order was put up in the station-house, previous to my being in Norwich, prohibiting interference unless in flagrant cases.

2021. Lord *Lovaine.*] You have said that no information is to be laid without having previously undergone the sanction of the watch committee?—These instructions were given. I took the responsibility of laying informations against some houses.

2022. And brought them direct before the magistrates of the city?—Yes. In some cases the parties were fined.

2023. Mr. *Fitzroy.*] Is Sunday trading carried on to a great extent at Norwich?—Not so much now as it used to be.

2024. What are the principal offences which are committed by the public-house and beershop-keepers in Norwich?—It is said that in the city of Norwich there are 200 houses that are used for the purposes of prostitution; it is difficult to supervise them.

2025. *Chairman.*] Do you mean that those houses are the resort of hired prostitutes?—The resort of prostitutes; some of those houses are kept by returned convicts, or by men who have been convicted of felony; and in many of those low public-houses crime is fostered; many of them I suspect to be receivers of stolen property; I recently found a quantity of stolen goods in the house of a returned convict, and also an illicit still.

2026. Did you take any measures in that instance to bring the offenders to justice?—Yes; I had the man taken before the magistrates; but one of the magistrates, who is a practising barrister, has two sons, solicitors, and his sons appear before the bench; he adjudicates in cases where his sons appear as solicitors; he was there that day, and he suggested that the case was got up by the police; that it was a set-up robbery.

2027. Was the case dismissed?—Yes.

2028. Upon the representation of the magistrate that it was a got-up robbery by the police?—I cannot say that it was dismissed upon that statement; that remark was made by that magistrate. The men vote at elections; there are generally from 20 to 30 men who vote at parliamentary and municipal elections; at the last election I submitted to the watch committee the impropriety of allowing the men to interfere in the election, directly or indirectly, only in the performance of their duties; that both parties were entitled to protection, one as much as the other. The committee met my proposition with a direct negative.

2029. Lord *Lovaine*.] Have you ever found it necessary to call in further assistance during elections?—No; my experience only extends to one election at Norwich, and there was no occasion then to apply for further assistance, excepting posse-men; the military were ordered to remain in barracks, and they were in readiness to come out if called upon. I had been informed that they were obliged to avail themselves of military aid when a disturbance took place. During the riots in Manchester in 1841 the military were called out; large bodies of special constables were appointed; I was detached with a party of police and special constables on three occasions; when called into action the special constables ran away; three active policemen were beaten; in a day or two afterwards they died in the hospital. It is my opinion that special constables are unequal to any emergency.

2030. Mr. *Fitzroy*.] On the occasion to which you refer, regarding Norwich, did those members of the police vote?—I am informed they always have done so.

2031. *Chairman*.] You have spoken of the expenses of the parish constables; have you any scale of fees?—Yes.

2032. What is the scale of fees?—It is laid down in this Form.

[*The Witness delivered in the same, which is as follows :*]

KENT.

TABLES of Fees and Allowances to the Clerk to the Justices for the County of *Kent*, for the performance of their Duties, under the Acts 5 and 6 Vict. c. 109, for the Appointment and Payment of Parish Constables, and 13 Vict. c. 20, for amending that Act, and to the Constables for the performance of their Duties.

JUSTICES' CLERKS' FEES.

	£	s.	d.
For every precept to high constable for convening a special petty sessions, —to be paid by each parish		1	—
Notices to justices when required,—to be paid by each parish		—	6
Precept and notice to overseers to return lists to special sessions, including abstract of duties,—to be paid by each parish		2	6
Each form of list of persons agreed to at vestry, when required by overseer		—	3
For every other precept and notice issued under these Acts		1	6
Verification and allowance of each list returned, including hearing objections thereto		2	6
Appointment of constable, if only one		2	6
Each additional constable in the same appointment		—	6
Copy of appointment for overseers,—one half.			
Every appointment of paid constables (exclusive of the stamp)		5	—
Every duplicate of the above, or copy, if required		2	6
Every summons and duplicate		1	6
Oath of office		1	—
Certificate		1	—
Lists of constables for justices and clerk of the peace, not exceeding 20 names		2	6
For every additional 10 names		1	—
For every order of justices to unite parishes, under sect. 4,—to be paid by each parish included therein		2	—
For every copy		1	—
For every information and examination, if in writing		2	6
For each witness examined on hearing, including oath		1	6
Confession		1	—
Conviction (as form is not prescribed)		5	—
Distress warrant		2	6
Commitment		2	6
Other orders and allowances not provided for		1	6

CONSTABLES' FEES.

	£.	s.	d.
Serving summons or written order of justice when within the parish	-	1	-
Executing warrant	-	2	6
Executing warrant to search	-	2	6
Distraining, when not otherwise directed by statute	-	2	6
Pressing carriages for baggage (up to 10) each	-	1	-
For every one in addition, to be paid by the county	-	-	6
For attendance in making a return, or obeying a legal order of justices	-	2	-
For attendance with prisoner	-	2	6
For assistance with prisoner when necessary	-	2	6
Travelling expenses actually incurred, when out of the parish	—		
For taking a prisoner into custody, or before a justice, per mile	-	-	3
Subsistence of prisoner, per day	-	-	9
Subsistence of constable, after one day	-	2	-
Assistant, when ordered, same as constable.			
Lodging of prisoner	-	-	9
Lodging of constable	-	2	-
Assistant to constable	-	2	-
For the performance of any occasional duty which may be required under a written order of a justice, or which having been performed without such order is afterwards sanctioned and allowed by justices in petty sessions, a sum not exceeding while actually engaged) per day	-	2	6
per night	-	3	-

At the annual general session holden by adjournment at Maidstone, in and for the county of Kent, on Monday the 14th day of October 1850, the above tables of fees and allowances were settled by the justices of the said county there assembled, subject to the approval of one of Her Majesty's Principal Secretaries of State.

(signed) *Wm. Deedes,*
Chairman.

Whitehall,
5 November 1850.

Approved,
G. Grey.

Witness.] I should refer to my experience during seven years in the Essex County Constabulary; I had an opportunity of making myself thoroughly acquainted with the working of that force, and the items of saving effected there, and comparing them with the expenses of the constabulary system in the county of Kent, I feel confident in saying that an effective police force could be carried out upon a similar principle to that of Essex at a less real cost to the county than a superintending constable system, giving to the poor man the protection which he does not enjoy under the parish constable system. If a man applies to a local constable he may have to pay him for the duty performed.

2033. Was not the police force in Essex very effective for the suppression of vagrancy?—Yes, most effective.

2034. Was the superintending constable system in the county of Kent efficient for the suppression of vagrants?—Certainly not.

2035. Why not?—Because the constables were seldom on duty, and the superintendent was unable to superintend the extent of ground placed under his supervision, therefore there was but little check upon vagrancy. Hordes of vagrants travelled from one part of the county to another; there was a regular migratory population which tramped from one county to another; previously to the establishment of the Surrey constabulary that county was infested with gangs of gypsies, and those parties immediately on the establishment of that force came into Kent, and in Kent the number of vagrants increased to a great extent.

2036. When you were appointed superintending constable in the county of Kent, was not it one of your duties, as far as you had the means, to suppress vagrancy?—It was my duty to suppress vagrancy, but in consequence of the want of efficient constables I had not the means to do so.

2037. Do you mean, having used your best endeavours during the period you were in Kent, that vagrancy was decreased?—I think the appointment of superintending constables, to a certain extent, did tend to decrease crime as regards the apprehension of offenders; but to suppress vagrancy was impossible; the man was utterly unable, both physically and morally, to perform the duties which were expected of him. In Essex the performance of the duty and the strict supervision of all grades of the officers, arises from the superior uniformity of the system laid down in that county.

2038. Lord *Lovaine.*] Would there be a very violent opposition on the part of the city of Norwich to their police being amalgamated with the rural police? —Not

Mr. *J. Dunne.*

3 June 1853.

—Not with the inhabitants generally. I do think there would be some opposition by the watch committee; I think they would feel the taking away from them the patronage; but that would ultimately subside, and the advantages derivable from the consolidation would render it a very popular thing with the public. In Cambridge I know the chairman of the watch committee is a brewer, and I know that there are orders that the superintendent shall not proceed against any public-house-keeper without previously having submitted the case to the committee.

2039. Mr. *Fitzroy.*] Have there been any complaints on the part of the inhabitants of Norwich with reference to the misconduct of the public-houses and the inefficiency of the police?—There was a very great complaint, when I went there, of the inefficiency of the police, and the want of assistance, without they were paid, exclusive of their regular pay. They were principally paid by fees, and they were allowed to receive all fees and rewards; there was a fee for the most ordinary duty.

2040. Is that system done away with now?—Entirely so. I recommended the watch committee to abolish that system, and I considered it essential, for the efficiency of the service, that I should have the appointment and promotion of the men, that is, the selection, and their ultimate promotion. I divided the men into classes.

2041. Lord *Lovaine.*] The Committee may conclude from what you have stated, that you would prefer yourself to be subject to the control of one individual, rather than be placed in the position in which you are with reference to the watch committee and the magistrates?—I would.

2042. Mr. *Fitzroy.*] Do you think the present method of appointing the police in Norwich tends much to impair its efficiency?—It does; I have often recommended men whom I have considered efficient, and instead of taking the man whom I recommended, the watch committee have chosen another man; I have recommended men for promotion from one class to another, and instead of taking the man I recommended they have taken others. At the election the Marquis of Douro applied to me for some protection; I was obliged to place men specially on duty to give him that protection which he required, and I believe the consequence of my doing so was to cause considerable opposition to me in the performance of my duties. As regards the expenses of prosecution in Essex, the average cost was between 7 *l.* and 8 *l.*; in the county of Kent it was considerably more; I find that in Norfolk it is less.

2043. Mr. *Burroughes.*] Do you know the relative proportion of the expenses of prosecution between the county prisoners and the city prisoners?—I am told the average expense of the prosecution of a city prisoner is one half more than a county prisoner.

2044. You are not speaking now upon any precise information?—No, from information I received from the auditor. With regard to the superintending constable system in the Dewsbury division in Yorkshire, there is a population of 80,000, and only a superintending constable with parish constables in substitution of the police establishment.

Jovis, 9° die Junii, 1853.

MEMBERS PRESENT:

Mr. Rice.
Mr. Sotheron.
Lord Advocate.
Mr. Fitzroy.
Mr. Burrroughes.
Lord Lovaine.

Sir John Trollope.
Mr. Moody.
Mr. Mackie.
Mr. Charles Howard.
Sir James Anderson.
Mr. Phillips.

EDWARD ROYDS RICE, ESQ., IN THE CHAIR.

George William Blathwayt, Esq., called in; and Examined.

G. W. Blathwayt,
Esq.

9 June 1853.

2045. YOU are a Magistrate for Gloucestershire?—I am a Magistrate for Gloucestershire, Somersetshire, Wiltshire, and the city of Bath.

2046. In which of those counties do you act?—I act as a magistrate for Gloucestershire,

Gloucestershire, Somersetshire, and the city of Bath regularly; I do not act in Wiltshire; I am constantly acting for Gloucestershire, and occasionally for the city of Bath.

G. W. Blathwayt, Esq.

9 June 1853.

2047. Are you chairman of the court of quarter sessions?—Chairman of the Bath division of Somersetshire petty sessional division.

2048. Do you reside on the borders between Gloucestershire, Wilts and Somerset?—Upon the borders of the whole of the three counties, about seven miles from Bath.

2049. Have you had some experience of the system of police, and the state of crime in those three counties?—In Gloucestershire and Somersetshire; I know but little of Wiltshire.

2050. In the county of Gloucester there is a police?—A rural police.

2051. Can you state at all what the expense of that police is in the pound?—Nine farthings in the pound; we have three halfpenny rates and a three-farthing rate.

2052. Are you acquainted with the police in the county of Wilts?—I know nothing of the police of Wiltshire, except that there is a police.

2053. Can you speak of the comparative advantages or disadvantages in the county of Gloucester where there is police, and in the county of Somerset where there is none?—I should say decidedly, that there is a very great advantage in the police. I will give an instance: at Lansdowne, which is about three miles from Bath, in the county of Somerset, there are annual fairs held; and the rioting at those fairs, and the felonies which were committed, were so bad that people were almost deterred from going. Being lord of the manor of Lansdowne I naturally took an interest in it, and summoned a quantity of special constables to attend; I found they were of little use to preserve order.

2054. Was there a riot?—The people at the fairs were regularly robbed at noon day; there was a riot upwards of four or five years ago.

2055. Was it in consequence of any riot or apprehended riot that you swore in special constables?—Yes, and upon sworn information.

2056. What number of special constables did you swear in?—Twenty-four, I believe.

2057. Did you call in the aid of any of the parish constables?—I summoned the parish constables and ordered the high constable to attend with them, and I found they did more harm than good.

2058. What was the effect of swearing in the special constables?—The special constables generally created disorder; I thought they did more harm than good.

2059. What class of people did you swear in as special constables?—People of all descriptions; I afterwards availed myself of the Act of Parliament; and with the assistance of another magistrate, upon some sworn informations, I called upon the city of Bath to send up a certain number of police; they have regularly attended the fairs and races since that time, which is now, I believe, about four or five years ago; the fairs are conducted quietly, and there is very little felony committed; at the races all the thimble riggers and all those vagabonds are completely got rid of, that is, by the assistance of the police of the city of Bath.

2060. Have you experienced any advantages from the establishment of police in the county of Gloucester?—A case took place last year: there was a very serious riot at Bridge Yate, in the county of Gloucester, at one of the polling-places; there was a magistrate there and some police; the police were brought in too small a number, and the riot was so bad that the police were severely beaten, and the magistrates could do nothing. Sworn informations were taken afterwards against some 27 of the ringleaders of the riot, and the magistrates sent a special messenger to the chief of the police at Cheltenham, who ordered 50 men down that night, and 23 of the 27 rioters were taken in their beds, brought before the magistrates, and the whole 23 were sent for trial, with the exception of two that were let off, because they were not shown to have been so bad or actively concerned in the riot; 21 out of the 23 were tried at quarter sessions and were convicted. The consequence has been, that that part of the country has since been quiet, and I am certain that that could not have been done by parish constables.

2061. What distance had you to send for the police?—We sent by rail to Cheltenham, which is about 30 miles.

2062. Can you state how soon you got them down?—As soon as we wanted them; and the police executed the warrants in the night.

2063. You think you could not, without having had those policemen from

G. W. Blathwayt,
Esq.
———
9 June 1853.

Cheltenham, have maintained the peace, by swearing in special constables, or by calling in the assistance of parochial constables?—Certainly not; these parties would have resisted the parish constables.

2064. What is your opinion of the efficiency of parochial constables?—Parochial constables are very well in their way, but they are very inferior to the police. Some of them do their duty very well. I do not mean to say one word against the parish constables, but they are very far from being efficient; they are changed in Somersetshire almost every year; a fresh batch comes in, which makes them of very little use.

2065. Are you aware whether the parochial constables are still appointed in Gloucestershire?—Yes, certainly; in the month of March.

2066. Do you ever make any use of them?—The men come and are sworn in; they get their certificate and are paid their fees, but their services are seldom required.

2067. Is there any expense and trouble in swearing in the parish constables? —They are summoned to attend at the petty sessional divisions; there they are sworn in; and that is all we hear about them. The Act of Parliament obliges us to do it. They act as a sort of reserve in the case of a riot. The police know upon whom to call in the case of riots.

2068. Mr. *Moody.*] What is the expense paid on swearing in?—Three shillings and sixpence; being the scale of allowance of the quarter sessions.

2069. Mr. *Burroughes.*] Do you know the precise annual expense of swearing in those parish constables in Gloucestershire?—No, I cannot tell the cost; we only do it for our own division.

2070. What is the expense in your division?—It varies very much; some parishes have two, and some half a dozen. There are 25 parishes in our division.

2071. What does each constable cost?—Each constable costs 3 s. 6 d.; they give the man 3 s. for the loss of his day's work, and there is 6 d. for the clerk for making out the order to him.

2072. There is a police in the county of Gloucester, but there is no police in the county of Somerset?—No.

2073. Do you think the police in the county of Gloucester would be more efficient if you had the assistance of a similar system of police in the adjoining counties?—Undoubtedly; a link in the chain is broken; and if a thief gets into Somersetshire he is often lost sight of, because you cannot depend upon the parish constables for information. My idea is, to have no police in Gloucestershire, or have them in all three counties.

2074. Have you found any evil to arise from the continuance of the parish constables in Somersetshire?—No, I cannot say that we have. I think there is not so much crime detected by the parish constables as by the police; and I think there is a less amount of crime altogether.

2075. Do you think the proportion of undetected crime is much greater in Somersetshire than in Gloucestershire?—Certainly.

2076. Mr. *Moody.*] Have you any particular data upon which you give that answer?—I go upon the returns which I have had from the police in Gloucestershire, that the amount of undetected crime has decreased about 15 per cent. the last five years. For the last two or three years we have not had a single case of sheep-stealing or cattle-stealing. I believe there have been cases in Somersetshire, from all I can learn.

2077. Have you had any similar return from Somersetshire?—No; mine is only the police return from Gloucestershire.

2078. *Chairman.*] Do you know whether there are many cases of sheep-stealing in the county of Somerset?—There are cases. There are large farms in Somersetshire, and lately I heard of half-a-dozen being stolen from near a magistrate's house; Captain Scoble's house. I merely heard in Bath that six sheep had been stolen, and the people had never been heard of.

2079. Were they Captain Scoble's sheep?—It was in his neighbourhood. Perhaps the Committee will allow me to mention a case of sheep-stealing which occurred in Gloucestershire, about three years ago. I remember the time, because it was the very year that I was sheriff of Somerset. A Gloucestershire policeman was upon patrol at night, and against my park wall he saw a very large bonfire; he quietly darkened his lantern, and went up; he found a bonfire of faggots with a sheep roasting whole. He very quietly went to a neighbouring village,

G. W. Blathwayt, Esq.

9 June 1853.

village, and knocked up half-a-dozen able-bodied men; the party came down, and surrounded those men, and took them all into custody; they found the skin, and he discovered from my bailiff to whom the sheep belonged. Those fellows were all taken off to the assizes and were convicted, and thus a gang was broken up just by the individual exertions of that young policeman.

2080. Mr. *Sotheron.*] Can you give the date of that case?—It was in the year 1849; it was during the spring assizes. I remember it perfectly well, because I happened to be sheriff of Somerset at the time.

2081. *Chairman.*] Do you think that the want of a police force is felt more by the poorer classes of society than any other?—I think it is in this instance; if a poor person wants a summons executed he must look up his halfcrown to the parish constable; whereas, if there is a policeman to serve it, he does it at once for nothing. I do not mean to charge the parish constables with neglect of duty or being unnecessarily harsh; but I know that that is the case.

2082. If an offence is committed and pursuit is necessary, that pursuit must be paid for by the parties robbed in the first instance?—Yes; the parish constable will not move till he gets his halfcrown.

2083. A poor man has not the facility of paying him that a rich man has?—No.

2084. Has not a rich man an opportunity of employing other parties, such as gamekeepers or servants, to aid the parish constables?—Yes.

2085. Therefore a rich man has facilities in the detection of crime if he is robbed, which a poor man does not possess, excepting under a good police system?—Certainly.

2086. Have you ever considered the subject of an uniform system of police being established throughout the country; do you think it would be desirable?—I think so; I have had an opportunity of seeing the working of the Irish constabulary, and I have often thought it was a pity that we had not an universal police on the same system all over England.

2087. If there were an uniform police system all over England, and crime was diminished in consequence, do not you think that in all counties the expense of the staff might be decreased?—Most decidedly.

2088. If it were universal, it would be generally cheaper?—I think so; I believe our police in Gloucestershire is considered an expensive police; in Gloucestershire the sub-constables range from 15 s. the second-class men, to 18 s. the first-class men, and 1 l. the serjeants. The chief constable has 506 l. 2 s. 6 d.; he has one deputy who has 116 l. 12 s. Three superintendents at 148 l. 11 s. each; seven inspectors at 135 l. 5 s. each, which includes a horse to each of those persons, which they provide themselves. Then there are 55 serjeants at 20 s. a week each; 120 first-class constables at 18 s.; and 55 second-class at 15 s.; which with clothing, boots and hats, amounts to about 16,500 l. per annum; that is about $2\frac{1}{4}$ d. in the pound, which is more than equal to the county rate.

2089. What boroughs are there in the county of Gloucester which have a police force?—I do not think there are above two that have a police force; Tewkesbury and Gloucester.

2090. Are the police force of any of those boroughs consolidated under the Act of Parliament with the police of the county?—Cheltenham, Stroud and Cirencester are; Gloucester and Tewkesbury stand by themselves.

2091. Can you state which of those boroughs was first consolidated with the county?—I believe all; Cheltenham is the head quarters of the police, where the chief constable resides.

2092. How soon after the establishment of the police in Gloucestershire was Cheltenham consolidated with the county?—I think about two years afterwards.

2093. When was Stroud consolidated with the county?— I think about the same time; the police was established before I became a resident magistrate in the county, two or three years.

2094. Do you think it would be desirable, if there were an uniform system of police, that the boroughs should be consolidated with the county?—I should say so, decidedly; we have a police in Bath; I have been a borough magistrate, and have acted occasionally, I do not act so much as I did. There was a very good police, but I do not think it is so good as it was; I think if that police were consolidated with the county it would be better for both the borough and the county.

G. W. Blathwayt,
Esq.

9 June 1853.

2095. Is not the Bath police under the direction of the watch committee?—It is, and I do not admire the direction; I think there is too much jobbing.

2096. Mr. *Sotheron.*] Is not the Bath police under a chief constable?—It is under a chief constable, but the chief constable is the subordinate of the watch committee.

2097. Do you suppose that the advantage of consolidating the police of the city of Bath with the police of the county would be, that the force would be placed under the superintendence of the chief constable, or under a different set of magistrates?—I think if the police of the city and the police of the county were all one it would work very well, as it is part of the county; the division for which I act is frequently obliged to avail itself of the assistance of the police at Bath.

2098. Mr. *Howard.*] Have you any check in Gloucestershire by which you ascertain that the policemen are upon night patrol?—We have; I will explain it: in each division probably there are at least three constables, that is, one serjeant and two men; those men are sent out to patrol six hours in the night. When a man goes out he is furnished with a ticket; this ticket is entered in a book; he is desired to go a particular house and leave this ticket, and two days following another policeman goes round to collect those tickets; those tickets are brought back and filed. In the course of the week the superintendent visits the station, and examines all the tickets in order to see that they are all delivered; my servant, if it is brought to my house, writes his name upon the back of it. Those particulars are stated in the reports, and then the reports are brought before the magistrates in petty sessions once a fortnight, and all the journals are open to their inspection.

2099. Do you find that there is much evasion of the duty?—No; there have been evasions; I recollect one evasion, in which an Irish serjeant sent a boy round with the tickets; the fraud was discovered, and the man was dismissed immediately. I consider the Gloucestershire policemen work very hard indeed; they are out every night for six hours, and they are frequently out on patrolling duty during the day. I should say that the district for which I act extends over an area of about 60,000 acres, containing a rural population of about 14,000; we have only 16 policemen at different stations, three and four to a station.

2100. Mr. *Sotheron.*] Are the Committee to understand that the Gloucestershire police is founded on the model of the Irish police?—Yes.

2101. Does not that system consist of having certain stations distributed over the county, and a certain number of policemen, under a superintendent, at each of those stations?—Yes; a serjeant or superintendent.

2102. Therefore the police stations would not necessarily be in the different parishes?—No.

2103. The parishes in fact come into a circle drawn round from the centre of the station; is that the Irish system?—I fancy it is.

2104. Have you had any experience in any other form of rural police, such as distributing the policemen in the different parishes?—I am not aware of that system.

2105. Therefore you are not in a condition to make a comparison between the two systems?—No.

2106. Speaking of that which is in Gloucestershire, you think it works very well?—Yes.

2107. Supposing a parish were four or five miles from a station, and a poor man lost a duck, in what way would he proceed to recover his property or detect the offender?—Frequently a man comes to me, and I give an order to the police, or he goes himself direct to the policeman.

2108. Whether you give him an order, or whether he goes himself, he would have to travel four or five miles in some cases?—Yes.

2109. So far as the distance is concerned, he is not so well off as when he had a parish constable at home?—He has a parish constable at home now to go with him.

2110. Have you had complaints made from persons who have suffered loss of having so far to go?—No, I have not.

2111. You do not think, taking a broad view of the system, that that is a disparagement to the efficiency of the police?—I do not think it is.

2112. With the same amount of efficiency, would you consider it an improvement to establish a policeman in every parish, or nearly so?—Certainly, the poor
would

G. W. Blathwayt, Esq.

9 June 1853.

would be benefited by that, if it did not make the policeman idle; probably the policeman would have too little to do.

2113. The efficiency of the force is the first point; supposing it could be shown that in a neighbouring county the policemen are found in the different parishes, would you think that was an improvement?—I do not think in our district each man is more than three miles from the station; I would observe that Mr. Lefroy, who has the charge of those police, and who has framed them upon the Irish constabulary, was for 20 years in the Irish constabulary.

2114. Mr. *Moody*.] In a large area of 60,000 acres, are all the police of the district concentrated at one point?—No, at different stations; a serjeant and two men at each station; at some stations there are more.

2115. What is the greatest distance which the night patrol would have to go?—I suppose he would patrol between three and four miles each way from the station.

2116. Lord *Lovaine*.] In the case which has been suggested of a poor man losing some trifling article, would it not be perfectly possible for him to apply to the policeman at the time he was making his rounds in the day?—It might happen that he would not come in the daytime.

2117. If he did he could make his case known?—Yes; and at all events he would have only three miles to go to the station.

2118. Mr. *Mackie*.] You are of opinion that a general system of police would be very desirable in England and Wales?—Decidedly so.

2119. Do you think a system of police such as that would enhance the value of property?—I think so.

2120. By giving greater security?—I think it would.

2121. Mr. *Moody*.] Do your parish constabulary serve any processes?—No; the police serve all the summonses, and everything; the only thing which the parish constabulary do is to give notice to the coroner for an inquest; if there is a case requiring an inquest, the parish constable is sent off by the church-wardens.

2122. Mr. *Phillips*.] Are you acquainted with the town police in Gloucester-shire?—In the town of Gloucester they have a police of their own. I do not know anything of them. I merely see them when I am going to the assizes.

2123. Mr. *Moody*.] Are not the police sent annually from Bath to Lands-downe fair?—We do so now.

2124. Who pays the police in that case?—They are paid by the borough, but the parishes make some allowance for refreshments in the case of the fair; but at the races the whole of the expense is paid from the race fund.

2125. Under a special Act?—The Bath police are employed under the 76th sec. 5 & 6 Will. 4, c. 76.

2126. Lord *Lovaine*.] Have you any personal knowledge of the manner in which the lighting and watching committee influence the management of the police in Bath?—I should say that the police in Bath are entirely in the hands of the watch committee.

2127. What are the evils of that system?—In the first place, I think that one of the greatest evils in Bath is, that the police there still retain their right of voting both at municipal and Parliamentary elections; the consequence is, that there is a good deal of jobbing, I had almost called it. I remember an instance in which a member of the watch committee had canvassed a policeman, and told him, "If you will support me as a member of the town council, I will do what I can to get you promoted when I get into the council."

John Thomson Gordon, Esq., called in; and Examined.

J. T. Gordon, Esq.

2128. *Chairman*.] YOU are the Sheriff of the City of Edinburgh?—I am.

2129. And Mid-Lothian?—Yes; the jurisdiction runs over both city and county.

2130. Will you shortly state to the Committee what the system of police generally in Scotland is?—The system of police in Scotland is different in the cities and the counties; the large cities, like Edinburgh and Glasgow, have police statutes of their own, under which their police is constituted. In the year 1839 there was an Act passed which permitted, but did not enjoin, the counties to levy assessments for maintaining a constabulary force; that was only permissive, and some counties have adopted the Act, and others have not.

J. T. Gordon, Esq.

9 June 1853.

2131. By whom was that discretion exercised?—By the commissioners of supply of the county.

2132. What are the duties of the commissioners of supply?—They are the proprietors; they are the heritors of the counties; freeholders, in fact.

2133. They are not necessarily magistrates?—No.

2134. In what counties under your immediate observation has that Act been adopted?—I know that a police force exists in Mid-Lothian, in Aberdeenshire, in Fife, in Stirling, in Dumfries, and, I believe, in many other counties.

2135. In which of those counties has that system of police come most under your observation?—In Mid-Lothian.

2136. What is the nature of the force in Mid-Lothian, and its extent?—The force in Mid-Lothian consists altogether of 31 persons.

2137. Will you state the population of Mid-Lothian?—The population of the county may be about 260,000, but from that number must be taken about 130,000 or 140,000 for the city of Edinburgh.

2138. The remainder would be rural district?—The remainder will be the rural district; that is about 120,000; but this includes several small towns or burghs, as Dalkeith, Musselburgh, Portobello.

2139. How many men have you for this district?—Thirty-one; there is one superintendent, one inspector and clerk, one serjeant, one criminal officer, two police serjeants, two first class constables, 18 second class constables, and four probationers; those are men that are on the move for promotion; and one messenger; that is the whole establishment.

2140. Has the superintendent the appointment of the subordinate officers?—Yes.

2141. What you call the superintendent would be the same description of officer as the chief constable of the counties in England?—I suppose so; perhaps I had better state, when it is resolved in any county (I am now speaking more particularly of Mid-Lothian) to raise this constabulary force, a county meeting appoints what is called a police committee, and that police committee appoints a superintendent, the head of the police, and maintains a general superintendence over the whole force, although practically it never interferes with any of his appointments, unless there is some gross case of mismanagement to call for their interference.

2142. The appointments would rest with the superintendents, subject to the approbation of this committee?—Yes; I may perhaps as well say also, that practically the appointments are made with the approbation of the sheriff of the county, who is the chairman of the police committee.

2143. Is the chairman of that committee appointed from the commissioners of supply?—Yes.

2144. What number of commissioners of supply is there in Mid-Lothian?—I can hardly tell you; they are a very numerous body; the police committee varies from 12 to 14 members; a list of the commissioners of supply I think is annually published.

2145. Lord *Lovaine*.] What are the duties of the criminal officer?—His duty is principally, I think, that of a detective officer.

2146. Does the criminal officer go round to all the courts of petty sessions?—There are only two places in which courts are held for the trial of offences in Mid-Lothian, one in Edinburgh and the other in Dalkeith, about eight miles from Edinburgh.

2147. Can you explain a little further the duties of the criminal officer?—His duties being regulated under the direction of the superintendent, I cannot precisely define them.

2148. Mr. *Fitzroy*.] Does this man take any part in the duties of the constabulary?—He is employed when he is needed; he is generally resident in Edinburgh.

2149. You have stated that the Edinburgh police was a separate body?—Quite.

2150. But still under your jurisdiction?—In combination with the magistrates of the city.

2151. Lord *Lovaine*.] Does not there arise considerable confusion and impediment in the administration of justice from those two separate bodies being engaged in the same purpose?—No; because under the Act of Parliament, a copy of which I have here, constituting the city police, the police boundaries are so clearly marked that there is no conflict of jurisdiction or any annoyance.

2152. Is

J. T. Gordon. Esq.

9 June 1852.

2152. Is there any jealousy existing between the forces?—I dare say there is a little jealousy; I am bound to say that the county police are much superior men to the city police.

2153. From what does that arise?—From the greater care in the selection of the men, from higher pay, and also from the superintendence generally of the whole body being very different in the one case from the other.

2154. From which I conclude you are of opinion that the body which has the power of appointing and managing the police in Edinburgh is not a proper one?— I do not think it is a proper body for that purpose.

2155. On what account?—It is a body called the police commission, consisting of 32 members, who are annually elected to represent different wards in the city; it is a body elected every year by a popular election, and although the head of the commission is stated in this Act to be the Lord Provost, or, in his absence, the sheriff of the county, there is much divided superintendence, not very easily reconcilable with the duties of a very efficient police force.

2156. Do you apprehend that a considerable amount of jobbing goes on?—I should not certainly use the word jobbing; but there are obvious reasons to show that it is an improper body to manage the police; and that the superintendent of the city police is necessarily subject to influences from which such an officer should be free.

2157. Do you believe that 31 constables are sufficient to carry on their duty in a population as large as 120,000?—I should say it is not a sufficient force; especially for night patrolling, if that were necessary.

2158. Do you believe night patrolling to be necessary?—I think certainly it is very necessary.

2159. Is there much complaint of the weight of the assessment?—No, there is not; the whole amount of the assessment is 2,047 *l.* 14 *s.* 6 *d.* for the whole expense of the establishment of the county constabulary.

2160. Amounting to a rate in the pound of how much?—I cannot exactly tell you what the rate is; but I think 2 *d.* in the pound sterling.

2161. Mr. *Mackie*.] Are not the assessments in Scotland laid upon the old valuation?—Yes, generally, I believe they are.

2162. The assessment of 2,000 *l.* odd is passed on the 30th of April annually? —Yes.

2163. Upon what property is that laid?—It is laid upon all the landward part of the county, excluding Edinburgh and Leith and Portobello.

2164. Is it not chiefly upon the landed property?—Yes.

2165. What does a shopkeeper in Edinburgh, with 1,000 *l.* or 1,500 *l.* worth of goods in his shop, pay upon that assessment?—Nothing; but a shopkeeper in Edinburgh has to pay for the city police; the burden undoubtedly falls upon the land.

2166. Is not that the principal cause of some of the most important counties in Scotland not having adopted the police system?—I dare say that is one of their main reasons.

2167. Did not that cause operate in Lanarkshire and Renfrewshire?—Lanark-shire I know has refused to adopt the police over and over again.

2168. Lord *Lovaine*.] Has the establishment of police caused a great diminu-tion of crime in the county of Mid-Lothian?—I have not a doubt that the estab-lishment of police in the county of Mid-Lothian has been attended with a great repression and diminution of crime.

2169. What counties are there adjoining Mid-Lothian, which have not a police force?—Lanark.

2170. Confine yourself to the county of Lanark, where there is no police; do you think there is more crime in that county, where there is no police, than in Mid-Lothian, where there is a police?—I have not the slightest hesitation in say-ing that I think there is a greater amount of crime over the border; it is not very easy to exaggerate the state of matters upon the borders of the county.

2171. Lord *Advocate*.] The county of Lanark adjoins Edinburgh?—Yes; I am now speaking of the parts of Lanark which adjoin Mid-Lothian.

2172. What is the state of matters there?—There are seasons of the year when there are very large bands of poachers, who come regularly across the border from Lanark into Mid-Lothian and commit great depredations. I am not entitled to speak from my personal knowledge, but I believe the depredations that are carried on in that part of Lanark upon the farm-houses and dwellings about the country are to an extent that it would be very difficult indeed to exaggerate. That I speak of upon the report of Lanarkshire gentlemen, not of my own knowledge.

2173. *Chairman.*] Have you reason to believe that that is the fact?—Every reason.

2174. *Lord Advocate.*] Do you find that criminals escape across the border from your jurisdiction into Lanarkshire?—Unquestionably they do; and that thieves come thence into Mid-Lothian

2175. Are not those parts of Lanark and Peebles the haunts of thieves who have been expelled from the countie   ere there is a police force?—Very frequently indeed.

2176. *Mr. Fitzroy.*] Is the superintendent of the police of the city of Edinburgh removable by the police committee?—He is appointed and removed by the Lord Provost and the Sheriff of Mid-Lothian; if they differ, then the ultimate decision of the appointment rests with the Lord Advocate of Scotland; he is the arbitrator between the two.

2177. Is the superintendent totally free from the control of the police committee?—So far, that his appointment is made not by the police commission, but by those two magistrates.

2178. Has he the power of nominating the men under his control?—Yes.

2179. And of dismissing them?—Yes.

2180. Irrespective of any recommendation or advice from the police committee?—Certainly.

2181. Lord *Lovaine.*] Under those circumstances, if he is a perfectly independent officer, it does not appear that there should be any pressure which would affect him?—It is not perhaps very easy to explain in a few sentences how it is, but there are so many masters in one respect holding the purse-strings, with a superintendence going on at all times of the different departments of the institution, that it is not very difficult to see that the superintendent of police is not so independent as in my opinion he should be.

2182. Mr. *Fitzroy.*] Does his salary depend upon the police commission?—The minimum of the salary is fixed by the Act of Parliament; by the 73d section of the statute it is enacted, that the salary to be paid to the superintendent of police shall not be less than 300 *l.* per annum.

2183. What does he now receive?—Three hundred and fifty pounds.

2184. Who fixed that increase?—That increase was fixed by the vote of the police commissioners, but upon the recommendation of the Lord Provost and the sheriff.

2185. Would the police commissioners have the power of reducing his salary to the minimum?—They cannot reduce it lower than 300 *l.* a year, but to that sum they may at any time reduce it.

2186. Lord *Lovaine.*] What power have the police commissioners over the private constables and the serjeants?—The superintendent has the entire control, speaking generally; but the number and remuneration of the force may be altered at any time by the commissioners.

2187. Mr. *Sotheron.*] You think that there is grea disorder in Lanarkshire, at least on its borders, as compared with Mid-Lothian?—Unquestionably; I should say so.

2188. You say that the proposition for establishing a paid police in Lanarkshire has often been mooted and always rejected?—So I have understood.

2189. Can you give the Committee any reason why it should have been so rejected, except upon the ground of expense?—I do not know that   am entitled to speak to the reasons which have actuated the landholders in Lanarkshire; I have no connexion with that county whatever; I know at this moment as a fact, that they very often send in times of trouble requisitions to the city police of Glasgow to obtain assistance from them, which would have been hardly required if there had been a constabulary force constituted in the county.

2190. Are the Committee to understand that whatever the expense may be of this paid police force, it is entirely raised from the land, as distinguished from trades or houses?—Yes.

2191. Consequently, the 2,000 *l.* paid in Mid-Lothian, though a very small amount of rate in the pound, is not paid by those persons exclusively who obtain the advantages to be derived from the existence of a police force?—No.

2192. Is not that one great reason why they do not establish a police force in Lanarkshire?—

Lanarkshire?—I think I have already said that that operates in some counties as *J. T. Gordon, Esq.* a reason for not establishing a police force.

2193. Mr. *Mackie*.] Are you of opinion that an uniform system of amalgamated police force in the whole of Scotland would be desirable?—I have not the least doubt of it.

9 June 1853.

2194. In your opinion would it enhance the value of property, from giving greater security?—I can state that in the county of Mid-Lothian property has risen in value, and that sales have been effected upon the strength of the police reports made on the state of the district. As to the uniformity of the system, perhaps you will allow me to mention, that at present, as I said before, there are various counties in Scotland which have adopted the Act of 2 & 3 Vict. c. 65; the rates of payment or remuneration of the police are very different; it has frequently occurred that an application has been made to Mr. List, the superintendent of the county of Mid-Lothian, for men to be drafted to other counties, in consequence of their experience and training enabling them to do good elsewhere; the answer has been frequently on the part of those men, " We are not going to change from a very good force into one that is much worse, and where the pay is so much lower, and there is no hope of promotion."

2195. Mr. *Fitzroy*.] What is the number of police in the city of Edinburgh?—Three hundred and twelve.

2196. *Chairman*.] Can you tell the Committee the amount of police assessment for the city of Edinburgh?—The amount of police assessment for the city of Edinburgh, for the year ending Whit Sunday 1852, was 35,963 *l*. 19 *s*. 5 *d*.; but this includes cleaning, lighting, and other departments, besides watching.

2197. Mr. *Fitzroy*.] You are nominally the head both of the watching committee and also the head of the police commission, but you state that jealousies do exist, you think, to a certain extent between the two forces?—I think they may to a small extent.

2198. Do you think that jealousies exist to a sufficient extent to frustrate the ends of justice?—Certainly not.

2199. Do you think that the jealousy would be very much done away with if they were both put under the same superintendent?—I do not think I can safely say that jealousy exists to that extent; I do not feel it would be a very easy thing to amalgamate those two forces under one head, because in such a city as Edinburgh the duties of the superintendent of the city police are so onerous, that I should hesitate a little before adding to the duties which now devolve upon him.

2200. You think the charge of 342 men and the area of ground which those men cover would be too much for one head constable to superintend?—As the office is at present constituted I think it would, on this account, that the superintendent of the city police is also the public prosecutor of all police cases; he is obliged at the end of each day to prepare the charges which are to be brought into the police court the next morning, and superintend the prosecution of those cases before the Judge. I know that that is a task which takes up a very great deal of time, and often tries his strength very much.

2201. Supposing that the chief constable remained with his existing duties in Edinburgh, and that there were an assistant superintendent who acted under him to superintend the whole of the force, do you think that would facilitate the administration of justice?—I do not know that there would be practically any objection to that; it might get rid of some of the jealousies which do exist, though I do not think they are very serious at this moment.

2202. Do you not think that the detection of crime would be very much facilitated by the two forces working thoroughly in a good spirit together?—I cannot doubt that it would be so.

2203. That would be very much brought about by the forces being placed under one head, would it not?—I beg to state that personally I have no objection to seeing the two forces under one head.

2204. Do you think the facilities in the detection of crime would be so much increased as to enable a reduction in the number of constables to meet the extra expense of an assistant superintendent?—I am not prepared to say that there could be much reduction, because I for one believe that the establishment of the city police is by a great deal too small in point of number.

2205. Sir *J. Anderson*.] Do you think it an advantage to have the city police under the police commission rather than under the town council or the magistrates?—

J. T. Gordon, Esq.

9 June 1853.

trates?—I am bound to say that it is my firm belief that it would be for the public advantage if the police commission did not exist.

2206. *Lord Advocate.*] In your opinion, is not the police commission a body very little calculated to manage the police department with efficiency?—I think I have already stated that it is not by any means the body the best calculated to administer such affairs as those of police.

2207. Mr. *Fitzroy.*] Is there any qualification requisite to enable a person to serve upon the police commission?—Commissioners must be electors within the ward, whose houses, shops, &c. are valued at least at 15 *l.* of actual yearly rent.

2208. Sir *J. Anderson.*] Do you think the power of the police commission should be vested in the town council?—I have not the least hesitation in saying that it ought, in preference to a separate police commission.

2208. Mr. *Fitzroy.*] Are any of the members of the town council members of the police commission?—They are.

2210. *Lord Advocate.*] Will you state to the Committee generally your view of what a uniformly organised system of police throughout Scotland ought to be, and on what principles it should be maintained?—I should say if you still keep for the great cities a separate police, it would be better to let that be administered by a committee, consisting of magistrates of the city, and the sheriff, and one of the sheriff substitutes; that in each county there should be a police committee; and I should almost like to propose, if it were possible, that *ex officio* the Lord-advocate and the Solicitor-general should be members of every such committee throughout Scotland, or that the sheriff, who might communicate with them directly, should be *ex officio* chairman, because, I was going to conclude by saying, that I think there ought to be a certain payment out of the Consolidated Fund for the establishment of an uniform system of police, and if that were so, there would require to be some kind of control, and some means of knowledge on the part of the Crown as to how the funds were administered, and how the force was maintained.

2211. Lord *Lovaine.*] What powers would you give to the watching committee?—Very much the powers which they now have.

2212. Would you give them the power of interfering with the pay of the private constables, or the pay of the superintendents?—You cannot very well regulate it in any other way, unless you leave it in the discretion of some single public officer, which I am afraid is not a very easy thing to manage.

2213. Sir *J. Anderson.*] Would you suggest that the committee should be selected by the commissioners of supply?—They should be appointed as they are in Mid-Lothian; each committee is nominated on the 30th of April.

2214. If you propose to make the assessment more general, do you think the commissioners of supply would still be the proper body to appoint?—If you are going to change the basis of the assessment, and bring it upon the shops and other tenements, that would open a larger question; I am only speaking of things upon their present footing.

2215. *Lord Advocate.*] Do you think a general system would be much more economical, as well as more efficient, than the system which prevails at present?—I have no doubt it would.

2216. Mr. *Fitzroy.*] You have stated that in Mid-Lothian the assessment is not complained of as being too heavy?—I am not aware that it is.

2217. In the event of a general system being introduced throughout the whole of the kingdom, would not a reduction of the police be the necessary consequence in many counties, so that the assessment would be comparatively lighter?—Everything might be easier than at present, when many counties have no police, or a different assessment.

2218. Consequently there is much greater difficulty, and a more arduous duty falling upon those constables who are appointed?—Unquestionably, and upon the counties which have a police, in the rating to maintain the constabulary.

2219. You have stated that the value of land is enhanced by the establishment of a police force?—Yes.

2220. Taking those two facts into consideration, is not it to be inferred that the advantages to be derived from a general system would more than counterbalance any extra charge upon the counties?—I should say so, without any hesitation.

2221. Mr. *Howard.*] What system is adopted in the counties where a police force has not been introduced; are constables appointed?—There are some sheriff officers, and there may be parish constables in those counties.

2222. Mr.

J. T. Gordon, Esq.

9 June 1853.

2222. Mr. *Sotheron.*] Do you mean that in Lanark there is no constabulary force of any description?—In a large part of Lanark there is no police such as we have been speaking of; Glasgow has a large force; in the upper ward of Lanark they frequently send messengers to Glasgow for assistance to check disturbances.

2223. In those counties in Scotland where there is no paid police force, what is the ordinary constabulary force for the administration of justice?—There are, as I said just now, some sheriff officers, and perhaps parish constables.

2224. Mr. *Howard.*] You have said that you thought it would be desirable to introduce an uniform system all over Scotland; do you think that is requisite in the thinly peopled districts?—I should say so; even under the Act to which I have before referred, there is a clause enacting that it shall be lawful for one or more counties to unite in taking measures for establishing a county force; if the system were still more uniform than that, you might make arrangements by which two counties, by combining together, would have a force applicable to each other.

2225. You have said that a good system of patrols is required; do you propose to establish patrols over the moors?—That must be judged of very much by the superintendent of the police of the district.

2226. Lord *Advocate.*] It is only at certain times of the year, and under certain circumstances, that you would require patrolling in the moors?—Yes.

2227. Mr. *Howard.*] Would it not be necessary in those districts to build a great number of stations?—That will depend upon the nature of the county the police have to traverse; if it is a thinly inhabited county, and there is nothing very tempting to depredators, it may not be necessary to have those stations so numerous or the patrols so frequent.

Edwin Corbett, Esq., called in; and Examined.

2228. *Chairman.*] ARE you a Magistrate for Cheshire?—I am.

E. Corbett, Esq.

2229. Are you the chairman of the Court of Quarter Sessions?—No, I am not; I have acted as vice chairman for some few years.

2230. Have you taken considerable interest in the police in Cheshire?—Yes; we have two Acts in Cheshire; in consequence of finding how ineffectual the first was for the purpose for which it was intended, last year I prevailed upon the magistrates to apply for a revision of the Act, and we obtained a new Act in 1852.

2231. Will you state the date of the first Act?—The 1st June 1829; this Act was passed with the approbation of Sir Robert Peel, who at that time was very anxious to introduce a police force into the country, and he was glad of this experiment being tried in Cheshire, and he gave all the encouragement he could to the passing of this Bill.

2232. You are perfectly aware that your Act of 1829 having been in operation 10 years in the year 1839, was one material element in the information which was given to the Commission which was appointed, of which the Speaker was the chairman?—I presume it was.

2233. Will you state what the system of police was, under that first Act?—Under this first Act, and it is similar now, we have no general superintendent of the police, but we have one special high constable for each hundred, or each petty sessional division; in the hundred of Macclesfield there are three high constables; that is a very populous manufacturing part of the county. The petty sessional divisions are divided into three, and there is one for each division; we have one high constable for each of the other hundreds in the county. The appointment of the constable is rested upon the recommendation of the magistrates in petty sessions to the quarter sessions, and then they are appointed for certain townships, but at the time of the passing of this Act there was a considerable jealousy on the part of some gentlemen in Cheshire. In 1829 there was a good deal of opposition made to the Bill, in consequence of their thinking it not right that the townships should be charged for the payment of the constables except with their own consent. The impression was that there should be limited payment in each township. I beg to observe, that the parishes in Cheshire are many of them extremely large; the townships are similar to parishes in other counties, in every respect; the poor rates, highway rates, and everything else, there being a jealousy in charging the township, without the approbation of the township itself. The payment of each constable was limited to 20 *l.*, and the consequence was that

E. Corbett, Esq.

9 June 1853.

the force was very ineffective, as I can show by the population and the value of the property in particular townships; some townships were unfairly charged, to make up the salary of a constable, but not in the same proportion according to the value of the property; they were forced to be charged a higher rate to make up the salary of 50 *l.* a year to the constable. Therefore I suggested to the magistrates in quarter sessions last year, that it would be very desirable to pay the constables by a hundred rate. I can state many instances where it operated very unfavourably; and perhaps it would be as well that I should state the particulars now before I go on, if it is the wish of the Committee. I can show an instance where a township is valued at a very large sum, namely, at 63,000 *l.* a year; and another township is attached to that which is only assessed at 16,000 *l.*; it would be impossible to put any rate upon that township proportionately to make up the salary for the constable. Therefore we went to Parliament last year, and we obtained another Act which makes it a hundred rate, and not a township rate, and we find it works remarkably well. It was originally paid out of the poor's rate; now by the hundred rate the hundreds are assessed according to their proportion, and I think it seems to have given very general satisfaction as a system of working the police. I have got a letter from the clerk of the peace which he wrote to me unasked, in which he says that it acts a great deal better than where the constables are under a superintendent for the whole county. They are therefore separate jurisdictions, the high constables being of course in constant communication with the magistrates of the hundred; the police of every hundred is entirely a separate thing, the constables under the Act of 1829 were forced to be appointed for particular townships. Now they are appointed for the whole hundred, and the magistrates appoint the particular districts to which they are immediately to give their attention; for instance, in some cases, two constables will have a jurisdiction in the same township. We do that from local knowledge, so as to make the police as effective as possible.

2234. Mr. *Phillips.*] How many hundreds are there in the county of Chester?—Seven; one hundred is in three divisions.

2235. Mr. *Sotheron.*] In each of those hundreds are the police under the superintendence of one chief constable?—We have no chief constable at all, nor do I think it is at all requisite. I think it works well as independent jurisdictions, the circumstances of the several divisions being so different. From the experience I have had for many years, I do not think it is possible for any police force to work better than it does.

2236. *Chairman.*] You say it works independently; what is the distinction between the hundreds?—In the first place, some of them are entirely agricultural districts; they do not vary so much in point of size, but I will show the difference of value of the different hundreds, which perhaps will give you some information.

2237. Will you take the case of a manufacturing hundred and an agricultural hundred?—The Macclesfield hundred is rated at 537,699 *l.*; it is divided into three divisions; the lowest is Broxton, which is wholly an agricultural district; in point of acreage there is very little difference. Broxton hundred is rated at 118,281 *l.*

2238. Mr. *Sotheron.*] Will you be so good as to state generally the difference of the acreage between those two hundreds?—Macclesfield hundred is 110,113, Broxton is 68,793.

2239. Therefore, in order to make a comparison, you ought to look at Broxton as about 200,000?—No, it will not be double by a great deal.

2240. *Chairman.*] That is on account of the difference of the population, the one being purely a manufacturing hundred and the other an agricultural hundred; you think it is desirable that they should be under separate jurisdictions?—I think if they were all agricultural it works better, and more within itself, and more satisfactorily in general, than if they were always subject to one superintendent. I do not know it from experience, but I cannot conceive that one superintendent can have that supervision of the force which is requisite.

2241. Have you had any experience of one superintendent over a county force? —No further than what I have heard, from which I do not think I am much in favour of it.

2242. Have you a separate police for each hundred?—Yes.

2243. Who is at the head of that police?—The high constable.

2244. Is he a paid officer?—Yes, appointed under this Act of Parliament.

2245. Do

2245. Do you employ parochial constables at all?—Very little indeed; the police do all the work.

2246. You rely entirely upon the paid constabulary?—Entirely; in fact we have done so since the year 1829.

2247. Mr. *Phillips.*] Can you give the population of those two districts?—Not under the last census. At the census of 1841 the Macclesfield hundred was 178,117, and Broxton was 16,233; the population has not extended to any great degree; if anything, it has a little increased in Broxton, but it would be very much increased in the Macclesfield hundred.

2248. Mr. *Sotheron.*] Will you state to the Committee, shortly, the mode in which the constables in the different hundreds are disciplined, and under what supervision they are placed?—They are under the supervision of the high constable, who visits them very frequently; I believe not less than once a week.

2249. Is he a paid officer?—Yes, he is a paid officer. In the Macclesfield hundred the salaries are rather higher. If the Committee wish, I can give the number of the police constables in the several hundreds. In the Broxton hundred there is one high constable at a salary of 80*l.*, and an allowance of 60*l.* for the purchase of a horse and cart, and the keep of the horse. There are six assistant petty constables at 52*l.* a year each. In the Macclesfield hundred, Prestbury division, there is one high constable at 170*l.*, including the horse; he has eight assistant petty constables at 60*l.*, and one at 52*l.* In Macclesfield hundred, Stockport division, you observe the constables are not quite so numerous as you would be led to suppose are requisite. Stockport and Macclesfield have their own separate police; the special high constable has 170*l.*; eight petty constables, 60*l.*; and one, 10*l.*; this man is also paid a salary as lock-up keeper under the county rate.

2250. *Chairman.*] You have mentioned that Stockport and Macclesfield have an independent police; will you tell the Committee whether under the Act of last year, or under the Act of 1829, you have any power of incorporating the police of those boroughs with the county police?—The boroughs that have a separate police do not pay towards the constabulary rate of the hundred; in the Macclesfield hundred, Hyde division, the high constable has 190*l.* a year; five petty constables at 60*l.*; three at 50*l.*, and one at 40*l.*

2251. Mr. *Sotheron.*] Do those three divisions constitute the hundred of Macclesfield?—Those three divisions constitute the whole of the hundred of Macclesfield.

2252. Have you now given the force for the Macclesfield and Broxton hundreds?—Yes.

2253. Mr. *Fitzroy.*] What is the number of the Macclesfield borough police?—Macclesfield has 13; Stockport, 11; Birkenhead, 30; Chester, 20; and Congleton, 8. The total of our constables are 9 high constables and 69 petty constables. The way in which the other Act worked in the Hyde division, in fact, generally speaking, in the Macclesfield hundred, it was impossible, from the salary in each township or parish being limited to 20*l.*, that they could appoint as many constables as they positively required. In Dukinfield, where they have no constable in their own township, they have only a part of one; two or three other townships were forced to contribute to have a petty constable; our petty constables amount to 91.

2254. Lord *Lovaine.*] Are they all governed by the same internal regulations?—Yes, they are. I have a book, which perhaps the Committee may desire to retain, being the instructions which are issued by the court of quarter sessions to the constabulary force. (*The Witness delivered in the same.*)

2255. Is not the force of 12 policemen for Stockport ridiculously small?—I think it may be; but the county have nothing to do with it.

2256. Are you of opinion that it would be an advantage to the public if these boroughs were placed under the same management with regard to the police as that which the county is under?—I do not know that it would, because there is a sufficiency of constables in the county; I am not well acquainted with the Macclesfield hundred, but I should think there were enough constables to do all the rural work; those parties who are wanted for the town police I should conceive are always better under the control of the town, which, if it were made a general thing for the whole of the county, they could not be.

2257. Are you aware that the metropolitan police force comprises a distance of 13 miles around London?—That is a regular organized police, and more completely organized than we should be able to establish in the rural districts.

E. Corbett, Esq

9 June 1853.

E. Corbett, Esq.

9 June 1853.

2258. Mr. *Fitzroy*.] Do none of those 91 police constables do any duty in the boroughs?—I fancy not in the boroughs; they are not precluded from the boroughs; they are not under the control and the authority of the boroughs, but only of the county magistrates.

2259. Are there no instances in which they act with the borough police?—I think they do upon particular occasions; I cannot speak positively about that. Chester has a separate jurisdiction, and the county constabulary has no power within the city of Chester.

2260. *Chairman*.] In your opinion you would prefer a system of constabulary separate in each hundred in your county, under a superintendent, to having a a consolidated county police under one head?—I think it decidedly operates better.

2261. Mr. *Sotheron*.] Will you state to the Committee the reasons why you think so?—I think you have always a responsible officer upon the spot, and a man who is only acting under one general superintendent in the county is not in a position to be so responsible to his superiors, though there should be a super-intendent of police, for not doing his duty. I do not think he would be so independent a person; he could not act upon his own authority if he was under a superintendent.

2262. Did you not say that you thought the circumstances of the county of Chester rendered this institution advisable, although it might not be advisable elsewhere?—I think it is the best system of police, in my opinion, that can be established.

2263. Are you of opinion that in an entirely rural county a division in hun-dreds, with a separate police in each division, would be better than having the police all under one authority?—I think so, because the officers are under the superintendence of resident magistrates; and from the reports which the men are obliged to make, the magistrates see whether those people are active and attend to their duty; they see the magistrates constantly, and I think they are better acquainted with what is going on than one superintendent of police in a county could be with what his subordinates were doing.

2264. Do you mean that practically the magistrates are acquainted with all the movements of these constables from week to week?—No, not exactly; I know, as far as my hundred goes, we hear from time to time whether the constable is visiting his different posts from different parties, and from personal inquiries.

2265. Do you know whether your constables patrol at night?—Yes, they do.

2266. Who ascertains whether they perform their duties at night?—The only way in which it is done is this: they are obliged to keep regular routes of what they do, and of such parties as they meet; those are received by the high con-stable every week, and if he has any opportunity he makes inquiry of those parties; or if he has any reason to believe they are not doing their duty, he then would go to those parties whom the constable says he has met upon the road; that is frequently done; I mean from the different residents in different parts of the country, where the constables have attended upon their duties. They go round to farm-houses. An instance was mentioned to me the other week, that a man had not locked up his cheese-room; fortunately there were no rogues there, but there might have been; and the constable called him up, and told him of it.

2267. Are the regulations of the different hundreds identical?—Yes. I have just handed in a copy of the orders and regulations of the police; there was one drawn up by a barrister, a chairman of the court of quarter sessions, and we had a committee some time ago to revise the rules; they were printed the year before last.

2268. Is there any supervision over the high constables of the different hun-dreds to see that they adhere to these rules?—None, but of the magistrates of the hundreds.

2269. Practically, you trust to the magistrates of the different hundreds to see that the high constables and the other constables under them are doing their duty?—Yes; I have every reason to think that that supervision is well attended to.

2270. *Chairman*.] Do you know the cost of the whole force?—£.6,461.

2271. Do you know what the rate is in the pound?—I cannot tell you exactly; I can tell you what the amount of the valuation is, which is only waiting for confirmation at the next quarter sessions; it amounts to 1,675,458*l*.

2272. Mr. *Burroughes*.] What is the amount in the pound?—I cannot tell you; I have given you the total.

2273. Sir *J. Trollope.*] Have you not some other source from which you derive a portion of those payments?—No; it is from the hundred rate entirely.

2274. Do you raise each rate from the hundred separately?—Yes.

2275. Not equally in the whole county?—No; some of these hundreds require a more expensive police; in the rural districts they pay less.

2276. Is that the reason you give the preference to the system which you have adopted in Cheshire?—In fact, there was no reason for adopting this particular plan in the year 1829, any further than it was considered requisite that there should be a police force; we had further powers by the Act of last year, and we had found it work extremely well, and I know that it is the opinion of the magistrates of the county; they prefer it to the Rural Police Act. I was so taken by the passing of the Rural Police Act, that I brought a proposition twice before the quarter sessions that it should be adopted in the county of Chester, and I was beaten by a large majority. There is one objection, I think, to the Rural Police Act, namely, that the policemen should be in uniform. It may be very useful in towns, where there a great number of police always parading about, but in the country, where they are only moving about the county, and particularly when they have any object in view, they should pass unobserved, which at other times they would not. I know several instances in which constables have gone to watch at night, when a burglary has been suspected, and where they have been successful in apprehending the burglars; if two or three policemen had been found coming to a given point, there would have been an alarm raised, but a man in coloured clothes could come without exciting any observation.

2277. Lord *Lovaine.*] Is it not rather an advantage that a burglary should not be committed?—Decidedly; but you cannot apprehend a man that is going to commit a burglary.

2278. May you not prevent it?—I do not know; if four or five extremely bad characters were seen going to a particular place, and it was suspected that they were about to commit a robbery, if they met a policeman in uniform I dare say they would turn round and go home. It strikes me as much more advisable, if these men are bent upon committing a burglary, that they should be apprehended. Another burglary was proved against these men, which had been committed a short time before, a few miles off.

2279. Mr. *Burroughes.*] Do you not think it better that crime should be prevented by the fear of detection, than that it should be committed and the criminal apprehended?—Decidedly; if you can by moral force prevent the perpetration of crime, it is extremely desirable; I think there can be no doubt about it.

George Kitson, Esq., called in; and Examined.

2280. *Chairman.*] ARE you a Magistrate for the county of Somerset?—Yes.

2281. And also have been Mayor of Bath?—Yes; and I am a member of the watch committee of the city of Bath, and have been for years.

2282. Is not the police of the city of Bath entirely under the control of the watch committee?—Entirely.

2283. Is the police of Bath in an efficient state?—I should say it is; my own opinion would be, that a short time since it was more efficient than it is at present.

2284. Have you found, as a member of the watch committee and mayor of Bath, any inconvenience to arise from the police being under the control of the watch committee?—When I was the mayor of Bath it was under the old system, before the Municipal Act.

2285. As a member of the watch committee, are you of opinion that there is any practical inconvenience from the police being under the control of the watch committee?—Practically I believe the inconvenience to be little. It is unnecessary to state to the Committee, that in all boroughs political bias will obtain; and in Bath we have as much to do with politics as most other places; still my opinion is, that under all the circumstances, whether one party or another were supreme in the town, there has been so much discretion shown in the election of the members of the watch committee, that I am not aware of any considerable inconvenience arising from the mode in which the police is conducted.

2286. Mr. *Fitzroy.*] You stated just now that the police had been, in your opinion, more efficient than they are at present; can you give any reason for the

G. Kitson, Esq.

9 June 1853.

falling off in its efficiency?—We have reduced our police somewhat, though not considerably, but below what I should consider to be well.

2287. What was the cause of that reduction?—Merely a wish for economy, and nothing further.

2288. When was that reduction made?—It has been but a slight reduction, within the last year.

2289. Do you attribute any alteration in the efficiency of the force to the change of the superintendent, or simply to the reduction of the number?—My own opinion is, that our late superintendent was peculiarly fitted for his position. He was a man in every way particularly well qualified. I do not know that you have a right to expect that all men in that situation should be as well qualified as I consider him to be. I do not consider our present superintendent to be inefficient, but I cannot consider him to be so efficient as our late superintendent.

2290. To what amount have you reduced the force?—Not above three during the last year. I should state that the late superintendent made a reduction in point of number, and with the full sanction of the watch committee; but the watch committee considered that the duty was quite as efficiently performed with fewer men on Mr. Oakley's suggestion as before with a greater number.

2291. You do not find that the duty is as efficiently performed now?—Perhaps that would be going too far; I think the number is lower than it should be.

2292. Was it in consequence of any representation from the inhabitants of Bath that you reduced the number?—No, certainly not; it arose from this, that there were out-stations, one of which it was considered might be given up; at that out-station there was a man, having the rank of a sergeant, whom we withdrew, and one police constable, and there was also one man reduced from another station which was not discontinued.

2293. What is the amount of your police rate in the pound?—Four-pence farthing. I must take care not to mislead the Committee in this respect; the police rate is assessed at, say 4¼d. in the pound, but that does not cover the whole expense of the police; the police rate and the borough rate are in fact assessed on the same property; there are 4,423 l. regularly collected in the form of police rate; the deficiency I believe, amounts to between 500 l. and 600 l. a year, which has been paid from the borough rate. The Committee will understand that the parties contributing to each rate are the same, and the properties are assessed in the same way; it is a mere difference in name.

2294. What is the object in having that distinction?—I know it has been from the very commencement; I will leave the Committee to understand why it is done under the Municipal Act; and we have had the sanction of our legal advisers.

2295. Has there been any objection made to the amount of the police rate as it stands now?—No, I am not aware that there has; there will be always people who object to expenses of every kind; there has been no decided objection to the police rate, or to the manner in which this rate has been levied; it has been done so, I might say, from the commencement, and the deficiency in the 4,400 l. has been collected as a borough rate. I am not quite sure that it may not arise from another circumstance. There is a neighbouring ward, the ward of Lyncombe and Widcombe, where they had not originally watching or lighting, and the council took upon themselves to furnish a watch and light in the parish of Lyncombe and Widcombe, and assess the parish at a certain amount, and certainly for some years (it no longer exists) the borough was assessed, I might say illegally, for lighting the adjoining parish of Lyncombe and Widcombe; it is very likely between 500 l. and 600 l. a year; I know that it came to that; and the deficiency may be accounted for in that way.

2296. Was any objection made on the part of the members of the watch committee to the reduction of the men?—None whatever; it was done with the full consent of the watch committee, at the recommendation of the chief of police.

2297. How are the watch committee appointed?—Under the Act of Parliament, by the council.

2298. Are they elected?—The town council are called on every year to elect the watch committee; that watch committee has discretionary power; they are elected for that year, and have the supreme power over the police, I might say, except over the funds; for the expenses they must have the sanction of the council.

2299. Is there any qualification necessary to becoming a member of the watch committee?—

committee?—No further than the qualification of a councillor; any alderman or councillor is qualified for the watch committee.

G. Kitson, Esq.

9 June 1853.

2300. Lord *Lovaine*.] Has there been any reduction of the police subsequently to the appointment of your new superintendent?—Yes; it has been done within the last year, arising from the circumstance of one of the police stations being given up, and one man taken from another station.

2301. The reduction was not made upon the recommendation of the late superintendent?—It was done on the recommendation of the present superintendent.

2302. Mr. *Fitzroy*.] What was your force prior to the reduction?—The force is at present 84; 87 was the force before the reduction; that includes the superintendent, serjeants, and everything.

2303. What is the population of Bath?—According to the late census, we have not much increased in population; between 50,000 and 60,000.

2304. Have the watch committee anything to do with the appointment of the police constables?—Strictly speaking, they have not. The watch committee appoint the chief constable, and it has been the custom for the chief constable to appoint the subordinates, submitting them to the approval of the watch committee. There is a printed paper in which every man's name is entered who is a candidate for the place; he is bound to give certain certificates of conduct, and to state how he has been employed, and so on. The chief constable selects the men, and he brings them up for the approval of the watch committee. After they have been examined by the surgeon, it is not usual for the watch committee to object to any man whom the chief constable brings up; but they have the power to do it if they think proper, but they do not do it.

2305. They have a veto upon his appointment, but no power to appoint themselves?—In point of fact, the men are appointed by the watch committee, on the recommendation of the chief constable; they do not interfere with the nominations of the chief constable, but they have the power to do so should they think fit.

2306. Is that power ever exercised?—I do not recollect that it ever has been; the regular mode is this: the man is brought up with his recommendation by the chief constable; he has been examined by the surgeon, and he is then submitted to the watch committee. It has occasionally happened that some of the members of the watch committee thought that the man could not read or write well enough, and that he did not appear to be sufficiently educated for the police, and he has been objected to on that ground.

2307. In those cases has the man been refused?—Wherever the watch committee think fit to refuse a man they have full power to do so.

2308. Did not you say that the watch committee have not exercised the power, except in cases where a man has appeared not sufficiently educated, and that he has been rejected?—Certainly, but that has been rarely the case.

2309. Although he has been recommended by the superintendent?—Certainly.

2310. Can you tell at all in what number of instances that has occurred within the last few years?—I should say very few indeed; I could not call to my mind more than one or two during the time I have been on the watch committee. I must say it has never been capriciously exercised, but that the superintendent has been in all the cases I can call to my mind quite satisfied that the watch committee have come to a just decision; that is to say, that circumstances have come out before the watch committee of which he himself was not aware.

2311. Do you think the superintendent himself thinks it is a better system that the nomination of the police constables should be subject to the veto of the watch committee than that he should have the sole and entire control over them?—I apprehend he has never had any reason to be discontented; I have never heard any dissatisfaction on his part. You will have an opportunity of examining the late superintendent, and you will find that he has not been dissatisfied, nor is the present superintendent.

2312. Have the watch committee the power of suspending and dismissing the police?—Yes, they have full power to do so. The mode in which the business is done is this: if any misconduct is reported by the chief constable to the watch committee, the case is considered by them, and they determine what penalty should be inflicted.

2313. Then the superintendent or chief of the police has no voice with respect

G. Kitson, Esq.

9 June 1853.

to the suspension or dismissal of the men?—None; he may recommend, but he has no positive power to dismiss; it is not very often that the committee would interfere with him; I should say that his opinion is nearly always followed, but that the decision rests with the watch committee.

2314. Then, in fact, the whole power of appointment of the police constables rests with the watch committee at Bath?—Decidedly so; I believe, by the Act of Parliament, it is intended that it should be so; that is the way in which we read the Act at Bath.

2315. Is there any restriction as to the position in life of the watch committee, or as to the trade they follow?—Nothing more than what the Act of Parliament points out as the qualifications for a town councillor; the watch committee is indiscriminately selected from the council, whether aldermen or councillors.

2316. Would there be any objection to a brewer forming a part of the watch committee?—None whatever.

2317. Would there be any objection to a publican being on the watch committee?—No, supposing he was in the town council.

2318. Are there any persons in either of those trades forming a part of the watch committee?—I think no brewer; but certainly but one publican has ever been on the watch committee since I have been. I have been a member of the council from the commencement; I think I can state from memory that there never was but one publican; I do not know whether there has been a brewer, but I believe not.

2319. Is there any brewer upon the watch committee now?—Certainly not; the watch committee is selected from the council, consequently if there were no brewer in the council there would be no brewer on the watch committee.

2320. Of what number does the watch committee consist?—Fifteen.

2321. *Chairman.*] You have referred to the administration of police under the former chief constable; was there any different system of appointing the constables under the administration of the former chief constable to what there is now?—I should state, that on the late chief constable coming into office, the watch committee were fully aware that things were not in the state in which they ought to have been, and that a change must take place; the change was deferred till the appointment of another chief, from deference probably to the feelings of the then chief constable. I am speaking of the appointment of the late chief constable, Mr. Oakley. Before Mr. Oakley's appointment, for some time the more active members of the watch committee were satisfied that things were not on the best footing; many of the men were superannuated, and were taken from the old constabulary force, when the new force was formed, and they were unfit for their situation. There were some other circumstances which the watch committee, or the more active members of it, considered it would be necessary to reform, but they thought it best to leave those matters till we had a new chief constable. I may state, that on the appointment of that new chief we found we had a man thoroughly conversant with his business, a man who submitted to us such a statement in writing, that although we were a committee composed of the most heterogeneous materials, all his propositions were carried unanimously by the watch committee, and also when submitted to the council. Whatever propositions it was necessary to submit to the council were equally approved by them.

2322. Is there any publican on the watch committee now?—None whatever; I believe I am correct in saying so. There is no publican, strictly speaking, in the corporation; no common public-house keeper since I have been in the council has ever been in the corporation.

2323. Is Mr. Hancock a publican?—No, he is a spirit dealer and a wine merchant; he is an alderman, and has been in the council from the commencement; he does not keep a public-house.

2324. Is he a member of the watch committee?—Yes, an old member.

2325. Is any member of the watch committee a pawnbroker?—There is one pawnbroker on the watch committee, and a very active member. I did not quite understand the question with respect to a publican. I understood the question to refer to the keeper of a public-house. Mr. Hancock does not keep a public-house; he is a wine merchant, and has a spirit-shop under a licence.

2326. Do you mean a retail spirit-shop?—He has a retail licence.

2327. Mr. *Fitzroy.*] Does he sell spirits over the counter by the glass?—Yes; he is not merely a man who has a gallon licence, but he sells glasses.

2328. In

2328. In fact, he keeps what is commonly called a gin-shop?—Yes, you may call it a gin-shop.

2329. Mr. *Sotheron*.] You do not call a man conducting such a business as that a publican?—I do not consider him as ranking in that class; he has a gin-shop, and sells by retail, it is true; there is a difference between a man that has a licence to sell by the gallon, and a licence which is granted by the magistrates to hotel-keepers, which enables them to sell spirits if they like.

2330. When you say there is no publican on the watch committee, you mean that there is no person keeping an inn or a public-house, but you do not include in that description a person selling spirits?—No; this man is a spirit dealer, and also a wine merchant; the licences of wine merchants in general are such, that they may sell spirits if they like.

2331. Mr. *Howard*.] Where are your assizes held?—At Taunton, Bridgwater, and Wells.

2332. When the Bath policemen go to the assizes, do they receive fees?—They receive no fees, they only receive their travelling expenses. I should state, on the score of fees, there is a decided order that no policeman should receive any fee or gratuity whatever beyond his general wages, which order I think was made when Mr. Oakley came into the force; what they have for attending the assizes is what they pay for their expenses, necessarily incurred in going.

2333. Are they paid by the county?—They are paid by the county their travelling expenses.

2334. Are they paid for the conveyance of their own prisoners?—They have nothing to do with the prisoners after they are committed; there is much to be said on that score; the prisoner does not go to the assize towns till he is committed, and then he is in the custody of the gaoler, and the police have nothing to do with him.

2335. Mr. *Sotheron*.] For what purpose do your policemen go to the assizes?—To give evidence.

2336. They do not go in charge of the prisoners?—No.

2337. Mr. *Howard*.] Have there been complaints of prisoners having been sent for trial to the assizes instead of the quarter sessions?—No, I think not; the Act of Parliament determines that there are certain offences which must go before a judge.

Captain Samuel Meredith, called in; and Examined.

2338. *Chairman*.] ARE you Chief Constable of Wiltshire?—I am.

2339. Will you state to the Committee of what your force consists?—It consists of 200 men, one chief constable, 10 superintendents, 10 inspectors, 25 serjeants; the remainder are in two classes, but not any stated number to each; they are simply termed first and second-class constables.

2340. What proportion do the men bear to the population?—The population is 240,000, and there are 1,200 inhabitants to each constable.

2341. What is the cost of that force?—The average cost for the last 10 years has been 10,833*l.* 1*s.* 11*d.*, as charged to the police-rate; the average proportion to each man is 54*l.* 3*s.* 3¾*d.*; that is the average cost to the county of the whole force; it is the lowest in England.

2342. Do you find that force sufficient?—Yes, we find that force quite sufficient.

2343. Are the boroughs in the county of Wilts all consolidated with the county?—There are five boroughs in the county, four of which are consolidated.

2344. What are the four boroughs which are consolidated with the county?—Chippenham, Devizes, Marlborough and Calne.

2345. Which is the borough which is not consolidated with the county?—Salisbury.

2346. What is the reason that Salisbury has not joined the county?—They had a force of their own, established some years before the county police was formed, and I believe they are attached to their own force.

2347. Do you know the number of the force in Salisbury?—A superintendent and 10 constables.

2348. If Salisbury were consolidated with the county what number should you have there?—Six men would perform the duty

2349. Therefore you think they have a sufficient number now?—I think if they were to consolidate with the county there would be a considerable saving, and the force would be efficiently worked.

G. Kitson, Esq.

9 June 1853.

Captain
Samuel Meredith.

Captain
Samuel Meredith.

9 June 1853.

2350. How would the county be affected ?— I think we might engage, without any additional expense to the county, to take charge of Salisbury.

2351. You have four boroughs consolidated with the county ; you think there is great economy in that arrangement, and you think if that arrangement were carried out to Salisbury, it would be a saving to that borough, and also to the county?—There would be no increase of expense to the county ; I think it could be done by the same force which we have now.

2352. Mr. *Fitzroy.*] You state that the duty would be more efficiently performed if Salisbury were under your charge ; and at the same time you state that the number of men which is now employed is more than sufficient for the purpose ?—No, I do not think I stated so.

2353. Did not you say there were . policemen in Salisbury?—I think eight men might perform the duty ; we have a great number of men round the suburbs, and of course they might assist in the performance of the duty ; we should have our head-quarters of the county force there, and they would act with the borough force ; the county force around the borough would come into it to assist when required, without stationing so many men in the borough.

2354. At all events, you think you have a sufficient number of men to perform the duty ?—Yes.

2355. In what way do you mean that the duty would be more efficiently performed if you had Salisbury under your control?—The whole of the force of that division would co-operate with each other; at present they are under distinct governments.

2356. Have you found any difficulty from want of co-operation ?—Yes.

2357. Will you state the chief difficulties which have occurred in consequence of that want of co-operation ?—Felons and other offenders from the county escape into the borough, and we have not the means of tracing them out, from the want of local information ; we do not know the parties to whom to apply ; there is also a little jealousy always existing between one force and the other.

2358. Lord *Lovaine.*] Do you think, if a system of consolidation were carried out throughout the counties of England, there would be consequently a diminution of the police force ?—I think so, and also a very considerable diminution of crime.

2359. Do you mean that diminution would take place, owing to the superior efficiency of the police acting as one body ?—Yes.

2360. Mr. *Sotheron.*] Can you give the Committee any account of the state of crime before your force was established and what it has been since ?—I can give you the state of crime since the force was established ; you will then see the working of the force. To save the time of the Committee, I have just made an extract of the number of serious offences. In the year 1841, immediately after the force was established, there were 12 highway robberies committed, three were brought to justice, and nine escaped ; there were 19 burglaries, eight were brought to justice, and 11 escaped ; there were four cases of housebreaking, neither of which were brought to justice ; there were nine cases of cattle-stealing, each of which was brought to justice, and the cattle recovered ; 12 cases of horse-stealing, six were brought to justice, and six escaped ; there were 95 cases of sheep-stealing, 26 were brought to justice, 69 escaped. In 1852 the returns are only made up to the end of the year : there were three cases of burglary, which were brought to justice ; there were 12 cases of housebreaking, six were brought to justice, six were undetected : those were small articles stolen from the cottages of poor people, which were entered in their absence, such as a shirt, or a coat, or something of that sort ; there were two cases of cattle-stealing, both of which were brought to justice ; there were three cases of horse-stealing, two of which were brought to justice, and one escaped ; there were eight cases of sheep-stealing, five of which were detected, and three were undetected. The number of persons charged in 1842 were 3,006 in the county ; the whole number of persons charged which came under the cognizance of the police in 1852 was 2,350. The Committee will be pleased to recollect that we had taken charge of the boroughs subsequently to 1842, and there were nearly 20,000 inhabitants thrown upon the service of the police ; the actual deduction is much greater than shown in the figures. The number of offences which were reported to the police in which the parties were not taken into custody in 1842 amounted to 147, in 1852 there were 34, taking into account the increased population of the boroughs which I have before mentioned.

2361. *Chairman.*]

Captain
Samuel Meredith.
———
9 June 1853.

2361. *Chairman.*] When there were 147 cases undetected, the four boroughs were not included, and now the four boroughs are included, the number of cases undetected is 34?—I have given here the number of persons brought under the cognizance of the police.

2362. Do you think there have been any complaints in those boroughs in which the police has been adopted?—No; I have in fact received testimonials of the highest character from each of the boroughs.

2363. Mr. *Sotheron.*] Can you state to the Committee what has been the difference of expense to those boroughs?—I cannot.

2364. Do you know whether, to the inhabitants of those boroughs which have been consolidated with the county police, there has been a saving in expense?—There has been a very large saving in the borough of Devizes; the saving amounts to 100 *l.* per annum; they pay 150 *l.* per annum to the county for the services of the police, and formerly they paid 259 *l.* per annum; the 150 *l.* includes the whole cost of their police protection.

2365. Sir *J. Trollope.*] What is the number of men in Devizes?—Three men exclusively for the borough; the head-quarters of the force is established there also.

2366. Do you shift your men often in the boroughs?—Occasionally.

2367. Do you shift them in the rural districts?—Yes.

2368. Do you permit men to reside for any lengthened period in the boroughs?—That depends entirely upon circumstances; if it is found that a man is getting too intimate with the inhabitants and not sufficiently attentive to his duty, another man is selected; and that is the case in the rural districts; if a man is found to be too intimate with the inhabitants, he is removed at once.

2369. *Chairman.*] Those arrangements could not take place if the police were under the management of the different magistrates of the division?—Certainly not.

2370. Mr. *Fitzroy.*] Do you find it necessary to change the men often?—No, not very often.

2371. How long do you leave the men stationed in the borough?—Sometimes two years; we have one inspector in Devizes who has been there five years; he has charge of the town, and when an offence is committed he knows where to put his hand upon the party; he has nothing to do with the watch committee; he is entirely under my directions, and subject to the superintendent, who resides in the borough; the superintendent having charge of the whole division.

2372. The borough authorities have nothing to do with the government of the police?—Nothing whatever; that was the understanding, that the boroughs should not interfere with the government of the police when they incorporated themselves with the county; that the police were to be placed under the authority of the chief constable.

2373. *Chairman.*] What counties joining Wiltshire have no police?—Somersetshire and Berkshire.

2374. Can you give the Committee at all an idea of the difference in crime within the borders where there is a police force, and over the borders where there is no police force?—I can give a statement of the number of prisoners committed for trial in the adjoining county of Somerset for the year 1852; namely, Somerset 585; Wilts 283.

2375. Are you aware that there is a great number of vagrants over the border of the county?—Yes; we do not allow gypsies in Wiltshire to pitch their tents, or squat about the roads; if you go into Somersetshire or Dorsetshire, where they have no rural police, you will find hundreds along the borders.

2376. Have you got rid of vagrants in Wiltshire?—The superintendents of police, in 11 out of 17 unions, have been appointed assistant relieving officers; a return has been made to me showing a reduction of 6,000 during the years they have been in operation on the applications which have been made to them.

2377. Mr. *Sotheron.*] Do you mean an annual reduction?—That is the reduction altogether from the first year when they commenced operations up to this last year.

2378. How many years is that?—Since 1847; five years.

2379. Mr. *Phillips.*] Have you a superannuation fund?—We have.

2380. *Chairman.*] Do you give rewards to any of your constables for apprehending offenders?—No, except in two cases; there have been rewards given to them by the judges of assize; now they can be given by the court of quarter sessions.

2381. Mr. *Fitzroy.*] Do your police give notice to the coroners in cases of death?—They do not generally; that is casually done by the parish constables.

2382. *Chairman.*] Do your men act as inspectors of weights and measures?—Yes; they took charge of the weights and measures in 1845, and in the following year there were 14,942 found defective; 408 prosecutions took place, the fines amounting to 152*l.* 2*s.* 6*d.* In 1852 there were five informations, and the fines inflicted amounted to 4*l.* 0*s.* 6*d.*; that is the difference in seven years.

2383. Mr. *Sotheron.*] Can you state what has been the saving to the public by the police taking charge of the weights and measures?—The salaries paid to the former inspectors of weights and measures were smaller in Wiltshire than in other counties; it is the saving of the salaries of the different inspectors, about 160*l.* a year.

2384. Lord *Lovaine.*] Were the inspectors reduced at once?—All except one; they had been recently appointed, with an understanding they would be required to resign when the police were appointed; there is one of the old inspectors in the neighbourhood of Salisbury acting as inspector of weights and measures.

2385. Mr. *Sotheron.*] What is the general system of the arrangement of your police; is it the same as in Gloucestershire and in Ireland; with respect to the stations, or in any other way?—I ought to state to the Committee that I commanded districts of the coast-guard for six years before I took the appointment in the Wilts constabulary, and on forming the force I adopted what appeared to me to be the best system for the protection of the public; it is a system entirely my own. I stationed the men in the rural districts, giving each man, as near as I could, a beat of a certain extent. I divided the county into nine police divisions; those were again subdivided into a certain number of subdivisions, at the head of which there is an inspector or serjeant; the men were placed in districts, and each man was responsible for the good order of that district, the men meeting at points given to them, varying every night. The inspector or serjeant is expected to visit those points occasionally during the week; and if anything has occurred during the day to prevent a man attending to the night meetings at the proper point, he would have to report the cause; and it would be the duty of the serjeant to ascertain that his statement was correct.

2386. Do you place your policemen in different parishes, or do you put them in different stations?—In different parishes, in proportion to the population; in some there are two or three.

2387. In what manner do you combine those different policemen in the different parishes?—They are to be on duty 12 hours out of the 24; during that time they have to visit the different places or farms in their district, to see if there have been any depredations or complaints. The patrols at night are arranged so as to go sometimes in one direction and sometimes the other, so as to meet the other constables; but these meetings vary nightly.

2388. Do they practically in the 24 hours meet the neighbouring constables, so as to keep up the chain of communication?—Yes, every night.

2389. In what manner do you ascertain that the men have properly performed their duty?—The man has to state his reasons in a book why he was not at the place of meeting; the serjeant's duty is to satisfy himself that his statement is correct; there is a night meeting every night; the serjeant of the subdivision has the whole list of the meetings weekly; he goes to the spot, and if he does not find his men there, he invariably reports them; it is also the duty of the other constable to report that the meeting has not been kept.

2390. Lord *Lovaine.*] Is not that a better system than the Gloucestershire system?—I think so; no other county in England has adopted the Gloucestershire system. The same system as my own has been adopted by Captain MacHardy, who is an old coast-guard officer, and by other chief constables who had not had the advantage of serving in the coast-guard.

2391. Mr. *Sotheron.*] Is there not an advantage if you are able to collect your men readily at any particular part of the county where there may be any emergency?—In two hours we can throw a body of 50 men into any part of the county. A case occurred some time ago of a strike of labourers for wages at West Lavington; a man came to me on horseback at midnight, and in two hours I had 35 men in the place; and in a short time the remainder came up.

2392. How many parishes are there in Wiltshire?—Three hundred.

2393. Consequently, you have not a constable to each parish?—No.

2394. You arrange, as well as you can, to place your constables for two or three

three parishes, as the case may be ?—Yes; so as all may be visited regularly by the constable.

2395. Mr. *Fitzroy.*] Do you take the parishes as the basis of your arrangment ? —Yes; the men are strictly ordered to visit the outlying farms; the superintendent also visits them to know if there is any complaint.

2396. Mr. *Sotheron.*] If a poor man loses any article, will he, under your system, have a distance of three or four miles to go before he can meet with a policeman ?—Certainly not; all the constables are especially ordered to give every possible protection to the cottages of the poor when the occupiers are absent.

2397. Do you find that is practically an advantage ?—Every case is reported to the policeman; at once he makes his inquiries, and follows up the offender immediately; to that system I attribute our good fortune in keeping down crime. Every constable is responsible for his district; if an offence is committed, and he does not give a satisfactory account of it, he is suspended, or if I find he has been negligent in the discharge of his duty he is immediately suspended, and probably dismissed.

2398. Lord *Lovaine.*] Captain MacHardy, in his evidence, has said that it was an immense advantage to keep the men in stations ?—That, I apprehend, is where there are station-houses built, and one or two constables are residing in them, in order that the prisoners may be properly visited. I have had no communication with Captain MacHardy on the subject; but I apprehend his view is this, that where there are prisoners they should be regularly visited during the night, and that a man should be always ready for any emergency.

2399. Mr. *Sotheron.*] I believe when the force was established it was complained of on account of the expense ?—It was; and a very powerful opposition organised.

2400. Were not some motions made at quarter sessions for its reduction ? —Yes, frequently.

2401. At that time what was the feeling amongst the farmers generally about the police ?—The objection was not to the force itself, but to the expense; and this was very general.

2402. Do you consider that that feeling has altered ?—I think it has entirely subsided; I think if the county were canvassed you would find six to one in favour of the police, by the occupiers of the land; a case came under my observation some short time ago when the subject was mooted in a rural Board of Guardians.

2403. *Chairman.*] What Board of Guardians ?—The Devizes Board of Guardians; I am informed that the farmers at once said, " We will not reduce the police; that is money very well bestowed;" and they resisted the motion.

2404. Lord *Lovaine.*] Comparing the amount which is raised for the police rate with that which is raised for all other county purposes, is it about the same, or not ?—It is about the same.

2405. Therefore the establishment of the police in that county doubled the county rate ?—It did, or nearly so; the county rate is now very much reduced.

2406. Notwithstanding that, you are still of opinion that the farmers who contribute towards this rate are satisfied to continue to make that payment ?—From the information I have obtained, I am of that opinion.

2407. Are you aware of any attempt having been made within five or six years to make any proposition at the court of quarter sessions for a reduction of the police force ?—Not any.

2408. Mr. *Fitzroy.*] What is your police rate in the pound ?—Two-pence farthing. In speaking of cost, perhaps the Committee will permit me to place before them this statement; I have made a rough estimate of what the county was paying, under different heads, for protection before the police force was established. (*The Witness delivered in the same.*)

2409. Lord *Lovaine.*] What do you reckon the average payment to the parish constables ?—Nine pounds.

2410. Mr. *Burroughes.*] How do you arrive at that result ?—From an estimate of the number of summonses which they served, and the fees they received; they received money of course from individuals; but taking the average, they received about 9 *l.*

2411. Is the 9 *l.* an assumed sum ?—There is no means of getting at the money they were paid; they were paid largely out of the poor's rate for the services they performed.

Vide Appendix.

2412. Sir *J. Trollope*.] Do you include the expense of fetching the coroner?
—Yes; that is paid by mileage.

2413. Mr. *Burroughes*.] Do you know what the exact fees are, assuming that
the parish constable does nothing at all, and is called upon to perform no duty;
what are the fees of the clerk of petty sessions necessary for his appointment?—
One shilling is usual for swearing him in; the fee for the notice and precept I
think is about 2 *s.* 6 *d.* altogether; I think for each parish constable, in some
places, he is allowed a certain sum for coming to be sworn in.

2414. Lord *Lovaine*.] Do the police perform the services gratuitously, as
assistant relieving officers?—There is a small allowance made to men who are
appointed assistant relieving officers.

2415. Suppose a policeman had to pursue a man who had absconded, leaving
his family chargeable on the parish, whom would you charge for those services?
—A constable who is employed on that service makes out a bill, which is submitted to me, and signed by me; he then takes it to the union, and is there paid
his expenses. The intention of the bill being submitted to me is, that there should
be one uniform system of charge throughout the county.

2416. Mr. *Sotheron*.] Will you state in what mode your constables proceed
who have been appointed as assistant relieving officers, with regard to vagrants;
supposing a vagrant comes to the town of Devizes, what is the course pursued?—
He has to apply immediately to the assistant relieving officer, whose duty it is to
ascertain that he has no means of providing for himself, and then he is authorised
to find him food and a bed for the night.

2417. Where does he do that?—There is a place provided in the union. I
understand there is a room fitted up, which is cut off from the union altogether,
but still under the same roof to a certain extent; he visits that place frequently
during the night; there is a separate place for males, and another for females.

2418. What happens the following morning?—He receives his breakfast, and
then he is seen out of the place, and handed over to the other constables, and so
he is followed out of the county.

2419. Do you mean that the constable sees him fairly out of the town?—He
sees him fairly on his route.

2420. Do you know whether your constables have ever detected any money on
the persons of those vagrants?—Very frequently, in large sums; as much as 23 *l.*
was found on an Irish vagrant who applied for relief; we generally find a considerable sum of money upon the females.

2421. Mr. *Phillips*.] Was not it a case where one person was bearing the
purse for a number?—It was; that is a common practice; if they have no other
means of concealing their property, they send one of the party down to a lodging-
house with their property. It is the duty of the police to go down to these lodging-
houses where the parties are, and, as far as they can, to discover who belong to the
same gang that may be lodging there.

2422. Whatever may be the result, has not experience shown that the vagrants
do not like this system?—We rarely see any vagrants now in Wiltshire, the
numbers are so much reduced from the surveillance that is kept up by the police;
there is a great reduction of thieves, also, as well as vagrants. Wherever a
vagrant finds a poor cottager's house left, or insecurely fastened, they enter it,
and they carry off the little bread and cheese from the cupboard, the clothing,
or something or other. A large portion of the offences committed in our rural
districts were committed by vagrants; at one session we had as many as 14
vagrants committed for trial for robbing cottagers' houses during the time
that the occupiers were at work in the fields. There is another point which I
omitted to mention to the Committee, with respect to the expenses of police constables and parish constables. A case came before the magistrates of Devizes on
the 14th of last month. A boy had stolen a pair of boots from a barge; he was
followed up by the party that lost them into Somersetshire, and there he was
apprehended and handed over to a parish constable; he brought him to Wiltshire,
and the boy was convicted under the Juvenile Offenders' Act, which only authorises 40 *s.* to be paid for expenses; the parish constable's expenses amounted to
4 *l.* 16 *s.* 7 *d.* I have a copy of the bill here. Now, the party had to pay the
difference between 2 *l.* and 4 *l.* 16 *s.* 7 *d.*; consequently, it operates as a rejection of
justice to a certain extent. The man said he would rather have lost the boots than
paid

paid the constable. This is the sum which the parish constable says he should
have been allowed if he had apprehended the party in Somersetshire.

[The same was read, as follows :]

	£.	s.	d.
To apprehending prisoner - - - - - - -	-	2	6
Maintaining ditto two days - - - - - -	-	3	-
Guard watching ditto one night - - - - - -	-	2	6
Conveyance of prisoner at 9 *d.* per mile, and allowance to constable, 8 *d.* per mile (37 miles) - - - - -	2	12	5
Three days' loss of time - - - - - - -	-	15	-
Hire of conveyance, coach and other fares - - - ·	1	1	2
£.	4	16	7

2423. Mr. *Sotheron.*] Is the difference between these two sums the difference
between the cost of the same amount of protection in a county which has a rural
police, on the one hand, and a county with only local constables, on the other?—
The 40 *s.* is regulated by Act of Parliament; you cannot make the costs of a
juvenile case more than 40 *s.*; therefore the complainant had to pay the difference
between 2 *l.* and 4 *l.* 16 *s.* 7 *d.*

2424. What is the inference that you draw from the statement you have now
made?—The inference is that the parish constable making his own charges in his
own county is a much more costly person than a police constable.

2425. Lord *Lovaine.*] Do not parish constables charge 9 *d.* a mile, whether
they go by railway or not?—I believe so; this bill appears to be the cost of
taking a prisoner into custody in his own county and taking him before a county
magistrate in another.

2426. Sir *J. Trollope.*] Do your men convey prisoners out of your district into
other counties?—Not frequently; but when they do there is a regulated charge.

2427. How is that charge regulated?—They are allowed their actual costs
for conveyance; each constable, when out of his district, is entitled to 2 *s.* 6 *d.*
per day in addition to his travelling expenses; if he travels by rail he is allowed
1 *d.* per mile; all constables can travel on the rail at 1 *d.* per mile.

2428. That is by Act of Parliament?—Yes.

2429. Are you allowed to make out a bill against the county to which the
prisoner is taken for trial?—Yes; that is the usual practice.

2430. Upon what scale do you make out that bill?—On the scale I have
before mentioned.

2431. Do the men receive their pay in full, and the 2 *s.* 6 *d.* in addition?—Yes;
when they attend at the sessions they are allowed 5 *s.* a day, and their pay
is stopped; when they are employed as witnesses in Wiltshire they are allowed
5 *s.* a day, the same as an ordinary witness, and their pay as constable stopped.

2432. With regard to rewards, you have stated that judges of assize order
certain sums to be given to policemen occasionally; have you known any instances
in which private persons have tendered reward?—Very frequently.

2433. Do you permit your men to receive them?—Yes; under certain regulations.

2434. Whatever the sum may be?—If it is a moderate sum.

2435. Do you require the rewards to be reported to the superintendent?—
To me, on all occasions.

2436. Is it left to your discretion whether the men have the whole or a part of
the reward?—Yes.

2437. What is your practice with respect to rewards?—No constable can
receive any money over and above his pay without the authority of the chief
constable.

2438. Is it your practice to permit the men to receive rewards?—When I
consider their services have been such as to entitle them to receive rewards, I
permit them to receive rewards.

2439. Are not rewards sometimes offered by associations for the prosecution of
offenders, and at other times by private individuals; in that case does the reward
go to the policeman?—The policeman would receive two-thirds, and the other
third is carried to a fund to meet contingencies which cannot be charged in any
other way.

2440. To the sick fund?—No.

2441. Have you a sick fund ?—We have not a sick fund.

2442. Supposing a man is disabled, either by accident or sickness, is he permitted to receive the whole or a portion of his pay ?—If a man is wounded in the execution of his duty he receives the whole of his pay.

2443. What fund have you besides that ?—A superannuation fund ; a great portion of our men belong to a county club, from which they receive a certain sum in illness, and medical assistance.

2444. Is that under your control ?—I manage that part which our men belong to.

2445. In what way have you invested the superannuation fund ?—£. 5,000 is lent to the county.

2446. On the security of the county rates ?—It is lent for the purpose of building a lunatic asylum.

2447. What number of lock-ups have you ?—We have some hired places, which we use for lock-ups. We have not expended anything in Wiltshire upon the building of lock-ups.

2448. Have you recommended the building of lock-ups ?—Yes, I have.

2449. Have the magistrates rejected your recommendation ?—No ; it will be decided at the next quarter sessions.

2450. Will not that add materially to the expense of the police force ?—Not materially ; the amount of expense will be very small, because we shall save the rents we are now paying.

2451. Do you intend to have magistrates' rooms attached to the lock-ups ?—To some of them.

2452. And lodgings for the men ?—Yes.

2453. Has any estimate been made of the cost of those lock-ups ?—It has.

2454. Are they to be on one uniform scale ?—They are to be nearly on a uniform scale ; there are to be first and second-class stations.

2455. What is the cost that you propose for each ?—About 1,500 *l.*, or something like it, for the first-class stations.

2456. What is the total number of first-class stations ?—The total number at present proposed is five.

2457. How many second-class stations, and at what cost are these to be ?—Only one, at a cost of about 800 *l.* ; I am not prepared with the items ; I have no estimate of the amount ; it is a rough calculation which I have made.

2458. Mr. *Fitzroy.*] What number of men do you propose to lodge in these lock-ups ?—A head superintendent and two constables will be lodged, and they will pay rent for those stations.

2459. What rent ?—According to the rank of the officer ; we have three classes of superintendents ; the first class will pay 10 *l.*, the second 9 *l.*, and the third 7 *l.*

2460. Mr. *Sotheron.*] What will be the amount of money payable to the county in the shape of rent for the outlay in building these stations ?—I should estimate the rent at about 30 *l.* a year altogether for each station.

2461. Mr. *Phillips.*] Upon what plan are those lock-ups to be built ?—The lock-ups must be all the same. The Secretary of State's regulations distinctly apply to all lock-up houses ; they must be built with concrete, and with heated flues. There is a plan sent by the Secretary of State from which you cannot deviate if they are built under his authority.

2462. Mr. *Howard.*] Do you think your police is sufficient for other services than those they have to perform as policemen ?—In Wiltshire they have recruited three-fourths of the militia ; they are also employed as inspectors of nuisances and lodging-houses. I think the police might be employed in recruiting for the army with great advantage, both to the country and to the army, if they were so employed.

2463. It has been suggested that the police should inspect the roads ?—That is a subject to which I have not turned my attention ; but I think it would require practical men.

2464. Mr. *Fitzroy.*] You say that your men were employed in raising recruits for the militia ?—We raised three-fourths of the militia in Wiltshire, and served all the notices gratis.

2465. Have the police received the bringing-money ?—They have received the bringing-money which is allowed to every person who brings a recruit, but all the other duties connected with the militia have been performed gratis.

2466. Mr.

Captain
Samuel Meredith.

9 June 1853.

2466. Mr. *Sotheron.*] What is your opinion with regard to putting your men in uniform; it has been suggested that in some cases it would be much better that they should not be clothed in uniform?—I think it is important that they should be in uniform, and it checks many irregularities, which could not be checked otherwise. A policeman has no right to be in public-houses; if a policeman is in uniform, and he goes into a public-house, every one knows that that man is a policeman, and that he has no right there.

2467. Therefore the conduct of the men is to some extent checked by their being in uniform?—Yes; and I think also that crime would not be more efficiently detected by a man in plain clothes than by men in uniform, in the present state of crime throughout the country.

2468. Do you think that the presence of a policeman in uniform contributes very much to deter people from crime, or making a riot or disturbance?—Yes, most certainly.

2469. *Chairman.*] Would it not give him more authority in suppressing a riot? —No question; I think it would be utterly impossible to conduct a police establishment properly without the men being in uniform, or to enforce discipline.

Sir *Baldwin Leighton*, Bart., called in; and Examined.

2470. FOR what counties are you a Magistrate?—For Shropshire and Montgomeryshire.

Sir *B. Leighton,*
Bart.

2471. Have you a police force in Shropshire?—In both counties; Shropshire and Montgomeryshire.

2472. Have you always taken a great interest in the subject of police?—I have always taken a great interest in the subject. I am chairman of the police committee in Shropshire; I am a member of the police committee of Montgomeryshire, and chairman of the court of quarter sessions in Montgomeryshire.

2473. Can you state to the Committee of what the police force consists in Shropshire?—The force in Shropshire is 58 men, including the chief constable and all the officers, excluding the boroughs which do not belong to the rural police; we have two boroughs which have joined us, therefore the 58 men include the whole of the rural police and the police which serves the two boroughs.

2474. Was the number of the police force increased when these boroughs joined the county?—Yes; the borough of Wenlock joined in 1842; we then applied to the Secretary of State for an increase of seven men; we did not increase the force to that extent, although we got the order to do so; we increased the force four, but afterwards we have increased the force three more, one of which went to Bridgnorth when that borough joined us; we have increased the force for the county, I may say, four, since it was originally formed, and three for the boroughs that have joined us.

2475. What is the expense to the county of the whole of that force?—The expense is about a penny in the pound in Shropshire; during the 12 years we have had eight rates at a penny, three years a penny farthing, and one year at three farthings, which I ought to say includes the expense of the lock-ups, which have come rather heavy.

2476. Do you think the force which you have in Shropshire is sufficient?—I think it is quite sufficient.

2477. Mr. *Fitzroy.*] What is the population of Shropshire?—199,467.

2478. Does that include the two boroughs which have joined with the county? —Yes.

2479. Mr. *Burroughes.*] What is the amount of assessment upon which the rate is raised?—£. 1,027,000.

2480. *Chairman.*] What is the number of the force in Montgomeryshire?—The number in Montgomeryshire is 14.

2481. Mr. *Phillips.*] What is the total cost of the force in Shropshire?—The total expense last year was 4,865 *l.*; but I ought to say that we deduct from that 879 *l.* which the police treasurer received in actual cash from the constables for duties performed, and that would leave what he paid about 4,000 *l.*

2482. *Chairman.*] Do the 4,000 *l.* with that 800 *l.* constitute the sum raised by the rate of a penny in the pound?—Besides that, there is a saving of about 500 *l.* a year, which is not carried to account, for conveying prisoners to gaol, and for keeping courts of quarter sessions, and the serving of jury lists; the 4,000 l. includes the lock-ups; 200 l. is for lock ups.

2483. Mr. *Burroughes*.] Is that sum merely the current outlay, or for building the lock-ups?—It includes what was spent upon the building, which I find was about 200 l. for that year.

2484. *Chairman*.] Have you made any calculation of the comparative expense of your present system and that of the parochial constable system?—I tried to form some estimate before the police was established; but putting aside the diminution of crime, the police force is an expense to the county; that is a thing you cannot calculate; there is no data of that sort, I fancy, in any county before the police was established, to enable you to know what the amount of crime was, because the number of prisoners in gaol affords no data of the amount of felonies actually committed.

2485. Do you think the amount of property which has been saved by having an efficient police force is equal to the cost of the police in the county?—I have no data which will enable me to answer that question.

2486. Do you think there has been a great saving of property?—I think so.

2487. Mr. *Fitzroy*.] Do not you think it would be very desirable to increase the number of your police force?—Perhaps the best answer I can give to that question is, that two years ago an inspector of weights and measures died; we had to appoint one temporarily; I said to our chief constable, " I think the man in our neighbourhood can be spared; you had better appoint him for three months, and if he does his duty well, he can be appointed as inspector of weights and measures; if not, you can keep the place open for him." There was not the slightest inconvenience, although that constable was taken away.

2488. *Chairman*.] Do you think you were able to spare that man from having had a well-organized police force for a considerable time?—When I was treasurer of a local police, before the rural police was established, we had only one constable, and that man did the duty perfectly well, whereas now we have two police officers. So efficient did I find that one man, that I was able to send him to other parts of the county in which parties applied for his assistance; during the last year he served in my hundred he was absent two months, the parties paying him the same wages that I paid him.

2489. Mr. *Fitzroy*.] Is the population less dense in your neighbourhood?—I find there is about one constable to 4,000 in the county; that is about the average in my hundred; my hundred is about 8,000.

2490. Do you think your force is sufficient?—I think it is more than sufficient in my neighbourhood.

2491. Do you think one policemen to 4,000 inhabitants is sufficient?—It must depend entirely upon the district; if you have a thinly populated district you have a great acreage; perhaps you would require more constables than where there was a dense population and less acreage. Allow me to say that Shropshire has districts containing a dense population, and districts just the contrary. We have mines, where the population is very dense; they are not quite towns, but there is a succession of villages, over eight or nine or ten miles; in other parts there are hills, where the population is very slight.

2492. Taking the whole of the country, do you think that 58 men afford sufficient protection?—Perfectly so, looking at the number of felonies; one man has a felony a month to look after; not a conviction, but an actual robbery committed.

2493. *Chairman*.] It appears by the return to which you have alluded, that previously to the appointment of the police, that in the hundred of Ford the number of robberies was 65; that is in 15 months; the amount of property lost was 139 l. 18 s. 6 d.; do you think the number of robberies which have been committed since the appointment of the police has been much less in that district? —It has in that district. I believe I have a return of the felonies which have been committed; it shows perhaps favourably to the police; it begins in 1841, when there were 554 felonies; it goes gradually down to 1846, when there were 334.

2494. In what year were the police appointed?—In 1840. In the year 1841 the number of felonies committed were 554; in 1842, 584; in 1843, 657; in 1844, 573; in 1845, 460; in 1846, 334; in 1847, 497; in 1848, 513; in 1849, 565; in 1850, 651; in 1851, 810; in 1852, 738. There are two reasons for that increase. Our railway works began in the year 1847, and we had a great number of offences committed by the railway labourers; we had a great many

crimes

Sir *B. Leighton*, Bart.

9 June 1853.

crimes committed in the county by the Irish labourers; we had also an immense increase of vagrancy, owing to the alteration made in the administration of the poor law; the workhouses were dreadfully crowded, and there were great complaints about the relief given to vagrants. I find that this increase of felonies commenced just about the time that those two things happened in our county, therefore that is the reason why there is that increase. Since 1851 they have decreased to 738. Since the railway has been opened to Shrewsbury there has been a very great increase of crime; in Shrewsbury there are an immense number of pickpockets; they can come from Wellington for a penny, and for sixpence from Wolverhampton; they constantly come to Shrewsbury on fair days.

2495. Shrewsbury not being incorporated with the county police, what police force is there at Shrewsbury?—The borough police amounts to 17 men, and they talk of increasing it to 20.

2496. Is that force under the corporation?—Under the watch committee of the corporation.

2497. Do you think the police force of Shrewsbury is sufficient?—I do not think it is; they do not work very well with the county, at least none of the boroughs do.

2498. They do not give reciprocal assistance?—No; I do not think they work nearly so well as the two counties of Shropshire and Montgomery; but perhaps I may say one reason is for my being an influential magistrate in each of the counties. I say to the men, "You must catch the thief; never mind which county catches him. We have just now come to an arrangement in Shropshire and Montgomeryshire to do away with the boundary of the counties, and to draw a line; the counties go in and out; there are one or two parts of Montgomeryshire which have never been patrolled; one owing to the borough of Poole surrounding it in a great measure, and the other, the county of Shropshire. In another part of Montgomeryshire one of our Shropshire policemen resides.

2499. In fact, there is a cordial co-operation between the police of the counties of Shropshire and Montgomeryshire?—Yes; I attribute it in a great measure to my being myself an influential magistrate over both the chief constables, and if they were not to work well they would know that I should report them to the quarter sessions; my office would carry considerable weight with it in either county. I am bound to say that the chief constables are working very well; I think the knowledge that there is a person interested in both counties is a very great tie over them.

2500. Do not you think a cordial co-operation between the two counties of Shropshire and Montgomeryshire enables you to do with a smaller force in Shropshire than if the adjoining county had no police force?—No doubt; I live on the borders, and I can order the Shropshire police to go into Montgomeryshire.

2501. And the Montgomeryshire police would come into the county of Shropshire if they were wanted?—Certainly. My Shropshire policeman lives two miles off, and my Montgomery policeman six miles off; that is the reason why I employ the Shropshire man more than the Montgomeryshire man.

2502. Do you think it would be desirable to establish a uniform system of police throughout the country?—It would be very desirable. Bridgnorth applied to the county to unite with us; the magistrates said, "We are willing to unite, and you shall pay the same rate as the county rate is." The agreement was signed; the borough authorities wanted particularly to appoint their own policeman. We said, "The county magistrates do not appoint their policemen themselves, but it is left with the chief constable to appoint them." It was agreed that if the Bridgnorth policeman was efficient he should be appointed. The chief constable reported to the police committee that he could not appoint the man because he could not read writing. We met the mayor of Bridgnorth, and there was a great discussion; the poor man wrote in our presence, and certainly very badly; the mayor said, "He is nervous." There was a letter written by the mayor lying on the table, and I said, "Let him read the mayor's letter, which is very plainly written." It was handed to him, but it was evident he could not read it. The mayor said, "I have nothing more to say, gentlemen, will you allow us to break our engagement, and not to unite with you?"

2503. You mean to say the mayor and corporation broke their engagement for the sake of that one man?—I can only say that they did break it; it was mutually understood that we did not want to hold them to their engagement. They had actually paid the first instalment of 20*l.* to our treasurer. We said we had no

U

wish to keep them to their bargain; it was merely on the part of the borough, from a good feeling towards the man, because he would have been sent to the right-about, and not know how to maintain himself. In six months after they found the man some other situation, and they asked us to join, and have joined us.

2504. Mr. *Burroughes*.] Your chief constable has the appointment of the police in the boroughs?—Yes.

2505. In a similar manner to the county?—Yes; with this proviso, that the mayor may report a man to the chief constable, and the chief constable is then bound to remove him, but not to dismiss him.

2506. Is there any proviso as to the appointment?—No; he must be approved of by the mayor.

2507. Sir *J. Trollope*.] Are your police officers allowed to assist as relieving officers to the unions by way of checking vagrancy?—Not generally. In my own union we have had a great deal of difficulty; at last it was agreed that if the governor of the workhouse had any doubts about any able-bodied tramp, he should send him to the policeman before he took him in, whoever gave the order. The policeman was then to countersign the order if he really thought he deserved to be admitted; if he could find any act of vagrancy against him he was to take him immediately to a magistrate; that has considerably checked vagrancy in the union. It was getting into a dreadful state; in the year 1840 we had three vagrants in the union house; it gradually increased, till in 1848 we had 250. Our workhouse is the country, in a hamlet. We had 56 this last year.

2508. *Chairman*.] Do you think the certainty of detection of crime is much greater now than it was before the establishment of the police force?—Certainly, very much greater; we detect about half the crime that is reported, or hardly half now; but I ought to say before the police was established I used to attend the quarter sessions very regularly, and I took an account of the number of vagrants who were tried, and they amounted to a third or a fourth of the total number of prisoners tried; at the last session and assizes they amounted to about one-ninth.

2509. Lord *Lovaine*.] Does it not militate against your opinion of the efficiency of your force, that so few detections should take place compared with the number of crimes which have been committed?—I am not aware what the proportion has been in other counties, but a good many of the crimes are committed by the trampers. The difficulty in our county is to take up vagrants legally; a man is not justified in taking up a tramper, and whenever they see a policeman they take care not to commit an act of vagrancy. Hardly any ratepayer will go to the trouble of prosecuting a vagrant, although it is no expense; even myself, I do not like the trouble, although an active magistrate; it is a great trouble; you must go and give evidence at the court four, five, six, seven, eight, or nine miles; of course that deters people from prosecuting a vagrant for merely asking for a halfpenny. There is one thing which has been mentioned by the last witness about recruiting for the militia; our force have been used a little in that respect; they have not brought up a great many men; however, they have been useful in it. In regard to the men wearing uniform I think there has been something stated to the Committee; my opinion is, that it is desirable to have the men in uniform. Our policemen are allowed, whenever they think proper, to go out of uniform, but they must write it down in their journal; if it is not written in the journal, it is an offence for which they will be fined; if it is entered in the journal, stating the reason, they are permitted to go out of uniform. They frequently come to my house out of uniform; I ask them the reason, and they give me the reason.

2510. Mr. *Fitzroy*.] You heard the statement made by the last witness as to the decrease of vagrancy in Wiltshire; do you think that the same system might not be adopted in Shropshire which has been pursued so successfully in Wiltshire for the suppression of vagrancy?—I always like to have figures; it is a matter of experience.

2511. *Chairman*.] Are your officers appointed assistant relieving officers?—No; my union extends a very large distance; I think we have only four constables; and the workhouse being in the country, I do not know how they could be appointed assistant relieving officers; the workhouse is 14 miles from my house.

2512. Sir *J. Trollope*.] How near is there a constable to the workhouse?—The man is a mile and a half off to whom we send our vagrants.

2513. If you appointed the police in the capacity of relieving officers to attend
the

the vagrants, they would be required to be in attendance daily at the workhouse? —No; we had only 56 applications in the year.

2514. Does it follow that that is the total number required in relief at your workhouse?—Yes.

2515. Were not there more than 56 that made application to the relieving officer?—Yes, a few more made applications.

2516. Were they rejected?—I ought to say that a vagrant seldom applies for relief where there is no union house.

2517. Perhaps your union house is not in the direct highway in their line of march?—We are the greatest highway out of Shrewsbury.

2518. Between Shrewsbury and Wales?—Yes, if there is no workhouse they never think of applying for relief; the workhouse is 14 miles off.

2519. *Chairman.*] Before the appointment of the police had you considerable experience of the efficiency of the local constables?—I had experience of their perfect uselessness.

2520. You think the parish constables were perfectly useless for the purpose of detecting crime?—Perfectly so; I consider it is a waste of money appointing them; it is a mere trifle to the county, but it is a great loss to the men themselves, because we do not pay them in my hundred; we appoint about 40 now, and those poor men lose, no doubt, 1 s. 6 d. a day by coming there, at least.

2521. Are they not paid for attendance the day they come in to be sworn?— No; that is a large sum for people of that class to lose. I think they are perfectly inefficient; and if I were to commit a prisoner from my own house, I should swear in my own gamekeeper to take him to gaol; I would rather trust my own servant to take him to gaol than a parish constable.

2522. Sir *J. Trollope.*] Are you not aware that under the last Local Constable Act that a gamekeeper is forbidden to be sworn in as a special constable?—I merely accidentally mentioned the gamekeeper, but I would swear in one of my garden labourers.

2523. *Chairman.*] With respect to the expense incurred by conveying prisoners by parochial constables, do you think, upon the whole, that the old system of parochial constables which you had in the county of Shropshire before the appointment of the police, was as expensive in point of money as the present system?—If you will put out of view the amount of crime and depredation that was committed; I think I reckoned the constables cost 800 *l.* or 1,000 *l.* a year; they now cost 4,000 *l.* a year, but I believe none of the magistrates would at all wish to do away with the police. We have frequent applications from the ratepayers to increase the police; we have been pressed very much for an increase by a parish in Montgomeryshire lately; we have had some very pressing memorials sent to increase the police.

2524. Then, in the opinion of the ratepayers, it is desirable to increase the force? —I find every one wants to have a policeman at his own door; that is the universal feeling throughout both counties.

2525. Mr. *Burroughes.*] Do you find that the ratepayers are willing to pay for the force?—As they memorialize us so often, I think they must be willing.

2526. *Chairman.*] So far as you are aware, in Shropshire and Montgomeryshire there is no complaint of the expense of the police?—No, not in the least.

2527. Mr. *Fitzroy.*] What proportion does the number of men bear to the population?—I think about the same proportion to the population as in Shropshire, but not to the acreage.

2528. What do they pay the superintendent?—I think 120 *l.*, and 50 *l.* for a horse.

2529. What is the pay of the chief constable in Shropshire?—£. 300, and 100 *l.* for a horse; 400 *l.* altogether.

2530. *Chairman.*] Do you wish to make any further statement to the Committee?—I think it is desirable to employ the police as much as possible; there is one thing in which they might be employed in courts of justice; at present the sheriff keeps the court at assizes with javelinmen; if the policemen were made to keep the courts, a great expense would be saved to the sheriffs.

2531. Mr. *Phillips.*] Has it ever been suggested that they should keep the toll-gates?—I do not think that is possible.

SECOND REPORT

FROM THE

SELECT COMMITTEE

ON

POLICE;

TOGETHER WITH THE

PROCEEDINGS OF THE COMMITTEE,

MINUTES OF EVIDENCE,

AND APPENDIX.

Ordered, by The House of Commons, *to be Printed,*
5 *July* 1853.

Martis, 26° *die Aprilis,* 1853.

Ordered, THAT a Select Committee be appointed to consider the Expediency of adopting a more Uniform System of Police in England and Wales, and Scotland.

Jovis, 5° *die Maii,* 1853.

And a Committee is nominated accordingly of,—

Mr. Rice.	Mr. Rich.
Mr. Sotheron.	Mr. Moody.
The Lord Advocate.	Mr. Mackie.
Mr. Walpole.	Mr. Brand.
Mr. Fitzroy.	Mr. Charles Howard.
Mr. Burroughes.	Sir James Anderson.
Lord Lovaine.	Mr. Philipps.
Sir John Trollope.	

Ordered, THAT the Committee have power to send for Persons, Papers, and Records.
Ordered, THAT Five be the Quorum of the Committee.

Jovis, 9° *die Junii,* 1853.

Ordered, THAT the Committee have power to report the Minutes of Evidence taken before them, from time to time, to The House.

SECOND REPORT.

THE SELECT COMMITTEE appointed to consider the expediency of adopting a more Uniform System of Police in England and Wales, and in Scotland, and who were empowered to report their Opinion, together with the Minutes of Evidence taken before them, to The House;——— HAVE further considered the Matters to them referred, and have agreed to report the following RESOLUTIONS, together with MINUTES of EVIDENCE.

Resolved, 1. THAT the Acts for the appointment of District Constables (2 & 3 Vict. c. 93, and 3 & 4 Vict. c. 88), commonly called the Rural Police Act, has (from the permissive character of its enactments), failed to provide such a general and uniform Constabulary Force as, in the opinion of Your Committee, is essentially required for the prevention of crime and security of property.

Resolved, 2. That in the districts in which the Rural Police Act has been adopted, its efficiency for the prevention of crime, by rendering the detection and apprehension of offenders more prompt and certain, has been proved to the satisfaction of Your Committee; that it has tended to the maintenance of order, and the improved habits of the population; that vagrancy has greatly decreased, and, more especially in combination with the casual relief order of the Poor Law Board, has been, in some places, almost entirely suppressed; and the effectual protection afforded to property peculiarly exposed to depredation, has, in the opinion of owners and holders of land, rendered its occupation more desirable. The adoption of the Rural Police, therefore, in the opinion of Your Committee, has proved highly advantageous to those districts, whether tested by moral, social, or economical considerations.

Resolved, 3. That the Superintending Constables appointed under the 5th & 6th Vict. c. 109, have proved useful as Police officers, to the extent of their individual exertions and services within their respective divisions, but that the appointment of a Superintending Constable in each petty sessional division provides no remedy for the inefficiency of Parochial Constables; and it is the opinion of Your Committee that any system of Police mainly dependent on the aid of Parochial Constables, must prove ineffectual for the protection of property, more especially that of the poorer classes, for the prompt detection and pursuit of offenders, the maintenance of order, and other duties of a Police Force, for which their necessary avocations and local connexions entirely disqualify them.

Resolved, 4. That the actual cost of the Rural Police Force is ascertainable by the ratepayers, while the great aggregate saving effected by it is not so generally known or appreciated. That it is, on the other hand, difficult to ascertain the full extent of the indirect and undefined expense of the Parochial Constables: it has, however, been proved to Your Committee, that it greatly exceeds the amount at which it is generally estimated.

Resolved,

Resolved, 5. That where the population of separate districts within the same county differs in amount and in the character of its employments, and consequently in its requirements for a Police Force, an equitable adjustment of the Police rate to meet those cases should be provided for by enactment, and that such an arrangement would tend to remove the objections now partially entertained against the adoption of the Rural Police Act.

Resolved, 6. That the efficiency of all existing Police Forces is materially impaired by the want of co-operation between the Rural Constabulary and the Police under the control of the authorities of boroughs, or other local jurisdictions. That, in order to secure that co-operation which uniformity can alone afford, Your Committee are of opinion, that the smaller boroughs should be consolidated with districts or counties for Police purposes, and that the Police in the larger boroughs should be under a similar system of management and control to that of the adjoining district or county, and (where practicable) under the same superintendence, by which arrangement a considerable saving would be effected in the general expenditure.

Resolved, 7. That, taking into consideration the aid afforded (hitherto partially and gratuitously) by the Rural Police for the protection of the revenue, the valuable services it has rendered for the maintenance of order, and in promoting the observance of the laws, in reducing the cost of prosecutions, and the effectual protection it gives to life and property of every description, by which the holders of a large amount of property not contributing to the Police Rate are greatly benefited, it is the opinion of Your Committee that it is a matter worthy the consideration of The House whether some aid should not be afforded by the Government towards defraying the cost of an improved and extended system of Police, without essentially interfering with the local management of that Force.

Resolved, 8. That it is the opinion of Your Committee, that it is most desirable that legislative measures should be introduced without delay by Her Majesty's Government, rendering the adoption of an efficient Police Force on a uniform principle imperative throughout Great Britain.

5 *July* 1853.

PROCEEDINGS OF THE COMMITTEE.

Veneris, 6° die Maii, 1853.

Members Present.

Mr. Rice.	Mr. Walpole.
Mr. Borroughes.	Mr. Mackie.
Sir James Anderson.	Mr. Moody.
Mr. Brand.	Mr. Charles Howard.
Mr. Philipps.	Mr. Rich.

Mr. Rice was called to the Chair.

[Adjourned to Thursday, 12 May, at 12 o'clock.

Jovis, 26° die Maii, 1853.

Members Present:

Mr. RICE, in the Chair.

Mr. Sotheron.	Sir J. Anderson.
Mr. Fitzroy.	Mr. Borroughes.
Sir J. Trollope.	Mr. Walpole.
Mr. Rich.	Mr. Philipps.
Mr. Mackie.	

Captain Harris, Chief of the Hampshire Constabulary, examined.

Sir William Heathcote, Bart, examined.

Mr. W. Hans Sloane Stanley, examined.

Mr. Fielder King, examined.

Mr. Henry Thompson, examined.

Dr. John Reynolds Beddome, examined.

[Adjourned till To-morrow, at 12 o'clock.

Veneris, 27° die Maii, 1853.

Members Present:

Mr. RICE, in the Chair.

Mr. Borroughes.	Mr. Philipps.
Mr. Mackie.	Mr. Rich.
Mr. Howard.	Mr. Sotheron.
Sir J. Anderson.	Lord Lovaine.
Sir J. Trollope.	Mr. Walpole.

Mr. Andrew Robert Fenwick, examined.

Sir R. Sheffield, Bart., examined.

Captain Harris, further examined.

Captain B. B. McHardy, R. N., examined.

Mr. Maurice Swabey, examined.

[Adjourned till Thursday next, June 2d, at 12 o'clock.

a 3

Jovis, 2° die Junii, 1853.

Members Present:

Mr. RICE, in the Chair.

Lord Lovaine.
Sir J. Trollope.
Mr. Burroughes.

Mr. Mackie.
Sir J. Anderson.
Mr. Moody.

Mr. James Parker, examined.

Mr. Robert Baker, examined.

Mr. William Hamilton, examined.

Mr. George Marris, examined.

Mr. G. Warry, examined.

Mr. Thomas H. Redin, examined.

Mr. Alfred Hughes, examined.

Mr. Charles Aaron Moody, a Member of the House, examined.

[Adjourned till To-morrow, at 12 o'clock.

Veneris, 3° die Junii, 1853.

Members Present:

Mr. RICE, in the Chair.

Mr. Burroughes.
Mr. Mackie.
Lord Lovaine.
Mr. Fitzroy.

Sir J. Trollope.
Mr. Howard.
Mr. Rich.
Sir J. Anderson.

Mr. T. H. Redin, further examined.

Captain J. Woodford, examined.

Rev. J. Holmes, examined.

Mr. H. Dover, examined.

Mr. J. Wyberg, Jun., examined.

Major G. F. White, examined.

Mr. H. F. Mackey, examined.

Mr. J. Wayte, examined.

Mr. J. Danne, examined.

[Adjourned till Thursday next, at 12 o'clock.

Jovis, 9° die Junii, 1853.

Members Present:

Mr. RICE, in the Chair.

Mr. Sotheron.
The Lord Advocate.
Mr. Fitzroy.
Mr. Burroughes.
Lord Lovaine.
Sir J. Trollope.

Mr. Moody.
Mr. Mackie.
Mr. Howard.
Sir J. Anderson.
Mr. Philipps.

Mr. G. W. Blathwayt, examined.

Mr. J. T. Gordon, examined.

Mr. E. Corbett, examined.

Mr. G. Kitson, examined.

Captain S. Meredith, examined.

Sir B. Leighton, Bart., examined.

[Adjourned till To-morrow, at 12 o'clock.

Veneris, 10° *die Junii,* 1853.

Members Present:
Mr. RICE, in the Chair.

Mr. Sotheron.	Lord Lovaine.
Mr. Fitzroy.	Sir J. Trollope.
Mr. Mackie.	Mr. Moody.
Mr. Howard.	Sir J. Anderson.
Mr. Burrougher.	Mr. Philipps.

Rev. E. Postle, examined.

Honourable and Rev. A. Talbot, examined.

Rev. W. G. Townley, examined.

Mr. J. Beadle, examined.

Mr. F. M. Mallalieu, examined.

Capt. E. Willis, examined.

Mr. E. B. Denison, a Member of the House, examined.

[Adjourned till **Thursday next, at 12 o'clock.**

Jovis, 16° *die Junii,* 1853.

Members Present:
Mr. RICE, in the Chair.

Lord Lovaine.	Mr. Rich.
Mr. Charles Howard.	Mr. Mackie.
Mr. Burroughes.	Mr. Philipps.
Sir J. Trollope.	Sir James Anderson.
Mr. Fitzroy.	

Mr. John Fawcett, examined.

Mr. Robert Brown, examined.

Mr. John Clayden, examined.

Mr. George Carrington, examined.

Mr. Oakley, examined.

Captain McHardy, examined.

[Adjourned till **To-morrow, at 12 o'clock.**

Veneris, 17° *die Junii,* 1853.

Members Present:
Mr. RICE, in the Chair.

Mr. Howard.	Mr. Fitzroy.
Sir John Trollope.	Mr. Sotheron.
Mr. Philipps.	Mr. Mackie.
Mr. Burroughes.	Sir James Anderson.
Lord Lovaine.	

Mr. Healy, examined.

Mr. Matthews, examined.

Mr. David Smith, examined.

Mr. George Martin, examined.

Mr. Edwin Chadwick, examined.

Sir John Walsham, examined.

Mr. N. Barnadiston, examined.

Captain McHardy, examined.

Mr. Oakley, examined.

[Adjourned till **Thursday, at Twelve.**

Jovis, 23° *die Junii,* 1853.

Members Present:

Mr. RICE, in the Chair.

Mr. Charles Howard.	Sir J. Trollope.
Mr. Burroughes.	Mr. Philips.
Mr. Fitzroy.	The Lord Advocate.
Mr. Mackie.	Mr. Rich.
Mr. Sotheron.	Sir James Anderson.

The following Witnesses were Examined:

Mr. George Irving.

Mr. Henry Clifford, Member of the House.

Mr. List.

Mr. Smart.

Mr. Murray.

Mr. Robert Macleod.

Mr. John Jones.

[Adjourned till To-morrow, at One.

Veneris, 24° *die Junii,* 1853.

Members present:

Mr. RICE, in the Chair.

Mr. Philips.	Sir J. Trollope.
Mr. Sotheron.	Mr. Burroughes.
Mr. Howard.	The Lord Advocate.
Mr. Mackie.	Mr. Fitzroy.
Sir J. Anderson.	Mr. Walpole.

The Committee deliberated with regard to their Report.

[Adjourned till Tuesday, July 5, at Twelve.

Martis, 5° *die Julii,* 1853.

Members present:

Mr. RICE, in the Chair.

Sir J. Trollope.	Sir James Anderson.
Mr. Rich.	Mr. Philipps.
Mr. Mackie.	Mr. Burroughs.
Mr. Brand.	Lord Lovaine.
Mr. Charles Howard.	

Motion made (*Chairman*), and question proposed, " That the Acts for the appointment of District Constables (2 & 3 Vict. c. 93, and 3 & 4 Vict. c. 88), commonly called the Rural Police Act, has (from the permissive character of its enactments), failed to provide such a general and uniform constabulary force as, in the opinion of your Committee, is essentially required for the prevention of crime, and security of property."

Amendment proposed (Sir *John Trollope*), " To leave out all the words from the word ' That,' to the end of the question, for the purpose of adding the words ' the present law with respect to the Rural Police Act, which is left to the option of magistrates of counties, for the adoption of its provisions or the contrary, according to the requirements of the locality, seems to your Committee most in accordance with the wishes of the ratepayers, and the spirit of the constitution,' instead thereof."

Question

Question, That the words proposed to be left out stand part of the question, put.

Committee divided :

Ayes, 7.	Noes, 2.
Mr. Burroughes.	Sir J. Trollope.
Mr. Rich.	Mr. Moody.
Mr. Mackie.	
Mr. Brand.	
Mr. Charles Howard.	
Sir James Anderson.	
Mr. Philipps.	

Original question put, and agreed to.

Motion made (*Chairman*), and question proposed, "That in the districts in which the Rural Police Act has been adopted, its efficiency for the prevention of crime, by rendering the detection and apprehension of offenders more prompt and certain, has been proved to the satisfaction of Your Committee; that it has tended to the maintenance of order, and the improved habits of the population ; that vagrancy has greatly decreased, and more especially in combination with the casual relief order of the Poor Law Board, has been in some places almost entirely suppressed ; and the effectual protection afforded to property peculiarly exposed to depredation, has, in the opinion of owners and holders of land, rendered its occupation more desirable. The adoption of the rural police, therefore, in the opinion of Your Committee, has proved highly advantageous to those districts, whether tested by moral, social, or economical considerations."

Amendment proposed (Sir *J. Trollope*), "To leave out the words, ' Whether tested by moral, social, or economical considerations,' for the purpose of inserting, ' As tested by moral considerations,' " instead thereof.

Question, That the words proposed to be left out stand part of the question, put.

Committee divided :

Ayes, 8.	Noes, 2.
Mr. Burroughes.	Sir J. Trollope.
Lord Lovaine.	Mr. Moody.
Mr. Rich.	
Mr. Mackie.	
Mr. Brand.	
Mr. Howard.	
Sir J. Anderson.	
Mr. Philipps.	

Original question put, and agreed to.

Motion made (*Chairman*), and question, "That the superintending constables appointed under 5 & 6 Vict. c. 109, have proved useful as Police officers, to the extent of their individual exertions and services within their respective divisions, but that the appointment of a superintending constable in each petty sessional division provides no remedy for the inefficiency of parochial constables ; and it is the opinion of Your Committee that any system of Police mainly dependent on the aid of parochial constables must prove ineffectual for the protection of property, more especially that of the poorer classes, for the prompt detection and pursuit of offenders, the maintenance of order, and other duties of a police force, for which their necessary avocations and local connexions entirely disqualify them." Put, and agreed to.

Motion made (*Chairman*), and question, "That the actual cost of the Rural Police Force is ascertainable by the ratepayers, while the great aggregate saving effected by it is not so generally known or appreciated. That it is, on the other hand, difficult to ascertain the full extent of the indirect and undefined expense of the parochial constables : it has, however, been proved to Your Committee, that it greatly exceeds the amount at which it is generally estimated." Put, and agreed to.

Motion made (*Chairman*), and question, "That where the population of separate districts within the same county differs in amount, and in the character of its employments, and consequently in its requirements for a police force, an equitable adjustment of the police rate to meet those cases should be provided for by enactment, and that such an arrangement would tend to remove the objections now partially entertained against the adoption of the Rural Police Act." Put, and agreed to.

Motion made (*Chairman*), and question " That the efficiency of all existing police forces is materially impaired by the want of co-operation between the rural constabulary and the police under the control of the authorities of boroughs, or other local jurisdictions. That, in order to secure that co-operation which uniformity can alone afford, Your Committee are of opinion, that the smaller boroughs should be consolidated with districts or counties for police purposes, and that the police in the larger boroughs should be under a similar system of management and control to that of the adjoining district or county, and, where practicable, under the same superintendence, by which arrangement a considerable saving would be effected in the general expenditure," put, and agreed to.

Motion made (*Chairman*), and question proposed, " That, taking into consideration the aid afforded (hitherto partially and gratuitously) by the rural police for the protection of the revenue, the valuable services it has rendered for the maintenance of order, and in promoting the observance of the laws, in reducing the cost of prosecutions, and the effectual protection it gives to life and property of every description, by which the holders of a large amount of property not contributing to the police rate are greatly benefited, it is the opinion of Your Committee that it is a matter worthy the consideration of The House whether some aid should not be afforded by the Government towards defraying the cost of an improved and extended system of police, without essentially interfering with the local management of that force."

Amendment proposed (*Mr. Rich*), " To leave out from the word ' That,' to the end of the question, for the purpose of inserting, ' Without entering on the question of the redistribution of local assessment, it appears to Your Committee, that to preserve the independence of the police force, it is expedient that it should be under the control of the local authorities, and therefore independent of all Government pecuniary aid,' " instead thereof.

Question, That the words proposed to be left out, stand part of the question, put.

The Committee divided :

Ayes, 8.	Noes, 2.
Mr. Burroughes.	Mr. Rich.
Lord Lovaine.	Sir J. Anderson.
Sir J. Trollope.	
M. Moody.	
Mr. Howard.	
Mr. Philipps.	

Original question put, and agreed to.

Motion made (*Chairman*), and question, " That it is the opinion of this Committee, that it is most desirable that legislative measures should be introduced without delay by Her Majesty's Government, rendering the adoption of an efficient police force on a uniform principle imperative throughout Great Britain," put.

The Committee divided :

Ayes, 7.	Noes, 2.
Mr. Burroughes.	Sir J. Trollope.
Lord Lovaine.	Mr. Moody.
Mr. Rich.	
Mr. Mackie.	
Mr. Brand.	
Sir J. Anderson.	
Mr. Philipps.	

Question, That the above Resolutions be reported to The House, put and agreed to.

Ordered to report Minutes of Evidence to The House.

To Report.

EXPENSES OF WITNESSES.

NAME of WITNESS.	PROFESSION or CONDITION.	By what Member of Committee Motion made for Attendance of the Witness.	Date of Arrival.	Date of Discharge.	Total Number of Days in London.	Number of Days under Examination by Committee, or acting specially under their Orders.	Expenses of Journey to London and back.	Expenses in London.	TOTAL Expenses allowed to Witness.
							£. s. d.	£. s. d.	£. s. d.
William Charles Harris	--Chief of Hampshire Constabulary.	Chairman	25 May	26 May	2	1	1 13 -	2 2 -	3 15 -
John Reynolds Beddome	M.D.	Chairman	26 May	26 May	1	1	2 2 -	3 3 -	5 5 -
J. B. B. M'Hardy	Captain, R.N.	Chairman	27 May	27 May	1	1	- 10 6	1 1 -	1 11 6
Robert Baker	Farmer and land-agent	Chairman	2 June	2 June	1	1	- 10 6	1 1 -	1 11 6
James Parker	Solicitor	Chairman	2 June	2 June	1	1	- 10 6	2 2 -	2 12 6
William Hamilton	--Superintending constable.	Chairman	2 June	2 June	1	1	1 - -	1 1 -	2 1 -
George Morris	Solicitor	Chairman	1 June	2 June	2	1	1 18 -	4 4 -	6 2 -
George Warry	Magistrate	Chairman	2 June	2 June	1	1	3 - -	1 1 -	4 1 -
T. H. Redin	-- Governor of Carlisle Gaol.	Chairman	1 June	3 June	3	2	6 5 -	3 3 -	9 8 -
A Hughes	Chief of Bath Police	Chairman	1 June	2 June	2	1	1 14 -	2 2 -	3 16 -
J. Wyberg	Magistrate's clerk	Chairman	2 June	3 June	2	1	6 12 -	2 2 -	8 14 -
R. Woodford	--Chief constable of Lancashire.	Chairman	2 June	3 June	2	1	6 1 -	2 2 -	8 3 -
F. White	--Chief constable of Durham.	Chairman	2 June	4 June	3	1	5 8 -	3 3 -	8 11 -
H. F. Mackay	--Chief constable of Sussex.	Chairman	2 June	3 June	1	1	- 15 -	1 1 -	1 16 -
J. Dunne	--Chief police officer of Norwich.	Chairman	2 June	4 June	3	1	2 18 -	3 3 -	6 1 -
G. W. Blathwayt	Magistrate	Chairman	8 June	9 June	2	1	4 - -	2 2 -	6 2 -
George Kitson	Magistrate	Chairman	8 June	9 June	2	1	- - -	2 2 -	2 2 -
Samuel Meredith	-- Chief constable of Wiltshire.	Chairman	8 June	10 June	3	1	2 10 -	3 3 -	5 13 -
Rev. E. Postle	Clerk	Chairman	9 June	11 June	3	1	2 18 -	3 3 -	6 1 -
Hon. & Rev. A. Talbot	Clerk	Chairman	9 June	10 June	2	1	4 11 -	1 1 -	5 12 -
J. Beadle	Agent and landholder	Chairman	10 June	10 June	1	1	- 14 -	1 1 -	1 15 -
E. Willis	--Head of Manchester Police.	Chairman	9 June	11 June	3	1	4 5 -	3 3 -	7 8 -
F. M. Mallalieu	Metropolitan Police	Chairman	9 June	11 June	3	1	- 5 -	3 3 -	3 8 -
Mr. George Martin	-- Superintendent of Police.	Chairman	17 June	17 June	1	1	Travelling expenses -		- 6 10
Mr. John Clayden	Landowner	Chairman	16 June	16 June	1	1	1 6 -	1 1 -	2 7 -
Mr. Robert Brown	-- Superintendent of Police.	Chairman	15 June	18 June	4	4	5 16 -	4 4 -	10 - -
Mr. Wm. Oakley	--Governor of Taunton Gaol.	Chairman	15 June	17 June	3	3	3 7 8	3 3 -	6 10 8
Captain M'Hardy	R.N.	Chairman	15 June	16 June	2	2	1 1 -	2 2 -	3 3 -
Mr. Richard Healy	-- Chief constable of the Hundred of Aveland.	Chairman	16 June	18 June	3	3	1 18 -	3 3 -	5 1 -
Mr. David Smith	--Superintending constable, Oxfordshire.	Chairman	16 June	17 June	2	2	2 2 -	2 2 -	4 4 -
Mr. A. J. List	-- Superintendent of Police in Mid-Lothian.	Chairman	22 June	24 June	3	3	7 12 -	3 3 -	10 15 -
Mr. James Smart	-- Superintendent of Glasgow Police.	Chairman	22 June	24 June	3	3	11 - -	3 3 -	14 3 -
Mr. David Murray	--Provost of Borough of Paisley.	Chairman	22 June	24 June	3	3	9 5 -	3 3 -	12 8 -
Mr. Robert Bruce Macleod	Landowner	Chairman	22 June	24 June	3	3	14 - 6	3 3 -	17 3 6
Mr. John Jones	-- Superintendent of Dumfriesshire Police.	Chairman	22 June	24 June	3	3	7 2 -	3 3 -	10 5 -
								£.	

LIST OF WITNESSES.

MINUTES OF EVIDENCE.

Veneris, 10° die Junii, 1853.

MEMBERS PRESENT.

Mr. Rice.	Lord Lovaine.
Mr. Sotheron.	Sir J. Trollope.
Mr. Fitzroy.	Mr. Moody.
Mr. Mackie.	Sir J. Anderson.
Mr. C. Howard.	Mr. Philipps.
Mr. Burroughes.	

EDWARD ROYDS RICE, Esq. in the Chair.

The Rev. *Edward Postle,* called in ; and Examined.

2532. ARE you a Magistrate for Norfolk ?—I am.

2533. What are the duties which you especially perform in the county of Norfolk ?—I am, and have been for the last seven years chairman of the gaol committee, which is not only the visiting committee of the county gaol, but the standing finance committee of the county, to examine the county bills.

Rev. E. Postle.

10 June 1853.

2534. Do you examine the expenses of the police among others ?—No, the police committee is a separate body.

2535. Are you a member of the police committee ?—Not now ; I was for two years. I may say, with regard to the police committee, two or three times when special committees have been appointed in conjunction with the police committee, I have been appointed as one of those magistrates to act with the police committee on such special occasions.

2536. What have those special occasions been ?—Drawing up rules and regulations, or rather conferring with the chief constable as to rules and regulations in 1852. This year a committee was appointed, which is now in existence, to take into consideration a report of the present chief constable, Captain Black.

2537. Was that report as to an increase of the force?—It was ; also as to building station-houses, and other matters in reference to a different system than heretofore.

2538. Has that committee yet decided upon the report ?—Yes ; and I think I am quite at liberty to mention the recommendations contained in our report.

2539. You have not made your report ?—No ; it will be made to the magistrates in quarter sessions in about three weeks.

2540. Have you any objection to state the substance of the report ?—Not at all ; we were perfectly unanimous ; the committee was composed of seven magistrates, added to the police committee at their request, in all fifteen ; one gentleman did not attend at all, and another gentleman once ; the others I may say attended nearly every meeting, and a more unanimous committee could not have been. We determined to report in favour of the recommendations of Captan Black, which were to the effect to increase the police force about 30 men ; the building of station-houses generally throughout the county ; the superintendents hitherto have found their own horses and carts, with a salary allowed them ; we propose to reduce that salary, and that the horses and carts should be found at the expense of the county ; that they should take upon themselves, also, the duties of inspectors of weights and measures. I think that is generally what we are about to recommend should be adopted in the county of Norfolk.

2541. I think you stated that you were a member of the finance committee ? —Yes.

O.71.

A

2542. Are

Rev. E. Pottle.

10 June 1853.

2542. Are you the chairman of that committee ?—Yes.

2543. Is every publicity given to the ratepayers as to expenditure ?—I may state, also, that I am one of the auditors of the county accounts, which are submitted to the gaol, which is also the finance committee; they examine the bills, and the auditors have only to examine the vouchers at the end of the year, which the treasurer holds, and to regulate the printing of the accounts, to be laid before the county at the beginning of each year. I hold in my hand the system which has been adopted since 1834, of publishing the accounts of the county of Norfolk, which includes the general accounts of the county, the police account, and the lunatic asylum account, in which every item is entered with the minutest detail.

2544. Are those printed accounts sent to the magistrates ?—They are; each magistrate has a copy sent to him, and every Board of Guardians have three copies sent to them, the several officers of the county have copies, and then there are a considerable number left for other ratepayers who wish to be furnished with a copy.

2545. When was your police established?—Our police was established in November 1840.

2546. Can you say whether that was after the establishment of a police force in the Isle of Ely ?—I cannot say; since I have been in this room a magistrate of the Isle of Ely has told me that their force was established a year after ours; might I just observe this with regard to the ratepayers, that when a contribution order is issued by the Board of Guardians, it is stated exactly what is the required contribution, for the poor so much, the county rate so much, and the police rate so much; therefore each overseer and each parishioner, if he pleases, can know exactly what it is that is required.

2547. Every ratepayer, if he chooses to apply to his own overseer, may ascertain exactly what he pays to the county rate and to the police rate ?—Yes; I am speaking of my own district.

2548. Can you state generally to the Committee what the whole of the expenditure in the county is; perhaps you will give the gross amount, and what it is in the pound, in the county on the assessment ?—In the year 1852, there was levied for general purposes a $1\frac{1}{2}$ d. rate, amounting to 11,084 l.; and for police a rate was raised at $1\frac{5}{16}$ d., being 9,698 l. 10 s.; in the year 1851 they were precisely the same, but the general expenditure is somewhat more than the police.

2549. Do you think the police does not cost the county of Norfolk more than $1\frac{1}{2}$ d. in the pound ?—No, certainly not.

2550. What number of policemen have you ?—Our force consists now, of a chief constable, a deputy chief constable, who acts as clerk, 12 superintendents, one inspector, and 132 constables.

2551. Taking the whole number, what proportion do the constables bear to the population ?—I believe now, it is one to 2,400.

2552. That is what the force is now, previous to your report being adopted ?—Yes.

2553. What difference will there be when Captain Black's recommendation is adopted ?—It will be about one to 2,000.

2554. From Captain Black's report, and from your own opinion and experience, do you think that will be sufficient for the preservation of the peace?—I think it will be sufficient for the preservation of the peace; I think the police force generally might be increased, by other duties being put upon them which they would find ample time to perform, and yet have the opportunity of superintendence which is necessary on the part of the police force.

2555. Do you think that the proportion of one policeman to 2,000 of the population will be sufficient to establish a night patrol ?—It is intended it should be so.

2556. Does Captain Black in his report contemplate that one to 2,000 will be sufficient for a night patrol ? — He does contemplate that that force will be able to patrol.

2557. Mr. *Philipps.*] What additional duties would you propose to impose upon the police?—It is a matter of opinion on my own part; hitherto we have not adopted, as in other counties, the relief of vagrants on the part of the superintendents; we recommend that they should become inspectors of weights and measures; I think that the superintendents of police might with great advantage be made district surveyors of highways, but this is not in our report.

2558. *Chairman.*]

Rev. R. Postle.
—————
10 June 1853.

2558. *Chairman.*] Have you any station-houses in Norfolk?—We have station-houses to the number of seven, which are small, but we advise the erection of station-houses on a general system throughout the county, in the report to which I have before referred, and which is about to be presented to the quarter sessions.

2559. Will that be an expense over and above the 1½ d. rate?—We propose to borrow 10,000 l., to be paid off in 10 years.

2560. Will the buildings pay rent?—Yes.

2561. Will the rent of the buildings pay the interest?—I should think not; the interest will be 400 l.

2562. Have you made any calculation of what the police will cost under the increased system?—Captain Black's recommendation was to raise the rate to 2 d., and then the cost of the erection of stations might be paid off in two years.

2563. Notwithstanding the increase of station-houses and of police, you calculate that the expense to the county will not exceed 2 d. in the pound?—Certainly I may say that.

2564. Mr. *Philipps.*] What is the gross amount of the expense of the police at present?—The gross amount was 9,763 l. 3 s. 2 d. in the year 1852.

2565. *Chairman.*] In what manner are the ratepayers of the unions informed as to the distribution of the expenses?—It refers only to my own union. I have for 15 or 16 years been the chairman or vice-chairman of an union. I can speak only to my own district, and what is the method which is adopted there. A precept is sent from the Board of Guardians, signed by three guardians, to the overseer to pay in his quarter's contribution, which in the case in my hand amounted to 6 l.; it includes the expenses of the union, the "contribution to the poor," the "county rate," which means county rate for general purposes, and the "police rate."

2566. Are your superintendents inspectors of weights and measures?—They are not.

2567. Do not you intend that they shall be so?—I hope the quarter sessions will adopt the recommendation.

2568. Do they attend to the relief of vagrants?—They do not.

2569. Do you think it is desirable they should relieve the vagrants?—Yes.

2570. Have you much vagrancy in the county of Norfolk?—The number of vagrants committed to prison in 1851 and 1852 was four times as many as in the two years antecedent to the formation of the police. I unhesitatingly say, that vagrancy has immensely decreased in the county of Norfolk; but the number of vagrants punished has increased.

2571. Do not you think that the adoption of the plan of making the police assistant relieving officers of vagrants, would tend further to decrease the number of vagrants?—I am confident it would.

2572. Do your men receive deputations from the Board of Customs?—Some of them do.

2573. Have they rendered any efficient assistance to the coast-guard?—I do not reside on the coast, and therefore I am not able to say.

2574. Is it not their duty to do so if they can?—An application was made to the magistrates at quarter sessions to allow the men to hold deputations; they agreed to the application, and that is all I know about it.

2575. Mr. *Burroughes.*] Do not you think it probable they will all hold those deputations ultimately?—I think it is most likely.

2576. *Chairman.*] From your experience, do you think it would be desirable to establish a more uniform system of police throughout the kingdom?—I do; I think it is a misfortune that the rural police are not under uniform rules and regulations. It has fallen to my lot to communicate with a great many gentlemen holding the office of chief constable in the counties of England and Wales, with the view of ascertaining what their rules and regulations were. In 1851, I had occasion to write to the Home Office to ask for copies of the rules and regulations which governed the police; the answer I received was, that they were drawn up entirely and solely by the magistrates of the respective counties. I applied to the chief constables of the counties for a copy of their rules and regulations. I received a great many; and, excepting in Cambridgeshire and Hampshire, which both seemed *verbatim* to have adopted the excellent rules established in the county of Essex, the other rules, from Lancashire, Leicestershire, Suffolk, Northamptonshire, and others, vary most widely, although the Act of Parliament under

Rev. E. Postle.

10 June 1853.

under which they are established, states it is "expedient" that there should be one "uniform" system.

2577. Have you high constables?—We have high constables, but not paid high constables; the hundred constables are still appointed.

2578. Do they perform any duties?—They do.

2579. What are those duties?—They are the persons to whom are directed the precepts for jurors; and they have to send out the precepts with regard to licensing ale-houses and public-houses; they have not now the duty of collecting the county rate; until 1846 the high constables collected the county rate; on that occasion, having made inquiry about the matter in the county of Essex, which county had adopted a system which was afterwards carried into Norfolk, I found there was a saving to the county of Essex of several hundred pounds a year, by placing the collection of the county rate on the Board of Guardians.

2580. Whatever remaining duties are now performed by the high constables, do not you think they might be performed by the police?—Yes, certain Acts of Parliament state that the high constables are to perform those duties, but the police are ordered to assist them in issuing the precepts; the high constables now receive the precepts from the clerk of the peace; the policemen in the district are ordered to distribute them in the different parishes.

2581. If it were not for the Acts of Parliament to which you allude, do you think the policemen might perform those duties?—Yes.

2582. Do you still swear in parochial constables in the county of Norfolk?—We do.

2583. Do you make any use of them?—We make no use of them.

2584. Are they paid for their loss of time, in attending to be sworn in?—They are paid a mileage; they are really of little or no use.

2585. Might not all that expense be saved?—Most decidedly.

2586. Do you think with an increased police force, it would be desirable to get rid of parish constables, and the expenses attending them?—Yes.

2587. Are they not still an expense to the county?—From 15 s. to 1 l. per head, to the county.

2588. You think that expense might be got rid of entirely?—I think so; allow me to say on this head, I hold in my hand the 5 & 6 Vict. c. 109, which is called, "An Act for the appointment and payment of Parish Constables;" it is enacted by the 18th and 19th clauses, that where parishes adopt paid superintending constables, those parishes shall be exempt from the appointment of parish constables, whereas there is no such exemption in districts under the county constabulary: a great inconsistency, I think.

2589. Where paid constables are appointed under that Act no other parochial constables are to be appointed?—Yes.

2590. Are you aware of the Act under which superintending constables are appointed in divisions?—Yes, the 5th & 6th Vict. c. 109.

2591. Are you of opinion that the appointment of a superintending paid constabulary in each division of a county can render the parochial constables under the superintending constables efficient as a police?—I think, certainly not.

2592. Do you think if there were a chief constable appointed, as has been proposed, the superintending constables in each division, with the parochial constables, would then be an efficient police?—I think the police might perform all the duties of the parochial constables.

2593. Would the parochial constables be rendered efficient police by that means?—I think the worst system is the old parochial constable system; better than that is the paid superintending constable system, and best of all is the rural police.

2594. Mr. Burroughes.] You have stated that a considerable saving was effected in Essex by abolition of high or hundred constables; will you state what saving has been effected in Norfolk?—In Norfolk the exact saving was 689 l. a year; they were paid 1 l. a parish.

2595. How was that 689 l. raised?—By a county rate. I will explain it thus. Until the passing of the new Poor Law Act they were paid 5 s. each quarter from each parish, which amounted to 1 l. The auditors appointed under the Poor Law refused to allow the charge. The high constables were put on to the county rate with the general expenses of the county until 1846, when the payment ceased altogether.

2596. What inducement do you consider the high constables had still to

continue

Rev. E. Postk.

10 June 1853.

continue without pay the performance of their duties?—They are free from serving on juries, which is a very great inducement. I think also if they wish it, and they plead their duties as a reason, they are free from serving in any parish office; it is not a legal exemption, but the magistrates always attend to it if they come forward and plead it.

2597. Consequently the county has not suffered from the loss of their services? —Certainly not.

2598. *Chairman.*] As a ratepayer and a clergyman, should you prefer being subject to the police rate on your rentcharge, with the advantages which you think are derived from the police, rather than be spared the rate, and be without the police?—Individually, I have no hesitation in saying that I should greatly prefer paying it on the rentcharge, but, as a magistrate as well as a clergyman, perhaps that is a question which others might better answer than myself. I feel confident that the answer would be the same from the clergy generally in the county of Norfolk.

2599. Was there much objection to the establishment of the police in the county of Norfolk?—On the part of some individuals there was, but there was no great opposition to it.

2600. Do you think the ratepayers are now satisfied with the police in the county of Norfolk?—Decidedly, with the general working of the police they are well satisfied.

2601. Do you think the value of property is increased in the county of Norfolk from the establishment of a well-regulated police?—That is a question which I will not undertake to answer; the value of property must be necessarily increased in any place where there is better security for property, and I have no doubt there is better security under the rural police than under the parochial constabulary system.

2602. Do you not think, from the farmers' property being exposed to depredations, that they save much more than the rate in the value of the property they might otherwise lose?—I think they do.

2603. Mr. *Burroughes.*] Are you not aware that in Norfolk there were districts in which a police force was voluntarily paid for previously to the establishment of the rural police?—Previously to the appointment of the rural police in 1840 there were several districts in Norfolk where they established a paid constabulary of their own. In the parish of Wymondham there were appointed a superintendent and two constables; I may observe, that they first appointed a superintending constable to be at the head of the parish constables; he found it so impossible to do anything with them that he said, "If you will give me two men of my own selection they shall be as good as all the men that are now put under my charge."

2604. Can you give the relative expense of that force?—In the parish of Wymondham they actually paid to those men 230 *l.* per annum, and they had also to maintain a lock-up of their own. The charge now for the police rate is 188 *l.* 11 *s.* 1 *d.* They have had a new lock-up built in that parish at the expense of the county; in addition to that, many of the farmers in the district and the principal owners of property were contributors to one of those societies for the protection of property which existed previously to the rural police being established, and which have all died a natural death since.

2605. Mr. *Philipps.*] Have you any returns of the comparative amount of sheep stealing before the establishment of the police in Norfolk, and subsequently to it?—I have not.

2606. Is sheep stealing a common offence in Norfolk?—Not now.

2607. Was it so to the best of your knowledge before the establishment of the police?—Yes; I cannot give you any return, because, before the establishment of the police there were no statistical returns which I can refer to; I think before the establishment of the police, when the offence was committed, the chance was that the offenders would not be discovered; I think now if the offence were committed that chance is almost reduced to a certainty that the offenders would be discovered.

2608. Does the payment of your police force include a retiring allowance from the superannuation fund?—It does; with regard to that subject, I may mention that there is a superannuation fund, and a pension thereby for every member of the police force except the chief constable; and I must take the opportunity of stating that I think it a very great defect that the magistrates have not the power of granting a pension to the chief constable. I think a good officer deserves a pension;

Rev. E. Pestle.

10 June 1853.

pension; it is an act of justice to him, and it is a benefit to the ratepayers at large, that the magistrates should have the power of pensioning the chief constable; I think it is a defect in the Act of Parliament that the magistrates have not the power of so doing.

The Honourable and Rev. *Arthur Talbot*, called in; and Examined.

Hon. and Rev.
A. Talbot.

2609. *Chairman.*] YOU are a Magistrate for the county of Stafford?—Yes; I live in Staffordshire.

2610. Are you a magistrate for any other county?—No.

2611. Are you the chairman of the police committee?—No, not at this moment; I have been; I attend regularly, and I am at almost every meeting.

2612. Can you state generally what the police system is in Staffordshire?—We are divided into three districts; we have, first of all, a mining district; secondly, a pottery district; and thirdly, a rural district; they are rated at different rates for police purposes; our force now consists of about 279 men.

2613. Do you know the cost per man?—£.57. 16 s. 8 d. I believe it was last year.

2614. What is the gross amount of the police rate?—About 16,000 l. in round numbers.

2615. What is that on the assessment in the pound?—The rural district last year was assessed 1 d. in the pound; the assessment in the mining district last year, was 3 d. in the pound; and the assessment in the pottery district last year, was 5 d. in the pound.

2616. What boroughs have you in Staffordshire?—The boroughs of Wolverhampton, Walsall, Stafford, the city of Lichfield, and the borough of Newcastle-under-Lyne.

2617. Are any of those boroughs incoporated with the county?—The city of Lichfield is under contract with us; we find the police for them; they are incorporated with the county for police purposes; Wolverhampton has its own force; Walsall has its own force; Newcastle-under-Lyne has its own force; and Stafford has its own force.

2618. Sir *J. Trollope.*] Did not Stafford once belong to the county?—It did once, but it has declined to act with the county any longer; I looked into the banker's books yesterday, and I find we did it for 200 l. a year, and I understand that they have raised for police in this year 250 l. already.

2619. How long has Stafford been dismembered from the rural police?—About three years.

2620. *Chairman.*] Are the 279 men whom you have mentioned employed in the three districts, the potteries, the mining, and the rural district, and also the city of Lichfield?—Yes.

2621. Can you state to the Committee how the number of men is apportioned in those districts?—I think we have not had a return of the census for 1851; we have about 600,000 inhabitants according to the present census, as far as I can gather, in the old district belonging to us, independently of Wolverhampton, and those boroughs with which we have nothing to do.

2622. Can you state the population of the three separate districts, the mining, the pottery, and the rural districts?—In the mining district in 1841, there were 196,082.

2623. Can you state the number of men apportioned to that district?—There were 99 in those days, when we had the borough of Wolverhampton. In the rural district there were 192,042 population, and the number of men was 75. In the potteries district the population was 122,082, and we had 70 men there, and have now. In the mining district under our charge now, the population is about 225,000.

2624. Lord *Lovaine.*] That would give one man to about 1,600 or 1,700?—Yes.

2625. *Chairman.*] What would it give in the rural district?—We have now 98 men; we call them 200,000 inhabitants; that would be one man to about 2,000 inhabitants.

2626. What is it in the pottery district?—There are 70 men to about 140,000 population.

2627. Do you think that number is sufficient?—No, I do not think it is.

2628. Is is sufficient for a night patrol?—There is a night patrol, but the men are

are worked very hard; it was sufficient at the time when they were appointed, but the population has increased so much that we want more men.

Hon. and Rev. A. Talbot.

10 June 1853.

2629. You stated that there were a certain number of boroughs which were not incorporated with the county?—Yes; the borough of Wolverhampton, I believe, in the year 1847 was severed from the county; it became incorporated, and took command of its own police; at that time we transferred to the borough bodily the 22 men, who were then employed in the borough of Wolverhampton, reducing our force of 99 men by those 22. Immediately upon that reduction we found that it was necessary to increase our own force so as to place men at the different outlets of the town. The Committee must be aware that no borough or town police force and the county force work well together; there is always a jealousy; and it was so particularly in this instance, because the man who became the chief constable of the borough of Wolverhampton was our deputy chief constable, and did not agree with our chief constable; consequently the jealousy was very prominent. Upon the formation of that force we found it necessary to increase our force by five men; at this moment it has been found necessary to add to our force; our force instead of being what it was, 99, now is 92, so that, in point of fact, we have only reduced the force by seven men. I asked for a return from the chief constable of the borough of Wolverhampton yesterday, and I found that his force consists of 29 men, so that, in point of fact, it is very nearly surplusage of the whole of the Wolverhampton force.

2630. You think, notwithstanding this increase of 22 policemen, which there is now in your district and Wolverhampton taken together, Wolverhampton now having 29, and you only having decreased your force seven, that the police is not as efficient in that district, taking the two together, as it was before?—I do not think it is. I believe the chief constable of Wolverhampton is a very efficient officer, but still, from the different jurisdictions, I do not think the police force works so well. It is fair to say that the population has very much increased in all the districts round; but the probability is, that had the management remained as it was, it would not have been necessary to have so largely increased the force. I have no means of ascertaining what the present expenditure of the Wolverhampton district is. I know this much, that the chief constable, when he was our deputy constable, had 120 l. a year; he has now 250 l. and a house.

2631. Have those 22 men which were given up to Wolverhampton been continued?—Yes.

2632. Do not you think there is an advantage that the men employed in the police force in the county should be removable from those boroughs to other places?—We found it a very great assistance when we had the borough; it was a sort of depôt to us; and we used to put our men there to be broken in, as it was a large town; then as they distinguished themselves, or became efficient officers, they were sent out into the rural districts, where there is much less supervision over them. I do not think there is any advantage in moving the men very much from one place to another.

2633. Do not you think it is an advantage to have the power of removing them?—It is a great advantage to have the power of moving them.

2634. Can you give the Committee any information with respect to the boroughs which have not adopted the police?—In the borough of Stafford we had four men; and some years ago the mayor of Stafford was offended because he thought the officers were not sufficiently under the control of the borough magistrates; it was resolved in the town council that they should be removed from us. Under our contract we provided four men for 200 l., knowing that there was some small loss upon that force *per se*, but at the same time thinking it enabled us to keep less men in the adjacent district; therefore, it was an advantage to us to have the borough; actually it was no real loss of income to us, though apparently it was so; therefore we were very glad to have the borough of Stafford, so as to enable us to have fewer men around it.

2635. What number of policemen had you in the borough of Stafford?—Four, and they have now the same number. The chief constable was at breakfast with me yesterday morning. I asked him, without his knowing what my idea was, " Now, how far, supposing you had men in Stafford, could you manage to superintend the adjacent district?" He said, " I can take a circle from the town, six miles in and six miles out." We took a map of the county, and we found how far it would extend. I said, "Now we will take this country, and suppose you had the control of the borough of Stafford, how many men should you require?"

He

He said, "Twelve men." I took the county constabulary return, and I found that, with the police of the borough of Stafford, we had 17 men in that district; therefore, I suppose there is a surplus of at least five men in that district. We are obliged to watch all the outlets of those towns; the borough force gives us no assistance, consequently we do not know what is going on in the borough; we are obliged to watch the roads. If we knew the bad characters in the borough of Stafford, we should be able to manage the adjacent country with a much less force than we have.

2636. If all those boroughs were consolidated with the county, and were acting cordially with them, do you think the expense of the whole might be materially diminished?—Yes.

2637. Do you think an uniform system of police throughout the country is desirable?—I have no question of it. I have thought of it; and I have no doubt, were different arrangements made, it would be done at a little increase of expense to what is going on now, supposing there were to be a general system of police all over the country, which, in my opinion there ought to be, provided it is done by a general rate, an urban or suburban, and a rural rate.

2638. Sir *J. Trollope.*] Do you mean in the immediate precincts of the town, or the whole county?—I would have an urban, a suburban, and a rural rate. The question was asked the last witness whether as a clergyman he objected to paying upon his rentcharge in the same way; I also say that I do not, but I think it is a hardship that a property like a rentcharge, which can derive no benefit whatever from the police, should be charged with that rate. The living which I hold is rated at 700l. a year, and I pay upon that 700l. which can get no benefit from the police. A shopkeeper who has 500l. capital when he first begins, may have in that very village a house which costs him 10l. a year, so that he gets complete protection for 1s. a year, whereas I pay the rate upon 700l. for nothing.

2639. You mean your rentcharge is a property which is not exposed to any depredation whatever?—It is perfectly immaterial whether there is a police force or not. I get my rentcharge as usual, it is no benefit at all; I mean the evidence I have given, with reference to the different rates and the different districts, to show that the rural district ought not to pay the same amount as a town district does. Here you have the pottery district content to pay 5d. in the pound; and the mining district 3d. in the pound for their protection, and we are content to pay 1d. in the rural district. I think if there were a general rate all over the county of Stafford it would be 2¼d. in the pound, which would be hard upon the rural parishes.

2640. *Chairman.*] Do you think your observations would only apply to counties situated like your own?—I think I would go further than that; I think such towns as Leek, Cheadle, and places of that sort, where there must be a police station, where the rural districts have already built rural stations, ought to be classed in another category from a mining district, or a rural district like mine; I am a farmer, and I know that a great deal of the farmer's capital is invested in a manner which does not require protection, such as growing crops of corn, &c.

2641. In the case of a district of a purely rural character being divided into three separate divisions, do you see any inconvenience in rating them separately?—None at all; but no advantage. There is a power under the Act of Parliament of rating districts at different rates. I would put the towns, if there were a general rate with a certain population, at one rate; I would put places without that population at another; any town of, say 2,000 inhabitants, I would put that in the urban, and anything below that should go in the rural rate.

2642. Sir *J. Trollope.*] How do you manage to separate your three districts for financial purposes?—Under the Act of Parliament we were empowered to assess different districts for different purposes.

2643. Having so great a difference between the three districts, the rural, the mining, and the potteries, have you had any remonstrances as to the cost?—None at all, for this simple reason, that in the pottery district we do it cheaper than they did it themselves; they had a police force before; it is a small district, having 70 men; the area is very small, and, of course, the rate is high. I understood it was done under the chief bailiff in former times, and that we do it cheaper than they did. Instead of ever having a remonstrance from the Potteries, on several occasions we have had applications for increasing the force.

2644. With

Hon. and Rev.
A. Talbot.

10 June 1853.

2644. With regard to rating the pottery district, have you made a fresh valuation?—Yes, under the Assessment Act.

2645. At what period?—I think for county purposes; we valued it three years ago.

2646. Have you had any remonstrance as to the cost of the police from either of the other districts?—We had two gentlemen, who were active magistrates, who rather set themselves in opposition to the police in the rural district; they have had petitions against it from some of the ratepayers.

2647. To whom have those petitions been presented?—To the Court of Quarter Sessions.

2648. Have they been entertained?—Yes, they have been entertained and inquired into; within the last two or three years one of those gentlemen has fallen into ill health, and he has dropped his opposition, and we have heard nothing of any opposition to us since.

2649. Was that an individual opposition on the part of those magistrates, or at the instigation of the ratepayers?—The opposition in one instance was at the instigation of the magistrate himself; he got up petitions in his own parish, and the immediate neighbourhood.

2650. Was that gentleman always opposed to the system?—He went about canvassing the country in opposition to it; when a motion was brought forward to the effect that the police should be done away with, he was only supported by five gentlemen, two of whom lived out of the county.

2651. Has the rate in the rural district ever exceeded 1 d. in the pound?—Yes; at one time it cost 1½ d.

2652. Do you consider that 1 d. in the pound would be a sufficient assessment for the rural district?—For the actual maintenance of the force it is sufficient; we have built county police stations in a great many districts, and a rate of ½ d. in the pound is being raised for the purpose of paying the cost of those stations off; but the actual cost of the force is 1 d. in the pound.

2653. Still do not you consider that that is a contingent expense upon the force?—That is done.

2654. Is it paid for?—Not all.

2655. Is it done by way of debt?—Yes, the debt is paid off annually; we borrowed the money from the Loan Commissioners.

2656. That amounts to another ½ d. in the pound?—Yes.

2657. Does that ½ d. in the pound cover the whole county, or only the rural district?—Only the rural district.

2658. Is it not greater in other districts?—I do not remember.

2659. Have you got your whole system of lock-ups complete?—Very nearly; there are one or two others which ought to be built; whether we shall build them or not I do not know.

2660. Lord *Lovaine*.] Do you contemplate the necessity of a further increase of the force at no very distant period?—I think if all was done which is required, we should want an additional force of 10 or 15 men in the rural district, and perhaps eight or ten in the mining district.

2661. Sir *J. Trollope*.] Have you heard the reason why the Stafford authorities severed themselves from the rural police; was it in consequence of a riot which occurred some time ago, when the borough authorities thought that the police had acted in a partial manner; is that the case?— No, it was because the mayor thought he had not the power of calling upon his own men to act as he wished; he did not at all approve, upon that occasion, of the borough police being under the authority of the county magistrates.

2662. On that occasion would the riot have been put down by the police, if it had not been for the interference of the borough authorities?—No. If I must honestly tell the truth, I think the police in a great measure caused the riot themselves; they were excessively violent; if they had been quiet, and remonstrated a little, I do not think the riot would have taken place; I think it was the violence of the police which exasperated the mob; it is but fair to say that.

2663. Do you attribute that to the orders which were given to the police upon the occasion?—No, it was owing to the conduct of the superintendent at the time.

2664. Mr. *Philipps*.] Do you know the relative acreage of the mining, the potteries, and the rural districts?—No, I do not.

2665. *Chairman*.] With respect to the riot to which you have referred, was

Hon. and Rev.
A. Talbot.

10 June 1853.

your opinion shared in by the magistrates, that the police were to blame?—The rioters were tried, and the evidence that was given upon the trial, I think, convinced the jury and the judge that the police were very much to blame.

2666. Were any steps taken with regard to punishing the police?—It was a matter of discussion at the moment; and the man who was then in charge of the police has been quite lately, from another cause, suspended and removed.

2667. Lord *Lovaine*.] Was not it rather want of discretion than positive criminality?—Yes; the mob rushed out; the policemen hit them on the head with their staves; they hit them as they came down the steps.

2668. *Chairman*.] Were there only four policemen?—There were a good many rural police in the town at the time.

2669. Supposing there were now a riot at Stafford, as they have only four policemen of their own, must they not have recourse to the rural police for assistance?—Yes.

2670. Or otherwise, they would not have a sufficient force to repress a riot?—With 1,300 in the town, and four policemen, I will leave you to judge how well that could be done.

2671. Would not one of the advantages of the consolidation of the boroughs and the county be, that in case of peculiar circumstances like those to which you have referred, you could add a force to that already in the town?—No doubt that is happening every year to us in the Potteries, where there are 70 men. We did it at Mr. Ricardo's election the other day; we threw in 100 men in addition to what there were in that district. It was a strongly contested election; perhaps higher political feeling was never known, but we had not the case of a single man in custody for rioting.

2672. Lord *Lovaine*.] Is the feeling against the rural police very violent?—No; the opposition to the force has completely died away.

2673. Mr. *Howard*.] Have you found it necessary to call in the aid of the military since the police force has been established?—Not since the establishment of the police force; there was a body of military stationed at Newcastle-under-Lyne, but they have been removed.

2674. Mr. *Philipps*.] Does the expense of the police include the retiring allowance and the superannuation fund?—No; the chief constable, and all the other constables, pay 2½ per cent. out of their pay to the superannuation fund. The chief constable will be entitled to a pension at the end of his time, as well as any other officer in the force. I think I heard evidence given to the contrary, but that is a mistake; it was only yesterday I was talking to our chief constable upon the point.

2675. Lord *Lovaine*.] Since the establishment of the police, has there been a complete cessation in Staffordshire of bull fights, cock fights, and prize fights?—There has been a complete cessation of bull fights and cock fights, but not of all prize fights; there was a prize fight the other day in the county. Our county is so intersected by railroads, that it is almost impossible to prevent such occurrences; but all the local disturbances are done away with. I should like to call the attention of the Committee to this fact: we try in our county, on the average, about 1,000 prisoners in the year. I have had a good deal to do with the gaol; and I called for a return of the prisoners that came from the different districts and the different boroughs. Now the number of prisoners tried in 1852 from the mining district was 357. The Committee will bear in mind that there are 92 or 93 constables now employed in that district. From the Potteries, where there are 70 constables, the number of prisoners for trial was 181. From the rural district, where there are 90 odd constables, and which takes in all the towns, such as Leek, Cheadle, and the borough of Stafford, we had 235; from the borough of Wolverhampton, where there are only 30 constables, there were 187 cases. I called upon the treasurer yesterday, and I looked at the certificates of the cost of sending those prisoners to gaol; and I found that, generally speaking, they allow them 5 s. 3 d. per head from the borough of Wolverhampton to send them to gaol. The 17 miles by railroad, I believe the fare by third-class train is 1 s. 5 d. Supposing (which is not the fact) that a single constable were to bring each prisoner, there would be two tickets at 1 s. 5 d. each, and there would be another 1 s. 5 d. for the return ticket of the constable; so that there would be three times 1 s. 5 d. Therefore, there is a cost of 1 s. less than the 5 s. 3 d.; there is a profit to somebody of 1 s. in the case of every prisoner.

2676. Therefore, you carry that to your credit?—As far as the county goes, we

Hon. and Rev:
A. Talbot.

10 June 1853.

we only charge the actual cost; the borough force gets, for some reason or another, something in addition.

2677. Have you had any experience of the system of parochial constables?—In the first instance, in the year 1842, the force was established in the mining and pottery districts, as it is now; in the rural district, superintending constables were appointed under the Act. We tried that system for one year; and we found, in consequence of being obliged to keep a large number of horses, and to have constables of the first class at a high rate, we paid, for a nearly useless force (which it was), five-eighths of a penny, whereas now, for an efficient force, we only pay one penny.

2678. You were obliged to have a better class of local constables?—Of course, if you are to have a man to superintend others, you cannot have a man at 15 s. a week.

2679. Were those men only paid for the duties which they performed?—We had a certain number of superintendents, and we had a district appointed to them, with a man to instruct the parish constables in their duties, so as to preserve the peace of the county.

2680. Do you think a superintending constable in each division can make the parish constables efficient officers?—As a clergyman, intimately acquainted with a large parish, and from other circumstances knowing the county well, I have no hesitation in saying that they were of no manner of use, except what they did themselves; the superintending constables did, to a certain extent, protect the county, but as far as the parochial constables went, they were no manner of use.

2681. Had you only one for each division?—I should think there were eight or nine of them, or more than that.

2682. You think their usefulness was confined to themselves individually; that you had eight or nine useful constables, but beyond that, they were of no use whatever?—There was a jealousy between them; they would not cotton to them at all.

2683. Do you not think they rendered the parochial constables more efficient?—I think rather less so, because they said, " There are other people doing our work; we will not do it."

2684. Were the parochial constables persons engaged in business generally?—They were generally shoemakers and small shopkeepers, and people of that sort, whoever was appointed.

2685. Is not their time valuable to them?—Of course it is.

2686. Is not their loss of time a loss of money?—Yes.

2687. Therefore taking them away from their business is a money loss to them?—Yes.

2688. And so far an additional cost is thrown upon the county?—Yes.

2689. Mr. *Philipps.*] Do you change your men from the rural district to the mining district?—Yes; as the chief constable finds a man fit for that district he removes him. I would venture to make a remark, that I think the money which is now spent by the Government and by ourselves, if properly economised, might very nearly give an efficient police all over the kingdom. I hold in my hand the particulars of a case which was tried at our last sessions, which I think will go far to prove my assertion, that if there were a public prosecutor the expense of the trials would be very much diminished; and if the magistrates' clerks were paid by salary instead of fees, not half the cases which now come to sessions and assizes would be sent there, all of which the Government pays for. Here is the case of the expenditure in a trial, where in a neighbouring town to my own a drunken butcher fell down in the street; he was carried home, and by one of the people that carried him home I believe he was robbed to the amount of 20 *l.* in crowns and half-crowns. I believe it was a very simple case; it was taken before the borough magistrates; it was got up by an attorney; attorneys, generally speaking, are not employed in our county, except when the committing magistrate requests them to be employed. The culprit went to a town some distance off, where he bought several articles, for which he paid in crowns and half-crowns, in the very sort of money of which this man was robbed; they sent a policeman down to hunt up inquiries. The result was that the cost of the case to the Government was 67 *l.* 13 *s.* 4½ *d.*, and I will venture to say if there had been a public prosecutor, it would not have cost 10 *l.* certainly. I may remark that our force has been very useful to the Inland Revenue; we have for the last three years allowed our officers to assist in the discovery of illicit stills;

they have certificates from the Commissioners, and I called for a return the other day, and it appears that in the course of three years they have destroyed 80 stills.

2690. *Chairman.*] Therefore they have been of use to the Inland Revenue?— They have been of great use; in fact, the revenue officers could not do what they have done; they would have been afraid to act in the pottery district.

2691. Did the men receive those deputations at the request of the Commissioners of Inland Revenue?—Yes.

2692. Have they given you anything for those services?—They have given us nothing for them.

2693. Therefore you perform those services gratuitously?—I believe the men get something themselves.

2694. Mr. *Philipps.*] Are your men inspectors of weights and measures?—They are.

2695. Are there any other purposes for which you think the police could be employed?—No, I do not agree with the last witness, that the police could act as district road surveyors.

2696. Do you think that police could be employed as toll collectors at the tollgates?—No; I think the great value of a policeman consists in nobody knowing where he is. I think he should have no fixed duty to any place.

2697. *Chairman.*] If you had a well-regulated police, all those additional duties might be a matter for after consideration?—Certainly.

2698. Mr. *Philipps.*] You are decidedly of opinion, that it would be better that the men should do nothing but the business of policemen?—Exactly so; I would not let anybody know what they were doing.

2699. *Chairman.*] Are you of opinion that it is desirable that the men should wear uniform?—I have no doubt of it.

2700. Sir *J. Trollope.*] Do you ever employ the men as detectives out of uniform, by order of the magistrates?—Yes, I think it would be very useful; and I conceive the expenditure would be much less if there were a general force under the control of the Government. In the first place our chief constable has too high a rate of pay for his area; of course his salary swells the average of the pay very much. My belief is, that a good officer might do three counties instead of one.

2701. *Chairman.*] You are aware that under the Act he might do the duties of three counties adjoining?—Yes; but where will you get three counties to agree to it?

2702. Sir *J. Trollope.*] Would it not depend on the size of the counties?— My belief is, that Derbyshire, Warwickshire, and Shropshire might be under one chief constable, in addition to Staffordshire.

2703. Mr. *Philipps.*] What do you pay your chief constable?—£. 400 a-year, and 150 l. travelling expenses.

2704. What was he before he became your chief constable?—He was in the Irish constabulary.

2705. Is your police distributed by districts or by parishes?—By districts. Some of our magistrates, when the rural police was first placed in the rural district, made it a *sine quâ non* that they should be put, as far as possible, singly, in different parishes. The experience which I have since had I think tends to show that that system is wrong, and that it would be much better to have four or five or six men in a station, and give them a larger district. In the first place you would have a better officer over them, who would see that the men under him were moving about; every man in the district would know where to go for a policeman if the men were at a station, and then the proper supervision on the part of the chief officer would be so much easier.

2706. Sir *J. Trollope.*] In your three districts, have you a distinct superintendent for each?—Yes.

2707. Are they men of intelligence whom you pay at a superior rate?—Yes; and supposing that it were under one management, I think you would do away with those men; you would get a class of rather less good men, if the thing were all under one management. I think we pay these men 120 l. a year; I think if the thing were properly managed, you would get a class of men to perform the duties for 100 l. a year.

2708 Are those men allowed a horse?—Yes; we have not many horses and carts in our force; the business is chiefly conducted by railway; the Government have derived some benefit from that. In the year 1842, before the force was
established,

established, the cost of the conveyance of prisoners was 1,900l. odd; this year it was 343l.

2709. Did that arise from the extension of railways?—Partly from the extension of railways, and partly from the police constables.

2710. Lord *Lovaine*.] Of course you can insist upon economy being observed by the rural police which you could not carry out with parish constables?—Of course, as far as we are able to control the expenses by the police committee, we do so; we allow them at the sessions and assizes a fixed sum per day, and everything which they receive as witnesses from the Government allowance is taken off, as far as we can ascertain it, and put into the fund for the relief of the police rate.

Hon. and Rev.
A. Talbot.

10 June 1853.

The Rev. *William Gale Townley*, called in; and Examined.

2711. *Chairman*.] ARE you the Chairman of the Quarter Sessions in the Isle of Ely?—I am one of them.

2712. Do not the quarter sessions sit at Ely and Wisbech alternately?—Yes.

2713. Have you a rural police in the Isle of Ely?—Yes.

2714. When was that force established?—It came into operation about the same time as the Norfolk force, in 1840 or 1841.

2715. Is the police in the Isle of Ely rated in three separate districts?—Four.

2716. What are those four districts?—Whittlesea, Wisbech, Ely, and Chatteris.

2717. What is the population of the four divisions?—I have only a general statement here. The population, in 1841, was 53,080. That does not include the borough of Wisbech.

2718. Has the borough of Wisbech a separate police?—Yes.

2719. What proportion does the police bear to the population?—In 1841 the police force was 38; it is now 45. The population has increased to 58,571.

2720. When did that increase in the force take place?—In 1853. The expense originally was 2,600l.; it is now 3,100l.

2721. What is the average cost of your men?—It is very high; 68l.

2722. Can you state why the cost is so much higher than in other counties?—There is the formation of a large staff thrown into it.

2723. You mean that there is a large staff to the number of men?—Exactly.

Rev.
W. G. Townley.

[*The Witness delivered in the following Statement:*]

ISLE of ELY CONSTABULARY; instituted 1841.

1841:

Population, 53,080 (exclusive of the borough of Wisbech).
Acres, 221,138 - - - ditto.
Valuation, 355,000l. (less 65l.)
Number of Police, 38.
Expense of Police, 2,600l. per annum (about that sum).

1 Police Officer to 1,396 inhabitants.
                    5,819 acres.

Average Cost, about 68l. per man per annum.

1853:

Population - 58,571⎫
Acres - - - 221,138⎬ The borough of Wisbech not included.
Valuation £. 355,000⎭
Number of Police, 45. Has been gradually increased.
Expense of Police, £. 3,100 per annum (about that sum).

1 Police Officer to 1,301 inhabitants.
                    4,914 acres.

Average Cost, about 68l. per man per annum.

2724. You say the Isle of Ely is divided into four districts; do you think there is any advantage in that division?—We certainly think not. There was very great difficulty in establishing the force. Whittlesea, which is a very large district, objected entirely to the force; and it was with great difficulty that we got them in at all. It is now come in, and is quite satisfied.

Rev.
W. .. Townley.

10 June 1853.

2725. Do you think the feeling of opposition to the appointment of police, which existed in the division of Whittlesea, has entirely ceased?—Entirely.

2726. What means had they of apprehending offenders before the appointment of the police?—They lost a great number of sheep, and they kept some blood-hounds. I told them that I thought it was not a very constitutional force, and they had better join a rural police, and give up the blood-hounds.

2727. Are those divisions all under one chief-constable?—Entirely.

2728. Are those four districts all rural districts?—Yes.

2729. Do you think it would be much more convenient, and no injustice to them, if they were all united?—I think they are satisfied so themselves.

2730. Though you are chairman of the court of quarter sessions in the Isle of Ely, you reside in the county of Norfolk?—Yes, and act there as a magistrate. I can speak to both police forces.

2731. Does your district adjoin Lincolnshire?—Yes.

2732. How does the fact of your having police and their having none in Lincolnshire operate as to vagrancy?—It is a great inconvenience to us. Instead of organising their own force they take away our best men as superintendents. They have taken three of our best men. It is highly inconvenient. Huntingdonshire is the same. They have only an apology for a police.

2733. Sir *J. Trollope.*] For what purpose have they taken away your best men?—For the towns.

2734. For the rural police?—No; they have no rural police.

2735. In the municipalities in Lincolnshire?—Yes.

2736. *Chairman.*] Have they not been taken for superintending constables? I understand so.

2737. Sir *J. Trollope.*] Do you know where the men are stationed?—I think Alford is one station, the last near Spilsby.

2738. Lord *Lovaine.*] Are you of opinion that the police established in Lincolnshire, with the help of your men, is better than your own police in the Isle of Ely?—No. We have nobody to communicate with in the county of Lincoln; they join us, and the vagrants come into the Isle of Ely, which we wish to get rid of.

2739. In spite of the superintending constables?—Yes.

2740. But if their object is answered by going to merely the expense of superintending constables, why should they adopt your system, which is more expensive?—I do not believe it is, except so far as those particular spots go, where the superintending constables are stationed, but not throughout the county generally. I believe there is an expense of between 2,000 *l.* and 3,000 *l.* for those 12 towns; but the county, generally, is left to itself, I should say.

2741. *Chairman.*] Is it your opinion that a more uniform system of police is desirable?—I should say decidedly, so far as I am aware.

2742. Lord *Lovaine.*] What is the difference between the state of crime in Lincolnshire and the Isle of Ely?—Our crime has diminished most amazingly, but I cannot speak to Lincolnshire; though I am in the commission of the peace, I do not act for it.

2743. Mr. *Philipps.*] Do you keep many sheep in the Isle of Ely?—Yes.

2744. Are there many cases of sheep-stealing now?—No.

2745. Was there much sheep-stealing formerly?—At Whittlesea, particularly, they lost an immense number, and we could not for a great while be of any service.

2746. *Chairman.*] Are you aware whether sheep-stealing was general in the county of Norfolk?—Yes; it is not so much now. I may observe that they have great facility in the Isle of Ely for carrying them away by water.

2747. Have you large works going on in the Isle of Ely?—Large works have continually been carried on without any commotion whatever; 3,000 or 4,000 men sometimes have been employed within these five years, and merely by the contractors paying for six additional men, to work with ours, the whole thing has been carried on without any commotion; the works finished, the additional men were dismissed.

2748. Do you attribute the fact of such large bodies of men being employed at the Isle of Ely without any disturbance to the presence of the police?—Yes.

2749. Mr. *Philipps.*] What is the pay of the chief constable in the Isle of Ely?—£. 250.

2750. *Chairman.*] Has not the police force recently been adapted in the county of Cambridge?—Yes.

2751. Do you know the reason why they have adopted the police in Cambridgeshire?—

shire ?—There were a great many fires, and a great deal of crime. I believe everything has been going on very well since the establishment of the police.

2752. Do you know at all what is paid to the chief constable in Cambridge?—No.

2753. Sir *J. Trollope*.] Had you a police force in the Isle of Ely before the county of Cambridge?—Yes; the Cambridgeshire police has only been established two or three years.

2754. Is not the Isle of Ely under a separate commission of the peace, therefore you have jurisdiction though a part of the county of Cambridge?—We have a separate *custos rotulorum*.

2755. Is the borough of Wisbech within your limits?—Yes.

2756. How does your police work with the police of that town?—I believe they do not work very well together, but I have had no reason to complain.

2757. Do you think it would be better if the police forces were amalgamated?—I think it would; they do not work very well together.

2758. Mr. *Fitzroy*.] Are your opinions the result of actual experience?—Yes.

2759. *Chairman*.] Cambridgeshire and the Isle of Ely being comparatively a small county, do not you think they might be both under one chief constable?—It would be much better; there is always a jealousy.

2760. If that system were adopted, you think you would not only have a more efficient police, but save the salary of one chief constable?—Yes, certainly.

Rev.
W. G. Townley.

10 June 1853.

Mr. *James Beadel*, called in; and Examined.

2761. *Chairman*.] ARE you a large occupier of land?—I am.

2762. In what county?—In Essex, principally.

2763. Do you occupy land in any other county?—I have the management of land in other counties.

2764. Are you agent for property in other countries?—Many others.

2765. Have you a county constabulary in Essex?—We have.

2766. Are you the agent for large properties in any counties where there is no police?—In Huntingdonshire.

2767. Do you, as a landholder in Essex, derive benefit from the police?—I consider I do.

2768. Do you think that is the general opinion of the landholders and rate-payers?—I think it is; when the police was first established there was a great deal of opposition; I think that opposition has much subsided, and I think it is now popular, generally speaking.

2769. From your experience that opinion is altered, and you think favourably altered?—I do.

2770. Do you think, as an agent and occupier of land, that what you gain by the saving of property is equal to what you pay for your police rate?—Quite so; I think I would rather occupy in a county where we had a police, and pay the police rate, than occupy in a county where they had the old constabulary.

2771. Is that the case in the county of Huntingdon?—They have the old constabulary there.

2772. Will you state for what properties you are agent?—I am agent for Lady Olivia Bernard Sparrow's estate, in Huntingdonshire; I am agent for Lord Carington's estates, and I am agent for Mr. Williams, in Dorsetshire; I hold a great many agencies.

2773. Is there any police in Dorsetshire?—No; I think there is not.

2774. From your experience as an occupier of land in Essex, where there is a police established, and of Huntingdonshire and Dorsetshire, where there is no police, would you prefer renting and occupying land in a country where there is a police?—I should prefer occupying land in a county where there is a police, and paying the police-rate.

2775. Lord *Lovaine*.] Is that the general feeling amongst farmers?—I think it is, so far as I can judge.

2776. *Chairman*.] Have you the opportunity of judging of the opinion of the occupiers of land generally in Essex upon the subject?—I have.

2777. Mr. *Fitzroy*.] Have you heard of complaints from farmers in counties in which there is no rural constabulary, of the want of such a force?—I do not know that I have heard complaints of the want of such a force.

2778. Have you witnessed depredations committed on their farms which you think would have been checked by the establishment of a police force?—I do

Mr. *J. Beadel*.

not know that I have where I am agent, but I consider crime has very much diminished in Essex since the establishment of the police; we used to have a great number of sheep stolen, but now we hardly hear of it; horse-stealing was very prevalent, and now it is very rare. There used to be a great many more incendiary fires than there are at present. I do not mean to say that it is all owing to the establishment of the police. I think a great deal may be attributed to that, as compared with the old constabulary, because the police is a preventive force, whereas the old constabulary did not wish to prevent crime; their profit was in the commission of crime; they were paid for serving summonses and conveying prisoners to gaol, and they had no object in preventing crime.

2779. Do you think there is any disinclination in the minds of the farmers in the counties to which you have referred, to adopt the police?—Not from my experience, so far as I have had the opportunity of judging.

2780. You think such a proposition would be rather popular than the reverse? —Yes.

2781. You think they are beginning to open their eyes to the saving in the long run, which might be effected by the police?—Yes; when they looked into it, examined it, and thought it over, I think they would be very much like myself, they would become converts.

2782. Sir *J. Trollope.*] Has it in your presence ever been discussed by the tenants when you have met with them, whether they would require the police in those counties where it does not exist?—No.

2783. Have you not heard the question mooted?—No.

2784. In the rural counties in which you act as agent for estates, where there is no police, do you think crime is on the decrease or on the increase?—I think, generally, crime is on the decrease throughout England.

2785. Do not you think there are other causes at work which are likely to bring about a diminution of vice as well as the police?—No doubt.

2786. In fact, in your opinion, the credit of diminution of crime ought not to be given entirely to the police system?—Certainly not.

2787. Mr. *Fitzroy.*] Has vagrancy been abolished very much in Essex by the police?—Almost entirely.

2788. Does vagrancy exist in Dorsetshire to any large amount?—I am only occasionally in Dorsetshire, therefore I do not know.

2789. *Chairman.*] Would not one of the causes of the decrease of crime be the increased employment of labourers?—No doubt.

2790. Do you think that would not operate as much upon the class of persons who are vagrants as it does upon the industrious labourers?—No, certainly not.

2791. Therefore, although you do not ascribe the decrease of crime among the labouring classes entirely to the police, still the decrease of vagrancy you do ascribe in a great measure to the police?—Nearly entirely.

2792. Are you of opinion that the protection of property by a well-organised police is a sort of insurance on that property?—No doubt about it; it increases the value of the property.

2793. And therefore would make it much more desirable to rent?—Undoubtedly. I think the police force might be made a self-supporting force, almost entirely so. There are many duties which the police might perform. In Essex several things are done by the police which used to cost the county a considerable sum of money.

2794. Have you ever seen the report which was made by Captain M'Hardy, and which he gave in evidence?—I cannot say that I have read it carefully; I have read parts of it.

2795. From your own experience you are of opinion that the police may, to a certain degree, be made a self-supporting force?—Yes.

2796. Mr. *Philipps.*] Do you think there has been a decrease in the crime of sheep-stealing, greater than in other crimes?—Yes.

2797. In those counties where police have been established?—Yes; in sheep-stealing and horse-stealing.

Mr. *Francis Mayall Mallalieu*, called in; and Examined.

2798. *Chairman.*] IN what district of the Metropolitan Police Force are you employed?—Mine is called the R. Division; Greenwich is the head-quarters, but it includes a rural district, and contains altogether 28 parishes.

2799. Are

Mr.
r' M. Mallalieu.
——
10 June 1853.

2799. Are those parishes entirely in Kent?—Yes, entirely in Kent.

2800. What is the extreme parish of your district in Kent?—Crayford would be the extreme parish on the Dover Road; Farnborough, on the Hastings Road, and West Wickham, adjoining Surrey, would be the extreme in that direction.

2801. Are they all under one rate with the Metropolitan district?—Yes.

2802. What is the amount of the rate in the pound?—Sixpence in the pound.

2803. Have you had any complaints in the rural district as to the amount of that rate?—No; they seem well satisfied with it.

2804. What is the extent of your police division altogether?—I think it comprises about 50 square miles.

2805. What is the number of men employed in the district?—My district also includes the Government dockyards at Woolwich and Deptford, and the Arsenal at Woolwich. The total number of police of all ranks is 395.

2806. Mr. *Fitzroy.*] Are not the men employed in the dock-yards paid by the Government?—Yes, by the Admiralty.

2807. *Chairman.*] In the towns of Greenwich and Deptford, there is one uniform rate?—Yes.

2808. Therefore Crayford and Farnborough would pay the same rate as Deptford and Greenwich?—Exactly.

2809. Do they do that without complaining?—I hear no complaints, and believe the farmers are very well satisfied.

2810. Is it not the case, that the farmers in Farnborough and Crayford are content to pay this larger rate, because their property is so much more exposed to depredation from the bad neighbourhoods therein?—It may be so; I know they contrast their condition with the condition of the farmers who are living outside our district; and they think themselves well off.

2811. There must be some reason why the ratepayers in the rural districts which adjoin Deptford and Greenwich, cheerfully pay 6*d.* in the pound, while some counties refuse to adopt the rural police at a probable expense of 2*d.* in the pound?—I cannot give any other reason, except that they think their property is better protected.

2812. Mr. *Fitzroy.*] Whatever the reason may be, you are not aware of any dissatisfaction being felt by those farmers as to the amount of rate they pay?—No.

2813. *Chairman.*] Is it not the case that over the borders of the district there are great complaints of the want of protection to property, which is received by those residing within the boundaries of your district?—I might say there are every day complaints from the people living outside our district; they say we drive the depredators out of our district into theirs, which is unprotected.

2814. Have you ever made any attempt to act beyond the line of your district?—Occasionally there may be cases out of the district, which are connected with matters within the district; a successful inroad may be made, and offences committed by parties connected with places outside the district, in which cases the the duties of the constables compel them to go beyond the boundary line.

2815. Do you think there is a marked difference as to the amount of crime in your district and immediately beyond it?—Yes, I think so.

2816. Can you give any data for that opinion?—I should think there is not one-fifth of the crime in the metropolitan district to what there is outside, judging from my experience, and from all I know; but I have no positive data, no records being kept outside.

2817. Have you had frequent complaints?—Yes, frequent complaints.

2818. How are the prisoners conveyed to the gaol in your district; do you send them to Maidstone?—We send them to Maidstone; that is one of the difficulties we have had to contend with; the county gaol is 32 miles from the great mass of our population, and the expense of conveying prisoners has therefore been very considerable indeed. I think, before we undertook the conveyance of the prisoners, it must have cost nearly 3,000 *l.* a year from the district over which I have the charge.

2819. Before the establishment of the police?—No, not before the establishment of the force, but before the passing of the 2d & 3d Victoria for improving the police of the metropolis.

2820. You now convey the prisoners?—Yes.

2821. At what cost do you convey them now?—The cost does not exceed 650 *l.* a year now.

Mr.
F. M. Mallalieu.

10 June 1853.

2822. Have not the county objected to pay that 650 *l.* a year?—Yes, and unwisely in my opinion.

2823. Having paid 3,000 *l.* a year before, they object to pay 650 *l.* now?—Yes; the saving having arisen entirely through the management we have adopted.

2824. Mr. *Fitzroy.*] What has been the largest charge incurred in the county of Kent for the conveyance of prisoners since you undertook that duty?—£. 950; now reduced to about 650 *l.*

2825. Was that for the year 1852?—Yes.

2826. *Chairman.*] That amount the county has refused to pay?—Yes.

2827. Is not that matter settled now?—The decision of the Court of Queen's Bench is in our favour; the magistrates still withhold payment, but I believe it will be settled at the ensuing quarter sessions.

2828. Were not you a witness on Mr. Hawes's Committee in 1839?—Yes.

2829. What was the result of that Committee; was that previous to the Rural Police Act?—Yes; and previous to the Act of the 2d & 3d Victoria, which was passed for the improvement of our system of police.

2830. Had not that Act in a great measure reference to the Metropolitan Police?—Yes.

2831. Since your service in the Metropolitan Police, have you had frequent opportunities of seeing the advantage of a police force in times of popular commotion?—Yes. I may say I have been present at all the principal scenes of popular commotion for the last 20 years. I was present during the Reform riots, the Cold-bath Fields disturbances, and at the most recent public gatherings of people in 1848, on Kennington Common and Blackheath.

2832. Do you think the police was sufficient to prevent the employment of the military on those occasions?—The military have never been called out since the establishment of the police force; we have never felt the slightest doubt of being able to preserve the peace.

2833. Have you ever had any experience as to the police force in boroughs?—I had the charge of the Bristol Police in 1839, during the disturbances in Wales; I was there some months.

2834. Were you sent down as an officer from the metropolis?—I was sent down to take charge of the police temporarily during the excitement in Wales.

2835. Was there a police force at Bristol before you went there?—It had been established recently; the chief officer had suddenly died; it was to supply his place that I was sent down from the metropolitan establishment temporarily during the excitement in Wales; it was a great improvement upon the old system in Bristol, but it was still incomplete.

2836. Under what authority was the Bristol force?—The watch committee of the town council.

2837. Do you think it desirable that it should remain under the control of the watch committee?—I do not think that any high state of police efficiency can be obtained by any such system. I think the gentlemen acting at Bristol were about as respectable and energetic men as could be found; but I do not think a thoroughly efficient police can be obtained under such a system.

2838. What system do you think is better?—The control of one responsible officer acting under the magistrates, and appointing his own subordinates.

2839. Have they not one responsible officer at the head of the police at Bristol?—Yes; but he acts under the watch committee.

2840. Has he not the appointment of his subordinates?—No.

2841. You are decidedly of opinion that the head of the police in any district, county, or place should have the sole appointment of his subordinate officers?—I have no doubt about it.

2842. Have you had any experience of a police force in an entire county?—No; I was sent to the West Indies to organise a police force, which was necessary in consequence of the abolition of slavery; I organised the police in the Island of Barbadoes, and there I found it indispensable for good management to amalgamate Bridge Town, which is the chief town in the Island, with the rural districts. That is all my experience with reference to the management of police on a large scale. It appeared to me necessary that the rural districts should be united with the town in order to procure the highest state of efficiency in the police.

2843. In the district in which you are now employed, and of which you have the direction, is the police in the form of town police or rural police?—It partakes of the character of both.

2844. Are

2844. Are they all under your immediate direction ?—Quite so.

2845. Do you think that a police force works better under one control than under separate jurisdictions ?—Yes.

Mr.
F. M. Mallalieu

10 June 1853.

2846. Mr. *Fitzroy*.] Are some of the members of your force acting in rural districts?—Yes; the advantage of the police being under one control is very obvious to persons connected with police management; it affords opportunities of keeping the men under control in the populous parts of the district, and training them. They do not become efficient constables without training, and by having them at head quarters at first, drilling them, and ascertaining their qualifications, you are enabled to select for the rural districts men who are adapted to the particular wants of each district.

2847. Lord *Lovaine*.] Are not the advantages of your system felt as much in boroughs as in rural districts?—Yes; in any change, I think it would be of the utmost importance to amalgamate the police of the towns and boroughs with the rural force.

2848. Mr. *Fitzroy*.] Have you ever been employed in any situation to see the bad effects of conflicting systems?—As I said before, I went to Bristol in 1839, and there I had the opportunity of observing how much better it would have been if the police had been under the sole charge of one responsible person, in preference to the town council.

2849. Lord *Lovaine*.] Does your jurisdiction in Surrey extend as far as Kingston and Epsom?—Mine is exclusively confined to Kent, but our police district extends to Kingston, and beyond it.

2850. Do you think there is any want of unanimity felt between the rural police and the metropolitan police upon the borders of that jurisdiction?—I do not know that from my own knowledge; I think it is general; I never found it otherwise; I know wherever there is separate and independent jurisdiction there is always a jealousy. Kent has adopted the superintending constable system, which is a great failure.

2851. Is the system of rural police generally as efficient as that of the metropolitan police under good management?—It might be made so.

2852. You say that the present rating for the metropolitan police is 6 *d.* in the pound over the whole district over which the police extends?—Yes.

2853. Does not it fall very heavily upon the rural district?—It falls heavily upon the land.

2854. Do you think the suggestion made to the Committee by the Honourable Mr. Talbot, for urban, suburban, and rural assessments, could be carried out?—I think it is possible, and I thought it a valuable suggestion. It is, however, open to this objection: that in case of emergency, the police of rural districts, for instance, could hardly expect support from the town, which, paying the higher rate, would naturally expect the force so paid for to be employed exclusively in it. Our system, on the contrary, enables us to throw into any district an amount of force sufficient for any purpose; thus crime is met by unlimited means of repression, and the preservation of the peace amply secured. The rural parishes in Kent, under a separate and lower rating, could not maintain more than one-fourth of the force we employ in them.

2855. From the evidence which has been given before the Committee, it appears that in Surrey, a police rate of 3 *d.* in the pound for the rural police is sufficient to answer the purpose; whereas the metropolitan police rate is 6 *d.* in the pound. Is not the amount of protection which is enjoyed very nearly the same in Kent, and the increase of rate only owing to the necessity of assimilating the rural and town districts for the purpose of assessment?—I am not able to say what the difference would be in Surrey, nor am I able to say what the Surrey rural police is.

2856. Mr. *Fitzroy*.] Does not the amount of rate depend upon the number of men employed?—Precisely.

2857. Mr. *Philipps*.] Do you distribute your men in the rural district in parishes, or do you keep them in a body together, with certain districts assigned to them?—Our system partakes of both those arrangements; it is, to keep in the stations which are scattered over the district the single men in our force, who are exposed to temptations which we think it desirable to protect them from, if possible, and where they are subject to a certain degree of surveillance after their duty; that would apply, perhaps, to one-third of the force employed. The married men, I should observe, are the men most frequently sent to the rural districts,

Mr.
F. M. Mallalieu.

10 June 1853.

selected for that purpose as experienced steady persons; these we scatter over the villages to make them accessible to the greatest number of persons of all classes.

2858. Lord *Lovaine*.] Do your men patrol?—Yes, incessantly.

2859. Mr. *Fitzroy*.] Have your men been employed in giving notice to the coroners in cases of death?—We have not yet done so, but almost every other description of duty of which a police force is capable has been performed by us; we have served all the parochial summonses for the non-payment of poor rates; for the non-payment of church rates; and have executed distress warrants and all duties of that kind.

2860. Lord *Lovaine*.] Are those duties performed gratis?—Yes; we have done it for this reason (the Commissioners having given their sanction): there were great complaints from the ratepayers of the way in which it was done, and the magistrates determined that if the Commissioners would give their sanction the public would be better served. To give an idea of the amount of that sort of duty done by the constables in the year 1852, I would state that we executed more than 5,000 warrants and summonses in the district under my charge, including Greenwich.

2861. Have you lock-up houses at any police stations?—Not at all the police stations; I have 18, and at most of them there is a convenience for detaining the prisoners.

2862. Mr. *Fitzroy*.] If the notices to the coroners were to be made out and served by the police, would there not be a very great saving to the ratepayers generally?—A considerable saving, and the duty would be better done.

2863. There would be no difficulty in performing the duty, if you had authority to do so?—None whatever, without the increase of a farthing expense.

2864. Are the police employed in your division as inspectors of weights and measures?—No.

2865. Lord *Lovaine*.] Is there any objection to their being inspectors of weights and measures?—No; I should like to see it done as far as I am individually concerned.

2866. Mr. *Philipps*.] Do you think the men could be employed in any other duties beyond those of police duty, if the system were general?—Yes.

2867. What other duties could the police be employed for?—My impression is, that by the employment of the rural police for the relief of vagrants great advantage would arise; for instance, the relieving officer's duties might be more efficiently applied to the relief of the poor in the union over which he is the officer. I would have the relief of all the wayfaring mendicant class performed by the police; and I think that, if the police were general all over the country, and this system was applied, it would almost root out vagrancy; I do not see how it could exist to any large extent under a general system of police.

2868. Mr. *Fitzroy*.] How long is required to make a man an efficient policeman?—Certainly not less than two or three years, even if he has the requisite amount of intelligence; you cannot reckon him fit to be left to act upon his own authority in a case of emergency, at a distance from any other control or advice, earlier than that.

2869. How soon do you put the men upon a beat?—Almost immediately. The practice is this: a man is retained in the probationary section for two or three weeks, where he receives the rudiments of his police education and drill; he then joins a division, and he is employed usually at head quarters, on an average perhaps of 12 months, in the more populous parts of the district, in order that he may have an opportunity of frequenting the police courts to see how the police cases are managed; during that period he is also made more efficient in his drill. The men in the Metropolitan force are all now well drilled, and made efficient in the practice of the sword.

2870. Are there many old soldiers in the Metropolitan police force?—No, not so many; less than formerly.

2871. Had you not at the commencement of the force a large proportion of men who had been in the army?—Yes.

2872. Did you find that class of men desirable for the purpose?—I never considered them the most efficient men for the purpose; I have been rather disposed to think that the intelligent part of the agricultural labouring community after training make the best policemen.

2873. For how many years have you been in the Metropolitan force?—Twenty-two years.

Mr.
F. M. Mallalieu.
——
10 June 1853.

2874. Do you think the discipline of the Metropolitan force is improving, or the reverse?—I think we have made rapid strides within the last few years.

2875. Do you think upon the whole the discipline is better than it was?—Yes; I feel proud of the establishment, in comparison with what it was 15 years ago.

2876. *Chairman.*] What is the cost per man in the Metropolitan police force?—I am not very well conversant with the financial part of the establishment. I should think about 60 *l.* per year per man.

2877. Mr. *Howard.*] Are you able to carry on the duty with a comparatively smaller force than when it was first established?—No, the district increases in population; the time is rapidly approaching when the force will have to be increased, because building is going on at such an immense rate.

2878. Lord *Lovaine.*] Are you speaking of London, or of the district adjacent to London?—Of the vicinities or suburban districts of London.

2879. *Chairman.*] Is not that the case in your district very much?—Yes; the increase of building and the preparation for building is on a great scale. New streets and roads are laid out by the mile; I think I know of more than a hundred acres which are now laid out for building purposes, and which will very soon be covered with buildings.

2880. Then it would necessarily increase the number of policemen in your district?—It will.

2881. Would the increase be an additional cost to the rural districts in your division?—No; because with the increase of building and population our means of payment will increase.

2882. Mr. *Fitzroy.*] Will not that property when it comes into rating, contribute to the police?—Yes; and so the force will be increased; I should say we shall want more men, but we shall have more money to pay them.

2883. *Chairman.*] You already take a maximum rate of 6 *d.* in the pound; the rest is paid for by the Government?—Yes.

2884. So that the rural districts cannot be worse off than they are now?—They cannot be worse off as to payments, and they will be better off, inasmuch as each augmentation of police will increase their security.

2885. Mr. *Philipps.*] Have you made any sort of calculation with regard to the rural districts with reference to what the proportion of the population ought to be to one policeman?—I have; and I have heard gentlemen refer to it frequently in their evidence; I think that a policeman to each 800 of the population would not be too many.

2886. Mr. *Sotheron.*] Must not that depend upon whether the population is dense?—I am speaking of the average.

2887. Are you speaking of a thickly populated district?—I am speaking with reference to the sort of population which we should have in Kent to deal with generally.

Captain *Edward Willis*, called in; and Examined.

Captain E. Willis.

2888. *Chairman.*] ARE you the head of the police of the borough of Manchester?—Yes.

2889. Mr. *Sotheron.*] How long have you filled that office?—I have been in Manchester very nearly 11 years.

2890. *Chairman.*] What is your force in Manchester?—454 persons, of all ranks, with myself.

2891. What is the population of Manchester?—316,487.

2892. What proportion does your force bear to the population?—The proportion is 1 in 698.

2893. Do you think that is sufficient?—There is a proposition before the watch committee at the present time to increase the force 65 men in October; whether it will be granted or not I do not know; the population has lately very much increased, and during the last year there were 2,600 houses built in the borough.

2894. Mr. *Fitzroy.*] Is the proportion you have just now given to the Committee, taken upon the present rate of the population?—As calculated up to December last; the average annual increase of the population between the census of 1841 and 1851 has been at the rate of 6787 persons per annum.

2895. As the population now stands your proportion is 1 to 698?—Yes.

2896. Lord *Lovaine.*] Is not a large portion of the population of Manchester of a vicious and degraded description?—Manchester is generally a quiet and orderly town; and upon the occasion of the Queen's visit we had no barriers, and had very little trouble to keep order.

2897. *Chairman.*] What is the cost of the police?—The cost of the police force last year amounted to 25,510 *l.*

2898. Lord *Lovaine*] What is the rate in the pound?—About 5 *d.* three-eighths.

2899. Do you concur in the opinion of other witnesses that it is of great importance that the borough police and the rural police should be under one head, or amalgamated?—It must, I think, be in districts if it is done.

2900. *Chairman.*] You think it is desirable that Manchester should be taken as a separate district?—I think so.

2901. Have the adjoining districts a Manchester a police force?—The county of Lancaster has a constabulary police force under the Government Act, the 3d & 4th Victoria; and the incorporated towns, such as Ashton-under-Lyne and Blackburn, have also police forces, but very small in number, I think.

2902. Supposing they had a separate police and separate districts, taking Manchester as a separate county, do you think Lancashire and Manchester could be under the direction of one chief constable?—There is certainly at present a want of co-operation and a want of union; the police forces know very little of what each other is doing, and there is very little intercommunication except when very serious robberies are committed. I think it would be a benefit to the counties; as most of the thieves reside in large towns, from whence they go out to commit their depredations.

2903. Lord *Lovaine.*] Therefore whether the county police were amalgamated with the town police or not, it would be desirable to have a certain area round all large towns, which should be under the charge of the head of the borough police?—Yes; I think there is an evil in Manchester and Salford, where the river is not more than 100 yards wide which runs between them, having separate police establishments.

2904. *Chairman.*] Is the district round the Manchester police district half rural and half manufacturing?—Yes.

2905. In the vicinity of large towns, like Manchester, do you think those districts should be attached to the Manchester district?—I think so.

2906. Do you think it would tend to the prevention of crime?—I think it would.

2907. You say that the boroughs have but a few police of their own?—Some of them very few.

2908. Do they ever apply to you for assistance?—Blackburn applied to us at the election the other day for assistance, which, of course, we did not grant.

2909. Are prize-fights frequent in your neighbourhood?—Not within the borough; we have had however, once or twice, attempts; and also close without the borough.

2910. Do they call upon you for assistance?—They call upon us for assistance at times, and sometimes we go without a call, if it is close to the outside of the borough.

2911. Do you ever have the people turn out *en masse* in Manchester?—In 1842 we had a very serious turn-out, and a very long one.

2912. Was that in the district of Manchester?—I think the whole country turned out at that time round Manchester. I was in the Lancashire county police at the time, and not in the borough police.

2913. On that occasion, did the police of Manchester and Lancashire act cordially together?—I think they seldom had to work together in any way whatever. I had charge of the district immediately round Manchester at that time, and we never came into the borough to assist in the borough.

2914. On that occasion, would it not have been a convenience if the police had been all under one head?—I think so; communication, of course, is kept up so much better as to what is transpiring around; but although I was not a borough officer at that time, I knew what was going on in the town, as I was stationed in the immediate neighbourhood.

2915. Lord *Loraine.*] Do you ever meet with any obstruction or impediment in the management of the police from the manner in which they are selected under the Watching and Lighting Act?—No, the watch committee intrust to me the entire selection of the men; they have the final approval of them before they are sworn in, but they leave to myself the selection of the officers.

2916. Mr.

Captain *E. Willis.*

10 June 1853.

2916. Mr. *Fitzroy.*] Do they ever reject men who have been selected by yourself?—I do not recollect an instance of their rejecting a man who had been selected by myself.

2917. Do you dismiss the men?—They allow me to punish the men and to fine the men; but the final dismissal they reserve to themselves; they have never objected to any dismissal which I have recommended.

2918. Lord *Lovaine.*] In short, the power, as the watch committee have exercised it, has never been exerted in a manner detrimental to the force?—No, they have treated me with very great confidence ever since I have been under their command.

2919. *Chairman.*] Have you, on the occasion of a turn-out, employed the military?—In 1842 the military were employed, and acted against the mobs in several instances; in 1848 they did not act against the mob; the police were able to do it themselves, but the military were in the back ground to assist, in case of necessity.

2920. Do not you think it is much more desirable to employ policemen than soldiers?—Most decidedly, I quite object to the idea of employing soldiers, so long as the police can perform their duty.

2921. Why do you think the police should be preferred to the military?—I think the police can suppress a disturbance better, and the chance of danger to the inhabitants is so much less with police constables.

2922. Are not the police superior to the military in suppressing a disturbance in this respect, because they at all events can without orders go into the mob and persuade the people to desist, or they could lay hold of the ringleaders?—Decidedly, they need not be under the orders of the magistrate to do that.

2923. A soldier could not do that?—No.

2924. His musket employs both his hands?—Yes.

2925. Are your men drilled to the use of the sword at all?—They were, at the time of the excitement in 1848, drilled to the use of the sword; we do not drill them ordinarily to sword exercise, they are drilled to the common manual exercise.

2926. Mr. *Philipps.*] Where do you get your men from?—Chiefly from Derbyshire, Yorkshire and Cheshire.

2927. Are they agricultural labourers or townspeople?—Chiefly agricultural people.

2928. Have you a recruiting office?—No; I appoint a day once a week which is generally known throughout those counties; I have a book in which I put down the candidates' names who come; we have never had an insufficiency of candidates; it is generally known in the district, one man tells another. Sometimes we have had as many as 130 or 140 on the book waiting, we have now only about 25; they come to the general office at the town hall.

2929. *Chairman.*] Have you sworn in special constables on any occasion?—In 1848 there were special constables sworn in, also in 1842, but the special constables were not required to act against the people in 1848; they were placed in the station-houses, the town hall, and at the principal places in the town, in conjunction generally with the police.

2930. You did not call upon the special constables to act?—Not to act aggressively or to suppress disorder.

2931. Do you think the special constables would have rendered you any aid if they had been called upon?—I think they were very willing to have done so.

2932. Were they from the better class of persons?—The better and middle class of persons generally.

2933. Not from the class of persons from which parochial constables are selected?—Not those who assembled for general duty under the authorities; but the operatives in most of the large establishments were sworn in to protect their masters' premises, and generally remained on the premises for this purpose.

Edmund Beckett Denison, Esq., a Member of the House; Examined.

E. B. Denison, Esq.,
M. P.

2934. *Chairman.*] YOU are a Magistrate for the West Riding of Yorkshire? —Yes, I am.

2935. Are you the chairman of quarter sessions?—Frequently, not always. The West Riding of Yorkshire is divided into three divisions, and we have five or six chairmen of quarter sessions, each taking a part by rotation.

2936. What police is there in the West Riding of Yorkshire?—In the West

E. B. Denison, Esq.
M. P.

10 June 1853.

Riding the boroughs have their own police; viz., Leeds, Pontefract, and Doncaster. In Sheffield and some other towns there are policemen; how they are paid I do not know; they are not paid out of the county rate.

2937. What police is there in the rural districts of the West Riding?—There are no policemen, but latterly the magistrates have thought it right to build lock-up houses, and to have a certain number of superintending constables.

2938. Have you superintending constables in each division?—No, not in each division; the system of building lock-up houses, and appointing superintending constables, has only been lately and adopted; it is going on progressively, and probably will be extended.

2939. Mr. *Fitzroy.*] Is there no constabulary at all in the divisions of the West Riding, where there are not superintending constables?—No, not under the Rural Police Act, the 2d & 3d of Victoria.

2940. *Chairman.*] Are there only parochial constables?—Only parochial constables, excepting in the large towns. The subject of a rural police has been more than once discussed in the West Riding of Yorkshire. In 1840, shortly after that Act of Parliament was passed, the whole subject was taken into consideration. A number of magistrates entertained an opinion that the Rural Police Act, 2d & 3d Vict. ought to be adopted; a committee was appointed to inquire into all the bearings of the question, and to report. They did so report, and several meetings were held upon the subject, but it ended in the magistrates determining not to appoint a rural police under the 2d & 3d Vict., in consequence of the expense which it would cost, provided the Act were to be applied efficiently and generally.

2941. When was that committee appointed?—In 1840.

2942. Who was the chairman of that committee?—The late Lord Wharncliffe was in the chair when the magistrates met; a committee was then appointed, and Mr. Edwin Lascelles was the chairman of that committee; I was a member of it, and by that committee a report was afterwards made to the whole of the magistrates, and it ended in nothing being done

2943. Then the question was not raised as to the appointment of police?—Yes; the question was, whether the 2d & 3d Victoria should be applied to the whole of the West Riding of Yorkshire or to any part of it; and it ended in the Act not being applied to any part of the riding.

2944. Was the decision of the magistrates unanimous upon that subject?—No.

2945. To what extent did they differ?—There was a considerable majority against the proposition.

2946. Mr. *Fitzroy.*] Was any calculation made of the rate per pound which would be thrown upon the county to carry out the Act efficiently?—Yes.

2947. What would it be?—I am not sure what the rate per pound would have come to. The calculation was, that a police force, to be efficient for the whole of the West Riding, would cost at least 30,000 *l.* a year; that it would have taken 500 constables, at 60 *l.* a man.

2948. *Chairman.*] What would that be in the pound?—The calculation at that time was, that it would cost about 30,000 *l.*; the valuation of the county is now materially increased.

2949. What would it be now in the pound?—About 2¼ *d.*

2950. Mr. *Burroughes.*] Can you tell the Committee what the county rate is in the pound?—The county rate in the pound does not amount to 2 *d.* If the number of policemen to which I have referred were to be appointed at present, the county rate would be more than doubled. The county rate does not come to 2 *d.*, it is 1¾ *d.* at present.

2951. Lord *Lovaine.*] Do you include the boroughs and great towns in your calculations?—No, the boroughs are excluded; we have no control over them. This is a paper which I received from the clerk of the peace; it is a statement of the total expenditure of the West Riding for the years 1850, 1851, and 1852.

[*The same was read, as follows:*]

STATEMENT

STATEMENT of the EXPENDITURE of the *West Riding* for the Years 1830, 1831, and 1852.

E. B. Denison, Esq.
M. P.

10 June 1853.

1850.	£.	s.	d.	£.	s.	d.
Total expenditure - - - - - - -	-	-	-	52,903	7	5
Deduct amount received by the Treasurer from Government for prosecutions; from the boroughs for general expenses; for rent of cells in Wakefield House of Correction; expenses of convicted prisoners; fines and penalties; prisoners' earnings; convictions on short weights; sale of register of voters, and sundry small receipts - - - -	24,108	7	8			
Repayment of loans for New House of Correction and Asylum - - - - - - - -	4,000	–	–			
Interest on ditto - - - - - - -	1,631	–	–			
Income Tax - - - - - - -	53	13	4			
Lock-up houses - - - - - - -	50	3	1			
				29,843	4	1
Or 1½d. and half a farthing in the pound.			£.	23,060	3	4

1851.	£.	s.	d.	£.	s.	d.
Total expenditure - - - - - - -	-	-	-	52,992	1	5
Deduct amount received by the Treasurer from Government for prosecutions, &c. - - - -	21,067	13	2			
Repayment for loans for New House of Correction and Asylum - - - - - - -	4,000	–	–			
Interest and Income Tax - - - -	1,524	13	4			
Payments for lock-up houses - - - -	231	8	–			
New wash-houses, drying closets, and straw places at Asylum - - - - - - - -	331	19	4			
				27,155	13	10
Or 1¾d., and nearly 4-10ths of a farthing in the pound.			£.	25,836	7	7

1852.	£.	s.	d.	£.	s.	d.
Total expenditure - - - - - - -	-	-	-	52,795	17	–
Deduct amount received by the Treasurer from Government for prosecutions, &c. - - - -	20,609	4	10			
Repayments for loans for New House of Correction and Asylum - - - - - - -	4,000	–	–			
Interest and Income Tax - - - -	1,364	13	4			
Payments for lock-up houses - - - -	361	11	5			
New cow-houses at Asylum - - - -	250	–	–			
				26,585	9	7
Or 1¾d. and 4-10ths of a farthing in the pound.			£.	26,210	7	5

	£.	s.	d.
Average of the above three years - - - - -	25,035	12	9

Or 1¾d. in the pound.

1d. in the pound upon the Riding (£.3,402,067), *ex* the Boroughs, raises £14,175 15s. 7d.

2952. *Chairman.*] It amounts to this, that the average expense has been 1¾d., and you calculate that the estimated expense of the rural police would be 2¼d.? —Yes, rather above 2d. The establishment of an efficient police would double the county rate. The present expenditure is about 2d. in the pound, and an efficient police would also be 2d. in the pound. It is on that account that the majority of the magistrates have not thought it prudent to adopt the Rural Police Act, the 2d & 3d Victoria. My own opinion is, that the county rate is based upon a wrong principle. It is a property-tax, but the county rate is raised for purposes which depend upon the density of population. Prisoners of every description come from the most densely populated parts of the county or riding; the lunatic asylums are built for parties who come from the most populated parts of the riding or county. The money to be raised for the purpose of either prosecuting criminals (a cost that Government now takes upon itself, which it did not formerly), or for the conveyance of offenders to prison and their maintenance in prison, and also the expense of building asylums, is raised by a property-tax. The consequence is, that in

E. B. Denison, Esq.
M. P.

10 June 1853.

divisions of counties, or in counties which vary, as the west riding of Yorkshire does, between a manufacturing district on the one side and a purely agricultural district on the other side, the agricultural part of the riding is very heavily rated in proportion, because it is rated according to the value of the property, although it does not send criminals to prison to anything like the amount, according to the property, which they do from the most populous part of the riding. I found that an immense proportion of the prisoners whom I had to try, came from the most populated parts of the riding, especially from Sheffield, Bradford, and Huddersfield. Leeds is a borough town. When I came to compare the amount of money levied upon Sheffield and its neighbourhood, I found it bore no proportion to the number of prisoners sent to Wakefield for trial from that district. Sheffield has frequently cost the West Riding above 3,000 *l.* per annum, for the prosecution and maintenance of its criminals, more than it contributed to the county rate purse; but the money was raised in the agricultural parts of the riding, according to the value of the property, as if they had produced an equal number of criminals. That is the reason why I entertain the opinion that the county rate is a very unfair rate, particularly in a district, one half of which is exceedingly rich, more populous, and more criminal, sending a much greater proportion of criminals for trial than a rural part of the district. The manufacturing population increases the county rate in other matters; coroner's inquests are much more frequent in a manufacturing population than they are in an agricultural population, and those charges come to a very considerable sum of money in a population like ours, which is now, I think, 1,200,000; but, nevertheless, the whole of the property is rated in order to meet the charges which arise in the manufacturing districts, as well as for other matters. It is on that account that the agriculturists think a uniform county rate for police purposes would be very unfair, and I take that view of the case. I should not have felt any objection to 2 & 3 Vict. being applied to limited districts, instead of applying it to the whole of the Riding; I think that all parishes should be compelled to have an efficient police. Small parishes may combine under one Act, and have their own police; while it is optional they never will do it.

2953. Do you not think the objection as to the amount of crime, and therefore the amount of expense, being greater in the manufacturing districts of Yorkshire than in the rural districts, is met by an arrangement under the powers of the Act of Parliament similar to that in Lancashire, and also in Staffordshire, that though the rural police are under one head, still there are separate rates for the manufacturing district, for the mining district, and for the rural district?—That principle would meet the objection which I have stated. If the county were divided into districts, and the requisite number of policemen were appointed at the expense of each district, I should have no objection to the application of the Rural Police Act, 2 & 3 Vict.

2954. It has been stated to this Committee that Shropshire is divided into three districts, the mining district, the pottery district, and the rural district, and that each district pays a different rate; the mining district paying 3 *d.*, the pottery district 5 *d.*, and the rural district 1 *d.*; would the adoption of such a system in the West Riding of Yorkshire meet the objections which you have to the establishment of the rural police?—The objection I have felt to the police rate is, that it is a property tax, from which property of a certain description derives no benefit; the police ought to be established and paid for, in my opinion, according to the population. Suppose it had been settled that there should be 500 constables appointed for the West Riding, where would the policemen have been sent to? The greater proportion would have gone into the manufacturing districts; 500 would cost 33,000 *l.* Why are you to tax the property in the agricultural neighbourhood of Goole and that district to a county rate for paying the policemen who are to be stationed in the neighbourhood of Sheffield? If, as I said before, a circle had been drawn round Sheffield, or each manufacturing town, and they had been required to pay 3 *d.* or 6 *d.* in the pound according to the number of men they wanted, there would have been no objection; the objection was, that the property in the neighbourhood of Goole and Selby, which is a purely agricultural district, from whence but few criminals come, would have had to pay to the county rate towards the support of policemen in the manufacturing districts.

2955. Lord *Lovaine.*] Would not that objection be met by the adoption of the provision of the Act, which allows the rate to be assessed in such proportions as
may

E. B. Denison, Esq.
M. P.

10 June 1853.

may be agreed ?—Yes; my objection is to a general county rate, without reference to the wants of each part of the county.

2956. If the county had seen fit to adopt that provision of the Act, would it not have met your objection?—Yes.

2957. *Chairman.*] Has any proposition been made to adopt the Act?—The first proposition was, that the manufacturing districts should be put under the Police Act; that was not considered satisfactory. Then the proposal was that the whole of the Riding should be put under the Police Act, and that raised a very considerable objection to the whole scheme. The proposal to apply the Act fell to the ground, and it was not raised again till about a year ago, when it was discussed upon the same principle, and was negatived. Instead of adopting the Police Act, we have adopted the system of building lock-up houses in the various localities, and of having superintending constables. The principle of the objection is just the same as it was to the application of the Police Act; you take the money for building lock-up houses, and paying the superintending constables, not out of the immediate district, but out of the whole county rate; the principle is just as bad as it was before.

2058. Mr. *Burroughes.*] It has been stated in evidence that the rural districts benefit very much from the police watching the ingress and egress of bad characters in and out of those manufacturing places; do not you think that would justify the adoption of some measure?—I should be very sorry if those rural districts did not benefit, having the expense to bear. I can show the Committee what has been the state of crime in the West Riding of Yorkshire for the last eight or 10 years, notwithstanding we have no rural police.

2959. *Chairman.*] Is that a statement of detected crime?—Yes; the number of prisoners committed to Wakefield House of Correction from 1840 to 1852. In 1840 the number was 1,078; in 1841, 1,126; in 1842, 1,350; in 1843, 1,115; in 1844, 972; in 1845, 872; in 1846, 835; in 1847, 948; in 1848, 800; in 1849, 783; in 1850, 664; in 1851, 779; in 1852, 690.

3960. Is that the number of convictions or committals?—The total number committed for trial in each year. All that I mean to show by the return is, that although the population in the West Riding has increased very materially, crime has decreased.

2961. May it not prove also, that although you have the same number of rogues, you catch a less number every year?—There is an increased amount of vigilance adopted; the towns are certainly better served with constables than they were. There is a good police in the town of Leeds, and in the town of Pontefract, which is but a small place, and in several other towns; but, nevertheless, the number of prisoners committed for trial has decreased, and we, in the West Riding, rather flatter ourselves that our morals are improving than growing worse. I do not mean to say that the establishment of the new police, at an expense of 25,000 *l.* or 30,000 *l.,* would not decrease the number of prisoners. I should be exceedingly sorry that the money should be spent and no beneficial result arise. I think it would have been a remarkable thing in counties where the police have been established if crime had not decreased to a certain extent. Therefore it is a question of pounds, shillings, and pence. If the parties think it worth their while to spend their money in establishing the police, it is to be hoped that crime will be to a certain extent prevented, and the morals of the people improved; but the question is, whether, under the circumstances of the case, the magistrates think it worth their while to spend the money, and by what rule.

2962. *Chairman.*] It amounts to this, when, by your own showing, crime would be diminished, and the morals of the people would be improved, do you think you can view it merely as a question of pounds, shillings, and pence, and that you are justified in refusing to expend the money for the establishment of the police? —If I am asked as a magistrate of the West Riding of Yorkshire, I say it would be unwise and unnecessary in the magistrates having the county purse under their care, to expend 25,000 *l.* or 30,000 *l.* in establishing a rural police, taking into account that crime decreases, and that the Government pays a very considerable portion of the expense arising from crime; and they would, by establishing a rural police, be forcing upon a county the payment of a sum of money per annum which the Government has within the last few years taken upon itself to pay.

2963. Lord *Lovaine.*] It appears, then, that the Government is chargeable with a large proportion of the crime which is committed in the West Riding of Yorkshire?—I do not say so. I think the Government, having done what they have done, ought to appoint a rural police over the whole kingdom. In my opinion, everything connected with crime ought to be under the control of Government officers; and if Government, having gone so far as it has done (and I think wisely) in taking upon itself the expense of the prosecution, though not all the expense of the apprehension of criminals, I think they ought to go further. I think that the Government had better take the control of all the prisons and appoint all the officers. Having taken upon itself to relieve the West Riding from the payment of 20,000 l. for the prosecution of crime, it does not seem to me very logical that the Riding should be called upon to pay for the police, which is merely to prevent the crime which the Government has undertaken to prosecute.

2964. Then you would make the expense of the police a national charge instead of a provincial charge?—Decidedly. If such a system were carried out, it would cease to be a property tax, because the purse out of which the police would be paid would be provided by the population, and not by a rate upon the counties.

2965. *Chairman.*] Has this calculation of the total expenditure of the county rate reference to what is paid throughout the country generally?—Yes.

2966. Have you taken into account the money expended in the cost of parochial constables, and in other ways?—No.

2967. The question refers to the costs of proceedings before justices?—No.

2968. You have not taken that expenditure at all into account?—No.

2969. Have you ever considered the costs of the parochial constables which are paid out of the poor rates?—Not minutely.

2970. Lord *Lovaine.*] Are you aware that calculations were made in the county of Surrey as regards these expenses, and it was found that the sums actually paid to the parish constables out of the poor rates, as far as could be ascertained, and which formed but a small part of the money really paid to the parish constables, amounted to more than one-third of the sum which was expended for an efficient police force?—I was not aware of that fact.

2971. *Chairman.*] Are parochial constables ever employed in the West Riding of Yorkshire to watch under the orders of magistrates?—Never, I should think.

2972. Mr. *Philipps.*] You have said that superintending constables were appointed in the West Riding of Yorkshire, under the 5 & 6 Vict. c. 109?—Yes; and that system is being extended.

2973. What has that system cost?—It costs 1,200 l. per annum; it has not been carried to any great extent, and the same feeling prevails against that system as against the county rate; because the money, as I said just now, is called for to build lock-up houses and pay superintending constables out of the general county rate, and not out of the parish rate, or a limited locality. When the lock-up houses were first established, there was a greater outcry for them in the manufacturing districts than in the rural districts. Lord Beaumont lives in an agricultural district, and he has said frequently, " It is hard upon us at Selby that we should have to contribute to building lock-up houses at Halifax and other places, whilst we have not one." The answer to that was, " We must begin somewhere." And I believe at last it is settled that there is to be a lock-up house at Selby.

2974. It is like all taxation, it cannot apply equally under every state of circumstances?—That may be: but if the rate were paid according to the population, it would be infinitely fairer than it is at present. If a manufacturing district creates a necessity for a larger amount of county rate than a rural district does, surely it would be only fair that they who are getting rich in the manufacturing district should pay a tax in proportion to the crime which they create, and that they should not call upon the more innocent and more moral district to pay for their crime.

2975. Mr. *Fitzroy.*] Does not the 3 & 4 Vict. c. 88, by the 27th and 28th sections, already provide for the formation of police districts; and for each district paying for its own constables?—Yes.

2976. Would the 27th and 28th clauses of the 3 & 4 Vict. c. 88, which gives that power, meet your view as to the justice of the case, that the district requiring a greater number of constables should have a greater number of constables allotted to it, but paying proportionately a larger sum?—Yes.

2977. As a matter of arrangement, have you not the power of locating the police in such a manner as to avoid the injustice to which you refer?—Yes.

2978. As far as legislation is concerned, there is no necessity for any fresh legislation on the subject, inasmuch as the existing Act gives you the power of

raising

raising the rate in a fair manner, according to your view?—I think there is no E. B. Denison, Esq. occasion for further legislation, unless Parliament should think it desirable to M.P. establish a police force throughout the whole of the kingdom, for which the Government would pay. If they would do that I think they would act more 10 June 1853. wisely, and such a measure would receive my cordial support.

2979. *Chairman.*] If the present Police Act which gives these powers had been made compulsory instead of permissive, the probability is that you would have settled your arrangements in the county of York in a way which you think is much more fair?—If the Act of 2 & 3 Vict. had been made compulsory, that the whole county, or the whole riding, should be put under the rural police established by that Act, of course it would have been settled; but that would not have removed the injustice of an equal county rate.

2980. Would not you probably have settled the proportion of rating in the various districts in such a manner that the application of the Act would have been rendered satisfactory?—I am not quite sure that it would.

2981. Assuming that the police should be adopted by the whole of the West Riding of Yorkshire under one system, and under one head, and that those different districts should pay according to the number of constables they required: would that meet your objection?—That would require no fresh legislation, if the magistrates thought proper to do so.

2982. Mr. *Fitzroy.*] Do you mean that these two clauses should be made compulsory upon the magistrates, and that they should be compellable to form police districts?—If you made the Act of Parliament compulsory upon the magistrates to divide a county into police districts, and that, according to the number of constables fixed in the police district, the same district shall be rated, that would be more satisfactory.

2983. *Chairman.*] Are there any other observations which you wish to make to the Committee?—No; I was asked if I would give evidence as to what had passed in the West Riding upon the subject, and I wished to state to the Committee the reasons why the Rural Police Act had not been fully carried into effect in the West Riding of Yorkshire; it has been twice considered, and I think I am justified in saying that it would have been adopted but for the inequality in the application of the rate.

2984. Mr. *Fitzroy.*] Would not your objection be very much obviated, supposing those powers which are now permissive to allot police districts, were made compulsory?—Yes; I will go this length; if you choose to send down commissioners to say what shall be a police district, and who shall decide the boundary, and that the parties shall be chargeable with the maintenance of their police force, I should not have the slightest objection, because I am quite sure the commissioners must apportion such a number of constables as is requisite to the population.

2985. Would it be necessary to send commissioners into Yorkshire for this purpose, if the 27th and 28th clauses of the Act were made compulsory?—It might be done easily enough without, but the objections to a rural police have increased since the Government has repaid a part of the expense of the prosecution of felons; and I think the Government ought to apply that system still further.

Jovis, 16° die Junii, 1853.

MEMBERS PRESENT.

Mr. Rice.	Mr. Rich.
Mr. Fitzroy.	Mr. Mackie.
Mr. Burroughes.	Mr Charles Howard.
Lord Lovaine.	Sir James Anderson.
Sir John Trollope.	Mr. Philipps.

EDWARD ROYDS RICE, Esq., IN THE CHAIR.

John Fawcett, Esq., called in; and Examined.

2986. *Chairman.*] YOU are a Magistrate for the borough of Carlisle, I J. Fawcett, Esq. believe?—I am.

2987. And in the commission of the peace for the county of Cumberland?—I 16 June 1853. am am in the commission of the peace, although I have not qualified ; being a prac-tising barrister, I do not choose to throw that aside ; I have qualified for the borough for many years.

2988. Can you state to the Committee what the number of police is in the borough of Carlisle ?—It consists of a superintendent, and, I think, 18 men ; 16 was the force for many years.

2989. How are the police appointed ?—The police are appointed by the watch committee, under the Municipal Act.

2990. Are they entirely under the control of the watch committee ?—Almost entirely under the control of the watch committee ; of course, under the Act, the magistrates have the power of dismissing the police for misconduct ; that is the only control which the magistrates have over them, the entire control otherwise being in the watch committee.

2991. Do you think the police force which you have in Carlisle is sufficient ? Yes. I think in point of number, generally speaking, it is sufficient ; it is a very efficient and a very good force.

2992. Do you think that there is any objection to the system of control by the watch committee ?—Yes, I think that is highly objectionable ; the appointment and the control of the police being so much in the hands of persons who are, almost all of them, I will not say all, tradesmen, and some of them brewers or wine merchants, having public-houses ; this exposes them to the imputation of having an interest in preventing the officers from doing their duty in making reports. The superintendent has repeatedly complained of this, and other inter-ference by members of the watch committee. I understand also there is great favouritism in the appointment of the officers.

2993. What do you think would be a better arrangement ?—If the police force was extended over the county, and it was all amalgamated, I, myself, should like to see the appointment of the men in the chief constable, who should be appointed by the magistrates, and who should be responsible for the good conduct of his subordinates to the magistrates who appointed him.

2994. As they are in the counties which have adopted the rural police ?—Yes ; much in the same way as above, the rural constabulary force has been generally adopted.

2995. Mr. *Burroughes.*] There is no rural police in Cumberland, I believe?— In only one division ; in the Derwent division. The county of Cumberland is divided into five divisions ; one of the divisions has its rural police, and the effect has been most beneficial ; it has been found beneficial in many ways which I could mention, and the expense has not been very great.

2996. Is that police force upon an extensive scale ?—No ; it is only for one division, being about a fifth part of the extent of the whole county.

2997. Is there a superintendent ?—Yes.

2998. Your opinion seems to be that the appointment of the constables should be vested in the person who is responsible for their conduct ?—Yes, I think so.

2999. *Chairman.*] Having the police only in one division of the county, and only a superintendent and not a chief constable, is the appointment of the con-stables vested in the superintendent or in the magistrates ?—I rather think it is vested in the magistrates.

3000. Have you experienced much advantage from the adoption of the Lodging-house Act in the borough of Carlisle ?—Very great.

3001. Mr. *Howard.*] Do you find that the police examine the lodging-houses? —Constantly ; I do not at this moment remember the exact number of the lodging-houses, but there is a considerable number in the town and in the out-skirts within the Parliamentary borough, which consists of the old city, and the suburbs extending round the whole of the town ; these are all registered with the superintendent of police, and licensed to receive only so many, according to the size of the room or house ; the penalties inflicted by the Act are incurred by the lodging-house keepers offending, and having more persons than they are licensed for. They are also obliged to keep them cleaned, washed and ven-tilated at certain periods which are mentioned in their licenses. The police officers very carefully attend to see that those operations are performed. We have had several convictions against lodging-house keepers for having too many persons in their houses, and occasionally for not having sufficiently ventilated and cleaned them ; we have seldom had a repetition of the offence. I do not remember a second conviction.

3002. You think that great benefits have accrued from having carried the
Lodging-house

J. Fawcett, Esq.

16 June 1853

Lodging-house Act into effect with the supervision of the police?—Yes, very great; in a sanitary point of view the benefit must be very great.

3003. Do you think that that Act could have been carried into effect without an efficient police force?—I think it would have been impossible.

3004. Do you think that vagrancy is very general in the county of Cumberland?—Very general, indeed; and Irish vagrancy to a very great extent.

3005. Have you any opportunity of knowing whether there is less vagrancy now than there was before you had the police force established?—Yes; I can speak to that positively; in the Derwent division there is less than there was before the adoption of the police by a great amount. I know of my own knowledge that it is very much diminished indeed since the establishment of the rural police.

3006. Having given your attention to the subject as a magistrate, are you or not of opinion that vagrancy is the source of all crime in the rural districts?—Of all the ordinary minor crimes, of course putting aside more serious offences.

3007. Do not they proceed from small offences to greater ones?—There is not the least doubt in the world of that; I have taken a list of small offences which have come before the court of quarter sessions, and I find that a large proportion of the offences have been committed by vagrants and strangers. I have been very much struck with this fact: three-fourths of the persons who have been convicted at quarter sessions for passing bad money are Irish tramps; that is a remarkable circumstance which I have noticed for many years. It so happens that all those cases come through my hands, having the prosecution of such cases for the Crown, and I have noticed that they have almost all been committed by Irish tramps.

3008. Do you think it would be very desirable to establish a general system of police throughout the kingdom?—I have no doubt of it; it would be a very great saving of expense as well as a great preventive of crime. I always look at the rural police as being more beneficial as a preventive force than as a detective force; vagrants in the country are so much afraid of the very name of a police officer.

3009. Does not detection lead to prevention?—If you can prevent crime it is better than detecting it; no doubt if you detect an offender, for a while you prevent that person from committing that offence again.

3010. Have you turned your attention as to whether or not the police might be employed otherwise beneficially in any way than as policemen?—I have; I have repeatedly expressed the opinion that road surveyors under certain circumstances might be made most efficient rural police, without at all infringing upon their duties as road surveyors; I mean that they might carry out an efficient superintendence; I do not mean that they should be active officers of the rural police.

3011. Do you not think that that order of things might be reversed; instead of making the road surveyors policemen, that the policemen might be usefully employed in the inspection of roads?—It is merely an inversion of terms; I say I would make police officers district road surveyors. I know from my own knowledge the great benefit we have had in one or two districts, in the Abbey Holme, and also Sir James Graham's property at Netherby; those two large districts have been united under the statute for district road surveys, and they have found, from having the worst roads that there were in the county, now they have the best; and the saving of expense, I think, is more than one-third.

3012. Mr. Howard.] You are aware that in the other wards of Cumberland the police is very deficient?—It is very deficient indeed.

3013. In the Brampton district, are you aware that they send very often for the police to Carlisle, whenever they find it necessary to apprehend any offender? —Yes. I have known of their doing that several times; I do not know it of my own knowledge, but I have heard of it from the officers, that as far as Longtown Mr. Brown has been sent all the way from Cockermouth. The officers at Carlisle were constantly sent to Longtown until they had an officer of their own for that town; he is paid by a local subscription, which proves the feeling of the people there.

3014. Are you aware what the expense is of sending the officers from Carlisle? —There is no charge to the county; they are always sent at the cost of the persons requiring them.

3015. Is there any other purpose for which you would recommend the police force to be employed besides that of overlooking the roads?—I would give them a general superintendence over lodging-houses. I should like very much indeed to see the lodging-houses in the country placed under the same control as they are in the towns. We find that the lodging-houses in the country are worse than ever; there is no control over them; they are crowded to a degree, and they are in a much worse position than they were ever in. In the degree that you have a watchful care over the lodging-houses in the towns, so in an equal ratio the others become worse, and more full of vagrants; they hang outside the town, and dare not pass through. The recent enactment requiring all public-houses to be closed between the hours of 12 o'clock on Saturday nights and one o'clock on Sunday afternoons, has been of great service. The most respectable innkeepers consider the measure a great boon; but in the country it cannot be carried out for want of police. In some rural districts the public-houses are filled on Sundays by those who cannot get into ale houses or beershops in the towns. I would have this carefully attended to by a rural police.

3016. Was there not a considerable apprehension on the part of the ratepayers on the increase of the police?—Yes, there was a considerable battle at the sessions upon the subject; a resolution was carried in favour of a general police rate, and then at a subsequent sessions that order was rescinded.

3017. Owing to the representations of the ratepayers?—Yes, no doubt it would be so; I do not remember exactly whether it was on petition, or how it was. No doubt it would be from the ratepayers; some of the magistrates had a strong feeling against any police whatever.

3018. Do you think it would be possible, if the rural police were established in the county of Cumberland, to effect a system of patrols in the wild parts of the county?—I think it would, if you had surveyors in the way I suggest; they would necessarily patrol; the patrols must go over the roads in the district, and from the extent of the district which I would propose they should have, they must ride. The mere uncertainty of their movements would be the best preventive you could possibly have against ordinary depredations, from which we suffer so much in the county. I was inquiring of one of the surveyors who has a large district in the Abbey Holme division, if he could, consistently with his duties as a road surveyor, look after the roads, and inspect the lodging-houses in the district, and keep a sharp look-out upon vagrants and tramps. He said he should not find any difficulty in doing so, and that it would be a great advantage to him that he should be a police officer.

3019 Have you formed any calculation as to what number of men would be required for that service?—I have estimated that the saving of expense, even in road surveying for the county, would more than pay the expense of the police; and carrying that calculation out upon the same basis of what the expense would be in Cumberland, throughout the 52 counties, you would save as much as would establish a police force throughout the kingdom.

3020. Lord *Lovaine*.] Are you acquainted with the mining districts of Cumberland?—I am not at all acquainted with the lead mining district, but the coal mining district I am acquainted with, though not very extensively; I never was in Alston.

3021. Is it not rather a turbulent district?—So we have found. We have occasionally had to send troops to quell disturbances there, but this is some years ago.

3022. Would the occupation of that part of the district by the rural police enter into your view?—Certainly.

3023. Do you anticipate any impediment to the efficiency of the police from the nature of the occupation of the people?—No. not at all. I do not see that there would be any more difficulty in controlling them than in controlling coal miners, or weavers, or iron workers, or any other persons. They have only the advantage of being able to run to earth quicker than others.

3024. Mr. *Mackie*.] Is there a rural police force established in the county of Cumberland between Carlisle and the Scottish borders?—No.

3025. Are you not of opinion, that if you had a good rural police established in that county, it would materially check the influx of Irish vagrants which you speak of between the Scottish counties and Cumberland?—I have no doubt that a good rural police force, in whatever position it is, would check vagrancy very much indeed. I do not think that the Irish vagrants leave us or come to us so much through Scotland as by Maryport, Whitehaven, and the small port of Carlisle, where they find it cheaper to come by water.

3026. But still you would be of opinion that a good rural police force established in that district of Cumberland would have the effect of checking vagrancy, no
matter

matter whether the people came from Maryport or from Scotland?—Very materially.

J. *Fawcett*, Esq.

16 June 1853.

3027. Do you think that a national police force all over the country would have the effect of materially checking vagrancy?—I have not the least doubt of it in the world; I have a strong opinion upon that subject.

3028. Lord *Lovaine*.] Have you frequent recommittals of persons who have been under the law before?—Very seldom; and not only that, but we find that the vast proportion of the offences are committed by the vagrants; we very seldom have recommittals. I do not ever remember a third committal of the same person for vagrancy; because, if they are really very troublesome ones, we generally punish them in Carlisle pretty smartly, so that they do not trouble us again.

3029. Is the vagrancy of which you complain from a body of Irish, and similar persons passing from the port of Liverpool to Scotland, or are they a permanent class of vagrants who wander from one part of the county to another, perpetually passing and repassing through your district?—I am not aware that they are the same persons; very likely they may be; if they came often, the superintendent of police would know them, and they would take care to keep out of the clutches of the police and the magistrates; I have no doubt they do return very often, from the circumstance of the number which pass through the lodging-houses; but to that fact I could not speak so well as the police officer himself.

Mr. *Robert Brown*, called in; and Examined.

3030. *Chairman*.] ARE you the Superintendent of Police in the Derwent division of the county of Cumberland?—Yes.

Mr. R. *Brown*.

3031. By whom were you appointed?—By the magistrates.

3032. Were you appointed by the magistrates of the division, or the magistrates of the county?—By the magistrates of the county generally, and my appointment was confirmed by the Secretary of State.

3033. Have you the appointment of the subordinate officers under you?—I have, entirely.

3034. Have you the power of dismissing them?—I have.

3035. What number of men have you?—I have only three.

3036. What is the size of your division?—An area of 205 square miles.

3037. What is the population of the division?—The population is 31,960.

3038. Then you have in fact, exclusive of yourself, one policeman to about 10,000 of the population?—Yes.

3039. Do you find that a sufficient force?—It gives very great satisfaction. We have been the means of reducing vagrancy very materially by the system which I have adopted. Perhaps the Committee will allow me to show the system which I have adopted for the inspection of the lodging-houses.

3040. Can you tell the Committee what is the expense of that police force?—I have an abstract of the expense of the constabulary for the last four years. In 1849, the constabulary cost 256*l*. 14*s*. 4*d*.; in 1850, 263*l*. 3*s*. 3*d*., that was a clothing year; in 1851, the expense was 249*l*. 15*s*. 6*d*.

3041. The largest expense was 263*l*.?—Yes.

3042. What does that amount to in the pound?—It was three farthings in the pound for the year; there were three rates in the year at a farthing in the pound.

3043. Do you avail yourself at all of the assistance of the parochial constables?—I do occasionally, but I am very sorry to say that generally they are a very useless body.

3044. To what extent do you avail yourself of their services?—I wrote instructions for them to visit the public-houses in the district.

3045. Did you do that because your three men could not do that without their assistance?—Yes.

3046. Do the parochial constables inspect the public-houses efficiently?—No.

3047. You framed some instructions which you think are very good, but they have not been carried out?—They have not.

3048. Lord *Lovaine*.] Have you any means of enforcing those instructions?—No.

3049. *Chairman*.] Have you any means of punishing the parochial constable if he does not do his duty?—If I saw a neglect of duty, I should report him to the magistrates.

Mr. R. Brown.

16 June 1853.

3050. What could the magistrates do?—They could fine him for neglect of duty; the penalty is 10 *l.*

3051. Have you ever done so?—No, I have not.

3052. What increase of force in your division do you think would be sufficient to enable you entirely to dispense with the aid of parochial constables?—The increase would be about five more men; I could do it very satisfactorily with eight men.

3053. What would be the cost of that increase?—Each of the officers has 44 *l.* 4 *s.* and clothing; it would more than double the expenditure.

3054. Upon an average, it would cost about 600 *l.*?—Yes.

3055. What is your salary?—£. 80 and clothing.

3056. If your salary continued the same, and there were five more constables, that would be rather more than double the present expense?—Yes.

3057. It is now three farthings in the pound, and that would make it less than 2 *d.*?—Yes.

3058. Would a three-halfpenny rate pay the expense, do you think?—No, I do not think it would; something between that and 2 *d.*

3059. Lord *Lovaine.*] If you had the increased force which you propose, how many inhabitants would there be to each policeman?—About 4,000.

3060. *Chairman.*] You think you could do the duties efficiently with that force? —I could.

3061. Mr. *Howard.*] What towns are there in your ward which have any police?—I have one station at Keswick, one at Maryport, and one at Cockermouth; that is the centre division. Maryport has one policeman under the harbour trustees, to attend to the vessels and town.

3062. Lord *Lovaine.*] What is the population of Keswick?—About 3,000.

3063. What is the population of Maryport?—Between 7,000 and 8,000.

3064. Mr. *Howard.*] Are all the policemen in the ward under your control? —Yes.

3065. Do you find that it is difficult to proceed against offenders in the neighbouring wards?—I do.

3066. Do you find that you do not get much co-operation from the constables in the wards?—I do not, I am sorry to say. In case it is necessary for me to obtain any information, I have no person to apply to at all. To show the inefficiency of the police, I can state one case, which occurred some years ago. The Reverend William Graham met me in the street one day, and he said to me, "Brown, I should like to see you very well come to our neighbourhood." I said, "Well, sir, I should be happy to do so, if I could obtain leave from the committee." He said, "Depredations have been committed in our neighbourhood which are well known to the parochial constable." I said, "What is the reason he does not apprehend them?" He said, "I believe he is afraid of them." Accordingly, I obtained leave, and I went to Longtown, and apprehended those parties, and brought them before the magistrates; they were committed and convicted. The parochial constables were well aware that the parties were carrying on those depredations.

3067. What have been your proceedings under the Vagrancy Act?—I will state the system which I adopted in inspecting the lodging-houses. We have not the Lodging-house Act in our division. The system I adopt is, that an officer in each town, as in Maryport and Keswick, shall inspect the lodging-houses between the hours of six and nine o'clock in the evening. He makes a report of the number of males and females found in each lodging-house, and gives me the gross number that he finds there. In the year 1847, there were 42,386 vagrants and tramps; in the year 1848, there were 39,571, making a decrease of 2,815. In 1849, there were 29,835; decrease, 9,736. In the year 1850, 23,176; decrease, 6,659. In 1851, 17,648; decrease, 5,528.

3068. Do you inspect the vagrants at the union house?—No; they are inspected by me at the station-house before they go there. Those vagrants that go to the union-house for a bed for the night are inspected at the station-house first before they go there.

3069. Lord *Lovaine.*] How is that done; you have no right to do it, have you?—They apply to the relieving officer, and he sends them to the station-house; as I was appointed relieving officer by the Poor-law Commissioners.

3070. *Chairman.*] You have spoken of the inspection of the lodging-houses; do you entrust that inspection to the parochial constables?—Never.

3071. Do

Mr. R. Brown.

16 June 1852.

3071. Do you think them unfit for the duty?—I do; in the four years there was a decrease of 24,738.

3072. Mr. *Mackie*.] That is more than half?—Yes; it was 42,000 the first year. To show the good effect of my being appointed relieving officer, I have the power to give tickets, and if I find ablebodied men applying, I do not give them tickets. In 1848, the expense of relieving these vagrants with a ticket for the night was 18 *l.* 0 *s.* 9½ *d.* This last year it was 2 *l.* 11 *s.* 8½ *d.* in the whole division.

3073. Mr. *Howard*.] Do you inspect weights and measures?—I do not.

3074. Lord *Lovaine*.] Can you keep up a patrol with so small a number of men?—No; The district is dissected into three divisions; these men go round the division once a week in the coal mines; and in the mountain districts they go once a fortnight. They have a book of instructions, and have to call upon the most respectable ratepayers and magistrates in that district to sign the book. At the time the officer calls, in case a gentleman has any remarks to make, there is a column for that purpose, if he wishes the police to attend to any particular case.

3075. A night patrol is out of the question, is it not?—On Saturday nights we are on duty.

3076. *Chairman*.] Do not you think a night patrol is very necessary for the prevention of crime?—It is, certainly.

3077. Could you have a night patrol, if you had the increase of which you have spoken?—I could.

3078. Mr. *Philipps*.] What is the acreage of the district?—

3079. Lord *Lovaine*.] Is not there a large portion of the district which is thinly inhabited?—The neighbourhood of Keswick is thinly inhabited, the other district is very thickly inhabited.

3080. *Chairman*.] Have you a coal district in your division?—Yes.

3081. Is that very troublesome?—At times.

3082. Is it more troublesome than you could effectually control with your eight men?—It is not.

3083. Mr. *Howard*.] What is the police force at Whitehaven?—I believe it is ten men, one superintendent, and four supernumeraries; I believe that is the number.

3084. Do they cordially assist the county police?—The superintendent and myself act very well together; generally speaking, the county police and the borough police do not act well together; I should recommend the police to be amalgamated, and placed under one head, and then they would work well together.

Mr. *John Clayden*, called in; and Examined.

Mr. J. Clayden.

3085. *Chairman*.] ARE you a landowner and land occupier at Saffron Walden, in Essex?—Both.

3086. To a considerable extent?—I occupy about 1,500 acres in Saffron Walden and adjoining parishes, 700 of which are my own. I reside in the parish of Littlebury.

3087. What is the population of Saffron Walden?—Between 5,000 and 6,000, and its acreage is about 7,297.

3088. Are there any hamlets adjoining Saffron Walden?—There are three hamlets, with a resident population of about 400 people.

3089. Are they within the borough?—Yes. There is a considerable extent of road within the parish, from 25 to 28 miles of road, upon which there is a great deal of traffic.

3090. Are the public-houses numerous?—There are 16 public-houses, and about 21 beershops; there are four beershops in those hamlets out of the town, and 17 beershops in the town.

3091. What police force is there in Saffron Walden?—The present police force is two; a few years ago, the police was only the parish constables; after that there was one policeman appointed.

3092. To what degree of protection have you arrived now?—The first policeman was shot at his own door; then, in consequence of the representations of the ratepayers, we had two police, and one old man who acts as a beadle, walking about the town.

3093. Under what circumstances was the policeman shot?—In consequence of his being obnoxious to those around him. He had not strength enough under his control, and he was actually shot at his own door. He was not killed on the spot, but he died within a week.

3094. Mr. *Philipps.*] Was it known who shot him?—Yes; the man was tried.

3095. Your present police force is two men?—Yes; who are mostly confined to the precincts of the town.

3096. Under whose control are the police?—They are paid by the watch committee, I suppose; they are certainly not under very excellent control, for they may be about their duties, or they may not.

3097. Are they both on an equal footing?—I think not. I do not know what wages are paid; one man, is the superior officer, I think he is a pretty good fellow. The last policeman got into disgrace. I rather think there was a charge of drunkenness brought against him, and he sent in his resignation.

3098. Do you think your present police force satisfactory?—We do not.

3099. Is that opinion shared by others?—It is shared by others. We drew up a memorial, and handed it to the magistrates of the borough, memorialising them that the present force was considered altogether inefficient for the protection of the property, and for the defence of the borough. It was handed round to others for signature, and obtained 67 signatures, many residing in the town.

3100. What was the object of the memorial?—To obtain a more efficient system of police by forming a connexion with the county police.

3101. Was one part of the memorial a recommendation to consolidate the police of the borough of Saffron Walden with the police of the county?—Yes; under the 2d and 3d of Victoria.

3102. What was the result of that memorial?—The result was a document in which the town council said they could not see upon what ground the allegations in the memorial were based; and intimated that they were decidedly and unanimously opposed to a union with the county police. In my opinion, they wish to keep the patronage belonging to such appointments in their own hands.

3103. You mean to say that the watch committee differed from the memorialists, and thought that the police establishment was sufficient?—I do; the parties who signed this memorial did not consider so. There are a lot of persons loitering about the precincts of the borough; it is noted for having idle men standing about at all the corners who get their living by acts of pilfering and poaching.

3104. What benefit do the memorialists expect to derive from the consolidation of the borough police with the county police?—We expect that our property will be better watched than it is at present, in consequence of the borough police being so much confined to the town; the county police moving about would fall in with these idle characters, and act as preventers of robberies, if they did not apprehend them.

3105. Do you think from the inefficient state of the police of Saffron Walden it is the general resort of thieves and vagabonds?—I do not know that it is a resort for thieves, but it is a city of refuge for pilferers; the moment they come within the confines of the borough they are out of the hands of the county police; there have been two or three cases of sheep-stealing. I remember an instance in which some parties went out of the town and took a lamb out of a flock, carried it away, and cooked it; they were seen, and information was given to a county policeman who happened to be near the spot; it being, however, within the jurisdiction of the borough, he refused to act, and the parties decamped before they could be apprehended.

3106. Are you not of opinion, Saffron Walden being a sort of refuge for thieves, that the property immediately surrounding the borough is still more exposed to depredations than the property in the borough?—No; I do not think I ought to agree to that, because the county police come in there, and if depredations were committed, it would be their duty to apprehend the offenders.

3107. Is there no county police for these four hamlets?—No.

3108. I am speaking of the hamlets which immediately adjoin the borough; are depredations very frequent there?—Not very frequent; still there are depredations; there are numbers of dissolute persons always about.

3109. Have you sufficient force to keep the peace in case of a riot?—No.

3110. Have you ever had a riot?—No; at the last election the county police
were

Mr. J. Clayden.

16 June 1853.

were sent for, fearing that there would be an outbreak, and that there would not be a sufficient force to overcome it.

3111. Have you experienced any inconvenience from the absence of the policemen, while they have been conveying prisoners to gaol?—In the event of the committal of a prisoner, the chief constable is engaged in conveying him away to Chelmsford, 27 miles distant; therefore the town is left entirely without protection, except one constable and the old parish beadle; and until recently without even these.

3112. Where are your prisoners sent to gaol?—To Chelmsford, 27 miles off.

3113. Is there no nearer gaol?—No; our borough prisoners are sent to Chelmsford.

3114. How are they conveyed to the gaol?—The policeman conveys them in a cart.

3115. During the whole of that time you are left with one man?—Decidedly.

3116. You think that parochial constables are perfectly inefficient for police purposes?—Yes.

3117. Do you make use of the parochial constables at all?—They have a parochial constable in one of the hamlets.

3118. Do you find them useful there?—They are useful, but not so efficient as a general system of police acting in concert with each other would be.

3119. In your opinion, the best course that could be taken for the protection of the property of the ratepayers would be the consolidation of the police of Saffron Walden with the county police?—Yes.

3120. Lord *Lovaine*.] Would you be charged an extra rate in that case?—Not very much more than it costs at present.

3121. And you would be willing to pay the surplus?—Yes.

3122. Sir *J. Trollope*.] What is the rate that you now pay for the police force?—It goes into the corporation funds; we know nothing about it; the corporation has property.

3123. Are you rated at all for the police?—About 420 *l.* is annually paid to the corporation out of the poor's-rate, and the town council pay the constables thereout.

3124. Do you know what the weekly pay of each man is?—I should think the first man has 1 *l.*

3125. Are the men efficient as far as they go?—One is efficient; the first man is the best man we have had for a long while.

3126. Yours is chiefly rural property?—Yes.

3127. Are you rated for that upon the same footing as the houses; is there an equal property rate throughout the parish?—Yes; we pay as occupiers of land in the borough.

3128. It appears that your complaint is that the two policemen are used entirely for town purposes, and that the rural property is unprotected, although you pay equally with the others?—Yes.

3129. In short, your rate would be larger than the others?—Yes, and our property is more exposed to depredation in consequence of the roads branching out in every direction from the town; and the parish extending to 7,000 or 8,000 acres, there is a large amount of road to keep, and a great deal of traffic on the road.

3130. Are any of the owners of rural property members of the corporation of Saffron Walden?—Very few; this memorial is chiefly signed by the occupiers of land; consequently, not much by those who are connected with the corporation.

3131. Was that memorial signed by a majority of the owners, or a majority of the ratepayers within the borough?—Not a majority in number of the ratepayers, because there are many holdings in the town; it was not taken to many small occupiers.

3132. You consider if your police force were amalgamated with the county police, the cost would be more than it is under the present system, but that the protection would be better?—Yes.

3133. Lord *Lovaine*.] And you have said that you would be willing to pay an extra rate?—I do not expect that we should have much more to pay then than we have now. In consequence of Saffron Walden being made the head quarters of the police, I think our security would be much greater.

Mr. J. Clayden.

16 June 1853.

3134. Sir *J. Trollope.*] Should not you require more men for the parish and borough?—To be effectually done, it would require more men; but it would depend upon how the men were placed around; we should save in other respects, and perhaps at the end of the year the amount would not be much greater.

George Carrington, Junior, Esq., called in; and Examined.

G. Carrington, Jun. Esq.

3135. *Chairman.*] YOU are a Magistrate for the county of Buckingham, are you not?—I am.

3136. You have superintending constables appointed in each division of the county?—We have; we had them not at first for each division; in some cases, some were appointed for more than one division; we found that the divisions were larger than they ought to be; but at the last quarter sessions, except in the case of one of the hundreds, each division has its superintending constable.

3137. Have you adopted that system in the whole of the county of Buckingham?—Yes.

3138. As a magistrate, did you approve of the adoption of that system?—I did; it was not moved by me, but after it was carried at the quarter sessions, I became the chairman of the constabulary committee, and of course I became well acquainted with it.

3139. Do you approve of the working of that system in the county of Buckingham?—Yes; it has been in operation but a very short time, about 18 months altogether; and only one quarter since it has been made as efficient as it ought to be, by the appointment of one superintending constable to each division.

3140. You think the system has been made more efficient than it was by the appointment of one in each division?—Yes; in several cases we were applied to to have a man appointed; there was a good deal of feeling about it, and therefore the quarter sessions adopted it on our recommendation.

3141. How many have you now?—Fifteen; in the hundred in which there is only one for the two divisions, there is a superintendent of the lock-up, and his whole services are employed. There are 15 superintending constables, and one assistant.

3142. Putting the hundreds out of the question, there are 15 divisions?—Yes; there are 16 divisions of the county. Two of them have one superintendent constable between them, and the remainder have one a-piece; 15 superintendent constables, and one superintendent of a lock-up, whose whole services are retained.

3143. What is the largest division in the county which is under one superintending constable?—I think the two divisions of Newport Pagnell are the largest.

3144. Can you tell the Committee what number of parishes there are in those divisions?—I think there are 25 in one of the divisions, and 27 in the other. Those are the two largest divisions that we have, I think. I am not very well acquainted with the northern part of the county.

3145. Is there a parish constable in each parish, appointed by the magistrates?—Yes.

3146. Is he a parish constable or a paid constable?—There are no paid parish constables in our county but the superintendents of the lock-up houses, and occasionally, in large populous parishes, there is a private constable who is paid by a subscription of the inhabitants; except the one superintendent of the lock-up, who was a London policeman, and whose whole time is employed at Slough, and the superintending constables of the divisions, we have no other paid county constables at all in the county.

3147. Are you of opinion that the parish constables are efficient as police officers?—Some of them; they vary a good deal in their qualities.

3148. Do you think that generally they are fit for the purpose?—I have known some of them do their work very well; of course they vary. In small places there is no great choice of men.

3149. The parish constables are of no use, unless they are paid for the duties which they perform?—Of course not.

3150. If they perform the duties which they ought to perform, and they are paid by fees, would not they be more expensive than a paid constabulary?—I think it is difficult if you have a completely paid police force to diffuse it into every corner, and into every hamlet, without having men that are not fully employed;

they

they fall into idle, dissolute habits. There are a great number of hamlets and places where it is of no great use to have a man who is remunerated for occasional services, because the whole of his time is not required.

G. Carrington, Jun.
Esq.

16 June 1853.

3151. If you had a paid constabulary force in the county of Buckingham, in your opinion many of those men would be so little employed that they would be liable to contract drunken and dissolute habits?—I think if you had them to a sufficient extent to penetrate into every place wherever a man is required to keep order in a public-house disturbance, then I think they would often be without occupation; but I have no knowledge whatever of the working of a rural police force, therefore what I say is mere conjecture.

3152. You have a knowledge of the parochial system; do you find that the parish constables do penetrate into those places which you speak of, public-houses, beershops, and so forth?—I go a good deal by what the officers tell me; they think that some of them are efficient.

3153. Do the officers generally tell you that they can rely upon the parish constables for the superintendence of public-houses and beerhouses?—Upon some they can, and not upon others; that is the account they give to me.

3154. Do you not think generally yourself that their local connexions and their local interests would interfere with their efficiency in controlling beershops and public-houses?—No doubt, to a certain extent; but my doubt is, whether you can plant a man where you wish to have a constable, without a heavy expense, and without his having a good deal of idle time.

3155. The two objections which you have to a paid constabulary under the Rural Police Act would be, that if you have a sufficient force to pervade the country you would have too many, and they would contract idle, dissolute habits, and also that the expense would be too great?—These are not the only objections; although I think if you had them in sufficient frequency to have one everywhere where you now have a parish constable, you would find the expense very heavy.

3156. Do you know what is the expense of the superintending constables?—Yes; the superintending constables get 80 l. for themselves; they are all upon one uniform salary. We find a cart and harness at going off, and we should renew it when it was fairly worn out; they find and maintain a horse, for which they are allowed 30 l. a year; then there is about 10 l. for outgoings with their horse, payment to ostlers, and so on, when they are out. They have also a portion of the fees in the business of weights and measures.

3157. Then the whole cost, taking everything into consideration, is about 130 l. a year?—Yes. There would be, of course, some little outgoings when they sleep at an inn at the assizes, when lodging is higher, and there is a small allowance to them for that.

3158. Have not you a general allowance for such purposes?—When they are called upon in the actual discharge of their duty to be absent from home they have a slight allowance for the night's sleeping.

3159. Is there no fixed allowance; do not you allow them 2 s., 3 s., or 5 s. a day?—When they are detained at quarter sessions they are allowed a few shillings on each occasion. The actual salary is 80 l., finding a horse and the repair of the cart and harness at 30 l., the outgoings with the horse and cart 10 l., which was calculated at 4 s. a week, and outgoings when in charge of a prisoner for four hours previous and during the conveyance to a gaol, 2 s. 6 d.

3160. Mr. Burroughes.] Do you know what the parish constables cost upon the average?—No; I do not think I could give accurate information as to that.

3161. Have you any high constables or hundred constables?—No; the superintending constables perform all the duties of the high constables, and the inspection of weights and measures.

3162. Had you high constables?—We had, and they altogether cost 100 l. a year; for many years they used to have more than that; then upon the reduction of the work which took place some years ago some of their pay a year was struck off; finally, they were entirely superseded by the superintending constables.

3163. Therefore you save that expense entirely?—That is thrown in towards the expense of the superintending constables.

3164. Chairman.] Are the parish constables ever employed in watching?—They are; but there is not the proper means of remunerating them for being out watching.

G. Carrington, Jun.
Esq.

16 June 1853.

3165. Have not the magistrates the power of ordering payment out of the poor-rates, when they are watching under a magistrate's order?—Perhaps, strictly speaking, they have; I do not think practically they do that; a bill is submitted to the vestry, and if the bill comes to 2 l. or 3 l. more than is commonly the case, there is so much discontent about it, that it is discouraged by the inhabitants, I think.

3166. Do you mean that the bill is paid by the overseer of the parish?—If it is legally drawn out it is allowed; still it produces arguments with the vestry and with the inhabitants if much increase be observable.

3167. Do you know what the amount of those bills paid to parish constables is?—No; we used in Missenden to pay a man 10 l. a year, who was one of the constables, and there were two or three others besides to keep order in the parish, and the parish wishing to do away with that, paid him by fees; I calculated that they saved very little by that; it came to about 10 l.

3168. They contracted in one case for 10 l.?—Yes; they said they would pay for the actual work done; I supp— in Missenden parish it must come to 16 l. or 20 l. a year; the population of the parish is about 2,000, and there are distant parts of it which require some one in authority on the spot.

3169. Do you think that the average cost of parish constables would be 10 l. a year?—I should not like to say unless I had the facts; I only act in one petty sessional division.

3170. Do you know what the costs of parish constables in proceedings before the justices are?—It is all done by a scale of fees; Lord Chandos is more familiar with that than I am; I have not it with me; they have a shilling for serving a summons, and a shilling a mile when it is beyond the immediate place where they reside.

3171. But in many cases where there are informations before the magistrates, and the case is dismissed, are the costs paid to the constables by the plaintiff?—There has been a great deal of question in point of law about that; it is a great question how their costs shall be paid; we have taken legal opinions about it; in some cases the prosecutor pays, but in general the parish pays.

3172. Are the costs which the prosecutors have to pay settled out of court between the constables and the prosecutors?—I do not allow that where I act; I never allow a case to be settled without a reference in open court.

3173. Lord Lovaine.] Not a question of costs?—No; if the parties wish to make it up, they are not allowed to make it up except in the petty sessions to which they have been summoned.

3174. The question has reference to the payment of the expenses of the constable where the case is dismissed; do you allow that to be settled out of court?—We ask the constable, "What are your costs?" and we say what is fit to be given to him, and the parties sometimes say he has been paid, or that they have agreed upon it.

3175. Chairman.] You do not know what it amounts to?—The most usual thing is the summons, which is a shilling for serving, and a shilling a mile if he goes beyond the immediate village in which he lives; and he has sometimes, according to circumstances, from 3 s. to 5 s. when he comes to have the case heard.

3176. What are the constables paid for the conveyance of prisoners?—I think, under the present scale, it is a shilling a mile, including all charges, except the maintenance of the man; if it is 16 miles, it is 16 s., in addition to the maintenance of the man, or the cost of an assistant, if he has one.

3177. Do you know what the cost of conveyance of prisoners to gaol by local constables is at all?—I suppose, on the average, the superintending constables convey about half; they would nearly convey the whole where there is one to each division.

3178. Do your superintending constables, or the parochial constables, summon coroners' juries?—The superintending constables, I think; I will not be positive; sometimes a coroner's inquest happens upon such an emergency, that the nearest constable must do it.

3179. Do the superintending constables inspect weights and measures?—Yes.

3180. Mr. Philipps.] How much in the pound is paid for the superintending constables in the county of Buckingham?—There is 1,600 l.; and you may take in a rough way that there are 16 times 30 l. besides that, which is nearly 2,100 l.; from that we deduct 100 l., which the high constables cost under the old law; and

and 100*l.* to one inspector of weights and measures, who was inefficient from his too great extent.

G. *Carrington*, Junt. Esq.

16 June 1853.

3181. Sir *J. Trollope.*] How many of the old high constables were there?—About eight.

3182. Did they receive only 100*l.* amongst them?—Not since the recent instructions.

3183. Was that for collecting the county rate?—Yes.

3184. Mr. *Philipps.*] Can you give the Committee the largest amount of population and acreage that any one superintending constable looks after?—

3185. Sir *J. Trollope.*] The total cost of the superintending constables is a little more than 2,000*l.*?—Yes.

3186. Have you ever estimated, if the rural police were in full force, what would be the additional cost?—I do not know; I am not at all conversant with the rural police.

3187. Have you not made any calculation of the number of men that would be required, and the consequent cost?—No; I am not able to give any information as to that.

3188. Mr. *Philipps.*] Can you tell what is the amount of county rate which is levied?—

3189. *Chairman.*] Are you aware whether it is in contemplation, in the Act which is now before the House, to appoint a chief constable over all the superintending constables?—I am aware that there is an Act before the House; but from the first we saw that it was necessary to have some head.

3190. Is one of your superintending constables superior to the others?—No; we have appointed a committee before whom all the reports and books of the officers are laid; we meet once at least in every quarter, and more if need be.

3191. You have a police committee appointed?—A constabulary committee.

3192. Of which you are the chairman?—Yes.

3193. How often do you meet?—At least once a quarter, for looking over the men's accounts, before the quarter sessions, and oftener for revision of rules, new appointments. &c. &c.

3194. Have you reports from the superintending constables?—All the reports they lay before the magistrates.

3195. Will you state what is the course adopted?—Every constable has three books which he keeps in order, and lays before the magistrates of his own district. Whenever we assemble at our quarterly meetings, we see that the rules have been regularly observed, and compare those books with each other.

3196. Are there any other circumstances that you wish to mention to the Committee?—I think the superintending constables would be much more efficient if they had more means of giving remuneration to parochial constables when they are out watching at night.

3197. Do you think it would be desirable that they should have the opportunity of giving rewards to the parochial constables for the apprehension of offenders?—No; I think they should be able to give remuneration to the men who go out to watch at night, independently of the parochial authorities; I think it should be more in the hands of the magistrates legally to order a certain rate of remuneration to a parish constable for going out when he is ordered at night.

3198. You think it would be desirable in the first place that the magistrates should have the power of ordering constables to watch, and when they had watched, that they should order the remuneration to be paid by the parish officers?—Yes, I think there may be such a power desirable.

3199. Do you think those orders are acted upon generally?—Yes.

3200. And you think the power of the magistrates should be extended?—Yes; one of our superintending constables had a man in his service many nights last winter, and we all contributed towards his payment.

3201. Mr. *Burroughes.*] How long has the constabulary committee been appointed?—About 18 months.

3202. How often do they meet?—Once a quarter, before the quarter sessions, always one day, and they confine themselves to routine, looking over the men's accounts; and they meet if there is the appointment of a new officer, or any new officer to hear the rules.

3203. They do not generally superintend those constables as their head?—All the men attend on that day, and undergo an examination of the current events of the quarter.

F

3204. Do you give any directions as to their mode of patrolling the country?
—Yes; we have lately amended the rules; I have the rules here under which they all act.

3205. Do they act under your special supervision?—Yes.

3206. Sir *J. Trollope.*] It is not the fact that there is no system at all of over-looking those constables?—Those are the rules which I have here.

3207. Are not the superintending constables under strict rules, and also under the strict supervision of the magistrates of the petty sessional divisions?—They are primarily under the magistrates, and secondarily under the constabulary committee.

3208. How often do they re...t to the constabulary committee?—At least once a quarter.

3209. How often do they report to the petty sessional magistrates?—Every time they meet, they lay those three books before them, which account for all their conduct, where they have been, and what they have done; what places they have visited, and so on; all which comes before the petty sessions, and then the books are signed by the magistrates.

3210. Then in your judgment, your system is as complete as it is capable of being made under the Act of Parliament by which the superintending constables are appointed?—Yes.

3211. *Chairman.*] Do you think the magistrates having business at the petty sessions have time carefully to examine those books?—Yes.

3212. Do you think, generally speaking, they do examine the books?—Yes. I have often spoken to the magistrates about occurrences which have taken place; we go through the books regularly when we meet in my own petty sessions.

3213. Sir *J. Trollope.*] Have you reason to believe that since the establishment of the superintending constables, crime and vagrancy have been diminished in the county of Buckingham?—I know that in one district in my neighbourhood, in which I do not act, the district of Chesham, there is very far less sheep-stealing and pig-stealing than there was.

3214. As regards crime of a minor description, including misdemeanors, which generally come before the petty sessions, have they been diminished also?—A very good farmer, who occupies 400 acres of land, told me that the place was very different to what it had been before; he thought the man had been most active, and that there had been infinitely less depredation since he had been there.

3215. Have you put the parish constables under the superintending constables? —Yes; the law puts them under them.

3216. Do you think with good effect, as regards parish constables?—I do.

3217. How many lock-up houses have you completed under the charge of each superintending constable?—There is one at Slough, one at Newport Pagnell, one at High Wycombe, one at Beaconsfield, and there is one at Stoney Stratford, between Bucks and Northamptonshire; between the county of Hertfordshire and our county there may be one more.

3218. Do you contemplate furnishing all the petty sessional divisions with lock-up houses?—Yes. We have referred the consideration of the question of lock-up houses to the constabulary committee, and they have requested four more.

3219. Do you contemplate completing the whole number?—Yes, we contemplate completing the whole in every division.

3220. With accommodation for the lock-up housekeeper to reside on the spot? —Yes.

3221. Is he a separate officer?—He is by law.

3222. Have you separate constables besides the superintending constables?— Yes.

3223. When you have completed all your arrangements, do you think the police regulations which you have established in the county of Buckingham will be sufficient for the preservation of the peace and the protection of property?—I think they will; it is a question of time; it is a great improvement upon there being none before. I have no means of comparing it with any other system.

3224. Do you wish to extend the principle, so as to establish the rural police? —At present, I should wish to give this system a fair trial. I think no police officer is really efficient until he has been appointed four or five months; he does not know the people, nor do the people know him. I think the constables are
much

G. Carrington, Jun.,
Esq.

16 June 1853.

much more willing to act under these men; the constables are appointed knowing that there is a superintendent over them. I think you see in many places the inhabitants appoint a constable at the recommendation of the superintending constable. He points out to the constabulary committee who would be fit men to take, and by degrees, I think he gets something like parochial constables appointed at his recommendation in many places.

3225. Are those parochial constables paid?—In some instances, in the south part of the county, where there is a large and rich population. In some parishes they have paid constables, but the vestries in general have a great objection to anything like salaried constables.

3226. Do you think that if the Police Act were extended beyond the superintending constables there would be objections on the part of the ratepayers to the expense?—I believe there is great jealousy in reference to the county rate in many places.

3227. Do you think that feeling would be extended by incurring the expense of a police force?—I think it would; but I have no public meeting to refer you to; I believe there is a great unwillingness to extend the county rate.

3228. Lord *Lovaine*.] Would you be astonished if you were informed that the superintending constables who have been appointed under the Act 5th & 6th Victoria, chap. 109, who have been examined before this Committee, have invariably stated that the parish constables were of no use at all, but rather an impediment to the performance of their duties?—No, I should not be surprised at it; I think those men naturally wish for the discipline of a regular force; but that is their opinion, and I am only giving mine. The man who was examined from our county gave me a general idea, before he came to the Committee, what he was going to say; he came to me afterwards, and told me that he was asked whether he could say it was efficient; he said, he thought he could not say so. He has told me that some of the constables are efficient men, and ready to act with him; of course not so ready to act as men whom he might dismiss at a moment's notice. What he said was, "I can lead them, but I cannot drive them."

3229. *Chairman*.] Has the superintending constable any means of punishing the parochial constables?—No, except by taking them before a magistrate; there have been some instances in which they have been fined, or threatened to be fined, for neglect of duty, having been placed under the orders of a superintending constable.

3230. Mr. *Howard*.] You have stated as an objection to the rural police, that they would be liable to fall into idle habits for want of regular employment?—Yes, if you put one into every place where there is some one bound to keep order when any little disturbance takes place. I think the men often in such cases would want real occupation.

3231. Might not that be obviated by giving them the superintendence of the highways?—I do not think there would be any advantage from blending the two together.

3232. Mr. *Rich*.] You say that you think the rural police would be objectionable on account of their acquiring habits of idleness; might not that idleness be obviated by having fewer men?—I think the difficulty in a county, where there are large wastes and commons, is to have a sufficient number to be ready at each place, so that they can be conveniently sent for. In some places there is very little for a constable to do, but it is desirable to have a man in case of anything arising at the public-houses at night.

3233. You say the magistrates meet once a quarter. If any thing occurred in the county requiring the superintending constables to act, who would give them authority during the intermediate time in the case of their being called upon to act if a robbery was going on?—They have printed rules before them; they would require no orders as to their general conduct from quarter to quarter.

3234. Does each superintendent constable act independently of the others?—Yes, except when he is under orders to co-operate with the others.

3255. If three or four men were required, who would give directions to them as to the method of conducting their operations?—If a felony happened in the district, the first man to act would be the superintending constable of that district, and if he saw occasion he would call in the others to assist him.

3236. There could be no head; each one would act independently of the others?—Yes, of course, they are all on an equal footing.

G. Carrington, Jun., Esq.

16 June 1853.

3237. You say your constables are paid by fees?—The parochial constables in almost all instances are.

3238. Do you look upon the system of payment by fees as likely to supply a better class of persons than the payment by salary?—I should prefer a salary, but it may be occasional, for a certain number of days or nights.

3239. Would not the parochial constables, being paid by salary, become almost the same as the rural police in the counties?—So far as having remuneration by a settled payment.

3240. Do you think if the parochial constables were paid by salaries, they would be less serviceable than the police?—I think a salary a more respectable way of receiving renumeration, and puts a man upon a better footing; but now, by fees, the parochial constable cannot be paid for doing many things which we want him to do. If a parish becomes infested with depredators, and the superintending constable wishes him to be out for a night or so, the practice is not to pay him by fees for the time he is out; if the man has remuneration, it is only by some private subscription.

3241. On such occasions his services would be less efficient than those of a regular policeman?—In great cases of felony in large towns, you have very often efficient good men as parochial constables; but the practice is not to pay fees except upon actual working, like moving vagrants, attending the sessions, serving summonses, and so forth; but those fees do not apply to cases of going out to watch for sheep-stealers.

3242. The superintending constables themselves have no authority to order a night watch?—I think they have in point of law. The law says that the parochial constables are to be under their orders, and in some cases they do go out at night.

3243. The superintending constable of our district might consider the emergency sufficiently urgent to establish a night watch; and the superintending constable in the adjoining district might have a contrary opinion?—He might so.

3244. Therefore, you might have a night watch in one district and not in the adjoining district?—Yes.

3245. *Chairman.*] Supposing a felony were committed, and from the inefficiency on the part of the parochial constable the prisoner escaped, would not you have a great expense in pursuit?—Of course; and so there would be if the prisoner got away from anybody else.

3246. When a felony is committed, and a parochial constable is ordered to pursue the offender, if he goes in pursuit, and he does not catch the offender, by whom is he paid?—I think he brings in a parochial bill; the practice is to require the order of a magistrate; I think it is usually paid under the parochial bill.

3247. Is that bill paid by the parish officers?—Yes.

3248. Do you think that bill would be allowed under the circumstances where the offender was not apprehended; would not it fall upon the person who had lost the property, and employed the constables in pursuit to pay him?—There is no uniform practice as to payment in those cases. Now, in the case of a prisoner going to a distance, the superintending constable goes after him. We had a superintending constable sent down to Sunderland after a man; in any case where the distance was great, we should send the superintending constable, because his time belongs to the county.

William Oakley, Esq., called in; and Examined.

W. Oakley, Esq.

3249. *Chairman.*] ARE you Governor of the County Gaol of Somerset, at Taunton?—I am.

3250. Had you previously served as chief officer of the police force of the city of Bath?—I succeeded Admiral Carroll as chief of the police in Bath, in March 1849.

3251. Had you previously served in a county police force?—I served seven years in the Essex County Constabulary, under Captain M'Hardy, and nearly four years as chief superintendent at the head-quarter station.

3252. How long were you chief of the police at Bath?—Three years.

3253. Why did you leave Bath?—To take my present appointment as Governor of the County Gaol, which is better emolument.

3254. How long have you been at the county prison at Somerset?—Not quite two years.

3255. **What**

W. Oakley, Esq.

16 June 1853.

3255. What is the police force in the county of Somerset now?—Parish constables in the rural districts; and, in some of the towns, petty local police forces.

3256. Are superintending constables appointed in Somerset?—Not under the Superintending Constables' Act; there are one or two superintending constables in the towns.

3257. Has your present appointment afforded you peculiar opportunities of observing the working of the parochial constable system?—It has.

3258. In what way?—By coming constantly in contact with the parish constables, and also seeing them at the sessions and assizes. I have frequent opportunities of noticing them in various cases, and have had communications with superintending constables in other counties.

3259. From your experience in the rural police, in Essex, do you believe that the operation of a county rural police is beneficial?—I do.

3260. Will you state generally in what respects you think so?—In the prevention of crime by patrolling, and in the detection of offenders particularly, from the police obtaining a knowledge of suspected persons. The duties which they generally render are particularly beneficial in the preservation of order in cases of anticipated public outbreaks or public occasions. The patrolling of constables renders them useful in the prevention of crime.

3261. Do you think a night patrol is necessary?—Absolutely necessary.

3262. Do you think the system which is described as the rural police force system is capable of improvement?—Yes, I think it requires great improvement in many respects.

3263. In what respects?—Particularly as to the necessity for its general extension. It is of very little use establishing a police force in one county unless it is extended to adjoining counties; and the benefit is only partial, even to the county in which it is established.

3264. Does not your observation apply more to the necessity of a general uniform system?—Yes.

3265. Supposing a regular uniform system were adopted, do you think that the system which is now in operation, under the Rural Police Act, is capable of improvement?—Yes, it is; of much improvement.

3266. In what respects?—Particularly in the duties of the chief constables, the number of the officers, and performance of duties by the police, by which great saving may be effected.

3267. Do you think the number of officers is too great in proportion to the number of men?—I think the proportion of officers much too great.

3268. And, therefore, too expensive?—Exactly.

3269. You think the expense of the rural police might be diminished by reducing the number of the staff?—I do.

3270. Do you believe that the remuneration of constables by fees and allowances tends to frustrate the ends of justice?—It does; it tends to give them an interest in crime. I have known instances where there has been no doubt that the cases have been got up by the parish constables entirely for the sake of the fees. I have known it done by men who have been police officers, where they were not under control.

3271. Do you think that this objection to the payment of constables by fees applies particularly with regard to the detection of offences committed upon the poorer classes?—It does; it was impossible in many cases which I have known for a poor man to obtain justice, or to have an investigation into his complaint, where it would be necessary to provide the means to pursue the offender or to make an inquiry.

3272. Can you mention an instance of that description?—I have known several instances within my own knowledge, where it has been altogether hopeless for a poor man to think of obtaining the restitution of his property, or the apprehension of an offender, because he has not had the means of giving the constable the amount necessary for him to go in pursuit. I have memoranda of some cases which have recently come within my own knowledge, in which parish constables, where they have been paid by fees, have resorted to various means for obtaining money. I have with me a copy of letters, which I felt it my duty to address to the committing magistrates; one case occurred on the 23d of November; perhaps it will be right that I should not give the names. " It is my duty to report to you that A. was brought here this day, under a commitment signed by yourself and B., Esq. for bastardy, by two persons, C. and D., saying they were sent by E., a

constable,

constable, but had neither themselves been sworn, or had any authority as constables. The prisoner complained of being heavily double ironed, hand and leg together, for such a charge as bastardy, never having been in custody before, or made the least resistance." On the previous Sunday three prisoners were brought to the gaol " by the same persons, and all three prisoners were covered with vermin, which they say they must have got in the lock-up ; and the turnkeys inform me prisoners have frequently complained of getting not only vermin but the itch also." I referred to the Act, which prevented my giving a receipt to such persons when they were brought to the gaol. One of those persons, after delivering over the prisoners, asked to see another prisoner in the gaol. On making inquiry, he said, " He is my uncle." That man was sentenced for receiving stolen goods. In another instance, in December, a prisoner was brought to gaol under commitment by another person, whom I will call G. T., the keeper of a low public-house in the town ; he was not a constable, nor had he any authority beyond being requested by the driver of a coach to bring the prisoner in a case of felony.

3273. Is it your opinion that the description of persons who are usually appointed as parochial constables are capable of efficiently performing their duty ?— It is quite impossible ; I have known many of them to be respectable men, but from local connexions and their occupation, it is utterly impossible for them to perform the duties of constables. In some instances recently parish constables have prevented prisoners from getting bail entirely for the sake of the fees.

3274. Do you think that the instances you have mentioned of abuse of power on the part of constables, have taken place for the purpose of pecuniary profit ?— I do ; a parish constable sent a common labourer, not being a constable at all, that he might employ himself in some other way, solely to obtain the expense of conveying prisoners to gaol.

3275. Do you mean that they persuade the prisoners to refrain from obtaining bail ?—Yes, in order that they might obtain the expense of conveying them to gaol. I have here a copy of a constable's bill, as attached to the receipt, signed by the gaoler. In this instance the distance was only nine miles, and the constable's expenses, including assistant's lodging and subsistence of the prisoner, were 1 l. 9 s. 3 d.

3276. Lord *Lovaine*.] Is that bill made up of charges which could not be refused ?— Yes, I believe it is made up of charges that could not be refused by the committing magistrate, without a better knowledge of the circumstances than committing magistrates generally obtain from parish constables. I believe the present proceedings under the criminal law hold out peculiar facilities for parish constables to obtain money improperly, in the way I have stated. Cases are heard, unfortunately in many instances, by magistrates at their private residences. Information is given to the parish constable of an offence having been committed ; he goes in pursuit of some particular party ; he may fix, and often does, upon a person who has been convicted before ; if the evidence which comes before the magistrate, on the first and second examination, is not sufficient to justify a committal, the parish constable, unless he obtains the committal of a prisoner, will lose, not only all the expenses which he has been put to, but also his fees for attendance before the magistrate. If he strains the evidence just sufficient to obtain a committal, he will get all the expenses on a magistrate's certificate. When bills come before the grand jury, the grand jury have no depositions before them or means of testing the evidence ; and the constables take care to get the bills thrown out, because the evidence would not bear the test of an examination in court.

3277. *Chairman*.] Do you believe that the criminal returns afford any index to the state of crime in counties employing parochial constables ?—Certainly not ; it is apt to mislead ; I have here a return printed with the calendar of prisoners for the Lent assizes at Taunton, showing the number of prisoners committed under summary convictions in the county of Somerset for 10 years ; and a return of prisoners committed for trial from 1823 to the year 1852, a period of 20 years. From the return of the offences committed, I find in the year 1848, in the county of Somerset, there were 20 persons committed for trial for sheep-stealing.

3278. There were 26 committed to gaol for sheep-stealing ?—Yes ; but there were more than 26 sheep stolen. In all 33 sheep and lambs, for which the 26 persons were committed.

3279. In fact that number was apprehended ?—Yes, and committed, for the whole

W. Oakley, Esq.

16 June 1853.

whole county, which consists of 20 divisions; by a return which I had whilst I was chief of the police at Bath, I found, in the same year, that there were 43 sheep stolen in the Bath division alone.

3280. Is the Bath division much larger than any other division?—It is a fair proportion to the other divisions; I find it so, having recently prepared returns to the magistrates and the gaol committee.

3281. Mr. *Rich.*] Is the population in the Bath division much larger?—It does not include the city of Bath; it comprises only the rural districts of the division.

3282. *Chairman.*] I presume the number of sheep is not larger?—They are not likely to be in the division of Bath, in the neighbourhood of a town.

3283. You have expressed your opinion of parochial constables; do you think the appointment of superintendent constables will improve them as police officers?—Certainly not; it only increases the expense, and I believe also, increases the evils; I have not been able myself to ascertain that there is any advantage at all to be derived from the appointment of superintending constables.

3284. Lord *Lovaine.*] How does the appointment of superintending constables increase the evil of the parochial constable system?—It increases the evils by inducing the parish constables to set themselves in opposition to the superintending constable. I have known instances in which the superintending constable has given them directions to watch particular persons, or to watch particular houses, where it was believed they gave information to the very persons whom they were directed to watch; and the consequence was, that it frustrated the efforts of the superintending constables. The superintending constables being altogether uncontrolled and without supervision themselves, fall into habits which render them unfit for the proper performance of their duties. I know two or three instances in which the only effect of appointing superintending constables has been to spoil them as police officers, and render them unfit for the proper performance of those duties which they would be required to perform in an efficient police force.

3285. You do not believe that the magistrates can obtain, through the means of a police committee or themselves, any real supervision?—I think the police committee, appointed as a police committee of the magistrates to assist the chief constable, would have a very beneficial effect. I do not believe that the gentlemen who usually attend the petty sessions for the purpose merely of receiving reports, and who are only there occasionally, can by any possibility superintend or supervise the superintending constables.

3286. In your opinion, does the superintending constable gain any real advantage by having a voice in the appointment of the constables of the parishes?—I do not think he gains any advantage at all.

3287. *Chairman.*] Do you think that the existing want of uniformity amongst police forces in counties and towns prevent mutual co-operation?—It does. It tends to frustrate the ends of justice, and to facilitate the escape of offenders. I have known even cases of murder, where a want of co-operation has prevented the criminal being brought to justice. In a recent case, two police officers from different forces were acting, and parish constables were also acting; and instead of investigating the offence properly, they were watching one another.

3288. In what way do you mean they were watching one another?—To ascertain what the one or the other were doing. When the two police officers found that they were merely watching one another, they went and amused themselves. They found, while they were both together, they were frustrating each other's efforts, and there was no hope of securing the criminal.

3289. Was one of those officers a borough police officer?—Yes.

3290. What was the other?—A detective officer from the metropolitan police.

3291. Do you think that the restrictions of the powers of constables within certain limits is also prejudicial?—I do. In another case of suspected murder, I had no doubt that a woman had been wilfully drowned; and in consequence of the limited jurisdiction of the police, and the course of proceeding which was taken by the parish constable, and unfortunately also, in that instance, by the coroner, the offender escaped. I brought the case myself before the court of quarter sessions.

3292. Do you think that the establishment of a uniform system of police throughout the kingdom is practicable, and would be beneficial?—I have no doubt that it would be not only practicable, but in the highest degree beneficial. It would be beneficial as ensuring information being attended to; whereas under

W. Oakley, Esq.

16 June 1853.

the existing system, if information be sent to any borough or county throughout the kingdom, there are no means of ensuring that information being acted upon. In fact, I have found instances where no proceedings have been taken upon the information at all, while not only the stolen property, but the offenders themselves, have actually been within the locality. A uniform system of police would be of the greatest benefit in insuring the detection of offenders, in preventing their escape, and in ensuring the recovery of the property. It would prevent improper persons obtaining appointments, who had been dismissed from another force. I know one instance in which a man, who had been in one county police force, was dismissed for putting a marked sovereign into the box of another man, and charging him with stealing it. He obtained, by some false representation, an appointment in another county; he was dismissed in disgrace; he obtained a special appointment, in another county, to investigate cases of incendiary fires. At last his evidence became so doubted, that I believe, in one or two instances, a pardon was obtained for persons who had been convicted upon his testimony. That man afterwards, and, until very recently, held an appointment in a borough police force. If there were a uniform system throughout the country, it would be impossible for such a man to obtain employment in the police.

3293. From your knowledge of the metropolitan police, do you believe that an extension of that system would prove effectual or satisfactory?—I do not; and for this reason: in the rural districts the present system of the metropolitan police would take away entirely the interest of the local magistrates and gentlemen, who are most interested in the prevention of crime and the detection of offenders. I think the appointment of a local committee at the quarter and borough sessions, as an executive committee to control the chief constable, or chief officer of the district, to investigate complaints against police constables, and in the performance of other duties, would be in the highest degree beneficial; but there must be a centre of some kind to issue orders and regulations, and to ensure, what is above all important, that information should be acted upon when transmitted from one part of the kingdom to another.

3294. Have you had any experience of the advantage of employing policemen for any other purposes?—Yes. It would be a great advantage that the police should be employed on public occasions; for instance, when large assemblages take place, either for any public object or for amusement at races, fares, regattas, and things of that kind. I know a county town where they have only seven policemen in a population of 16,000 inhabitants; they have one honorary superintendent, who is a chemist and druggist, without pay; an inspector, a serjeant, and five constables, who are paid by public subscription, and who have to go round their beat once a week to obtain those subscriptions; and receivers of stolen goods and beerhouse-keepers are allowed to contribute, or not, as they please. The authorities recently applied for the assistance of a borough police 40 miles distant, to keep the peace during the election. Under the Municipal Corporation Act, the county magistrates have the power to order the police of a borough to go to any part of the county within seven miles of another county.

3295. Was an application ever made by the magistrates of the Bath division for the appointment of a rural police force in that division?—For several quarter sessions the matter was under discussion, and efforts were made to adopt the county constabulary, and more recently, the Superintending Constables Act. I prepared the paper which I now hold in my hand, showing the expense of superintending constables and parish constables as compared with the rural police.

Vide Appendix.

[*The Witness delivered in the same.*]

3296. Was the resolution which is contained in that paper signed by all the magistrates of that division?—It is signed by nine magistrates. There are about 24 magistrates in the Bath division of the county of Somerset, and all who attended were unanimous in signing that resolution. A committee had been appointed by the court of quarter sessions to consider the subject, and it was to that meeting that these papers were submitted. The resolution is as follows: " It having been resolved by the magistrates of this county, at the last Epiphany sessions, to establish the system of superintending constables under the provisions of the Acts 5 & 6 Vict., c. 109, and 13 & 14 Vict., c. 20, for the respective divisions; and the magistrates of the Bath division, having decided objections to the proposed scheme, on the ground of its inefficiency and expensiveness; and also on the ground that they consider the provisions of the 2 & 3 Vict., c. 93, and the 3 & 4 Vict., c. 88, would be more beneficial to the ratepayers, the following resolutions were

W. Oakley, Esq.

16 June 1853.

were adopted by them, and laid before the committee appointed at the last quarter sessions, to carry out the former Acts; and the magistrates of the Bath division have resolved on making application, at the next quarter sessions, to exempt the Bath division from the operation of the former Acts, and for the establishment of a divisional police in lieu thereof, under the said Acts of 2 & 3 Vict., c. 93, and 3 & 4 Vict., c. 88. The following are the data upon which the magistrates of the Bath division have come to this resolution, and they are now printed and circulated for the information of the magistrates generally and the ratepayers. It is desirable that the ratepayers of the respective parishes of the Bath division should, at as early a period as possible, consider the memoranda now laid before them; and if any difficulty should suggest itself, or explanation be required, the magistrates of the Bath division will be happy to confer with them on the subject."

3297. Were those memoranda which was submitted to the magistrates prepared by yourself in a great measure?—The memoranda were.

3298. Were they carefully examined by the magistrates?—They were examined particularly by a sub-committee appointed for that special purpose. The reason of their not being adopted was, that in the 33 parishes of the Bath division the parish constables got up meetings; I attended one or two at the request of some of the ratepayers. The feeling excited by the parish constables was such as to prevent the magistrates of the Bath division carrying out their intention of applying for a police. The question of the appointment of superintending constables was postponed from quarter session to quarter session, until now it is not upon the paper for the consideration of the county. The opinion has been very generally expressed at the quarter sessions, that no steps should be taken until some general measure should be introduced by the Government.

3299. Mr. *Rich.*] How did the parish constables influence the magistrates?— By getting meetings called in the different parishes.

3300. *Chairman.*] Were those meetings of ratepayers?—They were meetings of ratepayers and others, and the parish constables persuaded the ratepayers generally that the expense would be so great.

3301. Is not 250 *l.* a year, which you have put for the salary of the chief constable, a high salary?—It is the lowest according to the 3 & 4 Vict. c. 93.

3302. Are these figures all according to the usual payment of constables?—In the county police under the Act.

3303. The total expense, according to your statement, is 1385 *l.*; is that according to the scale usually paid?—Yes; from my judgment, and from the information I have obtained from other counties, and from my experience in Essex.

3304. On the other hand, you have the expenses under the superintending and parish constable system?—Yes.

3305. You have put the expense of conveyance of prisoners at 90 *l.*?—Yes; to that item I have appended this note: "The average amount in the two years 1849 and 1850, paid to parish constables out of the county rate, for conveyance and lodging of prisoners, was 95 *l.*; 5 *l.* is as much as should be incurred by a police for the expense of subsistence of prisoners in the division for a year, and the whole amount of conveyance and lodging would be saved; the prisoners being conveyed by the police in the carts necessary to be provided for the other duties of the police." I ascertained that that was the average amount for the years 1849 and 1850.

3306. Lord *Lovaine.*] Will you explain why the conveyance and lodging would be saved?—I propose that there should be police stations wherever there is a police force; the police must live somewhere; and the police would convey all the prisoners in the carts which are provided for their other duties.

3307. Have you entered anything on the debtor side of the account as to the cost of those stations?—I think they would cost the county nothing, from the rent and other sources of receipt. In order that my meaning may be clear, perhaps I may be permitted to read a note from the other side of that printed statement: "Another important advantage of establishing a police for the division would be the obtaining a station-house and strong rooms, with a proper room for the magistrates, and accommodation for all persons having business at petty sessions. The expense of such station-house would probably be the same under both the Superintending and Parish Constables Acts and the Police Acts. But under the Parish Constables Act the lock-ups must be paid for immediately at the expense of the

W. Oakley, Esq.

16 June 1853.

whole county, though the benefit may be only to a particular locality; while under the Police Acts there is power to borrow money for the erection of station-houses on the security of the rates of the district for which the station-house is erected; and the money so borrowed, with the interest, may be paid by the rents received from the members of the police force, and the amount of charges for lodging of prisoners received from Government as part of the expenses of prosecutions; thus making the buildings pay the cost of erecting them, by which means the county obtain the buildings by merely being security for the money borrowed."

3308. *Chairman.*] Will you read the next item?—"In the years 1849 and 1850 the average amount paid out of the poor-rates for constables' expenses in the 18 parishes of the Bath division included in the Bath union, as stated in the union accounts, was about 100 *l.* Adding 50 *l.* for the average in the same proportion for the other 10 parishes of the Bath division, the amount would be 150 *l.*"

3309. Lord *Lovaine.*] Those payments by the parish would be entirely abolished? —Yes; the duties would be performed by the police. The next item is, "The costs of proceedings before justices in the same years, as also stated, averaged about 99 *l.* for the same 18 parishes, paid out of the poor-rates. Adding 45 *l.* for the average of the other 10 parishes, the amount paid would be 144 *l.*, of which, for the appointment and swearing in of parish constables, and other charges made on their account, there is paid at least 100 *l.*" I ascertained also from the various accounts that those amounts were actually paid.

3310. Then as far as this item is concerned, you take credit for a saving of only 100 *l.* out of 144 *l.*?—Exactly; there would be some other costs of proceedings which might still have to be paid under the police.

3311. Is it not necessary by law that parish constables should be sworn in, whether there is a police or not?—As the law at present exists.

3312. So that the other amount must be struck out, unless you change the law?—Not more than the 44 *l.*, which I have allowed.

3313. *Chairman.*] Do not you think the swearing in of parish constables, where there is a rural police force, is an unnecessary expenditure both of time and money?—Quite so, and a very great hardship upon some of the parish constables; they are taken away from their ordinary occupations; I have heard many of them complain of it as a great hardship. The next item is " Estimated amount paid to parish constables for serving summonses and warrants, and by individuals, 30 *l.*" It is almost impossible to ascertain the exact amount of such a sum; upon going through the books of the clerk to the magistrates to the Bath division, I arrive at 30 *l.* as being as near a fair conclusion as possible.

3314. Lord *Lovaine.*] Going back to your first item, which is connected with this third item, you have included savings to be made in the union accounts; but the unions will nevertheless have to pay for services performed to a certain extent?—Under a uniform system of police, none of those expenses that I estimate would fall upon the unions.

3315. Suppose a man absconded and left his wife and children chargeable upon the parish, and a pursuit were necessary, must not the subsistence of the officer and his expenses upon the road be paid?—They must; some such expense as that must be paid.

3316. The third item is " Estimated amount paid to parish constables for serving summonses and warrants, and by individuals, 30 *l.*" Those payments would entirely cease, because individuals would have the right to the service of their warrants without paying anything for them; in fact, a person holding a warrant, would have nothing to do but put it into the hand of the police constable who had to perform the duty?—Precisely so. The next item is " Estimated amount paid to parish constables under orders of court, in cases of felony at assizes and sessions, 60 *l.*"

3317. Sir *J. Trollope.*] Are you sure that item is correct; would not the parish constable come in with a bill for the expenses of prosecution, which would be allowed by the county in the first instance, and be allowed by the Government afterwards?—I explain that in a note to that item: " Such amount being paid out of the county rate, and repaid to the county by Government as part of the expenses of prosecution. If the same allowances were made for the police, the amount might be retained by the county, and, therefore, saved. In the county of Essex, consisting of only 14 divisions, 380 parishes, and a population of 265,972, in which the county police are acting, the amount so received from Government

was

was for the last year 1,104 *l.* 12 *s.* 11 *d.*; the allowances being retained by the county treasurer from the amounts paid under orders of court, and the police never, under any circumstances, being permitted to receive any monies, except their salaries and expenses actually incurred, or rewards in very special cases."

3318. Can you tell the Committee what became of the 1,104 *l.* 12 *s.* 11 *d.* in the county of Essex eventually?—It was received by the county from the Treasury, and credited to the county.

3319. Lord *Lovaine.*] Is it not the case in Essex, that there is a certain allowance paid out of this 1,104 *l.* to the police constables, for expenses out of pocket?—No; the expenses of the police are paid out of the contingent accounts.

3320. Then the whole of this 1,104 *l.* is carried to the credit of the police rate?—Yes. The next item is, "Fines under penal statutes;" that I take from the books of the clerk of the justices, as having been about the amount. All fines under the rural police would be appropriated to the county. The next item is, "Summoning coroner's juries," &c.; that I ascertained as near as possible. The next item is, "Proposed salary to superintending constable, under 5 & 6 Vict. c. 109, and 13 & 14 Vict. c. 20, to be paid out of the county rate, 110 *l.*;" that was the amount proposed by the gentleman who brought forward the motion at the court of quarter sessions.

3321. *Chairman.*] It has been stated in evidence before the Committee to-day, that the cost would be 130 *l.*?—That evidence was given, not as to the actual amount; there are other things that would make up that sum in the shape of contingent expenses.

3322. You are satisfied that you are quite within the mark?—Yes. The next item is, "Contingent expenses at 2 *l.* 10 *s.* per month, as paid (out of the county rate) in the county of Kent for extra horse hire and tolls (the police are exempt from tolls under 3 & 4 Vict. c. 88, s. 1), taxes for horse and cart, shoeing horses, stationery, and postage, 30 *l.*"

3323. How did you get that amount from the county of Kent?—I got that from Mr. Dunne, who had served under me as inspector of police at Bath. Mr. Dunne gave evidence before this Committee, bearing out what I have stated here. Mr. Dunne also put in evidence the table of fees, from which I made out this estimate. The next item is ascertained from the same source: "Payments are made out of the county and poor-rates to parish constables under 5 & 6 Victoria, cap. 109, and 13 & 14 Victoria, cap. 20, for patrolling or occasional duty in charge of prisoners, or under the written order of a justice in Kent, according to the table of fees in that county, in addition to fees for serving summonses and warrants at 2 *s.* 6 *d.* per day and 3 *s.* per night, or 1 *l.* 18 *s.* 6 *d.* per week. Since the establishment of the system in Kent, 14th October last (only three months), it has been found necessary to have numerous constables employed for weeks together. If 15 constables only out of the 241 in this division were employed, and for only three days a week, at the same rate, the amount would be 643 *l.* 10 *s.* per annum. Deducting from that amount the above 150 *l.* estimated as now paid to parish constables, the additional expense probably to be incurred under the proposed system would be 493 *l.* 10 *s.*"

3324. Lord *Lovaine.*] Why did you select 15 constables and three days a week?—From information given to me by Mr. Dunne as to the number who had actually been employed.

3325. Why do you deduct 150 *l.*?—This amount would not be paid. These amounts were still paid in Kent under the superintending constables, but under rural police they would not be paid.

3326. Therefore a deduction of 150 *l.* must be made?—Yes; those are amounts paid out of the poor-rates; those amounts are actually paid in the division of Bath, and I deduct that amount. "In the county of Kent there is no saving in the conveyance of prisoners, the parish constable conveying prisoners, receiving the amount allowed, and mileage for conveying them; neither is there any saving on the inspection of weights and measures, relieving vagrants, or under the various heads of saving shown by a police." "Inspecting weights and measures I put down at 200 *l.* In the year 1848 the fines in the division under the Weights and Measures Act amounted to 138 *l.*, the inspector's salary 25 *l.*; fees for stamping, &c., not known. There appears to have been no inspection or fines since. If the duty were performed by the police, the saving in the division from fines, fees, &c. (the whole of the fines in such case being appropriated to the county), would be at least the amount named."

W. Oakley, Esq.

16 June 1853.

3327. *Chairman.*] Who received those fines?—The inspectors.

3328. Did the fines go wholly to the inspectors?—One-half went to the inspectors.

3329. What was the amount actually received by the county?—I think it is half 138 *l.* I ascertained that amount from taking an estimate of the sums actually received in the division of Bath, knowing that with the police the duty is efficiently done, and that there would be a great number more fines than under the old inspectors, because it appears that the present inspectors of weights and measures, according to the county returns, do their duty very inefficiently; there are numerous complaints of the duty being inefficiently done, and there is no source from which the poor suffer more than from false weights and measures.

3330. Lord *Lovaine.*] Have you a right to appropriate the whole of the fines to the county?—One half of the fines go to the inspectors.

3331. Did not the other half go to the poor-rate?—If the police did the duty, the whole would go to the county.

3332. By the Act of Parliament, is not half the fine given to the poor-rate?—I mean that the proposed saving is effected as a saving to the county, by being a saving to the ratepayer.

3333. *Chairman.*] The 69 *l.* is so far a saving to the ratepayer that it goes to the county?—It does. I make up the difference between an efficient performance of the duties and an inefficient performance between 69 *l.* and 25 *l.*, and 200 *l.*

3334. Is that the only item which you do not derive from any positive information?—I derive the whole of the amount partly from estimates, and partly from actual amounts.

3335. What is the amount which you derive from estimate?—£. 94.

3336. Lord *Lovaine.*] What are the fees for stamping?—The fees would also form a portion of the sum of 200 *l.*, which I could not ascertain.

3337. *Chairman.*] Leaving out of consideration altogether your estimated advantage, there is a clear saving of 100 *l.*?—More than that; taking into consideration the amount for stamping, there must be more than 100 *l.* I performed the duty of an inspector of weights and measures for some time in the county of Essex, and I am sure, without being able to call to recollection what the amount was, I should say it was more, perhaps 20 *l.* or 25 *l.* a year, were actually received in one division for stamping fees. The next item is " Relieving vagrants, 150 *l.*" In the county of Essex, it is shown to be 5,101 *l.*, as fully explained in page 2 of the printed " Report of the Chief Constable of Essex to the Magistrates in Quarter Sessions assembled, 15th October 1850."

3338. Sir *J. Trollope.*] How do you make out that amount?—I took it from Captain MacHardy's Report; the estimate I am now referring to is only for one division. I am able to give some information as to the advantage of the police relieving vagrants. On taking the command of the police at Bath, I re-organised the police force there; and I recommended the inspectors of police to be appointed assistant relieving officers for vagrants. I recommended their appointment under the 10 & 11 Vict. c. 110. Bath is very peculiarly situated as regards vagrants. There are an immense number of persons of very large property residing in Bath, in a bad state of health; they are often imposed upon by the number of vagrants that flock to that city. In order to put a stop to vagrancy as far as possible, and at the same time to ensure that a really destitute person should be relieved, a Refuge for the Destitute was established under an influential committee. I had the honour to be a member of that committee as chief of the police. I hold in my hand a report, prepared by the late Mr. Sutcliffe, of Bath. It appears from that Report, that there were relieved in the winter of 1843–44, 2,812 cases; in 1844–45, 2,403 cases; in 1845–46, 2,001. With the permission of the Committee, I will read a paragraph from the Report. Mr. Sutcliffe says: " At the suggestion of Mr. Oakley, the present chief of police, two officers of the police force have been appointed relieving officers for vagrants by the Board of Guardians; and the appointment has been confirmed by the Poor Law Board. Travellers pleading destitution will be examined by one or other of these officers, who will relieve in all cases not clearly improper, by sending the applicant to a house in Abbey Green, recently opened by the committee as a nightly refuge. In entire conformity with the uniform practice of the institution, the Refuge House will be open to all persons coming within the rules, who may be brought by the police, the committee reserving the power of admitting such other persons as they may

see

W. Oakley, Esq.

16 June 1853.

see fit, and retaining an entire control over the management of the house. It has been thought right to bring the dietary into general accordance to that of the workhouse, and a member of the police has been selected to act as resident superintendent and housekeeper." Then the result of that is shown in a " Report to the Watch Committee of the City and Borough of Bath, 4th of October 1850." No. 5, is a return of mendicants applying for and receiving relief at the central police station, since the appointment of the in-door inspectors as relieving officers for vagrants. The advantage of such appointment is clearly shown by a comparison with the only previous period of returns being kept, viz., between the 18th March and the 31st May 1849, in which time 991 persons received relief. From the date of the appointment of the in-door inspectors, 12th November 1849 to 1st October 1850, 998 applied for relief, and 961 received it ; the remaining 37, for various good reasons, were refused, showing a diminution (the different length of time being taken into account) of more than three-fourths. At the same time, the number of persons apprehended for begging during the latter period (notwithstanding the employment of the detective officers and men in plain clothes) has been only 139, showing, as compared with the year 1847, when 247 were apprehended, and the year 1848, when 232 were apprehended, a diminution of 30 per cent. But it will be impossible to effect anything like a permanent check to vagrancy, until the powers of section 66, Act 11 & 12 Vict., c. 63 (Health Act), be extended to this city, giving certain officers of the police power to inspect low lodging-houses, where, by Return No. 4, on an average 136 mendicants are to be found daily ; and as long as they can beg 2 d. to pay for their lodging, they will resort to such places. I should mention that the assistant relieving officer being, to a certain extent, under the control of that committee, the greatest possible care was taken that a really destitute person should be relieved, although there might be doubt as to the character of the applicant, or the propriety of giving that relief. I account for the difference in the comparative statement I make here between what I think would be the saving in the division of Bath, and the enormous saving effected in the county of Essex, by feeling that we should be compelled to give more relief in that locality than what I believe was given in the county of Essex.

3339. *Chairman.*] Then the 150l. for relieving vagrants, which is stated in your printed paper, is calculated upon the returns of the decrease of vagrancy in the county of Essex ?—Not entirely. I have put 150l., which is a very small proportion compared with 5,110l.

3340. Mr. *Howard.*] Might not that saving be effected by a superintending constable, if he were appointed an assistant relieving officer ?—I think it would not effect the same amount of saving.

3341. Mr. Brown told the Committee that the diminution of tramps going through the town of Keswick was half what it was in 1847, and that diminution was effected by his being appointed assistant relieving officer ?—I have no doubt it would check them to some extent, but not to the same extent as where the police are constantly looking out and constantly patrolling ; the vagrants have more fear, and I have known many instances where crime has been detected by the assistant relieving officer, from vagrants being recognised by the police. In cases where a police inspector is an assistant relieving officer, and has refused relief for good reasons, he has sent to watch the person who has applied, and found out that he was a known offender, and was, to use a police term, " wanted " for some offence which he had committed. I think the same benefit would not arise in the employment of superintending constables, because the superintending constables have no confidence in the assistance of the parish constables.

3342. Lord *Lovaine.*] Did you hear the suggestion, which was made by a witness who was formerly examined, as to the possibility of having three separate rates for urban, suburban, and rural districts ?—I did.

3343. Do you think that suggestion is capable of being carried out with advantage ?—I think it is ; I am still of opinion that the expense of a uniform system of police need not be more than what is now being actually paid to parish constables, local constables, and petty local police.

3344. You have said that you would give local magistrate the power to hear complaints against police constables ?—Yes.

3345. Would not it be dangerous to remove the power of controlling the men from the chief constable ?—I think not ; I think it would work with advantage. I have known instances, and one a serious one, where influences have operated upon the mind of the chief constable ; I know chief constables are apt to be led, and cannot help it, by the reports of the superior officers. I know that constables are afraid to state really the facts themselves where the power is entirely centred in one man. I am prepared to say from experience, from having the advantage, I will term it, of a watch committee in the city of Bath, that bad as the arrangements are under such watch committees, I believe it would be better to have even the control of a small watch committee, than to have no control at all over the chief constable; the powers of a chief constable are greater than almost any other one man possesses.

3346. *Chairman.*] Do you think it is desirable he should have the appointment of the officers?—I think so, subject to approval; I found in the borough of Bath evils arose from the police being under the control of the watch committee instead of the magistrates. I found, when I took the appointment at Bath, the force in as inefficient a state as I believe it possible for any force to be; there were two-thirds of the men locally connected, and before their appointment had been out of employment, or in low employment; a large proportion of them were working at their various trades; there were instances of dishonesty which were substantiated before the watch committee, on the part of members of the force; many were incapacitated, some unable to write; some, at the previous sessions, the Recorder had noticed as giving false evidence. I found a system of supernumeraries existing there, and many of them were living on the prostitution of women in the city of Bath. I have here an analysis of a return which I prepared for the watch committee of the town council. Of 98 officers I found two were above 70 years of age; one between 60 and 70; 14 between 50 and 60; 20 between 40 and 50; 31 between 30 and 40; 28 between 20 and 30; that six were then keeping shops; six were unable to write; 62 were natives of Bath. On a very careful consideration of the whole matter, I found 28 only efficient out of 98; 34 I entered as "doubtful;" most of those were disposed of afterwards; 20 I entered "not efficient," and 14 as "worn out." Upon my recommendation the numbers were reduced, in order that the others might be better paid; the old officers were superannuated; and, with increased efficiency (as appears by a resolution of the watch committee and town council), I effected a saving of 500l. a year. A very great evil then existed in the mayor's officers, who had the management of cases of felony, the police being directed to attend upon them, and go into evidence of cases of felony, without the control of my predecessor, Admiral Carrol. Instances were reported to have occurred, in which the mayor's officers sat quietly in their room, and obtained of thieves in their pay the information which was taken before a magistrate. The mayor's officers were entirely abolished, but there still remain in the borough very great evils from courts leet officers, and the conflicting jurisdiction of the magistrates and of the watch committee. In some instances the magistrates have given instructions to one effect, and the watch committee have given instructions to the contrary. I found that the influence exercised over the constables, from their still having the right to vote at Parliamentary and municipal elections, operated in a most serious manner, and to a certain extent it prevented either myself or other persons having any proper control over them. Notwithstanding the great evil of the control of borough police by watch committees, I believe the advantages counterbalance the evils; I believe it would be preferable to have a watch committee than to have no committee at all. I do not fear responsibility, and have in my position taken as much as most men; but I would strongly recommend that there should be a select committee of magistrates to act as an executive body.

3347. Do you mean that there should be a police committee in every county?—Yes.

3348. Sir *J. Trollope.*] Would you not propose a police committee for boroughs also?—Yes.

3349. Do you think, if an efficient rural police were established in the country, it would not be possible to dispense with the coroner's court?—I am quite sure it would; transferring the coroner's duties to magistrates. I have known a coroner's court to frustrate the ends of justice. In a case of suspected murder, which was brought under the notice of a court of quarter sessions, I believe, had it not been for the conduct of the coroner, the parties would have been brought to justice.

3350. Have you ever known in your experience that a coroner's court facilitated the ends of justice?—I cannot say that I have.

3351. Would

W. Oakley, Esq.

16 June 1853.

3351. Would not the abolition of coroners' courts be a still further saving of expense to all counties and jurisdictions?—No doubt. There were serious cases of murder at Bath, poisoning cases, where the greatest possible evils arose from the jurisdiction of the coroner conflicting with that of the magistrates; the examination was going on before the coroner for many weeks, and another examination was going on before the magistrates. I have no doubt that the proceedings, in one instance, tended to ensure the escape of persons who I believe were connected with the murder; one was convicted, and sentenced to death, but others escaped.

3352. Did you attribute that entirely to the interference of the coroner?—I did; to the coroner's court.

3353. Mr. *Howard.*] Have you not in other cases had suspicions raised in consequence of examinations before coroners?—I have, but I have had the same suspicions in consequence of examinations before magistrates; I think there must be an inquiry of some kind. I hope I may not be understood as suggesting for a moment the abolition of inquiry in cases of death; on the contrary, I think the investigations should be by magistrates or other competent authorities, but not as at present carried out by coroners' courts.

3354. Mr. *Rich.*] You have said that you would object to the county police having any communication with or being at all in subordination to the metropolitan police?—No; I said that I had had a great deal of experience of the metropolitan police; I have notes of cases from the time of its establishment in 1829; I am perfectly certain that it would not be found beneficial to the country if the present system of the metropolitan police were carried out. I am certain it is much more expensive than a uniform system of police need be. I am sure that the metropolitan system in the rural districts tends to remove all interest, on the part of the local magistrates and local gentlemen, in the police, the prevention of crime, or detection of offenders.

3355. Preserving a general superintendence by the magistrates of the counties, would you desire to cut off all intercommunication between the police of one county with another, and the county police with the metropolitan police?—Certainly not; it should be all under one control and one system of communication. I ventured to state most particularly that it was of the first importance that you should ensure acting upon information that might be sent to different parts of the country; there must be central control for that purpose; at present there is no check whatever: if information is sent from Scotland-yard, to Bath, Bristol, or Birmingham, there is nothing whatever to insure the information being acted upon; it is generally turned over to a detective officer, and it is only just when it suits his purpose that he acts upon it. I have known instances where there has been no doubt whatever that the property and the offender were within the locality, but no steps were taken to find the property or to apprehend the offender; and therefore it is of the utmost consequence that there should be some central body to receive reports of all information sent, and of the proceedings taken upon that information, to ensure acting upon all occasions.

3356. That is, you recommend county supervision, with some central direction?—Not only for that purpose, but there must be a system of routes established, and of proper rules and regulations, which are of the greatest importance. The great object of a police force should be to render crime difficult to commit, to ensure the apprehension of offenders, and to prevent the disposal of stolen property.

3357. Have you considered the subject of the application of the electric telegraph to the police stations throughout the country?—I have; I have known instances in which it has been of great advantage in its present state.

3358. Do you apprehend, by its general adoption, you would be able to reduce the number of constables?—It would effect a reduction to some extent. I have carefully considered the subject of a general system of police throughout the country. I had the honour of considering the subject with Captain MacHardy, in 1846, and of copying some suggestions made by him. I have here the original manuscript with his corrections, and from my consideration of the subject from time to time, since then, I am led to believe that the number of men required throughout the country, taking boroughs and rural districts together, would be about the number prescribed by the County Constabulary Act, namely, 1 to 1,000 of the population. I believe the expense of such a police, if all unnecessary expenses were avoided, would not be more than the present payment to parish constables and local police. I am perfectly certain that the amount to

W. Oakley, Esq.

16 June 1853.

be saved to the Consolidated Fund in the expense of prosecutions would be very considerable indeed, more particularly if some improvement were to take place in the present system of criminal trials, and also if some arrangements were made with the railway companies for the conveyance of police and the conveyance of prisoners. At present the charge of one railway is double what it is upon another; there is no uniform system at all. Railway companies themselves would find an advantage, and would save a great deal of time and trouble to their clerks and officers, if Government would enter into some arrangement with them for the conveyance of prisoners and police officers.

3359. The economy which you suggest could only be applicable with the general adoption of a similar system of police throughout the country?—There would be an advantage now in paying the actual expenses of the parish constables if they remain as they are, in preference to allowing them to make cases for the sake of the fees. I took the liberty of addressing a letter to Sir George Grey upon that subject in 1851, at the time the Expenses of Prosecution Bill was under consideration; I pointed out the great hardship to prosecutors, constables, and witnesses, in not being allowed their expenses out of pocket in cases of non-committal. My letter contains this paragraph: "Many instances have come under my notice, in which great hardship has arisen. Prosecutors incur expense to trace out the perpetrators of offences, and in some cases labouring men, to whom the loss of a day's work is of paramount importance, are compelled to attend as witnesses on examinations, and frequently adjourned examinations of prisoners, travelling long distances; and though the proceedings have been commenced under the warrant or order of a justice, the evidence being at length insufficient to justify a committal, there has been no means of reimbursing such prosecutors and witnesses. Prosecutors, witnesses, and even constables, knowing that without a committal they will not be paid expenses, and perhaps money disbursed out of pocket, are apt to strain or distort evidence so as to ensure a committal; but before the grand jury, or on trial, the case breaks down, and very heavy expense is thus unnecessarily incurred in prosecutions. Without for a moment intending to reflect on any magistrate, I may mention that, in some cases, when it is known expenses have been incurred, it may operate on the mind of the magistrate, who may be induced to commit a prisoner, and then allow him to be bailed, to ensure the payment of such expenses, it being upon committal only that he is empowered to grant a certificate.

3360. In your arrangements of police forces, have you had any military organisation?—The men have been drilled, and to some extent drilled to the use of the small sword. I believe, without any parade being made of it, it would be a very great advantage that the police should be drilled in the performance of their ordinary duties; it would not be an advantage that they should be intrusted with anything beyond a truncheon or a cutlass in the performance of ordinary duties. I think it would be dangerous to entrust the police generally with fire-arms. I know an instance where a police officer having a pistol with him at a time when he thought he was being interfered with in the execution of his duty, very serious evils arose from it; he fired at one of the men, but providentially the bullet merely grazed his temple. The policeman preferred a charge against the men at the magistrate's private residence; and if at this distance of time I recollect right, he told the prisoners' friends were to be examined at one magistrate's residence, whereas he took them to another; the men were committed upon his evidence for two months, with hard labour. By chance the real facts came out; and so strong did the magistrates consider the case, that they sent an order to the keeper of the gaol to discharge those prisoners, before the circumstances were reported to the Secretary of State.

3361. Lord *Loraine.*] You have stated that you think the police should be under general control?—Yes.

3362. Do you think you would leave them under the command of the chief constable?—Of the chief officers of counties or districts, controlled by local committees of magistrates.

3363. Do you think those committees of magistrates would interfere with the board of general management?—I should propose that the duties of the local committees should be similar to those exercised by the visiting justices to the county gaols. From experience I have known the visiting justices to be of very great assistance indeed, not only to the governors of gaols, but, I believe, to the Home Office.

3364. In

W. Oakley, Esq.

16 June 1853.

3364. In the case of visiting justices of gaols, the subordinate officers never come in contact with the magistrates, but a police officer comes in contact with the magistrates in the daily exercise of his avocation; would not you anticipate some danger in allowing his conduct to be subject to a police committee composed of magistrates?—I should not; I believe the appointment of a small committee of magistrates, at the court of quarter sessions, to act as executive, would be found to overcome every difficulty.

3365. What authority do you think the chief constable would possess, if the punishment he awarded might be negatived by the police committee?—I found by experience, during the time that I held the appointment of chief of the police at Bath, that I was generally sufficiently upheld by the watch committee. The watch committee enabled me to control the men, except now and then, when any political matter interfered.

3366. Sir *J. Trollope.*] Had you any interference with your men by the members of the watch committee?—I had; I have already taken the liberty of saying, that I think the watch committee a very improper body to control the police; but I would rather have a watch committee to control the police than leave it to chief constables alone. I believe a committee of magistrates to control the police, with the assistance of the chief constable, would be a very different body. I found a very great deal of assistance from the watch committee of the city of Bath, which certainly, as to respectability of its members, is, I believe, an exception to watch committees generally.

3367. Did the watch committee never interfere improperly with your men?—Members of the watch committee encouraged the men on two or three occasions to make complaints to them at their houses; I remonstrated with them, and finding that the remonstrance had not its effect, I told the committee, if the practice were repeated, that I should feel it my duty to place my appointment in their hands; a strong expression of opinion took place by the majority of the watch committee, which had the effect of checking it.

3368. You wished all complaints to come through yourself?—Exactly; and to be heard by the watch committee only as a committee, and not by individual members at their private houses.

3369. Were the watch committee influenced by the body which elected them in the borough?—Frequently; I have known members of the watch committee to consult their constituency; they used to ask them how they were to act in certain cases, and they have even obtained the adjournment of a particular case in order that they might do so.

3370. Mr. *Fitzroy.*] Is it from fear of arbitrary conduct on the part of the chief constable towards his men you have suggested that the control should be taken out of his hands?—To some extent; but also that the course of justice may not be interfered with.

3371. What are the evils which you believe exist now in consequence of the control being vested entirely in the hands of a chief constable?—The men are afraid to state the facts that are under their knowledge when complaints are made against them; it operates very seriously upon the officers in the police when the control is vested entirely in the chief constable, and from the power of the chief constable in other respects.

3372. What are the particular evils to which you refer, and how do they operate detrimentally to the officers from the power of control being vested solely in the chief constable?—The men are afraid to state the facts as they would wish to do to the chief constable alone. I know that the chief constable cannot, by possibility, prevent his mind being biased to a certain extent; and there takes place failure of justice in some cases, danger to the public in others, injustice and hardship to officers and men in the stoppage of promotion, their removal, punishment, or dismissal.

3373. Lord *Lovaine.*] You mean that the men are afraid to state any complaints of the superintendents, or inspectors, or sergeants to the chief constable?—Yes; if he made complaints, if he were not a marked man by the chief constable, he would be a marked man by the superior officers. I have known instances where a police constable has very creditably exerted himself in reference to certain cases, the inspector or sergeant has heard all the information, has acted upon that information, and has taken away all the credit from the constable, and the man dare not say a word upon it at all. In the instance I before referred to, I am perfectly sure that a man would have been prosecuted for perjury and maliciously wounding,

wounding, if there had been a committee of magistrates to act with the chief constable ; because the same influence which operated upon the mind of the chief constable alone, could not have operated upon the mind of the chief constable had he been acting with a committee of magistrates.

3374. You mean to say, that when a police constable lays a complaint before the chief constable, the chief constable judges of that complaint in a different manner to what he would if he were assisted by a committee of magistrates? —The chief constable would be afraid to take the odium of certain acts upon himself, when he would not be afraid to take the odium of those acts if he were assisted by a committee of magistrates. I am quite sure the power of the chief constable to remove the petty constables from time to time, and from place to place, without any control, operates very hardly and very severely upon the petty constables ; and that were the removals carefully considered before they took place by the chief constable, assisted by a committee of magistrates, those hardships would not arise.

3375. Mr. *Fitzroy.*] In what counties have you been most familiar with the rural constabulary?— I served eight years in the Essex county constabulary, during which time I was three years chief superintendent at head-quarters ; I believe to some extent I am acquainted with the system adopted in every county in England ; I have notes of cases which have come within my experience from the time of the establishment of the metropolitan police.

3376. Sir *J. Trollope.*] Have you ever served in the metropolitan police?—I have not ; but I was brought into frequent contact with it, from my father having served in it, and having been constantly in communication with its various members, from the chief officers to the subordinates.

3377. In Essex your force joined the London force?—It did. I was frequently sent by the chief constable to act in London, and in other cases to obtain the assistance of the metropolitan police. In one case in particular, very serious offences had been committed by an organised gang in the county of Essex. Men had gone about with fire-arms and committed various act of violence. In one case they put a woman on the fire ; in another case they put a rope round a man's neck and threatened to hang him, and set fire to a house ; great efforts were made to trace out these offenders, and sufficient information was at last obtained to justify an application for warrants, which were obtained. The appointment of parish constables to act with the police had this effect : a parish constable gave information to the parties, so that their escape was effected ; and it was not till some considerable period, and after, I may say, the extraordinary co-operation which we obtained on that occasion from the metropolitan police, under the direct orders of the Commissioners, that these parties were brought to justice ; showing the evil of parish constables in one respect, and the great advantage of cordial co-operation in another.

3378. Did you ever come in contact with the Hertfordshire police?—Yes.

3379. Were they on a different system to the Essex police?—It was somewhat different.

3380. Do you consider that the Hertfordshire police were as effective as the Essex police?—I had not a sufficient opportunity of judging of that ; a man is naturally biased in favour of the force in which he has served ; I consider from all I have seen that the Essex force is the most efficient in England.

3381. Mr. *Fitzroy.*] You think, from your experience of other bodies of police, the Essex police stands very high as to its efficiency, and so on?—I believe so, not only from what I have seen myself, but from what I have heard from ratepayers in different counties. I have been in communication with the ratepayers in Essex, going there from time to time ; and have also had a great deal of communication with ratepayers of other counties, who were not aware that I was at all interested in the police. My present appointment has brought me in contact with leading ratepayers, and I think the system adopted in Essex, taking it altogether, is the most efficient.

3382. Notwithstanding your knowledge of the efficiency of that system, and your experience of its good working, you think it would be desirable to introduce so very important a change as to take away the control of the chief constable, and to vest it in a police committee?—I am bound to say that I do ; but it is hardly a fair question in the presence of that gentleman.

3383. Sir *J. Trollope.*] You do not mean the whole of his power as regards the appointment and removal?—I think the chief constable should have the

nomination

nomination of every man; that the committee should never name one, as it is to a certain extent in Essex now. I think no man should be punished, discharged, or removed without investigation by a committee of magistrates.

3384. With regard to removals, is not the chief of the police a much better judge than a police committee could be of the desirability of removing a man from his locality?—He is; at the same time it would be found more beneficial for all parties, if the facts which are within the chief constable's knowledge were considered by local committees.

3385. You would make the local committees a sort of court of appeal between the men and the chief constable?—No; appeals should be to a central Board. I would recommend that no dismissal or removal should take place by order of the chief constable, without the cognisance of a committee of magistrates.

3386. Lord *Lovaine*.] Would you not, in that case, make the committee of magistrates a standing body?—Very nearly the same as the visiting justices of the county gaols.

3387. Mr. *Fitzroy*.] You would leave the power of dismissal and removal of constables with the committee of magistrates, although nominally with the chief constable?—I would recommend that he should be controlled by a committee of magistrates.

3388. *Chairman*.] Do not the visiting justices meet only at the time of the quarter sessions?—They should meet at least once a week; in point of fact, I am prohibited from sending returns or a communication to the Home Office, except in some instances; they must all go through the visiting justices.

Captain *J. B. B. M'Hardy*, R.N., called in; and further Examined.

3389. Sir *J. Trollope*.] YOU have heard the evidence of the last witness, Mr. Oakley?—Yes.

3390. He has stated that the sum of 1,104*l.* 12*s.* 11*d.*, in the particular year which he named, had been paid by the Government for prosecutions in the county of Essex, and for the services of the men in your force who were called upon to attend to those prosecutions. Will you inform the Committee how that sum has been appropriated?—The 17th section of the Act of 3 & 4 Vict. c. 88, directs that it shall be appropriated to putting the Act into execution; that money is therefore retained by the treasurer of the county, and credited to the police account; therefore that amount lessens the sum which is levied upon the ratepayers.

3391. Credit is taken for 5,101*l.* by decrease of vagrancy; how do you make out that very large sum as an item of credit?—Anticipating this question, I have prepared the different items, because I have no doubt it strikes the Committee, as it strikes everybody, with astonishment, that the Essex police is a self-supporting force; it surpasses the comprehension of every one. If my report is read carefully, it will appear that I only ask to be credited for two-thirds of the savings and earnings by the police; therefore the Essex police only costs, at most, one-third of its apparent expense, 15,886*l.* With the permission of the Committee, I will read the document which I have prepared.

[*The same was read, as follows:*]

SAVINGS and EARNINGS effected by the ESSEX COUNTY CONSTABULARY.

	£.	s.	d.
Annual saving by the conveyance of prisoners, calculated from the actual expense in 1839, the year preceding the establishment of the police -	991	—	—
Annual saving by the inspection of weights and measures -	584	11	8
Annual earnings under sect. 17 of the Act 3 & 4 Vict. c. 83, viz.: from Government, under orders of court, coroners, petty sessions, and other jurisdictions - - - - - - - - - - -	1,286	10	8
Annual payment of interest and instalment on money borrowed for the erection of police stations, which are a permanent investment for the benefit of the county - - - - - - -	1,150	17	1
Annual saving by the abolition of Halstead, Newport, and Colchester District Gaols, besides the consequent advantage of centralised prison discipline - - - - - - - - -	1,000	—	—
Rent paid by members of the constabulary for such parts of the police stations as are occupied by them, - - - - - -	332	11	—
Annual amount of fines credited to the county rate under penal statutes, where proceedings have been taken by the police - - -	24	—	—
Carried forward - - - £.	5,569	10	5

W. Oakley, E.

16 June 1853.

Capt. J. B. B. M'Hardy, R.N.

Capt.
J. B. B. M'Hardy,
R. N.

16 June 1853.

	£.	s.	d.
Brought forward - - - £.	5,669	10	5
Annual saving in postage by the police delivering official parcels to the magistrates and parochial authorities - - - - - -	40	—	—
Annual saving of payments to special constables, calculated from actual sums formerly paid, using as an index the average annual payments in the 10 years preceding the establishment of the police - - -	366	6	—
Annual saving in magistrates' clerks' fees, in consequence of the diminution of business at petty sessions, calculated at a reduction of one-third on the average; although it is proved that in the Chelmsford division the fees have decreased from 546 l. in 1842 to 304 l. in 1852, being a decrease of nearly one-half - - - - - - - -	913	14	6
Annual saving in payments to parochial constables by the 380 parishes, by poor-law unions, private individuals, and other sources, taking as an index the average annual payments of each parish of one division, which was 10 l., without considering the extra payments under the other heads mentioned - - - - - - - - -	3,800	—	—
Making the ascertained savings and earnings annually - - - £.	10,789	10	11

Annual savings, of which the pecuniary value cannot be correctly ascertained, but which may be fairly estimated as under; viz.

	£.	s.	d.		£.	s.	d.
By the decrease of vagrancy, considering the immense decrease of 21,905 in six months, proved by the Poor-law returns: but as the fact that the same vagrant visits many unions might raise a question as to this index, it will be more safe to take the lowest possible estimate, by taking credit for expelling half the number proved to have been previously relieved at one union, viz., Chelmsford, where the numerical decrease of 5,101 was effected in one year, and estimating the average expense of each vagrant at 1 l., which gives - - - - - - -	2,550	—	—				
By the protection and recovery of property, which will best be ascertained by taking the lowest estimate of eminent land-valuers as to the increased value of land, and in consequence of the effectual protection of property by the police. Taking this index, 884,680 acres, increased in value 1 d. per acre, give - - - - - -	3,686	3	4				
					6,236	3	4
					17,025	14	3

Annual savings effected by additional duties since 1850 :

	£.	s.	d.		£.	s.	d.
By serving notices on the volunteers of the Essex Militia, at 1 s. each - - - - - - - - - -	160	—	—				
By performing certain parochial duties transferred to the police in 1852; viz., making returns of overseers and assessors, and serving precepts, saving at least - -	200	—	—				
					360	—	—
Making the annual amount of ascertained and estimated savings and earnings - - - - - £.					17,385	14	3

Duties performed and savings effected, for which no credit is taken :

1. Effectual protection afforded to the public revenue by the police holding Custom-house deputations for the seizure of contraband goods and the suppression of illicit stills.

2. Savings and benefits derived by members of the police acting as inspectors of nuisances and common lodging-houses, under the local authorities.

3. Legal expenses in criminal prosecutions diminished by the assistance of the police in procuring evidence.

4. Saving to the public by rendering payments to local associations for protecting property and prosecuting offenders less necessary.

5. Saving of the expense formerly levied for the erection and repair of parochial cages or lock-ups, in 380 parishes.

3392. You take the expenses at 10 l. a parish?—Yes; and my report in Appendix will show my index to this sum : any difference of opinion is met by my not having included what the unions paid, and also what private individuals paid, lest some persons might suppose that 10 l. was too much; that makes a total of 11.789 l. 10 s. 11 d. Then there is this other item of what is saved by the decrease of vagrancy; there was a reduction of 40,000 in the number of vagrants in one year;

Capt.
J. B. B. M'Hardy,
R. N.

16 June 1853.

year; the same parties apply frequently in the different unions. I take the reduction in one union, namely, Chelmsford, where the reduction was 5,101 in one year, and I only ask credit for one-half.

3393. How do you charge them per head?—I take them at 1 *l.* a head. Every one that is acquainted with the money which is spent in low lodging-houses will know that these persons spend as much as any labourers in passing over the country. It is a fair calculation to say 1 *l.* per head. It is quite a matter of opinion as to the increased value of property. Then there are five items shown for which I take no credit. I leave them as a set-off against the other items, against which I have set different sums to meet difference of opinion. It may be readily admitted that I am entitled to a credit of at least 10,000 *l.*; and if that be the case, the police only costs one-third of its apparent expense. I had a difficulty in my report not to make it balance, and I threw off 84 *l.* from my credit. I say, I am comparing a county with a police with a county without a police, and am satisfied the introduction of the police has entailed no expense on Essex.

3394. You have taken credit for the lock-up houses as a valuable investment for the county?—Yes; and I have arranged them so, that if the police should be disbanded at any time, they will make delightful dwellings. Some of them are built in the Elizabethan style, affording the greatest accommodation and convenience at the least expense, and including proper accommodation for holding petty sessions.

3395. Lord *Lovaine.*] You have credited the parishes in this account with an average saving of 10 *l.*, which payment was entirely made to parochial constables from the parishes?—Yes.

3396. Afterwards you take another credit for performing certain parochial duties transferred to the police in 1852?—When I made that calculation, as shown in my report dated October 1850, the duties referred to were performed by the parochial constables. You will observe, by the scheme of items which I have produced, that in 1852 those duties were transferred to the police. That report of October 1850 has reference to 10 *l.* a year, calculated as therein shown; that is the reason why I say "subsequent duties."

Veneris, 17° die Junii, 1853.

MEMBERS PRESENT.

Mr. Rice.
Mr. Mackie.
Mr. Sotheron.
Mr. Burroughes.
Mr. Fitzroy.

Sir James Anderson.
Sir J. Trollope.
Lord Lovaine.
Mr. Charles Howard.
Mr. Philipps.

EDWARD ROYDS RICE, Esq., IN THE CHAIR.

Mr. *Richard Healy,* called in; and Examined.

Mr. R. Healy.

17 June 1853.

3397. Sir *J. Trollope.*] YOU are Chief Constable of the Hundred of Aveland, in the parts of Kesteven, Lincolnshire?—I am.

3398. Have you been so for several years?—I think for 24 or 25 years.

3399. In the parts of Kesteven there is a separate jurisdiction from the other portions of the county?—Certainly.

3400. It is under a separate commission of the peace?—I believe so.

3401. You have no police in that district, have you?—We have not.

3402. Or superintending constables under the Act of 1842?—No; in the southern division of the parts of Kesteven we have not; there is a man stationed at Slaford, in the northern division; Kesteven is divided into two parts, south and north.

3403. In the northern part of Kesteven there is one man of that description?—In the northern part there is one man of that description.

3404. Are the ordinary parish constables under your orders and management?—They are, partly; I apprehend, as chief constables, we have not a great deal of control over them; generally speaking, if we are applied to for advice or assistance, we give that advice or assistance.

3405. In your district, is the state of crime on the increase or diminution?—I should say that latterly it has been very much upon th. diminution. I con-

Mr. R. Healy.

17 June 1853.

sider that the habits of the people are much more regular and orderly than they were.

3406. Do you consider that a large proportion of the crimes committed in that district go undetected or not?—I think not; as far as regards ordinary crimes, they are, generally speaking, well looked after. I am not aware that there is anything, in respect of the detection of crime, that could be much or materially improved to what it is at present.

3407. In case of crimes, such as offences against property, such as sheep-stealing, or any crime of that kind, what steps are usually taken in that district to apprehend offenders?—In the first place, there are several local associations for the prosecution of felons; if parties are members of those associations, we go to the clerk of the association for instruction and information, and every means is taken, by advertising, by handbills, and by the application of the parties themselves, to detect a criminal, if possible.

3408. Is there much sheep-stealing now in the parts of Kesteven?—I should say there has been a very great diminution of sheep-stealing the last three or four years.

3409. Do you recollect a case in which a gang of persons were concerned in sheep-stealing, who were apprehended by the exertions of the local authorities?—Yes, I do; we had an extraordinary case, where a very large gang was broken up in consequence of the exertions of the individual who had his sheep stolen, and also the exertions of the constables and parties.

3410. Has the district where that instance occurred been free from the offence since that gang has been broken up?—I think to a great extent it has. For my own part, having been a very large occupier of land, I have had the good luck never to have had a prosecution for sheep-stealing. I think I never have had, in the course of a very long period, more than one or two cases of sheep-stealing at the most in my life, out of something like 500 or 600 sheep annually.

3411. Sheep-stealing is not an offence which is committed to a great amount in that neighbourhood?—I think not.

3412. As chief constable, have you not been called upon by the magistracy to take some steps to organise a police force, in reference to a large fair held at a place called Stowe Green?—Yes, I have.

3413. Will you describe to the Committee the nature of that fair, where it is held, and what steps you have taken to repress crime at that assemblage of people?—The Stowe Green fair is a very large assemblage of country people of the middle and lower classes, who come from a great many miles round; it is held upon a green where there is no town, church, beer-shop, or public-house, or anything of the kind; but it is frequented by traders of almost every description, who encamp in booths. The green is a very considerable area, and it appears at fair time as if it were all covered over with cloth. At that time there are a great many public-houses, and houses for refreshment, tea, and different things.

3414. By houses, you mean the booths where those things are sold?—Yes. Formerly, when I was first chief constable, there used to be a great deal of dissipation and drunkenness. I am happy to say, of late years that has almost entirely disappeared, as far as regards the country people. We have had, I think, for the last four or five years, exceedingly quiet fairs; we have not found it necessary to take up any persons for felony, or for misdemeanors, or misconduct, or drunkenness, or anything of that kind. I think, for the last four or five years, we have never troubled the magistrates with offenders from Stowe Green. It is a fair to which people come in carts, waggons, and in all sorts of conveyances; on foot and on horseback, and in every way. There are not less than 10,000 people congregated in the afternoon of the 4th of July at Stowe Green fair.

3415. You have had no committals from Stowe Green fair recently?—I think we have had no committal for five or six years.

3416. People congregate of all descriptions from the surrounding country?—From the surrounding country. It is rather a thinly-populated country; the people come from a great distance for a great many miles round. Stowe Green fair is the great holiday of the country.

3417. Amongst this assemblage, are there not people who are not connected with the district, who require looking after on the part of the police, such as gipsies, tramps, and idlers of all sorts?—Yes; there is a great deal of trade, and almost everything is to be purchased at Stowe Green fair; all descriptions of furniture, all sorts of agricultural implements, and all those kind of things. If it were not for the chief constable and the police attending at that fair, very serious depredations

depredations would be committed, and have been committed in former years, before preventive steps were taken.

Mr. R. Healy.

17 June 1853.

3418. Have you the charge of the police at that fair?—The sessions publish an order, in which they state that Stowe Green fair is under the direction of the two chief constables of Aveland, who are to take as many constables from their separate divisions as they think necessary to keep the peace; it was formerly the case that there used to be from 20 to 30 constables summoned to attend the fair at Stowe Green.

3419. Are those parish constables selected from the parishes in the surrounding neighbourhood?—Generally; it has been the habit of me and my colleague, the other chief constable, to select the most useful men from the parish constables in the immediate neighbourhood; our present practice is to summon 10.

3420. Do you find that number sufficient for your purpose?—We have always found it amply sufficient, so far; our position has been almost a sinecure of late years.

3421. Have you any building that you use as a station during the continuance of the fair?—A small cottage house stands upon the green, the only house which used to be inhabited upon it. There were great objections to the house on the part of the occupiers and landed proprietors, from the circumstance of its standing alone. In consequence of that it is now uninhabited, with the exception of the fair day. It is used as a police station; it is divided into two rooms, in one of which we have a sort of lock-up; we have a form with staples, and anybody we have to take up and secure we handcuff, and put into that room. In the other room the chief constables and the petty constables continue, from 12 o'clock of the fair day till 12 o'clock at night, or two the next morning, as circumstances arise.

3422. Have you found those selected parish constables sufficient for the purpose of keeping order at this assemblage of 10,000 people?—We have, hitherto.

3423. Have you generally had the same constables?—We very frequently have had the same constables; it occasionally happens, when there is a change of constables in the parishes that are near, we do not think the new constables are as efficient as the old ones. The practice of my colleague and myself is this: out of our number of parish constables, I think I have about 14, and Mr. Osborne has about 10, we select those men whom we think are the most effective men; consequently, where they continue the constables in their parishes one year after another, we continue them. The men from Hanby and from Bourn we always had. There is a constable from another large agricultural village, called Rippingale, who is a blacksmith, whom we have always had; we find it better to have men who have been in the habit of attending than to have fresh men.

3424. From your experience of parish constables in this duty, which requires men of some discretion and knowledge, are you of opinion that parish constables could, by a proper selection and by proper remuneration, be made as effective a police force as the requirements of a rural district would demand?—I do think so. It is also right to state that, in addition to the parish constables, we have had a man from Sleaford, who is a police constable resident at Sleaford; we have had that man to assist us in managing the constables under us, and in managing the fair generally.

3425. The question is with regard to their efficiency for other purposes; if the parish constables were put upon a better footing, do you think they would be so capable of improvement in the execution of their duties as to be sufficiently effective for all purposes in your district?—I do. I think the selection of parish constables might be improved; it is rather too much the practice, occasionally, that persons in the middle class of life at the vestry appoint, in different parishes, persons who are not so proper as otherwise. If the selection of constables was given to the magistrates, the chief constable would, at the same time, be able to report who would or not be proper to be appointed as parish constables.

3426. Should you think it advisable that they should be remunerated on a fixed plan for their services, either by a salary or by fees?—I think they should be paid better than they are at present, and have less difficulty in getting their money.

3427. Do you think, under such circumstances, you could get an effective constabulary?—Ours is the quietest district in the county; we are all agriculturists; we have not a manufacture of any sort or kind; consequently it is an exceedingly quiet country. It is a country where the working classes are exceedingly well off; and, what is a still more important thing, generally speaking, it is a very fertile district, and I have always found that all descriptions of persons, great and small, do the best upon the best land.

3428. You

3428. You have stated that there are a number of persons assembling at this periodical fair who do not belong to the locality, such as gipsies and tramps; have you serious difficulty with them?—Not a serious difficulty; at the same time, I should say we have more trouble with the gipsies than all the rest of the people put together; they are more disorderly, and more disposed to get drunk, and get up fights, and things of that kind; we find our principal trouble is the management of those people, and to keep the peace with them. The country people are uncommonly orderly, respectable, and respectful in their conduct, and much more sober than they were when I was first chief constable; drunken people formerly was the rule, now it is quite the exception. In the 10,000 which I believe are congregated together on the afternoon of the 4th of July, it is very rare indeed to see a man who is the worse for drink.

3429. You said that tea had been introduced as a beverage instead of beer and spirits?—There are booths in which they find tea for 1,000 people.

3430. Are those tea-booths much frequented by the people of the district?— They are very much frequented by all descriptions of people, particularly by the cottagers and labourers, and their wives and families.

3431. Can you give the Committee some statistics as to criminals in your own district?—In consequence of receiving a summons to attend this Committee, I went to the house of correction last Tuesday; I took a statement from the house of correction, showing the committals for the last eight years.

3432. When do you commence them?—Mr. Mare, the governor of the house of correction at Falkingham, offered to give me returns for a great many years backwards; I thought the last few years would be sufficient.

[The same was read, as follows:]

COMMITTED.				COMMITTED.		
1844 to Michaelmas 1845.	Felons	80	1849	Felons	77
	Assaults	27		Assaults	28
	Vagrants	20		Vagrants	41
	Misdemeanors	38		Misdemeanors	42
	Game Laws	21		Game Laws	54
		186			242
1846	Felons	74	1850	Felons	90
	Assaults	21		Assaults	23
	Vagrants	14		Vagrants	30
	Misdemeanors	39		Misdemeanors	39
	Game Laws	27		Game Laws	84
		175			266
1847	Felons	69	1851	Felons	129
	Assaults	17		Assaults	35
	Vagrants	23		Vagrants	42
	Misdemeanors	39		Misdemeanors	54
	Game Laws	32		Game Laws	76
		180			336
1848	Felons	103	1852	Felons	87
	Assaults	23		Assaults	30
	Vagrants	14		Vagrants	32
	Misdemeanors	47		Misdemeanors	35
	Game Laws	24		Game Laws	58
		211			242

1851—From 29 September to June 14 - - - - 211
1852 - Ditto - - ditto - - - - 144

3433. There

Mr. R. Healy.

17 June 1853.

3433. There appears to be a greater number in the years 1850 and 1851 than in the preceding years; can you assign any reason why there was an increase at that time?—I think I can show one very strong reason. In the first place, the increase of offences under the Game Laws, in the year ending 1850, increased from 54 the year before, and 24 the year before that, to 84, which was in consequence of the execution of some railways in the vicinity of Grantham; the Great Northern from Stamford to Grantham going across our division. In consequence of that there was a very great increase of crimes, and also of offences against the Game Laws. There was one occasion when 16 men were brought in one batch.

3434. Since the execution of that railway, has not the number of committals greatly decreased?—Yes.

3435. The number was diminished from 336 in 1851, to 242 in 1852?—Yes, just so. There is one thing more striking even than that; because at the end of 1851 to 1852, these railways were not quite finished, and consequently there was still a great number of poachers, 58, but the committals are made up from Michaelmas to Michaelmas. From the 29th of September 1851 to the 14th June 1852, there were in the whole 211 committals; but from the 29th of September 1852 to the 14th of June 1853, last Tuesday, there have been only 144, being a diminution in that neighbourhood from 211 to 144.

3436. Therefore there is a diminution of about 80 per cent.?—Yes. This is a report which I had from the books of the governor at the house of correction. I have also the convictions for felony for seven years. In 1845, there were tried and convicted, 58; in 1846, 59; in 1847, 52; in 1848, 88; in 1849, 63; in 1850, 67; in 1851, 107; that was the year we had a great influx; and in 1852, 78; making an average of 71 each year for the eight years.

3437. Is it your opinion that the bulk of offences against property and person in this district is detected and brought to justice by the present means?—My opinion is, that the great bulk of offences is so detected; in fact, ours is a country, with the exception of two or three considerable towns, which is almost without serious crime. It is very rarely indeed that we have committals to the assizes. During the time that I have lived in the county, now for five or six-and-thirty years, I should say it was an exceedingly quiet, moral and respectable country, as far as regards the working classes of the people. I believe I may say, to the credit of the farmers in the county, that their labourers are well paid, and, I believe, the labourers are satisfied that they are well paid.

3438. Are you acquainted with the amount of rate which is now levied for county purposes in your district?—I took the opportunity, before I came from home, of looking at the assessment of the county rate for the two divisions of the county. From my having to collect the rates, and to pay in the rates for the county, I am acquainted with the amount of rate and the gross value of the property. For the south division of Kesteven the assessment is upon the value of 238,545 *l.*; for the northern division the assessment is 425,459 *l.*; making a total of 664,004 *l.* That is the gross assessment for the parts of Kesteven.

3439. What is the amount of rate levied upon that assessment?—The amount of the rate upon those assessments is, in the south division, 372 *l.* 14 *s.* 6 *d.*; in the north division, 664 *l.* 15 *s.* 6 *d.*; that is the quarterly assessment; making a total of 1,037 *l.* 10 *s.* quarterly, or an annual rate of 4,150 *l.*, which is within a very small decimal of 1½ *d.* in the pound, for the whole county rate for the year. The quarter's rate is a farthing and half a farthing, consequently it is 1½ *d.* in the year.

3440. *Chairman.*] That is for the two divisions?—Yes, the two divisions of Kesteven; they are both charged at the same rate, though they are under different jurisdictions.

3441. How many hundreds are there?—There are four hundreds in the south division of Kesteven.

3442. Sir *J. Trollope.*] The present county rate assessment being 1½ *d.* in the pound, have you ever considered what the establishment of a rural police force would cost the county, supposing it were carried out in its full efficiency?—I am perfectly unable to answer that question; I can give no guess at what the increased expense would be, not the slightest.

3443. Have you ever taken into consideration what number of men would be probably appointed?—I have not the slightest means of judging, our district only consisting of agricultural villages, with one or two small market towns; there is one considerable market town in our division, the town of Bourn.

3444. Is it your opinion that your division of the county of Lincoln requires a

Mr. R. Healy.

17 June 1853.

rural police at all?—I certainly am of opinion that it does not; it would be a very unpopular measure in our district; the farmers of the district and the rate-payers are exceedingly well satisfied with things as they are.

3445. They do not wish to incur the additional cost?—I never heard any one express a desire to have the rural police.

3446. Did the magistrates hold a general county meeting to consider the adoption of that Act when it was first carried?—I heard of it some years ago, but I cannot speak to it in any other way than as a mere floating idea and rumour being prevalent. I do not know it of my own knowledge at all.

3447. Lord *Loraine*.] Have you any idea what is paid by the parishes to the constables?—As far as that goes, I have very little evidence whatever; I am at present of opinion that the parish constables are badly paid; I think they are not paid sufficiently to make them so efficient a body as they otherwise would be.

3448. What do you think the place of a parish constable is worth to him now? —As far as that goes, it almost entirely depends upon the size of the parish, and the amount of business that there is in that parish for the constables. I have lived almost the whole of my time in a very small parish indeed, where I believe the parish constable's duties have been nominal, and his pay nominal. We have a population of only 100 persons in our parish, consequently the parish constable has nothing to do.

3449. Cannot you form a guess what the constables receive?—I have not the least idea. They are paid regularly in some parishes; in some parishes they allow a payment to a parish constable. I consider, in those parishes where they keep the constables for years together, those constables become by far more efficient than in places of small population, where they appoint a man a constable, and it is a mere nominal office.

3450. Are the constables paid by fees?—Partly by fees; they are paid by fees for certain things they do. They are in some parishes also paid a small stipend from the parish.

3451. Where they get both fees and stipend, do they make up a living?—No; I do not know any instance of any village where the constable gets as much as makes him a comfortable livelihood; I am not aware of it; the village in which I reside is a village of 1,200 inhabitants; we have an intelligent parish constable; I am very little connected with the parish; I do not believe he gets more than 4 *l*. or 5 *l*.

3452. You say that gypsies commit depredations in your neighbourhood; do you think a farmer paying 100 *l*. a year rent would object to pay 17 *s*. for complete protection against them?—I really do not know what the farmer could do; I am aware that the gypsies are a very considerable nuisance; I presume that though that nuisance might be abated, it would not be abolished by the appointment of police.

3453. The question is, whether for the service of summons and warrants, and matters of that sort, the pursuit of a thief, the prevention of the depredations by gypsies, a farmer paying 100 *l*. a year rent would not be willing to pay 17 *s*. a year? —I really feel great difficulty in answering that question. All I know upon the subject is, that we have nothing of the kind to complain of in a usual way. I am quite sure that the feeling of the farmers would be against increased expenses.

3454. Do not you think that a farmer paying 100 *l*. a year rent very often expends between 15 *s*. and 1 *l*. in payments to parish constables for different thefts? —I should say not, in a general way. Will you permit me to say, that ours is rather a peculiar district of country; we have very large parishes in extent, but very small population; it frequently happens that our parishes are sometimes, perhaps, 3,000, or 4,000, or 5,000 acres, with a very small population; I should think that our district of country is as free from crime as any district in the kingdom.

3455. You do not think, in your parish, that for all services performed by the constable year by year, including losses, the farmer pays 17 *s*.?—I should say nothing of the kind.

3456. Mr. *Howard*.] Can you state how much is contributed to the local associations for the prosecution of felons?—I think, generally speaking (I have not been a member of one of those local associations myself), 5 *s*. a year is contributed to the local associations; but the subscribers, I should say, to some of those local associations probably may be 150 members; some not so many.

3457. Do those associations give rewards to the constables for the detection of offenders?—They offer rewards to the constables, and the clerk of the association

sees

Mr R. Healy

17 June 1853

sees to the management of the prosecution of offenders. I do not think myself it is considered much advantage to the parties; for my own part I have had only one prosecution for the 35 years I have been in the county, and that did not cost me a farthing.

3458. Would those local associations give money for the detection of an offender who did not offend against a member of the association?—They would not give rewards for the apprehension of offenders who had committed offences against non-members.

3459. Mr. *Philipps.*] Are the subscriptions regularly paid?—I have no means of knowing.

3460. Sir *J. Trollope.*] Was not the origin of those associations with the view of saving the members of the association from the expense of a prosecution?— That was the case before the law was altered; before the Government and the county paid the expenses of prosecutions, they used to fall entirely upon the individuals prosecuting. That was the origin of the mutual associations. I remember them as far back as 50 or 60 years; but since the expenses of prosecutions have been either borne by the county or Government, individuals are not put to unnecessary expenses in prosecutions.

3461. Mr. *Philipps.*] Have you heard of any of those voluntary associations breaking up from the non-payment of the subscriptions?—Never; they are generally in the hands of solicitors, and very frequently leading solicitors, who are pretty astute in looking after those things.

3462. Sir *J. Trollope.*] Have they they not an annual meeting and a dinner, which keeps them together?—They have a dinner, which keeps them together.

3463. Lord *Lovaine.*] You have given the Committee a return of the crime which was detected and punished; have you any return of the crimes which have been committed, where the persons committing them have not been brought to trial?—No, I have no other return than the one I have given. There is a return of committals from year to year. This is a return of the convictions; and consequently the difference would be, the parties who either afterwards were released by the magistrates, or there was no bill found against them upon trial.

3464. *Chairman.*] You are the chief constable for the hundred of Aveland?— For the hundred of Aveland.

3465. Is Caistor in the southern division?—No.

3466. Is Heckington?—No; Heckington is in the northern division of Kesteven.

3467. Is crime as small in amount in the northern division of Kesteven as in the southern division?—I think it is not quite. The returns I have been giving are for both the northern and southern divisions.

3468. Do you know Heckington?—Yes.

3469. Did you ever hear of a great extent of sheep-stealing there?—I heard some years ago of sheep-stealing there.

3470. Did you ever hear of sheep-stealing having been committed, where the parties in bravado nailed the sheep's heads on the church-doors?— I never heard that.

3471. Are you aware of highway robbery being committed in the parish of Heckington?—I am not aware of its having been committed at Heckington, though I do not reside very far from Heckington; it is across the district from me, and the farmers from the parts about Heckington do not attend the same markets that I do; consequently, I have not an opportunity of hearing what goes on there.

3472. If a person has been robbed in the parish of Heckington of his watch and other property, you are not aware of it?—No.

3473. You have stated the case of a sheep-stealing gang having been broken up; was not that gang broken up very much by the exertions of the person who lost his sheep?—Very much.

3474. Was he a large occupier of land, and a man of property?—Yes.

3475. What steps did he take in order to recover his property?—He took means to trace the footsteps of the parties, and he afterwards had reason to suppose that the depredators did not belong to our parts of Kesteven, but came from the parts of Holland.

3476. Whom did he employ?—The first steps were taken by himself and his own servants. Then, afterwards, he had some reason for supposing that the parties who had committed the felony lived in the parts of Holland, which is out of the division of Kesteven; the parts of Kesteven and the Parts of Holland are divided by a very large drain, which is called the Forty Foot, and in consequence of that

he

Mr. R. Healy.

17 June 1853.

he went to Spalding; he had the assistance of police constables from Spalding. From certain suspicious circumstances which came out, and from one thing being traced after another, it was discovered that those parties were the parties who stole the sheep; he prosecuted them to conviction. It was cleverly managed, principally by the prosecutor himself and his servants; I should say almost entirely by himself.

3477. Supposing, instead of being a man of property, he had been a poor man, would he have had the same facilities for pursuing the offenders?—In all probability, if he had been a poor man, he would not have had the means or the ability to have exerted himself.

3478. Lord *Lovaine*.] In all probability he would never have recovered his property?—Perhaps not; the property consisted in sheep, and being slaughtered, the skin was buried. The parties only desire to steal the mutton.

3479. *Chairman*.] Do you think it desirable to have a better class of constables than those which are employed?—I think there might be an improvement in the selection of the constables. I think some of the present constables are as good as is necessary.

3480. You think they ought to be better paid?—Yes.

3481. If you cannot tell what the cost of the present constabulary is, probably you cannot tell what the cost of the better men would be?—I cannot tell what the cost of better men would be. I know very little of the emoluments of the present constables. I know they very frequently complain to me, as the chief constable, that they do a great many things, and they have a difficulty in getting paid.

3482. How are your prisoners conveyed to gaol?—Our prisoners are conveyed to gaol by the constable. Almost the whole of our crime arises from parties who come into the district, such as vagrants, tramps, and people of that description.

3483. Do you know what the constables are paid by the mile for taking prisoners to gaol?—I do not.

3484. You have made no calculation of what is the cost of conveying prisoners to gaol?—The gaol is situated in the centre of the district; in our southern division the expense of conveying prisoners to gaol is not very important.

3485. Do you know what the cost of constables in proceedings before justices is?—No.

3486. Sir *J. Trollope*.] Do you know that there are regular tables of fees for mileage and allowances to constables?—I know such a table is stuck up in the town-hall at Bourn.

3487. *Chairman*.] Do you know what the expense of parish constables in your division is, for serving summonses, warrants, and so forth?—I think they are allowed 1 *s.* for serving a summons.

3488. You do not know what is the total cost?—I do not know.

3489. Have any of the chief constable's sheep been stolen?—They have not stolen many of them. I think I may have had two stolen. I know I had one stolen a few years ago.

3490. Mr. *Howard*.] Are you the relieving officer of the union?—No.

3491. Can you give the Committee any information about the number of vagrants relieved?—No, I cannot.

3492. You do not know whether the number of vagrants has decreased?—I really do not know whether the vagrants have increased or decreased. I should say, by the committal of vagrants at one time, they seem to have increased considerably, and then to have decreased again.

3493. Mr. *Mackie*.] Are your parish constables constantly employed in the detection and prevention of crime?—No.

3494. Do the constables follow any other occupations occasionally?—They are all persons who have other occupations.

3495. Are they tailors and shoemakers, and different trades?—Just so. The parish constable in the parish in which I live is a very intelligent man; he is a carpenter. Ours is a large agricultural parish.

3496. Then he follows his occupation of a carpenter generally, and occasionally performs the duties of a parish constable?—When he is applied to, he goes from his business of a carpenter to his duty as a parish constable.

3497. As the principal constable of the district, have you framed any regulations for the guidance of the parish constables?—In point of fact and reality, though we have the name of high constables, we have nothing at all to do with the parish constables in any other way than the management of Stowe Green fair, as to which I gave evidence. That is only once a year. I have nothing whatever to do with the parish constables in any other way than this. If a parish constable finds himself in a difficulty, he comes to me for advice.

3498. It is only once a year that you come in contact with the constables at all?—Yes; I come in contact with them in case they have any difficulties; they come to ask my advice; they come to me rather in the way of a friend; they know I have no control over them. I have nothing to do with them in any sort of way, only in the management of this fair.

3499. You said you considered 10 constables sufficient for that fair?—Ten constables is the usual number we summon for that fair; and during that fair we are in attendance to give directions to the constables.

3500. How many people are there at the fair?—Of course mine is only a guess; I believe there are 10,000 people.

3501. *Chairman.*] And even at this fair, you say the duties of the constables is almost a sinecure?—Of late years it has been; some years ago we used to have more difficulty; for the last four or five years we have had no difficulty.

3502. Therefore the constables are paid for a holiday?—They do not get a great deal for their holiday; they are paid 10s. for their services, out of which they are obliged to pay their own expenses, and to attend from 11 or 12 o'clock in the day to 12 or 1 o'clock in the morning.

3503. Mr. *Mackie.*] What salary do you get?—The salary I get is 24l. a year.

3504. Sir *J. Trollope.*] Is not the 24l. paid to you for collecting the county rate?—I consider that my principal duty is that of collecting the county rates, and also distributing the precepts to the constables, overseers, and churchwardens.

3505. Holding statutes for hiring servants is under your jurisdiction?—Yes.

3506. Mr. *Mackie.*] How are you remunerated for being high constable in that district?—The 24l. includes everything. The chief constable is the chief constable by name, but, in point of fact, he is everybody's boy, from the clerk of the peace to the magistrate's clerk.

3507. Sir *J. Trollope.*] Have you to attend at the quarter sessions?—We are always expected to attend at quarter sessions.

3508. Are you not charged with the superintendence of the arrangements to keep order in court?—We are.

3509. Now, in your experience at the quarter sessions, where you always attend, will you state to the Committee the description of prisoners from those rural districts; have they been natives, or persons who have wandered into the country from other districts?—I should say almost three-fourths are tramps, who come in for the purpose of picking pockets, or of stealing anything that is loose when they happen to be prowling about; it is a very rare thing that we have trials of any of the natives.

3510. Mr. *Burroughes.*] How many high constables are there in Lincolnshire?—I do not know how many there are in the county; in the south division of Kesteven there are two for each hundred.

3511. How many hundreds are there?—Four hundreds in the south division of Kesteven.

3512. Do each of the high constables have 24l.?—Yes. There are eight chief constables in the four hundreds of the south division of Kesteven.

3513. Is that money received for performing the duties appertaining to the office of high constable?—It is paid for the collection of the county rate; that is a part of the duty; the principal duty is, that we issue precepts to the overseers of the poor.

3514. Is it any part of the duties of the high constables to maintain order at the quarter sessions?—All I can say is, that it has been the custom with us.

3515. The high constable, or hundred constable, has certain specific duties to perform, but he has nothing to do with being the chief constable?—I mentioned the high constables as the chief constables, supposing them to be synonymous.

3516. Upon what ground do you say that part of the duties of the chief constables is to maintain order in the court of quarter sessions?—That is a duty which is thrown upon us, and which we are expected to perform; we do not do it ourselves; we sit in court. Our practice is this: we are called over at the beginning of the court, and we are expected to attend the court as long as it sits, unless we get leave from the magistrates to be set at liberty.

Mr. *Henry Mathews*, called in ; and Examined.

3517. *Chairman.*] WERE you formerly in the Metropolitan Police ?—Yes.

3518. In consequence of depredations committed in the parts of Lindsey, in Lincolnshire, were you, at the request of the tenants of Lord Yarborough, sent down from the metropolitan police force as a police officer for the detection of crime at Caistor, in North Lincolnshire ?—I was.

3519. When were you sent down ?—On the 14th December last.

3520. What did you find to be the state of crime in the district of Caistor and the neighbouring villages when you went down ?—I found that several premises had been broken open, and large bulks of property taken away.

3521. You mean that several burglaries had been committed ?—Yes ; and also several sheep had been stolen in that neighbourhood.

3522. Were the inhabitants of that neighbourhood alarmed in consequence of the depredations which had been committed ?—The inhabitants were very much alarmed ; they were afraid to go to bed at night, in many places ; the servants were kept up all night to watch, armed with pitchforks, fire-arms, and so on.

3523. During the time you were there, did you watch at night ?—I did.

3524. Did you receive any aid from the parochial constables ?—None whatever ; only on market-days, and occasionally visited the public-houses with me on Saturday nights and Sunday mornings.

3525. Was not there a superintending constable in that division ?—Yes.

3526. Did he live at Caistor ?—No ; he lived nine miles off, at Brigg.

3527. Had you any communication with or assistance from him ?—I had some communication with him.

3528. Had you any assistance from him ?—No.

3529. Did he never come to Caistor ?—He used to come generally on market day, once a week, on Saturday, and occasionally visited the public-houses and lodging-houses with me.

3530. During the time you were there, did the presence of a police officer check those depredations ?—There were no depredations scarcely committed.

3531. Were there many lodging-houses in Caistor ?—There were four.

3532. Did you inspect them ?—I did.

3533. Were you sworn in as a special constable ?—I was.

3534. Had you any legal authority to inspect the lodging-houses ?—I had not.

3535. You did that upon your own responsibility ?—I did.

3536. Do you think there is a great benefit to be derived from police officers inspecting lodging-houses ?—I do.

3537. You think they do good by it ?—I do.

3538. Have you any reason to think that crime has increased since you came away ?—Yes, I have.

3539. Have you had any communication of that sort from any person at Caistor ?—No, I have not.

3540. Sir *J. Trollope.*] Were you sent down first as a detective, or were you known to be a police officer on your arrival ?—I was first sent down on the application of the Earl of Yarborough ; I first went down dressed in private clothes ; no one knew I was coming, I believe, with the exception of the Earl of Yarborough, and one or two gentlemen in the neighbourhood.

3541. Were those gentlemen magistrates ?—I believe gentlemen farmers, not magistrates. I don't think the magistrates knew that I was there until an application was made to have me sworn in as special constable. I went from one place to another ; I was there about a month ; after that, I was sworn in as a special constable, and then it became known I was there ; previous to that time, it was not known.

3542. Did you dress in uniform after that time ?—No.

3543. How many months were you there ?—I was there from the 14th of December to the 2d of May.

3544. Can you tell the Committee how many persons you detected and brought to justice in that time ?—None.

3545. Not one ?—No.

3546. If you did not fulfil your mission by bringing to justice those parties who committed these numerous offences, in what way did you check depredation ? —I had no chance to detect robberies, because there were scarcely any robberies committed, and none in which I could obtain any clue.

3547. For

3547. For the first month, you were not known to be a detective?—I was not there particularly as a detective: it was merely to see the state of the country, and if possible, where those characters were located; to find them out.

3548. Did you find anything out?—I saw a great many idle people in the town and neighbourhood.

3549. Might that not have been from want of employment; do you set down every person whom you see out of work as a thief or a depredator?—Certainly not.

3550. You did not detect a single case?—No.

3551. Had you been for some years in the London police before you went down?—Eight years and a half.

3552. You have stated that there had been numerous offences against the law before you went; many had been committed very recently; did you detect none of those cases?—No; all clue was gone to bring any one to justice; there was nothing you could act upon.

3553. In fact, you did not effect any good in bringing parties to justice?—No.

3554. Was that the reason you were discontinued?—No.

3555. Why did they discontinue your services?—Because crime had so much diminished, and the magistrates refused to re-appoint me at the expense of the county; the gentlemen in the neighbourhood offered to keep me at their expense, but I declined to stop any longer.

Sir *John Walsham*, Bart., called in; and Examined.

3556. *Chairman.*] ARE you a Poor-law Inspector in Kent?—Yes.

3557. Of what counties does your district consist?—It consists of Norfolk, Suffolk, Essex, part of Kent, and part of Cambridgeshire.

3558. What was your district in 1847?—It consisted of Norfolk, Suffolk, Essex, Cambridgeshire and part of Hertfordshire; Kent has been added since then to my district.

3559. Have you any statement with regard to the amount of vagrancy in Essex in the different years from 1848 to 1851?—My attention, naturally, has been a good deal directed to the question of vagrancy in my district. All the poor-law inspectors were required to report on the subject of vagrancy generally some years ago, and from what I then observed of the effect of the employment of the police in Essex, I was very much struck when I came into Kent to find, that whilst vagrancy had almost disappeared in Essex, it still was in a very vigorous state in the 14 unions of the county of Kent which were attached to my district in 1851. In Kent, I understood there was no police, and any questions which I had to ask of the chairmen, when attending the boards of guardians, elicited the fact, that no police officers had been appointed, as in Essex, to act as assistant relieving officers for vagrants.

3560. Was the minute of the Poor-law Board, which was issued by Mr. Buller, subsequent to your report, or was your report subsequent to the minute?—The directions which were given to report were given in 1849, in order to see what the result of that minute had been.

3561. What was the substance of that minute?—The minute is rather a long one; vagrancy had increased very greatly, and become exceedingly burdensome in every part of the country. I happened recently to be casting my eyes over the Parliamentary Paper which had been presented in reference to the order obtained by Mr. Christie, which shows the number of vagrants up to 1845. Vagrancy was then progressively increasing very much; in 1848 it had still increased; and at that period, when Mr. Buller had become the President of the Poor-law Board, he issued this minute, the commencement of which is, "The Board have received representations from every part of England and Wales respecting the continual and rapid increase of vagrancy." The minute suggested, *inter alia*, certain modes of proceeding by means of the rural police.

3562. Was not one part of the suggestion a careful discrimination between those who were mendicants and those persons who were applying for relief through distress?—No doubt; previously to that, it had been generally supposed that every person who applied for relief, whom the relieving officer could not of his own knowledge know not to be in a state of destitution, must of necessity be relieved. Mr. Buller saw the evil tendency of such an arrangement as that, and he suggested to the boards of guardians not to relieve able-bodied persons, except during

Mr. H. Mathews.

17 June 1853.

Sir *J. Walsham*, Bart.

Sir J. Walsham,
Bart.

17 June 1853.

very inclement weather, or where they were accompanied by women and children; elderly persons, or persons stating themselves to be sick, might also be relieved.

3563. Although Mr. Buller did not direct that the police should be employed for the relief of vagrants, he suggested it to the unions, as having been a useful practice in some places?—In answer to that question, perhaps the Committee will permit me to read half-a-dozen sentences in the minute: "The relieving officer will have to exercise his judgment as to the truth of their assertions of destitution, and to ascertain, by searching them, whether they possess any means of supplying their own necessities. He will not be likely to err, in judging from their appearance, whether they are suffering from want of food. He will take care that women and children, the old and infirm, and those who, without absolutely serious disease, present an enfeebled or sickly appearance, are supplied with necessary food and shelter. As a general rule, he would be right in refusing relief to able-bodied and healthy men, though, in inclement weather, he might afford them shelter, if really destitute of the means of procuring it for themselves. His duties would necessarily make him acquainted with the persons of the habitual vagrants, and to these it would be his duty to refuse relief, except in case of evident and urgent necessity. A plan which has been adopted with success in some towns in different parts of England, is that of employing a trustworthy officer of the local police as assistant relieving officer for vagrants. As the habitual vagrant has generally rendered himself amenable to the law by criminal acts, he dreads being confronted with the police; and the effect of this arrangement, where it has been adopted, is said to have produced the speedy disappearance of the greater proportion of the usual applicants."

3564. That recommendation has been acted upon in the county of Essex?—Yes; through the strenuous exertions of Captain M'Hardy and the efficiency of the Essex police force, this recommendation has been most useful in Essex, in almost all the unions. I have by me letters which I might read, as to such being the actual result, in the opinion of the boards of guardians, even at this particular moment. The Committee will permit me to say further, that at Lady-day 1851, in the 14 unions in the county of Kent now in my district, I was very much struck, as I before mentioned to the Committee, by finding a great extent of vagrancy; in consequence of that, and perceiving that I did not make very much way with the boards of guardians, in inducing them to believe the results that had really taken place in Essex, Essex being merely over the river, and being a case, in my view, precisely upon all fours with the county of Kent, I selected 14 unions in the county of Kent and 14 unions in the county of Essex, representing pretty nearly an identical population, and compared the two groups.

3565. Will you state what the population of those 14 unions was?—The population of the 14 unions in Kent was 273,452; the population of the 14 unions in Essex was 265,503.

3566. Was not the date of Mr. Buller's minute 1848?—Mr. Buller's minute upon vagrancy was issued upon the 4th of August 1848.

3567. That comparative estimate is up to the end of the year 1851?—It takes in 1847–48, which was the year previously to the minute; 1848–49, which was partially under the operation of Mr. Buller's minute; 1849–50 and 1850–51, which were wholly under the operation of that minute. During that period, there was a considerable decrease of vagrancy in the county of Kent. The decrease of vagrancy in the county of Kent in 1850–51, as compared with 1847–48, the last year of the return, and the year previously to the issue of Mr. Buller's minute, was 20,508 vagrants, or 55¼ per cent. upon the whole number. This decrease was subsequent to the issue of Mr. Buller's minute, and was without the assistance of the police.

3568. What was the diminution in the county of Essex?—In the county of Essex, taking 14 unions, with a population as nearly as possible the same as in the unions in Kent, the diminution was 24,806, or 97 per cent.

3569. Taking per-centage as the test in the two counties, in Essex, where there is a police force, and where the recommendation of Mr. Buller was acted upon, as to making the police relieving officers of vagrants, the decrease was 97 per cent., and in Kent, where there were no police three years subsequently to Mr. Buller's minute, the decrease was 55½ per cent., therefore the difference would be 41½ per cent.?—Yes.

3570. Then the decrease of 55 per cent. in the county of Kent you would ascribe in some degree to Mr. Buller's minute?—In a great degree to Mr. Buller's minute; and in a great degree also to another obvious fact; the fact, which is

perfectly

Sir *J. Walsham,*
Bart.

17 July 1853.

perfectly well known, that every lodging-house where vagrants resort has statistics, if I may so speak, of the workhouses throughout the country. If, then, you stop vagrancy in its progress through any given counties, it must have a very great effect upon the counties beyond it; the circulation of vagrancy has been checked in a variety of places, and checked especially in the county of Essex.

3571. Ascribing in a great measure the decrease of 55 per cent. in Kent to Mr. Buller's minute, and to the other causes of which you have spoken, the difference between 55 per cent. in Kent, where there is no police, and 97 per cent. in Essex, where there is a police, might be fairly ascribed to the beneficial effects of the Essex police?—I should be unwilling to say that there might not be other differences in Kent which are not within my knowledge; there might be reasons why vagrancy should be greater in the county of Kent, though I am not aware of any such reasons, nor do I suppose that there are any such reasons.

3572. Have you also a return of the vagrancy in the county of Kent, up to 1853?—I have; I had it drawn out the other day; and in Essex also.

3573. Should you ascribe the difference in the per-centage of decrease between Essex and Kent, viz., 42 per cent., in a great degree to the efficiency of the police in Essex?—Perhaps the Committee will permit me to read what my impressions were in 1851, when I wrote a letter on the subject to the boards of guardians in Kent: "My attention" (I wrote) "having been attracted to the large number of vagrants relieved in many of the workhouses of those unions which the Poor-law Board placed under my charge in March last, I have prepared the annexed tables, for the purpose of illustrating the progressive decrease of vagrancy in 14 Kent unions, south of the Thames, as compared with 14 Essex unions, north of that river. From these tables, it would appear, that whilst vagrancy has nearly become extinct in the Essex unions, which I have quoted in Table 2, its decrease (though considerable) in Kent, falls far short of the decrease effected on the opposite side of the river, and leaves what may be called a large balance still to be provided for in vagrant wards. It is right, however, I should add, that I attribute the almost total disappearance of tramps in the great majority of the Essex unions to the aid afforded by the Essex constabulary force, members of which are employed as assistant relieving officers for the relief of vagrants. Table 3, indeed, demonstrates that where Captain M'Hardy's rural police have no authority, as in the Colchester and West Ham unions, vagrancy continues to be comparatively vigorous."

[*The Witness delivered in the following Tables :*]

COMPARATIVE STATEMENT showing the Total Number of VAGRANTS admitted into the Vagrant Wards of the undermentioned Unions of *Kent* and *Essex,* during the four Years ended 25 March 1851.

TABLE I.—KENT.

Nos.	Names of Unions.	Population in 1851.	Number of Vagrants Relieved in			
			1847–48.	*1848–49.	1849–50.	1850–51.
1	Blean - - - -	14,679	98	128	287	344
2	Bridge - - - -	11,164	143	214	417	517
3	Canterbury - - -	14,097	3,250	3,441	2,624	2,307
4	Dartford - - -	27,342	3,517	2,430	417	160
5	Dover - - - -	28,324	1,324	1,471	1,328	1,305
6	Eastry - - - -	25,162	974	1,179	1,048	1,108
7	Faversham - - -	16,684	1,492	1,769	1,335	1,273
8	Gravesend and Milton -	16,635	9,509	8,423	3,834	2,085
9	Hoo - - - -	2,845	-	-	-	3
10	Medway - - -	42,798	8,576	5,685	2,753	2,597
11	Milton - - - -	12,025	1,882	1,778	809	736
12	North Aylesford - -	16,569	4,066	1,892	1,115	1,716
13	Sheppey - - -	13,360	741	937	434	428
14	Thanet - - - -	31,793	1,119	812	756	704
	TOTALS - - -	273,482	36,691	30,159	17,155	16,183

Decrease in 1850–51, as compared with 1847–48, 20,508, or 55¼ per cent.

* Mr. Buller's Minute of Instructions to Guardians for the suppression of vagrancy was dated 4 August 1848.

TABLE II.—ESSEX (A.)

Nos.	Names of Unions.	Population in 1851.	Number of Vagrants Relieved in			
			1847–48.	1848–49.	1849–50.	1850–51.
1	Billericay - - -	13,780	2,295	1,496	35	3
2	Braintree - - -	17,576	1,067	1,167	44	61
3	Chelmsford - - -	32,300	5,755	3,000	119	90
4	Dunmow - - -	20,483	3,277	2,085	362	158
5	Epping - - - -	15,632	1,710	1,495	11	15
6	Halstead - - -	19,252	1,373	1,510	60	49
7	Lexden and Winstree -	21,665	838	631	20	15
8	Maldon - - - -	22,138	1,495	1,311	16	9
9	Ongar - - - -	11,857	2,102	1,738	85	41
10	Orsett - - - -	10,492	1,939	2,045	35	35
11	Rochford - - -	15,825	219	115	33	6
12	Saffron Walden - -	20,708	1,071	1,746	87	98
13	Tendring - - -	27,711	160	196	90	67
14	Witham - - -	16,084	2,132	1,402	54	70
	Totals - - -	265,503	25,523	19,937	1,051	717

Decrease in 1850–51, as compared with 1847–48, 24,806, or 97 per cent.

TABLE III.—ESSEX (B.)

Nos.	Names of Unions.	Population. in 1851.	Number of Vagrants Relieved in			
			1847–48.	1848–49.	1849–50.	1850–51.
1	Colchester - - -	19,443	2,952	2,374	1,169	739
2	Romford - - -	24,592	4,704	4,644	747	33
3	West Ham - - -	34,378	4,619	7,066	4,350	5,053
	Totals - - -	78,413	12,275	14,084	6,266	5,825

Decrease in 1850–51, as compared with 1847–48, 6,450, or 52½ per cent.

3574. Have you returns which continue the comparative statement up to 1853?
—Yes. I thought it desirable, as the comparative table merely goes to 1851, to extend a similar sort of inquiry, so far as time permitted, to 1853, by writing to the various clerks of the Kent and Essex unions, the results of which I beg to place before the Committee.

[The Witness delivered in the following Tables:]

QUERIES addressed, on the 11th day of June 1853, by Sir *John Wakeham*, Bart., Poor Law Inspector, to the Guardians of the undermentioned Unions, in the County of Essex.

Nos.	NAMES of UNIONS.	1848.	1849.	1850.	1851.	1852.	1853.	Have the Guardians, with the consent of the Poor Law Board, appointed any Police Officer (whether attached to the Rural, Municipal, or Parochial Constabulary), to assist in the relief of Vagrants?	If an Assistant Relieving Officer for Vagrants has been appointed from the Police, give the Date of the first Appointment of such an Assistant.	State, in general terms, what effect in the Number of Applications from Vagrants (in the way of diminishing or otherwise) the assistance of the Police is considered to have produced.
		\multicolumn{6}{c}{How many Vagrants have been admitted into the Workhouses during the Years ended the 25th of March}				
1	Billericay	2,295	-	-	-	-	37	-- Yes; two officers of the Essex Constabulary: one for Brentwood, and one for Billericay.	October 1848	-- The appointment of the police as relieving officers for vagrants has produced a rapid and progressive diminution in the number of vagrants relieved.
2	Braintree	199 (Half-year ended 25 March 1848.)	-	-	-	-	28	Yes -	30 October 1848	-- 199 have been admitted during the half-year ended 25 March 1848, and 28 during the year ended 25 March 1853; the effect has been a diminution in proportion of 28 to 398, or nearly 1 to 15.
3	Chelmsford	5,873	-	-	-	-	52	-- Mr. John May, superintendent of the Essex County Constabulary.	24 October 1848	-- "The effect" here asked, may, in "general terms," be stated to have been most extraordinary, the diminution having been from hundreds to units! a diminution of from 111 per week to 1 has actually taken place in the number of vagrants admitted in the union house since the appointment above mentioned was made.
4	Colchester	2,965	-	-	-	-	618	-- Yes; the superintendent of the Municipal Police of the borough of Colchester.	Michaelmas 1849	-- A very great difference in the number of vagrants admitted to the union house has been the result. The admissions have decreased to about a fifth of what they were in 1848, and the lodging houses are not now much used by tramps. The average number of admissions weekly during the year, to Lady-day 1853, was 11 and 44-52ths, whereas to Lady-day 1849, there were 57 and 1-12th.
5	Dunmow	3,277	-	-	158	-	172	Yes.	November 1849	-- The appointment of a police constable to assist in the relief of vagrants was followed by an immediate reduction in the number of applications from that class of paupers, and ever since, the number of such applications has been inconsiderable, as compared with the number of applications previous to such appointment.
6	Epping	1,710	1,495	38	20	33	33	No -	Nil -	-- The manner in which the guardians put a stop to the practice of vagrancy was by authorizing the master of the workhouse to admit no vagrants upon either a relieving officer or overseer's order unless the same was accompanied by a medical certificate, stating that the applicant was suffering from some illness, or unable to bear exposure to cold, &c. The news spread rapidly amongst the vagrant fraternity, and the result is evident from the above statistics. We have rarely an application, except it be a *bonâ fide* case of illness.
7	Halstead	Upwards of 1,000	-	60	51	78	43	-- There are two police officers appointed as assistant relieving officers for vagrants (one for each relieving officer's district), viz.: Mr. Banks, inspector of police, Halstead, and Mr. Ray, superintendent of police, Castle Hedingham.	-- 24 November 1848.	-- The effects have been extraordinary. In the three-quarters of the year ended Christmas 1848, there were 806 vagrants admitted. In the following quarter, ended Lady-day 1849 (after the appointment of the police), there were six only.
8	Leyden and Wanstead	No record	-	-	-	-	None	No -	Nil -	Nil.
9	Maldon	1,812	-	-	-	-	29	-- A police officer appointed as assistant relieving officer for vagrants.	February 1849	-- The number of applications made since such appointment has diminished to the amount of about 80 per cent.
10	Ongar	2,120	1,738	82	50	8	18	-- A police constable has been appointed as assistant relieving officer, so far as concerned vagrants, from the police for the county of Essex.	12 June 1849	-- It will be seen by the above statement that the number of applications in the half-year previous to the appointment of a police constable as assistant relieving officer, had decreased from 1,613 for the half-year to Michaelmas 1848, to 132 to the half-year to Lady-day 1848. Since which time the number of vagrants admitted into the workhouse has decreased.
11	Orsett	1,342	-	-	-	-	23	-- A police officer (of the Essex Constabulary Force) to assist in the relief of vagrants, with the consent of the Poor Law Board.	-- About February 1849.	-- The above statement will sufficiently show the advantage of appointing the police as assistant relieving officers; the above 23 cases were all persons in really destitute circumstances.
12	Rochford	219	-	-	-	-	24	-- The guardians (with the consent of the Poor Law Commissioners) appointed the superintendent of the Essex Constabulary Police stationed at Rochford, relieving officer for vagrants.	January 1849	-- The number of applications from vagrants has greatly diminished since 1849, but much depends on the vigilance of the officer. The number of admissions at the workhouse appear to have rather increased in this union during the past year, as compared with the year ended 25 March 1852.
13	Romford	-- Several hundred died.	-	-	-	-	None	No -	Nil -	Nil.
14	Saffron Walden	2,073	-	-	-	-	57	No -	Nil -	*Vide* Enclosure (A.)
15	Tendring	No record	-	-	-	-	33	No -	Nil -	Nil.
16	West Ham	4,623	-	-	-	-	2,382*	No -	-- No assistant relieving officer been appointed.	-- So far as the guardians are acquainted with the subject, they are of opinion that the interference of the police with vagrants in this union has not in any degree tended to diminish the number of applications for admission to the workhouse.]
17	Witham	2,123	-	-	-	-	101	-- The guardians have appointed the superintendent of the Essex Constabulary at Witham, the inspector of ditto at Coggeshall, and a police constable at Kelvedon, relieving officers for vagrants.	-- Three appointments were made on 13th November 1848.	-- The appointment of the police has tended to almost put a stop to vagrancy in this union, as will be seen from the foregoing figures. During the first half of the year in which they were appointed, the number of vagrants relieved in-doors was 1,092; but during the half-year then the police acted, the applications dwindled down to 296.

* First quarter, 1,374; second, 274; third, 228; fourth, 506; in all, 2,382. In this year the guardians altered their regulations for the admission of vagrants, and the result is seen by the diminished numbers in the three last quarters.

QUERIES addressed, on the 11th day of June 1853, by Sir *John Walsham*, Bart., Poor Law Inspector, to the Guardians of the undermentioned Unions in the County of *Kent*.

Nos.	NAMES of UNIONS.	How many Vagrants have been admitted into the Workhouses during the Years ended the 25th of March						Have the Guardians, with the consent of the Poor Law Board, appointed any Police Officer (whether attached to the Rural, Municipal, or Parochial Constabulary), to assist in the Relief of Vagrants ?	If an Assistant Relieving Officer for Vagrants has been appointed from the Police, give the Date of the first Appointment of such an Assistant.	State, in general terms, what effect on the Number of Applications from Vagrants (in the way of diminution or otherwise), the assistance of the Police is considered to have produced.
		1848.	1849.	1850.	1851.	1852.	1853.			
1	Blean - - -	98	–	–	344	–	-	No - - -	Nil - - -	Nil.
2	Bridge - - -	147	–	–	–	–	365	No - - -	Nil - - -	Nil.
3	Canterbury - -	3,250	–	–	–	–	2,118	No - - -	Nil - - -	Nil.
4	Dartford - -	3,250	–	–	–	–	117	No - - -	Nil - - -	Nil.
5	Dover - - -	970	–	–	–	–	1,113	No - - -	Nil - - -	Nil.
6	Eastry - - -	974	–	–	–	–	658	No - - -	Nil - - -	Nil.
7	Faversham - -	1,492	–	–	–	–	856	No - - -	Nil - - -	Nil.
8	Gravesend and Milton	9,509	–	–	–	–	2,226	- - Police assist as to relief to vagrants, but no appointment by the guardians.	Nil - - -	Reduced one-fourth.
9	Hoo - - -	None.	–	–	–	–	None.	No - - -	Nil - - -	Nil.
10	Medway - - -	8,576	–	–	–	–	1,795	No - - -	Nil - - -	Nil.
11	Milton - - -	1,883	–	–	–	–	388	No - - -	Nil - - -	- - The police have not assisted in this union, but I think such assistance would tend to diminish the number of applications from vagrants.
12	North Aylesford -	3,321	–	–	–	–	1,133	No - - -	Nil - - -	Nil.
13	Sheppey - - -	974	–	–	–	–	264	No - - -	Nil - - -	Nil.
14	Thanet, Isle of -	1,119	--	–	–	–	650	No - - -	Nil - - -	- - The superintendents of police, both at Margate and Ramsgate some years since, undertook to assist in affording relief to vagrants. No salary was allowed them. Their services gradually ceased ; and I think I may state, they had no effect in diminishing the number of applications.

Witness.] The majority of the boards of guardians in Essex, it will be seen, unquestionably attribute the great decrease of vagrancy in those unions to the employment of the police as assistant relieving officers. The results in Kent show, however, a tendency in vagrancy still to diminish, but very nearly, I think, in the same proportion to Essex, as in 1851. There is still a diminution in the Essex unions, and there is also a diminution in the Kent unions. But, from the reasons I stated a little while ago to the Committee, I am of opinion that the effect of checking vagrancy in various parts, in addition to the great improvement at present in the demand for labour, must exercise a beneficial effect in the ultimate reduction of vagrancy. No doubt the facts are as I have stated, that there has been a greater decrease in Essex, where the police are employed as relieving officers, as compared with Kent, where there is no police.

3575. If you are of opinion that checking vagrancy in one district decreases it in another, do not you think if it were checked by a general system of police throughout the kingdom, it would be greatly decreased ?—I see no reason why the same results should not be produced in England generally as has been produced in the county of Essex.

3576. Mr. *Philipps.*] What, in your opinion, would become of the vagrants, supposing you had a uniform system of police ?—They would cease to become vagrants; they would be absorbed.

3577. **You**

Sir J. Walsham,
Bart.

17 June 1853.

3577. You think that vagrancy is not only shifted, but entirely subdued?—A few years ago, I had to look a good deal into this subject, and it would have astonished the Committee to have seen the sort of persons that went upon tramp; most distressing cases of young people belonging to respectable families. Those individuals knew perfectly well that they could have a lodging every night at the union-house, and therefore they could calculate (in whatever parts of England they pleased to go on tramp) on having these lodgings. They knew in what unions they were well treated, according to their view of good treatment, and in what unions they were ill treated. There are still some vagrants in Essex, but I do not see myself why they should not be checked everywhere quite as much as in Essex. In former times I suppose there were great pleasures in that vagabond life; but the numbers of persons who really require to go upon tramp are very few indeed.

3578. Your opinion is, that if vagrants were watched in all directions, they would turn their attention from vagrancy, and seek some more reputable mode of obtaining a living?—In 95 cases out of 100, that is my decided opinion.

3579. You think it might not merely be shifted, but that it could be destroyed?—At the period when I found this extraordinary diminution in the Essex unions, I was rather alarmed lest I should find that though they did not come to the union-houses, they were circulating in the districts, going to the lone farm-houses and lone cottages; but I ascertained, by reference to Captain M'Hardy, that crime had diminished; that the number of vagrants had diminished; and that there were much fewer committals of vagrants at that particular period, although previously there had been very many. I might also state, that the only other occasions on which I have been brought necessarily into contact with the police has been when there were disturbances in workhouses; there have been such disturbances occasionally in those parts of my district where happily there was a rural police force; and my firm persuasion is, that these workhouses might have been pulled down, or nearly destroyed, if we had not had the assistance of the police. This has occurred in different Suffolk unions, where the police has afforded the most valuable and prompt assistance.

Nathaniel Clarke Burnardiston, Esq., called in; and Examined.

N.C. Burnardiston,
Esq.

3580. *Chairman.*] ARE you the Chairman of the Quarter Sessions in the county of Essex?—I have been one of the four chairmen of quarter sessions in the county of Essex since January 1844.

3581. Had you acted as a magistrate before and subsequently to the establishment of the police?—I have acted for 28 years, I think.

3582. How long has the police been in operation in Essex?—The Essex constabulary was established in 1840.

3583. Will you state to the Committee the advantages or disadvantages which are derived from the establishment of the police in Essex?—As a magistrate and as an inhabitant, I should say, we have day by day seen the advantages, and the continual growth, I should say, of those advantages.

3584. Has that opinion of yourself and brother magistrates been recorded in any resolutions at quarter sessions?—Yes; from time to time the rate-payers have noticed the expense, and the magistrates have looked closely into it. Upon the various petitions which have been presented from time to time we have looked accurately into them; the matter has been discussed at the Court of Quarter Sessions, and resolutions have been taken at the Court of Quarter Sessions.

3585. When the rural police was first established in Essex, was not there a prejudice on the part of the rate-payers against it, on the ground of expense?—Yes, at times there have been.

3586. Do you think that feeling has decreased from experience?—I think decidedly so. I think some of the rate-payers, because they did not see actually and numerically the police walking about the county, might not think that they were sufficiently protected, or that the man could superintend the area over which he went, or that he could practically protect the property; but I think now, from the experience of the effects, the opinions are decidedly changed of many who were opposed to it.

3587. In consequence of the objections to the expense in the first instance, did you attempt to carry into effect the system of local constables under superintending constables?—We did. The idea of the magistrates was, that we had not a fair number of police constables to produce a sufficient effect. Before any

N. C. Burnardiston,
Esq.

———

17 June 1853.

increase to that number took place, the magistrates were ready, with the aid and assistance of Captain M'Hardy, in every way to choose from the parishes the best persons we could procure for local constables, to act with the then existing force. I think, at the special sessions for the appointment of these constables in the county of Essex, as many as 600 cr 700 were appointed; but though men of credit and farmers were ready to come forward and say, " I will serve this year," expecting some one else would be ready to come forward to take their turns, it failed; and I think in the following year there were not above half that number appointed; the system failed, and we could not get an efficient addition to the constabulary by local constables.

3588. You are aware that there has been a report from Captain M'Hardy, of the savings and earnings effected by the police in Essex ?—Yes; Captain M'Hardy put forth a very elaborate report.

3589 It is headed " Savings and Earnings effected by the Essex County Constabulary;" are you acquainted with the items contained in that report ?—Yes.

3590. The first item is, " Annual saving by the conveyance of prisoners, calculated from the actual expense in :839, the year preceding the establishment of the police, 991 *l.* ;" do you think tha a correct estimate ?—I believe it is fairly calculated.

3591. The next item is, " Annual saving by the inspection of weights and measures, 584 *l.* 11 *s.* 8 *d.* ;" is that correctly estimated ?—Yes, I think so; it cost the county very nearly 900 *l.* or 1,000 *l.* under the old system.

3592. Is the 584 *l.* the difference between the present cost and the cost under the old system ?—Yes.

3593. Then there is, " Annual earnings under section 17, Act 3 & 4 Vict., c. 88, viz., from Government, under orders of court, coroners, petty sessions, and other jurisdictions, 1,286 *l.* 10 *s.* 8 *d.* ;" was that sum actually paid ?—Yes, according to the table of fees under that Act of Parliament.

3594. The next item is, " Annual payment of interest, and instalment on money borrowed for the erection of police stations, which are a permanent investment for the benefit of the county, 1,450 *l.* 17 *s.* 1 *d.* ;" how is tha item made out ?—That money was borrowed, and used for the purpose of building the station-houses, which have now become the permanent property of the county.

3595. How is the cost of erecting those buildings repaid ?—The money is repaid by instalments, and when consequently that money is repaid, the station-houses will become the property of the county, producing a rental to the county, being inhabited by the superintendents and constables.

3596. The next item is, " Annual saving by the abolition of Halstead, Newport and Colchester district gaols, besides the consequent advantage of centralised prison discipline, 1,000 *l.* ;" is that an actual saving ?—We used to have the expense of those buildings, as well as the establishment of officers in those buildings, and they were very expensive, I have no doubt; I believe, if it were clearly worked out, we could show a greater saving than 1,000 *l.* ; I think it is decidedly low.

3597. Then there comes the item. " Rent paid by members of the constabulary for such parts of the police stations as are occupied by them, 332 *l.* 11 *s.* ;" that is the money actually received from the officers ?—Yes.

3598. " Annual amount of fines credited to the county rate under penal statutes where proceedings have been taken by the police, 24 *l.* ;" is that the actual amount received ? —Yes.

3599. That went to the parochial constables, or to the informers ?—The moiety of the fine payable to the constables would not go to the constables; it would go to the superannuation fund.

3600. The other moiety now would go to the county ?—To the general fund.

3601. " Annual saving in postage, by the police delivering official parcels to the magistrates and parochial authorities, 40 *l.* ;" is that too large amount, do you think ?—There are a great many precepts and orders; all the accounts are delivered quarterly, and every document of that sort is now delivered by the police, which otherwise would have been posted; I do not think that that amount is at all too large.

3602. The next item is, " Annual amount of payments to special constables, calculated from actual sums formerly paid, using as an index the average annual payments in the ten years preceding the establishment of the police, 366 *l.* 0 *s.* 6 *d.* ; is that an actual payment ?—That is according to figures; that can be proved; that is the average of ten years.

3603. " Annual saving in magistrates' clerks' fees, in consequence of the diminution

tion of business at petty sessions, calculated at a reduction of one-third on the average, although it is proved that in Chelmsford division the fees have decreased from 546 *l.* in 1842, to 304 *l.* in 1852, being a decrease of nearly one-half, 913 *l.* 14 *s.* 6 *d.*;" do you think that is a moderate estimate of saving?—It is very fairly taken; I should say there was a greater diminution, if you took the whole of the divisions through the county.

3604. " Annual saving in payments to parochial constables, by the 380 parishes, by poor-law unions, private individuals and other sources, taking as an index the average annual payments by each parish of one division, which was 10 *l.*, without considering the extra payments under the other heads mentioned, 3,800 *l.*?" —That is an item very difficult to estimate; if you look into the parish accounts, you find that for years past the sums vary very much indeed, perhaps from 1 *l.* up to 40 *l.* or 50 *l.*, taking the way in which the constables were paid; under the parochial system they expected their 5 *s.* a day, as well as all the fees and payments by the table of fees.

3605. Having gone through all these items, in your opinion, is 11,789 *l.* 10 *s.* 11 *d.* a moderate amount of saving?—Yes.

3606. Do you concur in that statement entirely?—I think the calculation is not above the mark, and is very fairly worked out.

3607. Then there are other calculations as to vagrancy, which is put at one-half, 2,550 *l.*; that must be a matter of opinion, and not a matter of fact?—Yes. I feel confident, from my own knowledge in every way, both in unions, towns and parishes where the police have acted, that an immense expense has been saved. I believe we have nearly practically annihilated vagrancy, compared to what it was before the police was established.

3608. This estimate is based upon the calculation of each vagrant costing 1 *l.*? —Yes; it is very difficult to say what is the actual saving in money.

3609. It must also be a matter of opinion as to the two items in the last part of the account as to the protection and recovery of property; you think there has been a great saving by the decrease of vagrancy, and in the protection of property, but you think in both cases it must be a matter of opinion?—I consider that the police is a preventive force, which certainly saves property immensely.

3610. To these two items, of course, you cannot speak positively?—In my own mind I have no doubt there is a great advantage; it is very difficult to give a calculation of the actual saving in figures.

3611. Have not the police been of great service in the protection of the revenue?—Yes, decidedly; we have found out that smuggled goods have passed the outer barrier, and we have frequently had occasion to pursue the parties.

3612. There is no credit taken for that?—No.

3613. Neither do the Government pay anything for it?—No; we have only within a short period had authority to act in matters connected with the revenue.

3614. Do the police act as inspectors of common lodging-houses, and inspectors of nuisances?—Some towns have not adopted them; though they have taken up the Bill of Health; in some the police have been made relieving officers for vagrants. I do not practically myself know in what way most of the towns are carrying it out.

3615. Do you think there is a great saving in prosecutions?—There has been a diminution of crime decidedly, and of late our calendars at quarter sessions have been most happily diminished.

3616. Do you think there is a great benefit derived by the owners of property from the police?—I think so, decidedly, with regard to sheep-stealing, and the higher felonies, but we cannot close our eyes to the calendar; we find some men charged with pilfering their master's corn, and so on; at the same time, I think now, from the vigilance of the police, many prisoners being detected actually in the fact at night, the labouring classes are very cautious how they attempt the more concealed crimes.

3617. Do you think a night patrol is essential for the prevention of crime?— Yes, the police is a night patrol. Many people say, " We do not see the police;" many people complain of the expense, and they say, " I do not see the policeman about." I say, " You may be quiet in your beds, but we who try the prisoners find that the man who was robbing you or your fellow-farmer has been actually detected in the night." They are often detected on a winter's evening after the people had retired, or early in the morning. I have tried criminals within this last year, where the police have actually taken people in the night. I recollect

N. C. Burnardiston,
Esq.

17 June 1853.

last year we had one or two cases of burglary, when the offenders were detected in the act of breaking in.

3618. Do you think sheep-stealing is diminished?—Immensely.

3619. Have you had gangs of sheep-stealers effectually broken up by the police?—Decidedly. When the police were first instituted, a number of dissolute men were living in the neighbourhood who, I am confident, used at certain times to steal sheep to an immense amount.

3620. Can you state any particular case in which a gang was broken up by the activity of the police?—I recollect in my own neighbourhood, Hedingham, a superintendent with his constables broke up a family who had every winter, I have no doubt, been living in a great measure by sheep-stealing. I recollect one of our superintendents, who is now governor of Carlisle gaol, Mr. Redin, by intelligence and firmness breaking up a family of sheep-stealers; he entered the house at night, and found the old father of the family actually boiling down the fat, while some of the family were out depredating; they were watched; the house was entered, and Redin took the old man, though the old man was ready with a coulter in his hand to fly at him.

3621. Was the man armed in any way?—He had a coulter down by his side. Mr. Redin being a firm man, pulled a pistol out, and said, " You are my prisoner;" the family were desperate characters.

3622. Were the sons taken?—I think two or three of the family were convicted. I believe, since then, that part of the country has been very free from sheep-stealing.

3623. Do you suppose that would have been effected by parochial constables? —I think not. In that district, if the farmers find they lose their sheep, and they have active sons, they lie out and watch.

3624. Mr. *Philipps*.] You said that there was a marked diminution in those crimes which could fairly be cognisable by the police, but not of those crimes of which the police could not be supposed to have cognisance, crimes involving breaches of trust?—I say of late, though crime, generally speaking, has diminished, still we find farmers are robbed by being pilfered by their servants of small quantities of corn carried away in their pockets, and so on. I have no doubt those crimes are diminished by the vigilance of the police, who know the characters of those men. I tried a case this year, where the fact of the man spending a good deal of money at a public-house, and in various other ways, created a suspicion in the master's mind that there was something wrong; a watch was kept, and that man was found actually coming from his master's premises with the corn upon him.

3625. *Chairman*.] Do you think the powers given to the chief constable under the Constabulary Acts are more than sufficient for the proper performance of his duties?—No; I think under the Act of Parliament, and the way he is appointed by the magistrates, he ought to have that power.

3626. Do you think the chief constable should have the power of appointment and dismissal of all the officers under him?—Yes; he ought to have the selection of the material he is to work with; he ought to exercise his own judgment whether such a man is fit for the service. If he selects a bad man he is responsible for so doing. I think he ought to use his own judgment.

3627. Mr. *Howard*.] Have cases come to your knowledge of improper conduct on the part of the police?—If by chance a policeman has been guilty of drunkenness or any misconduct, it has come immediately, by a report through the superintendent, to the knowledge of the chief constable, and that man has been suspended directly.

3628. You think, if there is misconduct, it is sure to be known and punished? —I think so, looking at the way in which the Essex force has been managed. If you appoint a good chief constable to work the force, in the same manner as the captain of a ship, or the colonel of a regiment, the misconduct of any man under his command comes to his knowledge immediately. I have known cases where knowledge of misconduct has come to the chief constable, and the man has been suspended before it was notified to me that such a man had misbehaved himself.

3629. *Chairman*.] Do you think there would be any advantage in having a police committee of magistrates?—We have a police committee for general purposes, namely, with regard to building station-houses, and working out the minutiae; we have always a standing committee of magistrates.

3630. Mr. *Burroughes*.] Is that committee of magistrates appointed to revise the

N.C. *Burnardiston,*
Esq.

17 June 1853.

the accounts?—They look through every item of account, and report those accounts to the court of quarter sessions quarterly, having examined all the vouchers and all the accounts previously. The police committee, I think, meets monthly; I live 25 miles off; I have not acted upon what is called the police committee generally. But I do not think their control should extend beyond the accounts; I would not give the committee any control over the chief constable. The court of quarter sessions appoints the chief constable, and he is answerable to the court of quarter sessions.

3631. Is there time at the quarter sessions to look into the minutiæ of the accounts?—There is always a standing committee, and under the Act of Parliament the chief constable makes his returns. There is a monthly return, besides the quarterly return, describing the force, and that committee is always ready to answer any question, or to hear any complaint.

3632. Mr. *Philipps.*] Does the police committee interfere at all with the movements of the men, or does it leave the distribution entirely to the chief constable? —The chief constable makes a report of the distribution of his force, but the magistrates do not interfere with him. When a good officer, either a private or a superintendent, has been some time in a neighbourhood, and notice has been given to the man that he is to remove to other quarters, I have had a brother magistrate and other persons come and say, "I wish you would interfere; Captain M'Hardy is going to move this good man away." I have said, "Depend upon it, Captain M'Hardy has some good reason for removing the man; I dare say he is going to put the man into a locality where his services will be more useful; he will send another man." I have declined to interfere in such cases. I recollect a case, when Mr. Oakley was moved from Castle Hedingham to Chelmsford, a magistrate came to me, and said, "Captain M'Hardy is going to move Oakley." I said, "That may be, but the Captain is responsible for what he does; I dare say he has some good reason for it, and I shall not interfere."

3633. You think any interference on the part of the magistrates with the movement of the men would be prejudicial to the efficiency of the force?—I think it cramps a chief constable in the same way as control would cramp the colonel of a regiment.

3634. *Chairman.*] You think unlimited confidence should be placed in the chief constable?—Yes; let the county choose a really good chief constable; if you do not, you cannot place confidence in him.

3635. Do not you think the county is responsible for the selection of a proper chief constable?—Yes.

3636. Having selected a good chief constable, do not you think unlimited confidence should be placed in him?—I think so.

3637. Mr. *Philipps.*] Have the magistrates been called upon to act as arbiters between the chief constable and the policemen in cases of alleged grievances?— I do not recollect any case at this moment. Perhaps a man has said to me, "I hope, sir, I shall get something, I have been so many years in the force." I have said, "The chief constable knows your merits, and he will do what is right." I may say this, I have frequently been talking with men who have been in the force, who have left the force and taken other occupations, but I never heard any man say that he had not been treated in the most fair and open way possible. If there is any real grievance, I think it would come before the magistrates immediately.

Edwin Chadwick, Esq., c.b., called in; and Examined.

E. Chadwick, Esq.,
c.b.

3638. *Chairman.*] WERE you one of the Commissioners in 1839 who were appointed to inquire into the best means for establishing a constabulary force?— I was. In 1835, when we were carrying out the organisation of the parishes into unions under the Poor Law Amendment Act, there were frequent riots, instigated, as was ascertained, by those who thought they would lose money by the change of system; as by small farmers, who expected they would have to give more wages on the discontinuance of the allowance system, and by small shopkeepers, who expected the loss of the parish supplies. There were riots in Suffolk, Sussex, and several other counties. On these occasions, we were requested to send down a force for the preservation of the peace; and the ground of the application invariably was, the utter inefficiency of the local constabulary. On these occasions it was my duty to go to the Home Office, and I generally had to communicate with the Home Secretary to make arrangements for sending a sufficient force, generally of police, sometimes of military, or of coast guardsmen.

E. Chadwick, Esq.,
c. b.

17 June 1853.

This experience of the local deficiencies of means for the preservation of the peace, (of which indeed we had previous experience in the agricultural riots and fires of 1830) as well as for the ordinary service of a constabulary in various counties, appeared to me to make it my duty to represent to Lord John Russell, who was then the Home Secretary, the importance of the issuing a Commission to inquire whether the like deficiencies prevailed throughout the country. In consequence of these representations a Commission was issued in 1836 to the present Speaker of the House of Commons, the late lamented public officer, Sir Charles Rowan, and to myself. The result of the investigations of that Commission was the recommendation of the establishment of a paid constabulary or police force in the counties of England and Wales. It was one of the primary conditions of that recommendation, that by whatsoever county it was adopted, it should be a constabulary for the whole county, including the boroughs. We stated emphatically, " That any administration of a paid constabulary on a less scale than for a whole county does not comprehend a sufficiently wide basis for ultimate and complete efficiency and economy, either as to the county regarded separately, or in its general relation to the rest of the kingdom."

3639. Have you had occasion to observe the practical operation of the 2 & 3 Vict. c. 93, which is commonly called the Rural Police Act, since it was passed?—I have had frequent occasion; I was much consulted by magistrates about its introduction into several counties, and I have, of course, watched its operation with great interest. Moreover, in taking part in the consideration of the new local administrative organisation of nearly 200 towns, required for the sanitary measures under the Public Health Act, I have had continued practical occasion to observe the deficiencies of organisation and action of the police force in towns for sanitary as well as other purposes.

3640. Have the results of that Act been in accordance with the views and the expectations of the Commissioners?—They have. I mean that, considering the measure has been carried out partially, and exclusively of the proper centres of the working of a police—the towns;—the working of the fragmentitious county forces, has, on the whole, been much more satisfactory than we anticipated.

3641. In what respect?—Most prominently first, in the immediate and marked difference between those districts where there is a police, and those where there is none; and, in the next place, although we were prepared for the introduction of much eventual economy by the action of a properly constituted police force, we were not prepared for the extent to which even the partial county forces instituted have been, by the collateral services which they have rendered, been made nearly, if not entirely, self-supporting.

3642. You think it is a defective measure, because it has not been uniform?— Yes; because it was adopted in only a part of the counties; because it was not constituted uniformly in the several counties where it was adopted; because it was not arranged for concurrent action with contiguous counties or upon any general system; but, above all, because within the counties, the most important centres and portions of a properly acting county force, the town forces, are left separate and uncombined; which state of separation commonly means, a state of hostility as well as of inaction for any general purpose. I am clearly of opinion that, if the proper amalgamation of the borough forces were effected with the rest of the county forces, the proportionate expenses might be lessened, whilst, without any increase of expense, the efficiency and public service of the force would be more than doubled. I am very confident that, even now, if there were an amalgamation of the forces existing in some of the counties where the County Constabulary Act has been adopted, very small, if any, additional forces would be required, most probably none eventually, for the purposes of penal administration. To take the example of the county of Lancaster: there are now in the county only 355 policemen, but there are, in Manchester, between four and five hundred; in Liverpool, upwards of 700, and in the whole of the county, according to the last returns, a force of nearly two thousand policemen. By the last returns there were 1,393 policemen in the boroughs, and in the whole county, 1,918 men. There were originally 500 policemen in the county under the County Constabulary Act, but at the spring sessions of 1842 the magistrates, acting no doubt on such information as their own districts, exclusive of the larger towns, gave them, which was such as the event displayed, determined to reduce the force to 350, and on the first day of the month the reduction took place. From the 9th to the 12th of the same month there was a general outbreak in the towns, which overspread the whole of the rural districts, put all property at the mercy of the mobs, which

only

E. Chadwick, Esq.,
c. b.

17 June 1853.

only wanted leaders with ability commensurate with the powers at their disposal to have done wide-spread and irreparable mischief. Now I was in the county at the time, and observed the outbreak as a constabulary force commissioner; and I had no doubt whatsoever, that had the whole of the force in the county been under one proper organisation, that every large town, which was then driven to rely on military force, would have been secure without any addition, and that the outbreak would have been repressed at its commencement. To advert to a more recent and smaller instance. The borough of Blackburn had been under the county police force, when 22 policemen were stationed there. It obtained a town council, when they reduced the force to 11. At the recent election, riots, disgraceful to the whole country, occurred; the town was in possession of the mob, and it became necessary to send for a military force. Now the 22 county policemen, if they had remained there, would, in all probability, have suppressed the riots at the outset. But if they had not sufficed, a hundred more might have been sent, as similar forces were sent with effect to Bury and Wigan from the existing county force.

3643. You think there is no doubt that the non-adoption of the Police Act in many counties in England is a cause of expense?—Yes; it is a cause of expense for indifferent and bad service; for a force which is paid by fees and emoluments for apprehensions, and has an interest in facilitating the commission of offences which lead to emoluments, rather than in preventing them;—of expense for the maintenance of the hordes of delinquents and mendicants at large who obtain more than honest labourers—of expense also for the maintenance of many thousands of habitual delinquents equal to a large army, always in confinement in prisons; but whose careers are preventible—and it is a cause of that insecurity of property which, amongst persons in the lower conditions of life, makes it unsafe to have or to hold moveable property.

3644. Are you of opinion, that a uniform system of police throughout the kingdom would render the expense of the force less in each county, than if partially adopted, as at present it is?—Yes; the same effects could be produced at much less cost. In the opinion of my colleagues and myself, the action of an efficient police for the rural districts must centre in the towns. In the towns the hand must be placed, from which fingers may be extended and withdrawn according to the need. I have had frequent practical observations of such extensions into the rural districts, and of withdrawals from them. We have had local applications for such bodies, as nine or ten, or five or six policemen, to be sent to large villages which were in state of chronic disorder and lawlessness. After a time the disorder has been reduced; then it has been announced that the police force might be reduced, and half has been withdrawn; two policemen, or one policeman was found to suffice for the permanent service, where four or six were required in the first instance. Without adopting implicitly these proportions of reductions, which the pressure of the whole expense would make too immediate, and without regard to important collateral sources against less gross and less alarming evils, yet I should have the support of much concurrent evidence, in saying that, in the first instance, a larger force would be required for most rural districts, than would be needed eventually for the purpose of penal administration. After the large villages, or the beershops and the outlying common lodging-houses had been brought into order, it is possible that, in thinly populated rural districts, the contiguity to the police station in the town, and the liability to immediate extension and action from it, would suffice for prevention as well as repression. These economies of force, and the varying adaptations required, are all obstructed by the disconnection of forces. I have examined the police arrangements in Essex with some interest; and I am satisfied that if the borough forces there were amalgamated with the county force, from the better watching and regulation of the common lodging-houses there would be a more complete diminution of vagrancy than has yet been effected even there (and by extension of the concurrent action on the whole lines of vagrancy through several counties, the evil might possibly be entirely extirpated); whilst the pecuniary savings in all the items enumerated in the evidence of Mr. Barnardiston, the chairman of the Essex Quarter Sessions, might be increased.

3645. Did you recommend, in your report, that the system of police should be under general supervision in London?—Yes; to obtain the efficiency and economy of general action against wide-spread and shifting evil there must be a general supervision, and that administrative supervision and direction, like the

E. Chadwick, Esq.,
C. B.

17 June 1853.

legislative supervision of Parliament, must be in the metropolis. But I would here beg leave to state a modification of the views set forth in our first report. We proposed that when the Act was adopted for any county, and adopted, as we contemplated, for the county in its entirety—for the towns as well as for the rural districts—that it should be by an extension of the metropolitan police force, and supplied from thence with a detachment of trained constables, and appointed serjeants and inspectors. It was then, however, our opinion that it would be eventually found necessary to direct a national police force, whensoever it was adopted, from several distinct centres, each centre comprising several counties. At the time we made our report there was no other trained force known in England, to which we might refer as to what was meant, or as a resource for trained men. But the circumstances have much changed in that respect. Moreover, the special adaptations of the metropolitan force and its habits of action, which render it less fit for provincial service, have increased. The late Sir Charles Rowan expressed to me his view in concurrence with me, that it would now be better to leave the metropolitan force as a special district, by itself, of course under general supervision in common with other districts, rather than attempt its extension. His successor, Captain Hay, has expressed to me a similar opinion which I would submit as of much weight; inasmuch as he first became connected with the police in consequence of the efficient part he took in the organisation of some forces for rural districts. The consultation of local feelings and conveniences, and (within proper limits) of the feelings of private individuals, is necessary to conciliate the support required for the efficient action of any police. This support for direct police purposes, as we have shown in our report, was largely obtainable by collateral local services. The seaboard counties, for example, would require very special arrangements for maritime traffic and the prevention of wrecking; and Captain M'Hardy has rendered an important service by the adaptations he has made, proceeding upon the basis of the experience of the coast guard service, which, for such districts is better for the purpose than that which happens to be influenced by purely military habits. We, however, contemplated the drill of the county constabulary, and its use as a defensive force, or in aid of one; and the importance of that view has been made subsequently more distinct and prominent.

3646. Do you think, with a view of saving expense, and giving increased co-operation, it would be practicable or desirable to place more than one county under the same head or chief constable?—We thought so then, and the reasons for doing so have greatly increased since we made our first report; namely, from the rapid extension and close ramification of railway communication, which, in truth, for the purposes of communication, brings four counties within the scope of one heretofore; and to those means of communication must be added another, namely, the electric telegraph, which may also, I have no doubt, be made wonderfully subservient to a general police.

3647. There was a great mass of valuable evidence in the report of the Commissioners, which led to the recommendations which you have described for the establishment of a police force: can you state the leading points in that evidence which led the Commissioners to that conclusion?—The leading points, so far as I can state them, were the general state of crime; in relation to which, it was shown that almost every doctrine current as popular principles of legislation were widely erroneous. Thus, as to the causes of crime, the prevalent notion amongst writers and politicians was, that "Poverty was the mother of crime;" that habitual depredation chiefly arose from the pressure of unavoidable distress, or from the assumed pressure of population on the means of subsistence; whereas, we found the operation of such causes as unavoidable distress in impelling persons of previously honest habits to crime so rare, as to be almost unknown, and that, whatever wages were obtainable in the lower walks of labour by honest industry, that in consequence of the facilities for escaping detection or pursuit, much more was usually obtained by depredations committed by persons of the same class. In respect to the number or amount of crimes committed, we showed that the inferences derived from statistical returns of criminal commitments and convictions were widely erroneous, and that crime prevailed often to a far greater extent even than policemen were aware of, or magistrates were informed upon. Our principal conclusions were as follow: and I would recall the attention of the Committee to the evidence on which they were founded, as being as applicable now to those districts where there has been no new police force established, as they were then, not excepting the examples of the practice of wrecking. (The Witness delivered in a Paper.)

Vide Appendix.

3648. Do

E. Chadwick, Esq.
c. b.

17 June 1853.

3648. Do you think that the police have been the means of materially decreasing the expense of prosecutions and the number of prosecutions?—In several places, where a tolerably complete force has been established, there have been striking exemplifications of how much may be done for the reduction of expense. On the general topic of the expense of the force, I must be permitted to say that very large additions would be needed to the existing expenditure for fragmentitious forces. We estimated that 450,000 l. would give a police force of about 8,000 men for England and Wales, or one policeman to every 1,700 of the population. Since 1839 the population has largely increased; allowing for that increase, and for some other contingencies, the estimate then made would be available now. But there are already 6,770 policemen in towns and in the counties under the County Police Act. The total expenditure for these separate and fragmentitious forces is already within one-ninth of what we estimated; it is 418,000 l., of which 228,000 l. is expended by boroughs, and about 190,000 l. by counties; and to these amounts may be added the expenditure for prosecutions.

3649. What is the amount paid for prosecutions by the Government?—The amount now paid for England and Wales is 237,000 l., and for Scotland it is 62,000 l. To meet any probable financial obstacles, the local ratepayers, or the parties locally interested, might well ask, as a means to the adoption of a general and efficient police, to have the application of that large amount of money changed from the prosecution of crime to the prevention of crime. By the improvement of the procedure conducted by a properly-trained police, the expenses of prosecutions would be reduced, I believe, one half. What is of primary importance to the efficient action of a police, is the diminution of the annoyances of prosecutions to parties and witnesses, which occasions the reluctance to give information for fear of being compelled to attend and prosecute, and other annoyances which prevail and militate against the operations of a police to a greater extent than is known by those who have not paid close attention to the subject. By a good county police these annoyances would also be diminished. By the application of the money to a preventive police, an effect would be produced which would be felt and appreciated by the population, who would be largely freed from the expense and from the crime which they are now called upon to prosecute. For this proposed application of the expenditure there would be an efficient check in the power of the Government. At present there is little or no check on the expenditure for prosecutions.

3650. You mean, that now, the expenses of prosecutions being paid by the Government, there is no check upon the cost of the prosecutions?—Yes.

3651. But if they were still paid by the county, and the money paid by the Government, namely 300,000 l., were given to the police, the counties would then be parties concerned in reducing the costs of the prosecutions?—Yes; the motive which now exists—which is a most dangerous, and indeed, improper motive, which exists on the part of the legal adviser of the magistrates to get up prosecutions and urge commitments for the sake of emolument—would be withdrawn. I do not apply these observations to the expenditure for prosecutions in Scotland. I had occasion to examine the penal procedure in Scotland, which I found had many features which we intended to propose for consideration and adoption as improvements in the penal administration and procedure in England; though in all cases the proper prosecuting officers should be paid by salaries, and not by fees.

3652. While the Government would be no losers by appropriating this 300,000 l. a year, as you suggest, towards the payment of the police force, the counties, on the other hand, might be gainers from a decrease in the expense of prosecutions by the appointment of a good police force?—Undoubtedly; if the 300,000 l. now paid by the Government were added to the 418,000 l. now paid locally, and all extensively misapplied, for the establishment of an efficient police force, beside such measures as Lord Shaftesbury's Act for the regulation of common lodging-houses, the first measure perhaps which has reached the lowest depths of society, we were prepared to report on other measures, which could only be executed by the agency of an improved and intelligent police, under educated and responsible direction: mendicancy, vagrancy, and habitual out-door depredation would be suppressed; a state of things would be producible of which the Legislature or the public can have no conception, even from the best of the police forces now instituted. In respect to the estimates as to the force needed, I would observe that we calculated on the aid of the relieving officers, and some others of the union officers, as auxiliaries of the police. On consideration of the

E. Chadwick, Esq.,
c. b.

17 June 1853.

working of the arrangements promoted by Captain M'Hardy in Essex, I should now recommend, as the preferable course, that the police should, in cases of vagrancy, act as relieving officers, and as auxiliaries to the officers engaged in poor-law administration. In the change of the application of the grants of money from the Consolidated Fund now paid in aid of the expenses of local administration, I should, from my own knowledge, recommend to be included all the sums now paid for poor-law purposes (except those towards the payment of schoolmasters), which, accompanied as it is by tests as to the fitness of the masters, serves to ensure a better order of education to the classes most in need of it, and considered in a police view, is really an application of money of a highly preventive character.

3653. It was stated in your report that the average career of a thief was five years; do not you think that a good police would be a great saving to the country, by shortening the career of thieves and depredators?—Yes; and by shortening their careers to drive them into honest courses. For that purpose it will suffice not that there should be absolute certainty of conviction in every case, however desirable in itself, but that a larger proportion of offences committed should be made known to the police, and the offenders pursued and prosecuted. A man who should start the career of a highwayman might even now probably commit some 12 or 20 offences, and if he were not subjected to a particular pursuit, like the case of a murder, or crime attended by shocking circumstances and exciting public attention, he might escape. But those chances, with a mounted patrol and turnpikes, are too narrow, and even under the existing arrangements, though absolute certainty of conviction is by no means attained, that species of offence is prevented. In the course of our investigations we were tendered, in confidence, the evidence of persons who had formerly followed particular lines of depredation, house-breaking, for example, but who had, on the new police coming into action, given up their careers; not that the house-breaker might not now commit a certain number of burglaries and probably escape, but that the chances were so much narrowed, the labour to evade the police was so great, that they said the careers "did not pay," or pay better than ordinary and recognised occupations, and accordingly the illegal courses were abandoned. Crimes of passion, the offences of a domestic character, must be met by religious and moral training, and by those sanitary measures which prevent the heaping of the population of both sexes together, in such a manner as to frustrate all the effects of such training. But all of what may be termed the out-door and professional delinquency; all that is pursued as an occupation; all the crime committed by persons who rise in the morning to obtain by depredation the means of the day's or the week's subsistence, which must be obtained by numerous repetitions of crimes for long periods of time; all juvenile delinquency and mendicancy, and vagrancy, are within hand. I am confident that the whole of it may be suppressed, though the suppression, or the prevention, more properly speaking, would, no doubt, require various measures and considerable labour proportioned to the magnitude of the evil.

3654. In your opinion, would not the adoption of a uniform system of police throughout the kingdom be a great advantage, both in an economical and in a moral point of view?—Allow me to give my answer in the following terms of our Report: "That the pecuniary saving from the services of such a force would be considerable; that independently of the saving to individuals of the greater proportion of the money or produce now taken by habitual depredators, there would be much saving effected on upwards of two millions of money now expended chiefly in the cost of repression and of punishment in various ways; amongst others in the maintenance of delinquents in gaols, in transports and in the penal colonies, as well as in the prevention of frauds upon the revenue. The principles embodied in our recommendations being based on extensive experience, we feel confident that, however they may for a time be impeded by adverse interests, those interests and the prejudices engendered by them will yield before the light of future experience, which will lead to the ultimate adoption of measures on the principles of those we propose; if one uniform and trained force be efficiently directed to the prevention or repression of crime, we cannot doubt of success. What has been done partially in particular places, may be done generally and more completely throughout the country, by the more efficient application of the like means. If a constabulary force were well appointed, and trained on a uniform system, and were placed under trained and responsible direction for the whole country, it would, we are assured, soon enable all Your Majesty's subjects to sleep under a feeling of security from midnight plunder and violence; it would give protection to the industrious classes in the enjoyment of property,

perty, and by enhancing its value, create additional motives to industry and frugality; it would give freedom and security to travellers on the roads, and humane succour to natives, and hospitality to strangers thrown by shipwreck on our coasts; it would free the country from mendicancy and vagrancy, and the various evils that follow in their course; it would free the industry of the manufacturing labourers, and increase the inducements to the investment of capital by protecting them from lawless violence; it would tend to secure the people from the alarms and dangers of riotous disturbances of the peace, by affording a powerful means of repressing them without the risk of military execution and bloodshed, without putting hostile parties in array against each other, without engendering animosities by arming neighbour to conflict with neighbour, and master with servant. All this, and much more beneficent service, it might be made to render at an immediate expense of less than one-fourth of the sum recently saved by one amendment in local administration; or, as we feel confident, all these great objects may be accomplished with an ultimate saving of the whole expense from upwards of two millions of money now chiefly expended on what have been proved before Committees of both Houses of Parliament, and pronounced by them to be ineffective or demoralising systems of punishment."

3655. Where the Rural Police Act has been adopted, do you think those opinions have been fully borne out by the results?—Yes, fragmentitious and imperfect as those means have been; but I would submit a topic not touched upon as deserving of the grave consideration of the Committee. We have now constantly under confinement, in the prisons of Great Britain, a force of able-bodied men, equal to an army of about 30,000, numerically greater than the British force which fought at the battle of Waterloo. A large proportion of this delinquent force consists of depredators who, at the termination of a long career in this country, will be shifted and disposed of by transportation to the colonies. Now resistance is being made to this shifting of the evil and to colonisation with selected delinquents, and this resource for our population bred up in crime must be eventually closed. This resistance will eventually succeed; these numbers of convicts, heretofore regularly shifted from this country, will be discharged with the almost certainty that the greater proportion of them must renew their careers, which they will have extensively open to them for renewal, unless preventive measures of a general and complete nature be adopted.

3656. Would not that be balanced by the great amount of emigration that has taken place?—To some extent that may be so; but it is to be considered that the greater proportion of the discharged convicts are about the last persons who will be able to obtain the means of emigration. Superior officers of police and very competent persons view the prospect of an unguarded change of practice with very serious alarm.

3657. Mr. *Philipps.*] How would you propose the rates to be levied for the support of the police; by an uniform rate on the county or in districts?—By rates in districts. The graduation of the rates was a subject upon which we found a little difficulty at the time; our conclusion was, that distinctions should be made, and settled upon local inquiry between rural and town districts.

3658. *Chairman.*] Would you also make a distinction between rural and manufacturing districts?—Yes, that would be equivalent.

3659. Mr. *Philipps.*] Are you acquainted with the mode of rating in Staffordshire, with reference to which evidence was given by Mr. Talbot; in the pottery district, the rate is 5 d. in the pound, in the mining district 3 d. in the pound, and in the rural district 1 d. in the pound?—Yes, I am aware of the grounds for distinctions. These are questions about rating which might be accommodated by previous local inquiries and adaptations, as is done now in the introduction of the Public Health Act.

3660. Do you think there would be any difficulty in defining the lines of demarcation between those districts?—No; but to do it satisfactorily, it must be done by an independent authority; the parties interested are the worst judges for the adjustment of burthens. There is one reason for a distinction with respect to the towns, namely, in that large and crowded towns there are many services required from the police in maintaining order, in street-keeping, in meeting fires, accidents, and calamities, and a variety of services which are little if at all needed in the rural districts. I apprehend, if you were to prevent entirely, supposing such a thing possible, all crime in the metropolis, that for a great variety of public and private services, which would be probably extended, a large staff of police would still be needed.

3661. Mr. *Howard.*] Can you suggest any means by which the jealousy between

E. Chadwick, Esq., c. b.

17 June 1853.

E. Chadwick, Esq.,
c. b.

17 June 1853.

between the town and county authorities, with reference to the appointment of the police, could be overcome?—I have always found that there really was less local jealousy and difficulty on the part of one local authority in giving up power to a Government authority than to another local authority. The towns would less readily give up their authority to the county magistrates, or the county magistrates to the towns. In other administrative changes which I have been called upon to take part in preparing, I have generally advised as a principle, local initiation with central supervision. If the change in question be impartially and dispassionately considered, and the necessity of shifting high constables and forces from district to district, and varying their numbers as circumstances require, and the need for economy as well as efficiency of extended concurrent action be kept in view, it will be admitted that the principle of administrative action will here require to be reversed, to central initiation and local supervision. We have shown that that local supervision and aid is essential to the efficient action of a police. I must say, however, that the appointments of high constables to the county forces have, on the whole, been as good as may reasonably be expected to be made by any authority. I think these appointments, and the manner in which they have been made, are highly honourable to the county magistrates.

3662. *Chairman.*] You think that those appointments have answered the expectations of the Commissioners who have recommended them?—In a very high degree. There is one observation I may be permitted to make: I think, in respect to the metropolitan police, I have seen reason to believe that it would be improved if there were more men of education as officers; I think it was impossible to get any other service at the time; I believe, however, that the men would act better, and that the action would be better directed, if the force comprised more educated superior officers.

Mr. *David Smith*, called in; and Examined.

Mr. *D. Smith.*

3663. *Chairman.*] WHAT are you?—A superintending Constable in Oxfordshire.

3664. When were you appointed?—Two years back.

3665. What is your salary?—£. 110 a-year.

3666. Is there a superintending constable in each division of Oxfordshire?—Yes.

3667. Is there a lock-up in each division?—No; I have got one, but it is not a general thing throughout the county.

3668. Under whose care is the lock-up in your division?—In mine.

3669. Did you ever serve in any police force before?—In the Essex county constabulary, for 10 years.

3670. What assistance have you in the detection or in the pursuit of criminals in your division?—The parish constabulary.

3671. Do you find them efficient for the purpose?—Not at all.

3672. How many parishes are there in your district?—Thirty. There are between 60 and 70 parish constables. I consider myself, that six of the Essex county constabulary that I had under me previous to coming to Oxfordshire would be equal to the 70 parish constables now under me.

3673. Can you give the Committee any opinion as to the cost of those 70 parish constables individually to the county?—No, I cannot exactly do so; some of them are pretty well paid.

3674. Mr. *Howard.*] Have not you anybody to assist you, except parish constables?—No, I have not.

3675. *Chairman.*] Would the cost of those constables be put too high, if it were put at 10 *l.* a piece?—I think they cost about 10 *l.* a piece to the parishes.

3676. By indirect payment?—Yes.

3677. That would amount, at 10 *l.* a year each, to 700 *l.*?—Yes.

3678. What would your six policemen cost?—About 60 *l.* each.

3679. Should you want horses for those six men?—Only one for myself.

3680. Should not you want horses and carts for your six men to make them efficient?—Only for each division; I should only want a horse and cart for the conveyance of prisoners.

3681. What would be the cost of a horse and cart?—About 40 *l.* a year.

3682. Then the account of the expense would stand thus, according to your showing: the 70 parish constables, at 10 *l.* each, would cost 700 *l.* a year; your six policemen would cost 360 *l.*, and your horse and cart 40 *l.*, which makes just

400 *l.*?—

oo *l.*?—Yes. For the conveyance of prisoners in the county of Oxford, the arochial constable receives 9 *d.* a mile for each prisoner, and 5 *s.* a day. I am stant 20 miles from the county gaol, and that amounts to 1 *l.* for each prisoner.

3683. Mr. *Burroughes.*] Do you include the conveyance of prisoners in the 700 *l.*? —No.

3684. Consequently, the expense of the conveyance of the prisoners will be extra the 700 *l.* a year ?—Yes.

3685. Mr. *Howard.*] What are the expenses which you include in the 10 *l.*?— Payments to constables for serving summonses and warrants. That is a rough calculation ; I should consider 10 *l.* is the average.

3686. *Chairman.*] There is also their payment for assisting in the apprehension of offenders, and different things ?—Yes.

3687. Are the constables paid by bills by the overseers of the parishes ; those bills may vary from 5 *l.* to 10 *l.*?—Yes.

3688. You think 10 *l.* a year is not more than the average cost ?—I think not.

3689. You think it would be less, rather than more ?—I should say so.

3690. Considering the efficiency of the rural police, as compared with the inefficiency, as you have described, of the parochial constables, which system do you think is the cheapest ?—In my opinion, the rural constabulary is the cheapest of the two, taking everything into consideration.

3691. Do you find the parish constabulary generally efficient ?— Not at all.

3692. Are they willing, as far as they can, to render you assistance ?—They are willing, as far as they can, but they are not adapted for police purposes.

3693. Do you think their habits and occupations render them unsuitable for the purpose ?—Yes, some of them can neither read nor write. Some time ago I had occasion to place a warrant in the hands of a constable ; he asked me what it was ; I told him to look at it again ; he did, and he said he could not read it. I had no effectual means of discharging him ; my only remedy was to report him at the next annual re-election.

3694. If you had a better class of parish constables, or more educated men, they might be small shopkeepers, might they not ?—Yes.

3695. Would it not be inconvenient to them to be taken from their businesses to perform the duties of constables ?—Yes.

3696. Their time is a money value to them ?—Yes.

3697. Would it not be a considerable tax upon them to be obliged to leave their businesses ?—Yes.

3698. If you get an inferior class of men, they are unfit for the duty ?— Wholly.

3699. Have you the means, as superintending constable, of punishing the paro-chial constables for neglect of duty ?—No, not effectually.

3700. Could not you lay an information before the magistrates ?—I always do so, and they are punished, but not immediately ; I make a memorandum, and bring it before them at the annual re-election of constables.

3701. Have you any night patrols for the prevention of crime ?—Not one.

3702. Do you think your presence in that district, as superintending constable, renders the parochial constables more efficient ?—I do, to a certain extent ; they are not at all efficient, and never can be under that system.

3703. Have any of the boroughs or towns in Oxfordshire separate police forces ?—Yes.

3704. What are those boroughs ?—There is the small borough of Chipping Norton, which is in my division ; the population is about 3,000.

3705. Are they under your control ?—They are ; I have got the borough of Chipping Norton.

3706. Are there any boroughs not under your control ?—Not in my division.

3707. Are there in the county ?—Yes, there is Banbury, Woodstock, and the city of Oxford.

3708. Do you know, of your own knowledge, whether the superintending con-stables have ever rendered any assistance in those boroughs ; have you ever been called upon to go there ?—Frequently.

3709. Into what boroughs have you been ?—Into the boroughs of Banbury and Woodstock, which is a very small borough.

3710. Are those boroughs out of your division ?—Yes.

3711. From your experience in the police in the county of Essex, do you think

.Mr. D. Smith.

17 June 1853.

property is much more efficiently protected than it is in Oxfordshire?—I decidedly do.

3712. Did you ever hear any complaint on the part of the rate-payers of the want of increased protection?—No, I think not.

3713. You think they are satisfied with things as they are?—I think they have been more satisfied since the appointment of the superintending constables.

3714. You think the superintending constables, at all events, are useful as police officers, as far as their individual services go?—Yes.

3715. Can you state any other duties which you recollect than those strictly belonging to the police which were performed in Essex?—I was relieving officer of vagrants.

3716. What was the course you adopted with regard to vagrants?—The vagrants made application to me for relief: I gave them an order, or otherwise refused them; I examined them minutely before I would give them an order, and if I found they were not in want of relief, I at once refused the order.

3717. Do you think there was a greater disinclination on the part of vagrants to apply to you, knowing you to be a police officer, than if you had been simply a relieving officer?—I do.

3718. Therefore you think the employment of police as assistant relieving officers acted as a moral check upon vagrancy?—Very great indeed; in the year 1849 I was inspector of police at Orsett, Essex, and was also assistant relieving officer of vagrants for the Orsett Union; I reduced their numbers in that year from 2,542 to 51, and the cost of relief from 63 *l.* 11 *s.* to 1 *l* 5 *s.* 6 *d.*

3719. Have you many vagrants in Oxfordshire?—Yes, a great many.

3720. You have not the same means of checking vagrancy with parochial constables as you have with efficient paid police officers?—Certainly not.

3721. Has vagrancy been on the increase, do you think, since your appointment?—On the increase; I think there is a great deal of it at the present time.

3722. Do you think, from your experience as a police officer for many years, that vagrancy is one of the great sources of crime?—I do.

3723. Have the counties adjoining Oxfordshire any rural police?—Gloucestershire, Worcestershire, and Northamptonshire.

3724. Does your division join Gloucestershire?—It does.

3725. Do you think the effect of having an efficient rural police in Gloucestershire is to drive a certain number of bad characters over the border into your division?—I have found it so.

2726. Mr. *Howard.*] In other unions, where the policemen were not assistant relieving officers, there you find there were more vagrants?—A great many more.

Mr. *George Martin* was called in; and Examined.

Mr. G. Martin.

3727. *Chairman.*] WHAT are you?—I am Superintendent of the G. Division of the Metropolitan Police in Clerkenwell.

3728. Were you sent into Wales at the time of the Rebecca riots?—Yes.

3729. What did you find the state of the country when you went there?—There was very great disorder; there were regularly organised gangs breaking down the turnpike-gates all over the country, and there was no police of any kind whatever, except one policeman at Carmarthen, and two or three at Haverfordwest.

3730. Did you receive any assistance from the local constables?—No.

3731. Did you take any men with you?—Yes; I went into Carmarthenshire with 22 men; I went into Pembrokeshire with a party of 100; I took a detachment of 32 men to be stationed in Pembroke; two serjeants and 30 men.

3732. Mr. *Howard.*] Were you mounted?—I had a horse.

3733. *Chairman.*] What time were you there?—Ten months.

3734. What counties were you in?—Pembrokeshire. I was in Carmarthenshire previously to going to Pembrokeshire.

3735. Was there any rural police in either of those counties?—No, not in Carmarthenshire; there has been a rural police since established for the county of Carmarthen.

3736. Was that force established immediately after the disturbances?—Immediately; and I think chiefly in consequence of the gate-breaking.

3737. Were you ever employed anywhere else as a detective officer?—Yes, I was at Huddersfield in 1837.

Mr. G. Martin.

17 June 1853.

3738. In consequence of what?—In consequence of an application being made to the Secretary of State, I went down with 12 men; there was great excitement in opposition to the poor laws; a very serious disturbance took place; the Riot Act was read, and several of my men got much injured, and myself as well. We had a great many special constables sworn in, about 400; we had a very serious fight, and the special constables ran away, with the exception of one only who remained with us.

3739. They were not injured, were they?—They did not stop long enough.

3740. Then the whole of the brunt of resisting this riot was thrown on yourself and your fellow constables?—Yes. They had a small police at Huddersfield of six men, and they behaved very well and remained with us.

3741. Were those police paid officers?—Yes.

3742. Had you any special constables sworn in in Wales?—Yes.

3743. What did they do?—They were not called into service, but they were so intermixed with the people that I could get no information from them, and all the captures I made was from what I was obliged to find out myself. I could get no information from them whatever. I had 30 men there.

3744. Were you at Huddersfield before you went to Wales?—Yes; I was at Huddersfield in 1837.

3745. When you were at Huddersfield, 399 of the 400 special constables having run away from you, when you went into Wales you had special constables, but you did not make use of them, from your experience of special constables at Huddersfield?—In Carmarthenshire I had a great many special constables under my command, and I used to have them out at night, but we never fell in with any gate-breakers in Carmarthenshire. From what I saw, I saw enough to satisfy me that it would be very doubtful, if the special constables were called upon, whether they would have acted. I was satisfied they were mixed up with the gate-breakers, and knew who they were from their peculiar dress.

3746. Notwithstanding your belief that they were acquainted with the parties engaged in gate-breaking, still you could get no information from them?—No.

3747. Therefore you had no reliance upon them?—Very little. They were a better class of men for constables, because they were chiefly selected from old pensioners; but they lived in the neighbourhood, and had been living there for a great many years, and they had got very intimate with the farmers, and could not be depended upon to act, especially in a case of disturbance.

3748. Have you been anywhere else in cases of riots?—I was in Dewsbury, in the year 1838.

3749. On what occasion were you sent to Dewsbury?—There was a great excitement against the Poor-law.

3750. What number of men did you take to Dewsbury?—Thirty.

3751. Was there a serious riot there?—Yes; and we apprehended several of the rioters.

3752. Was there a great deal of violence?—There was stone-throwing, and the mob were armed with bludgeons.

3753. Did you, or any of your 30 constables, sustain any material injury?—Nothing very serious; we had some cut heads from brickbats being thrown.

3754. Did you receive any aid from special constables there?—No. I posted them at a place on the side of the bridge near to a meadow, where the magistrates had a meeting, to keep the field clear, so that there should be no stones thrown at the magistrates. After the meeting was over, when I came out of the inn, they had every one of them left.

3755. How many were there?—Two hundred, I should say, all over the town. I posted about 10 in this field; my party and myself escorted the magistrates to the hotel, a distance of about 50 yards, and the mob pelted the magistrates. After I got the magistrates inside, I went to Colonel Campbell, and suggested to the magistrates the propriety of reading the Riot Act, and giving the publicans an order to close their houses, and not to draw any more drink till the streets were clear. One of the magistrates was mounted, and the Riot Act was read, and myself and my men took several of the ringleaders into custody. Then I thought it would be very prudent to clear the public-houses, so that the mob should not get drunk; in doing so, I found most of my special constables upstairs in the public-houses enjoying themselves, and apparently quite glad of the opportunity of getting out of the disturbance; they did not like to make themselves obnoxious by interfering; I found them in places of greater security.

Mr. G. Martin.

17 June 1853.

3756. Were the military called out at either Huddersfield or Dewsbury on the occasion of the riots of which you have been speaking?—Yes, in both cases.

3757. What aid did you derive from the military?—At Huddersfield there was an election, and they made a very desperate attempt to get hold of the books; we succeeded in keeping the mob out of the booth; the streets were densely crowded with a mob; we got the Riot Act read; and I then suggested that the military should parade the streets with the police in front, who should apprehend the ringleaders, and give them over to the military as we proceeded. That was done, and we got the streets clear. If they had had a police in Yorkshire, they could have concentrated a force, and there would have been no necessity for the military, or for us either.

3758. There is no rural police in Yorkshire, is there?—They have superintending constables in some of the districts. ,

3759. Had they at that time?—No.

3760. Is it your opinion, if there had been a rural police force as there is in Essex and other counties, those riots could have been prevented?—They would have acted as we did, but there would have been no need of military being called out.

3761. Would not they have acted more effectually than the military?—Yes; they could draw a great number into a town on an emergency.

3762. On those occasions you think there would have been no occasion for calling in the military?—No.

3763. You have had considerable experience in riots; do not you think that the policemen are much more efficient for the suppression of riots and the dispersion of a mob than the military?—Decidedly so; and more especially when they get to know the people; if a constable knows a number of these low characters, he can do more than a dozen strange constables; they do not like to resist for fear of the after consequences.

3764. Is not this one reason, that a soldier cannot leave his ranks without the orders of his officer, whereas a policeman can go into a mob with his truncheon, and he has one hand at liberty with which to seize an offender?—Yes; by apprehending the ringleaders, I have prevented a riot by taking them, and persuading others to go away.

3765. Would not you go into a mob to induce them to desist from riotous proceedings, and endeavour to seize the ringleaders?—Yes.

3766. Should not you have more facility for so doing with a truncheon than a soldier would, whose hands were occupied with his musket?—Yes; I could handle a truncheon with one hand, whereas a soldier's musket is as much as he can manage, and lends him no assistance.

3767. The only weapon you have is a truncheon, which you can use without occasioning loss of life; but if a soldier uses his musket, he cannot do it without probable loss of life?—No.

3768. Notwithstanding his using his weapons, do not you think a policeman is more efficient in suppressing riots and apprehending offenders in riots than a soldier?—There is no comparison; if a soldier is called upon to act he is obliged to charge or fire, and by doing so he stands a great chance of killing the parties, and cannot apprehend them very well.

3769. Mr. Howard.] And very often might kill the wrong parties?—Yes.

3770. Chairman.] Were the military which were employed at Dewsbury cavalry or infantry?—We had some of both; we took the same means at Dewsbury as we did at Huddersfield.

3771. Were the military called upon to act?—No; they merely accompanied us,; we delivered our prisoners over to them, and they took possession of the prisoners whom we apprehended.

3772. You apprehended them?—Yes.

3773. When you were in Wales, had you any military?—Yes; I had them out with me one night to assist us.

3774. Were they cavalry or infantry?—I had a party of marines out with me.

3775. Mr. Philipps.] On what occasion was that?—It was one night, when I apprehended about 30 men, in the neighbourhood of Fishguard, between Haverfordwest and Fishguard. I was also at Birmingham before the police was established there; I went down in 1839, I think. There was a very serious riot in the Bull Ring with the Chartists. Things would not have got to the head they did there, if there had been a good police in the town, as they have now.

3776. Chairman.]

Mr. G. Martin.

17 June 1853.

3776. *Chairman.*] What force did you take with you to Birmingham?—Sixty men; and we were reinforced the following day by about 40 men; we had about 100.

3777. Mr. *Burroughes.*] Were the additional 40 men sent from London?—Yes.

3778. *Chairman.*] Was that a very serious riot?—Yes; and I was very seriously injured. I think about 14 of my men were taken to the hospital that night.

3779. Were there any military employed?—They were in barracks; the magistrates thought it best not to call them out until we had had a great deal of fighting.

3780. Did you apprehend any number of offenders?—Yes, several of whom were committed for trial; there were two or three of my men stabbed with knives and daggers; it was at the time the Chartist affair was at its full height.

3781. Mr. *Burroughes.*] Of course, at Birmingham, you had not the benefit of local knowledge?—No; we were not in the town an hour before we went into action.

3782. You consider that it would have been more beneficial if there had been a local force?—Decidedly so; a great many of the men who threw brickbats at my men, would not have done so if they had known they would be liable to be recognised.

3783. *Chairman.*] Were you in uniform when you were at Huddersfield?—Yes.

3784. Were you in uniform when you were in Wales?—No; the men had their uniforms with them, but they chiefly wore their private clothes; they were detached in Wales with small parties of military, to form a sort of chain round the mountainous district; they ran in twos and threes, but they were well known to be police; all the inhabitants knew that we were metropolitan police.

3785. In all those cases in which you were called out in order to repress riots and disturbances, is it your opinion, if there had been an organised paid constabulary, not only the services of the military, but your services would have been unnecessary for the suppression of the riots?—I think so decidedly; I have always thought so; I went down to Lewes about two or three years ago; it struck me then, if the Brighton and the county constabulary had been under one head, they could have drawn their men from Brighton to Lewes, and have rendered the assistance which we afforded to them.

3786. Is there a police force at Lewes?—Yes.

3787. The authorities thought it was not sufficient on that occasion?—No.

3788. You think they might have had sufficient aid from Brighton, if there had been a readiness on their part to act?—I understand they have 50 men at Brighton; if they had sent half that number to Lewes, it would have been sufficient.

3789. How many men did you take to Lewes?—Sixty; but half the numb would have been sufficient, I think.

3790. You think, if there had been a desire to co-operate with the county police in Sussex on the part of the police at Brighton, and they had sent over 30 men, that would have been sufficient for the purpose?—Yes.

3791. And that would have saved the expense of your going down?—Yes.

3792. Mr. *Fitzroy.*] Was the riot at Lewes ever more formidable than a mere bonfire mob?—No; it had led to a great inconvenience the year previous. I believe they had so large a bonfire in the middle of the town that it singed the sashes of the windows, and I believe they threatened to throw a gentleman into the river for interfering with them. The magistrates gave orders for the streets to be cleared, or a riot would be attempted; we formed line across the streets by sub-divisions; we faced each way, and the mob walked away quietly.

3793. *Chairman.*] From your experience, that disturbance might have extended very much?—No doubt; the mob had every inclination to carry out the having of the bonfire, if there had not been a sufficient police force to prevent them.

William Oakley, Esq., called in; and further Examined.

W. Oakley, Esq.

3794. *Chairman.*] IS the statement contained in your printed report, with regard to the expense of a police force for the county of Somerset, exactly similar to the statement of the expense of a police force for the division of Bath, with respect to its details?—It was published at the same time. This note, with reference to the county of Somerset, was added: " As the establishment of a police for one division only would naturally be at a higher rate in that division, than if the same were adopted throughout the country, the following calculation of the rate at which it might be so carried out is also submitted." The items upon which the calculation is founded for the county are not precisely the same as those upon which the calculation was founded for the division. I believe they are more strictly correct for the whole county. I have compared them with a calculation recently made for the gaol committee now sitting in the county of Somerset, with reference to the expense of the conveyance of prisoners by constables. By that comparative statement I show that there would be a saving of 6,000 *l.* a year between the expense of superintending constables and an efficient police force for the county.

3795. Is that statement made out exactly upon the basis of the statement upon which you were examined yesterday?—Except some items, which I took from the accounts for the whole county. In both pages of this comparative statement I have a note that " The figures shown are not set forth as strictly correct, but merely estimated from such data as could be obtained."

3796. Mr. *Fitzroy*.] Are not the salaries for the officers low?—I have taken them from salaries actually paid.

3797. You put the inspectors at 28 *s.* a week?—They are paid less in some counties.

3798. In what counties?—They are paid in Essex less than that.

3799. (*To Captain M'Hardy.*) What is the rate of pay to your inspectors?—They are paid exactly the same as a serjeant in the metropolitan police, viz. 25 *s.* a week.

3800. (*To Mr. Oakley.*) You will observe that the salaries in Essex are higher than those you have put down in your statement; you put serjeants at 23 *s.* per week; they receive in Essex 25 *s.*; your seven inspectors would be in the third class superintendents, would not they?—There are no serjeants in Essex. I have put the superintendents at a larger amount than they receive in the county of Essex; the highest class superintendents in Essex receive 100 *l.* a year. I have put them at 120 *l.*

3801. Does this calculation include clothing for the men?—Yes.

3802. What is the average of Somersetshire as compared with Essex?—I am unable to give the average from any papers here; it consists of 480 parishes; the population is more than Essex.

3803. What is the population of Somersetshire?—The " population of Somerset, excluding Bath and Bridgewater (exempt under the 2d & 3rd Vict. c. 88, s. 24, having separate quarter sessions), is 372,000, according to the census of 1841." You will observe, below that estimate of expense, the average number of constables to the population, not only in various police forces, but also in Scotland.

3804. It appears by this note, that you do not propose that the amount of force in Somersetshire should be anything like that in Essex?—Not quite so large in proportion to the population.

3805. Why not?—It is a more rural district, distant from London. A note will be observed that " The above estimate for the county of Somerset is given at a moderate rate, allowing one constable to every 1,750 of the population; and such a force would be less expensive than superintending and parish constables, afford much greater protection to property, be more likely to prevent crime and detect offenders, in addition to providing a body of disciplined and efficient men. To put the force in this county on a satisfactory footing at the outset, it might be advisable to add 35 constables to the above number, giving one constable to every 1,500 of the population, at an expense of 1,736 *l.* per annum, which would still show a saving of 4,273 *l.* 4 *s.*, as compared with the superintending and parish constable system. The number of 250 for the whole county may appear too low to those who have looked on the duties of a police as a mere patrol; but the aim of a county policeman should be less to watch property than to watch thieves." I also state, in another note, that in some police forces there are too many inadequately paid officers in proportion to the number of men; Essex is one to which I allude.

3806. You state that the population of Somerset is greater than that of Essex, and you propose to limit the constables to one in 1,500; upon the basis on which you form your calculation for an efficient rural police force, you may reduce the expenditure to any amount; this calculation, to be worth anything, should be placed in comparison with some existing force?—I do compare it with Essex.

" In

W. Oakley, Esq.

17 June 1853.

" In the county of Essex, the police were established in the year 1840, with one constable to about every 1,750 of the population; in 1842, the force was increased 50 men, giving one constable to about every 1,325 of the population. In the county of Surrey, the police have been established this year, at about the latter proportion of constables to the population." At the time I made this calculation, I was not aware that there were petty local police establishments in some towns of Somerset, such as Taunton, Chard, and one or two other small towns. I believe if I were now to prepare a detailed statement of the comparative expense of superintending constables and a police, I should show the difference to be still greater.

3807. What police force is there in the town of Chard?—About three or four men. How they are paid I am not aware.

3808. The Taunton constabulary are under no control, and recognise, I believe, no authority?—Not under any proper supervision, but they were only established by the inhabitants for the want of better.

Captain *J. B. B. McHardy*, R. N., called in; and further Examined.

Captain J. B. B. McHardy, R. N.

3809. *Chairman.*] HAVE you received an application from the mayor of Harwich for assistance?—I have this day received a letter from the mayor of Harwich for assistance, in consequence of an election which is about to take place. Owing to their own inefficiency, they have applied to me for 20 policemen, with the necessary number of officers, for the purpose of keeping the peace during the approaching election.

3810. What steps do you take in Essex when you receive information of a felony having been committed?—Immediate information is given, of course, all over the county.

3811. In what manner?—In whatever division the felony occurs, the superintendent immediately spreads the information by the patrols. A route is sent off over the county, as well as by post; and the particulars are supplied to the "Police Gazette," and the electric telegraph sometimes used. The difficulty is from the want of unity of action between the counties; it facilitates the escape of offenders. If a man commits an offence, and he goes down to Liverpool, we get no assistance unless as a personal favour; there is no unity of action between the local police and others. The other day a clerk went away with 1,000 l.; he went down to Liverpool and took a passage in a ship; I found out the ship in which he had engaged a passage, and from the circumstance of my knowing the officer of Customs at Liverpool, I got an order for the river force to assist me in apprehending the party. I think it would be a great advantage if all the officers who are employed by the Customs afloat were made special constables, and required to co-operate with any police in the apprehension of offenders who were about to leave our sea-ports.

3812. You mean to say, that as your men assist in the protection of the revenue, the Customs' officers ought to assist you in return?—Yes; I think if they were appointed peace officers for the purpose of detecting offenders who are leaving the country, it would be a great advantage. The assistance I obtained in the case to which I have referred was a matter of personal favour.

3813. Mr. *Fitzroy.*] Do you propose, in the event of a increase in the police force generally, and its adoption under one central authority, that power should be given to the constables of each force to act in all the counties, without reference to their belonging to the particular county?—Yes; and there is a great disadvantage from the delay in getting warrants backed, as well as an expense. Until the passing of Act 11 & 12 Vict. c. 42, none of our officers could execute a warrant in another county, except by being accompanied by a constable of that county, he merely acting as an auxiliary. I think if a uniform constabulary were adopted, and the officers were all armed with the powers necessary for the protection of the public revenue, it would be but fair that, by a clause in the Act of Parliament, all the revenue officers should be appointed peace officers, for the purpose of unity of action.

3814. Having turned your attention to the necessity of establishing a uniform police force throughout England, in your opinion is it of importance that the officers should have the power to act indiscriminately in all counties?—I think it would be a very great advantage, and in fact I think it indispensably necessary.

Jovis, 23° die Junii, 1853.

MEMBERS PRESENT.

Mr. Rice.
Lord Advocate.
Mr. Mackie.
Mr. Burroughes.
Sir J. Trollope.
Sir J. Anderson.

Mr. Sotheron.
Mr. Philipps.
Mr. Howard.
Mr. Rich.
Mr. Fitzroy.

EDWARD ROYDS RICE, Esq., in the Chair.

Lieutenant-Colonel *Henry Morgan Clifford*, a Member of the House; Examined.

Lieut.-Col.
H. M. Clifford, M.P.

23 June 1853.

3815. ARE you a Chairman of the Court of Quarter Sessions of Herefordshire ? —Yes.

3816. Did not you, in conjunction with Mr. Deedes, bring in a Bill this Session for the amendment of the Act for Superintending Constables ?—Yes.

3817. The Committee may therefore presume that your opinion is favourable to the system of superintending constables ?—Of superintending constables, it is.

3818. Perhaps you will state to the Committee the grounds of your opinion ? —In the year 1841, crime having much increased in the county of Hereford, the then chairman of the quarter sessions, Mr. Barnaby, was very desirous to introduce the system of rural police which had then just come forward ; he failed in getting the whole county to adopt it, but one district of the county, the district of Kington, with a population of about one-tenth of the whole county, did adopt it, and they continued to maintain the new system for nine years ; about three years after its first adoption in that district the other parts of the county determined upon having the superintending constables.

3819. What was the population of Herefordshire at that time?—The population of Herefordshire at that time, when there was first a question about the police, was nearly 100,000, exclusive of the town of Hereford ; none of the other towns had a police of their own.

3820. Is Hereford the only town that has a corporation ?—Hereford is the only town that had a police ; the town of Leominster has now a police ; at that time it, I think, had not ; these have now a police separate from that of the county.

3821. What other boroughs are there in Herefordshire ?—Kington, Ross, Ledbury, and Bromyard ; they are each towns of from 2,000 to 4,000 population ; and the smaller borough of Weobley.

3822. Are the only two boroughs in Herefordshire which have a police of their own, Hereford and Leominster?—Yes. With regard to the superintending constables, as soon as it was determined to have them, the court of quarter sessions voted that each petty sessional district, if they thought fit, might adopt them ; however, only three at first did so, and finding the system to answer very well in these districts, it has ultimately been extended to each of the nine petty sessional divisions of the county ; for some time the Kington district went on maintaining its separate rural police at the same time with the superintending constables.

3823. Are there lock-up houses in each division ?—In most of the districts ; but that has nothing especially to do with the superintending constables. I keep the lock-up houses out of the question, as they have reference to either system: the rural police or the superintending constables.

3824. What are the salaries of the superintending constables ?—The superintending constables' salaries have varied. Each man now has 50 guineas a-year, his clothing, and some contingencies which amount to, perhaps, about 15*l.*; that would make it 67*l.* 10*s.* and 20*l.* for the keep of a horse, making 87*l.* 10*s.* When first established they had more than that ; each man had 75*l.* besides the other contingencies ; now they have a guinea a week, which is 50 guineas a year. I would proceed to state, as the grounds for my favourable opinion of the system of superintending constables, in opposition to that of a rural police, that the district of Kington, after going on with the rural police for nearly nine years, found that

the

Lieut- Col.
H. M. Clifford, M. P.

23 June 1853.

the crime there was about the same average as the crime throughout the rest of the county, and that they were put to a much greater expense than other parts of the county; they determined therefore to give up the system. To give an idea of what the increased expense to the district of Kington was, with a population of little more than 9,000 they were paying at the rate of 260l. a year, levied upon that district only, being a rate of about 1½d. in the pound a year in that one district; the superintending constables for the whole county, including the Kington district, which is now upon the same footing, does not cost above 750l. a year upon an average, with a population of about 100,000. The cost of the nine superintending constables, with all the *et cæteras*, amounts to about 750l., clothing, contingencies, and horses. From that expense of 750l. may be deducted more than 150l., which has been saved to the county by the conveyance of prisoners to gaol; that is included in this expenditure.

3825. Do the superintending constables convey all the prisoners to gaol?—Yes, with the carts and horses which are found by the county; therefore, in fact, the whole of the expense of the county is not above 600l., and that is defrayed by a rate of a farthing in the pound upon the whole county.

3826. Do you employ the parochial constables?—We should employ a parochial constable, if the superintending constable were absent on duty, but that does not very often happen.

3827. What is the largest division of the county of Hereford?—The divisions run from about 10,000 to 12,000 inhabitants.

3828. What is the number of parishes in the largest division?—The number of parishes varies; Kington is the largest; Kington has 18, the others are generally from 12 to 15; but there is so much difference in the size of the parishes that it does not give much notion of the size of the division.

3829. Have you made any estimate of the payments, in various ways, to parochial constables?—In the payments that come before us every year, at quarter sessions, we have hardly any payments to make for parochial constables. .

3830. Are the parochial constables never employed?—A very little; we know hardly anything of them at quarter sessions.

3831. Do not they attend at quarter sessions?—No, not the parochial constables often.

3832. Do not they attend at petty sessions?—No, I think they do not; I am not able to say much with reference to the petty sessions in the county of Hereford, but I do not think they attend very frequently.

3833. Mr. *Mackie*.] Do you think eight superintending constables are sufficient to keep 100,000 of the population in good order?—We find them quite sufficient; the diminution in crime is very great.

3834. Supposing there were a riot or a tumult in the county of Hereford, and those eight men were too few to suppress it, to what would you have recourse?— We should immediately call in the parish constables. We have at this moment three railways in the course of construction in the county of Hereford. Each of those railways has in the neighbourhood of Hereford one police constable; he is hardly ever called upon to act in such cases, for our superintending constables are perfectly able to compete with anything that occurs.

3835. Mr. *Howard*.] Have the superintending constables any men under them? —No; but under the powers of the Act of Parliament they can call upon the parish constables to assist them.

3836. *Chairman*.] Therefore, the whole of the paid police force which you have for the county of Hereford is eight superintending constables?—Yes. Previous to the time when the Kington division gave up their police, they had five applicable to a population of 9,000. but allow me to state this one fact. During the two years since that force at Kington has been done away with, crime in that district has actually diminished, at least our knowledge of crime; we have fewer cases than we had before.

3837. By "knowledge of crime," you mean the number of people apprehended? —Yes.

3838. Do you think the number of people apprehended is any proof of the amount of undetected crime?—I do. I think I should be sure to hear of it if crime were committed.

3839. Do you think the number of persons apprehended by a small number of policemen, is a test of the amount of undetected crime?—I do; because I think our superintending constables are extremely active, quite sufficiently active and

Lieut.-Col.
H.M.Clifford, M.P.

13 June 1853.

ready to look out for every possible case of crime that occurs. I do not think they leave anything not inquired into ; they ride about their districts, and they have the means of traversing the district from one end to the other.

3840. What is the extent of the largest division, which you say contains 18 parishes ?—About 12 miles long, by about 4 miles wide.

3841. Where does the superintending constable reside ?—At Kington, which is central ; the superintending constable who is there has a cart and horse ; the force which was there before had no cart and horse.

3842. Do you think, supposing a felony were committed, that the parochial constables are efficient for the purposes of pursuit ?—I think the system works in this way ; where a crime is committed, the parochial constable is the man who first hears of it ; he is despatched in pursuit of the superintending constable, who is brought to the spot as quickly as possible to investigate the case. I think that is the great use of the superintending constables.

3843. In the first instance, if a felony is committed in a parish in this district, which is 12 miles long, the parochial constable does not himself go in pursuit of the offender, but goes in pursuit of the superintending constable ?—That would depend upon the instructions which were given to him by the party who called him in. I think, generally speaking, he would do so.

3844. Then the superintending constable, if he were disengaged, would go back to the parish where the offence had been committed ; what aid would he have in pursuing the offender ?—He has the aid of the parish constables, and the parties injured ; I think there is no difficulty in procuring assistance.

3845. Supposing the party injured was a person of property, he would have the means of affording sufficient aid to the superintending constable, by sending one of his own servants, or one of his keepers, in order to apprehend the offender ?—Yes.

3846. But supposing it was the property of a poor man which had been taken, and the offender was not apprehended, who would have to pay the expenses of the pursuit ; that is to say, the parish constable's expenses ?—That is a point which is not settled ; that is one of the points which Mr. Deedes and myself wish to settle in our Bill before Parliament.

3847. Do not you think that the practice, at all events till that point is settled, is, that the expenses of the parochial constables must be paid by the party who orders the pursuit ?—No doubt about it.

3848. The present system, therefore, under these circumstances, would afford protection to the property of a rich man, but it would not afford protection to the property of a poor man ?—I do not see how it would do that at all ; the superintending constable is paid for his services, and he must go.

3849. Do not you think, as far as the services of the parochial constables go, if they are not paid they are very useless ; and, if they are employed, they are very expensive ?—Yes ; but in practice you will find that it never occurs. I should mention that there is no instance of a parish constable hesitating to go, even in the case of the humblest cottager ; the probability is that he will be paid by somebody ; he never refuses to go, I suppose, because he might not be paid his expenses, although the loss had happened to the humblest cottager. Crime in Herefordshire, at one time, took that line considerably, and it was very common for cottages to be broken open, in which case the humblest and poorest people were the parties injured ; it has diminished now very much.

3850. Do you think, in the inspection of public-houses and beershops, the parochial constables are efficient ; are they directed by the superintending constables to perform that duty ?—Yes ; our rules require that every superintending constable shall, within his district, visit from time to time, at least once a month, all the public-houses in his district, or at any other time that he pleases ; he is in constant communication with the parish constables, who are desired to report to him, from time to time, the results of their inspection, and they will be paid by the court of quarter sessions for any special services performed, which the magistrates at petty sessions sanction.

3851. Do you think the reports of the parochial constables to the superintending constable are to be depended upon ?—They do not come before us ; the superintending constable is the person who makes his report to the magistrates ; where he derives his information from we do not look into ; further than of course to investigate the statements which he makes to us.

3852. Mr.

Lieut.-Col.
H. M. *Clifford*, M.P.

23 June 1853.

3852. Mr. *Burroughes*.] Is it the custom in your county to appoint substitutes for the parochial constables?—That has not hitherto been the case; but in the regulations which lately we have authorised in each district, we have suggested that every superintending constable shall have the best constable he chooses to select as his substitute, who is to be paid for special services when employed.

3853. I alluded to the provision in the Act of Parliament for the appointment of substitutes as parochial constables. Do the parties liable to serve as constables avail themselves of that provision?—I think they do in certain parishes, chiefly in the town parishes, where the class of constables selected are of a rather different description.

3854. Are not the parochial constables generally men in trade?—In the agricultural districts they are, generally speaking, labourers; we find very few mechanics appointed as constables; sometimes there may be a mason or a carpenter.

3855. Are not bricklayers and carpenters appointed as constables?—We have very few of them; I think, generally speaking, they are agricultural labourers.

3856. Are not bricklayers and carpenters men whose time is of value to them?—Yes.

3857. *Chairman*.] Are not the better class of constables generally persons engaged in business?—Yes, they are, generally speaking.

3858. Then if they are so employed, is not their time of money-value to them?—Certainly it is.

3859. Is it not a cost and an inconvenience to them to be appointed as parish constables?—Yes, supposing they were not allowed a due remuneration for their services. I think there are few instances, if any, where a man does not get his expenses.

3860. Ought they not to be paid in proportion to the value of their time?—They are, in fact, when a prisoner is committed; and I think there are rare instances where a pursuit has taken place without the detection of the offender.

3861. In cases of informations before magistrates, in which conviction does not take place, are not the expenses paid by the plaintiff?—Yes.

3862. How are the expenses of the parish constable in that case paid?—He would be paid by the person employing him; and of course, upon the supposition that the party employing him is too poor to pay, he might lose his expenses; but that is a rare occurrence.

3863. Have you made any estimate of the cost of parish constables in that respect?—No.

3864. You have stated the exact expense of the superintending constables, but you have made no estimate of the amount of the expense of parochial constables whatever; it is, however, little or much?—No; in fact I have no means to make any estimate of the sort.

3865. Mr. *Howard*.] Is Herefordshire much infested with vagrants?—A good deal.

3866. Have they increased?—In the last three years they have sensibly diminished.

3867. Do you employ the superintending constables as assistant relieving officers?—No, we do not.

3868. Do not you take any steps upon the vagrants going to the union house?—No; we have taken no particular step. In the two towns of Hereford and Leominster the police may have more to do with that.

3869. Do the superintending constables work well with the town police?—Yes; exceedingly well.

3870. *Chairman*.] Is there a large police force in Hereford?—Yes; I think they have six or eight.

3871. Is that force under the corporation?—Yes; and they are paid by the county for any services performed by them. Of course, it often happens that a crime is committed in the rural districts, and the parties are actually taken in the town of Hereford, where the property is taken to be disposed of, and the town police are the parties who apprehend them.

3872. Is there anything further which you wish to state to the Committee?—No, I think not; the object I had in giving evidence was simply to show that, as far as the rural district of, Herefordshire was concerned, I think the object of the prevention of crime is entirely met by the comparatively small number of superintending constables we now have there, and that the introduction of the rural

Lieut.-Col.
H. M. Clifford, M.P.

23 June 1853.

police for the sole purpose of the prevention of crime, looking to that object only, would be an unnecessary expense to us. I am taking only that limited view of the matter. If the object is to make a national police force, then it becomes not a subject for local taxation, but general taxation. I think local taxation is perfectly reasonable for the defence of our own property; but if we are satisfied with the superintending constables, we should think it a grievance to have to pay for a general rural police.

3873. You do not know what the cost of your present system is?—If you mean as regards the parochial constables, I am satisfied it is much too small to take into the consideration in any way; although I do not act as a magistrate in petty sessions, I know it is extremely limited; I know that, generally speaking, crime has been on the decrease. At the Hereford quarter sessions now coming on it is on the increase; but on looking over the calendar I see that is owing to some few crimes in addition which have been committed by the railway navigators.

3874. As far as the services of the superintending constables go individually, you find them very efficient?—Extremely; as efficient as possible.

Mr. *Alfred John List*, called in; and Examined.

Mr. A. J. List.

3875. *Chairman.*] WHAT office do you hold in the police in Scotland?—I am superintendent of the county police in Mid Lothian.

3876. Does that include Edinburgh?—Not the town; only the suburban part of Edinburgh.

3877. What is the police force which you have in the county of Edinburgh?—We have 31 in the county; consisting of one inspector, who acts as a clerk; one office serjeant, two serjeants, three first-class constables, six constables who have been above two years in the force, 18 constables who have served under two years and one messenger. I have a return of the rates of pay to the constabulary.

Vide Appendix.

(*The Witness delivered in the same.*)

3878. What is the population of the county?—The rural population is 51,218, but for police purposes we take in two small towns which have no police.

3879. What is the whole of the population?—Sixty-two thousand, eight hundred and thirty-six.

3880. What is the proportion of the population to each policeman?—One to 2,027.

3881. Do you think that a sufficient force?—Most assuredly not.

3882. Is it sufficient for a night watch?—No.

3883. Do you think a night watch is absolutely necessary?—Immediately around Edinburgh I think patrols would be necessary.

3884. With the present force have you not the means of so patrolling?—No, I have not.

3885. Were you ever employed in any other police force before?—I was in the metropolitan police force, and held the rank of inspector.

3886. How long were you in the metropolitan police force?—I joined at its formation, and left in the year 1832. I have been 20 years in Scotland last October.

3887. What is the whole cost of the police in the county of Mid Lothian?—I have an abstract of the revenue accounts; the expenditure of the county for police purposes only is 2,061 *l*. 18 *s*. 3 *d*.

3888. What is that in the pound on the assessment?—Twopence in the pound.

3889. Mr. *Mackie.*] Is not the assessment in Scotland upon the old valuation?—Yes, it is in other counties; in our county it is upon the valued rent; four-fifths of the valued rent of the county pay the assessment.

3890. *Lord Advocate.*] Not upon the actual rent?—No.

3891. Do you know what the real rent of the county is?—I have a table here, taken from the poor-law statistics, made up three or four years ago by the Board of Supervision in Scotland, in which they give the valued rent of every county, and the real rent of every county; the real rent in that year was 246,350 *l*.

3892. Can you tell the Committee the proportion of the police assessment to the real rent?—No, that being more the duty of the clerk of supply.

3893. Mr. *Mackie.*] Who has the appointment of the county police in Scotland?—The Commissioners of Supply.

3894. How

Mr. *A. J. List.*

23 June 1853.

3894. How are the police paid?—From what is termed the Rogue Money Fund.

3895. Is not that an assessment entirely upon landed property?—Yes.

3896. Does it consist with your knowledge that the assessment being entirely upon the landed property in Scotland, is one cause why the police have not been originally appointed in other counties in Scotland?—It is, and for this reason; that house property is not assessed to the tenants, but only to the proprietors.

3897. Suppose a shopkeeper in Edinburgh has a large quantity of goods in his shop, say 1,000 *l.* or 1,500 *l.* worth, how much does he pay towards the assessment for the police?—If in the county part, and he does not happen to be a proprietor, he pays nothing.

3898. How much does a shopkeeper with goods in his shop pay towards the police assessment?—Nothing at all, if situated as above stated.

3899. *Chairman.*] That is, if he occupies the property, but does not own the property?—Yes; the property pays; the practice in Scotland is that the proprietor bears the public burthens. I may state here at this period, that in populous villages, where there are a number of such houses as those which have been mentioned, the parties subscribe and come to us to give them an extra policeman for their protection.

3900. *Lord Advocate.*] That does not enter into your estimate of expenditure? —No; I have four or six of those men.

3901. In such a case as that, do you appoint one of your own men?—The police committee who manage these matters say, " If you will meet us with a certain sum, we will give you a man, but he must be upon our force"; the cost of a man is about 45 *l.*; they may subscribe 20 *l.* or 30 *l.*, and we make up the difference; they have no control over the man; he is attached to the establishment.

3902. Does the number of policemen which you have given include those men?—Yes; there are four or five extra men.

3903. Do they enter into the general account?—Yes, they enter into the general account; we have the money which is subscribed, and take credit for it in our revenue account.

3904. What is the average cost of each of your policemen?—I should say, including clothing, lodging, and pay, about 57 *l.*

3905. Still, with only 31 men, the cost is a twopenny rate on the assessment? —Yes.

3906. That assessment is very nearly the actual value?—Within one-fifth of the valued rental.

3907. What number of men should you think would be sufficient for a night watch in the district of Edinburgh?—I proposed a plan for six pairs of patrols, to patrol within four miles of Edinburgh on certain roads and cross-roads; that would be 12 men on that duty.

3908. Do you think that an increased force for the rural districts of Mid Lothian is necessary on account of its vicinity to the town of Edinburgh?—I do, in consequence of Edinburgh being, as is the case with all large towns, the centre for a great many bad characters who assemble there, and migrate into the country.

3909. Are you, yourself, acquainted with the police in Edinburgh?—Yes; I have paid attention to it for the last 14 years, particularly since I have been resident in Edinburgh.

3910. Under what management are they?—They have a local Act and a Board of Commissioners of Police.

3911. They are not under the corporation?—No.

3912. How is that Board of Commissioners appointed?—From the constituents of the wards. There are 32 wards in Edinburgh, and each ward returns a commissioner.

3913. Are the commissioners elected by the ratepayers?—Yes.

3914. Do you think that fit persons for the purpose are generally elected?— They are respectable men in their sphere as shopkeepers, some publicans and brokers, but they are not calculated to have any knowledge of matters of police; in fact, it is their interference which causes the establishment to be not so effective as it otherwise would be.

3915. Do you think the want of efficiency is on account of the appointments being made by the commissioners of police?—Most assuredly not; the commissioners do not make the appointments, the superintendent makes the appointments; but the commissioners recommend men too frequently, these men look to the commissioners as their employers. They also interfere with the men in doing their duty.

3916. Have the commissioners the power of dismissing the superintendent?—No; his appointment is vested in the Lord Provost and the Sheriff of the county, and they have no power of removal.

3917. Then the superintendent is entirely independent of the commissioners?—He is; but then there is a clause in the Act of Parliament which enacts, that although they cannot dismiss him, they can interfere with his pay; and in other respects they worry and so annoy him as to make his situation very unpleasant. I have seen four changes during 12 years; two were deaths.

3918. Mr. *Mackie.*] Do you find that there is any jealousy existing between the county police and the Edinburgh police?—At one period there was a jealousy, but I have endeavoured to prevent it with the heads; there is a good deal with the subordinates, and had it not been for my close intimacy with the heads of the establishment, we should not have worked so well.

3919. If the city of Edinburgh police and the county police were amalgamated, in your opinion that jealousy would cease?—Yes.

3920. *Lord Advocate.*] Should you think it desirable that they should be amalgamated?—I think so, and for this reason; on every public occasion when there has been an outbreak in Edinburgh, I have paid strict attention to the way in which the police have performed the duty in suppressing disturbances, having been concerned a good deal in that duty in the London service. The sheriff of the county having a cumulative jurisdiction in the city, he has on all those occasions required me to act; and I act in that case, not as an officer of the town police, but as an officer of the sheriff. In April 1848, at the time of the chartist riots at Glasgow, as well as at Edinburgh, I took charge of a number of special constables; for on such occasions the police have not a sufficient force to contend with the mob; and, before taking charge of the constables, I asked the sheriff if I was to disperse the mob if we encountered them; he said that we were; and in consequence of that order, I took charge of the special constables, and we dispersed the mob. That gave me an opportunity of seeing that the Edinburgh mobs were such that if there was a bold front, and proper determination, they could be suppressed; but in consequence of the police being so hampered by the commissioners, they are afraid to act in a determined way.

3921. Do the commissioners give orders to the police?—They frequently do. I have seen it myself in the case of a very recent street disturbance; a policeman was interfering; a commissioner happened to come up, and I met the commissioner. He said, "Mr. List, do you see that disturbance"? I said, "I see the mob." He said, "I saw a policeman going to take a man to the police-office, and I told him not to do so. I said I was a commissioner of police, but the man did not respect my orders." My reply was, that "he acted very properly, and you had no right to interfere."

3922. Is the interference of the commissioners a matter of frequent occurrence? Of late it has not been of so frequent occurrence as formerly; the present superintendent has been very determined in resisting it.

3923. Do you find that private influence and interest interferes much with the proceedings of the commissioners?—I have heard so; I do not know much from my own knowledge; I have frequently heard that it does.

3924. Do you know any instance of that sort?—Yes; I do in the way of supplying articles to the force. Some time ago I was applied to for a particular article of clothing for policemen in the northern part of Scotland, and not having such articles by me, I went down to the police-office; I asked for a pattern of the article; I had one shown me of a lot which they had got for their own men, of which I at once disapproved. I said, "That will not do, that is not the kind of thing I want; who supplied them?" "Mr. So-and-so; he is a brother to one of the commissioners." I told the clerk that the commissioners, I understood, were not allowed to supply articles either directly or indirectly to the force, and if they did it was highly improper. I have every reason to believe there is a good deal of jobbing carried on.

3925. Mr. *Mackie.*] Are there any counties adjoining Edinburgh which have not adopted the police force?—Yes, the upper ward of Lanark.

3926. Do you find great inconvenience from that circumstance?—Very much so. From the upper ward of Lanark, at certain seasons of the year, particularly

towards

Mr. *A. J. List.*

23 June 1853.

towards the grouse-shooting season, in August, we have large bands of men coming from the colliery districts which are in the upper ward, and they completely scour our county. Two years ago it was so bad, that I went out with the proprietors to one or two of the villages, and made an inquiry as to the cause of these depredations; and the inhabitants said, " It is because we have no policemen here." I then went on to Glasgow, and saw the sheriff, but he could afford no assistance. I pointed out the necessity of doing something, and that it was very annoying to the ratepayers in Mid Lothian to have these people infesting the neighbourhood, as they did a great deal of mischief. The proprietors applied to me for a man, and they assessed themselves to pay him. I stationed a man in the village, where we had gone to make inquiries. I have recently had a letter from the gentleman who accompanied me, in which he states, that immediately the constable was stationed in the village of Forth, the poachers put away their guns, and some killed their dogs, and the place in the course of a month assumed a different aspect; altogether arising, as he said, from the presence of that man. I may state that I went into the houses in the village, and I asked one of the leading shopkeepers, who was a very intelligent man, how it was that the village of Forth was so very notorious; he said, " Because we have nobody here to look after it; I would cheerfully pay for a police; the people run to riot, and they do as they like." The village remained quiet so long as the policeman remained, but in six months the funds fell short, and the man was discontinued, and now it is as bad as ever.

3927. In fact you found the upper ward of Lanark to be the great district for poachers, thieves, and vagabonds of every description?—Yes. I should state that near Biggar they have had a man from me for the last 15 months, and the accounts I have received are exceedingly favourable; some five or six parishes have united, and subscribed for this man; they were infested in that district with camps of gypsies and muggers, as they are termed in Scotland, who steal the property of the inhabitants. In fact there was one instance I thought very strange; Mr. Sim in that neighbourhood had a quantity of turkeys carried off prior to this man being there; he had that part of the country scoured, got the thieves, and sent them down to Lanark; he had to pay for apprehending them, for their conveyance, and for everything, besides losing his turkeys; but now they have rarely a theft.

3928. *Lord Advocate.*] Were not these depredators at one time in the habit of taking up the potatoes in the autumn to a great extent?—Yes, very much so.

3929. Do you know how it has happened that the rural police has not been adopted in the upper ward of Lanark?—There are three wards in Lanark, and the upper ward being entirely a rural ward, they objected to pay the same rate of assessment as the other wards. They say, " We do not require so many policemen as you do in the lower and middle wards, where you have coal-works and iron-works, and we shall be assessed to supply your wants. We have no objection to have the police, if the assessment could be divided according to the requirement of each ward."

3930. Is it not the case that the proprietors of the upper and middle wards have voted for the rural police at the county meetings, and that they have been outvoted by the lower ward?—They have recently, on two occasions, been outvoted.

3931. *Chairman.*] Which are the two wards in which there are collieries?— The lower and middle wards; the middle ward embraces most of the coal-works; the upper ward is almost entirely a rural district.

3932. You say that the upper ward objected to the appointment of the police, because they would be rated generally with the other two wards?—Yes.

3933. Is not the property much more valuable in the other two wards, and would not the assessment therefore be much higher in those wards?—I do not know how they make their assessments, or whether the manufactories are assessed at the same rate as the land, but that has been the reason assigned to me.

3934. You think, generally speaking, the objection to adopt the rural police in Lanark is on account of the unequal assessment?—Yes.

3935. If the assessment were fairly adjusted, you think that objection would no longer exist?—Exactly.

3936. Do not you think it would be a fair thing so to adjust the assessment that that objection should be obviated?—Yes; that has been my objection to the mode of assessment in other parts of Scotland.

3937. Mr. *Howard.*] Would it be necessary to have a system of patrols?—

Mr. *A. J. List.*

23 June 1853.

Not in the rural parts of the country; but in all those parts where there is a large population I think it would be necessary. In our Scotch counties we have an advantage over the English counties in not having our men so thick; I do not see the use of having beats for patrolling a rural district in the same manner as you would in town.

3938. Mr. *Mackie.*] From your knowledge, are you aware that property in Scotland has increased in value in consequence of the establishment of a police force?—I can speak more particularly of our own county. Property has decidedly increased in value round Edinburgh; I hear from the proprietors, and also from the farmers, that they find their crops and everything much better protected, and they have less hesitation in taking a farm now near to Edinburgh than they used to have, in consequence of the protection afforded them. A few years ago a gentleman bought a property in that part of the county, called Gala Water, towards Roxburghshire, and he told me he was induced to buy the property in consequence of looking at my annual table of crime and finding that the parish of Heriot was so free from crime and vagrancy, he was induced to buy the property.

3939. You have no doubt whatever that if a good police force were established in the upper ward of Lanark, it would enhance the value of the property in that district?—I am fully impressed with that idea.

3940. *Chairman.*] What is the character of the police in those districts of Scotland where there is no rural police?—Parish constables; but the rate of pay is such that it does not insure a class of men fit to do the duties.

3941. *Lord Advocate.*] From what class are they generally appointed?—Generally from the agriculturists, or with tradesmen.

3942. *Chairman.*] How are they appointed?—By the commissioners of police.

3943. From lists furnished from the different parishes?—Not exactly lists; but from persons named by respectable inhabitants.

3944. The question referred to the appointment of parish constables?—The parish constables are appointed by the justices of the peace for the county, and they are paid by fees when they are employed.

3945. Mr. *Mackie.*] Do not the parish constables attend to their own occupations, except when they are called upon to go out in pursuit of offenders or otherwise?—Yes; and they give them a retaining fee of 1 *l.* or 2 *l.* a year, and so much when they are employed; generally a very dissipated class.

3946. Do you consider the parish constables of any use whatever in the prevention of crime, or in the detection of offenders?—No; they are neither fit for one nor the other.

3947. *Chairman.*] Do you employ any?—No.

3948. Are they still appointed?—They are appointed in some counties where they have no police.

3949. Are the parish constables appointed where there is a rural police?—Not generally.

3950. *Lord Advocate.*] What proportion of the expenses of the police of Mid-Lothian is repaid by fees from the Exchequer and reported cases?—I cannot tell the amount; I believe the total amount paid for what is called sheriff's accounts in Scotland amounts to about 50,000 *l.*; that embraces the whole; not merely the criminal cases; some part is for other duties.

3951. Are not the civil cases paid for from what is called rogue money?—No.

3952. Can you tell the Committee what amount is paid by each, distinguishing the latter from the former in the police assessment?—No.

3953. Mr. *Mackie.*] Have you any return of the police in the counties of Scotland in general, with their expenses?—I have a table before me which I have made up, giving under different heads the names of the counties, the population of the county in 1851, the number of parishes, the real rent of the county in 1841, the rate of assessment, the area of the county in square miles, the number of police, the rate of pay to the police, the annual cost of constabulary (I was anxious to show what portion they got from the Crown, but was unable to get it), proportion to population, inhabited houses. (*The Witness delivered in the same.*)

Vide Appendix.

3954. *Chairman.*] Can you state from that return what number of counties in Scotland have adopted the rural police force similar to that in Mid Lothian?—Yes; according to this return, only four counties are without a police force.

3955. How

3955. How many counties have adopted it?—I have 26 counties which have adopted it. Bute has no police; from Caithness I have had no return; I have 30 constables at Airdrie; but I can explain that; in the Airdrie district they applied for a local Act of their own; that is the only part of Lanark where they have a police force.

3956. Can you tell the Committee what number of counties in Scotland have adopted a police force similar to that which you have in Mid-Lothian?—Twenty-six; but they are not all organised similar to Mid-Lothian, some only remove beggars.

3957. Mr. *Sotheron.*] How many counties have adopted it partially?—Only Lanark. Renfrew is marked "No police." I have joined one or two counties together; Elgin and Nairn, Clackmannan and Kinross; Orkney and Shetland: those adjoin, and have no police; Ross and Cromartie are united; I have a return from them of 13 constables; the head quarters at Dingwall.

3958. *Chairman.*] Will you now state the names of the counties which have not any police?—Bute, Lanark, with the exception I have given of the Airdrie district; Orkney and Shetland, and Renfrew.

3959. *Lord Advocate.*] Do you think it would be desirable to make the rural police act imperative instead of permissive?—I think so; there is no uniformity of action, in the case of escapes, or of information being sent from one part of the county to the other. I have no guarantee, at least for my own county, that such informations are attended to; and recently for the purpose of ensuring it, I got from every county the police station where the men were placed, so that I could send direct from Edinburgh, not depending upon others to send to every part of Scotland where it was likely the party might go.

3960. If a compulsory Act were introduced, have you any suggestions to make by way of improvement upon the present Act?—I prepared a plan a short time ago, which I submitted to the commissioners of supply and the justices of the peace; and perhaps I may be permitted to read that part of the report as to a uniform system of police in Scotland; I said, " In proposing a uniform system of county police, I would suggest that an average be made of the sums paid by Exchequer to each county for the summary cases, so also for the reported ones, as very large sums are drawn by sheriffs and criminal officers in some counties for this duty, varying from 100 l. to 600 l. each. The Lord Advocate will understand that the Crown pays for the reported cases, and by the order of the Treasury in the year 1852, 30,000 l. was set aside for the summary cases in Scotland, which were not paid for by the Crown; then a fixed annual sum to be paid to each county from the consolidated fund, and all fees to officers abolished; a general Police Act brought in, compelling every county to have a force; the assessment not to exceed a fixed rate per pound on the valued rent, which, with the sums receivable from Exchequer, would establish an efficient and uniform police force."

3961. Do you mean a fixed sum, or a fixed per centage?—A fixed rate of assessment; at that time I thought two-pence over the whole of Scotland would be quite ample.

3962. *Chairman.*] Do you think one penny upon the rental would be sufficient to establish a uniform system of police in Scotland?—Yes; with the sums to be paid by the Crown, but 2 d. would be the safest calculation. Then I say, "Its government should be under an officer attached to the Crown Agent's Office, with a sub for the north, and another for the south of the Tay; and as many counties are small, and others entirely rural, two or three should be united together for police purposes, under the charge of a superintendent or inspector; all orders or instructions to emanate from the chief constable, and periodical reports to be made by him to the Lord Advocate; the local magistracy to have a control as at present, and the chief officer being attached to the Crown Agent's Department would obviate the necessity of creating a centralising Board in Edinburgh."

3963. Mr. *Mackie.*] Do you think that a uniform system of amalgamated police force would be a great improvement in Scotland?—I do think so.

3964. *Lord Advocate.*] If there were a uniform police system well organised, with central management, might it not be more efficiently and cheaply managed than by each county maintaining its own police force, as is at present the case?—Yes; there would be fewer staffs, and more unity of action.

3965. *Chairman.*] Have you formed any estimate of the number of men which would be required for Scotland?—No; I have not gone into the details.

3966. Sir *J. Anderson.*] You propose to amalgamate the town and county

Mr. A. J. List.

23 June 1853.

police throughout Scotland; and you say you think an amalgamation of the county police with the city police of Edinburgh would be an advantage; do you think the same observation would apply with respect to Glasgow and Lanark?—Yes; I think several staffs could be dispensed with, and the system could be economised.

3967. In whom would you vest the management of the police?—I would vest the management of the police, as in the metropolitan police, in paid commissioners under the Crown, and answerable to the Lord Advocate; but of course, in cases of towns with a liberal grant from the consolidated fund, as in the Metropolitan and Dublin forces.

3968. Would you exclude local management entirely?—I would.

3969. Mr. *Mackie.*] In a large city like Glasgow, you would have the management the same as in a county?—Yes.

3970. Sir *J. Anderson.*] Then you would set aside entirely the commissioners of supply, and all kinds of local management?—No, I would not set aside the commissioners of supply, but I would not allow them to interfere with the men; they should have only certain duties to perform, and should not interfere with orders emanating from the head of the police.

3971. Do you find the commissioners interfere with your management of the police force in Edinburgh?—No, I do not. I consider Edinburgh is quite an exception; we have no interference; I am held responsible and I have been very comfortable in the appointment, in consequence of non-interference; but such is not the case in every county.

3972. In the event of an amalgamation of the town and county police, would you consider the commissioners of supply the proper body in whom to vest the management of the police for the town; or in connexion with whom would you recommend that the appointment of the men should be vested?—In the chief constable, appointed by the Government as a commissioner or inspector-general.

3973. How would the Government deal with the details of the police?—The head would appoint the officers under him as superintendents in different localities, and those superintendents would have to report to the chief, and receive all orders from him.

3974. Is it your opinion that the appointment of superintendents superseding the commissioners of supply in their local management is a thing which would be received with anything like favour?—As I stated before, I would not supersede the commissioners of supply; but I consider for police purposes it would be very advantageous that superintendents should be appointed over districts, and would be cheaper in the course of a few years.

3975. Do you think such a great change is necessary in order to secure a uniform system of police?—I do; because a great many things are not attended to; there are a number of Acts of Parliament which have become dead letters, because the commissioners of police do not choose to meddle with those things. I may illustrate by referring to a recent Act, namely, the Cruelty to Animals Act; the town police never take cognisance of that Act, but I take cognisance of it in the county; people may commit cruelty to animals in the town, but in the county they are prosecuted.

3976. *Lord Advocate.*] Substantially you would approve of the police managing the criminal department, as in Scotland?—Yes.

3977. Is there any difficulty in the management of criminal cases by the police?—With the exception of paying by fees; I think fees are apt to give the officials and other officers an interest in offences; I would have salaries in all the departments.

3978. There would be no difficulty in the commissioners of supply continuing to manage police affairs, provided they did not interfere with them in the execution of their duty?—No; but there is the difficulty.

3979. *Chairman.*] Supposing the appointment were left, as it is now, with the commissioners of supply and the magistrates of Edinburgh, do you think that in the county of Mid-Lothian and in the city of Edinburgh the two police forces might be placed under the direction of one chief constable or superintendent, whichever he was called?—I think so, advantageously.

3980. Still the local appointments would remain the same, but the superintendence would be by one officer?—I am afraid if you left the local appointments to be made as before, they would be clashing with one another.

3981. *Lord Advocate.*] Supposing your plan were carried out of having one central

Mr. *A. J. List.*

23 June 1853.

-central officer in Edinburgh, who should be the head of a general police system, would there be any difficulty in working that system, although the local officers were appointed by local commissioners?—I think not; I would not allow them to give any orders.

3982. Sir *J. Anderson.*] Are you speaking merely of a criminal police?—No: I think prevention of crime is one of the principal duties of the police.

3983. Are not you aware that the Edinburgh police have much more to do than to deal merely with criminal matters; that they have to deal with sanitary matters; would it not be necessary to separate the prevention and detection of crime from the duties of the police, connected with sanitary matters, and various other things connected with the proper conducting of a large municipality?—As regards Edinburgh, from a residence of 14 years, I am not aware that the police perform any very onerous duties connected with sanitary matters.

3984. Do not the police give information with respect to pavements and drains under the local Act?—They have a separate officer at the head of each department.

3985. Do not they employ the police?—The same thing is done in the metropolitan police, in London, they attend to a variety of duties, and so also in county forces.

3986. Do the county police consider it any part of their duty to look after the sanitary matters connected with the county?—Yes, the county police perform duties of that description; for instance, in the first three years, the rural police acted as road police, and effected a saving of nine road officers, at an expense of at least 250 *l.* per annum to the road trustees, and during the first three years of the establishment, there were 1,255 convictions under the Turnpike Act. In all cases, the constables investigate, collect evidence, report thereon; and in summary cases, by an arrangement made in June 1841, by the sheriff, they cite witnesses, execute sheriff's criminal warrants for the fixed salaries they receive; and perform all the duties in such cases that used to be performed by the sheriff's criminal officers. During the first three years of the county police being in operation, there were 860 summary convictions, &c.; from the procurator-fiscal's criminal records, there appears to have been 355 summary convictions for the three years previous to the county police being established. I do not consider, from the increase of summary convictions, that crime has increased, but that it is attributable to many offences having been passed over unnoticed. There is another circumstance which, during the former of these periods, has increased the number of convictions: from the superior training of the police force, cases are more correctly reported than formerly, and convictions are, therefore, more certain; fewer cases break down at trial, as the evidence, from the accuracy of preliminary inquiries, seldom fails. Under the Nuisance Removal Act, in all the parishes they act as assistant inspectors. I consider that the police can be trained o perform many other duties which at present they do not perform.

3987. Is it your opinion, supposing the commissioners of supply to have the entire management of the police, that it would be a suitable arrangement in a large town to supersede all local authorities?—I think so, on public occasions when a body of men are required. I have done duty in different parts of London before I left the metropolitan force. I found we could act with a properly trained body of men, and suppress a riot without the aid of the military; but I find in Scotland, whenever there was any outbreak, the inhabitants were forced to enrol themselves as special constables, and then to apply to the Commander-in-Chief for military assistance; the police are merely lookers-on. In the year 1846 the county police were called in to suppress an outbreak at the construction of a railway. I took a large body of the Edinburgh police in two omnibuses to the place, and actually the Highlanders and Irish were burning the navvy huts, and the police were running in all directions. I was asked by Sheriff Jameson where the police were; I said, "Taking care of themselves. If I was in London, and had a similar body of the A Division with me, we would have stopped this."

3988. Mr. *Sotheron.*] What was the difference in the number of the police that so ran away compared with the A Division?—I said, if I had had a similar number of the A Division.

3989. What was the number that so ran away?—They were none of them efficient; I could not get them assembled together; I could not get them to fall in.

3990. Do you suppose there were 20 that ran away?—There were full 20;

Mr. A. J. List.

23 June 1853.

some of my own men ran away; we had not drilled them; but now I have endeavoured to drill them as much as I can.

3991. Do you attribute their running away to want of discipline and training, more than to the smallness of their number?—I do.

3992. Mr. *Fitzroy*.] Are not the Edinburgh police drilled?—Now they are. The superintendent is doing what he can to make them effective, but the drilling is not palatable to the Honourable Board of Commissioners.

3993. Mr. *Mackie*.] Are they trained to the use of arms?—No, only to marching drill, not to the use of arms; I think they should be trained to arms.

3994. *Chairman*.] Are they drilled to the use of the cutlass?—No.

3995. Mr. *Mackie*.] Do not you think it is advisable they should be drilled? —Yes.

3996. *Chairman*.] Do not you think that the employment of the military is vey objectionable in the case of an apprehended riot?—Yes; the military should be employed only in very extreme cases.

3997. Do not you think a police force is very much more efficient for the purpose of quelling a riot than soldiers?—I think so.

3998. A policeman can leave his ranks and go into the mob and use persuasion, which a soldier cannot do?—Yes.

3999. Mr. *Mackie*.] A policeman can use his baton with his right hand, and seize a ringleader with his left?—Yes; police officers possess many advantages, when drilled and trained, over soldiers in the suppression of a riot.

4000. *Chairman*.] Is not his local knowledge of some use?—Yes.

4001. If a soldier is called upon to act, it can only be with the probable loss of life?—Yes.

4002. *Lord Advocate*.] Do you act as criminal prosecutor?—Only in statutory offences, where fines are imposed, not for offences at common law.

4003. Mr. *Mackie*.] Do you think it is advantageous to move policemen from one station to another?—Yes.

4004. In the case of an amalgamated force, do not you think it would be very advantageous to move the policemen from one county to another, with a uniform system of pay at the same time?—Yes; at present, in consequence of the want of uniformity, we are not enabled to train our men. We are obliged to put the men on important duties without proper experience.

4005. Is there any further information which you desire to give to the Committee?—Another duty, which I consider a public and important one in Scotland, is the inspection of the lodging-houses. In consequence of the want of police, we do not attend to that. I have a list of the number of lodging-houses, showing how necessary it would be that the police, by having a uniform system, might check vagrancy in a great degree, and thus prevent a great deal of crime. The vagrants travel from one county to another. The other counties have a similar number of lodging-houses to what we have in Mid-Lothian. At present there is no control. The neighbouring county of East-Lothian have recently established a vagrant police, and they have five or six men who attend entirely to the removal of vagrants, and passing them through their county. I am assured, by the superintendent there, that since the plan has been adopted there have been scarcely any cases of crime at all, showing that the petty crime has been uniformly committed in that county by travelling vagrants.

4006. Have you any superanuation fund?—No.

4007. Do not you think it would be very advantageous to have a superannuation fund?—Yes; it would induce men to join us, and to remain with us when they are well trained, and also to perform hazardous duty with more determination.

Mr. *James Smart*, called in; and Examined.

Mr. J. Smart.

4008. *Lord Advocate*.] YOU are the Superintendent of the Glasgow Police, are you not?—Yes.

4009. How long have you been so?—Four years; I am superintendent now of the whole of the police; I was for many years superintendent in one of the separate boroughs, called Calton.

4010. How long have you been in the police force altogether?—Twenty years; I joined in 1832; I was six months in the Metropolitan force before that.

4011. By whom are the police of Glasgow appointed?—The Lord Provost, the

magistrates

Mr. J. Smart.

23 June 1853.

magistrates of the city, and the sheriff of the county appoint the chief superinten-dent, who appoints all the others, and promotes or dismisses them.

4012. Under whose orders is the superintendent?—Under the orders of the magistrates and of the sheriff, to a certain extent.

4013. How far does the police extend; to the boundaries of the borough?—The Parliamentary bounds; the police extends over the whole of the bounds; and to the north, the ancient royalty extends beyond the Parliamentary limit, which we also take in, making a district of 12 square miles.

4014. Does the city police extend beyond the Parliamentary bounds?—It does.

4015. What is the amount of the force?—Six hundred.

4016. Is it supported by assessment?—Yes.

4017. What is the population of Glasgow?—About 347,000.

4018. Do you consider your force sufficient?—Yes; I had an addition of 20 men to it about a month since.

4019. How long before that was the last addition?—I got an addition of six men last year at my own request, and 20 this year; the city is increasing very fast.

4020. What is the rate of assessment?—The rate of assessment is laid on to cover three or four different objects; it amounts to 1s. 2d. in the pound; that includes the police, detective and preventive; it includes lighting, cleansing, fire-engines, and there are sums in lieu of petty customs which are abolished; they are all put together.

4021. Is the whole of the force under your direction and orders?—The whole.

4022. Is there any police in the county?—There is in the western suburbs, namely, Partick, which is a part inhabited by the merchants of Glasgow; they took advantage of the General Police Bill for Scotland last year, and they have now a police of their own; the borough of Airdrie has a police, and there is the district of the county round Dundyvan and Gartsherrie ironworks, who have also a police.

4023. That is under a local Act?—Yes; under an Act for enabling the pro-prietors of public works to assess a certain district to establish police; those are all the places in Lanarkshire which have a police.

4024. Are Dundyvan and Airdrie in the middle ward?—No; they are in what used to be the middle ward; it is now called the Airdrie district.

4025. In the rural part of the middle ward there is no police, and none in the upper ward?—No.

4026. Will you state what is the effect of there being no police in those dis-tricts?—The Glasgow police are very much annoyed in the detection of criminals who have committed crimes beyond their jurisdiction; it also gives facilities to our thieves to carry stolen articles out of the city, and we have the trouble of going after them.

4027. That facility is greatly used, is it not?—Greatly; there is scarcely a farm-house that is not stripped of its lead, or a barn-yard that is not robbed of its poultry; the shirts, or anything that is left out of doors, are dragged off, and there is nobody to look after the thieves.

4028. What is the reason they have not adopted the Police Act?—The three districts could never agree about it; what the particular reason was I never could learn.

4029. *Chairman.*] Was not money the difficulty?—I have no doubt that cash was the difficulty.

4030. *Lord Advocate.*] Do you think there would be any injustice in making the Act compulsory?—None whatever; it would be a great improvement. The city of Glasgow police apprehended last year no less than 34 criminals, all belong-ing to different counties, who come into their hands; and on all the principal public occasions which have occurred in four or five different counties round Glasgow, the Glasgow police have been called upon to go out. On the Queen's visit 160 men were sent down. Our men are sent to races, colliers' strikes, Orange meetings, and elections of Members of Parliament all over Ayrshire, Renfrewshire and Dumbartonshire. The Glasgow police have sent 514 men on various occasions during these two or three years.

4031. If there were a uniform system of police, all that would be saved?—Yes; all that shows the necessity of a police.

Mr. J. Smart.

23 June 1853.

4032. Sir *J. Anderson.*] Are not your men sent under the power in the local Act, which authorises the sheriff to require you to send your men to other places in cases of emergency?—The sheriff of the county of Lanark has, under the Act of Parliament, the power to apply to the Lord Provost, and we are allowed to send any number of the Glasgow police to any part, as the Lord Provost may think fit.

4033. The parties requiring assistance paying the expense?—Yes.

4034. Mr. *Rich.*] When you say that it was the fear of expense which induced some districts not to adopt the police, do you consider that that was a well understood economy?—I do not; it is much the reverse; I may state that Glasgow is growing very fast; all the villages round the city are left wholly without police protection. I have just now in Renfrewshire, at Pollockshields, which is a suburb of Glasgow, three men watching who are paid by the people themselves, and I have one man at Upper Pollock.

4035. Did you not say that you considered your force was large enough?—Yes, for our own district.

4036. Sir *J. Anderson.*] You have stated that the force consisted of 600 men; those men are not all employed in the detection and prevention of crime; have you included in that number, the men who are employed for other purposes?—No; the strength of the Glasgow police is 600 men; that includes 40 men in the dock and harbour police, but they are under my control, the same as the others.

4037. Lord *Advocate.*] Do you think a night patrol is essential for the protection of property?—No doubt of it.

4038. Have you a night patrol at present?—All our roads are patrolled within our own bounds.

4039. Would it not be useful to have a patrol beyond the bounds?—Yes, I have not the least doubt of it.

4040. *Chairman.*] Supposing Glasgow were made a separate district for police purposes, would it be desirable to extend the district to the suburbs further than it is at present?—I think it would, the suburbs in the immediate neighbourhood of the city of Glasgow require in addition to the patrolling, lighting, and other privileges; then again, nearly all the Glasgow thieves go out to the country, and the city police would be the best parties to be on the spot, to be able to receive them, and to check their operations.

4041. In that case, however the police are appointed, would it not be better that the police of Glasgow, and the police of the county of Lanark and the adjoining county, should be under one head?—No doubt of it; we have one circuit court district, which embraces the three counties of Lanark, Dumbarton, and Renfrew; all the high crimes and offences are tried in one court, which is held in Glasgow.

4042. Whatever uniform system of police were adopted, would not it be desirable also, for the purpose of co-operation, and for the purpose of diminishing the expense, to reduce the staff, by having as many districts as possible under one superintendent?—No doubt.

4043. Would not such an arrangement, in your opinion, give greater efficiency to the police, and also diminish the expense?—No doubt it would save the separate staffs.

4044. Mr. *Mackie*] Is there any county police in Renfrewshire?—None.

4045. Do you find that a great inconvenience?—Yes; portions of Renfrewshire are within our municipal bounds; beyond that it is one of the worst places in Scotland for crime. No doubt they want a police very badly. They had one for several years, but they quarrelled regarding the expense, and gave it up.

4046. Would you recommend a uniform system of amalgamated police force for Scotland generally, and particularly embracing the counties of which you have spoken? With proper divisions, I think it would be an improvement.

4047. Sir *J. Anderson.*] You have stated that you have the entire control of the men, with reference to their appointment and dismissal; in whom is vested the management of the details of the Glasgow police?—In the committee of the town council, consisting of 28 members, the Lord Provost and magistrates being *ex officio* members.

4048. Do you find that you are interfered with at all in the management of your force by this committee of the town council?—I have never once been interfered with by any one party.

4049. They do not interfere with your appointment of the men, or show any favouritism?

favouritism ?—Never. I am held responsible for everything that is done. I have the full management of the concern.

Mr. J. Smart.

23 June 1853.

4050. In obtaining the clothing for the men, and other articles, all that is done by contract, so that there can be no jobbing or favouritism in the management of such matters at Glasgow ?—There is none at all.

4051. Was not Glasgow divided, until within a few years, into four separate boroughs ?—We had four separate boroughs in Glasgow within the Parliamentary bounds. We had the harbour police under a separate management. There were then separate magistrates, separate superintendents of police, and separate establishments, and it was found to work very ill indeed.

4052. In 1846 all these separate boroughs were joined together; and in the separate police forces there has been an amalgamation, and it is now under the management of a committee of the town council; is not that so ?—Yes.

4053. You are aware that that has been a very great improvement in the police of the city of Glasgow ?—No doubt of it.

4054. So that you have had experience of amalgamation in the city of Glasgow ? —Yes.

4055. Mr. *Mackie*.] If the principle of amalgamation were extended over the counties of Dumbarton and Renfrewshire, the adjoining counties, do not you consider that that would be a great advantage ?—No doubt, in conjunction with our Glasgow police, those three counties I have mentioned could be easily managed at a very little cost indeed.

4056. Sir *J. Anderson*.] In whom would you vest the management of the police, supposing the county police were amalgamated with the city police ?— I could not wish for a better management than that which the city police is under at present; it might be necessary, were it extended to other counties, to have a small police committee of perhaps the sheriff of each county, and one or two commissioners of supply.

4057. To act in union with the town council ?—Yes; as any detached police establishment, not part or parcel of Glasgow, where all the criminals come from, would be of exceedingly little use, as they would require to go into Glasgow for information.

4058. *Chairman*.] Have you the appointment of all the officers under you ?—Yes.

4059. Have you the power of dismissing them ?—Yes.

4060. Do not you think that is an indispensably necessary power for the chief officer to have ?—Yes.

4061. Whatever local arrangements may be made as to the management of the police, still you think they should be, as far as possible, under one head ?—Yes, I think they should be all under one head.

4062. Sir *J. Anderson*.] You have had experience of suppressing riots in Glasgow on various occasions, by means of a police force, have you not ?—Yes; I have been connected with the suppression of many riots in Glasgow; the disturbance of the cotton-spinners in 1837; and I was engaged in that of 1848 also.

4063. Mr. *Howard*.] Was it not necessary to call in the out-pensioners ?—Yes; I had charge of a party of out-pensioners on that occasion.

4064. Sir *J. Anderson*.] Have you not been able on several occasions to suppress a considerable disturbance, without the aid of the military ?—During all my experience in Glasgow, the riots of 1848 was the only case when the military were called in.

4065. *Chairman*.] On the occasion when the pensioners were called out, were they armed ?—Yes, with the usual muskets and bayonet.

4066. Mr. *Rich*.] Were the pensioners under your orders ?—No.

4067. Did they receive their orders from the military officer in command ?— Yes.

4068. Sir *J. Anderson*] Do not you act as procurator-fiscal in the police ?— Yes, I am the procurator-fiscal of the police court

4069. Do not you consider that that affords great facility for the speedy disposal of offences against the Police Act, and for the punishment of petty offences ?—It is a great improvement over the English system; there is no expense in the first place incurred in getting up the case; one of the great disputes in Renfrewshire was, that they had not summary jurisdiction, and when they had an efficient police, that that increased the fiscal charges for prosecuting; that was one of the worst grievances they felt.

4070. *Chairman.*] Have you ever been in any other police force?—I was in the metropolitan force before I went to Glasgow.

4071. *Lord Advocate.*] Do you consider it would be desirable that in a general system of police, the police should be under the same control as the procurator-fiscal is?—I do not see any objection.

4072. Does not it work perfectly well as regards the procurator-fiscal?—You are aware that the procurator-fiscal in Glasgow for instance, is appointed by the magistrates and paid by the magistrates.

4073. Is not the county procurator-fiscal, as well as the borough procurator-fiscal, under the orders of the Lord Advocate?—At Glasgow, we are not amalgamated as to criminal jurisdiction for the higher offences; we have two jurisdictions, which do not work so well.

4074. *Sir J. Anderson.*] Are your men extensively employed in detecting offences against the Public-house Act?—That has been one of the duties performed by the police; my attention was turned to it when I took charge of the force; I considered the arrangement of the public-houses in Glasgow one of the most important branches of public duty.

4075. *Mr. Howard.*] Do the men in your force inspect the lodging-houses?—Yes; and the Glasgow police inspect the weights and measures, and take charge of the licensing of all the hackney coaches and cabs, and of the public-houses also.

4076. *Sir J. Anderson.*] Do they not give a great deal of their attention to sanitary matters?—Hitherto the time of the Glasgow police has been more taken up in keeping the city in proper order than with reference to crime or criminals.

4077. *Chairman.*] You are well acquainted with the system of the metropolitan police?—Yes.

4078. Have you any acquaintance with the rural police in England?—I cannot say that I am intimately acquainted with any other police in England.

4079. Do you know what the system of rural police is in the counties in England, and how they are appointed?—I cannot say that I am much acquainted with it.

4080. *Sir J. Anderson.*] Do you think that if the local management were entirely set aside, and a general police system were adopted under the management of the Crown, that system would be received with anything like satisfaction by the people?—In such a city as Glasgow I am quite sure it would not be.

4081. *Chairman.*] In the city of Glasgow the police is so large that there is really no interference with your management; it is entirely under your control?—Completely.

4082. In your opinion it is desirable that it should be so?—Yes.

4083. Supposing in other towns there is interference by the committee of the corporations, do not you believe that such interference would be injurious to the ends of justice?—No doubt of it; I am perfectly aware of the mischief.

4084. *Mr. Philipps.*] You say that our force has been augmented; under what circumstances did that augmentation take place?—I represented to the police committee the necessity for an increase, first, of the police establishment of 20 men, and also that an increase of pay was wanted to each man in the force, both of which recommendations were acceded to unanimously, which added an expense of 3,500 *l.* to the annual outlay.

4085. *Chairman.*] Supposing there were a uniform system of police in England and Scotland, can you tell the committee any difference or distinction which you think it would be desirable to draw between England and Scotland, as to the police?—There are a number of differences in England, although I cannot explain them to the Committee, such as the different method of paying constables, and the sources from which the assessments are derived. I can see no reason why the police should not be conducted in the same way as in England.

4086. You think the same principle might be adopted with a difference as to the means of paying the men?—Yes, suitable to the locality.

4087. What do your men cost a year?—About 50 *l.* a head, clothing and all.

4088. *Mr. Mackie.*] Does that include your salary?—Yes.

4089. *Mr. Philipps.*] Have you any superannuation fund?—Unfortunately, there is no superannuation fund; that is one great want.

4090. *Mr. Mackie.*] You consider that it would be very desirable to have a superannuation fund for the police?—It is indispensable; had I remained in the metropolitan

metropolitan force, I should have been entitled to two-thirds of my pay for life. In Glasgow, I am not entitled to one farthing.

4091. *Chairman.*] Do you give any rewards to your men for the apprehension of offenders?—Yes.

4092. In what way do you give rewards?—A portion of the fines inflicted on the constables for neglect of duty is set apart as a reward for those who are active in the execution of their duty.

4093. Sir *J. Anderson.*] Is that a private arrangement of your own?—Yes.

4094. The committee of the town council do not object to it?—The committee do not interfere with it.

4095. Mr. *Philipps.*] Do you think it would add materially to your power of enforcing discipline with your men, if there were a superannuation fund?—Yes.

4096. *Chairman.*] By whom are those fines inflicted?—By myself; I inflict the fines.

4097. Then they are not fines inflicted by information laid before a magistrate? I do not take my constables before a magistrate at all; they are brought before me; I am the magistrate so far as that is concerned.

4098. Have you had any objection on the part of the men who have been so brought before you, to pay the fines which you have so inflicted?—No.

4099. Sir *J Anderson.*] What is your salary?—£.400.

4100. Mr. *Mackie.*] Does that include everything?—It includes everything; I have no fees; the Glasgow police receive no fees of any sort; they used to get a fee on reporting a public-house for a contravention of the Licensing Act; I thought it was not good, and it is abolished.

4101. *Chairman.*] You say that you inspect the lodging-houses?—Yes.

4102. Do not you think that that is a very necessary duty?—It is essential with the licensed lodging-houses; we inspect them; we apply the Removal of Nuisance and the Prevention of Disease Act. I did so last year, and compelled the landlords to clean out the staircases and the dwelling-houses.

4103. How long has that existed?—Glasgow was the first place that obtained the power to license lodging-houses; in 1840 we got the first Bill.

4104. Mr. *Philipps.*] What per-centage of your pay was appropriated in the metropolitan force to the superannuation fund?—Two and a half per cent. is the maximum; but I believe there is seldom so much as that taken off.

4105. *Chairman.*] Will you state to the Committee the gross cost of the police at Glasgow?—The total amount expended in wages, for watching, clothing, and so on, in the criminal, preventive, and detective departments in Glasgow, was 26,085 *l.* 17 *s.* 3 *d.*

4106. Is that strictly for police purposes?—Yes.

4107. What is that in the pound?—About 5 *d.* in the pound; that includes, however, 81 *l.* 4 *s.* 6 *d.* paid for the maintenance of prisoners in the various station-houses. There is to be deducted 2,748 *l.*, being the fines recovered by the police force.

4108. Sir *J. Anderson.*] Have you not a number of sub-superintendents under you?—Six.

4109. What are their salaries?—They range from 200 *l.* paid to the superintendent of the central district, down to 100 *l.*, the one last appointed.

4110. Do your superintendents act in the different districts?—They act each in his own district.

4111. Do they act under you?—Yes; they take charge of the district.

David Murray, Esq., called in; and Examined.

4112. *Chairman.*] WHAT situation do you hold?—I was Provost and Chief Magistrate of the burgh of Paisley from 1844 to 1850.

4113. *Lord Advocate.*] Did you not adopt the rural police in Renfrewshire at one time?—We had the police at one time for a short period, for about two years.

4114. In what year was that?—Several years ago.

4115. Why was the police given up?—The expense, I fancy, was the reason of its being given up.

4116. What has been the result of abandoning the police system?—The result has been that the county is, in a great measure, without protection; the only detective

D. *Murray*, Esq.

23 June 1853.

detective force is some constables employed under the procurators-fiscal in the different districts.

4117. How are they paid?—By fees charged against the county; but in the districts of Pollockshaws and Johnstone the inhabitants have, within the last year or two, made a voluntary subscription to augment the sum allowed by the county, in order to obtain a more efficient police force.

4118. In your opinion, would it be desirable to make the Police Act compulsory?—I think so.

4119. What was the rate in the pound, when you had a police force?—The amount was about 850 *l.* per annum, which I think would be a little more than a penny per pound on the real rental, after the usual deduction for repairs.

4120. Do the proprietors in Renfrewshire find that too heavy a burthen to continue?—I believe there was a little party feeling mixed up with the question of expense.

4121. Would you recommend that all those feelings should be overridden by a general compulsory Act?—Yes, decidedly.

4122. Do you think local management or central management the most desirable?—Excepting for a criminal or detective police, I do not see any advantage to be derived from a general management.

4123. In your opinion, a local management would be sufficient?—There are a great many duties devolving upon the police, which I do not think would be efficiently discharged by central management, especially in towns.

4124. Mr. *Mackie.*] Do you think an uniform system of police throughout all Scotland would be desirable?—I think an uniform system of police force, if it were made compulsory upon every county and district to provide a police force, would be a very proper thing.

4125. Would you recommend the same rate of pay all over Scotland?—I do not see any advantage to be derived from that.

4126. *Lord Advocate.*] Do not you think for a detective system, it would be a great advantage if a person at Edinburgh or Glasgow were able to communicate with the police in any part of the country?—As far as the criminal or detective police is concerned, I think it would be a great advantage.

4127. Sir *J. Anderson.*] Can you separate one set of duties from another, with advantage, which the police perform in the towns?—Not in the towns; and it is in the towns where the other duties of the police are more numerous than in the country.

4128. Have you formed any notion as to the management of an amalgamated police system?—I have never been able to see my way to a proper system of amalgamated police.

4129. That is, the union of the borough and county police?—I fear that is in a great measure impracticable, so far as I am able to see.

4130. *Lord Advocate.*] Why should you fear it to be impracticable?—I do not see any advantage to be derived from it; besides the different duties which devolve on a town and county police, there would be a difficulty in adjusting the rate of taxation.

4131. The question is whether it is impracticable; you have a separate procurator-fiscal for the borough of Paisley?—We have a fiscal for the justices of the peace, and a fiscal for the magistrates of the borough.

4132. Besides the county fiscal?—Yes.

4133. Would there be any difficulty in the sheriff's fiscal doing the work of the borough fiscal too?—No, I do not think there would.

4134. Is it not rather an inconvenience having two officials for the criminal work. In order to give you an illustration of what is supposed to be the uniform system of police contrasted with a local police?—In so far as the district is concerned there should be one prosecutor.

4135. Is there any difficulty in the same way in having one police for the borough and county?—I think there are a great many duties devolving upon the police in towns that must be under local management; I do not see how those are to be separated in large municipalities.

4136. In Glasgow the superintendent of police is practically under local management, but he is the despot of the police; he does as he pleases; is not that much the best position for such a force to be in?—Yes, in so far as the detection of criminals is concerned; but I apprehend that the superintendent of police in Glasgow

Glasgow does take instructions, in so far as other duties with respect to sanitary and municipal regulations are concerned.

4137. Sir *J. Anderson.*] You think it is necessary to have a local body to direct the superintendent in regard to sanitary matters, and matters not connected with the criminal departments?—Yes.

4138. *Lord Advocate.*] Supposing you had that local management, it does not follow that there is any difficulty in having one police for the town and county?—I do not see the advantage to be derived from it.

4139. *Chairman.*] Supposing there were a reservation of local management for the police in the borough and in the county, do not you think there would be an advantage from their co-operating as far as possible?—Yes.

4140. Do you not think co-operation between two bodies of police in adjoining counties is an advantage for the purpose of detecting offenders?—Certainly.

4141. Do not you think, reserving the local management, which in your opinion is necessary, it is desirable that they should be placed under one head?—I think, if some such arrangement could be devised in conjunction with local management, it would be advantageous.

4142. Sir *J. Anderson.*] Is it your opinion that in Paisley the police, though under local management, might send men into the county?—I think Paisley might, at all events, take the upper ward of the county. There is also Greenock, another large municipality, with a police force, which might take its surrounding district, provided the force was sufficient, and the county willing to bear the proportion of the cost.

4143. Do you think it is an advantage placing the management of the police under the commissioners of supply?—Either with them or some other local body.

4144. What is the state of the Paisley police?—It is very defective; we are still working under the old local Act obtained in 1806; it is very defective in many respects; there is a body of commissioners of police elected by 5 *l.* ratepayers, and I must say they do not exactly co-operate with the magistrates; there is a sort of official status, which makes the members of two local bodies jealous of each other.

4145. Are not the commissioners a popularly elected body, which is subject to local influences?—Yes, a certain number are elected annually; I do not think it is advisable in any municipality to have two bodies in charge of the police; I think it is better that the police should be under one body.

4146. *Lord Advocate.*] If the police were under the orders of the sheriff alone, would there be, in your opinion, any objection to that?—I still see the difficulties with respect to the other duties devolving on the police; I see none in regard to criminal matters.

4147. Would not the sheriff be as good and competent an authority in directing such matters as any local body could be?—I think he has already enough to do.

4148. Is not he as well acquainted with the local wants as the magistrates?—I do not think he is.

4149. Has not your sheriff-substitute at Paisley as good an opportunity of judging of the wants of the borough as any other inhabitant of Paisley?—I do not think he has the time to devote to it; I think there must be some body upon whom the consideration of these matters must devolve.

4150. *Chairman.*] As I understand, you think the police should be under local management; but that the body having the management of the police should not be an annually elected body?—Not exactly that; I think the appointment of the chief officer of police, as in Glasgow, should be vested in the sheriff and chief magistrate; I do not think it is desirable that the office of the chief of the police should be under the control of a popularly elected body; but there are a great many matters connected with the police, which, for well-regulating the community, require a local board to attend to.

4151. Sir *J. Anderson.*] In your opinion, the sheriff could not give his attention to such matters as lighting and cleaning, but that a municipal body could. You think the sheriff is not a suitable person to have the management of the police?—No, except in criminal matters.

4152. *Chairman.*] Is not the prevention of crime and the preservation of order a great part of the duty of the police?—Yes; the detection of crime is one of the principal duties of the police, certainly; but there are a great many other duties in every community to be attended to.

4153. Sir *J. Anderson.*] Do not you think the well-being of a community

D. Murray, Esq.

23 June 1853.

depends very much upon the proper regulation of lodging-houses and the putting down of vagrancy?—Yes.

4154. And attention to the sanitary condition of the town, as well as to the suppression of crime?—Those are some of the principal objects; there are a great many others which require the attention of a local body.

4155. *Chairman.*] Do you think those matters require the interference of a local body?—I think questions will arise connected with those subjects which will require to be from time to time considered, discussed, and decided by a local body.

4156. *Lord Advocate.*] Take the case of Glasgow; do you suppose Mr. Smart has instructions generally from the corporation with regard to the inspection of lodging-houses, lighting, cleaning, and so forth?—I have no doubt that Mr. Smart from time to time makes his reports and gets instructions.

4157. Do not you think, substantially he does a great part of the work himself without instructions?—Yes.

4158. Do not you think the duty is probably better performed than if he had to go for instructions to the corporation?—I think there must be responsibility to some local authority.

4159. *Chairman.*] Would the police being subject to a local authority, tend to interference on the part of that local body?—No, I should not think so.

4160. *Sir J. Anderson.*] Are you aware that at Glasgow there is fortnightly a meeting by Act of Parliament of this committee of the town council, which manages the police?—I do not know how often they meet; I know they meet at short intervals of time for the consideration of public business.

4161. Is it not their duty to give instructions to the superintendent on any matter requiring the cognisance of the police?—Yes, quite so.

4162. Does not he take his instructions from them?—Yes.

4163. *Mr. Philipps.*] Have not you said that there were some constables in Renfrewshire who were supported by voluntary subscription?—Yes; the operation is this: in certain districts, where there is a procurator-fiscal stationed, when information is lodged with him of the commission of some crime, it is his duty to look after it, and he employs a constable; the county have allowed certain expenses for that, but the principal inhabitants in the neighbourhood, with the view to make that more efficient, have voluntarily assessed themselves in addition, in order to secure the services of an efficient police.

4164. Do you find the payments fall off from time to time?—I believe they are principally raised by one or two influential parties, owners of large public works, or parties who have a great interest in the locality, and who take the trouble of collecting them.

George Vere Irving, Esq., called in; and Examined.

G. V. Irving, Esq.

4165. *Lord Advocate.*] ARE you the proprietor of an estate in the upper ward of Lanarkshire?—Yes.

4166. You have not adopted the Police Act in the upper ward, have you?—No, we have not; we have had a great deal of discussion about it; we have not adopted it in the county at all.

4167. From what causes has the non-adoption of the Act proceeded?—We began the discussion about the time of the introduction of the Act; at that time I was an advocate for it; seeing its advantages, and hearing what the judges at the Dumfries circuit said of it, I voted at first for it, until I saw the details of the plan. I found that the proposed plan of a police for the county of Lanark was 40 police for the lower ward, 20 for the middle ward, and 7 for the upper ward. I am speaking from recollection, to show its proportion. I have here a return of the whole of the property in those wards: in the upper ward the value of the property is 135,649*l.*, in the middle ward, 450,915 *l.*, and in the lower ward 157,438 *l.*, so that, in fact, the upper ward, with its seven policemen, would pay as much as the lower ward, with its 40 policemen.

4168. Are you now speaking of the valued rent of the three wards?—No; the real rental under the last Rogue Money Act.

4169. In consequence of that inequality the upper ward rejected the proposition for the police?—Substantially this was the reason why it was rejected by the county, not by the upper ward alone. The matter has assumed various bearings. Latterly the upper ward has been anxious to establish a police for itself, and

endeavoured

G. V. *Irving*, Esq.

23 June 1853.

endeavoured to have the 5 & 6 Vict. c. 109, extended to Scotland; but this proposition was negatived by the rest of the county. There were other reasons, however; one reason was, that even supposing the upper ward had seven or eight constables given to it, which would be as many as would find employment, a large number would have been idle loungers. This would have done very little good to the upper part of the upper ward, because we can more easily communicate by the railways with the town of Lanark, than with the villages, where the constables would have been placed; and we should still have had to pay as much as the other wards, where there were many more men.

4170. Substantially, the reason why you did not adopt the police was, that you thought you would have had to pay a great deal more than the police you required would cost?—Yes; but we should have less objected to it, provided we could have had the advantage of the neighbouring counties' police to have worked with us.

4171. What is the state of the neighbourhood in the upper ward?—My neighbourhood has not suffered so much as the district immediately lower down, because being a wild country, the vagrants pass through it towards Biggar, where they have been obliged to establish a voluntary police.

4172. Do not a great many vagrants harbour in your district?—I do not think they harbour with us; they harbour lower down, but they pass through our district to an enormous extent.

4173. It is the receptacle for all the scoundrels of the country?—Yes.

4174. Do not they commit great depredations?—Lower down they do, but not so much with us.

4175. Mr. *Mackie*.] Do you consider a uniform amalgamated police force for Scotland would be a great advantage?—I should be satisfied with no amalgamated police, unless it were a national police, and the police in the neighbouring counties would act together. I had a great deal of opportunity for observing the want of unity between the police forces during the construction of the Caledonian Railway. I found that the police on the railway and the police in the neighbouring county did not work cordially together; there was a great deal of jealousy between them.

4176. If there were a national police force, you would be able to depend upon Dumbarton assisting you?—Yes; we would mutually assist each other.

4177. Mr. *Howard*.] Would the seven men whom you have referred to have been able to patrol the district?—The upper ward is such an immense district that the men would not have been able to patrol it efficiently, unless they were mounted, and even then it would have been very doubtful. As the crime chiefly arises from vagrants, the best arrangement would be to station the men so that they might command the leading roads.

4178. Sir *J. Trollope*.] Do you contemplate that a national police force should be paid for by the country?—I should certainly say so, or at least the assessment should extend to moveable property. The present system of payment by real property alone, not exactly landed property, because it includes a great deal of other property, is most unjust, because that description of property derives almost no benefit from the police at all. The offences against it are not properly those which fall under the duty of the police, such as perjury, arson, &c., with the exception of malicious mischief, the cases of which are insignificant. The bulk of cases occur in the defence of moveable property, which escapes entirely from taxation.

4179. Mr. *Mackie*.] At present, the landed property in Scotland pays the whole of the cost of the police?—There is a power under the Police Act to assess other property; but this only extends to other classes of fixed property which pays the whole cost of the police, while it is not affected by the ordinary crimes.

4180. Thieves cannot carry the fixed property away?—It is impossible. I may mention an instance in illustration of the subject, in our county, which struck me forcibly at the time: during one of the riots I was an officer in the yeomanry, and we were obliged to be upon duty at Hamilton; when it was stated by the sheriff and other magistrates that the value of property in the palace there in the shape of pictures and articles of vertù, was such, that if the palace had been sacked by the mob, the damage would have been more than the county could have been able to replace; yet that property, though liable to be stolen, entirely escaped any taxation at all.

Robert Bruce Macleod, Esq., called in; and Examined.

4181. *Lord Advocate.*] YOU are the proprietor of a considerable estate in Ross?—Yes.

4182. What is the state of your county with regard to police?—The county is divided into three districts, the east district, the west district, and the district of Lewis. In the district of Lewis I am not aware whether they have a police force or not; in the eastern district we have a police force of three men; in the western district a police force of six men and a superintendent; besides that, there is one man at the borough of Dingwall and another man at the borough of Tain, which makes just 12 men.

4183. Do you consider that force at all sufficient for the wants of the county? —It is sufficient with regard to the present state of the county; there is usually very little crime in the county; I may say it is sufficient for the present purpose, but occurrences occasionally happen when it is perfectly inadequate for the preservation of the peace. In the year 1843, at the time of the Free Church riots, we had no police in the county; we then resorted to the old constables, and when they were rolled out they were found perfectly incapable of action. We then had recourse to special constables and pensioners; we found the special constables would not act, and the pensioners were incapable of acting from age and infirmity; the consequence was, that the magistrates, in two separate places, were entirely deforced and left at the mercy of the mob, and the military were sent for. Again, in 1846, the year of the Famine riots, there were disturbances, and there being no police in the county, we were obliged to send for the military again, and by the military order was re-established, at a very considerable expense to the county. Last year, at the time of the election, at Dingwall, further riots were apprehended; the sheriff had not sufficient confidence in the police of the county, and applied again for the military; the military were sent from Fort George to Fortrose, to be in readiness to act in case they should be required.

4184. So that, in case of any extraordinary emergency, you are quite helpless? —Yes. I believe, three months ago, on the property of the Marquis of Stafford, the tenantry had refused either to pay rent or to receive warrants of ejectment, and the Government then refused the aid of the military, and the people remained in a perfect state of insurrection.

4185. Have not the officers been deforced on various occasions, at Coigeach and Loch Broom?—Yes.

4186. You say, the military have been refused; do you think sending the military would have had any effect, seeing that they could not remain in the district? —The military would have effected the object for which they were sent doubtless, but they would have had a most demoralising effect.

4187. In your opinion, it is not desirable to send for the military in cases of disturbance?—I think the employment of the military is to be avoided in every case where it is possible.

4188. Will you tell the Committee what you would recommend or suggest for that state of things?—The only state of things I can recommend, is an uniform police, to act over the kingdom.

4189. So that you might send to neighbouring counties when you required assistance?—Yes; we should do away with the ridiculous demarcations of counties, and the same body could act wherever it was required. If there were a depôt at Inverness, for the northern districts, and we had reason to apprehend riots, men could be sent for from the depôt.

4190. Supposing the system were not so extensive as a national police, but supposing you had an uniform system of police in all the adjoining counties, and a good understanding existed between them, if a greater force were wanted occasionally in one county, then it could be supplied from the others?—I think you would find great difficulty in getting the heritors and commissioners of supply to agree.

4191. Supposing two or three counties were placed under one superintendent, do you consider it would be an advantage?—I think it would be very advisable; I think they would require to be under one principal, and not left entirely under the magistrates of the county.

4192. You think a local management would not be so efficient as a general management?—I think in my own county it would be very little good.

4193. Have

4193. Have you any suggestion to make with respect to the alteration of the law, which would remedy such a state of things as that which exists at Coigeach and Loch Broom?—The only way would be to increase the establishment of police in the county.

4194. Does not that lie with the commissioners of supply?—It does.

4195. Who have not taken any steps to do so?—It belongs to the western districts; we have no occasion for it.

4196. In the western district there have been no steps taken?—I have a report from the clerk of the western district, which shows that they have six policemen and a superintendent employed.

4197. Mr. *Mackie.*] You consider an amalgamated system of police all over Scotland would remove the difficulty?—I do.

4198. Do you think a general amalgamation would do away with the necessity of having so many men as would be required under separate jurisdictions?—I think it is the natural consequence, that large bodies will be better organised than small ones. If you had one officer to command the men of sufficient experience and capacity, I think the diminution of crime would in a very short time reimburse the county any extra expense to which they are put at the outset.

4199. Mr. *Mackie.*] Do not you consider if a police force were generally adopted all over Scotland, from the greater security it would give to property that it would enhance the value of property?—I cannot answer that; I should think it would if we may judge from analogy; perhaps in my part of the county it would not.

4200. Mr. *Howard.*] Is there much sheep-stealing in Ross?—There is a good deal of petty pilfering; serious crimes are of very rare occurrence; smuggling is very nearly suppressed.

4201. Mr. *Philipps.*] Is there much sheep-stealing in the Highlands?—In the western district there is a considerable amount of sheep-stealing. There is a great deal of difficulty experienced from the thieves driving the sheep off to other counties. A suggestion came from the county of Inverness last year, that the different northern counties should combine to have a police solely for the prevention of sheep-stealing; but as there are few sheep in Eastern Ross, and we were not concerned in the matter, we declined to co-operate.

4202. *Lord Advocate.*] You have not been able to agree upon it?—No; it did not concern us; there was a recommendation of that sort from Inverness.

4203. In some parts of Ross, is not the present state of things such that a warrant cannot be executed?—It is quite true. The sheriff has been deforced more than once, and the factor has been beaten in attempting to serve warrants.

4204. Have the adjoining counties to Ross adopted the rural police?—Yes, Sutherland, and also Inverness.

4205. Have you ever applied to them for assistance?—In 1843, we were obliged to apply to Inverness for assistance during the time of the Free Church riots.

4206. Did they render you efficient assistance?—I may say hardly. It was the military that established order; we had a detachment of military sent from Edinburgh, I believe.

4207. Mr. *Burroughes.*] Is your police force employed in assisting the revenue officers in the prevention of smuggling?—No, not at all.

Mr. *John Jones*, called in; and Examined.

4208. *Chairman.*] WHAT situation do you hold in the Police of Scotland?—I am the Superintendent of the Dumfriesshire Constabulary.

4209. How long have you held that office?—Nine years.

4210. Were you in any other police force before you went to Dumfriesshire?—I was 10 years in the metropolitan police force.

4211. Was the police force established in Dumfries before you went, or did you go before it was established?—There was a superintendent, but he was quite unacquainted with police matters, and he did not appear to give satisfaction, from what I can understand; and from the state I found the police in, both as regards the apprehension of offenders, and the state of the county in general, I should say they were useless; indeed, they did not perform the duty of police officers in criminal matters.

R. B. Macleod, Esq.

23 June 1853.

Mr. John Jones.

Mr. *John Jones*.

23 June 1853.

4212. What is the rural population of Dumfriesshire ?—The population, by the last census, is 78,123, and the number of square miles 1,800.

4213. What is the proportion of each policeman to the population ?—One man to 3,421.

4214. Do you think that is sufficient ?—In the present state of the county, I must confess we have very little crime ; but if railroads were to be formed through any part of the county again, or if any disturbance took place in any part of the county at a distance, and the men were dispersed throughout the county, and could not be collected together quickly, they would be perfectly ineffectual. I should like to have three or four more men.

4215. What does each man cost now ?—I have a return of the cost of the police from 1841–42 to the present date, 1853. Including my own salary, it is 850*l.* 15*s.* for last year ; which is, considering the extent of the county and population, an exceedingly low sum.

4216. What is that on the assessment in the pound ?—The assessment itself is a difficult matter to explain. In Scotland the property is assessed by merks ; the assessment is 12*s.* to every 100 Scotch merks ; 100 merks Scots represent 122*l.* sterling ; the rental is 290,000*l.*, which represents, in point of fact, 237,000 merks Scots. I may explain to the Committee that I did not myself understand what the 100 Scots merks meant. I obtained the information from the clerk of supply, and I made myself satisfied that the statement I have given is correct. The police assessment is for rogue-money, as well as police ; it is not police-rate alone in Dumfriesshire ; in some counties I understand it is. I have a return of the number and cost of the police force. In Scotland the Committee should be aware that the Exchequer pays certain sums of money, for business performed in what are termed Exchequer cases. About two or three years ago the Lords of the Treasury were memorialised, and the Lords of the Treasury ordered that county cases, that is, cases not reported to Crown counsel, should also be paid to the county. In the county of Dumfries, where we do the whole criminal business, the return in 1843–44, was 32*l.* 19*s.*, that is, when I commenced to take charge of the police ; in 1844–45, 119*l.* 9*s.* 11*d.* ; in 1845–46, 230*l.* ; in 1846–47, 300*l.* ; in 1847–48, 355*l.* 1*s.* ; in 1848–49, 264*l.* 6*s.* 10*d.* ; in 1849–50, 271*l.* 1*s.* 2*d.* ; in 1850–51, 308*l.* 1*s.* 1½*d.* Those sums went in reduction of the cost of the force, in point of fact.

4217. Supposing the police had not been established in your county, would those payments have been made by the Government in the same way ?—They would be paid by fees to the sheriff's officers, for performing the duty ; certainly not nearly so cheap as we perform it. The cost cannot be so much ; because, instead of the officer living at the place where the criminal warrant was to be served, he might have to go a distance of eight or ten miles, and being paid by fees, he might go three or four times. I am speaking of what I knew to be the fact when I first took charge of the force at Dumfries, and for a good reason, they got paid for every time they went ; and if the men had nothing else to do, and did not want to apprehend the prisoner, they returned and went again. The men cannot do so now many times without being found fault with.

4218. You mean that they made work for themselves ?—Just so ; besides it was not efficiently performed. When I took charge of the Dumfriesshire police, there were about 20 warrants then unexecuted on parties living in the county ; I may also mention that I am the public prosecutor of all statutory offences before the justices of the peace, and the fines which I received last year for road offences alone, I think amounted to above 100 *l.*, which were deducted from 850 *l.*, leaving 750 *l.* A number of fines were received from public-house cases ; I think somewhere about 50 *l.* ; half of those fines go to a charity, and I find I paid 31 *l.* 10 *s.* 6 *d.* to the charity, and the remaining half would go to the police funds ; that would leave about 700 *l.* ; the police have no constables' fees, or sheriffs' officer's fees, of any description.

4219. You mean that what was paid to the local constables before, now goes in reduction of the cost of police ?—Yes ; the principal part of the business done in Scotland, is done by the police, they are both criminal officers and police constables.

4220. Are there no civil officers employed in your county ?—No, they never interfere, because the county look to me to pay attention to all those cases as superintendent ; the procurator-fiscal sends me down all the warrants, and I have to see them executed.

4221. Supposing

Mr. *John Jones*.

23 June 1853.

4221. Supposing the cost of the police to be 700 *l.* a year, setting aside those indirect savings which you cannot exactly calculate, what is that upon the assessment in the pound?—It is difficult to state that; being an Englishman I am not so well versed in the Scotch mode of assessment; it is 12 *s.* on 122 *l.* on the rental of land, not on the houses.

4222. *Chairman.*] The real rental is 290,000 *l.* ?—Yes.

4223. What does 700 *l.* come to in the pound, on that?—About a halfpenny in the pound.

4224. Sir *J. Trollope.*] Is the assessment on the old valuation?—Yes.

4225. Mr. *Howard.*] Is there any police force in the town of Dumfries?—Yes; I was requested to take charge of it about six or seven months after I joined, and I continued to take charge of it for five years. I may also say that I received no remuneration for doing so; I took charge of it simply because I thought that the two forces working together would be of very great advantage, both to the county and to the town.

4226. Have you found any inconvenience from a different system being established in Cumberland?—In the parts of Cumberland, especially bordering the county of Dumfries, where there are no police, the vagrants are extremely numerous; and they assemble in the part of the county called Bewcastle in bands of some hundreds.

4227. Sir *J. Trollope.*] What are those vagrants?—Tinkers, vagrants, and travellers; men who go about stating that they are looking for work, and men who go about pretending to sell things; but they are regular known vagrants. I can hardly describe the class of characters, but amongst the police we call them travellers. I may state that travellers include all classes; some are actually in want, and cannot get work; some of them have been thieves all their lifetime; others beggars all their lifetime; and those men assemble in that part of Cumberland to an amount quite incredible; I cannot count them as they come across the borders to us; they infest our county, and, in fact, the whole of the thefts on the border are committed by parties coming from Cumberland.

4228. Mr. *Howard.*] Do you think if a sufficient police force were established in Cumberland it would check the depredations committed by those parties?— If we acted together, certainly; if I may judge of the amalgamation of the police in the town of Dumfries with the county police, when I had charge of both forces, I should state they are a very inefficient body compared to what they ought to be, and would be, if there was a general system; I think if there were some regular code of rules applied to the counties and burghs of Scotland, the police would be more efficient.

4229. Do you attempt to patrol the county with your force?—We patrol regularly.

4230. Do you patrol the whole county?—Once a week every part of the county is visited.

4231. *Chairman.*] Have you any return of crimes and offences?—I have a return of crimes and offences committed in the county of Dumfries, ending the 30th of December last.

4232. Do you think the number of offenders apprehended is any test of the amount of undetected crime?—Yes, I have a table which shows the amount of property stolen; I should think the amount of property recovered is about as much as ever is recovered.

4233. Can you state the amount of property lost and recovered in one year?— In the year 1852 the amount of property lost, reported to the police, was 255 *l.* 19 *s.* 9 *d.*; and the amount of property recovered was 103 *l.* 10 *s.* 10 *d.* I have a note at the end of the table, explanatory why some part of that property could not be recovered; it was from a number of sheep being stolen, amounting to a considerable sum; those sheep were not reported to us for four months afterwards, consequently we had no means of recovering them.

4234. Is sheep-stealing general?—No; there are a great number of large sheep farms in Dumfriesshire, and it sometimes happens that four or five, or a dozen sheep may be lost; it can be hardly called sheep-stealing, because it arises from a mistake of the shepherds in dividing them, or that they get loose into other flocks.

4235. Are the towns assessed to the police, in Dumfriesshire?—No, they are not; that is one of the points from which I consider very great evils arise in the police system in Scotland. In Annan there is a population of 3,426; they have

Mr. John Jones.

23 June 1853.

the power, under an Act, to assess themselves if they think proper. I think two-thirds of the inhabitants have the power of meeting, and, if they agree, to assess themselves at a certain rate, for a proper police; but they have never done so, and the result is, that they get the advantage of the county police without paying for it, because the county police reside in the town, and they are obliged to look out after the thieves in the town for the purpose of preventing their going into the country.

4236. Do not you think it probable that one of the reasons why, in some of the counties in Scotland, the rural police has not been adopted, has been on account of the unequal mode of payment?—I cannot speak generally for the counties in Scotland; I can speak for Dumfriesshire, and I should take it as a pretty fair description of the whole of Scotland. There are no less than nine boroughs, towns, and little villages, and none of these are assessed; there is one-third of the population gets the advantage of the police without paying assessment. My opinion is, that the whole of those small boroughs and villages should be liable to be assessed at a certain rate according to the rental; I will say 10 *l*. and 5 *l*. rentals; that they should pay a certain sum, and that they should be compelled to take the advantage of the police. At Langholm there is a population of about 2,000 persons; it is a very thriving village, and they pay nothing towards the police; if any offence is committed they complain to me just as if they paid for the policemen; whereas, in point of fact, they do not pay a single farthing; the policeman is obliged to pay attention to the business in the town, neglecting, of course, his duties throughout the country, because he is compelled to remain in the town.

4237. Sir *J. Trollope*.] Your opinion is that the rural districts bear the burden, and the towns derive the benefit?—Yes, clearly; so paying nothing for it; that is the case in the county of Dumfries.

4238. Could that be obviated by a new mode of assessment?—Yes.

4239. What would you propose?—My proposition would be, that all houses of a rental above 10 *l*. should pay a certain assessment, say a halfpenny in the pound.

4240. You would not exempt the land?—No; I should let the land be assessed by the same mode as it is now assessed.

4241. *Chairman*.] You would rate all property to the police, with the exception of houses under 10 *l*.?—Yes.

4242. Mr. *Howard*.] Do you look after the smugglers?—We have no smuggling.

4243. Is not there a good deal of smuggling between Dumfries and Cumberland?—There may be occasionally bottles of whiskey smuggled across. I never found the excisemen work well with the police; there exists a jealousy of the police interfering with smuggling matters; I never found them assist me at all.

4244. *Chairman*.] Have you ever considered whether there is any advantage to be derived from a uniform system of police in Scotland?—I have turned my attention to that, and I think in England a uniform system of police might be adopted, because the counties are under the same mode of assessment, and therefore there would be no difficulty about it. Scotland is different in many ways; there are the jurisdictions of the sheriffs over the counties, and the jurisdictions of the magistrates over their particular towns; but I think that a uniform system might be carried out in Scotland to this extent, without Government having the sole control of the police. I do not think Scotland is prepared, neither do I think it is necessary, that the Crown should have the whole government of the police there. The impression on my mind is, from the experience I have obtained, that if all the counties in Scotland were compelled to have a sufficient police force by Act of Parliament, it would be a great advantage. I think, if they were compelled, by orders issued by the Lord Advocate, or the Crown counsel, and those orders were sufficiently numerous and extensive to embrace the general rules and regulations to be adopted by all the police in the counties, it would tend very much to facilitate the administration of justice. I still think the counties should have the management of their own police, under the direction of a police committee; but I think the appointment of the chief constable should be with the sanction of the Secretary of State. I find throughout Scotland and England a number of persons are appointed to manage police matters who understand nothing whatever about it. I believe it requires that a man should be trained to police business before he can take the superintendence of police.

4245. How

Mr. *John Jones.*

23 June 1853.

4245. How were you appointed?—I was appointed by the police committee. I went down from London under the auspices of the Duke of Buccleuch, who is the largest landed proprietor in the county; above one-third of the county belong to him. We have very little difficulty in that county as far as police matters are concerned. There is great attention paid to police matters, which is not paid in some other counties.

4246. Do you think it is desirable that other counties should be under the same system?—Yes; I think also the superintendents of police should be procurators-fiscal, to act in certain cases, namely, statutory offences, cruelty to animals, offences under Licensing Acts, and for vagrancy; that is, if there is an Act to punish vagrancy; and the offences that go before justices.

4247. Sir *J. Trollope.*] That would enable him to be the public prosecutor?—Yes. before the justices of the peace, if appointed by them.

4248. You would recommend the superintendent of police to be that person?—Yes.

4249. Are you a procurator-fiscal?—I am, before the justices.

4250. How many meetings of magistrates have you in the county to attend in the course of a week or a month?—In Dumfriesshire, if there are a sufficient number of cases occurring, such as breaches of the peace, which could be brought before a local court, the clerk of the peace calls the magistrates together.

4251. There is no fixed time for meeting?—I do not know that a fixed time would suit the purpose.

4252. How often do those meetings take place?—About once in two months in some districts.

4253. Do you know what number you have to attend in the course of the year?—I think last year I attended about 40 in the different districts.

4254. Does not that take you a great deal away from your police duty?—No; I am looking after my men at the same time as I go through the country; I think it is part of the duty of the superintendent, and that he is not an efficient superintendent unless he prosecutes those cases. I may state also, that I am inspector of weights and measures, and that the whole of the police officers are billet-masters.

4255. For troops moving about the country?—Yes; of course all that saves expense.

4256. Have you any communication with the railway police in your county?—I took charge of the railway police during the time of the formation of the railroads. The sheriff has the power of appointing a certain number of constables at the request of the justices, and he appointed me to superintend them.

4257. Have you been in charge of the police since the railways have been completed?—No; I am in communication with the companies constantly; I prosecute under their local Act.

4258. Do they give you any information, or communicate with you, if persons are passing along the line of railway who have committed offences?—I have no doubt they would do so.

4259. Have you found them act cordially with you?—I have never found any difficulties.

4260. *Chairman.*] Do you think generally, from your experience, the railway authorities would object to have their police placed under the direction of the chief constable of the county?—The Glasgow and South-western Railway passes through the greater part of Dumfriesshire; they have no police whatever on the line.

4261. Sir *J. Trollope.*] Have they no authority to apprehend persons who have committed offences?—No.

4262. *Chairman.*] They depend upon your police?—Certainly.

4263. Supposing they had a police force of their own, would they object to their policemen being placed under your superintendence?—From what I have seen of the Glasgow and South-western Company, I should say they would be most happy to do so.

4264. Do you think it would be advantageous to have the police of the county and the police of the railway under one superintendent?—Yes, but it would be difficult, because the line extends from one county to another.

4265. Would it not be advantageous, so far as your own county is concerned?—I see a difficulty in the matter; in some counties the railway goes in and out, and passes from one county to another. I do not think it would work well; I think there would be constant collision between the county authorities and the railway authorities.

4266. Why should there be collision?—They would fancy that the police of the county paid more attention to railway matters, or that the railway police paid more attention to county matters.

4267. Do not you think there might be mutual co-operation between them?—There should be mutual co-operation; an efficient police system never can be carried out unless there is co-operation.

4268. Would not it be better secured by their being under the direction of one head?—Clearly; I do not mean to say it would not, but there would be a difficulty in carrying out the system.

4269. Mr. *Philipps.*] Have you any superannuation fund in your police force?—We have not, and we feel the want of it. I have lost the whole of my service in the Metropolitan force; and had I known as much as I do now, I would never have left the chance of superannuation.

4270. Sir *J. Trollope.*] How long had you paid?—Ten years.

4271. What rank did you hold in the Metropolitan force?—I was an acting inspector when I left the Metropolitan force. I paid about 8 *d.* a week out of my pay to the superannuation fund.

4272. Mr. *Mackie.*] What is your present salary?—My stated salary and emoluments would amount to somewhere about 300 *l.* a year, but I am not quite clear to every item.

4273. Sir *J. Trollope.*] Are you allowed to take fees?—Only sometimes in petty cases of prosecutions under the Game Acts. The whole fines, in police cases, are returned to the county funds. The police of the county do not look after the game. I am public prosecutor before the justices. The proprietors get me to attend to the game cases, because it saves them a great deal of trouble. Such cases have no connexion with police matters.

4274. And for that service they pay you a gratuity?—Yes. There are very few cases that I do not pay attention to.

4275. Can you give the Committee any information with regard to vagrancy in Dumfriesshire?—Vagrancy has somewhat diminished in consequence of the decrease of other crimes, perhaps, in the county of Dumfries, but still it is exceedingly bad in the hill districts. In the Eskdale part of the county they go in bands of from five to six, or seven persons, and they steal wool to a very great extent.

4276. Do you mean that they pull it off the backs of the sheep?—Yes, pretending to pick it up. The officers have detected frequently as much as five pounds or six pounds in one person's possession; and that, at the present price of wool, is a theft very prejudicial to the farmers. It is carried on to an enormous extent.

4277. Is it done by men or women?—Men, women, and children; they appear to have turned their attention to stealing wool.

4278. What numbers have you detected?—Last year the number that the constables challenged for vagrancy was 4,257; it is quite impossible to estimate the total number of vagrants. I should not think the number the policemen reported to me would amount to one-twentieth or one-thirtieth part of the total number.

4279. Does the Common Lodging House Act extend to Scotland?—It does not.

4280. Do you take any cognisance of tramps lodging houses?—I do; I have no right to enter those houses, but I look into them for our own protection.

4281. Do you inspect those houses on the plea of searching for persons who have committed offences?—I do it on the principle, that the police officer has a right to look after thieves in any place. In certain villages I manage it in this way: when we find a vagrant two nights in a place, I get an officer to watch and annoy him, and annoy the lodging-house keepers by visiting them frequently, and they are very glad to comply with the rules rather than be annoyed.

4282. Do you know the number of people who have been apprehended for the particular offence you have named?—The defective state of the law is a bar to our apprehending any of them. I understand, in many counties, they will not convict for vagrancy; in Roxburghshire they convict, and in Dumfriesshire they convict; but it is doubtful whether we have the power to convict. There are a number of old Scotch Acts with reference to vagrancy; there is the Act of 1661, c. 38; 1693; 1695, c. 43; and also the 9th of Geo. 2, c. 5. By the

Mr. *John Jones.*

23 June 1853.

the old Scotch Acts the parties were allowed to be apprehended; the old punishment was whipping then; that punishment has fallen into desuetude; the law authorities have decided that it cannot be now put in force. The second time, it appears from the Acts, they were punishable by boring them through the ear with a hot iron; that clearly has fallen into desuetude. The Poor-law authorities has the advantage of those Acts, but then they are amended; they make use of them to apprehend persons who desert their wives and families in Scotland; that power is not extended to the apprehension of persons who go about tramping. Perhaps I may state two cases in illustration of the want of power to apprehend vagrants: about four years ago I found some men with about 2 lbs. or 3 lbs. of silver in their pockets, trying to sell it; I detained these men, but I did not know what to do; in England I should have taken them before a magistrate; I have no doubt that the magistrate would have committed them for having the silver unlawfully in their possession, and they would have got three months' imprisonment at least; the result was, that I was obliged to resort to a trick, and prosecute these men for hawking without a licence; we kept them in prison for 14 days, but I did not find the owner of the silver. A case occurred very recently; a house in Haddington was broken open, and a quantity of property was taken away; the men were apprehended in Dumfries, with the property in their possession, but we had no means of detaining them; I was quite satisfied the property had been stolen, but we were obliged to let the men go about their business; we detained the property.

4283. Does not the Scotch law enable you to detain any person who has property in his possession which you consider to be stolen?—No, it does not.

4284. Mr. *Philipps.*] Your opinion is, that the law in Scotland, applicable to vagrancy, is defective?—I may state, that the police committee of Dumfriesshire have turned their attention to this subject; Mr. Trotter, the sheriff-substitute of Dumfriesshire, has had an elaborate report prepared; it is not yet printed, but it has been adopted by the commissioners of supply, at a meeting held on the 30th of April last, and the sheriff authorized me to state that he would be most happy to forward the report to the Committee.

4285. *Chairman.*] From your experience in Scotland, do you think that vagrancy is a great source of crime?—My opinion is, that were we empowered to deal with those vagrants crime would diminish at least one-half; in fact, the most of the crime is now committed by travellers and Irish vagrants, and persons from England; the Scotch people themselves are not a thieving population. It would be a great advantage if we were at liberty to deal with these vagrants; the vagrants are turned out of the burghs into the county; and in the county, if the officers turn them out from one district to another, it is not suppressing vagrancy; they are merely a little annoyed; the parties just walk across a field if an officer comes in sight, or sit still.

4286. Mr. *Howard.*] Are the vagrants relieved at the workhouse?—We have no workhouse in Dumfries; we have no communication with the relieving officer of Dumfries; I think there is no relief given unless a man is broken down or is ill.

4287. Sir *J. Trollope.*] Have you any stations for your men?—Yes; I believe no police force can be efficient without stations; we have a lock-up with two cells attached to most of the stations.

LIST OF THE APPENDIX.

Appendix, No. 1.

Appendix, No. 1—continued.

Appendix, No. 2.

Appendix, No. 3.

Appendix, No. 4.

Appendix, No. 5.

APPENDIX.

Appendix, No 1.

PAPERS delivered in by Captain *J. B. B. M·Hardy*, R.N., 27 May 1853.

REPORT of the Chief Constable to the Magistrates of the County of *Essex*, in Quarter Sessions assembled, 5th April 1842.

My Lords and Gentlemen,

I HAVE the honour to lay before this Court the Returns (*vide* Appendix) numbered from 1 to 19, with the view of showing the state and operation of the Essex county constabulary, and the state of crime in the county. And as the expediency of augmenting the present number of county constables, together with the efficiency of the present force, is to be this day taken into consideration, I trust I shall anticipate your wishes by briefly remarking on the said returns, and such other points as I consider worthy your attention.

The Tabular Returns numbered from 1 to 7 show the state of crime in the different divisions of the county ; and a comparison of the number of offenders in the quarters for the year 1841, with those in the corresponding quarters for 1840, will be an index to the increased duties performed by the police, and its progressive advancement to efficiency.

The columns headed Vagrancy will show that in the last year the extraordinary number (337) of these pests of the county were brought before the justices, who committed 241. This has tended in a great measure to reduce the incredible sum which has usually been extracted from the poorer inhabitants, frequently by vagrants using intimidating means ; and I am satisfied the vigilance of the police in checking the system of plunder heretofore carried on by vagrants, has driven them to seek temporary relief in the union-houses. I do not expect the county can effectually be relieved from vagrants, without a legislative enactment, rendering it necessary that all low lodging-houses should be licensed, and subject to regulations formed by the justices in special sessions. The class of persons denominated gipsies, has, since the introduction of the police, decreased in a greater proportion than other vagrants.

A reference to the Return numbered 8, containing an abstract of the calendars for the last three years, will show, that in the early part of 1840, and prior to the operation of the police, there was a prospect of a comparative reduction of prisoners throughout the year, but evidently from offenders going undetected ; because when the police came into operation, the calendars at first gradually increased, until the desired effect produced by the numerous causes attendant on a police in preventing crime evinced itself by the numbers in the calendars decreasing, as is shown by comparing the Epiphany Sessions of 1840 with that of 1839. By comparing the numbers apprehended by the police, as in the columns marked (P.), with those apprehended by parish, local constables, metropolitan police, railroad police, and others, as contained in columns marked (O.), the gradual comparative increase in the apprehensions made by the police will at once show its advancement to efficiency.

At the Epiphany Sessions of 1840, the number apprehended by the police was about two-thirds of the whole ; but early in 1841, the swearing in of a large number of local constables, as per Document No. 9, tended in a great measure to lessen for a time this great superiority.

For the better detection of known offenders, a part of the police are employed in plain clothes.

By comparing the sentences passed on the prisoners at the different sessions in the respective columns of the Return No. 10, it will be shown that the offenders apprehended by the police are for more serious crimes than those apprehended by other parties, inasmuch as their sentences have been the most severe, viz., of 67 sentences in 1841 to transportation for a term of and above seven years, 46 were brought to justice by the police ; and a comparison

parison of the sentences passed at the two most important sessions, viz. Michaelmas 1840
and 1841, will be an index to a decrease of crime at the latter period, as the sentences in
Michelmas 1840, considered aggregately, amount to nearly four times what they do in 1841.

It is difficult on the early formation of a police to procure an index to the decrease of
plunder since its establishment, but, as I have reason to believe, an impression prevails that
sheep-stealing has not decreased, which I attribute to the publicity which is given to the
missing of sheep, but not to their restoration.

I have to refer you to the Returns Nos. 11 and 12, by comparing which you will observe
that in two divisions of the county, Epping and North Hinckford, more sheep were lost in
the year preceding the introduction of the police (1839), than in the 14 divisions of the
county during the last year. I have selected these divisions, because they are rural districts,
and are not materially affected by the several thousand labourers who have been introduced
by the railroad works. The great influx of men consequent on the works of the Eastern
Counties' Railway has seriously increased the duties of the police, for the introduction of
such a number of persons, who are occasionally thrown out of employment for many weeks
together, must tend to increase crime; and the facility which will be rendered by the railroad to the London thieves, who are operated on by the metropolitan police, will evidently
augment crime in this county, without some efficient means are taken for its prevention.
I trust that the preceding evidence will satisfy you that the conviction of offenders has
been but a small part of the benefit derived from your constabulary, and you must be aware
that there are many instances of merit on the part of the members of the force, which never
come before the public; and that as the force procures a knowledge of idle and disorderly
persons, who are living without any visible means of support, it will, by a careful watching
of their proceedings, be enabled to effect the great end of a rural police, namely, the prevention of crime. I could, in proof of this, name many characters who have been already
traced out of the county.

The returns which the respective superintendents transmit to me of every public-house
and beershop in their divisions, represent them, with few exceptions, as being well conducted, and I have no complaint on the subject of want of order at public assemblages.

I have also a register of all low lodging-houses.

Document No. 13 shows the distribution of the force.

I have also respectfully to refer you to Document No. 14, containing some of the points
which, with the state of crime, influence me in the distribution of the police, and I
wish distinctly to explain, that in the absence of extraordinary circumstances, I deem it my
duty to make the number of constables paid for by each division my leading feature in that
distribution.

I have not failed to lodge with the clerk of the peace, at the termination of each month,
the return directed by the 31st section of the Amended Constabulary Act, showing the
daily distribution of the constabulary force under my command.

I had hoped that the example set by the towns of Chelmsford and Romford, which have
taxed themselves to provide, under the Constabulary Act, an additional force for their protection, would have been followed by other towns, more particularly those which, prior to
the establishment of the police, had night patrols.

With reference to the accompanying book, containing a copy of general orders issued
by me since the last quarter sessions, I have to acquaint you, in order that the magistrates
may be earlier apprised of them, that the respective superintendents are instructed to lay
before the chairman, at every petty sessions held in their divisions, the book containing
all orders issued by me, together with the journal, and contingent account book of their
divisions, that the justices may exercise their pleasure as to making themselves acquainted
with their contents, which will afford them every particular connected with the constabulary.

Although this force has been two years under organisation, it is still in its infancy, from
the circumstances not only of the constables, but also the officers, requiring to be trained
to their duties; and the great difficulty which exists in procuring proper material, more
especially as the qualifications of applicants cannot be known until they have been tried.
This is proved from 11,000 persons having either resigned or been dismissed from the
metropolitan police during the first eight years of its formation.

Experience has proved in the navy and army, coast-guard and police, that sentinels and
patrols must be constantly visited by night as well as by day by a superior, to guard
against sleeping, inattention, connivance, and drunkenness; and wheresoever neglect
may take place, the superior should be able at all times to point out the very person who
may be in fault, and thereby cause every member of an organised force to feel that he is
not liable to be charged with the neglect of others. Hence arises the great difficulty in a
generally dispersed force of effecting these requisites to discipline, and shows the necessity

of introducing a variety of grades, to promote emulation, and insure the supervision of a superior, who is a responsible individual.

I therefore recommend the superintendents being placed in three classes, as also the private constables; more particularly as such an arrangement will be attended with economy.

Notwithstanding my having expressed to this court my conviction that it was impracticable to provide efficient parish constables, and introduce a cordial co-operation between them and the county police, it became my duty on the passing of Act 3 and 4 Vict. chap. 88, to endeavour to do so, and on the generally supposed difficulty, arising from a want of proper remuneration, being removed by this court establishing, under the 17th section of the said Act, the liberal scale of fees and allowances, as per Document No. 15, I resolved to take such steps as would enable me to satisfy this court, when the question respecting the expediency of augmenting the county constabulary should arise, that every exertion had been used to avoid such a necessity, by the provision of a body of efficient peace officers, under the appellation of local constables, and thereby afford a powerful auxiliary. I therefore addressed to the magistrates and clergy of this county a circular, as per Document No. 16, soliciting their assistance in procuring efficient local constables, and explaining to them, that on the success of this measure would depend the decision relative to the necessity of augmenting the county police; and the better to insure proper persons, and a correct register of them, each individual was recommended agreeably to Form No. 17.

The result was, that with the additional assistance rendered by parish meetings and the superintendents, I was enabled early last year to submit for the county 670 local constables, as per Document No. 9, having previously provided for them a set of printed instructions, showing their powers and duties; but I have been enabled this year to submit only about half that number, as specified in Document No. 9, most of whom are the old parish constables. I shall not comment on the result of this attempt, but confine myself to expressing my sense of the willing assistance I have received in my endeavour, more particularly from such of the yeomen as have condescended to fill the office for the benefit of the county, and with a view of encouraging respectable and efficient persons to follow their example.

Thomas Tucker, No. 3, a private constable of the Essex County Constabulary, having under creditable circumstances apprehended Joseph Smith and Stephen Hills, who on the night of the 4th February last committed a burglary, and as Thomas Tucker, at the risk of his life, resisted their attempt to escape from his custody, until assisted by Philip Tiffin, I have the honour, agreeably to section 10, Act 3 and 4 Vict. cap 88, to recommend this court to grant to Thomas Tucker a small gratuity out of the fund formed by the constabulary, under the said section; and to reward the good conduct of Philip Tiffin.

The particulars of this case are fully known to the chairman of this court.

In conclusion, I have to refer you to Return No. 18, showing that the annual expense of your present police will be about 8,726 l., after deducting the following sums, which will in all probability be saved :—

1st. £.500 annually, by the abolition of Newport and Halsted houses of correction, with the advantage of improved prison discipline.

2d. £.722 by conveyance of prisoners in county carts during the year 1841.

3d. £.630 by orders of court, and received by the treasurer during the last 12 months, for the purpose of assisting in defraying the expense of the police.

4th. £.336 earned by serving warrants and summonses, under 17th section of Amended Act, during the year 1841, and received by treasurer, to be applied as before stated.

A reference to Return No. 19 will show that the mere expense of prosecuting each of the 574 prisoners, in the year 1841, was 10 s. 8½ d. less than in the year (1839) preceding the introduction of the police, which would amount in the whole to a saving of 307 l. 6 s. 7 d.

I have the honour to be,
My Lords and Gentlemen,
Your very obedient servant,
J. B. B. McHardy,
Chief Constable for Essex.

APPENDIX.

No. 1.—ESSEX CONSTABULARY.

RETURN of the Number of PERSONS Apprehended and Summoned, Offences Committed, and Results, from 7th April to 30th June 1840.

No. 2.—ESSEX CONSTABULARY.

RETURN of the Number of PERSONS Apprehended and Summoned, Offences Committed, and Results, from 1st July to 20th October 1840.

No. 3.—ESSEX CONSTABULARY.

RETURN of the Number of PERSONS Apprehended and Summoned, Offences Committed, and Results, from 21st October 1840 to 5th January 1841.

No. 4.—ESSEX CONSTABULARY.

RETURN of the Number of PERSONS Apprehended and Summoned, Offences Committed, and Results, from 6th January to 6th April 1841.

No. 5.—ESSEX CONSTABULARY.

RETURN of the Number of Persons Apprehended and Summoned, Offences Committed, and Results, from 7th April to 20th June 1841.

No. 6.—ESSEX CONSTABULARY.

RETURN of the Number of Persons Apprehended and Summoned, Offences Committed, and Results, from 30th June to 10th October 1841.

C. Convicted.

D. Discharged.

No. 7.—ESSEX CONSTABULARY.

RETURN of the Number of PERSONS Apprehended and Summoned, Offences Committed, and Results, from 20th October 1841 to 4th January 1842.

(Wide return, divided by Divisions — Brentwood, Chelmsford, Colchester, Dengie, Dunmow, Epping, Freshwell, North Hinckford, South Hinckford, Ongar, Rochford, Tendring, Walden, Witham — with "Apprehended and Summoned" (Males, Females, Total), numerous offence columns each shown as C. Convicted / D. Discharged, under the heading INFORMATIONS, and columns "Committed for Trial" (Felony, Assaults, Vagrants, Night Poaching, Rape, Arson).)

Offence column headings under INFORMATIONS include:
Felony; Vagrants; Trespass; Assaults; Disorderly; Drunk; Drunk and Disorderly; Drunk and Assault; Wilful Damage; Unlawful Possession of Property; Using Threatening Language; Deserters; Suspicious Characters; Furious Driving; Uttering Counterfeit Coin; Cruelty to Animals; Illegally Pawning; Fraud; Arson; Dog Stealing; Cutting and Wounding; Public House; Beer House; Driving without Reins; Refusing to pay Rates; Refusing to pay Wages; Deserting Families; Non-compliance with the Rules of a Benefit Society; Fraudulently using unjust Weights; Neglecting to support Parents; Leaving Work unfinished; Having no Names on Carts; Sunday Trading; Neglecting to pay a Loan; Refusing to pay Toll; Causing an Obstruction.

C. Convicted.   D. Discharged.

The Number of Commitments shown in the Tables, numbered from 1 to 7, differs from the Abstract of the Calendars, in consequence of some of the parties committed having been tried, as shown at the foot of Return No. 10.

No. 8.—ESSEX CONSTABULARY.

A BSTRACT from the CALENDARS for the undermentioned Years.

(Table by YEARS — 1839, 1840, 1841 — with columns for each Sessions: Epiphany, Adjourned, Assizes, Easter, Adjourned, Summer, Adjourned, Assizes, Michaelmas, Adjourned, Assizes, Adjourned, Epiphany (January 1842); each subdivided into P and O.)

P. Apprehended by the Police.   O. Apprehended by others.

No. 9.

RETURN showing the Number of Persons selected to act as Local Constables in the County of Essex, for the Years 1841 and 1842.

DIVISIONS	Number of Parishes and Hamlets	Number of Persons selected for 1841			Number of Local Constables selected for 1841			Number of Local Constables selected for 1842		
		Served before	Not served	TOTAL	Served before	Not served	TOTAL	Served before	Not served	TOTAL
Brentwood	59	55	22	77				32	9	41
Chelmsford	30	21	8	29				12	3	15
Colchester	33	64	32	96				23	8	31
Dengie	23	17	4	21				15	3	18
Dunmow	24	22	40	63				9	9	18
Epping	18	24	22	46				19	4	23
Freshwell	8	15	9	24				10	4	14
North Hinckford	27	26	13	39				18	5	23
South Hinckford	24	45	17	63				31	9	40
Ongar	26	18	8	26				16	4	20
Rochford	30	39	19	51				10	6	16
Tendring	34	35	9	44				23	4	27
Walden	33	37	12	40				18	4	22
Witham		59	6	44				12	9	14
TOTAL	394	450	220	670				248	74	322

No. 10.—COUNTY OF ESSEX.

RETURN of the Number of PRISONERS Committed for Trial, as shown by the Calendars for the Years 1840 and 1841, detailing the Sentences, and defining those Apprehended by the County Police from the Metropolitan Police, Railway Police, Local, Parish Constables, and others.

	A. Apprehended by County Police.	B. Apprehended by Metropolitan Police, Railway Police, Local Constables, Parish Constables, and others.	TOTAL.	Death Recorded.		Transportation for Life.		22 Years.		15 Years.		14 Years.		10 Years.		7 Years.		3 Years.		2 Years.		18 Months.		12 Months.		9 Months.		8 Months.		6 Months.		4 Months.		3 Months.		2 Months.		1 Month.		Under 1 Month.		Acquitted.		Bills Ignored.		Traversed to another Session.		Transferred to the Assizes.		Admitted Evidence for the Crown.		Fined and Discharged.		Bound in Recognisances to keep the Peace.		Whipped and Discharged.		Absconded.		At Large.	
				P	O	P	O	P	O	P	O	P	O	P	O	P	O	P	O	P	O	P	O	P	O	P	O	P	O	P	O	P	O	P	O	P	O	P	O	P	O	P	O	P	O	P	O	P	O	P	O	P	O	P	O	P	O
Adjourned Session - February 1840 -	-	67	67	-	-	-	The County Police not in Operation.																																														
Lent Assizes, - - - March „ -	-	38	38	-	-	-																																															
Easter Session - - April „ -	-	45	45	-	-	-																																															
Adjourned Session - May „ -	6	58	64	-	-	-	-	-	-	-	-	-	-	-	1	-	4	-	-	-	-	-	1	1	4	-	-	-	1	..	11	-	-	2	5	-	-	-	6	1	5	-	15	2	5	-	-	-	-	-	-	-	1	-	-	-	-	-	1	-	-
Midsummer Session - June „ -	20	33	53	-	-	-	-	-	-	-	-	-	1	1	2	1	2	-	-	-	-	-	-	2	-	-	1	-	-	..	4	-	-	1	2	1	2	1	4	3	3	5	6	2	4	-	-	-	1	-	1	-	-	3	-	-	-	-	-	-	-
Summer Assize - - July „ -	5	23	28	-	4	-	-	-	-	-	2	-	-	-	1	-	2	-	-	-	-	-	-	1	4	-	-	-	-	-	1	-	-	-	3	1	2	1	-	1	-	-	3	1	-	-	1	-	-	-	-	-	-	-	-	-	-	-	-	-	-
Michaelmas Session - October „ -	69	79	148	-	-	2	4	-	-	-	2	-	1	6	3	4	4	-	-	-	-	-	-	-	3	-	-	-	1	2	5	-	2	5	5	7	3	4	10	7	13	13	17	4	4	-	-	3	-	-	-	-	-	12	2	-	-	-	-	-	-
Adjourned Session - December „ -	37	35	72	-	-	1	-	-	1	2	-	-	1	2	2	3	-	-	-	-	-	-	-	1	1	-	-	-	-	3	2	-	1	2	2	1	-	4	7	5	6	8	8	3	4	-	-	-	-	1	-	-	-	-	-	-	-	-	-	1	-
Epiphany Session - January „ -	36	14	50	-	-	-	-	-	-	-	-	1	-	6	-	1	1	-	-	-	-	-	-	2	1	-	-	-	-	3	-	-	-	3	-	-	2	5	2	2	3	8	5	4	-	-	-	-	-	-	-	-	-	-	-	-	-	-	-	1	-
Adjourned Session - February 1841 -	49	32	81	-	-	-	-	-	-	-	-	2	1	1	2	2	2	-	-	-	-	1	-	1	3	-	-	1	-	1	2	2	-	3	1	1	-	7	2	5	4	10	4	8	6	-	1	4	2	-	2	-	-	-	-	-	-	-	-	-	-
Lent Assizes - - - March „ -	35	23	58	-	-	3	2	-	-	2	1	3	-	-	-	-	-	-	-	-	-	-	-	2	3	2	-	1	-	3	6	-	2	1	1	1	1	1	-	6	-	5	2	3	1	-	-	2	-	-	-	-	1	-	-	-	3	-	-	-	-
Easter Session - - April „ -	32	14	46	-	-	-	-	-	-	1	-	-	-	1	-	1	-	-	-	-	1	-	-	3	1	-	-	-	-	1	1	-	-	3	1	3	1	1	-	7	5	10	3	-	1	-	-	-	-	-	-	-	-	-	-	-	-	1	-	-	-
Adjourned Session. - May „ -	46	13	59	-	-	-	-	-	-	2	-	-	-	2	1	-	-	-	1	-	-	-	-	2	-	-	-	-	-	6	2	2	1	8	2	1	-	5	-	6	3	8	2	4	-	-	1	-	-	-	-	-	-	-	-	-	-	-	-	-	-
Midsummer Session - June „ -	43	23	66	-	-	-	-	-	-	-	-	1	1	1	-	2	1	-	-	-	-	-	-	1	-	-	-	-	-	4	1	2	-	6	3	1	2	1	8	7	2	9	4	8	-	-	-	-	1	-	-	-	-	-	-	-	-	-	-	-	-
Summer Assize - - July „ -	14	16	30	-	1	-	-	-	-	-	-	-	-	2	-	-	-	-	-	1	-	-	-	-	3	-	-	-	-	2	6	-	-	2	1	-	-	2	-	2	-	3	3	-	2	-	-	-	-	-	-	-	-	-	-	-	-	-	-	-	-
Michaelmas Session - October „ -	64	44	108	-	-	-	-	-	-	1	-	-	-	2	-	2	1	-	-	-	-	-	-	1	-	-	-	-	-	3	2	3	1	2	2	5	1	3	6	7	13	21	12	14	3	-	-	-	1	-	1	-	-	-	1	-	-	-	-	-	-
Adjourned Session - November „ -	54	22	76	-	-	-	-	-	-	2	-	1	-	1	1	1	1	-	-	-	-	-	-	-	1	-	-	-	-	7	1	1	-	2	2	5	-	10	1	4	[illegible]	13	5	7	2	-	-	-	-	-	-	-	-	-	1	-	-	-	-	-	-
Epiphany Session - January „ -	46	29	74	-	-	-	-	-	-	1	-	4	3	2	2	4	-	-	-	-	-	-	-	1	3	-	-	-	-	2	3	-	-	4	2	1	-	2	3	6	4	8	6	7	1	-	-	-	-	-	1	1	-	-	-	-	-	-	-	-	-

The Columns marked P. show the Sentences passed on the Prisoners contained as in Column A., and the Column marked O. the Sentences on those contained as in Column B.

In addition to the numbers contained in the above Return, the county police have apprehended the following prisoners, whose trials took place at the courts opposite their respective numbers:—14, Liberty of Havering Sessions, Romford. 1, Colchester Sessions. 1, Central Criminal Court. 5, Suffolk Assizes. 1, Hertford Sessions. 12, For trial at the coming Lent Assize.

No. 11.—RETURN of the Number of SHEEP and the Value of PROPERTY which came to the knowledge of

DIVISIONS.	JANUARY.			FEBRUARY.			MARCH.			APRIL.			MAY.			JUNE.		
	Amount of Property		Sheep Stolen	Amount of Property		Sheep Stolen	Amount of Property		Sheep Stolen	Amount of Property		Sheep Stolen	Amount of Property		Sheep Stolen	Amount of Property		Sheep Stolen
	Stolen.	Recovered.		Stolen.	Recovered.		Stole.	vered.		Stolen.	Recovered.		Stolen.	Recovered.		Stolen.	Recovered.	
	£. s. d.	£. s. d.		£. s. d.	£. s. d.		£. s. d.	£. s. d.		£. s. d.	£. s. d.		£. s. d.	£. s. d.		£. s. d.	£. s. d.	
Brentwood	8 – –	5 – –	1	17 7 6	3 4 3		1 9 –	1 – –		7 2 –	– 12 –	3	20 – –	20 – –	3	5 – –	3 – –	
Chelmsford	– – –	– – –		6 5 –	– – –		4 – –	– – –		6 – –	– 2 6		30 – –	– 5 –	3	1 15 –	– 5 –	
Colchester	6 – –	– – –		– 12 –	– – –		1 10 –	– – –		– – –	– – –		3 – –	– – –		1 15 –	– – –	
Dengie	3 16 –	– – –	1	4 3 –	– – –	1	1 2 –	– 13 –		4 10 –	– – –		1 10 –	– – –		2 – –	2 – –	
Dunmow	9 5 6	– – –		5 – –	– – –		– 15 –	– – –		– 15 –	– – –		3 17 3	3 7 3		– – –	– – –	
Epping	– 14 6	– – –		1 1 –	– – –		2 14 –	– – –	1	1 2 10	1 2 10		7 – –	2 10 –		– – –	– – –	
Freshwell	– 8 10	8 10 –		– 13 –	– 13 –		– 11 –	– 6 –		– – 6	– – 6		– 16 6	– – 6	1	3 3 –	3 3 –	
North Hinckford	– 17 –	– – –		2 – –	– – –	2	– – –	– – –		2 9 –	– – –		1 5 –	– – –	1	– – –	– – –	
South Hinckford	– 17 –	– – –		4 3 –	– – –		3 10 –	– – –		– – –	– – –		33 10 –	– – –		– – –	– – –	
Ongar	– – 2	– – 2		1 18 –	– 4 –	1	2 4 –	– 7 –	1	5 6 6	4 14 –		– 2 6	– 2 6		53 3 –	39 – –	
Rochford	– – –	– – –		1 15 –	– – –		3 10 –	– 10 –		– 3 –	– 3 –		16 16 –	6 1 –		1 15 –	– – –	
Tendring	4 7 –	1 10 –		3 13 –	– 5 –	3	2 7 1	1 2 1		– 3 –	– – –		2 8 –	1 3 –		72 2 –	20 – –	
Walden	7 17 –	– – –		36 6 6	35 – –		– – –	– – –		2 1 –	– – –		– 15 –	– – –		– – –	– – –	
Witham	– – –	– – –		– – –	– – –		– – –	– – –		– – –	– – –		– – –	– – –		– – –	– – –	
TOTAL £.	42 3 –	6 19 –	2	85 19 –	39 6 3		23 12 1	3 18 1	5	39 11 1	6 6 7	6	121 – 3	33 9 3	5	138 15 –	46 10 –	

* Twenty-nine sheep stolen in the Witham Division, in February, having been

---

No. 12.

RETURN of the Number of SHEEP Stolen during the Year 1839, in the *North Hinckford* and *Epping* Divisions.

NORTH HINCKFORD.		EPPING.	
Names of Parishes.	Number of Sheep Stolen.	Names of Parishes.	Number of Sheep Stolen.
Ballingdon	2	Epping	6
Belchamp Otten	4	North Weald Bassett	5
Belchamp St. Paul's	2	Thoydon Garnon	6
Belchamp Walter	2		
Bulmer	2	Harlow	4
Birdbrook	3	Little Parndon	2
Foxearth	24	Latton	1
Castle Hedingham	3		
Sible Hedingham	19	Hatfield Broad Oak	4
Lyston	10	Sheering	4
Great Maplestead	2	Roydon	8
Pentlow	16		
Stambourne	1	Nazing	1
Sturmer	1		
Toppesfield	8		
TOTAL	99	TOTAL	41

Sheep stolen at North Hinckford   99
Sheep stolen at Epping   41

TOTAL   140

the Essex Constabulary, either by Report or Inquiry, as having been Stolen during the Year 1841.

JULY. Stolen.	JULY. Recovered.	JULY. Sheep Stolen.	AUGUST. Stolen.	AUGUST. Recovered.	AUGUST. Sheep Stolen.	SEPTEMBER. Stolen.	SEPTEMBER. Recovered.	SEPTEMBER. Sheep Stolen.	OCTOBER. Stolen.	OCTOBER. Recovered.	OCTOBER. Sheep Stolen.	NOVEMBER. Stolen.	NOVEMBER. Recovered.	NOVEMBER. Sheep Stolen.	DECEMBER. Stolen.	DECEMBER. Recovered.	DECEMBER. Sheep Stolen.	Total Number of Sheep Stolen.	Total Amount of Property Stolen.	Total Amount of Property Recovered.
£. s. d.	£. s. d.		£. s. d.	£. s. d.		£. s. d.	£. s. d.		£. s. d.	£. s. d.		£. s. d.	£. s. d.		£. s. d.	£. s. d.			£. s. d.	£. s. d.
57 10 –	40 – –	–	9 3 –	- -	1	54 17 –	13 2 –	–	24 4 –	– 11 –	2	7 12 3	– 15 3	3	46 – –	- -	7	20	258 4 9	57 7 6
13 – –	- -	1	15 13 –	3 13 –	–	4 13 –	- -	1	8 – –	- -	5	5 – –	- -	3	37 2 –	– 14 –	3	20	130 8 –	4 10 6
5 5 –	- -	[illegible]	40 – –	- -	–	3 18 6	- -	1	12 8 –	- -	8	12 10 –	- -	6	13 – –	- -	7	23	108 3 6	—
37 10 –	18 – –	[illegible]	3 11 6	– 1 6	[illegible]	– – 8	– – 8	–	61 10 –	.. -	1	– 17 6	45 2 6	–	5 9 9	– 4 9	[illegible]	12	123 15 5	47 2 3
– 12 –	- -	–	1 10 –	- -	-	28 10 –	– 7 7	6	1 1 –	- -	–	75 19 3	16 11 9	1	1 10 –	– 7 –	1	10	118 17 –	29 15 7
6 5 7	1 5 7	1	12 1 –	7 17 6	–	7 14 –	– 4 –	–	12 9 –	12 9 –	–	3 3 –	– 13 –	1	1 – 6	– 8 –	–	3	55 5 5	26 9 11
- -	- -	–	- -	- -	–	– 1 –	– 1 –	–	- -	- -	–	- -	- -	–	4 4 –	– 12 –	–	1	6 13 10	1 16 4
– 8 –	- -	–	1 5 –	- -	1	22 – –	- -	–	1 15 –	- -	1	- -	- -	–	2 14 6	1 – –	1	6	34 8 6	1 – –
1 8 –	- -	–	10 – –	10 – –	-	- -	- -	–	7 6 6	3 15 –	–	7 12 –	- -	–	1 10 –	- -	1	1	72 19 6	16 18 –
– 11 6	– 10 –	–	1 – 6	1 – 6	.	– 5 11	– 5 11	–	6 12 –	– 8 –	4	26 16 –	26 – –	1	11 18 –	- -	–	6	50 12 1	31 2 1
25 8 –	– 8 –	–	1 8 –	- -	[illegible]	21 – –	21 – –	–	5 3 4	- -	1	3 2 11	– 6 5	–	8 8 6	2 10 6	1	4	141 11 3	63 3 11
- -	- -	–	2 – –	- -	–	- -	- -	–	- -	- -	–	4 5 –	- -	3	3 1 –	– 11 –	2	8	14 11 –	1 1 –
10 7 5	– 7 5	–	– 10 –	– 10 –	–	3 12 6	- -	–	– 5 6	– – 6	1	4 16 9	2 11 9	1	30 2 6	1 – 2	3	9	61 9 10	8 12 11
- -	- -	–	1 10 –	- -	1	4 – –	- -	–	8 10 –	2 10 –	3	3 16 –	- -	2	17 10 –	3 10 –	1	10*	150 7 6	61 – –
158 5 6	60 11 –	4	139 11 –	23 1 6	6	140 12 7	35 1 2	8	149 4 4	19 16 6	26	152 10 8	92 – 8	21	183 16 9	10 17 5	30	133	1,337 10 10	373 9 –

recovered by the police and the offender convicted, are omitted in this Return.

No. 13.—RETURN of the Distribution of the Essex County Constabulary; 5th April 1842.

DIVISIONS.	STATIONS.	Superintendents.	Inspectors.	Constables.
BRENTWOOD - -	Brentwood - - - -	1	–	2
	Billericay - - - -	–	1	1
	South Ockendon - - -	–	–	1
	Grays - - - -	–	–	2
	Collier Row - - - -	–	–	1
	Hornchurch - - - -	–	–	2
	Romford * - - - -	–	1	3
	Orsett - - - -	–	1	–
		1	3	12
CHELMSFORD - -	Chelmsford † - - -	2	1	10
	Ingatestone - - -	–	1	1
	West Hanningfield - -	–	1	–
	Danbury - - - -	–	–	1
	Writtle - - - -	–	–	2
	Waltham - - - -	–	–	2
		2	3	16
COLCHESTER - -	Stanway - - - -	1	–	1
	Peldon - - - -	–	–	1
	Great Horkesley - - -	–	–	2
	Dedham - - - -	–	–	2
	Fordham - - - -	–	1	1
	Mount Bures - - -	–	–	1
	Brightlingsea - - -	–	–	1
		1	1	9
DENGIE - - -	Latchingdon - - -	1	–	1
	Southminster - - -	–	1	1
	Purleigh - - - -	–	–	1
	Tillingham - - - -	–	–	1
	Burnham - - - -	–	–	1
	Bradwell - - - -	–	–	1
		1	1	6
DUNMOW - - -	Dunmow - - - -	1	1	2
	Takely - - - -	–	1	–
	Thaxted - - - -	–	–	1
	High Easter - - -	–	–	2
		1	2	5
EPPING - - -	Epping - - - -	1	–	2
	Harlow - - - -	–	–	2
	Roydon - - - -	–	–	1
	Abridge - - - -	–	–	2
	Hatfield Heath - - -	–	1	–
	Great Parndon - - -	–	–	1
		1	1	8
FRESHWELL - -	Great Bardfield - - -	1	–	1
	Steeple Bumpsted - -	–	–	1
	Weathersfield - - -	–	–	1
		1	–	3

DIVISIONS.	STATIONS.	Superintendents.	Inspectors.	Constables.
NORTH HINCKFORD	Sible Hedingham - -	1	–	2
	Walter Belchamp - -	–	–	2
	Foxearth - - -	–	1	1
	Toppesfield - - -	–	–	1
	Bulmer - - - -	–	–	1
		1	1	7
SOUTH HINCKFORD	Braintree - - -	1	1	3
	Halsted - - - -	–	1	2
	Earls Colne - - -	–	–	2
	Stisted - - - -	–	–	1
		1	2	8
ONGAR - - -	Chipping Ongar - -	1	–	1
	Blackmoor - - -	–	–	1
	Passingford Bridge -	–	–	1
	Matching Green - -	–	–	1
	Willingale Doe - -	–	–	1
		1	–	5
ROCHFORD - -	Rayleigh - - -	1	–	1
	Rochford - - -	–	–	2
	Great Wakering - -	–	1	–
	Southend - - -	–	–	1
	Prittlewell - - -	–	–	1
	South Benfleet - -	–	–	1
		1	1	6
TENDRING - -	Thorpe - - - -	1	–	1
	Manningtree - - -	–	1	1
	St. Osyth - - -	–	1	1
	Great Oakley - - -	–	–	1
	Ardleigh - - - -	–	–	2
	Elmsted - - - -	–	–	2
		1	2	8
WALDEN - - -	Newport - - - -	1	1	1
	Ashdon - - - -	–	1	1
	Stansted - - - -	–	–	1
	Chrishall - - -	–	–	2
	Great Chesterford -	–	–	1
		1	2	6
WITHAM - - -	Witham - - - -	1	–	2
	Coggeshall - - -	–	1	1
	Tolleshunt D'Arcy - -	–	–	1
	Heybridge - - -	–	–	1
	Hatfield Heath - -	–	–	1
		1	1	6
	TOTAL of the foregoing - - -	15	20	105

* The town of Romford is taxed additionally for two of these constables.
† The town of Chelmsford is taxed additionally for three of these constables, and most of the others are recruits.

Appendix, No. 1.

No. 13—*continued.*

AUTHORISED NUMBERS.		Chief Constables.	Secretary.	Superintendents.	Inspectors.	Constables.
Appointed by the County		1	1	15	20	100
" by the Town of Chelmsford	Under 19th section 3 & 4 Vict. cap. 88	–	–	–	–	3
" by the Town of Romford		–	–	–	–	2
TOTAL		1	1	15	20	105

No. 14.

RETURN referring to that Part of the County subject to Police Rate.

NAMES OF DIVISIONS.	Size in English Statute Acres.	Population, 1831.	Number of Parishes.	Sum raised by One Penny County Rate.	Proportion of Constables paid for by the respective Divisions.
				£. s. d.	
Brentwood	104,310	22,110	46	483 11 7 3/4	12
Chelmsford	79,570	26,531	29	426 10 1	10 5/8
Colchester	65,930	17,606	32	285 18 1 3/4	7 1/8
Dengie	58,520	10,979	21	283 – 10 1/4	7 1/4
Dunmow	54,400	13,042	24	190 16 6 1/2	4 3/4
Epping	51,110	13,733	19	251 8 6 1/2	6 1/4
Freshwell	27,340	6,562	8	86 7 2 1/4	2 1/8
North Hinckford	50,090	15,897	27	194 9 8 1/4	5
South Hinckford	56,770	24,506	24	236 15 9	5 7/8
Ongar	42,820	10,474	24	212 16 10 1/2	5 1/4
Rochford	61,890	14,663	26	278 10 1 1/4	7
Tendring	77,950	21,002	30	360 12 10 1/4	9
Walden	76,980	17,804	34	272 17 3 3/4	6 3/4
Witham	72,530	21,870	33	318 19 2 3/4	8
	880,210	236,779	377	3,882 14 9 3/4	97
LIBERTY OF HAVERING.					
Havering	- -	- -	- -	10 5 1 1/4	1/4
Hornchurch North Ward	- -	- -	- -	25 2 3 1/2	5/8
Hornchurch South Ward	- -	- -	- -	25 2 3 1/2	5/8
Romford Town	15,863	6,812	3	30 19 9 1/4	3/4
Collier Row Ward	- -	- -	- -	10 3 4 1/4	1/4
Harold's Wood Ward	- -	- -	- -	16 9 1 1/2	3/8
Noak Hill Ward	- -	- -	- -	5 19 7 1/4	1/8
TOTAL	896,073	243,591 *	380	4,006 16 4 1/4	100

The last column is also an index to the expense borne by each division in support of the other members of the force and its contingent expenses.

* The census taken last year not having been officially received, has not been applied, or this total would amount to 268,509.

No. 15.

TABLE of FEES and ALLOWANCES, made pursuant to the 17th Section of the 3 & 4 Vict. c. 88.

To each local constable executing a warrant, 5 s.; and if more than one day be necessarily occupied in the performance of the duty, then the constable shall be paid at the rate of 5 s. for each day so occupied.

	s.	d.
To every such constable serving a summons - - - -	1	—
For attending before the justice with return of summons - -	5	—

But if the constable, when attending before the justice, shall have two or more returns of summonses to make, then the sum of 5 s. shall be divided and paid equally and proportionably by the parties liable to pay them.

To each local constable acting under the orders of a justice of the peace, or the chief constable, or his deputy, if the distance travelled does not exceed five miles, 5 s. per day; but when the distance shall exceed five miles from his residence, then such constable shall be paid at the rate of 6 d. for every additional mile beyond the five miles, but nothing for returning.

	s.	d.
For each night - - - - - - - - -	2	6

For conveying one offender from the justice to prison, 10 d. per mile; for conveying two offenders, 7 d. per mile for each; for conveying three or more offenders, 6 d. per mile for each.

For every day during which such constable shall be under the necessity of keeping such offender or offenders in custody after commitment, for his loss of time and trouble, 5 s., and for every night 2 s. 6 d.; and the sum of 2 s. 6 d. for every day, and 1 s. 3 d. for every night to each assistant, if ordered by the committing justice.

For the subsistence of each prisoner whilst in custody after commitment, 1 s. per day, and 1 s. 6 d. for a day and night, if lodging is not provided; and 2 s. 6 d. for a day and night if lodging is provided.

No. 16.

Chief Constable's Office, Chelmsford,
22 October 1840.

Gentlemen,

By the 16th section of the Amended Constabulary Act, it becomes my duty, as chief constable of this county, to submit to the justices of each division of it a list of persons qualified and willing to serve as local constables. The great object of this is to provide at least one efficient peace officer in each village and hamlet in the county, who by a cordial co-operation with the county police, may render it truly efficient, without incurring the necessity of increasing the county police.

I am therefore induced to request you will be pleased to assist me in this very important part of my duty, by furnishing me with the names and addresses of such persons as you may think advisable to recommend, and who are willing to serve as local constables.

I attach, for your information, a Table of Fees and Allowances to be granted to such local constables.

I am, &c.

To the Magistrates and Clergy of the County of Essex.

J. B. B. McHardy,
Chief Constable.

No. 17.

Division.—County of Essex.   Day of   184 .

RETURN of Persons qualified and willing to serve as LOCAL CONSTABLES.

Names.	Ages.	Calling or Occupation.	Parish, Township, or Place, for which Parties are willing to serve.	Address, stating the nearest Post Town.	Has the Party ever served as Constable? if he has, state the Time.	Signature of Party Recommending.	Remarks.

Note. — Candidates should be capable of reading, writing, and keeping accounts, and reside where willing to serve for.

No. 18.

RETURN of the Probable ANNUAL EXPENSE of the *Essex* County Constabulary.

	PRESENT FORCE.	Pay.	Clothing.	Appointments.	TOTAL.
		£. s. d.	£. s. d.	£. s. d.	£. s. d.
1	Chief Constable - -	400 — —			
	Allowance under 18th Section - - -	160 — ··			
1	Secretary - - -	100 — —			
15	Superintendents, at 80 *l.* per annum - -	1,200 — —	135 — —		4,351 17 6
	Forage for 18 Horses -	657 — —			
	Stabling, shoeing, &c. -	117 — —		13 2 6	
20	Inspectors, at 65 *l.* per annum - -	1,300 — —	209 15 —		
50	Constables, 1st Class, at 21 *s.* per week - -	2,730 — —			
50	Constables, 2d Class, at 19 *s.* per week - -	2,470 — —	525 — —	37 10 —	5,762 10 —
	Annual Contingent Expenses - - -	- - -	- - -	- - -	800 — —

Total Outlay - - - £. 10,914 7 6

Total probable Saving :

Sum Saved by county carts -   -   -   -   -

„ Raised under 17th section -   -   -

„ Saved by orders of court -   -   -   -   2,188 3 6

„ Saved by abolition of gaols -   -   -

Probable Annual Expense of the present Force - - - £. 8,726 4 -

Note.—Table No. 14 shows that a nine-farthing county rate would raise the required sum, 9,000 *l.*; whereas, if the rate were collected on the parochial assessment, taking the county generally, I believe a six-farthing rate would raise the same sum.

No. 19.

RETURN of the PAYMENTS made to Prosecutors and Witnesses.

	1839.		1840.		1841.		1839.			1840.			1841.		
	Number of Prisoners.	Number of Indictments.	Number of Prisoners.	Number of Indictments.	Number of Prisoners.	Number of Indictments.	£.	s.	d.	£.	s.	d.	£.	s.	d.
Epiphany Sessions - -	53	53	79	61	50	47	496	5	4	513	8	3	256	15	9
Adjourned ditto - -	70	77	67	56	81	72	575	13	7	418	6	10	396	13	7
Lent Assize - -	41	36	38	38	58	49	426	17	–	378	9	1	465	8	4
Easter Sessions - -	55	49	45	43	46	55	357	11	6	299	15	5	356	8	10
Adjourned ditto - -	50	49	64	58	59	55	313	6	2	337	19	3	414	4	2
Midsummer ditto - -	37	32	53	53	66	58	198	17	2	265	17	11	449	1	4
Summer Assize - -	21	18	28	24	30	22	181	10	4	306	5	2	219	18	–
Michaelmas Sessions -	101	79	148	123	108	103	490	6	10	922	12	8	634	17	8
Adjourned ditto - -	54	45	72	73	76	60	280	3	8	452	14	6	453	10	10
	482	438	594	529	574	521	3,320	11	7	3,907	9	1	3,646	18	6

		£	s	d	£	s	d	£	s	d
Average Expense of each Prisoner -		6	17	9½	6	11	6¾	6	7	1
Average Expense of each Indictment -		7	11	7⅓	7	7	8¾	7	–	–

(*End of Report, dated 5th April* 1842.)

REPORT of the Chief Constable to the Magistrates of the County of *Essex*, in Quarter Sessions assembled, 15 October 1850.

See *Scheme, No. 7, in Appendix, submitted to Government in* 1846, *for an efficient National Police.*

My Lords and Gentlemen,

HAVING received, by order of this court, a copy of a Report made to it by a committee appointed to consider the subject of the county expenditure generally, I trust I shall be anticipating the wish of this court if, before particularly noticing the said Report, I respectfully lay before it, for its information, a brief statement, accompanied with Returns (*see* Appendix, as described in the margin*) of expenditure connected with the department intrusted to my supervision, more particularly lest anything should have gone abroad which would justify a suspicion of a want of the most rigid economy.

I feel satisfied the Essex constabulary is, by its savings under a variety of heads, a self-supporting establishment, which I shall endeavour to put in evidence by tables showing sums saved and earned by the police.

On my being appointed chief constable I deemed it my duty to submit to this court such arrangements as would, in my opinion, tend to render the limited number of the force placed

at

---

* No. 1. Return, showing gross Annual Expenditure and Distribution of the Force, 1849.

No. 2. Extract from Report, recommending providing Police Stations and Strong Rooms.

No. 3. Return, showing Expense incurred in the Conveyance of Prisoners prior to the Establishment of the Constabulary.

No. 4. Return, showing the Expense and Revenue produced by the Police Stations.

No. 5. Return, showing the Saving by Inspection of Weights and Measures.

(A.), (B.), and (C.) Return, showing the Decrease of Vagrancy.

No. 6. Return, showing Expense of Constabulary in Ilford Division.

No. 7. Scheme for an efficient Constabulary.

No. 8. Return of the Parishes and Places forming the seven Police Districts, under sections 27 and 28, Act 3 & 4 Vict., c. 88.

No. 9. Return, showing the present Distribution of the County Constabulary.

at my disposal as efficient as practicable, and at the least possible *net* expense; I therefore directed my attention to two points connected therewith; namely,

First, the best mode of economising, by auxiliaries, the time of the force, and thereby adding to its efficiency *physically* without doing so *numerically*.

Secondly, by transferring to the constabulary duties acknowledged to have been previously inefficiently performed by others, by which means a considerable saving has been effected, and the duties have been satisfactorily executed.

With reference to the first point, viz., economising the time of the force, I found that nearly 1,000 *l.* per annum (*see* Table No. 3) had been paid by the county for the conveyance of prisoners. I therefore submitted, that, as each of the superintendents had already been necessarily supplied with a horse, by incurring the trifling expense of furnishing the respective divisions for which they acted with a light cart and harness, they would be enabled to convey all the prisoners, and at the same time the carts would be useful for the occasional concentration of the force and a variety of other purposes; which recommendation you were pleased to approve. And as all the expenses attendant on these carts are included in the gross expenditure shown in Table No. 1, I have no doubt it will be readily admitted, that a credit of a saving of about 900 *l.* per annum may be taken in favour of the constabulary under the head of the Conveyance of Prisoners against the gross expenditure shown in Table No. 1.

I next laid before your court a Report (*see* Appendix No. 2), and strongly recommended the erection, to a certain extent, of police stations (capable of extension) as being indispensably necessary to the efficient organisation of a constabulary, which you were also pleased, by degrees, to carry into effect.

Now, without taking into consideration the expense which has been saved to the respective parishes in the repair or erection of "cages," (places which were always unfitted for the temporary confinement of prisoners) or the facility and economy thus afforded in carrying out the recent Act of Parliament for providing suitable accommodation for holding petty sessions, I take leave to refer you to Table No. 4, showing that the revenue produced by the police stations during the last five years (without taking into account various savings also shown in the same Table), not only pays the interest, but nearly two instalments out of five on the money borrowed; thereby showing that the county has gained all the incalculable advantages of these stations by paying the balance of 2,555 *l.* 9 *s.* 2 *d.* in five annual *investments* of 511 *l.* 1 *s.* 10 *d.* I consider that the advantage derived from stations adds more to the efficiency of the force than double that sum would have done laid out in adding to it *numerically*, because this sum applied in wages to increase the force numerically would provide only nine additional constables; and this plan has the further advantage of being a *permanent investment* for the benefit of the county. I wish the court further to observe, that the payments for interest on money borrowed is annually decreasing, and ultimately the instalments will also annually decrease, the sums having been borrowed at different periods, and in a few years the debt will be entirely absorbed; and so satisfied am I, from experience, that the light carts and police stations add so essentially to the efficiency of the force, that, were I left to the alternative, I would part with 20 constables rather than be deprived of those auxiliaries.

Secondly, with reference to transferring to the constabulary duties inefficiently performed by others, I first submitted for your pleasure the advisability of transferring to the force under my command duties connected with the inspection of weights and measures, of which you were also pleased to approve. I now take leave to refer you to Table No. 5, which shows an average annual saving, by the adoption of this plan, of 584 *l.* 11 *s.* 8 *d.* to the county during the last six years, when compared with the expense during the previous six years. Therefore, it must be admitted, that a credit of 584 *l.* 11 *s.* 8 *d.* per annum may be taken in favour of the constabulary under the head of Inspection of Weights and Measures, against the gross expenditure shown in Table No. 1.

Next, finding that professional mendicancy was, by the indiscriminate relief granted by the relieving officers of the unions in the county, increasing to an alarming extent, I, with your permission, invited the respective unions to try the effect of appointing some members of the county constabulary relieving officers for "casuals;" and, having succeeded in inducing four unions to try the experiment, the immediate effect was such as to remove objections and induce six other unions, which had previously declined, to follow their example. And I am happy to know that, by the discreet conduct on the part of the members of the constabulary on whom this most responsible and delicate duty devolved, the number of vagrants relieved in the unions of Essex in the half year ending Michaelmas 1849 is reduced from 24,882 to 2,977, thereby making a difference, in one half year, of 21,905, when compared with the half year ending Michaelmas 1848, as shown by Tables (A.) and (B.) taken from a Report made to Parliament by the Poor Law Board.

Although these tables are an index to such an incredible decrease of vagrancy in the county, viz., 21,905 in half a year, I do not ask you to credit this arrangement with having rid the county of about 40,000 of these annual visitors, because I know the same vagrant often makes his appearance at several unions; but I may reasonably ask you to give it credit for having relieved the county of at least the difference between 5,276 relieved in the single union of Chelmsford in 1847, and 175, the number relieved in 1849, thereby showing, in this one union, the surprising difference of 5,101; and, admitting that each of these vagrants of which the county has been rid gleaned in different ways in passing slowly over it 1 *l.* each,

each, it must be admitted that the constabulary, acting as relieving officers, has effected an annual saving of at least 5,101 *l*., and which should be taken in favour of it, under the head of Decrease of Vagrancy, against the *gross* expenditure shown in Table No. 1 ; exclusive of the moral effect gained by the riddance of so great a pest to society. And I am happy to find that what I recommended in my report in 1842, the New Health Act, now introduced into some of the towns in this county, will bring into operation, viz., the registering and licensing lodging houses to accommodate according to capacity, subject to rules formed by the Board, and thereby evils will, I hope, be checked which there exist, and which common decency forbids me to describe.

The next item I submit is, that the constabulary ought to be credited for saving annually 500 *l*. by the abolition of the two district gaols, Halsted and Newport; which, from their construction, admitted of the introduction of no systematic discipline. And when I observe that in one year the constabulary have conveyed from the northern part of the county to the county gaol 808 prisoners, it will, I have no doubt, be acknowledged that without an organised police the abolition of these gaols would have been attended with great inconvenience, if not altogether impracticable.

As there are 380 parishes in the county under the supervision of the constabulary, I have endeavoured to ascertain what sum was paid by each of these parishes to their constables prior to the establishment of the county constabulary, but I found this vary so much, not only in parishes, but in the same parish in different years, that it was impossible to ascertain the exact amount to which many parishes were subjected. In some instances more than 50 *l*. was thus annually expended; in others less than 1 *l*. Therefore, estimating the average expense to each parish to have amounted to so low a sum as 5 *l*., the expense under this head would be annually 1,900 *l*. ; and, to exclude the possibility of it being supposed that I have put this sum too high, I include what was previously paid by the poor-law unions and private inviduals.

I am led to this estimate from having succeeded in procuring a correct comparative return from a petty sessional division of this county, showing what was paid by each parish in the three years (1837, 1838 and 1839, preceding the introduction of the county constabulary, with the last three years (1847, 1848, and 1849), of the establishment of the constabulary, which, taking the mean, gives to each parish an annual saving of 10 *l*. 18 *s*. 4 *d*.

It is impossible to ascertain what was formerly paid by private individuals and the poor-law unions to parish constables, or what has been saved to the public by the police from the diminution of crime or business at petty sessions. And I also submit to your consideration the great advantage derived by the protection and recovery of property ; and, to illustrate this, I would refer you to a Report which I laid before this Court in 1842, by which it appears that 140 sheep were stolen in the North Hinckford and Epping petty sessional divisions of this county in the year (1839) preceding the adoption of the constabulary, a number far exceeding that stolen in any year in the whole 14 divisions since the establishment of the police ; whilst loss by horse-stealing, which was formerly very prevalent, is now almost unknown. But I have the authority of one of the first land valuers in this county, occupying nearly 1,000 acres, for stating, that he considers that land is increased in annual value by the establishment of the police from 1 *d*. to 2 *d*. per acre.

Before I enter into a summary of the different savings effected by the police, I beg the Court will bear in mind that the sum of 1,450 *l*. 17 *s*. 1 *d*, shown in Table No. 1, paid for interest and instalments on money borrowed for the erection of police stations, is annually decreasing, and will ultimately cease ; therefore, in considering the expense of the police, it should be deducted from the *gross* sum, as it is an *investment* in property for the permanent benefit of the county ; and I have also to draw its attention to the sum of 1,286 *l*. 10 *s*. 8 *d*. in Table No. 1, received for services performed by the constabulary, and that of 332 *l*. 11 *s*., received from it for rent, as well as 24 *l*. credited to the county rate from proceedings taken by the police under penal statutes ; and I may with confidence state, that the police annually save the county at least 40 *l*. by their delivering small official packages from the clerk of the peace's office to the parochial authorities, and quarterly to the magistrates. But I do not ask this Court to credit the police with 84 *l*. saved annually in allowances for stabling and offices in consequence of the erection of the police stations, for I am not here comparing the expense between a police with stations and a police without stations, but I am comparing the expense of the police with what the county would pay if there were no police.

There are still small payments made to parish constables, which amount in the aggregate to a large sum, and might be saved by employing the police.

I now submit a summary of the items saved and earned by the constabulary under different heads, which ought to be credited against its gross expense of 15,886 *l*. ; and I might further observe, there are items now charged against the police which were formerly paid by other parties, and I trust you will not add to the *apparent* expense of the constabulary by placing to its account the sums which you have authorised, and may be pleased to appropriate for providing accommodation for holding petty sessions, directed by Act 12 Vict., c. 18, s. 2, to be paid out of the county rate.

	£.	s.	d.
By the conveyance of prisoners - - - - - - - -	900	–	–
By the inspection of weights and measures - - - - -	584	11	8
By the decrease of vagrancy - - - - - - - -	5,101	–	–
By the abolition of Halsted and Newport Gaols - - - -	500	–	–
Interest and instalment on money borrowed for the erection of police stations - - - - - - - - - - -	1,450	17	1

Received from magistrates' clerks, under 17th section - £. 141 19 6 ⎫
Received from coroners, under 17th section - - 10 19 – ⎪
Received from other jurisdictions, under 17th section - 28 19 3 ⎬ 1,286 10 8
Received from the Government under Orders of Court - 1,104 12 11 ⎭

	£.	s.	d.
Rent for such parts of the station-houses as are occupied by members of the constabulary - - - - - - - - -	332	11	–
Amount of fines credited to the county rate under penal statutes - -	24	–	–
Amount saved in postage by the police delivering official parcels to the magistrates and parochial authorities - - - - - -	40	–	–

Probable sum formerly paid annually to parish constables - - - - ⎰ By the 380 parishes - ⎱
⎱ By the Poor-law unions - ⎰ 1,900 – –
By the private individuals -

Saved to the public by
The diminution of business at petty sessions -	Although a diversity of opinion must naturally exist in
The protection and recovery of property -	the absence of a direct index to the sum saved under these
Non-contributions to associations for the prosecution of offenders -	heads, I venture to estimate the annual increased value in land
Non-payments to special constables - - -	at 1 d. per acre on the 884,680 acres under the supervision of the police - - - -

3,686 3 4

	£.	s.	d.
	15,805	13	9

By referring to the foregoing summary, supported by the Tables in Appendix, it will be seen that the police, speaking generally, is a self-supporting force.

	£.	s.	d.
The gross annual expense being - - - - -	15,886	–	–
The savings and earnings - - - - - -	15,805	13	9
NET COST of the Police to the County - - £.	80	6	3 *

And I am satisfied that this Court will readily acknowledge, although there may be in the minds of a few a difference of opinion on some of the items now submitted, that the Essex constabulary does not actually cost the county one-third of its *apparent* expense. And I take permission further to observe, that Table No. 6 will show that the Metropolitan Police in one petty sessional division of this county, namely, Ilford, which is within the metropolitan district, cost last year 8,361 l. 10 s. 8 d., which is much more than half the *gross* expense of the remaining 14 divisions forming the county constabulary.

I regret that the constabulary is not, as at present organised, so nationally beneficial as it would have been rendered if the scheme I drew up in 1846 had been adopted.—(See Appendix, No. 7.)

I am prevented, by the present length of this report, from submitting observations showing that the provisions of the present Parish Constables' Act were virtually tried in this county in 1841, as shown in my report to this Court in 1842, under the powers given in the Constabulary Act, 3 & 4 Vict., c. 88, for providing "local constables," and that any attempt to form a constabulary under the present Parish Constables' Act would not only be much more expensive than under the Acts now in operation in this county, but would fail in efficiency principally from being a disjunct instead of a conjunct force; and its members having an interest in crime, and being shackled by local connexion.

I have not failed to lodge with the clerk of the peace, at the termination of each month, the return directed by the 31st section of Act 3 & 4 Vict., c. 88, showing the daily distribution of the constabulary; and I have also deposited with him quarterly a tabular abstract of the charge-sheets, showing the state of crime in the respective petty sessional divisions. In referring you to Return No. 8 (see Appendix), showing the parishes and places comprising the seven police districts into which you have been pleased to form

(under

---

* No credit is here taken for the effectual protection which has been afforded to the public revenue by arming the Essex constabulary (200 in number) with the powers given under section 33, Act 8 & 9 Vict., c. 87, for that purpose; although a large item might be credited when it is known that the coast guard (coast police), 127 men on the coast of Essex, solely for the protection of the public revenue, costs the Government 9,000 l. per annum, exclusive of 3,000 l. for three small cruisers for the same purpose.

Neither is credit taken for an additional sum of 500 l. also saved to the county by the abolition of Colchester gaol.

(under sections * 27 and 28, 3 & 4 Vict., c. 88), that part of the county under the supervision of the county constabulary, I have to acquaint you, with reference to Return No. 9 (*see* Appendix), showing the present distribution of the force, that, in the absence of extraordinary circumstances, I deem it my duty to make the number of constables paid for by each division (*see* also Table No. 1), my principal guide in that distribution. And I am happy to say, that the fully carrying out the formation of police districts has removed all pretext for stating that the rural districts are taxed to protect the towns.

† And now with reference to the report, which I have received by your order, recommending for your consideration certain reductions in the pay and allowances made to the members of the constabulary intrusted to my command, I trust I shall be anticipating the wish of this Court in submitting for its consideration such information as my experience may in my humble opinion assist it in weighing the subject.

With reference to the reduction of 30 *l.* from the salary of 150 *l.* to the deputy chief constable, I have to acquaint you that the difficulty attendant in making it retrospective is removed by the deputy chief constable's resignation, and to explain what led to his salary being 150 *l.*, viz.:

For some years after the first establishment of the force, when the office duties were naturally considerably greater than latterly, this Court granted a clerk at a salary of 100 *l.* per annum. In April 1848, the person who then filled this office resigned, in consequence of being offered a more desirable appointment. I took that opportunity of suggesting to this Court that the office of clerk should be abolished, and that it should be pleased to grant an addition of 50 *l.* per annum to the salary of such superintendent as may be appointed deputy chief constable, in compliance with section 7, Act 2 & 3 Vict., c. 93, which enacts, "That the chief constable shall, subject to the approval of the justices in general or quarter sessions assembled, or at any adjournment thereof, appoint one of the superintendents to act as his deputy in case of his being incapable from illness or necessary absence from the county to perform the duties of chief constable of the county; and the deputy so appointed shall in such case as aforesaid, and also in case of any vacancy of the office of chief constable by death or otherwise, have all the powers, privileges, and duties of chief constable."

I submitted to the Court that by this arrangement a saving would be effected of 50 *l.* per annum out of the 100 *l.* then allowed for a clerk, and that it would facilitate the means of procuring a desirable person. The Court was pleased to agree to my suggestions, and on the 3d of August 1849 a deputy chief constable was appointed.

The next recommendation in the report is, that the pay of each constable in the several classes should be reduced 1 *s.* 6 *d.* per week.

I beg leave to call your attention to the fact that each constable, on the first establishment of the force, received 20 *s.* per week. In my reports I represented the great difficulty which existed in procuring proper individuals, and I stated that experience had proved both in the navy and army, coast guard and police, that sentinels and patrols must be frequently visited by a superior in order to insure a faithful discharge of duty, so that wherever neglect takes place, the superior should be able to point out the person who is in fault, thus convincing every member of an organised force that he is not liable to be charged with the neglect of others.

I also represented in my report (April 1842) that the difficulty in effecting these requisites to discipline were much augmented in a county police from its being generally dispersed.

I therefore recommended the introduction of a variety of grades, which I propose to effect by placing the 15 superintendents in three classes, as also the private constables, in order to assist in ensuring the supervision of a superior, who would be a responsible individual;

---

* *Formation of Police Districts.*

XXVII. And whereas the number of constables needed may be different in different parts of the same county; be it enacted, that it shall be lawful for the justices of the peace for any county in general or quarter sessions assembled, if they shall be of opinion that a distinction ought to be made in the number of constables appointed to keep the peace in different parts of the county, to divide the county or any part thereof into police districts, consisting of such parishes and places, or parts of parishes and places, as shall appear to them most convenient, and to declare the number of constables which ought to be appointed for each police district, and from time to time to alter the extent of such police districts, and the number of constables to be appointed for each: and a report of every such proposed division or alteration, and of the number of constables proposed for each police district, with a estimate of its extent and population, and of any other circumstances upon which the determination of the justices shall have been grounded, shall be sent to one of Her Majesty's Principal Secretaries of State, and if approved by the Secretary of State, such division or alteration shall be deemed to be completed.

Each Police District to Pay for its own Constables.

XXVIII. And be it enacted, that if the Secretary of State shall approve of such division of the county, or of any part thereof, into police districts for the purpose aforesaid, the expense of putting the said Act into execution in such county, or part of such county, shall be classed under two heads, of general expenditure and local expenditure; and the general expenditure shall be defrayed in common by all the districts, and the local expenditure, consisting of the expense of the salaries and clothing of the constables appointed for each district, and such other expenses as the justices, subject to the approval of the Secretary of State, shall direct to be included under this head, shall be defrayed by each police district separately; and the police rates shall be assessed and levied in each police district accordingly: Provided always, that, notwithstanding the division of any county, or part of any county, into police districts, the constables of all such districts shall continue as part of the same force, and be subject to the same authority, and be liable, if required, to perform the same duty, in any part of the county or elsewhere, as if no such division into police districts had been made.

† This scheme for reduction was abandoned, and the following unanimous vote of the Court passed: "That the Essex constabulary is highly valuable, and is essentially necessary to the protection of property, and the proper administration of public justice."

vidual; such an arrangement, I stated, would have the effect of promoting *emulation*, and would be attended with economy.

The Court was pleased to comply with this recommendation by adding 20 *l.* per annum to the salary of each of five of the superintendents, and 10 *l.* per annum to the salary of each of five others, thus increasing the expense to the county by 150 *l.* per annum, at the same time the constables (not retrospective) were placed in three classes at a weekly pay of 17 *s.*, 19 *s.*, and 21 *s.*, thereby effecting a saving of 1 *s.* per week on each constable, and an annual saving of 423 *l.* 16 *s.* on the present establishment of 163 private constables, consequently, after deducting the increased expense of 150 *l.* per annum from the saving of 423 *l.* 16 *s.*, a net saving of 273 *l.* 16 *s.* would be effected.

Of the numerous advantages attendant on this arrangement of classification, the effect of that powerful incentive *emulation* thus introduced has been most felt in improving the standard of excellence of the material forming the force. By carefully weeding the force, and in consequence of the fall in the price of the necessaries of life tending to increase the value of the appointment, and enabling me to raise the standard of excellence of the candidates, I have succeeded in raising the character of the material of the force to a satisfactory state, notwithstanding even now I never get an application for employment from an eligible party who does not admit that it is in consequence of being out of employment, but after making the police for a short time his profession the prejudice against the employment subsides.

The difficulty of procuring proper men for county policemen is apparent from the qualifications required being not only high character and physical power, but also great energy and intelligence; for in consequence of the dispersed state of the force, a county policeman is generally less under supervision and more called on to judge and act for himself, than a serjeant in the metropolitan police, who receives the same pay as an inspector in this force (viz., 25 *s.* per week), who while exercising supervision discharges also all the duties of a private constable.

My great aim has been to raise the members of the force by every means in my power to that standard of excellence requisite for the proper discharge of their responsible duties, and thereby to insure discreet conduct, and avoid unbecoming zeal, and thus by elevation of character to earn a proper respect for an establishment which is indispensably necessary for the proper carrying out of the law; for I assure you that a large portion of the private constables are really sagacious, intrepid and valuable men, who would do credit to any establishment. Good men are tempted to enter the force on the lowest class, not merely for the 17 *s.* per week, but by the hope that by doing their duty they may rise to the 19 *s.* and 21 *s.*, in fact to the highest offices in the force, and secure to themselves a permanent situation and salary, which I feel it my duty to inform you is the consideration most valued.

With reference to the recommendation that the 20 inspectors be reduced to 15 when vacancies occur in that office, I have to acquaint you that two having resigned to join another police on improved salaries, I have refrained from filling their vacancies, as well as that caused by the resignation of the deputy chief constable, until your pleasure be known. With reference to the recommendation that the forage allowance of 2 *s.* per day made to the respective superintendents for each horse be reduced to 1 *s.* 6 *d.*, I take leave to draw your attention to the expenses which they are subjected to in visiting different parts of their respective divisions, which duties make it requisite they should have some allowance; and I can suggest no plan so economical as to place it to the forage account, which in fact is a payment for moving duty. At the time forage was much higher than it is now, some of the superintendents stated it did not cover their expenses. Notwithstanding this, as soon as the price of forage fell I availed myself of the opportunity of excluding them (under a regulation approved of by this Court) from any special service allowance for duties performed within eight miles of their residence, which was practically excluding them from any allowance for duties performed within their respective divisions. I have also to bring under your consideration the additional duties which have been by my recommendation placed on the superintendents, and the very efficient manner in which they have been performed, together with the great saving thereby produced to the county. I have to acquaint you that I encouraged the officers discharging the highly responsible duties of relieving officers for casuals, to believe that after they had put in evidence the benefit thus arising to the county, I would submit them to the favourable consideration of this Court; this I felt myself more particularly called on to do in consequence of some of the Boards of Guardians having officially applied to me to permit them to grant pecuniary reward to the officers of the constabulary appointed by them to discharge the duties alluded to; but while the applications were as gratifying to me as creditable to them, I felt myself painfully called on to object, in consequence of its being enacted by the 10th sect. of Act. 2 & 3 Vict. c. 93, "That all chief or other constables appointed under this Act shall be restrained from employing themselves in any office or employment for hire or gain other than in the execution of their duties under this Act." And as an index to the care which has been bestowed on the 18 county horses, I have to observe that taking the mean of the last five years, the expense of remount (interchanged to keep them efficient) has cost annually but 3 *l.* 7 *s.* 9 *d.* per head.

I have the honour to be,
My Lords and Gentlemen,
Your very obedient servant,
J. B. B. McHardy,
Captain R.N., and Chief Constable.

APPENDIX.

TABLE, No. 1.

RETURN, showing the Number of POLICE CONSTABLES in the County of *Essex*, under Act 2 & 3 Vict., c. 93, distinguishing each Class or Denomination, and the Rate of Payment made to each; including, also, a Return of the Number of Police Constables stationed in each Petty Sessional Division in the said County, with the Name and Population of such Divisions, and the Amount Paid to the County Police-rate by each Division, together with an Account, in detail, of the several Items of Expenditure in 1849.

AUTHORISED FORCE.

	£		
1 Chief Constable	400 per annum.		
1 Deputy Chief Constable	150 "		
4 Superintendents, 1st class	100 "		
5 " 2d "	90 "		
5 " 3d "	80 "		
21 Inspectors (1 under 19th sec.)	65 "		
52 Constables, 1st class	21s. per week.		
58 " 2d "	19 "		
52 " 3d "	17 "		
6 * Paid for under 19th section.			

RECEIPTS.

	£	s.	d.
Sum contributed by Police-rates	14,206	18	4
Fees and Allowances for Services performed by the Constabulary	1,286	10	8
Rent for such parts of the Station-houses as are occupied by members of the Constabulary	332	11	–
£	15,880	–	–

DISBURSEMENTS.

	£	s.	d.
Rates and Taxes	132	5	5
Repairs to Police Stations	98	5	4
Painting seven Police Stations	64	10	1
Pay, including allowance for boots	11,230	1	7
Clothing, including hats	700	11	–
Forage for 18 horses	657	–	–
Renount of 18 horses	53	–	–
Horse hire	45	18	6
Veterinary Surgeons	4	14	9
New harness and repairs to saddlery	40	15	10
Interest on Money borrowed to erect Police Stations	009	12	1
Principal paid off on Money borrowed for the like	841	5	5
Special Service Allowance under 18th sect.	430	5	–
Subsistence of Prisoners	100	–	–
	172	10	8
Carried forward £	15,247	1	7

	£	s.	d.
Brought forward	15,247	1	7
Coals	34	1	7
Candles	17	2	9
Oil	109	10	7
Appointments	7	7	4
Furniture and occasional necessaries	44	18	6
Postage	33	6	1
Printing and Stationery	48	5	9
Clerk of the Peace	155	3	9
Deputy Treasurer, for salary	10	9	2
" Receipt Stamps, Postage &c.			
Purchase and repairs of 18 carts	54	5	8
New sackings for Constables' bedsteads	5	14	–
Magistrates' Clerks' fees	7	13	6
Miscellaneous Items	5	1	–
TOTAL £	15,880	–	–

* At the January Session, 1850, the County was formed into seven Districts under section 27, by withdrawing the Liberty of Havering and Parish of Chelmsford from District No. 5, and four of the Constables under the 19th section were discharged.

C. 71.

T 2

No. 2.

HAVING received frequent complaints from the magistrates and others, of the very ineffi-cient state of the lock-up houses (cages), in different parts of the county; and being persuaded an impression exists that a much greater real expense will fall on the county, in carrying out the desirable object of erecting station-houses and strong rooms, than in reality will arise, I deem it my duty to submit the following remarks:—

It is quite clear that strong rooms and accommodation of some description or other, are necessary for the Police Force at the points at which it is located.

Two important questions are connected with this subject; viz., the comparative advantages and disadvantages, as far as discipline and efficiency are concerned, in allowing the officers and men to provide themselves with lodgings, or their being required to live in public build-ings provided for them by the county.

Secondly, how all the objects required can be conveniently combined in erecting a station-house, and what would be the comparative expense, either to the county or the individual, between the two methods.

With respect to the first, it will readily be admitted that the efficiency of a force, and the proper discharge of its duties, mainly depend (for various reasons) upon its members being placed in public buildings; and that no argument whatever, save that of a *belief* of economy, can be adduced in favour of their being independently in private lodgings.

The only real question, therefore, is, whether so important an advantage can be obtained without entailing a disproportionate expense on the county.

I believe it not practicable to efficiently carry out the Act in all its bearings, with the whole force in private lodgings.

It remains, therefore, to be considered, what number of stations and extent of accom-modation will be required; and whether the expense of building would be so great, that a rent to cover the interest on the outlay would prove to be more than the individuals occu-pying could afford, and in such a case whether the difference to be made up by the county is out of proportion to the advantages secured.

In order to come to a conclusion on this point, it is necessary in the first place to inquire what class of persons will probably fill the situations of constable, inspector, and superin-tendent, and what description of accommodation would be required for each.

It may fairly be assumed, that the constables will ultimately be all intelligent, trustworthy men, capable of reading and writing, and of a class much above the common labourer. The inspector will be admitted to be at least a degree above a constable, but not of a station in life to require superior accommodation.

The superintendent, from holding a most responsible situation, requiring some knowledge of legal proceedings, with a variety of qualifications to fit him for the discharge of his duties, will obviously be of a superior grade to the inspector and constable, and will require to be provided for in a suitable manner.

With regard to the more general question of the stations, it is assumed—

1st. That the county is divided into divisions, and each division subdivided into districts or detachments, *not* with reference to the purposes contemplated in the 27th, 28th, and 29th sections of the amended Constabulary Act, but for the more efficient working of the various duties devolving on the force.

2d. That each division has a principal or head quarter station.

3d. That the permanent force at most of such principal stations consists of not less than one superintendent and two or three constables.

4th. As it must be admitted without any comment, that two strong rooms *at least* are indispensably necessary at the head quarters of each division, I here attach a plan capable of extension at pleasure, showing the expense of erecting a divisional station, with the probable annual cost to the county in securing the numerous advantages attending the erection of such a building in each division, the guard-room attached to each division being at the disposal of the justices, as a proper place for holding their petty sessions, with the superintendent's office for the accommodation of their clerk, thereby remedying the great evil and expense of the justices assembling at public-houses.

The question, therefore, for consideration and decision, appears to me to resolve itself into whether the numerous advantages to be derived by the county by such an investment, with that of the annual sum which will be saved by effectually carrying out the 33d section of the Amended Act (committing to the nearest police station, and the police conveying prisoners to gaol), are such as to justify such a step. For the latter-mentioned service, I here attach an abstract of the expenses incurred by the county for the year preceding the introduction of the Constabulary Acts referred to, viz., from Easter 1839 to Easter 1840.

TABLE,

TABLE, No. 3.

Number of Prisoners conveyed.	Allowance to Constables for			TOTAL.
	Mileage.	Loss of Time.	Subsistence and Lodging of Prisoners.	
	£. s. d.	£. s. d.	£. s. d.	£. s. d.
1,234	476 – 10	236 6 3	36 11 9	748 18 10
Sum paid in the Year to the Governor of Ilford Gaol -	-	-	-	62 11 6
„ „ „ Colchester Gaol	-	-	-	54 2 2
„ „ „ Halsted „	-	-	-	62 1 2
„ „ „ Newport „	-	-	-	63 12 10
		TOTAL - - - £.		991 6 6

bearing in mind that such an arrangement would also avoid the evils attendant on the governors of district gaols being taken from their more important duties for the purpose of conveying prisoners, and by transferring this duty to the police constables secure to them generally a knowledge of offenders.

TABLE, No. 4.

RETURN of MONIES BORROWED for the Erection of Police Stations.

Years.	Amount.	Interest.
	£. s. d.	
1841 - - - - - - -	1,300 – –	4½ per cent.
1842 - - - - - - -	3,700 – –	4½ „
1843 - - - - - - -	4,650 – –	5 „
1844 - - - - - - -	1,675 – –	5 „
„ - - - - - - -	3,000 – –	4½ „
1845 - - - - - - -	1,000 – –	4½ „
1847 - - - - - - -	1,500 – –	4½ „
1849 - - - - - - -	1,500 – –	4½ „
TOTAL Sum Borrowed - - -	18,325 – –	
Paid off at 5 per cent. £. 2,130 } „ 4½ „ £. 3,100 }	5,230 – –	
Present Debt - - - - -	13,095 – –	

RETURN showing the REVENUE and SAVINGS produced by the Police Stations. Also the Annual Interest and Instalments paid on Money Borrowed to erect them, in the Years 1845, 1846, 1847, 1848, and 1849.

YEARS.	Rent, including Allowance for Office and Stabling.	Cash received from Government for Prisoners remanded.	Cash earned, but not received in consequence of Prisoners being discharged for want of Evidence.	Mileage saved in consequence of Prisoners being remanded to the Police Stations, instead of the Gaol.	Total Amount earned and saved by the Police Stations.	Amount of Interest paid, and Instalment of Principal paid off on Money borrowed for the Erection of Police Stations.	
						Interest.	Instalment.
	£. s. d.	£. s. d.	£. s. d.	£. s. d.	£. s. d.	£. s. d.	£. s. d.
1845 -	385 11 4	371 11 8	146 – 6	228 9 2	1,131 12 8	627 2 6	716 5 –
1846 -	400 10 1	431 11 7	274 13 4	325 2 –	1,431 17 –	638 6 3	766 5 –
1847 -	407 19 10	615 3 5	251 7 3	302 6 2	1,576 16 8	602 5 1	766 5 –
1848 -	425 4 8	442 3 10	224 7 6	212 4 2	1,304 – 2	633 13 10	841 5 –
1849 -	416 11 –	590 8 2	233 17 3	216 11 7	1,457 8 –	609 12 1	841 5 –
	2,035 16 11	2,450 18 8	1,130 5 10	1,284 13 1	6,901 14 6	3,110 19 9	3,931 5 –
Rent -		2,035 16 11				Interest	3,110 19 9
TOTAL Sum Received -		4,486 15 7		TOTAL Sum paid in the Five Years - - - £.			7,042 4 9

TABLE, No. 5.

RETURN showing the different SUMS received in the undermentioned Years for "Comparing, Examining, and Stamping" Weights and Measures. Also the Sums received under the head of Fines, together with the Annual Expense to which the County was subjected, exclusive of these Sums.

YEARS.	Monies received for Examining, Comparing, and Stamping.		Fines Received.		Annual Expense connected with Weights and Measures.
	Western Division.	Eastern Division.	Western Division.	Eastern Division.	
	£. s. d.	£. s. d.	£. s. d.	£. s. d.	£. s. d.
1838 - -	11 11 8	23 14 5	5 13 –	2 9 7	522 3 –
1839 - -	19 18 9	32 5 10½	17 12 3	49 18 9	548 1 6
1840 - -	13 7 7½	34 19 1½	4 12 7	24 10 –	540 9 –
1841 - -	8 9 –	44 7 2	– – –	30 – 11¾	556 16 2
1842 - -	12 10 –	37 17 4	17 3 10	15 19 5½	654 4 6
1843 - -	13 4 5½	44 15 9	20 13 10½	27 6 1¼	663 2 4
	79 1 6	217 19 8	2) 65 15 6½	2) 150 4 10½	6) 3,484 16 6

	6) 405 1 4	Average of 6 Years' Expenses	580 16 1
Average of 6 Years' Receipt -	67 10 2		
		Subtract Average Receipt -	67 10 2
	TOTAL Annual Expense to the County - - - £.		513 5 11

The police having discharged the duties of Inspectors of Weights and Measures, has benefited the county 5,000 l. during the last nine years.

RETURN showing the same Results since the Duties have been performed by the County Constabulary.

YEARS.	For Comparing, Examining, and Stamping.	Fines Received; Half appropriated to the County.	Expenses connected with the Discharge of these Duties.
	£. s. d.	£. s. d.	£. s. d.
1844 - - - - -	326 6 10	61 2 3	154 – –
1845 - - - - -	123 10 –	95 18 6	141 – 2
1846 - - - - -	148 8 10	306 6 4	134 11 –
1847 - - - - -	113 8 3	36 2 1	126 14 6
1848 - - - - -	114 14 4	48 1 6	138 10 –
1849 - - - - -	108 9 5	89 14 6	131 – –
	934 17 8	2) 637 5 2	6) 825 15 8

	6) 1,253 10 3 { - - Average of 6 years' expenses - }	137 12 7
Average of 6 Years' Receipts - - -	208 18 4	
Subtract Average Annual Expense - - -	137 12 7	
TOTAL Annual Saving to the County	£. 71 5 9	

Average Annual Expense to the County of the 6 Years preceding the above Duties being performed by the Constabulary - - - - - -	513 5 11
Average Annual Saving to the County of the 6 years the above Duties have been performed by the Constabulary - - - - - -	71 5 9
TOTAL Annual Saving to the County - - - £.	584 11 8

Appendix, No. 1.

TABLES (A.), (B.), and (C.)

TABLE (A.)—County of *Essex.*—RETURN of In-Door Vagrants.

Number.	NAMES OF UNIONS.	Number of Vagrants Received into each Workhouse during the Half-Years ending Michaelmas.		Decrease.	Increase.
		1848:	1849:		
1	Billericay	1,302	13	1,289	
2	Braintree	1,342	68	1,274	
3	Chelmsford	2,605	79	2,526	
4	Colchester	1,597	803	794	
5	Dunmow	1,886	357	1,529	
6	Epping	1,424	11	1,413	
7	Halsted	700	45	655	
8	Lexden and Winstree	2	14	-	12
9	Maldon	1,236	17	1,219	
10	Ongar	1,613	78	1,535	
11	Orsett	1,694	16	1,678	
12	Rochford	101	27	74	
13	Romford	3,244	616	2,628	
14	Saffron Walden	1,656	42	1,614	
15	Tendring	216	62	154	
16	Witham	1,093	12	1,081	
17	Bishop Stortford	1,805	406	1,399	
	TOTALS	23,516	2,666	20,862	12
	Number of In-Door Vagrants relieved in 1849	2,666			
	TOTAL Amount of Decrease in 1849	20,850	= 90 per Cent.		

TABLE (B.)—RETURN of Out-Door Vagrants.

Number.	NAMES OF UNIONS.	Number of Vagrants Relieved out of the Workhouse during the Half-Years ending Michaelmas.		Decrease.	Increase.
		1848:	1849;		
1	Billericay	Not known	52	-	52
2	Braintree	—	—	—	—
3	Chelmsford	15	24	-	9
4	Colchester	—	—	—	—
5	Dunmow	331	13	318	—
6	Epping	2	1	1	—
7	Halsted	—	—	—	—
8	Lexden and Winstree	—	—	—	—
9	Maldon	7	7	—	—
10	Ongar	6	11	-	5
11	Orsett	—	—	—	—
12	Rochford	9	14	-	5
13	Romford	832	146	686	—
14	Saffron Walden	-	1	-	1
15	Tendring	22	-	22	—
16	Witham	135	36	99	—
17	Bishop Stortford	7	6	1	—
	TOTALS	1,366	311	1,127	72
	Number of Out-Door Vagrants relieved in 1849	311			
	TOTAL Amount of Decrease in 1849	1,055	= 77 per cent.		

TABLE (C.)

COMMITMENTS of VAGRANTS to the undermentioned Prisons in this (*Essex*) County, during the Half-years ended Michaelmas 1848 and Michaelmas 1849.

NAMES OF PRISONS.	Half-Year ending Michaelmas, 1848. Number of Vagrants Committed.					Half-Year ending Michaelmas, 1849. Number of Vagrants Committed.					Decrease.	Increase.
	For Trial at Sessions.	For Begging.	For other Acts of Vagrancy.	For Workhouse Offences.	TOTAL.	For Trial at Sessions.	For Begging.	For other Acts of Vagrancy.	For Workhouse Offences.	TOTAL.		
Ilford Gaol, Essex :												
Metropolitan District	-	3	13	1	17	-	33	11	-	44	-	27
Essex Constabulary District	-	-	3	1	4	-	1	-	7	8	-	4
Colchester District Gaol :												
Borough	-	3	12	4	19	-	5	4	4	13	6	—
County	-	12	9	14	35	-	10	14	22	46	-	11
Essex County Gaol (Springfield)	4	12	39	72	127	7	12	48	26	93	34	—
TOTALS	-	-	-	-	202	-	-	-	-	204	40	42

1 per cent. Increase.

The remarkable decrease of vagrancy in Essex, amounting (it will have been perceived) to 90 per cent. in the number of in-door, and 77 per cent. in the number of out-door vagrants, is mainly due to the admirable arrangements adopted by the very able and zealous chief constable of the Essex constabulary force (Captain M'Hardy), and to the support which those arrangements have received from the magistracy and guardians.

It is to be observed, however, that the guardians of the Epping, Lexden, Romford, and Tendring Unions, have not availed themselves of the services of policemen as assistant relieving officers, although they must have reaped indirectly the benefit of those services in the neighbouring unions; that in Colchester Union the county police have no authority; and that a great portion of the Romford Union is within the metropolitan district, from which (it is also to be observed), that more than five times the number of vagrants have been committed to Ilford gaol than by the agency of the Essex constabulary. I understand, likewise, that the number of commitments from the West Ham Union (which, although in Essex, is not in my district), even exceeds the commitments from Romford.

I am moreover informed, by Captain M'Hardy, that some years ago he tried what effect sending vagrants to gaol would have, and caused about 1,000 to be committed in three years; but it only led to expense in fees, subsistence, &c., without producing any favourable result.

On the other hand, whilst the enforcement by the police of Mr. Buller's minute has diminished the number of vagrants to an almost incredible extent, and nearly destroyed professional mendicancy in Essex, the increase in the commitments of 1849 over 1848 is only 1 per cent.; there is an absence of any complaints; the rates are, of course, greatly relieved; and, in Captain M'Hardy's opinion, the decrease of vagrancy has tended generally to lessen crime.

John Walsham,
Inspector of Poor Laws.

RETURN, No. 6.

LIST of the PARISHES of the County of *Essex*, within the Metropolitan Police District, showing the Sum contributed by each in the Year 1849 towards the support of the Police, which costs an 8 *d.* Rate, Three-fourths being borne by the Parishes and One-fourth by the Government.

NAMES OF PARISHES.	Total of the Rate for the Year at 8 *d.* in the £.			Charged upon the Parishes at 6 *d.* in the £.			Paid by the Treasurer at 2 *d.* in the £.		
	£.	*s.*	*d.*	£.	*s.*	*d.*	£.	*s.*	*d.*
Barking Town Ward - - - ⎫									
Ditto Chadwell ditto - - ⎪									
Ditto Great Ilford ditto - - ⎬	1,471	–	–	1,103	5	–	367	15	–
Ditto Ripple ditto - - - ⎭									
Chigwell - - - - -	414	2	8	310	12	–	103	10	8
Chingford - - - - -	201	4	8	150	18	6	50	6	2
Dagenham - - - - -	477	7	4	358	–	6	119	6	10
Ham, East - - - - -	395	7	4	296	10	6	98	16	10
Ditto, West Church-street Ward ⎫									
Ditto, „ Plaistow - ditto - ⎬	2,151	19	4	1,613	19	6	537	19	10
Ditto, „ Stratford - ditto - ⎭									
Little Ilford - - - -	95	18	8	71	19	–	23	19	8
Loughton - - - - -	213	10	8	160	3	–	53	7	8
Low Leyton - - - -	596	2	8	447	2	–	149	–	8
Waltham Abbey and Town, including ⎫ Holyfield, Sewardstone, and Upshire ⎬	774	9	4	580	17	–	193	12	4
Walthamstow - - - -	845	18	–	634	8	6	211	9	6
Wanstead - - - - -	291	8	–	218	11	–	72	17	–
Woodford - - - - -	433	2	–	324	16	6	108	5	6
TOTAL - - - £.	8,361	10	8	6,271	3	–	2,090	7	8

No. 7.

SCHEME for an EFFICIENT CONSTABULARY and DEFENSIVE FORCE throughout England and Wales, Co-operating with the Coast Guard; affording increased Protection to the Public Revenue; Improving the present System of Recruiting for the Army; Obviating necessity of enrolling the Militia; Supplying Crews for the advanced Ships; an efficient Sea Fencible; and checking the rapid Increase of Vagrancy.

THE benefit to be derived by the establishment of county constabularies, under Acts 2 & 3 Vict. c. 93, and 3 & 4 Vict. c. 88, having been proved by the adoption of the said Acts in half the counties of England and Wales, and the strong prejudices which existed against such a force having now worn off, its *apparent* expense being the only barrier to its universal adoption; it is evident that great advantages would be obtained, as well as efficiency secured, were Parliament to render the force general, under a uniform system throughout England and Wales; by which, with co-operating with the coast guard, it would not only be a valuable defensive force for the country, but would also more effectually protect the revenue, avoid the expense of the recruiting establishment for the army, and curtail that attendant on raising the militia. I am therefore emboldened to submit the following scheme, lest it should be deemed worthy of attention:

That an Act be passed authorising the Government to establish a uniform constabulary throughout England and Wales, with a clause limiting the number as in the present Act, to one constable to a population of 1,000 (except under an Order of Council), which would afford for England, independent of the Metropolitan District, 13,000, and for Wales 1,000, making a total of 14,000; the annual expense of which would be about 950,000 *l.* including the mounting of 1,000. And by the Government paying half this expense, and the remainder being defrayed by local police rates, the scheme would be popular, and the Government enabled to make use of it in various departments, by which the Government would be considerably reimbursed.

If the Act under which such a force should be established armed it with the power given to the coast guard for the prevention of smuggling, the difficulties of smuggling would be so much increased, that it would be seldom if ever attempted, by which the revenue would undoubtedly be improved, and a numerical reduction of the coast guard warranted.*

As Government now pays al   e expense of bringing criminal offenders to justice, as also that attendant on prosecutions, a saving would be effected by appointing chief constables as public prosecutors, and solicitors on a salary, in each county, to conduct prosecutions, with a strict investigation of sums paid to witnesses and others, under orders of Court, and a proper system of communication in a well-disciplined constabulary distributed throughout the kingdom, would insure facility in detecting offenders, and great reduction of expenditure in bringing them to justice.†

Were the police to recruit for the army, the present expense of 22,000 l. per annum, for the general staff of the recruiting service, and 6,000 l. per annum to the 45 sub-divisions, exclusive of the pay of the officers and privates so employed, would be saved; and they would be enabled to remain with their regiments, and all the evils attendant on their recruiting would be avoided. ‡

A well-trained constabulary of one constable to a population of 1,000 would afford an efficient and respectable defensive force of 14,000 men (exclusive of the Metropolitan police), which, in cases of emergency, could be augmented and armed, as may appear most desirable; and by the Government directing at its pleasure (through the proper authorities) the police to enrol and train, at the respective petty sessional divisional stations, such numbers for the militia as it may deem expedient, not exceeding a limited number to the population, as by enrolling five men out of every 1,000, a force of 70,000 would be raised, making, with the standing constabulary of 14,000, a total of 84,000, which would be more than double the number authorised by the present Militia Act (40,963). From the constabulary being of necessity generally dispersed, such facility would be afforded for enrolling and training the men for the militia, that the expense would be considerably less than any other system; and the men so enrolled would, from being brought in contact with the constabulary, render it more efficient, and afford a source from which to complete or augment the constabulary or standing army, and provide special constables on their being required; and as the militia staff would necessarily be kept up to a certain extent, the respective adjutants could supervise the general training, and it is evident that an efficient constabulary, together with the facility it would afford for embodying a militia, would render the postponement of enrolling privates less hazardous.

§ By the seamen serving in the coast guard being made available for ships of war, the Government would have at its disposal at least 3,000 seamen for cases of emergency, out of 6,000 or 7,000 officers and seamen now employed in that service. With this reserve, and by placing in time of peace in Her Majesty's ships in commission only half the present complement of marines, and bearing seamen in lieu, who could be withdrawn in cases of need, and the war or present complement of marines replaced, such an arrangement would place at the disposal of the Government, crews for eight advanced ships of the line, which could with ease be at sea in 10 days; and by the coast guard enrolling the seafaring men on the coast, in like manner as I propose the constabulary to enrol the militia, a formidable sea fencible force might be provided for defending the coast when required, either in block ships, steam vessels, or otherwise.

‖ That members of the county constabulary be appointed relieving officers for vagrants, which by checking indiscriminate relief, and other reasons, would put a stop to professional mendicancy, and that the discipline of the poor-law unions be not disturbed, accommodation for "casuals" be provided under the charge of the constabulary; the expense of all "casuals" to be defrayed out of the consolidated fund; and that all low lodging-houses be, under a legislative enactment, licensed and subject to regulations formed by the justices in special sessions.

J. B. B. Mc Hardy,
Captain R.N., and Chief Constable of Essex.

---

* Since this was drawn up in 1846, the coast mounted guard has been disbanded, and the revenue cruisers reduced, which renders this more desirable; and I would recommend the sailing cruisers being succeeded, as opportunities offer, by small (wood) steamers, particularly as one of the latter would be as efficient as three of the former, and thus no additional expense would be incurred. One wood steamer has recently been provided, and each member of the constabularies of the maritime counties has, upon my suggestion, been armed with a deputation from the Board of Customs, under sect 33, Act 8 & 9 Vict., c. 87, for the protection of the public revenue, thereby also rendering the withdrawal of the coast guard, in time of need for naval purposes, less hazardous to the protection of the public revenue.

† When this was drawn up in 1846, the Government paid only half. *See* Parliamentary Return of Expense.

‡ The attempt to recruit for the army by means of the pensioners has proved a failure.

§ This has been partially carried out by making the seamen of the coast guard available for ships of war; but the time has arrived for doing more.

‖ This has been successfully carried out in Essex; *see* pages 151 and 152.

No. 8.

AUTHORISED FORCE.

GENERAL FORCE.

1 Chief Constable.
15 Superintendents.
20 Inspectors.

LOCAL FORCE.

Parishes and Places, or Parts of Parishes and Places, forming Police Districts under the 27th and 23th sec. Act 3 & 4 Vict., c. 88.	Population.	Amount raised on a Penny Rate.		Number of Constables.	Probable Annual Rate to meet General and Local Expenditure.
		£. s. d.	£. s. d.		
District, No. 1.					
Braintree - - - -	3,670	49 17 4	} 105 7 9	4	3
Bocking - - - -	3,437	55 10 5			
District, No. 2.					
Halstead - - - -	5,595	57 18 2	57 18 2	3	3¼
District, No. 3.					
Great Coggeshall - -	3,408	30 4 4	} 40 4 6	2	3¼
Little Coggeshall - -	443	10 - 2			
District, No. 4.					
South Weald - - -	1,450	39 2 6			
Brentwood - - -	2,362	24 16 7			
Great Warley - - -	596	16 13 4			
Little Warley - - -	216	8 11 3	} 130 3 4	5	3
Shenfield - - -	983	26 6 11			
Ingrave - - - -	530	8 9 -			
Childerditch - - -	247	6 3 9			
District, No. 5.					
Chelmsford - - -	6,789	104 11 8	104 11 8	6	4
District, No. 6.					
Havering - - - -	425	14 5 6			
Hornchurch - - -	2,399	72 7 -	} 192 16 9	8	3¼
Romford - - - -	5,317	106 4 3			
District, No. 7.					
Parishes and Places not comprised in the above Districts - - -	228,105	5,494 6 10	5,494 6 ?	135	2¼
Total - - -	265,972	6,125 9 -	6,125 9 -	163	—

The Burnham Oyster Company provide an inspector and two constables under the 19th sect. Act 3 & 4 Vict. c. 88.

TABLE, No. 9.

RETURN of the Distribution of The Essex County Constabulary, 15th October 1850.

Division	Station	Superintendents.	Inspectors.	Constables.	Division	Station	Superintendents.	Inspectors.	Constables.
	District, No. 4.					**Part of District, No. 7.**			
	South Weald	–	–	1		Latchingdon	1	–	1
	Brentwood	1	–	3		Southminster	–	–	1
	Great Warley	–	–	1		Steeple	–	–	1
	Little Warley	–	–	–		Purleigh	–	–	1
	Shenfield	–	–	–	DENGIE	Woodham Walter	–	–	1
	Ingrave	–	–	–		Woodham Ferris	–	–	1
	Childerditch	–	–	1		Althorne	–	–	1
						Tillingham	–	–	1
	District, No. 6.					*Burnham	–	1	3
	Havering	–	–	1			1	1	11
	Hornchurch	–	–	2					
	Romford	–	1	3					
	Collier Row	–	–	2		**Part of District, No. 7.**			
BRENTWOOD						Dunmow	1	–	2
	Part of District, No. 7.					Takely	–	–	1
	Billericay	–	1	1		Hallingbury	–	–	1
	Grays	–	–	1		Felsted	–	–	1
	Crays Hill	–	–	1	DUNMOW	Stebbing	–	–	1
	South Ockendon	–	–	1		Leaden Roothing	–	–	1
	Aveley	–	–	1		High Easter	–	–	1
	Heron Gate	–	–	1		Broxted	–	–	1
	Orsett	–	1	1			1	–	9
	Rainham	–	–	1					
	Horndon	–	–	1					
	Corringham	–	–	1					
	West Tilbury	–	–	1		**Part of District, No. 7.**			
	Mountnessing	–	–	1		Epping	1	–	1
	Upminster	–	–	1		Thoydon Garnon	–	–	1
	Laindon	–	–	1		Lambourn	–	–	1
		1	3	28		Roydon	–	–	1
					EPPING	Parndon	–	–	1
	District, No. 5.					Nazing	–	–	1
	Chelmsford	–	1	6		North Weald Bassett	–	–	1
						Harlow	–	1	1
	Part of District, No. 7.					Sheering	–	–	1
	Springfield	1	1	2		Hatfield Broad Oak	–	–	1
	Ingatestone	–	–	1			1	1	9
	Stock	–	–	1					
CHELMSFORD	Writtle	–	–	1					
	Roxwell	–	–	1					
	Danbury	–	–	1		**Part of District, No. 7.**			
	Great Waltham	–	–	1		Great Bardfield	1	–	1
	Great Baddow	–	–	1		Steeple Bumpstead	–	1	1
	Great Leighs	–	–	1		Weathersfield	–	–	1
	Boreham	–	–	1	FRESHWELL	Finchingfield	–	–	1
	Rettenden	–	–	1		Old Sampford	–	–	2
	Margaretting	–	–	1		Thaxted	–	–	1
		1	2	19		Sturmer	–	–	1
							1	1	7
	Part of District, No. 7.								
	Colchester	1	–	1					
	Stanway	–	1	–					
	Wivenhoe	–	–	1		**Part of District, No. 7.**			
	Great Horksley	–	–	1		Castle Hedingham	1	–	2
	Dedham	–	–	1		Sible Hedingham	–	–	1
COLCHESTER	Mount Bures	–	–	1		Foxearth	–	–	1
	Great Tey	–	–	1	NORTH HINCKFORD	Walter Belchamp	–	–	1
	Layer Bretton	–	–	1		Toppesfield	–	–	1
	West Bergholt	–	–	1		Bulmer	–	–	1
	Peldon	–	–	1		Ridgewell	–	–	1
	Abberton	–	–	1		Lamarsh	–	–	1
	Elmsted Market	–	–	1			1	–	9
		1	1	11					

* The Burnham Oyster Company pay for one inspector and two constables under 19 sect. Act 3 and 4 Vict. c. 88.

SELECT COMMITTEE ON POLICE.

Division.	Station.	Superintendents.	Inspectors.	Constables.
SOUTH HINCKFORD	**District, No. 1.**			
	Braintree } Bocking }	1	1	4
	District, No. 2.			
	Halstead	–	1	3
	Part of District, No. 7.			
	Earls Colne	–	–	1
	Colne Engaine	–	–	1
	Cressing	–	1	1
	Gosfield	–	–	1
	Pebmarsh	–	–	1
	Stisted	–	–	1
		1	3	12
ONGAR	**Part of District, No. 7.**			
	Chipping Ongar	1	–	1
	Navestock	–	–	1
	Passingford Bridge	–	–	1
	Blackmore	–	–	1
	Toot Hill	–	–	1
	Fyfield	–	–	1
	Moreton	–	–	1
		1	–	7
ROCHFORD	**Part of District, No. 7.**			
	Rochford	1	–	1
	Rayleigh	–	1	–
	Southend	–	–	1
	Prittlewell	–	–	1
	Leigh	–	–	1
	South Benfleet	–	–	1
	Wickford	–	–	1
	Canewden	–	–	1
	Foulness	–	–	1
	Hadleigh	–	–	1
	North Benfleet	–	–	1
	Hockley	–	–	1
	Great Wakering	–	–	1
		1	1	12

Division.	Station.	Superintendents.	Inspectors.	Constables.
TENDRING	**Part of District, No. 7.**			
	Thorpe	1	–	1
	Manningtree	–	1	–
	Ardleigh	–	1	–
	St. Oysth	–	–	1
	Great Clacton	–	–	1
	Great Bentley	–	–	1
	Kirby	–	–	1
	Bradfield	–	–	1
	Great Oakley	–	1	–
	Ramsay	–	–	1
	Lawford	–	–	1
	Brightlingsea	–	–	1
	Great Bromley	–	–	1
	Mistley	–	–	1
		1	3	11
WALDEN	**Part of District, No. 7.**			
	Newport	1	–	1
	Clavering	–	–	1
	Stanstead	–	1	–
	Henham	–	–	1
	Quendon	–	–	1
	Great Chrishall	–	–	1
	Great Chesterford	–	1	–
	Manuden	–	–	1
	Radwinter	–	–	1
	Debden	–	–	1
	Littlebury	–	–	1
	Ashdon	–	–	1
	Wenden Lofts	–	–	1
		1	2	11
WITHAM	**District, No. 3.**			
	Great Coggeshall	–	1	2
	Little Coggeshall	–	–	–
	Part of District, No. 7.			
	Witham	1	–	3
	Kelvedon	–	–	1
	Fairsted	–	–	1
	Great Totham	–	–	1
	Heybridge	–	–	1
	Hatfield Peverel	–	–	1
	Tolleshunt D'Arcy	–	–	1
	Messing	–	–	1
		1	–	12
	TOTAL of the foregoing	14	19	168*

* Three Constables borne in lieu of Deputy Chief Constable, and two Inspectors.

Appendix, No. 2.

HANTS CONSTABULARY.

RETURN of the Number of VAGRANTS relieved in the undermentioned Unions of the County of *Hants* during the Years 1848 and 1852; the Year 1848 being the last Year previous to the Constabulary undertaking the Duties of Assistant Relieving Officers for Vagrants.

YEAR.	U N I O N S.								
	Alton.	Andover.	Basingstoke.	Alverstoke.	Havant.	New Forest.	Ringwood.	Romsey.	Whitchurch.
1848 -	2,954	2,606	1,782	1,705	797	1,810	1,188	2,368	1,287
1852 -	274	55	166	77	111	81	50	4*	144

* The relief of vagrants by the constabulary has been only one quarter in operation in the Romsey Union.

HANTS CONSTABULARY.

RETURN of the Number of Cases of SHEEP STEALING that have occurred in the County of *Hants* between the Years 1847 and 1852, both Years inclusive.

1847	72
1848	83
1849	44
1850	50
1851	30
1852	33

Appendix, No. 3.

PAPER delivered in by *W. Oakley*, Esq.

No. 1, Fountain-buildings, Bath, 8 February 1851.

IT having been resolved by the Magistrates of this county, at the last Epiphany Sessions, to establish the system of Superintending Constables, under the provisions of the Acts 5 & 6 Vict., cap. 109, and 13 & 14 Vict., cap. 20, for the respective divisions; and the Magistrates of the Bath Division having a decided objection to the proposed scheme, on the ground of its inefficiency and expensiveness, and also on the ground that they consider the provisions of 2 & 3 Vict., cap. 93, and 3 & 4 Vict., cap. 88, would be more beneficial to the ratepayers: the following Resolutions were adopted by them, and laid before the Committee appointed at the last Quarter Sessions to carry out the former Acts; and the Magistrates of the Bath Division have resolved on making application at the next Quarter Sessions to exempt the Bath Division from the operation of the former Acts and for the establishment of a Divisional Police in lieu thereof; under the said Acts of 2 & 3 Vict., cap. 93, and 3 & 4 Vict., cap. 88.

The following are the data upon which the Magistrates of the Bath Division have come to this resolution, and they are now printed and circulated for the information of the Magistrates generally, and the ratepayers.

It is desirable that the ratepayers of the respective parishes of the Bath Division should, at as early a period as possible, consider the memoranda now laid before them; and if any difficulty should suggest itself, or explanation be required, the Magistrates of the Bath Division will be happy to confer with them on the subject.

(signed)   *Charles F. Bampfylde*, D.L.   *C. D. Bailey.*
             George Norman.   *Samuel W. Bythesea.*
             George Kitson.   *P. C. Sheppard.*
             N. Duff.   *R. W. Brown.*
             William Long.

The

The Committee of Magistrates appointed at the meeting, held at Fountain-buildings, on the 6th day of March 1850, for the purpose of ascertaining the best means of providing a proper lock-up for the division of Bath, of ensuring the appointment of efficient constables for the better protection of property, detection of offenders, and prevention of crime, and considering the suggestions of Mr. Oakley, chief of the Bath police force, in reference thereto, are unanimously of opinion that the provisions of the Acts 5 & 6 Vict., cap. 109, 11 & 12 Vict., cap. 101, and 13 & 14 Vict., cap. 20, for appointing a superintending constable and parish constables, would be altogether inadequate to the requirements of this division.

That a joint lock-up for the use of the Bath police and the parish constables of the division would be unadvisable and impracticable, from the class of persons from which parish constables are, of necessity, appointed, and their habits; and the means by which they are paid, creating an interest in crime, and there being no provision for ensuring a proper control or supervision of them.

That from the peculiar position of the division of Bath, the county of Gloucester and city of Bristol on one side, the county of Wilts on the other, and the city of Bath nearly in the centre, each having an efficient police, offenders are driven into the division of Bath, and commit offences, almost with impunity, from the inefficiency of the parish constables.

The Committee earnestly recommend that a representation be made to the Committee of Magistrates, appointed at the last Quarter Sessions, requesting their consideration of sec. 19, 2 & 3 Vict., cap. 93, and sections 12 & 13, 3 & 4 Vict., cap. 88 (County Police Acts), authorising the appointment of a police for any division of a county, and providing station-houses and lock-ups, with a view to the application of those clauses to this division, as the Committee are strongly of opinion, that the appointment of a superintending and parish constables would cause considerable expense, without any more efficient means for the better protection of property, prevention of offences, or detection of offenders in this division.

The Committee recommend that a return be obtained of the number and value of sheep, and other property, stolen in the division of Bath during the last three years, and also a return of the amount paid to parish constables, in the division, under magistrates' certificates and orders of court; for serving summonses and warrants, by individuals, by the union, or as salary, and the amount paid for the conveyance and lodging of prisoners; it being the opinion of the Committee that those amounts, and the cost of inspecting weights and measures, and relieving vagrants, together with the proposed salary to a superintending constable, with the fees and expenses, of necessity to be incurred under the Superintending and Parish Constables Acts, would be sufficient to meet the expenses of an efficient police for the division; and that, in any event, a saving would be effected to the rest of the county, as any rate for the necessary expenses of a police is directed to be levied on the division in which such police is established, while under the Superintending and Parish Constable Act, the whole county has to bear the expense of putting the Act in force in any particular district.

(signed)   *N. Duff.*
William Long.
C. D. Bailey.

Bath, 11 January 1851.

At a meeting of the Magistrates of the Bath Division, holden on Saturday, 11th January 1851, it was unanimously resolved that the Report of the Sub-Committee be received and adopted; and that a copy thereof be transmitted to the Chairman of the Committee appointed at the last Quarter Sessions, with an intimation that some members of the Bath Division, with Mr. Oakley, will be happy to have an opportunity of entering more fully into their reasons for coming to these conclusions.

(signed)	*N. Duff.*	*W. V. Jenkins.*
	P. C. Sheppard.	*S. W. Bythesea.*
	William Long.	*C. D. Bailey.*
	G. W. Blathwayt.	*W. T. Blair.*
	H. D. Skrine.	*George Norman.*
	R. W. Brown.	*C. F. Bampfylde,* D. L.
	George Kitson.	

At a meeting of the Committee, at Bridgewater, on the 1st day of February instant, the following documents were submitted:

STATEMENT of the Estimated Comparative Expense of Superintending and Parish Constables, under 5 & 6 Vict., cap. 109, and 13 & 14 Vict., cap. 20, and a Police under 2 & 3 Vict., cap. 93, sec. 19, for the Division of Bath.

PROBABLE EXPENSE under Superintending and Parish Constable System.

	£.	s.	d.
Conveyance of Prisoners - - - - - - - - - - -	90	—	—

The average amount in the two years 1849 and 1850, paid to parish constables out of the county rate, for conveyance and lodging of prisoners, was 95 *l.*; 5 *l.* is as much as should be incurred by a police for the expense of subsistence of prisoners in the division for a year, and the whole amount of conveyance and lodging would be saved; the prisoners being conveyed by the police in the carts necessary to be provided for the other duties of the police.

	£.	s.	d.

In the years 1849 and 1850, the average amount paid out of the poor-rates for constables' expenses in the 18 parishes of the Bath Division, included in the Bath Union, as stated in the Union accounts, was about 100 *l.* Adding 50 *l.* for the average in the same proportion for the other 10 parishes of the Bath Division, the amount would be   -   -   -   -   -   -   -   -   **150   -   -**

The costs of proceedings before justices in the same years, as also stated, averaged about 99 *l.* for the same 18 parishes (paid out of the poor-rates). Adding 45 *l.* for the average of the other 10 parishes, the amount paid would be 144 *l.*; of which, for the appointment and swearing in of parish constables, and other charges made on their account, there is paid at least -   -   -   -   **100   -   -**

Estimated amount paid to parish constables for serving summonses and warrants, and by individuals   -   -   -   -   -   -   -   -   -   **30   -   -**

Estimated amount paid to parish constables, under orders of court, in cases of felony, at assizes and sessions -   -   -   -   -   -   -   -   -   **60   -   -**

Such amount being paid out of the county rate, and repaid to the county by Government, as part of the expense of prosecutions. If the same allowances were made for the police, the amount might be retained by the county, and therefore saved. In the county of Essex, consisting of only 14 divisions, 380 parishes, and a population of 265,972, in which the county police are acting, the amount so received from Government was, for the last year, 1,104 *l.* 12 *s.* 11 *d.* The allowances being retained by the county treasurer from the amounts paid under orders of court, and the police, never, under any circumstances, being permitted to receive any monies except their salaries and expenses actually incurred, or rewards in very special cases.

Fines under penal statutes -   -   -   -   -   -   -   -   -   -   **20   -   -**

Amounts received by constables, as informers under the Alehouse, Beer, Highway, and Turnpike Acts, &c., being, under a police, appropriated to the county.

Summoning coroners' juries, &c. -   -   -   -   -   -   -   -   -   **5   -   -**

Proposed salary to superintending constable under 5 & 6 Vict., cap. 109, and 13 & 14 Vict., cap. 20, to be paid out of the county rate   -   -   -   -   **110   -   -**

Contingent expenses at 2 *l.* 10 *s.* per month, as paid (out of the county rate) in the county of Kent, for extra horse hire, tolls (police exempt from tolls under 3 & 4 Vict., cap. 88, sect. 1), taxes for horse and cart, shoeing horses, stationery, and postage   -   -   -   -   -   -   -   -   -   **30   -   -**

(It is proposed that the system in this county should be the same as in Kent.)

Payments are made out of the county and poor-rates to parish constables under 5 & 6 Vict., cap. 109, and 13 & 14 Vict., cap. 20, for patrolling or occasional duty in charge of prisoners, or under the written order of a justice in Kent, according to the table of fees in that county (in addition to fees for serving summonses and warrants) at 2 *s.* 6 *d.* per day, and 3 *s.* per night, or 1 *l.* 18 *s.* 6 *d.* per week. Since the establishment of the system in Kent, 14th October last (only three months), it has been found necessary to have numerous constables employed for weeks together. If 15 constables only out of the 241 in this division were employed, and for only three days a week at the same rate, the amount would be 643 *l.* 10 *s.* per annum. Deducting from that amount the above 150 *l.* estimated as now paid to parish constables, the additional expense probably to be incurred under the proposed system would be   -   -   -   **493   10   -**

	£. 1,088	10	-

In the county of Kent there is no saving in the conveyance of prisoners, the parish constable conveying prisoners receiving the amount allowed and mileage for conveying them; neither is there any saving in the inspection of weights and measures, relieving vagrants, or under the various heads of saving shown by a police.

To the above items may be added the following, which, if a police were established instead of superintending and parish constables, may be saved, viz.:—

Inspecting weights and measures   -   -   -   -   -   -   -   -   **200   -   -**

In the year 1843, the fines in the division under the Weights and Measures Act amounted to 138 *l.*; the inspector's salary, 25 *l.*; fees for stamping, &c., not known. There appears to have been no inspection or fines since. If the duty were performed by the police, the saving in the division from fines, fees, &c. (the whole of the fines in such case being appropriated to the county), would be at least the amount named.

Relieving vagrants   -   -   -   -   -   -   -   -   -   -   -   **150   -   -**

In the county of Essex it is shown to be 5,101 *l.*, as fully explained in page 2 of the printed Report of the Chief Constable of Essex, to the Magistrates in Quarter Sessions assembled, 15th October 1850.

	£. 1,438	10	-

Credit

Credit is not taken for any amount for the additional protection and recovery of property by a police, or the increased value of land.

In the county of Essex, it is considered that land is increased in annual value, by the establishment of a police, from 1 d. to 2 d. per acre, as shown by the following extract from the before-mentioned printed Report of the Chief Constable of Essex :—

" It is impossible to ascertain what was formerly paid by private individuals and poor-law unions to parish constables, or what has been saved to the public by the police from the diminution of crime or business at Petty Sessions ; and I also submit to your consideration the great advantage derived by the protection and recovery of property ; and to illustrate this, I would refer you to a Report which I laid before this Court in 1842, by which it appears that 140 sheep were stolen in the North Hinckford and Epping Petty Sessional Divisions of this county, in the year 1839, preceding the adoption of the Constabulary, a number far exceeding that stolen in any year in the whole 14 divisions since the establishment of the police ; whilst loss by horse-stealing, which was formerly very prevalent, is now almost unknown. But I have the authority of one of the first land-valuers in this county, occupying nearly 1,000 acres, for stating that he considers that land is increased in annual value, by the establishment of the police, from 1 d. to 2 d. per acre."

[The figures shown in the above are not set forth as strictly correct, but merely estimates from such data as could be obtained.]

EXPENSE of a POLICE FORCE for the Division of *Bath*.

	£.	s.	d.
1 Chief Constable or Superintendent, per annum - - -	* 250	–	–
1 Inspector, 28 s. per week - - - - -	72	16	–
1 Serjeant, 23 s. per week - - - - -	59	16	–
15 Constables, in three grades, averaging 19 s. per week - -	741	–	–
18 Total.	1,123	12	–
Chief, Horse, and Travelling Expenses - - - -	50	–	–
1 Horse for Inspector - - - - - -	30	–	–
Remount - - - - - - - -	5	–	–
Repair of Carts - - - - - - -	5	–	–
Clothing Inspector - - - - - - -	6	–	–
Clothing Serjeant and 15 Constables, at 4 l. 10 s. each - -	72	–	–
Oil and Cotton, for 15 Constables, at 1 s. 6 d. per month each -	13	10	–
Stationery - - - - - - - -	30	–	–
Sundries - - - - - - - - -	50	–	–
Total Expense - - -	1,385	2	–
Annual saving by the establishment of a police, instead of superintending and parish constables, with additional protection of property, and other benefits derived from a police - - - -	53	8	–
£.	1,438	10	–

Population of Division of Bath (exclusive of the city parishes), 20,891, according to census of 1841.

28 Parishes, 241 constables, now annually appointed.

Acreage,

A farthing rate raises 103 l. 8 s.

A threepenny rate for the whole year on the division would, therefore, meet the expenses of an efficient police, and the saving shown in the other column would effect a proportionate reduction in the present county and poor-rates. The rate would be levied quarterly, and in equal proportions.

The County Police Acts limit one constable to every 1,000 of the population. The number above proposed would give one constable to about every 1,160 of the population. A larger proportion, it is believed, than in any other county, but necessary where established in only one division of a county.

By the establishment of a police, unity of action, subordination and discipline, with a proper system of communication, are secured, and local influences, and jealousies which the employment and method of paying parish constables engender, avoided. Strict supervision, and payment by fixed salaries, ensure the due performance of their duty by a police, while under

* This sum is named as the lowest authorised by the Secretary of State under 2 & 3 Vict., cap. 93, sect. 3, for a chief constable.

under the superintending and parish constable system, fees being received, and the constables only employed when offences are committed, or expected to be committed, an interest in crime is created. The police constantly patrol at night, afford more certain means of protecting property, prevent offences, and being properly disciplined and trained, are better able to detect offenders.

Prior to the re-organisation of the Bath Police Force, the majority of offenders in the Division of Bath were detected by the Bath police; since the re-organisation, information of a very small portion only of the offences committed in the county division has been given, but there are reports in 1849 and 1850 of five burglaries, six highway robberies, 13 sheep stolen, and 35 petty larcenies. Several sheep have been recently stolen, and highway robberies and other offences committed. The following letter from Mr. Eve, agent to the Property Protection Society, till 1848, will give some idea of the state of crime in the Division of Bath, and the inefficiency of parish constables:—

" Dear Sir,   " Bath, 31 January 1851.
I feel much pleasure in giving you all the information I can touching the several robberies, burglaries, &c., which have come under my notice as agent to the Property Protection Society during the year 1848.
" There were stolen 43 sheep and lambs, 56 fowls, 14 sacks of potatoes, one saddle, some harness, and farm implements on several occasions; six burglaries, and plate of great value stolen; 50 or more petty thefts, three incendiary fires, slaughter-houses frequently broken open, and meat stolen in large quantities. In addition to this, I have no hesitation in saying I could furnish you with the names of several farmers in the neighbourhood of Bath who have lost annually four or more sheep, and I believe I am within bounds when I say that there are not less than from 80 to 100 sheep stolen yearly from the villages round us; during the winter months it is no unusual thing for the farmers at Wellow, Southstoke, Tunley, Dunkerton, Timsbury, Newton, Corston, &c., to find a sheep stolen, and the skin and entrails left in the field.
" In the year 1848 there were many other robberies, &c., which did not come under the notice of our society; we had only 143 agricultural subscribers. I believe this society caused six or eight sheep-stealers to be transported, and many to be apprehended, but seldom convicted, principally caused from the slovenly manner in which the officers got up their evidence.

                                                                                                    " I am, &c.,
" Wm. Oakley, Esq., Chief of Police, Bath.   (signed)   " Henry Eve."

The average value of sheep and other property stolen, damage to fences and growing crops, and wood-stealing, in the Division of Bath, during the years 1849 and 1850, may be estimated from such sources, as information could be obtained, at 750l. per annum. By the establishment of a police, the ratepayers would save at least three-fourths of that amount. And, although the statements in the above accounts are given only as a comparison between the expense of the proposed superintending and parish constable system and a police, by its savings under the various heads, a police may, with economy, be made a self-supporting establishment; it would certainly do more, and that more efficiently than the present parish constables, at less real expense, if the saving of property be taken into account: the simple difference would be that the amount required for a police would be levied in a direct manner by a police-rate, while, at present, the ratepayer indirectly, and by county and poor-rates, actually pays nearly the same.

It is believed many ratepayers are under the impression that in some counties where a police has been established, the county and poor-rates have increased instead of diminished, as they should be, in consequence of such establishments; whereas, such increase is more likely to have been caused by the erection of lunatic asylums, or other county improvements, as regards the county rates; and the expense of the union houses and poor-law unions, as regards the poor-rates; and therefore should not be attributed to the police, without whom the expense would probably have been much greater, particularly in those counties where members of the police force have been appointed assistant relieving officers for vagrants.

Another important advantage of establishing a police for the division would be the obtaining a station-house and strong rooms, with a proper room for the magistrates, and accommodation for all persons having business at petty sessions. The expense of such station-house would probably be the same under both the Superintending and Parish Constables Acts and the Police Acts. But under the Parish Constables' Acts the lock-ups must be paid for immediately, at the expense of the whole county, though the benefit may be only to a particular locality, while under the Police Acts there is power to borrow money for the erection of station-houses on the security of the rates of the district for which the station-house is erected: and the money so borrowed, with the interest, may be paid by the rents received from members of the police force, and the amount of charges for lodging of prisoners received from Government as part of the expenses of prosecutions, thus making the buildings pay the cost of erecting them, by which means the county obtain the buildings by merely being security for the money borrowed.

As the establishment of a police for one division only would naturally be at a higher rate in that division than if the same system were adopted throughout the county, the following calculation of the rate at which it might be so carried out, is also submitted:—

STATEMENT

STATEMENT of the Estimated Comparative Expense of Superintending and Parish Constables, under 5 & 6 Vict., c. 109, and 13 & 14 Vict., c. 20, and a Police, under 2 & 3 Vict., c. 93, and 3 & 4 Vict., c. 88, for the county of Somerset.

Appendix, No. 3.

PROBABLE EXPENSE under Superintending and Parish Constable System.

	£.	s.	d.
Conveyance of Prisoners	1,100	–	–

By the county accounts for 1849 and 1850, 1,238 l. 14 s. appears to be the average amount paid out of the county rates (exclusive of conveyance from prison to trial and back), 138 l. 14 s. is as much as should be incurred by a police for the expense of subsistence of prisoners. Deducting which leaves 1,100 l., the amount of conveyance and lodging which may be saved by the prisoners being conveyed by the police in the carts necessary to be provided for the other duties of the police.

Payments to parish constables, if paid in other parts of the county, as in the Division of Bath	3,000	–	–
Costs of proceedings before Justices, if in like proportion	2,000	–	–
Estimated amount paid to parish constables for serving summonses and warrants, and by individuals in like proportion	600	–	–
Constables attending assizes and sessions	102	–	–

(Average shown in county accounts for 1849 and 1850.)

Estimated amount paid to parish constables under Magistrates' certificates and orders of court, in cases of felony, at assizes and sessions	1,200	–	–

(See note in page 160.)

Fines under penal statutes	200	–	–
Summoning coroners' juries, &c.	100	–	–
Proposed salary to 20 superintending constables, at 110 l. per annum each	2,200	–	–
Contingent expenses, as explained in page 160, at 2 l. 2 s. per month each, for the 20 divisions of Somerset	600	–	–

Payments to parish constables, as also explained in page 160; if 10 constables only were employed in each of the 20 divisions of the county, and for only three days a week, at the same rate (5 s. 6 d. per day and night), the amount would be 8,580 l. per annum; deducting from that sum the above 3,000 l., estimated as now paid to parish constables, the additional expense probably to be incurred, under the proposed system, would be - 5,580 – –

	16,682	–	–

To the above items may be added the following, which, if a Police were established, instead of Superintending and Parish Constables, might be saved, viz. : —

Inspecting of weights and measures, per annum	800	–	–

As by the county accounts for 1849 and 1850, the average amount paid to the present inspectors appears to be 234 l. 10 s., the amount of penalties stated to be received is under 70 l. By the police being employed, five times that amount, it may be estimated, would be received by the county. No account is shown of fees for comparing, examining, and stamping weights and measures; at least 200 l. per annum should be earned.

Relieving vagrants, per annum	2,000	–	–

In the county of Essex, as mentioned in page 160, it is estimated at 5,101 l.

Postage and carriage, by the police delivering official parcels to magistrates and parochial authorities	50	–	–

	£. 19,532	–	–

Credit is not taken for any sum as saved by a police in the additional protection and recovery of property, or the increased value of land.— *Vide* extract from Report of Chief Constable of Essex in page 160.

[The figures shown in the above are not set forth as strictly correct, but merely estimates from such data as could be obtained.]

Expense of a Police Force for the County of *Somerset.*

		£.	s.	d.
1 Chief constable, per annum		350	–	–
Horse and travelling expenses		150	–	–
1 Clerk and storekeeper		100	–	–
1 Superintendent		150	–	–
2 Ditto — at £.120 – – per annum		240	–	–
2 Ditto — „ 110 – – „		220	–	–
2 Ditto — „ 100 – – „		200	–	–
7 Inspectors „ 1 8 – per week		509	12	–
14 Sergeants „ 1 3 – „		837	4	–
185 Constables in three grades, averaging – 17 – „		8,177	–	–

215 Total.	£.	10,933	16	–
6 Superintendents' clothing – at £.12 – – each per annum		72	–	–
7 Inspectors' ditto – „ 5 – – „ „		35	–	–
199 Sergeants' and constables' ditto „ 4 10 – „ „		895	10	–
20 Horses – „ 30 – – „ „		600	–	–
„ Remount „		80	–	–
Repairs of carts „		60	–	–
185 Constables' allowance for oil, cotton, &c., 1 s. 6 d. per month each		166	10	–
Stationery		200	–	–
Sundries		300	–	–
Depreciation of stock		180	–	–

Total expense	13,522	16	–

Annual saving by the establishment of a police instead of superintending and parish constables, with additional protection of property, and other benefits derived from a police - - - - - - - - - 6,009 4 –

£. 19,532 – –

Population of Somerset, excluding Bath and Bridgwater (exempt under 2 & 3 Vict., cap. 88, sec. 24, having separate Quarter Sessions), 372,000, according to census of 1841.
20 magisterial divisions.
480 parishes.
Acreage,
A farthing rate raises 2,029 *l.* 0 *s.* 3¾ *d.*
1¾ *d.* rate for the whole year, on the whole county, would therefore meet the expenses of a police, and the savings shown above, would effect a proportionate reduction in the present county and poor-rates. The rate would be levied quarterly and in equal proportions.

The County Police Acts limit one constable to every 1,000 of the population (*see* 2 & 3 Vict., cap. 93, sec. 1). In the county of Essex, the police were established in the year 1840, with one constable to about every 1,750 of the population; in 1842, the force was increased 50 men, giving one constable to about every 1,325 of the population. In the county of Surrey, the police have been established this year, at about the latter proportion of constables to the population. In the county of Edinburgh, there is only one police constable to about 3,000 of the population. Although there may be a difference between England and Scotland as to the state of crime, portions of the system now in force in Scotland might with advantage be introduced into the English counties.

It is believed that the unpopularity and unsatisfactory working of some of the police forces in England, arises from the employment of too many inadequately paid officers in proportion to the number of men. Few officers well paid and more men elevates the character of a police force, and promotes efficiency.

The above estimate for the county of Somerset is given at a moderate rate, allowing one constable to every 1,750 of the population: and such a force would be less expensive than superintending and parish constables, afford much greater protection to property, be more likely to prevent crime, and detect offenders, in addition to providing a body of disciplined and efficient men. To put the force in this county on a satisfactory footing at the outset, it might be advisable to add 35 constables to the above number, giving one constable to every 1,500 of the population, at an expense of 1,736 *l.* per annum, which would still show a saving of 4,273 *l.* 4 *s.*, as compared with the superintending and parish constable system. The number of 250 for the whole county may appear too low to those who have looked on the duties of a police as a mere patrol; but the aim of a county policeman should be less to watch property than to watch thieves.

If the police of the boroughs were consolidated with the county force, it would afford greater protection with less expense; the boroughs and large towns being formed into districts, under 3 & 4 Vict., cap. 88, sec. 27, and having a proportionate number of constables allotted to each district.

Appendix, No. 4.

RATE of PAY to the CONSTABULARY, as approved of by the Sub-Committee;

Namely,

	s.	d.
1 Inspector and Clerk, at - - - - - - - -	24	–
1 Office Serjeant, at - - - - - - - - -	22	–
2 Serjeants, at - - - - - - - - - -	19	–
3 First Class Constables, at - - - - - - -	17	6
6 Constables who have served above two years, at - -	16	6
17 Constables under two years, at - - - - - -	16	–
1 Messenger, at - - - - - - - - -	15	6

Allowance to the Constabulary attending Courts, as approved of by the Sub-Committee.

	s.	d.
1st. When necessarily out of their District a night, in search or pursuit of a delinquent, and not on their regular tour of duty - - - - - -	1	–
2d. Going out of County, above 12 miles from their station, on special duty -	1	–
3d. Going out of County, above 12 miles, a day and night - - - -	2	–
4th. Going out of District, above 12 miles, on special duty - - -	1	6
5th. Ditto day and night, on ditto - - -	3	–

(Railway or Coach Fares, if considered necessary, will be allowed.)

	s.	d.
6th. Attending as Witnesses, 7 miles and under 10 - - - - -	1	–
7th. Ditto - - ditto, 10 miles and under 17 - - - - -	1	6
8th. Ditto - - ditto, 17 miles and under 25 - - - - -	2	6
9th. Ditto - - ditto, 25 miles and above - - - - -	3	6

The above Rates include Fares.

No allowance for going from a District on the borders of the county a few miles into an adjoining one, or from one District to another, for the purpose of consulting with a brother constable, lodging information, or patrolling with him.

Note.—Constables attending Road Courts, whose stations are 4 miles and under from said courts, will receive no extra allowance. All others will be paid both for Road Courts and other Courts, as witnesses, agreeable to No. 6 of the above scale. Those stationed 4 miles and under, when attending as witnesses in summary cases, will be allowed No. 6 scale of payment.

By Order,
(signed) *J. M. Balfour,*
Clerk to Commissioners of Supply.

1852, } COPY of REPORT laid before COMMISSIONERS of SUPPLY and JUSTICES of
Sept. 30. } PEACE of County of EDINBURGH, on Subject of Uniform Police throughout
Scotland.

I beg to make a few remarks on vagrancy, &c., and then to lay before your honours what I consider would be an efficient system of Police for Scotland.

In reference to that class termed vagrants, I am compelled to say, they are invariably thieves, having great facilities, under the pretence of begging, of acquiring a knowledge at every house they visit; where places are locked and unlocked, they reconnoitre and ascertain from whence articles might be stolen.

A large number, and principally Irish, travel about and encamp at night, not always on the road sides, but in bye-lanes and on private property, for the purpose of evading turnpike statutes.

During the last two years in the Lothians, Roxburghshire, Berwickshire, Peeblesshire and Selkirkshire, there has not been less than 100 thefts of farm servants' wearing apparel from stable lofts, in which they sleep; the majority of these thefts are traceable to gangs of Irish, travelling from one county to another, and encamping in woods and unfrequented places.

A few detections have been made ; but owing to the want of organisation and general efficiency in the police establishments, with power under statutory law to deal with this vagrant tribe, the evil has not been cured.

In the county of East-Lothian they have appointed extra constables, and most of the parishes have contributed, for the purpose of passing vagrants out of the county; all persons found selling small wares, are taken hold of by these constables, passed along from one to another, until they are fairly out of the county; at Dunbar, Tranent, and Haddington they have receiving-houses, where they, at times, keep them for a night. Since this system has been adopted, petty thefts have very considerably decreased.

I question the legality of such a procedure, and have therefore not adopted it. In the county, and immediately beyond the city police boundary, thimble-riggers ply their avocation with impunity; more particularly on Arthur's Seat, and around the Queen's Drive; but having no law to reach them the police cannot interfere.

The only recent Act that touches on vagrancy is the Poor Law Amendment Act, 8 & 9 Vict. c. 83, ss. 79 & 80, and this falls back on Statute 1579, c. 74, intituled "An Act for Punishment of strong and idle Beggars, and Reliefe of the Pure and Impotent." Two small volumes containing the abridged Acts of those days, namely, 1666 and 1670, refer to vagrancy, but the punishment to be imposed is of that description which I fear could not in these enlightened days be inflicted. The English Act 5 Geo. 4, c. 83, contains ample provisions against all kinds of beggars, both in town and county. *See* Chitty's Office and Duty of a Constable.

In the year 1840, after I published my Prize Treatise on Rural Police, the draft of a General Police Act was prepared under my direction; the experience I have acquired since convinces me that some such Act is required.

Uniform System of Police.

I find the charges for the constabulary, rates of pay to constables, &c., to be according to the statement in the annexed Table, p. 167.

Counties will now be relieved of the charge against the rogue-money, for all their summary prosecutions. The sum laid aside by the Treasury for the first year is 30,000 *l.* As will be seen by the Table, I have been unable to get the sums charged against each county : this may be ascertained at the Exchequer Chambers.

Although we do not require an armed force in Scotland, I still think the men should be provided with, and trained to the use of arms; upon special occasions numbers might be drawn together, and act with unity of purpose in dispersing a mob and suppressing a riot.

In illustration of the present inefficient state of the police, both in town and county, I can first refer to the Autumn of 1842, when the colliers struck work for an increase of wages: constables of both town and county establishments were taken to a certain part of the county, and being undisciplined, they fled before the mob, and the military were obliged to be obtained. Again, in the year 1846, when the Edinburgh and Hawick Railway was under construction, a quarrel ensued at part of the works near Fushie Bridge, among the Irish " Navvies," in which a policeman was killed; on the following day a large body of both town and county police constables were taken to the spot, for the purpose of apprehending the murderers; a considerable number of Highlanders, who were engaged on the adjoining contract of the work, to be revenged, had gone down to drive the Irish off the ground, and burn down their huts; in the midst of this a body of both town and county police arrived at the spot under the charge of Sheriff Jamieson and myself, and from their inefficient state, being untrained and without arms, they fled in different directions apparently to take care of themselves, and numbers of the huts were burned down before our faces by the infuriated Highlanders. An express had to be sent off 12 miles for the military, and before they arrived the contractors had suffered considerable loss by the destruction of huts and other property.

At the Chartist riots in Edinburgh (in 1848) property was destroyed by the mob, and the police were perfectly useless and unable to act without the aid of the military; so also with the Annuity Tax affair.

In proposing a uniform system of county police, I would suggest that an average be made of the sums paid by Exchequer to each county for the summary cases; so also for the reported ones, as very large sums are drawn by sheriffs' and criminal officers in some counties for this duty, varying from 100 *l.* to 600 *l.* each; then a fixed annual sum to be paid each county, and all fees to officers abolished; a general Police Act brought in, compelling every county to have a police force; the assessment not to exceed 1 *d.* per £. valued rent. which, with the sums receivable from Exchequer, would establish an efficient and uniform police force.

Its government should be under an officer attached to the Crown Agent's office, with a sub for the north and another for the south of the Tay; and, as many counties are small, and others entirely rural, two or three should be united together for police purposes under the charge of a superintendent or inspector; all orders or instructions to emanate from the chief, and periodical reports to be made by him to the Lord Advocate.

The local magistracy to have a control, as at present; and the chief officer being attached to the Crown Agent's department, would obviate the necessity of creating a centralising Board in Edinburgh.

Alfred John List, General Superintendent and J. P. Fiscal.

STATISTICAL RETURN of SCOTCH COUNTIES, with Population, Rental, Area, Police, Rate of Pay, Rate of Assessment, Cost of Constabulary, &c. &c.

No.	NAME OF COUNTY.	Population of County in 1851 (Oliver & Boyd.)	(Landward Part.)	Number of Parishes (Suburban).	Real Rent of County in 1841.	Rate of Assessment.	Area of County in Square Miles.	Number of Police.	Rate of Pay (Weekly) — Sergeants. (s. d.)	Rate of Pay (Weekly) — Constables. (s. d.)	Annual Cost of Constabulary. (£.)	Probable Amount from Exchequer for Summary Cases. (£.)	Proportion to Population.	Inhabited Houses.
1	Aberdeen	151,445	120,618	82	400,630	— 13 s. 6 d. per 100 l. Scots.	1,985	37	None	12 6 / 12 3 / 10 -	1,583	300	1 to 4,201	24,587
2	Argyll	79,012	71,018	34	227,403	1¼ d. per 1 l. real rent	3,800	24	15	14 - / 14 6 / 13 6	1,208	150 to 200	1 to 3,317	14,136
3	Ayr	155,014	83,718	46	417,900	1 d. per 1 l. real rent	1,000	20	20	15 6 / 14 6 / 13 -	1,220	50 to 100	1 to 7,750	19,236
4	Banff	54,171	42,536	23	99,000	10 s. 6 d. per 100 l.	500	9		16 -	540	150	1 to 6,016	9,233
5	Berwick	35,192	28,102	32	220,986	No police	446	8		16 -	750	250	1 to 4,399	6,169
6	Bute [1]	16,608	8,867	6	23,000	No return	257	No police			No police	No return		2,335
7	Caithness	31,087	20,070	10	35,000	1¼ d. per 1 l. real rent	618	5	15	15 -	230	"	1 to 6,397	6,067
8	Clackmannan [1] { Kinross	41,405	11,979 / 4,729	9	87,009	— 12 s. per 100 Merks Scots.	131	8	12	12 -	300	Nil	1 to 5,187	6,207
9	Dumbarton	39,658	48,448	12	110,017	No return	260	9	14	14 6 / 14 -	640	No return	1 to 4,406	4,479
10	Dumfries	64,957	52,546	43	272,217	— 8 s. 8 d. per 100 l. real rent.	1,800	14		14 6	1,146	130	1 to 4,739	10,546
11	Edinburgh	62,836	51,218	31	246,358	— 8 s. 7¼ d. per 100 l. valued rent.	360	31	19	17 - / 16 6 / 16 -	2,061	250	1 to 2,029	9,005
12	Elgin and Nairn	39,601	23,859	24	111,319	No return	680	8	19	12 -	400	Nil	1 to 4,950	7,203
13	Fife	139,710		61	403,709		504	40	19	17 - / 16 - / 15 -	2,180	80	1 to 3,492	18,001
14	Forfar	64,101	70,018	53	279,073	No return	840	19	19	12 - / 12 -	899	No return	1 to 3,377	12,418
15	Haddington	28,002	20,506	24	214,778	1 d. per 1 l. Stg.	250	11	19	10 - / 12 -	862	70	1 to 2,600	5,433
16	Inverness	83,707	81,385	31	152,078	No return	4,000	28	16 6	11 6	988	No return	1 to 2,993	15,832
17	Kincardine	33,664	20,279	10	120,000	"	317	12	15 6	11 -	455	"	1 to 2,805	6,465
18	Kirkcudbright	30,087	30,031	28	210,000	1 d. per 1 l. Stg.	882	11	20	15 -	545	"	1 to 3,635	6,527
19	Lanark [1]	165,485	122,852	41	539,307	No police	870	30		16 -	No police	Nil	1 to 4,121	22,169
20	Linlithgow	24,727	18,745	13	100,000	— 18 s. 0 d. per 100 l. Stg.	112	6	18	16 -	424	Nil		3,569
21	Orkney and Shetland [1]	53,082	51,123	31	52,000	No police	1,325	No police						10,877
22	Peebles	10,738	8,756	14	75,405	— 15 s. per 100 l. Scots.	360	6		14 -	370	Nil	1 to 1,789	1,708
23	Perth	107,804	95,009	74	624,274	10 s. 6 d. per 100 l.	2,588	35	17	16 - / 14 - / 13	2,000	No return	1 to 3,080	19,182
24	Renfrew [1]	66,610	31,141	17	151,701	No police	241	No police			No police			5,068
25	Ross and Cromarty	75,632	61,832	33	126,137	No return	2,830	13	10	10 -	900		1 to 5,810	14,723
26	Roxburgh	48,027	33,208	32	266,314	— 10 s. 10 d. per 100 l. Scots.	715	14	10	15 - / 13 -	960	358	1 to 3,430	6,853
27	Selkirk	9,800	8,845	4	46,000	12 s. per ditto	263	6	15	14 -	330	100	1 to 1,639	1,331
28	Stirling	61,444	45,472	24	250,350	No return	489	15	14	14 -	660	No return	1 to 4,097	8,743
29	Sutherland	25,194	25,194	13	38,774		1,754	5	12	12 -	170	"	1 to 5,038	4,834
30	Wigtown	33,878	20,091	17	135,810		451	11	14	14 -	425	"	1 to 3,070	5,494
		1,850,646		821	6,037,719		31,834	435			20,412		1 to 4,254	

[1] These counties have no Police Establishments.

[2] Taken from a Return made up by the Board of Supervision under the Poor Law Amendment Act.

[3] Population that the Rural Police take charge of. The figures in first column population including small towns, &c. At Airdrie they have a Police in virtue of an Act of Parliament, but in no other part of the county.

A RETURN showing the Number of PLACES, beyond the Municipal Boundary, to which the *Glasgow* Police have been sent to preserve the Peace, at various Times since the Year 1847.

TOWN or PLACE.	COUNTY.	OCCASION.	Number employed at each Place.			
			Super-intendents.	Lieu-tenants.	Inspectors.	Constables.
Dumbarton - - -	Dumbartonshire -	Queen's visit - - -	2	-	2	50
Lochgilphead - -	Argyleshire -	- - „ - - -	1	-	1	50
Paisley - - -	Renfrewshire -	Races - - - -	-	-	2	30
Airdrie - - -	Lanarkshire -	Colliers' strike - - -	-	-	2	40
Provan Mill - -	- - „ -	- - „ - - -	-	-	1	19
Cambuslang - -	- - „ -	- - „ - - -	-	-	1	19
Airdrie - - -	- - „ -	Orange meeting - -	2	-	1	30
Ditto - - -	- - „ -	Election of M. P. - -	1	-	2	60
Kirkintilloch - -	Dumbartonshire -	Races - - -	-	-	1	13
Mary Hill - -	Lanarkshire -	Cattle show (yearly) -	-	-	-	5
East Kilbride -	Renfrewshire -	- - „ - -	-	-	-	6
Nitshill - - -	- - „ -	Colliery explosion - -	2	1	-	84 *
Hamilton - -	Lanarkshire -	Cavalry review (yearly) -	-	-	1	20
Bosgside - -	Ayrshire -	Races - - -	-	-	-	8
Ayr and Kilmarnock -	- - „ -	Election of M. P. - -	-	-	1	20
Ayr - - -	- - „ -	Races (yearly) - -	-	-	1	15
Greenock - -	Renfrewshire -	Election of M. P. - -	-	-	1	20
Ardrossan - -	Ayrshire -	Races - - -	-	-	1	8
Baillieston - -	Lanarkshire -	Cattle show (yearly) -	-	-	-	4
Bishopbridge - -	- - „ -	- - „ - -	-	-	-	2
Hellensburgh -	Dumbartonshire -	Opening new quay - -	-	-	1	11
			8	1	19	514

TOTAL - - - - - - - 542.

* This number was employed for eight days, varying from 12 to 6 each day.

Note.—In addition to this, they are often called out to preserve order at ploughing matches, &c.

STRENGTH of the City of *Glasgow* POLICE FORCE, 20 June 1853.

RANK.	General.	DIVISIONS.						TOTAL.
		A.	B.	C.	D.	E.	☉	
Chief - - - -	1	-	-	-	-	-	-	1
Superintendents - -	-	1	1	1	1	1	1	6
Lieutenants - - -	-	3	2	2	2	2	2	13
Detective { Inspector -	-	1	-	-	-	-	-	1
Department { Sub inspector -	-	2	-	-	-	-	-	2
{ Detective officers -	-	8	2	2	2	1	1	*16
Production keeper and clerks -	-	2	-	-	-	-	-	2
Court officer - - -	-	1	-	-	-	-	-	1
House officers - -	-	11	2	2	2	-	1	18
Day inspectors - -	-	5	1	1	1	-	1	9
Night ditto - -	-	3	1	1	1	-	1	7
Day sergeants - -	-	7	2	2	2	-	1	14
Night ditto - -	-	7	4	4	3	-	2	20
Day constables - -	-	83	25	24	17	-	16	165
Night ditto - -	-	144	60	58	48	-	14	324
	1	278	100	97	79	4	40	599

* One vacant.

Note.—The inspectors, sergeants, and constables of E. Division are classified with those of their rank in A. Division, the arrangements for detaching it from the A. Division not being yet complete.

Cost of the Glasgow police, for the year ending 15 May 1853 - - - £. 23,337. 17*s*. 3*d*.
   (After deducting the amount of fines received - £. 2,748.)

Dock and Harbour Police cost - - - - - - - £. 2,858. 9*s*. 3*d*.

Appendix, No. 4.

RETURN of Persons Apprehended by the *Glasgow* Police, charged with Crimes committed in other Counties, between 1st January 1852 and 1st June 1853.

Date when Apprehended.	NAME.	CRIME.	
1852:			
5 January -	James Kean - - -	Housebreaking, and theft of silver plate - - -	Greenock.
" -	George Tennant - -		
9 January -	Mary Sawers or M‘Lean -	Theft of clothes - -	Ayr.
10 January -	Peter Brewster - -	Theft of yarn - - -	Airdrie.
" -	Susan Brewester - -		
5 February -	Margaret Morrison - -	Theft of clothes - -	Paisley.
15 February -	Peter Currie - - -	Theft of a coat - -	Stirling.
19 February -	Mary Paterson - -	Theft of a carpet - -	Edinburgh.
" -	Margaret Elder - -		
15 March -	James Bryce - - -	Theft of 17 *l.* 10 *s.* - -	Edinburgh.
17 March -	John Haugh - - -	Theft of clothes - -	Wigton.
29 March -	Alexander M‘Intyre - -	Theft of a plaid - -	Inverness.
7 April -	Alexander Harrison - -	Theft of wright's tools -	Edinburgh.
27 April -	Jane Thomson - -	Theft by housebreaking -	Stirling.
1 June -	Margaret King - -	Theft - - -	Airdrie.
7 June -	Archibald Currie - -	Assault - - -	Argyllshire.
7 September -	James Webster - -	Theft - - -	Arbroath.
10 September -	Andrew Brand - -	Theft of a bale of goods -	Falkirk.
"	Henry Murphy - -		
16 September -	William M‘Donald - -	Theft of silver plate -	Lanark.
" -	Mary Blackwood - -		
21 September -	Thomas M‘Gee - -	Theft - - -	Stirling.
8 October -	Isabella Black - -	Theft - - -	Greenock.
18 October -	Margaret Harris - -	Theft - - -	Londonderry.
19 October -	John Moffat - -	Theft - - -	Edinburgh.
" -	Mary Stewart - -	Theft - - -	Dumbarton.
15 November -	Joseph Reid - -	Housebreaking and theft -	Kirkcudbright.
27 November -	James Aitkison - -	Theft - - -	Edinburgh.
9 December -	William Gillespie - -	Theft - - -	Stirling.
1853:			
20 January -	Thomas Donnelly - -	Theft of shawls - -	Falkirk.
27 January -	John Brown - -	Theft of a saddle - -	Stirling.
28 January -	J. Cunningham - -	Theft - - -	Linlithgow.
8 February -	Duncan Blair - -	Theft - - -	Greenock.
16 February -	Helen Douglas - -	Theft - - -	Stirling.
4 March -	John Broadie - -	Theft - - -	Manchester.
" -	Alexander Taylor - -	Housebreaking and theft -	Paisley.
16 March -	Hugh M‘Intyre - -	Theft of clothes - -	Oban.
" -	Isabella Todd - -		
" -	Hugh M‘Lean - -	Cattle-stealing - -	Stirling.
" -	John Cosh - -		
" -	Walter Walker - -		
12 April -	Andrew Inglis - -	Theft of beef - -	Haddington.

ABSTRACT.

Lanarkshire - - - - -	3	Argyllshire - - - -	2
Renfrewshire - - - -	5	Forfarshire - - - -	1
Ayrshire - - - - -	1	Dumbartonshire - - -	1
Stirlingshire - - - -	9	Linlithgow - - - -	1
Edinburgh - - - - -	5	Manchester - - - -	1
Wigtonshire - - - -	2	Haddington - - - -	1
Inverness - - - - -	1	Londonderry - - - -	1
			34

RETURN of Number of POLICE within the County of *Dumfries*, and the CHARGES of the same, since the year 1842–43 to 1852–53.

YEARS	Superin-tendent.	Clerk.	Criminal Officers or Ser-geants.	District Con-stables.	TOTAL Strength of Force.	Amount of Charge.	Received for Exchequer Fees.	Gross Charge.
						£. s. d.	£. s. d.	£. s. d.
1841–42	1	- -	3	10	14	656 10 –	- none -	656 10 –
1842–43	1	- -	3	10	14	689 8 4½	- none -	689 8 4½
1843–44	1	1	2	11	15	639 13 4	32 19 –	606 14 4
1844–45	1	1	2	11	15	1,023 12 1½	119 9 11	904 2 2½
1845–46	1	1	2	12	16	1,095 8 10⅓	230 – –	865 8 10⅓
1846–47	1	1	2	13	17	1,316 17 3½	300 – –	1,016 17 3½
1847–48	1	1	2	13	17	1,598 18 7½	355 1 –	1,243 17 7½
1848–49	1	1	2	13	17	1,389 10 –	264 6 10	1,125 3 2
1849–50	1	1	2	14	18	1,262 2 6½	271 1 2	991 1 4½
1850–51	1	1	2	14	18	1,118 17 4	308 1 1½ Account for this year not yet paid, but likely to be got.	810 16 2½
1851–52	1	1	2	15	19	1,150 15 –	300 – – Account for this year only about to be ren-dered, and sup-posed likely to be got.	850 15 –
1852–53	1	1	2	15	19	- - -	230 – –	—

Appendix, No. 5.

PAPER furnished by *E. Chadwick*, Esq., C. B.

1. THAT the public information as to the number of crimes committed, inferred from the extent of crimes judicially pursued and punished, is widely erroneous.

2. That there is an average of upwards of 100,000 commitments annually to the gaols of the able-bodied population of England and Wales for criminal offences.

3. That there are from 11,000 to 20,000 persons constantly in the criminal gaols, of which number a large proportion are persons known as living wholly by habitual depredation; and from inquiries made in a large number of the individual cases of prisoners confined for thefts in these gaols, we find that, on the average, such prisoners in the rural districts, where there is no trained constabulary, have been at large, living by depredation during average periods upwards of five years; and that the criminal prisoners in the gaols in the towns, where there is a paid and trained force, have not been able to pursue their depreda-tions more than half that time. But that nevertheless, in either districts, prisoners are liberated with the prospect and the temptation of a career of unknown but long duration for the future, before permanent removal by process of law or by natural causes.

4. That with relation to the particular crimes committed by such habitual depredators, no information is possessed by the unpaid constables.

5. That it results from a special investigation of the habits of the classes of habitual depredators, that a large proportion of them are migratory; that they migrate from town

to

to town, and from the towns where they harbour, and where there are distinct houses maintained for their accommodation, they issue forth and commit depredations upon the surrounding rural districts, the metropolis being the chief centre from which they migrate; and that they harbour in provincial towns in proportion to their magnitude, and in proportion to the facilities for plunder, or to the absence of protection in the surrounding districts.

6. That judging from particular cases in which we have made inquiries, a large proportion, if not always the majority, of prisoners in the county gaols, for offences committed within the rural districts, are persons who have migrated from the towns to the rural districts.

7. That from the impunity enjoyed by the classes of depredators, migrant or resident, property is rendered insecure; in some places so much so, on the part of the labouring classes, as greatly to impair the value of property to them, and their motives to industry and frugality.

8. That in the rural districts agricultural produce is subjected to extensive depredation, which often interferes with the most advantageous course of production.

9. That a large proportion of the highways are left without any protection whatsoever from any constabulary or other civil force.

10. That on the highways of a large part of the country, commercial travellers and strangers who travel singly, otherwise than by public conveyances, and carry money about them, abstain from travelling after dark, from fear of robbery and violence; and that farmers return from market in company, from the like fear, after dark.

11. That the products of commercial industry *in transitu* on the highways, being almost entirely without protection from any civil force, are subject to extensive and systematic depredation.

12. That in the absence of due protection, property carried by sea in ships which are wrecked on those parts of the coast where shipwrecks occasionally or frequently occur, is subject to extensive habitual depredation; and life is endangered or lost under circumstances of barbarity disgraceful to a civilised nation.

I N D E X

TO

REPORTS

FROM

THE SELECT COMMITTEE

ON

POLICE.

Ordered, by The House of Commons, to be Printed,
5 July 1853.

ANALYSIS OF INDEX.

ALPHABETICAL and CLASSIFIED LIST of the PRINCIPAL HEADINGS in the following INDEX, with the Paging at which they will be respectively found.

I N D E X.

[N.B.—In this Index the *Numerals* following *Rep.* ii., *p.* refer to the page of the Second Report; the *Figures* following the Names of the Witnesses refer to the Questions of the Evidence; and those following *Rep.* ii., *App.* to the page of the Appendix to the Second Report]

AGE. There is no definite age at which men cease to be policemen in the county of Hants, *Harris* 229, 230.——*See* also *Superannuations.*

Agricultural Property. Decrease of depredations on agricultural property since the establishment of the police in Hants, *King* 338-342; *Thompson* 466, 467. 473——Witness saves double the amount of his rate, if all kinds of property is taken into consideration, *King* 338-345.——*See* also *Sheep Stealing.*

Allerdale Below Division. See *Cumberland.*

Allowances. See *Extra Allowances. Fees and Allowances.*

Amalgamation of Counties. Suggestion for the amalgamation of two or three adjoining counties, including the boroughs under one system of police and one superintendence; there would be no difficulty in working the force on a more extended scale in the country, *Redin* 1383-1405. 1453-1457——With a view of saving expense, and giving increased co-operation, it is desirable to place more than one county under the same head or chief constable, *Chadwick* 3646.

See also *Districts. Government Control. Uniformity of System.*

Andover. The five men in the borough of Andover are constantly changed, *Harris* 40—— Consolidation of the police of Andover with the county in 1846, *Stanley* 280; *Thompson* 425-427——Improved condition of the borough of Andover since they have joined the county police, *Stanley* 280——Bad state of the town of Andover as to crime, previously to the establishment of the police, *Thompson* 428-434——The expense of the police to the borough is greater now than it was before the consolidation with the county, but the benefits are more than equal to the additional expense, *ib.* 435-448——Number of cases convicted before the magistrates in petty sessions at Andover, and of committals for trial in each year, 1843 to 1852 inclusive; causes of the great decrease of crime, *ib.* 449-460 —— Return of the cost of crime at Andover, from 1841 to 1852, showing the expenses of sessions, prosecutions, maintenance of prisoners, &c.; since the establishment of the police the expenses have rapidly decreased, *ib.* 460, 463.

See also *Lodging Houses. Public Houses. Rate,* 2. *Removals.*

APPOINTMENTS:

    1. *Generally.*
    2. *Suggestion that the Appointments should rest with the Chief Constable.*

  1. *Generally:*

The appointment and control of the police in Bucks is very inefficient, *Hamilton* 1026-1028—— Remarks upon the system of appointment and dismissal of constables in Bucks, *ib.* 1107-1113——The objection entertained on the part of the boroughs to join in the county constabulary, is the fear of losing their patronage in the police appointments, *Woodford* 1630-1632——The present method of appointing the police in Norwich tends much to impair its efficiency, *Dunne* 2042——Difficulty with respect to the appointment of the police; the appointments by the county magistrates are as good as can be expected; there would be less jealousy if the appointments were with the Secretary of State, *Chadwick* 3661, 3662.

APPOINTMENTS—continued.

2. *Suggestions that the Appointments should rest with the Chief Constable.*

The magistrates and authorities of the boroughs which have coalesced with the county constabulary of Hants have no voice in the appointment, promotion, or dismissal of the constables ; they are all county constables, and the chief constable of the county has the sole jurisdiction over them, *Harris* 45, 46——Opinion in favour of the appointments being left solely with the chief constable, *Harris* 47–52; *Mallalieu* 2841 ; *Oakley* 3344–3248. 3370–3374; *Burnardiston* 3625–3637; *Smart* 4056–4061. 4081–4083——The appointment of the police by the chief constable in Hants has worked very satisfactorily ; the appointments should not be transferred to Government, unless the expense of the force is defrayed out of the Consolidated Fund, *Stanley* 316–320——Objections to the appointment of the constables resting with the local authorities in boroughs, *M'Hardy* 803–805 ——Appointment and removal of the police of Shropshire by the chief constable, *Sir B. Leighton* 2504–2506.——*See also Bath.*

Apprehension of Offenders.   See *Capture of Offenders.*   *Customs' Officers.*

Arming and Training.   Great benefit would result from training the police to the use of arms, *Harris* 166–168. 212–227. 231, 232 ; *Woodford* 1669–1674——The police in Essex are not trained to arms, some of them are armed to assist the coast-guard in the prevention of smuggling, *M'Hardy* 771, 772——It would be a great advantage if the police were drilled in the performance of their ordinary duties ; they should not be intrusted with anything beyond a truncheon or cutlass, *Oakley* 3360.

Ashton-under-Lyne, Lancashire.   Different systems of police existing in the division of Ashton-under-Lyne ; under such different systems it is impossible they can act with effect or cordiality, *Woodford* 1622–1629. 1648–1650.

Assaults.   Diminution in the number of cases of ordinary violence and petty assaults since the establishment of a permanent and perfect police force in Essex, *M'Hardy* 795.

Assessments.   See *Rate.*

Assizes.   Attendance of the superintendent constables at assizes and sessions in Lincoln ; allowance made them for such attendance ; this is included in the expenses of the prosecution, *Sir R. Sheffield,* 620–634——When the Bath police go to the assizes to give evidence they receive their travelling expenses, but nothing on the score of fees, *Kitson* 2331–2337.

Audit of Accounts.   The expenditure of the Hants police is regularly brought before the court of quarter sessions, and the accounts are audited by the finance committee, *Stanley* 331–333——Manner in which the county accounts are audited and published by the finance committee of Norfolk, *Postle* 2541–2544.

B.

Baker, Robert.   (Analysis of his Evidence.)—Farmer and land-agent at Writtle, near Chelmsford, Essex, 951–956——Great benefits which have resulted from the establishment of the police in Essex; the offences against persons and property have both decreased, 957–962——The increased expenses of the police have been more than repaid by the advantage derived from their services, 963. 1003——Increased value of landed property since the establishment of the police in Essex, 964, 965. 1003——The improvement of the condition of the parish of Writtle is not entirely owing to the system of police, though that may be considered as the main instrument, 965–977. 977–1000—— Remarks relative to the expense of the present system of police as contrasted with the old system of constables, 978–989——Decrease of sheep, horse, and poultry stealing since the establishment of the police, 990–996——Prevention of the spread of crime by the present system of police ; such a system of watching was never practised with the old constables, 1001, 1002.

Bath.   Statement as to the strength of the police force of Bath ; the force has always been found sufficient for the maintenance of the public peace, *Hughes* 1207–1212. 1220. 1309, 1310; *Kitson* 2283, 2286–2303——Ready assistance given by the city of Bath police to the forces of the adjoining counties, *Hughes* 1216–1219——The police are under the control of the magistrates and the watch committee ; inconvenience arising from the existence of the two jurisdictions, *ib.* 1226–1238. 1277–1285. 1322–1324——The present method of appointment and payment of the police of Bath militates against its efficiency ; it would be a good thing to give jurisdiction over the city police to some authority who would also have under his authority the police of the surrounding counties, *ib.* 1272, 1273. 1322——
Remarks

Bath—continued.

Remarks as to the police in Bath; witness does not admire the mode of direction'; there is too much jobbing, *Blathwayt* 2094-2097. 2126, 2127——Efforts which have been made in the Bath division to obtain the county constabulary, but without success, *Oakley* 3295 *et seq.*——Particulars as to the adoption of the Superintending Constables' Act in the Bath division of Somerset, *ib.* 3295-3300 ——Statement of the estimated comparative expense of superintending and parish constables, under 5 & 6 Vict., c. 109, and 13 & 14 Vict., c. 20, and a police under 2 & 3 Vict., c. 93, s. 19, for the division of Bath, *Rep.* ii. *App.* 159-161.

See also *Fines.*   *Pay of the Police.*   *Rate,* 2.   *Watch Committee.*

Beadel, James. (Analysis of the Evidence.)—Large occupier of land in Essex, and agent for property in many other counties, 2761-2706——Advantage derived by the land-holders of Essex from the police; the gain by the saving of property is equal to the amount of the police rate, 2767-2770——Witness would prefer renting and occupying land in a county where there is a police to where there is no police; this is the general feeling amongst farmers, 2771-2784——Crime is on the decrease throughout England; the credit of the diminution ought not to be given entirely to the police system, 2784-2789. 2796, 2797——Decrease of vagrancy in Essex; this is nearly all ascribed to the police, 2787-2791——The protection of property by a well organised system of police increases its value, 2792, 2793——Opinion that the police may, to a certain degree, be made a self-supporting force, 2793-2795.

Beddome, John Reynolds, m.d. (Analysis of his Evidence.)—Justice of the peace, residing in Romsey; has held the office of mayor four times, 501, 502——Romsey is under the old Municipal Act; they have no sessions at present, 503——Unsatisfactory condition of the police of Romsey, 504-516——Exertions used by witness to induce the town council to amalgamate the borough police force with the county; memorials presented from the ratepayers; opposition which the proposal met with in council, and rejection thereof, 504 -511——The police establishment of Romsey would be more efficient if united with the county constabulary, 517-519. 523——The additional expenses of the police of Romsey, if amalgamated with the county, would be more than compensated for by the saving of property, 518-522——Great extent to which Romsey is infested with vagrants, 523.

Beer Shops. See *Public Houses.*

Birmingham. Remarks relative to a serious Chartists' riot in Birmingham in 1839, when witness and some of his men were sent down; had there been a good police in the town, things would not have gone so far, *Martin* 3775-3782.

Blathwayt, George William. (Analysis of his Evidence.)—Magistrate for Gloucestershire, Somersetshire, Wiltshire, and the city of Bath; chairman of the court of quarter sessions for the Bath division of Somerset, 2045-2048——Existence of a rural police force in Gloucestershire; amount of the rate necessary for the support of the force, 2049-2051—— Great advantages possessed by Gloucester, where there is a police, over Somerset, where there is none, 2053——Inconvenience arising from there being no police in Somerset-shire, 2053. 2123-2125——Special constables do more harm than good; instance in support of this opinion, 2053-2059——Advantages experienced by the county of Glou-cester from the establishment of the police, 2060-2063——Inefficiency of parochial constables as compared with the police; they are still appointed in Gloucester according to the Act of Parliament; expense of swearing in these constables, 2063-2071——The police in Gloucester would be more efficient if they had the assistance of a similar system of police in the adjoining counties, 2072, 2073.

The proportion of undetected crime is much greater in Somersetshire than in Glouces-tershire; reference to the cases of sheep-stealing, 2074-2080——The want of a police force is felt more by the poorer classes of society than any other; the parish constables will not move in pursuit of offenders until they are paid, 2081-2085——It is very desirable that an uniform system of police should be established throughout the country; if it was universal, the expense would be less, 2086-2088. 2118-2120——Recommendation that the borough police should be consolidated with the county constabulary, 2089-2097—— Remarks as to the police in Bath; witness does not admit the mode of direction; there is too much jobbing, 2094-2097. 2126, 2127.

Explanation of the check in Gloucestershire, by which it is ascertained that the police are upon night patrol, 2098, 2099——The Gloucestershire police is founded upon the model of the Irish police, and works very well, 2100-2106——How far it would be an improvement upon the system of police in Gloucester to have a policeman in every parish, 2104-2117——A general system of police throughout the country would enhance the value of property, 2118-2120——The Gloucester county police serve all summonses; the parish constables give notice to the coroner, 2121—— Evils resulting from the police of Bath being allowed to retain their right of voting at municipal and Parliamentary elec-tions, 2127.

BOROUGH POLICE :

1. *Generally.*
2. *Remarks as to the inefficiency of the Borough Police.*
3. *Evils resulting from the want of co-operation between the Borough and County Police.*
4. *Suggestions for their amalgamation.*
5. *Objections to a consolidation of the Forces.*
6. *Opinion that, in the event of a consolidation, Manchester and Liverpool should be considered separate Districts.*

1. *Generally :*

List of the principal boroughs in Hampshire ; boroughs in which the police force has been consolidated with the county police, *Harris* 23–25——Arrangement with respect to the payment of the force by those boroughs which have been consolidated with the county, *ib.* 26–29——Number of boroughs in Essex having separate police forces ; appointment of the police by the watch committee ; objection to consolidating with the county, as they would lose these appointments, *McHardy* 749–752.

2. *Remarks as to the inefficiency of the Borough Police :*

General inefficiency of the borough police, *McHardy* 752——Frequency of the police officers in boroughs being allowed to pursue their own trade and calling ; impossibility of their performing their duties under such circumstances, *Hamilton* 1033–1039—— Remarks relative to the boroughs in Lancashire having a police of their own separate from the county ; inadequacy of the borough police in the event of a disturbance ; applications made to witness for assistance by several boroughs at the time of the elections, *Woodford* 1541–1589. 1605——It is quite impracticable to establish an efficient police in any borough in accordance with the present system, *Dunne* 1938. 1987——Respects in which the police forces in the boroughs are deficient, *ib.* 1949 ——Boroughs in Stafford that have a police force of their own ; the borough police does not work so well as the county police, and is more expensive, *Hon. A. Talbot* 2616–2630.

3. *Evils resulting from the want of co-operation between the Borough and County Police :*

Opinion of the Committee that the efficiency of all existing police forces is materially impaired by the want of co-operation between the rural constabulary and the police under the control of the authorities of boroughs, or other local jurisdictions, *Rep. ii. p. iv*—— Inconvenience arising from the want of cordial co-operation between the county and borough police, *Harris* 34–39 ; *Stanley* 278, 279 ; *Sir W. Heathcote* 258–265 ; *McHardy* 721–726. 756, 757 ; *Hamilton* 1016–1025. 1040–1043 ; *Redin* 1383–1388 ; *Woodford* 1606 ; *White* 1852–1855 ; *Meredith* 2356. 2357 ; *Sir B. Leighton* 2497–2501 ; *Willis* 2901–2918 ; *Brown* 3061–3066. 3084 ; *Oakley* 3287–3290——It is very rarely that the superintendents of the borough police communicate with the superintendents of the county police in the event of the occurrence of a crime, unless it is a matter of importance, *Harris* 37–39——Want of greater union of action, not only between the boroughs, but between the counties themselves, *McHardy* 680–685.

4. *Suggestions for their amalgamation :*

Recommendation of the Committee, that in order to secure that co-operation which uniformity can alone afford, the smaller boroughs should be consolidated with districts or counties for police purposes, and that the police in the larger boroughs should be under a similar system of management and control to that of the adjoining district or county, and (where practicable) under the same superintendence, by which arrangement a considerable saving would be effected in the general expenditure, *Rep. ii. p. iv.*——Consolidating the borough police with the county force would be attended with the most beneficial results, *Harris* 34–39 ; *Sir W. Heathcote* 258–265 ; *Beddome* 517–519. 523 ; *Hamilton* 1106 ; *Hughes* 1249–1253. 1276. 1324 ; *Redin* 1383–1388 ; *Dover* 1784–1791 ; *Dunne* 1988 ; *Blathwayt* 2089–2097 ; *Meredith* 2343–2355. 2363, 2364 ; *Hon. A. Talbot* 2618. 2630–2633. 2636. 2671 ; *Townley* 2755–2758 ; *Mallalieu* 2842–2850 ; *Willis* 2901–2918 ; *Brown* 3084 ; *Chadwick* 3642——Growing feeling in some of the boroughs in favour of amalgamation with the county constabulary, *Woodford* 1607–1609——The police force of Saffron Walden should be consolidated with the county force ; memorial presented to the magistrates recommending the consolidation of the forces, *Claydon* 3099–3104. 3119–3134——Advantage would result from the amalgamation of the police of the burghs in Scotland with the county forces, *List* 3918–3920 ; *Jones* 4228.

5. *Objections to a consolidation of the Forces :*

No advantage would result from the incorporation of the borough police with the county police, and placing them under one head, *Corbett* 2250–2259 ; *Murray* 4127–4142——Impracticability of amalgamating the borough and county forces, *Murray* 4127–4142.

6. *Opinion*

Reports, 1852–53—*continued.*

BOROUGH POLICE—continued.

     6. *Opinion that, in the event of a consolidation, Manchester and Liverpool should be considered separate Districts :*

Suggestion that all large boroughs having a population of 100,000 should be considered as separate counties, and have a distinct force from the rest of the county, *Harris* 54–61 ——In the event of the amalgamation of the boroughs with the county police of Lancashire, Liverpool and Manchester should not be included, but each of those boroughs should be left as districts by themselves, *Woodford* 1590–1604——Suggestion that Liverpool should remain a separate police district, *Wybergh* 1814, 1815——Witness is not cognizant of the existence of a want of co-operation between the borough police of Liverpool and the Lancashire county police, *ib.* 1816–1819——In the event of the amalgamation of the borough and county forces, Manchester should not be included in the county, but taken as a separate district, *Willis* 2899–2914.

     See also *Andover. Appointments. Brighton. Colchester. County Constabulary. Crime. Expenses of the Force,* I. *Lymington. National Force. Norwich. Romsey. Salisbury. Shrewsbury. Stockton-upon-Tees. Wisbeach.*

Bridgewater Division, Somerset. Statement as to the expenses of the parish constables for the Bridgewater division of Somerset, *Warry* 1342–1344.

Brighton. Statement as to the police force of Brighton ; by whom managed, *Mackay* 1904–1908——Difficulty arising from the police of Brighton not readily co-operating with the county constabulary, *ib.* 1909——*See also Lewes.*

Bristol. Incomplete system of police at Bristol ; a high state of efficiency cannot be obtained whilst the control of the force rests with the watch committee, *Mallalieu* 2835–2841.

Brown, Robert. (Analysis of his Evidence.)—Superintendent of police in the Derwent division of the county of Cumberland, 3030——System of police adopted in the Derwent division ; extent of the force and expense thereof ; a slight increase of the force would render the police a very efficient body, 3031–3060. 3077–3082—— Uselessness of the parish constables generally, 3043–3052. 3070, 3071——Want of co-operation of the police of the towns with those of the Derwent division of the county, 3061–3066. 3084——Inspection of the lodging-houses in the division by the police, and beneficial effect thereof in the decrease of vagrancy, 3067–3072——A night patrol is very necessary for the prevention of crime, 3074–3077——The borough and county police should be amalgamated and placed under one head, 3084.

Buckinghamshire. The system of police adopted in Buckinghamshire is that of superintending constables ; number of divisions into which the county is divided, *Swabey* 824–832 ; *Hamilton* 1006, 1007 ; *Carrington* 3136 *et seq.*——The ratepayers of Bucks are satisfied with the present protection of property, and would be opposed to any alteration in the system of police, *Swabey* 853–859——Number of parochial constables under the superintending constables in Bucks ; amount of their pay and allowances, *Hamilton* 1049–1063——Efficiency of the parish constables under superintendents ; cost of the system, and good working thereof, *Carrington* 3136–3185. 3210. 3215, 3216——Appointment of a constabulary committee in Buckingham for the special supervision of the constables ; the superintending constables make quarterly reports to this committee, *ib.* 3189–3195. 3201–3212——The system in Buckingham is as complete as it is capable of being made under the Act of Parliament by which the superintending constables are appointed, *ib.* 3210.

     See also *Appointments,* 1.   *Lock-up Houses.*   *Rural Police.*   *Superintending Constables,* 2.

Buller, Mr. See *Vagrancy,* 1.

Burglaries. Suppression of burglaries and highway robberies in Hampshire since the establishment of the police ; formerly they were very frequent, *King* 405–414.

Burnardiston, Nathaniel Clarke. (Analysis of his Evidence.)—Chairman of quarter sessions in the county of Essex, 3580, 3581——Great advantages have resulted from the establishment of the police in Essex, 3582–3586——The objections of the ratepayers to the expense of the police has decreased from experience of its beneficial working, 3585, 3586——In consequence of the objections to the expense of a rural police in Essex, an attempt was made to carry into effect a system of local constables under superintending constables ; complete failure of that system, 3587——Saving effected by the Essex county constabulary, as compared with the expense under the system of parish constables ; accuracy of the calculations of Captain M'Hardy upon the subject, 3588–3615——The police is a preventive force, and saves property immensely, 3609. 3616.

Burnardiston, Nathaniel Clarke. (Analysis of his Evidence)—*continued.*

The police of Essex have been of great advantage in the protection of the revenue; frequency of their being engaged in the pursuit of parties who have passed the outer barrier with smuggled goods, 3611——Remarks relative to the crime of sheep-stealing in Essex; diminution of this description of crime since the establishment of the police, 3616-3623——The police of Essex are an efficient night patrol, 3617——Crimes of all descriptions have very much diminished since the establishment of the police, 3624—— The chief constable should have the undivided control, appointment and dismissal of the police constables; any interference of the magistrates or a police committee would be prejudicial to the efficiency of the force, 3625-3637.

C.

Caistor, Lincoln. Evidence generally relative to the frequent depredations committed in Caistor and its neighbourhood from there being no police for the protection of property, *Marris* 1117-1204——Representation made to the magistrates of the want of protection; memorials presented; refusal of the assistance applied for, *ib.* 1120-1138. 1162-1182—— Particulars generally as to the association formed at Caistor for the prevention of crime and punishment of offenders, *ib.* 1146-1152. 1183-1202——Evidence relative to witness being sent down from the metropolitan police force for the detection of crime at Caistor in North Lincolnshire, in consequence of the frequent depredations, *Mathews* 3518, 3519 —— Alarmed state of the district from the numerous crimes committed at the time of witness's arrival; great diminution of crime whilst witness remained in the district, *ib.* 3520-3530. 3538-3555——Witness did not receive any assistance from the parochial constables or the superintending constable whilst on duty at Caistor, *ib.* 3524-3529.

See also Rate, 2.

Calne. See Vagrancy, 3.

Cambridgeshire. Causes which led to the adoption of the rural police in Cambridgeshire, *McHardy* 687. 717-719; *Townley* 2749 *et seq.*——Opinion that the police of the Isle of Ely and Cambridgeshire might be united and placed under one chief constable, *Townley* 2749-2754. 2759-2760.

Capture of Offenders. During the time witness was in the Surrey County Police he apprehended many persons whom the parish constables would not have dared to seize, *Hughes* 1267-1271——Great difficulty in the detection and capture of offenders under the system of parochial constables, *Warry* 1335. 1338-1341. 1371, 1372.

See also Customs' Officers. Fugitive Criminals.

Carlisle. The police force in the city of Carlisle is established under the Municipal Corporation Act, *Redin* 1425-1427——Number of police in the borough; sufficiency of the force; *Redin* 1425-1427; *Fawcett* 2988-2991——Daily average of prisoners in Carlisle gaol for the years 1851, 1852, and part of 1853, *Redin* 1434-1436——The police force of Carlisle is entirely under the control of the watch committee; this is highly objectionable; the appointment and control should be in the hands of the chief constable, *Fawcett* 2989-2993. 2998.——*See also Lodging-houses. Vagrancy, 3.*

Carrington, George, Jun. (Analysis of his Evidence.)—Magistrate for the county of Buckingham, 3135——Adoption of the system of superintending constables in the county; efficiency of the parish constables under superintendents; cost of the system, and good working thereof, 3136-3185. 3210. 3215. 3216——Approval of the system of superintending constables, 3138——Objections to the establishment of a paid constabulary under the Rural Police Act in the county, 3150-3155. 3230-3232——The superintending constables act as inspectors of weights and measures, and also summon coroners' juries, and serve summonses, 3178, 3179——Appointment of a constabulary committee in Buckingham for the special supervision of the constables; the superintending constables make quarterly reports to this committee, 3189-3195. 3201-3212.

The superintending constables would be much more efficient if they had more means of giving remuneration to parochial constables when they are out watching at night, 3196-3200——The system in Buckingham is as complete as it is capable of being made under the Act of Parliament by which the superintending constables are appointed, 3210—— Since the establishment of the superintending constables, crime and vagrancy have been diminished in the county, 3213-3216——Number of lock-up houses under the charge of superintending constables; it is contemplated to furnish all the petty sessional divisions with lock-up houses, 3217-3222——When the arrangement of superintending constables has got thoroughly into operation in Buckinghamshire, it will be sufficient for the preservation of the peace and the protection of property, 3223-3225.

Unwillingness of ratepayers to incur the expense of a rate for the rural police, 3226, 3227——How far the superintending constable has any means of punishing the parish constables, 3228, 3229——Each of the superintending constables acts independently of the others;

Reports, 1852–53—*continued.*

Carrington, George, Jun. (Analysis of his Evidence)—*continued.*

others; they have printed rules for their guidance, 3233-3236——The parochial constables are paid by fees; witness looks upon the system of payment by fees as likely to supply a better class of persons than the payment by salary, 3237-3241——How far the superintending constables have authority to order a night watch, 3242-3244——Remarks relative to the payment of parochial constables in cases of the pursuit of prisoners where no apprehension takes place; there is no uniform practice as to payment in those cases, 3245-3248.

Centralization of Control. Witness is not favourable to a centralization of the police in London; for numerous reasons, it would be anything but advisable, *M‘Hardy* 730——There is no necessity that the system of police should be under general supervision in London, *Chadwick* 3645.——*See* also **Government Control.**

Chadwick, Edwin, C.B. (Analysis of his Evidence.)—Was one of the Commissioners in 1839 who were appointed to inquire into the best means of establishing a constabulary force, 3638——Particulars relative to the Commission; recommended establishment of a paid constabulary in the counties of England and Wales, 3638——The working of the Rural Police Act, considering the measure has been only partially carried out, has been more satisfactory than was anticipated, 3639-3642——Importance of the amalgamation of the borough with the county forces, 3642——A uniform system of police throughout the kingdom would be very advantageous, and would render the expense of the force less in each county than if partially adopted, as at present, 3642-3644——There is no necessity that the system of police should be under general supervision in London, 3645——In forming a national police, it should be formed in districts, with distinct centres; how many distinct centres would be a matter of arrangement, 3645.

With a view of saving expense and giving increased co-operation, it is desirable to place more than one county under the same head or chief constable, 3646——Statement of some of the leading points in the evidence taken before the Commissioners in 1839, which led them to recommend the establishment of a paid constabulary force, 3647——Opinion that the police, where adopted, have been the means of materially decreasing the number and expense of prosecutions, 3648-3652——A good police would be a great saving to the country, by shortening the career of thieves and depredators, 3653——The whole of the existing vagrancy might be put a stop to by means of a good system of police, 3653.

Conclusions set forth in the report of the Constabulary Commissioners, showing that the adoption of a uniform system of police throughout the country would be a great advantage, both in an economical and in a moral point of view, 3654-3656——Proposal that the rates for the support of the police should be levied in districts, a distinction being made between rural and manufacturing districts, 3657-3660——Difficulty with respect to the appointment of the police; the appointments by the county magistrates are as good as can be expected; there would be less jealousy if the appointments were with the Secretary of State, 3661, 3662——With respect to the metropolitan force, it would be improved if there there were more men of education as superior officers, 3662.

Chadwick, Mr. E., C.B. See *Crime.*

Cheshire. Evidence generally relative to the system of police in operation in Cheshire; each hundred has a separate police under the head constable; this system has been found to work well, and is the best system of police that could be established, *Corbett* 2230-2255——Reasons for witness preferring the system of police in operation in Cheshire to any other system, *ib.* 2260-2263. 2276-2279——The magistrates of the different hundreds practically see that the police perform their duties; the supervision is well attended to, *ib.* 2264-2269.——*See* also **Rate,** 2.

Chief Constables. Want of a chief constable over the superintending constables, *Swabey* 851——Having a chief constable at the head of the superintending constables would not improve the system; the parish constables cannot be made efficient police officers, *Dunne* 1962-1966——It is absolutely necessary that the chief officer should have the entire control of the force, *Dunne* 1989, 1990. 2039-2041; *Burnardiston* 3625-3637; *Smart* 4056-4061. 4081-4083——Objections to the chief constable having the undivided control of the police force, *Oakley* 3344-3348. 3370-3374.

    See also **Amalgamation of Counties.**   **Appointments,** 2.   **Dismissals.**   **Districts.**
      Essex, 2.   **Pay of the Police.**   **Watch Committee.**

Chippenden Union. Reduction in the number of vagrants relieved in Chippenham Union from the exertions of the police, *Wayte* 1926, 1927.

Claydon, John. (Analysis of his Evidence.)—Landowner at Saffron Walden, Essex, 3085. 3086——Inefficient state of the police in Saffron Walden; the expense is paid out of the corporate funds, 3087-3099. 3105-3115. 3122-3134——The police force of Saffron Walden should be consolidated with the county force; memorial presented to the magistrates, recommending the consolidation of the forces, 3099-3104. 3119-3134——Parochial constables are perfectly inefficient for police purposes, 3116-3118.

Reports, 1852-53—*continued.*

Clifford, Lieutenant-colonel Henry Morgan, M.P.   (Analysis of his Evidence.)—Chairman of the court of quarter sessions of Herefordshire, 3815——Witness, in conjunction with Mr. Deedes, brought a Bill into Parliament this session, for the amendment of the Act for Superintending Constables, 3816——Opinion in favour of the system of superintending constables, 3817——Beneficial working of the system of superintending constables in the county of Hereford; efficiency of the force; expense of maintaining the system, 3818-3874——List of boroughs in Herefordshire having a police separate from the county; the superintending constables work well with the town police, 3820-3822. 3869——The question of lock-up houses has reference to either system, the rural police or the superintending constables, 3823——Inspection of public-houses and beershops under the system of superintending constables, and general efficiency thereof, 3850, 3851 ——The introduction of the rural police force into the county would be an unnecessary expense, 3872-3874.

Clothing the Police. See *Uniforms.*

Coast Guard. Observations of the Committee on the aid afforded by the rural police for the protection of the revenue, *Rep.* ii. *p.* iv.——Suggestion that the constabulary should perform the duty of the coast guard in all maritime counties; great saving which would thus be effected; or they might be employed with great advantage as auxiliaries to the coast guard, *Harris* 139-165——Occasional employment of the constabulary of Essex as auxiliaries to the coast guard; neither the men nor the ratepayers make any objection, *Harris* 169-182; *Burnardiston* 3611——In the event of the police performing the duty of the coast guard, the Government ought to contribute to its maintenance from the Consolidated Fund, *Harris* 169-178——From the irregularities of the Essex coast, a large coast guard force is necessary, *M'Hardy* 813, 814.

    See also *Arming and Training.*   *Excise Officers.*   *Government Aid.*   *National Force.*

Colchester. Number of police in the borough of Colchester; number witness would consider necessary if the borough were consolidated with the county, *M'Hardy* 753-755—— Instance of the county constabulary being required to act within the borough of Colchester at the time of the election, *ib.* 758-762.

Commission of 1839. Witness was one of the Commissioners in 1839 who were appointed to inquire into the best means of establishing a constabulary force, *Chadwick* 3638—— Particulars relative to the Commission; recommended establishment of a paid constabulary in the counties of England and Wales, *ib.*——Statement of some of the leading points in the evidence taken before the Commissioners in 1839, which led them to recommend the establishment of a paid constabulary force, *ib.* 3647.

Commissioners of Police. The management of the police in Scotland should be vested in paid Commissioners under the Crown, as in the metropolitan police, and answerable to the Lord Advocate, *List* 3967-3981.

Commissioners of Supply. Remarks relative to the local management of the police by the commissioners of supply; there is no difficulty in their continuing to manage police affairs, provided they did not interfere with them in the execution of their duty, *List* 3970-3981——Advantage of placing the management of the police under the commissioners of supply, *Murray* 4143

Compulsory Act. There is no doubt that great advantage would accrue from having a compulsory Act for the establishment of police in those counties which have it not, *Sir W. Heathcote* 258-260; *List* 3959; *Smart* 4030-4032; *Murray* 4118. 4131—— It would be an advantage if all the counties in Scotland were compelled to have a sufficient police force, they having the management, under the direction of a police committee, *Jones* 4244-4246.——See also *National Force.*   *Uniformity of System.*

Consolidation of Force. See *Borough Police.*   *Co-operation.*   *National Force.* *Uniformity of System.*

Constabulary Force. Statement as to the number and cost of the present constabulary force in England and Wales, *Harris* 117-123.

Conveyance of Prisoners. Remarks relative to the conveyance of prisoners to Lindsey gaol; when the superintending constables are on duty they are conveyed to gaol by the parochial constables. *Sir R. Sheffield* 613-617——Decrease in the cost of conveyance of prisoners to gaol in Stafford; this is partly owing to the extension of railways and partly to the police, *Hon. A. Talbot* 2708, 2709——Great saving resulting from the prisoners being conveyed to Maidstone gaol by the metropolitan police instead of by the county, *Mallalieu* 2818-2827.

Co-operation. See *Amalgamation of Counties.*   *Borough Police,* 3. 4.   *County Constabulary.*   *National Force.*

Reports, 1852-53—*continued.*

Corbett, Edwin. (Analysis of his Evidence.)—Magistrate for Cheshire ; vice-chairman of the court of quarter sessions, 2228, 2229——System of police in operation in Cheshire ; each hundred has a separate police under the head constable ; this system has been found to work well, and is the best system of police that could be established, 2230-2255—— No advantage would result from the incorporation of the borough police with the county police, and placing them under one head, 2250-2259——Grounds on which witness would prefer a system of constabulary separate in each hundred of a county, under a chief constable, to having a consolidated county police under one head, 2260-2263. 2276-2279——The magistrates of the different hundreds practically see that the police perform their duties ; the supervision is well attended to, 2264-2269——Cost of the police force in Cheshire ; amount of the rate in the pound, 2270-2275.

Coroners. Observations as to the service of notices on the coroners by the Hampshire police ; saving which has been thereby effected, *Harris* 108-113——If an efficient rural police were established in every county, it would be possible to dispense with the coroner's court ; this would be a great saving of expense, *Oakley* 3349-3353.

    See also *Service of Processes.*

County Constabulary. It would be conducive to the efficiency of a county constabulary if the several forces were united with it, *Harris* 22——Summary of the number of constables proposed to be appointed in each county, provided the Rural Police Act were made compulsory, and the counties and boroughs were consolidated, *ib.* 123——Return showing the expense of carrying out that proposition ; explanation of that return, showing that 62 *l.* 17 *s.* 5 *d.* per man is the probable cost of the constables, if they were established throughout the whole of the kingdom, *ib.* 123-138——The establishment of county police forces has been attended with very beneficial results, *Redin* 1406, 1407——Necessity for the entire co-operation of the county forces with the metropolitan force, *Oakley* 3375-3379.

    See also *Appointments,* 2.   *Metropolitan Police.*   *Pursuit of Offenders.*   *Rural Police.*

County Rate. Statement of the amount of the county rate for the parts of Lindsey, from 1833 to 1853 ; if the Rural Police Act was put in operation, it would more than double the county rate, *Sir R. Sheffield* 637-640——The county rate is based upon a wrong principle ; a uniform county rate for police purposes is very unfair ; the police ought to be appointed and the rate levied according to the population of the various districts, *Denison* 2952 *et seq.*——See also *Rate.*

Crime. State of crime in the county of Cumberland ; in the average of the seven years ending 1852, the convictions are slight, *Redin* 1417-1422——The boroughs, as they are now managed, are the nurseries of crime, *Woodford* 1620——Paper furnished by Mr. E. Chadwick, c. b., with respect to crimes and commitments in the rural districts, *Rep.* ii. *App.* 170, 171.

    See also *Decrease of Crime.*   *Detection of Crime.*   *Metropolitan Police.*   *Petty Offences.*   *Vagrancy.*

Criminal Officer, Scotland. Explanation as to the office of criminal officer in Scotland ; nature of his duties, *Gordon* 2145-2148.

Cumberland. Particulars relative to the constabulary in Cumberland ; there is no rural police, but a system of superintending constables ; these are efficient, as far as they go, but the districts are too wide, *Redin* 1409-1416——Recommendation that the police force should be extended over the county of Cumberland, and the borough police amalgamated therewith ; beneficial effects resulting from the adoption of the rural police in the Allerdale Below division of the county, *Fawcett* 2993-2999——Deficiency of police in Cumberland ; opposition to the establishment of a police force for the county, *ib.* 3010-3014. 3016, 3017.——See also *Crime.*   *Mining Districts.*   *Vagrancy.*

Customs' Officers. Great advantage would result if all the officers employed by the Customs afloat were made special constables, and required to co-operate with the police in the apprehension of offenders who are about to leave the sea-ports of the country, *M'Hardy* 3811, 3812.

D.

Decrease of Crime. Decrease of crime since the establishment of the police in Hampshire, *Harris* 187-193 ; *Stanley* 281-283——Decrease of crime in Essex since the adoption of the police, *Parker* 887, 888. 903-907 ; *Baker* 957-962 ; *Burnardiston* 3624——Illustration of the material decrease of crime in Bath of late, *Hughes* 1222-1225——Decrease of crime in Lancashire since the establishment of the police, *Woodford* 1646, 1647—— The establishment of police in Mid Lothian has been attended with a great diminution and repression of crime in the county, *Gordon* 2168-2173——Diminution of crime which

Reports, 1852-53—*continued.*

Decrease of Crime—continued.

would result if a system of consolidation were carried out throughout the counties of England; decrease of crime in Wilts since the establishment of the police, *Meredith* 2358-2362——Diminution of crime since the establishment of the police in Shropshire; great saving of property effected, *Sir B. Leighton,* 2486. 2493. 2494——Decrease of crime, more particularly of sheep-stealing, in the Isle of Ely, since the establishment of the police, *Townley* 2742-2748——Crime is on the decrease throughout England; the credit of the diminution ought not to be given entirely to the police system, *Beadel* 2784-2789. 2796, 2797.

    See also *Agricultural Property. Andover. Burglaries. Hampshire. Kesteven. Petty Offences. Sheep Stealing.*

Denison, Edmund Beckett, M.P. (Analysis of his Evidence.)—Magistrate for the West Riding of Yorkshire, 2934, 2935——The only system of police in the West Riding is the parochial constables; in some districts superintending constables have been added, 2936-2940——The subject of the rural police has been more than once discussed in the West Riding of Yorkshire, but its establishment has never been determined on in consequence of the expense, 2940-2969——Statement of the expenditure of the West Riding for the years 1850, 1851 and 1852; 2951——The county rate is based upon a wrong principle; a uniform county rate for police purposes is very unfair; the police ought to be appointed and the rate levied according to the population of the various districts, 2952 *et seq.*——All parishes should be compelled to have an efficient police, 2952.

    If the county were divided into districts, according to the number of police that were required, and according to the expense which each district incurred, witness would have no objection whatever to the application of the Rural Police Act, 2953-2956. 2976——Statement of detected crime in the West Riding, notwithstanding there is no rural police; number of prisoners committed to Wakefield House of Correction from 1840 to 1852, distinguishing each year, 2058-2061——The magistrates of the West Riding would not be justified in expending 25,000 *l.* or 30,000 *l.* in establishing a rural police force, 2961, 2962——The Government having done what they have done, ought to appoint a rural police over the whole kingdom, and make the expense of the police a national charge instead of a parochial charge, 2963-2969.

    Expense of the system of superintending constables where introduced in the West Riding, 2971-2974——Carrying out the 27th and 28th clauses of the 3 & 4 Vict. c. 88, which provides for the formation of police districts, would meet witness's views of the justice of the case; the district requiring a greater number of constables should have a greater number allotted to it, but paying proportionably a larger sum, 2974-2982——The Rural Police Act would have been fully carried into effect in the West Riding of York but for the inequality of the application of the rate, 2983——In the event of the 27th and 28th clauses of the Act 3 & 4 Vict., c. 88, being made compulsory, it would be necessary to send commissioners down into the West Riding for the purpose of forming the police districts, 2984, 2985——By a general county rate a greater proportion of rates is thrown upon the agricultural than upon the manufacturing districts; this is the ground of witness's objection to a county rate, 2985.

Derwent Division, Cumberland. System of police adopted in the Derwent division, Cumberland; extent of the force and expenses thereof; a slight increase of the force would render the police a very efficient body, *Brown* 3031-3060. 3077-3082.

Detection of Crime. Comparison with reference to the proportion of the detection of crime in Hampshire as compared with the metropolis, also between London and Gosport, *Harris* 19-21——Readiness of the police of Hants to assist in every possible way, both in the detection and prevention of crime; how far they interfere in the apprehension of poachers and the preservation of game, *Stanley* 305-311——Greater certainty of detection of offences by the police as compared with the parochial constables, *Parker* 881-884; *Sir B. Leighton* 2508, 2509——Statement of detected crime in the West Riding of York, notwithstanding there is no rural police; number of prisoners committed to Wakefield House of Correction from 1840 to 1852, distinguishing each year, *Denison* 2058-2061——The bulk of offences against property and person in the parts of Kesteven are detected and brought to justice by the present means of parochial constables, *Healy* 3437——A good police would be a great saving to the country by shortening the career of thieves and depredators, *Chadwick* 3653.

    See also *Capture of Offenders. Horse Patrol. Mining Districts. of Offenders. Rewards.*   *Electric Telegraph. Night Patrol. Parish Constables.*   *Escape of Criminals. Pursuit*

Detective Police. See *Railway Termini.*

Discipline. Length of time necessary to make a man an efficient policeman; the discipline of the metropolitan force is rapidly improving, *Mallalieu* 2868-2875.

    See also *Arming and Training.*

Dismissals. The chief constable should not have the power of dismissal and removal of constables without an appeal to a committee of magistrates, *Oakley* 3282-3388.

     See also *Appointments,* 1.

Distribution of Force. Return of the distribution of the Essex county constabulary, on 5 April 1842, *Rep.* ii, *App.* 137, 138 —— Similar return on 15 October 1850. *ib.* 156, 157.

District Constables. See *Rural Police.*

Districts. As a remedy for the want of union between the counties, witness proposes that England be divided into four districts, that there should be a general constabulary and a chief constable for each district, *M'Hardy* 726-729 —— If the county were divided into districts, according to the number of police that were required, and according to the expense which each district incurred, witness would have no objection whatever to the application of the Rural Police Act, *Denison* 2953-2956. 2976 —— Carrying out the 27th and 28th clauses of the 3 & 4 Vict. c. 88, which provides for the formation of police districts, would meet witness's views of the justice of the case; the district requiring a greater number of constables should have a greater number allotted to it, but paying proportionately a larger sum, *ib.* 2974-2982 —— In the event of the 27th and 28th clauses of the Act 3 & 4 Vict. c. 88, being made compulsory, it would be necessary to send commissioners down into the West Riding for the purpose of forming the police districts, *ib.* 2984, 2985. —— See also *National Force.*   *Rate.*

Dock Police. See *Liverpool.*

Dover, Henry. (Analysis of his Evidence.)—Chairman of quarter sessions in Norfolk, 1767 —— Great advantage has resulted from the establishment of the police in Norfolk, 1766-1781 —— Vagrancy is one great source of crime, 1775 —— Under the old system of parochial constables pursuit could only be made after offenders by persons capable of paying them, 1776-1778 —— The establishment of a well-regulated police has increased the value of land, 1781 —— Improved mode of conducting prosecutions since the establishment of the police; saving of time and expense from unnecessary witnesses not being brought up, 1782, 1783 —— Considerable benefit would be derived from amalgamating the police of the towns and boroughs with the county police, 1784-1791.

Dumfries. Particulars as to the police of Dumfries; sufficiency of the force for the general wants of the county; expense of the police, *Jones* 4211-4225 —— Inconvenience experienced in Dumfries from there being no police in Cumberland; numerous bands of vagrants that assemble on the borders of the county, *ib.* 4226-4228 —— Patrol of the county of Dumfries by the police, *ib.* 4229, 4230 —— Crimes and offences committed in Dumfries; amount of property lost and recovered in 1852, *ib.* 4231-4234 —— Return of number of police within the county of Dumfries, and the charges of the same, since the year 1842-43 to 1852-53, *Rep.* ii. *App.* 170 —— See also *Lodging Houses.*   *Vagrancy,* 3.

Dunne, John. (Analysis of his Evidence.)—Chief officer of the police force at Norwich, 1929-1937 —— It is quite impracticable to establish an efficient police in any borough town in accordance with the present system, 1938. 1987 —— Inefficiency of the system of police at Norwich, although various alterations and improvements have been made therein, 1939-1946 —— The police rate of Norwich is 2 *d.* in the pound, 1947. 1948 —— Respects in which the police forces in the boroughs are deficient, 1949 —— Efficiency of the rural police in Essex, 1950. 2032 —— The system of superintending constables is most inefficient; it is quite impossible that it should ever become effective; difficulties attending the working of the system, 1951-1953. 1967-1986.

     Expense of the system under superintending constables; impossibility of arriving at the correct amount from the many indirect expenses, 1954-1961. 1974-1978 —— Having a chief constable at the head of the superintending constables would not improve the system; the parish constables cannot be made efficient police officers, 1962-1966 —— Consolidating the borough police with the county force would be attended with the most beneficial results, 1988 —— It is absolutely necessary that the chief officer should have the entire control of the force, 1989, 1990. 2039-2041 —— Inconvenience resulting from both the watch committee and magistrates of Norwich having jurisdiction over the police force, 1991-1993. 2042 —— Complaints of the inhabitants of Norwich that a sufficient supervision is not exercised by the police over the beerhouses; this evil is attributable to the influence of the brewers who are members of the town council and watch committee, 1994-2028. 2039.

     Large number of public-houses and beershops in Norwich; in many of the low public-houses crime is fostered, 1997-2002. 2024-2026 —— The police at Norwich vote generally at all parliamentary and municipal elections; witness's objection was overruled by the watch committee, 2028-2030 —— Tables of fees and allowances to the clerks to the justices for the county of Kent for the performance of their duties under Acts 5 & 6 Vict., c. 109, for the appointment and payment of parish constables, and 13 Vict., c. 20, for amending that Act, and to the constables for the performance of their duties, 2031, 2032:

Reports, 1852–53—*continued.*

Dunne, John. (Analysis of his Evidence)—*continued.*

——The police force of Essex is very effective for the suppression of vagrancy, 2032, 2033 ——An effective police force, upon the principle of that of Essex, could be carried out at a less cost than a superintending constable system, 2032.

Impossibility of suppressing vagrancy under a system of superintending constables, 2034–2037——Uselessness of special constables in cases of riots, 2037——How far there would be any opposition on the part of the city to their police being amalgamated with the rural police, 2038——The present method of appointing the police in Norwich tends much to impair its efficiency, 2042——Average expenses of prosecutions in Essex; from information witness has received, he finds that the average expense of the prosecution of a city prisoner is double that of a county prisoner, 2042-2044——With regard to the superintending constable system in the Dewsbury division in Yorkshire, there is a population of 80,000, and only a superintending constable with parish constables in substitution of the police establishment, 2044.

Durham. Remarks as to the Durham police; insufficiency of the force, *White* 1821–1827.

See also *Rate,* 2.

Duties of the Police. Nature of the supplementary duties performed by the police in Essex beyond the maintenance of the peace; additional duties which they might perform, *M'Hardy* 777–783——Beneficial results of transferring local duties to the county constabulary as experienced in Essex, *Redin* 1464——Nature of the supplemental duties performed by the Lancashire police; saving effected by this arrangement, *Woodford* 1674–1689——If a general system of police were adopted the men might be employed in other duties beyond those of police duty, such as inspectors of weights and measures, service of summonses, &c., *Sir B. Leighton* 2530, 2531; *Mallalieu* 2859-2867——It would be better that the police should do nothing but the duty of policemen, *Hon. A. Talbot* 2694-2698——The prevention of crime is only one of the duties of the police; varied nature of the duties performed by the metropolitan police, *List* 3982–3986.

See also *Inspectors of Weights and Measures. Surveyors of Roads.*

E.

Edinburgh. Edinburgh has a separate police under the jurisdiction of the sheriff, in combination with the city magistrates; the body which has the appointment and management of the police is not a proper one, *Gordon* 2149-2158; *List* 3920-3924——Number of police in Edinburgh, and amount of the police assessment for the city, *Gordon* 2195, 2196——Particulars as to the police force in Edinburgh; annual expense thereof; insufficiency of the force, *List* 3877-3888. 3909-3917.

See also *Lanarkshire. Mid Lothian.*

Elections. See *Voting at Elections.*

Electric Telegraph. If the electric telegraph were in communication with all the police stations throughout the country, it would be very useful in detecting and deterring crime, *Harris* 241, 242; *M'Hardy* 815; *White* 1846-1851; *Oakley* 3357, 3355.

Ely. Particulars as to the establishment of the rural police in the Isle of Ely; increase of the force in 1853; expense of maintaining the force, *Townley* 2713-2723——The Isle of Ely is divided into three districts; no advantage arises from that division; circumstances under which the division took place, *ib.* 2715-2717. 2724, 2729.

See also *Cambridgeshire. Decrease of Crime. Vagrancy,* 3.

Escape of Criminals. The escape of criminals is facilitated by the uncertainty of detection; a general and efficient system of police would tend to shorten the criminal career of offenders, *M'Hardy* 788, 789——The difficulty from the want of unity of action between the counties greatly facilitates the escape of offenders, *Hughes* 1261-1266; *M'Hardy* 3811——Escape of criminals across the border from the jurisdiction of the Mid-Lothian police in Lanarkshire, *Gordon* 2174, 2175.

ESSEX :

    1. *Generally.*
    2. *Papers laid before the Committee.*

    1. *Generally :*

Number of the constabulary force in Essex; it is calculated to insure the greatest amount of efficiency practicable under existing arrangements, *M'Hardy* 678, 679—— The adoption of an efficient constabulary in Essex obliged the adjoining counties, with the exception of Kent, to follow the example, *ib.* 686, 687. 713-716——Public expression of opinion on the part of the magistrates as to the Essex constabulary being highly
                                valuable

ESSEX—continued.

     1. *Generally*—continued.

valuable and essentially necessary, *Parker* 892-897——General efficiency of the Essex police, *Hamilton* 1069-1074; *Redin* 1380-1382; *Dunne* 1950. 2032; *Oakley* 3259, 3260. 3380, 3381; *Burnardiston* 3582-3586.

     2. *Papers laid before the Committee.*

Reports of the chief constable to the magistrates of the county of Essex in quarter sessions assembled, on 5 April 1842 and 15 October 1850, with respect to the police force, *Rep.* ii. *App.* 128-130. 141-146—— Return of the number of persons apprehended and summoned, offences committed, and results, from 7 April to 30 June 1840, *ib.* 131 ——Similar return, from 1 July to 20 October 1840, *ib.*——Similar return, from 21 October 1840 to 5 January 1841, *ib.* 132——Similar return, from 6 January to 6 April 1841, *ib.*—— Similar return, from 7 April to 29 June 1841, *ib.* 133——Similar return, from 30 June to 19 October 1841, *ib.*——Similar return, from 20 October 1841 to 4 January 1842, *ib.* 134——Abstract from the calendars for the years 1839, 1840 and 1841, *ib.*

Return of the number of prisoners committed for trial, as shown by the calendars of the county of Essex for the years 1840 and 1841, detailing the sentences, and defining those apprehended by the county police from the metropolitan police, railway police, local, parish constables, and others, *Rep.* ii. *App.* 135—— Return, showing the number of police constables in the county of Essex under Act 2 & 3 Vict., c. 93, distinguishing each class or denomination, and the rate of payment made to each; including, also, a return of the number of police constables stationed in each petty sessional division in the said county, with the name and population of such divisions, and the amount paid to the county police rate by each division, together with an account in detail of the several items of expenditure in 1849, *ib.* 147——Return of the authorised force in the county of Essex, *ib.* 155.

     See also *Borough Police,* 1.   *Coast Guard.*   *Decrease of Crime.*   *Distribution of the Force.*   *Expenses of the Force,* II. 1.   *Local Constables.*   *Lock-up Houses.*   *Metropolitan Police.*   *Night Patrol.*   *Rate,* 2.   *Rural Police.*   *Sheep Stealing.*   *Vagrancy,* 3, 4.   *Workhouse Riots.*

Excise Officers. The excise officers do not work well with the police of Dumfries; there exists a jealousy of the police interfering with smuggling, *Jones* 4242, 4243.

     See also *Illicit Distillation.*

EXPENSES OF THE FORCE:

     I. *Generally.*

     II. *In particular Counties* :

         1. Essex.
         2. Lancashire.
         3. Norfolk.
         4. Shropshire.
         5. West Riding of York.

     I. *Generally* :

Observations of the Committee as to the cost of the rural police force; the full extent of the indirect and undefined expense of the parochial constables, it is difficult to ascertain, but it greatly exceeds the amount at which it is generally estimated, *Rep.* ii. p. iii. ——How far the expense of the constabulary in the county and boroughs together would be increased by the union of the boroughs with the county, *Harris* 30-33——The expense of the police force would be diminished if there were one uniform system of police instead of one for each county, *Hughes* 1296-1298——Considering the question of efficiency, the expense of a well-organised police force is not greater than that of the parish constables, *Redin* 1449-1451——The amalgamation of the boroughs and the county would not necessitate an additional expense, *Woodford* 1619, 1620.

Remarks relative to the expense of the system under superintending constables; impossibility of arriving at the correct amount, from the many indirect expenses, *Dunne* 1954-1961. 1974-1978——An effective police force, upon the principle of that of Essex, could be carried out at a less cost than a superintending constable system, *ib.* 2032—— Calculation with respect to the expenses of police constables and parish constables, showing that the parish constable making his own charges in his own county is a much more costly person than a police constable, *Meredith* 2422-2431—— Statement showing the comparative expense of superintending constables and parish constables as compared with the rural police; examination thereon as to the data on which witness calculates the saving of the police force, *Oakley* 3295-3338——Considering the efficiency of the rural police, as compared with the inefficiency of the parish constables, the former system is the cheapest of the two, *Smith* 3690——The fear of expense, which has prevented certain districts from adopting the police, has been a very unwise economy, *Smart* 4034.

EXPENSES OF THE FORCE—continued.

II. *In particular Counties:*

1. Essex:

Total expense of the police in Essex in 1852, and amount of the set-off from allowances from Government and other sources, *Mc Hardy* 810–812——The increased expenses of the police have been more than repaid by the advantage derived from their services, *Parker* 899–901. 936–950; *Baker* 963. 1003; *Burnardiston* 3585, 3586——Remarks relative to the expense of the present system of police as contrasted with the old system of constables, *Baker* 978–989——Statement of the savings and earnings effected by the Essex county constabulary, as compared with the expense of the system of parochial constables, *Mc Hardy* 3389–3396; *Burnardiston* 3588–3615——Return of the probable annual expense of the Essex county constabulary, *Rep.* ii. *App.* 140.

2. Lancashire:

Division of the county of Lancaster into districts, each of which pays its police expenses separately, *Woodford* 1532–1537——The expense of the constabulary in Lancashire is rather under than over 2½ *d.* in the pound, *ib.* 1720.

3. Norfolk:

Great expense of the police in Norfolk; the ratepayers generally are not acquainted with the amount of rate which they contribute to the police force, *Holmes* 1725–1730.

4. Shropshire:

Although the expense of the police is larger than that of the parish constables, there have been no complaints by the rate-payers, as the advantage of the system is so much greater, *Sir B. Leighton,* 2523–2527.

5. West Riding of York:

Statement of the expenditure of the West Riding for the years 1850, 1851 and 1852, *Denison* 2951——The magistrates of the West Riding would not be justified in expending 25,000 *l.* or 30,000 *l.* in establishing a rural police force, *ib.* 2961, 2962——Expense of the system of superintending constables where introduced in the West Riding, *ib.* 2971–2974.

See also *Andover.*   *Audit of Accounts.*   *Borough Police,* 4.   *County Constabulary.*   *Districts.*   *Edinburgh.*   *Hampshire.*   *National Force.*   *Rate.*   *Scotland.*   *Superintending Constables,* 1.   *Uniformity of System.*

Extra Allowances. Manner in which the extra allowances of the constables in Hants are regulated, *Harris* 69–72.

F.

Fawcett, John. (Analysis of his Evidence.)—Magistrate for the borough of Carlisle, 2986, 2987——Number of police in the borough; sufficiency of the force, 2988–2991——The police force of Carlisle is entirely under the control of the watch committee; this is highly objectionable; the appointment and control should be in the hands of the chief constable, 2989–2993. 2998——Recommendation that the police force should be extended over the county of Cumberland, and the borough police amalgamated therewith; beneficial effects resulting from the adoption of the rural police in the Allerdale Below division of the county, 2993–2999——Advantage derived from the adoption of the Lodging House Act in the borough of Carlisle; constant examination of the lodging-houses by the police, 3000–3003. 3015——Great extent to which vagrancy exists in Cumberland; opinion that vagrancy is the source of all the ordinary minor crimes in the rural district, 3004–3007——It would be very desirable to establish a general system of police throughout the kingdom, 3008, 3009——The police might be usefully employed in the inspection of roads, as road surveyors, 3010, 3011——Deficiency of police in Cumberland; opposition to the establishment of a police force for the county, 3012–3014. 3016, 3017——Possibility of effecting a system of patrols in the wild parts and mining districts of Cumberland, if the rural police were established, 3018–3023——The establishment of a police force all over the country would have the effect of materially checking vagrancy, 3024–3329.

Fees and Allowances. Tables of fees and allowances to the clerks to the justices for the county of Kent, for the performance of their duties under the Acts 5 & 6 Vict., c. 109, for the appointment and payment of parish constables, and 13 Vict., c. 20, for amending that Act, and to the constables for the performance of their duties, *Dunne* 2031, 2032——The parochial constables are paid by fees; witness looks upon the system of payment by fees as likely to supply a better class of persons than the payment by salary, *Carrington* 3237–3241——Evils arising from the payment of parish constables by fees; frequency of

Fees and Allowances—continued.

of their making cases for the sake of the fees, *Oakley* 3270-3276. 3359——Table of fees and allowances, made pursuant to the 17th section of the 3 & 4 Vict., c. 88, *Rep* ii., *App.* 139——Statement of the allowances to constables for the county of Essex, *ib.* 149 ——Allowances to the constabulary attending courts in Scotland, *ib.* 165.

    See also *Assizes.*   *Extra Allowances.*   *Fines.*   *Pay of the Police.*   *Rewards.*

Fennick, Andrew Robert. (Analysis of his Evidence.)—Visiting magistrate of Northumberland, residing at Netherton, 524, 525——Evidence relative to the county police of Northumberland; number of men of which the force consists; efficiency of the force; decrease of crime since the establishment of the force, from offences being more frequently detected, 526-571——The parish constables are a very inefficient body of men, 546—— Employment of the police in the service of all warrants and summonses, 553-561—— The magistrates of Northumberland have occasionally applied to the police authorities at Newcastle for assistance; instance of this at the election last year at Hexham, 571.

Fines. Statement with respect to a place not far from Bath, where the police are allowed to fine the prisoners without their going before a magistrate; fees received from this source, *Hughes* 1316-1322.

Fires. Decrease of fires in Essex since the establishment of the police, *M'Hardy* 806-808.——See also *Incendiarism.*

Fugitive Criminals. Inefficiency of the police at present, from the difficulty of tracing a culprit from the country to the towns, *Harris* 237-240.

    See also *Customs' Officers.*   *Pursuit of Offenders.*

G.

Game Laws. How far the police of Essex are indirectly employed in the preservation of game, *M'Hardy*, 786, 787.——See also *Detection of Crime.*

Glasgow. Particulars as to the police force of Glasgow; extent of the force, and its sufficiency; rate of assessment, *Smart* 4011-4021. 4035-4039——It is only in certain portions of the county that the police have been adopted; reason why the whole of the districts have not adopted the Police Act, *ib.* 4022-4029——The control of the city police is vested in a committee of the town council, *ib.* 4047-4055——Cost of the police of Glasgow; rate of pay of the men, and salaries of the officers, *ib.* 4087, 4088. 4099, 4100. 4105-4111——Return shewing the number of places, beyond the municipal boundary, to which the Glasgow police have been sent to preserve the peace at various times since the year 1847, *Rep.* ii., *App.* 168——Strength of the city of Glasgow police force, 20 June 1853, *ib.*——Return of persons apprehended by the Glasgow police charged with crimes committed in other counties, between 1 January 1852 and 1 June 1853, *ib.* 169.

    See also *Lodging Houses.*

Gloucestershire. Existence of a rural police force in Gloucestershire; amount of the rate necessary for the support of the force, *Blathwayt* 2049-2051——Advantages experienced by the county of Gloucester from the establishment of the police, *ib.* 2053. 2060-2063—— The police in Gloucester would be more efficient if they had the assistance of a similar system of police in the adjoining counties, *ib.* 2072, 2073——The Gloucestershire police is founded upon the model of the Irish police, and works very well, *ib.* 2100-2106—— How far it would be an improvement upon the system of police in Gloucester to have a policeman in every parish, *ib.* 2104-2117.——See also *Night Patrol.*

Gordon, John Thomson. (Analysis of his Evidence.)—Sheriff of the city of Edinburgh and Mid-Lothian, 2128, 2129——Statement as to the system of police generally in Scotland; the system is different in the cities and the counties, 2130——Act passed in 1839, which permitted, but did not enjoin, the counties to levy assessments for maintaining a constabulary force; some counties have adopted the Act, 2130-2134——Nature and extent of the police force in Mid-Lothian; management of the force by the head of the police, subject to the control of the police committee, 2135-2144. 2176-2186——Explanation as to the office of criminal officer in Scotland; nature of his duties, 2145-2148——Edinburgh has a separate police, under the jurisdiction of the sheriff in combination with the city magistrates; the body which has the appointment and management of the police is not a proper one, 2149-2158——The county police in Scotland are much superior men to the city police; jealousy existing between the forces, 2151-2153.

    The assessments in Scotland are laid upon the old valuation; the chief burden of the assessment falls upon the land, and not upon trades and houses; this is one cause why the most important counties have not adopted the police system, 2159-2167. 2189-2191 ——The establishment of police in Mid-Lothian has been attended with a great diminution and repression of crime in the county, 2168-2173——Escape of criminals across the border from the jurisdiction of the Mid-Lothian police in Lanarkshire, 2174. 2175 ——Great

Gordon, John Thomson. (Analysis of his Evidence)—*continued.*

——Great disorder in Lanarkshire as compared with Mid-Lothian; the proposition for establishing a paid police in Lanark has often been mooted and always rejected, 2187-2192——An uniform system of amalgamated police force for the whole of Scotland would be desirable, 2193, 2194. 2224-2227——Since the establishment of police in Mid-Lothian the value of property has increased, from the greater security, 2194.

Number of police in Edinburgh, and amount of the police assessment for the city, 2195, 2196——The police commission is a body very little calculated to manage the police department with efficiency, and should be abolished; their power should be vested in the town council, 2197-2208——Principles upon which an uniformly organised system of police throughout Scotland should be maintained, 2210-2214. 2225-2227 ——A general system would be much more economical, as well as more efficient, than the present system; the advantages of a general system would more than counterbalance any extra charge upon the counties, 2215-2220——In those counties in Scotland where the police have not been introduced, parish constables are employed, 2221-2223.

Government Aid. Opinion of the Committee that, taking into consideration the aid gratuitously afforded by the rural police for the protection of the revenue, the valuable services it has rendered for the maintenance of order, and in promoting the observance of the laws, in reducing the cost of prosecutions, and the effectual protection it gives to life and property, it is a matter worthy the consideration of The House whether some aid should not be afforded by the Government towards defraying the cost of an improved and extended system of police, without essentially interfering with the local management of that force, *Rep.* ii. *p.* iv.——*See* also *Coast Guard.*

Government Control. The expenditure would be much less if there were a general force under the control of Government; one chief constable would be sufficient to superintend three counties instead of one county, *Hon. A. Talbot* 2700.

See also *Centralization of Control.   National Force.*

H.

Hamilton, William. (Analysis of his Evidence.)—Superintending constable, residing at Wendover, Bucks, 1004, 1005——The present system of police in Bucks is that of parish constables under superintending constables, 1006, 1007——Inefficiency of the system of superintending constables, 1008-1015——Remarks as to the police in boroughs; want of co-operation between the county and borough forces, 1016-1025 ——The appointment and control of the police in Bucks is very inefficient, 1026-1028——Great difficulty experienced by the superintending constables in getting any effectual assistance from the parish constables, 1028-1032——Frequency of the police officers in boroughs being allowed to pursue their own trade and calling; impossibility of their performing their duties under such circumstances, 1033-1039——Want of co-operation between the county and borough police, 1040-1043——Inefficiency of the parochial constabulary; the county force is far superior and less expensive, according to the efficiency of its members, 1044-1049. 1101, 1102.

Statement as to the number of parochial constables under the superintending constables in Bucks; amount of their pay and allowances, 1049-1063——The system of parochial constables under superintending constables cannot be made a perfect system of police, 1064-1078——General efficiency of the Essex police; it is better than the Herts police, 1069-1074——Observations relative to the lock-ups in Bucks, 1079-1091. 1103-1105 ——Frequency of the parish constables allowing motives of private interest to interfere with the performance of their duty, 1092-1093——Impossibility of the different systems of police in force in adjoining counties working well, 1094——Uselessness of special constables in cases of disturbance, 1095-1099——Witness knows of no plan by which the parish constables can be made effective under the present law, 1100——The police in rural towns and boroughs ought not to be independent of the rural constabulary; they would work better under one head, 1106——Remarks upon the system of appointment and dismissal of constables in Bucks, 1107-1113.

Hampshire. The adoption of the police under the Act has proved efficacious in Hampshire; documents proving that crime has decreased in the county since the police force has been established, delivered in, *Harris* 10-18——Summary of the number of felonies affecting property that have been committed in each year from 1847 to 1851, within the jurisdiction of the Hants constabulary, showing the amount recovered, first amount of loss, the number of persons committed for trial, and the number of undetected offences, *ib.* 18——Total number of the police force in Hampshire, *ib.* 60. 64-68——Counties bordering on Hampshire which have not a police force; inconvenience resulting to Hampshire from the bad characters congregated on the borders of the adjoining counties,

Reports, 1852-53—*continued.*

Hampshire—continued.

ties, *Harris* 82-85——Treasurer's account of the county of Hampshire, showing the receipts on account of the police force for 1852; amount of the expenditure, *ib.* 86-88—— Extract from the report of the committee on county expenditure; with respect to the saving effected by the establishment of the police force in Hampshire, *ib.* 115— —The police system as introduced into Hampshire has been universally successful, *Sir W. Heathcote* 244, 245——Circumstances attending the original establishment of the police in Hampshire; the whole of the county has been unanimous from the beginning to the end upon the subject of the adoption of the force, *ib.* 267——The present system of police in Hampshire is very satisfactory; anxiety of the population to get employment in the police; rate of pay, *Stanley* 321-330. 334.

See also *Appointments*, 2.   *Borough Police*, 1.   *Decrease of Crime.*   *Rate*, 2.
Sheep Stealing.   *Vagrancy*, 3. 4.

Harris, Captain William Charles. (Analysis of his Evidence.)—Commands the constabulary in Hampshire, 1, 2——Return of the several counties that have adopted the provisions of the Constabulary Act for the whole county, and for parts only, as also the counties which continue the system of parochial constables, 3-9 ——The adoption of the police under the Act has proved efficacious in Hampshire; documents proving that crime has decreased in the county since the police force has been established, delivered in, 10-18——Summary of the number of felonies affecting property that have been committed in each year from 1847 to 1851 within the jurisdiction of the Hants constabulary, showing the amount recovered, first amount of loss, the number of persons committed for trial, and the number of undetected offences, 18——Comparison with reference to the proportion of the detection of crime in Hampshire as compared with the metropolis, also between London and Gosport, 19-21.

It would be conducive to the efficiency of a county constabulary if the several forces were united with it, 22——List of the principal boroughs in Hampshire; boroughs in which the police force has been consolidated with the county police, 23-25——Arrangement with respect to the payment of the force by those boroughs which have been consolidated with the county, 26-29——How far the expense of the constabulary in the county and boroughs together would be increased by the union of the boroughs with the county, 30-33——Inconveniences resulting from the police of the boroughs not being incorporated in the police of the county; want of co-operation in the force, 34-39—— It is very rarely that the superintendents of the borough police communicate with the superintendents of the county police in the event of the occurrence of a crime, unless it is a matter of importance, 37-39——The five men in the borough of Andover are constantly changed, 40——The borough of Lymington has lately joined the county; benefits of the arrangement, 41.

State of crime in the borough of Romsey; this borough is not consolidated with the county, 42-44——Return of the number of felonies affecting property that have been committed in the Romsey division, the first amount of loss, the amount recovered, the number of persons committed for trial, and the number of undetected cases, between 1 January and 31 December 1850; 44——Return of the number of offences against property that have come to the knowledge of the Hants constabulary as having been committed within the borough of Romsey during the year 1850; 44——The magistrates and authorities of the boroughs which have coalesced with the county have no voice in the appointment, promotion or dismissal of the constables; they are all county constables, and the chief constable of the county has the sole jurisdiction over them, 45, 46 ——Appointments should be left solely with the chief constable, 47-52.

A valuation should be made of the boroughs, the same as of the county, and then they should contribute to one general rate, 53——All large boroughs having a population of 100,000 should be considered as separate counties, and have a distinct force from the rest of the county, 54-61——Total number of the police force in Hampshire, 58, 64-68——Amount of the police rate in the pound, 60——The consolidation of the borough and county police would lighten the rate, 62, 63. 77——Manner in which the extra allowances of the constables are regulated, 69-72——Amount of stoppage per head for the superannuation fund; age at which the men are entitled to superannuation, 73, 74——Extent of the police force in Southampton; insufficiency of the force, 75, 76——Importance of the constabulary being constantly shifted; impossibility of any man doing his duty if locally connected, 78-80. 91-93.

Counties bordering on Hampshire which have not a police force; inconvenience resulting to Hampshire from the bad characters congregated on the borders of the adjoining counties, 82-85——Treasurer's account of the county of Hampshire, showing the receipts on account of the police force for 1852; amount of the expenditure, 86-88 ——Manner in which the police force are lodged; divisional stations erected in Hampshire for their accommodation, 94-107——Observations as to the service of notices on the coroners by the Hampshire police; saving which has been thereby effected, 108-113—— Extract from the report of the committee on county expenditure, with respect to the saving effected by the establishment of the police force in Hampshire, 115.

Harris, Captain William Charles. (Analysis of his Evidence)—*continued.*

Number and cost of the present constabulary force in England and Wales, 117–123——Summary of the number of constables proposed to be appointed in each county, provided the Rural Police Act were made compulsory, and the counties and boroughs were consolidated, 123——Return showing the expense of carrying out this proposition; explanation of that return, showing that 62 *l.* 17 *s.* 5 *d.* per man is the probable cost of the constables if they were established throughout the whole of the kingdom, 123–138——Suggestion that the constabulary should perform the duty of the coast-guard in all maritime counties; great saving which would thus be effected; or they might be employed with great advantage as auxiliaries to the coast-guard, 139–165——Great benefit would result from training the police to the use of arms, 166–168. 212–227——Occasional employment of the constabulary as auxiliaries to the coast-guard; neither the men nor the ratepayers make any objection, 169–182.

In the event of the police performing the duty of the coast-guard, the Government ought to contribute to its maintenance from the Consolidated Fund, 169–178——Suppression of vagrancy in Hampshire since the establishment of the police, 183–186. 205–208——Decrease of both petty offences and crimes of a higher class since the establishment of the police in Hampshire, 187–193——Arrangements under which the constables take charge of the vagrants who apply to the union workhouses, 194–208——Popularity of the police force in the county, 209–211——Amount that might be saved in the cost of prosecutions by the establishment of a consolidated police, 228——There is no definite age at which men cease to be policemen, 229, 230——Forming the police into something like a military organisation would be the best thing for the country, 231, 232——If there were a national police there would be no jealousy whatever; want of co-operation between the borough and county police from the jealousy which exists, 233–236.

Inefficiency of the police at present, from the difficulty of tracing a culprit from the county to the towns, 237–240——In the event of a general police being established, great benefit would result from having a detective constable at the terminus of every railway, 241——If the elective telegraph were in communication with all the police stations throughout the country, it would be very useful in detecting crime, 241, 242.

[Second Examination.]—Evidence as to the efficiency of the county constabulary over the superintending constables in following in pursuit of criminals, 674, 675.

Harwich. Owing to the inefficiency of the Harwich constables, an application has been made for the assistance of some of the Essex police to keep the peace during the election for the borough, *M'Hardy* 3809.

Healy, Richard. (Analysis of his Evidence.)—Chief constable of the hundred of Aveland, in the parts of Kesteven, Lincolnshire, 3397, 3398——In the parts of Kesteven there is a separate jurisdiction from the other portions of the county, 3899, 3400——There are no police in the parts of Kesteven; there are only the ordinary parish constables, 3401–3404——State of crime in the parts of Kesteven; decrease of crime from the improved habits of the people, 3405–3411. 3464–3473——Remarks relative to Stowe Green fair; steps taken to organise the parochial constables, so as to repress crime at that assemblage, 3412–3123. 3428–3430. 3497——Parish constables could, by a proper selection and by proper remuneration, be made as effective a police force as the requirements of a rural district would demand, 3424–3427. 3479–3488——Statement of the number of committals to the house of correction for the parts of Kesteven, for the eight years, 1845 to 1852; causes to which the fluctuations therein are attributable, 3430–3436. 3463.

The bulk of offences against property and person in the parts of Kesteven are detected and brought to justice by the present means of parochial constables, 3437——Amount of rate which is levied for county purposes in the parts of Kesteven, 3438–3442——The Kesteven division of the county of Lincoln does not require a rural police; the ratepayers are well satisfied with the present state of things, 3444–3446——The parish constables are very badly paid; with better pay they might be made a more efficient body, 3447–3451. 3480——Farmers paying 100 *l.* a-year rent in Kesteven division do not pay 17 *s.* for the services performed by the constables, 3452–3455.

Particulars as to the local associations in the parts of Kesteven for the detection and prosecution of felons; witness never knew of one of these voluntary associations breaking up from the non-payment of the subscriptions, 3456–3462——Great difficulty of the poorer classes recovering property and pursuing offenders, 3473–3478——Remarks as to vagrancy in the parts of Kesteven, 3490–3492——The parish constables in Kesteven division are not constantly employed in the detection and prevention of crime; they follow their several occupations; the duties of the constables are almost a sinecure, 3493–3502——Nature of witness's duties as high constable of the parts of Kesteven; he has but little to do with the parish constables, 3497–3509. 3516——Number of high constables in the parts of Kesteven; amount of their pay, 3503–3506. 3510–3516.

Heathcote.

Reports, 1852-53—*continued.*

Heathcote, Sir William. (Analysis of his Evidence.)—Late Member for Hampshire, and late chairman of the quarter sessions, 243——The police system, as introduced into Hampshire, has been universally successful, 244, 245——The appointment of the police is a great economical advantage; the value of property is increased by an efficient police, 246, 247——Inefficiency of the parochial constables for the protection of property and the prevention of crime; they could not be rendered efficient except at great expense, 248-252 ——It is very desirable for the poorer classes of society that there should be a rural police; there are several aspects in which it is so, 253, 254. 268, 269——A uniform system of police would be very advantageous, 255——Diminution of petty offences since the establishment of the police in Hampshire, 256, 257——Great benefit would arise from the destruction of the subordinate jurisdiction of the boroughs as to the police; want of cordial co-operation between the borough and county police, 258-265——There is no doubt that great advantage would accrue from having a compulsory Act for the establishment of the police in those counties which have it not, 258-260——Circumstances attending the original establishment of the police in Hampshire; the whole of the county has been unanimous, from the beginning to the end, upon the subject of the adoption of the force, 267.

Herefordshire. Evidence generally as to the beneficial working of the system of superintending constables in the county of Hereford; efficiency of the force; expense of maintaining the system, *Clifford* 3818-3874.——*See also Superintending Constables,* 2.

High Constables. Existence of high constables in Norfolk; nature of their duties; these duties might be performed by the police, *Postle* 2577-2581. 2594-2597——Nature of witness's duties as high constable of the parts of Kesteven, *Healy* 3497-3509. 3516 ——Number of high constables in the parts of Kesteven; amount of their pay, *ib.* 3503-3506. 3510-3516.

Highway Robberies. See *Burglaries.* *Horse Patrol.* *Night Patrol.*

Holmes, Reverend John. (Analysis of his Evidence.)—Magistrate for Norfolk, 1721—— Existence of a police force in Norfolk since 1840; 1722-1724——Gross expense of the police in Norfolk; the ratepayers generally are not acquainted with the amount of rate which they contribute to the police force, 1725-1730——Extent of the police force of Norfolk, 1731——Recommendations of Captain Black, the chief constable of Norfolk for the erection of lock-ups and stations; great saving contemplated by carrying out these arrangements, 1732-1754——Expenditure on the police force; the expense is more than repaid by the great security of property, 1755-1764——There is no doubt that the establishment of the police has been of great advantage to the county, 1762. 1765.

Horse Patrol. A horse patrol is most inefficient for the detection of crime; witness would never recommend its introduction except for supervision, *M'Hardy* 796.

Huddersfield. Statement as to witness being sent down to Huddersfield in 1837, with some of his men, upon the occasion of a serious disturbance in opposition to the poor laws, *Martin* 3737-3741.

Hughes, Alfred. (Analysis of his Evidence.)—Chief of the police in the city and borough of Bath, 1205, 1206——Strength of the police force of Bath; the force has always been found sufficient for the maintenance of the public peace, 1207-1212. 1220. 1309, 1310 ——Remarks relative to the fees or rewards paid to the police for special services, 1213-1215——Ready assistance given by the city of Bath police to the forces of the adjoining counties, 1216-1219——Illustration of the material decrease of crime in Bath of late, 1222-1225——The police are under the control of the magistrates and the watch committee: inconvenience arising from the existence of the two jurisdictions, 1226-1238. 1277-1285. 1322-1324——Pay of the police of Bath; manner in which the officers are paid for pursuing offenders in the county, 1239-1248——Necessity for amalgamating the police of all the cities and boroughs with the county police, to insure uniformity of action, 1249-1253. 1324.

It is not possible to bring the system of superintending constables into effective operation, more especially in the county of Northumberland, 1254-1266. 1286——The rivalry and jealousy of the constables of the different police forces is extremely likely to conduce to the escape of a prisoner, 1261-1266——During the time witness was in the Surrey county police he apprehended many persons whom the parish constables would not have dared to seize, 1267-1271——The present method of appointment and payment of the police of Bath militates against its efficiency; it would be a good thing to give jurisdiction over the city police to some authority who would also have under his authority the police of the surrounding counties, 1272, 1273. 1322.

Existence of a great deal of crime in the county of Somerset, 1274-1276——Instance showing the necessity for a co-operative system of police, 1276——Amount of the watch rate in Bath, 1287, 1288——The evils of the absence of police in the surrounding counties are very largely felt in the towns, 1289-1293——Instances showing that the parish constabulary are not of the slightest use, 1293-1295——The expense of the police force

Reports, 1852-53—*continued.*

Hughes, Alfred. (Analysis of his Evidence)—*continued.*

would be diminished if there were one uniform system of police, instead of one for each county, 1296-1298——Disadvantage of the police being locally connected; in the event of the establishment of one uniform system, the men could be shifted, 1299-1304——The rural police system, as it is established in Surrey and Essex, is as perfect as the limited cost will permit, 1305——A uniform system throughout the country would be a great improvement upon the present system, 1306-1308——A very good and efficient police might be established in the county of Northumberland at almost the same cost as the parish constables, 1311-1313——With reference to Teignmouth, Shields and Newcastle, the police force is very insufficient; the amalgamation of such a district would be a matter of importance to all those places, 1314-1316——Statement with respect to a place not far from Bath, where the police are allowed to fine the prisoners without their going before a magistrate; fees received from this source, 1316-1322.

I.

Illicit Distillation. The police force of Stafford has been very useful to the inland revenue in the detection of illicit stills, *Hon. A. Talbot* 2689-2693.

Incendiarism. There have been no incendiary fires in Hampshire for several years past, *King* 382-384.——*See* also *Fires.*

Inspection of Lodging Houses. See *Lodging Houses.*

Inspectors of Weights and Measures. Advantage of the duties of inspectors of weights and measures being performed by the police, *Parker* 878-880. 932-935; *Woodford* 1674-1680; *Meredith* 2381-2384; *Postle* 2557. 2566, 2567——The superintending constables in Buckingham act as inspectors of weights and measures, and also summon coroners' juries, and serve summonses, *Carrington* 3178, 3179——Proposed employment of the police as inspectors of weights and measures; amount paid to the inspectors; if the police did the duty the whole amount would go the country, *Oakley* 3326-3337——Return showing the different sums received in the certain years for " comparing examining, and stamping" weights and measures in Essex; also the sums received under the head of fines, together with the annual expense to which the county was subjected, exclusive of these sums, *Rep.* ii. *App.* 150——Return, showing the same results since the duties have been performed by the county constabulary, *ib.*

See also *Duties of the Police*

Irish Police. See *Gloucestershire.*

Irving, George Vere. (Analysis of his Evidence.)—Proprietor of an estate in the Upper Ward of Lanarkshire, 4165——Discussion which has taken place relative to adopting the Police Act in Lanark; causes from which the non-adoption of the Act proceeded, 4166-4170 ——State of the neighbourhood of the Upper Ward of Lanark; establishment of a voluntary police, 4171-4174——Great advantage would result from the establishment of a national police paid by the country, 4175-4178——The present mode of assessment to the police rate in Scotland is very unjust; the landed property pays the whole of the cost, whereas the bulk of offences are against moveable property, which escapes entirely from taxation, 4178-4180.

J.

Jones, John. (Analysis of his Evidence.)—Superintendent of the Dumfriesshire constabulary, 4208-4210——Particulars as to the police of Dumfries; sufficiency of the force for the general wants of the county; expense of the police, 4211-4225——Inconvenience experienced in Dumfries from there being no police in Cumberland, 4226-4228——Advantage would result from the amalgamation of the police of the burghs in Scotland with the county forces, 4228——Patrol of the county of Dumfries by the police, 4229, 4230——Remarks as to the crimes and offences committed in Dumfries; amount of property lost and recovered in 1852; 4231-4234——The present assessment for the support of the police in Scotland is very unjust, as the rural districts bear the burden, and the towns derive the benefit, 4235-4237——Suggestion that all houses and property in Scotland, except houses under 10 *l.*, should be assessed to the police rate, 4238-4241——The excise officers do not work well with the police; there exists a jealousy of the police interfering with smuggling, 4242, 4243——In England a uniform system of police might be adopted, 4244——A uniform system might be carried out in Scotland without its having the government of the police, 4244.

It would be an advantage if all the counties in Scotland were compelled to have a sufficient force, they having the management, under the direction of a police committee, 4244-4246——The superintendents of police should be procurators fiscal, 4246-4255 ——Advantage would result from the railway police being placed under the control of the head of the county police, 4256-4268——Want of a superannuation fund for the

Dumfries,

Jones, John. (Analysis of his Evidence)—*continued.*

Dumfries police force, 4269-4271——Amount of witness's salary and emoluments as superintendent of the Dumfries police, 4272-4274—— Existence of vagrancy in Dumfries, though it has somewhat diminished, 4275-4278——The present law of Scotland applicable to vagrancy is defective; were the police empowered to deal with vagrants crime would diminish at least one-half, 4276-4286——Inspection of the tramps' lodging-houses in Dumfries by the police, 4279-4282.

Jurisdiction. It would be a great advantage, on the establishment of a uniform police force throughout England, that the officers should have the power to act indiscriminately in all counties; disadvantage arising from the delay in getting warrants backed, *Oakley* 3291; *M'Hardy* 3811-3814.

K.

Kent. See *Rate,* 2.   *Vagrancy,* 3.

Kesteven, Lincoln. In the parts of Kesteven there is a separate jurisdiction from the other portions of the county, *Healy* 3399, 3400——There are no police in the parts of Kesteven; there are only the ordinary parish constables, *ib.* 3401-3404——State of crime in the parts of Kesteven; decrease of crime from the improved habits of the people, *ib.* 3405-3411. 3464-3473——Number of committals to the house of correction for the parts of Kesteven for the eight years 1845 to 1852; causes to which the fluctuations therein are attributable, *ib.* 3430-3436. 3463——The Kesteven division of the county of Lincoln does not require a rural police; the ratepayers are well satisfied with the present state of things, *ib.* 3444-3446——Local associations in the parts of Kesteven for the detection and prosecution of felons; witness never knew of one of these voluntary associations breaking up from the non-payment of the subscriptions, *ib.* 3456-3462.

See also *High Constables.*   *Rate,* 2.   *Vagrancy,* 3.

King, Fielder. (Analysis of his Evidence.)—Farmer at Buriton, near Petersfield, Hampshire, 335, 336——Great benefit witness has derived from the establishment of the police in the county in the better protection of his property, 337-343——Decrease in the losses of agricultural property since the establishment of the police, particularly the loss of sheep, 338-345——In the western division of Sussex, the ratepayers are so convinced of the advantage of a police force that they have established a private watchman; this is a faulty system, and they would willingly see the man displaced by a general police force for the county, 346-366. 376-381. 403-405——Decrease of vagrancy in Hampshire since the establishment of the police; the vagrants are driven over the borders in Sussex, where they encamp, and commit numerous depredations, 367-372. 415-417.

Existence of sheep-stealing in Sussex, 373-375——There have been no incendiary fires in Hampshire for several years past, 382-384——General feeling among the farmers in Western Sussex in favour of a rural police; opposition of the lord-lieutenant to its establishment, otherwise it would have been carried out before now, 385-399——Improved condition of witness's parish since the existence of the police; the public-houses and beershops are better regulated, 400-402——Suppression of burglaries and highway robberies since the establishment of the police; formerly they were very frequent, 406-414——Witness pays double the amount for bad watching by a private watchman in Sussex to what he pays for good watching in Hampshire under the system of police, 418-420.

Kitson, George. (Analysis of his Evidence.)—Magistrate for the county of Somerset; member of the watch committee of the city of Bath, 2280, 2281——The police of the city of Bath is entirely under the control of the watch committee; very little inconvenience arises from this arrangement, 2282. 2284, 2285——Efficient state of the police of Bath; it may have been more efficient previous to the reduction of the force; circumstances under which that reduction took place, 2283. 2286-2303——Remarks as to the police rate in Bath; amount of the rate in the pound, 2293-2295——The power of appointment and dismissal of the police rests with the watch committee at Bath; the superintendent of the police has no voice in the matter, 2304-2314——Number of members of the watch committee; the committee is indiscriminately selected from the town council; there is no publican or brewer on the committee, and but one wine merchant, 2315-2330——When the Bath police go to the assizes to give evidence they merely receive their travelling expenses, 2331-2337.

L.

Lanarkshire. Great disorder in Lanarkshire, as compared with Mid-Lothian; the proposition for establishing a paid police in Lanark has often been mooted, and always rejected, *Gordon* 2187-2192——Inconvenience arising from the counties adjoining Edinburgh, which have not adopted the police force; instance of this in the Upper Ward of Lanark,

Reports, 1852-53—*continued.*

*Lanarkshire—*continued.

List 3925-3933——Discussion which has taken place relative to adopting the Police Act in Lanark ; causes from which the non-adoption of the Act proceeded, *Irving* 4166-4170 ——State of the neighbourhood of the Upper Ward of Lanark ; establishment of a voluntary police, *ib.* 4171-4174.

Lancashire. The Lancashire county police has worked very well since its establishment, *Redin* 1380-1383——Number of the force of Lancashire, and its classification, *Woodford* 1531, 1532——The arrangement of Lancashire into petty sessional divisions has answered very well ; the magistrates generally have appointed a sufficient number of men for their several districts, *ib.* 1613-1618.

 See also *Borough Police,* 2. *Decrease of Crime.* *Expenses of the Force,* II. 2. *Lock-up Houses.* *Pay of the Police.*

Leighton, Sir Baldwin, Bart. (Analysis of his Evidence.)— Magistrate for Shropshire and Montgomeryshire, 2470——Chairman of the police committee of Shropshire, chairman of the court of quarter sessions of Montgomeryshire, 2471, 2472——Number of the police force in Shropshire ; expense of the force ; sufficiency thereof, 2473-2479. 2481-2483. 2487-2492——Number of the police in Montgomeryshire, 2480——Diminution of crime since the establishment of the police in Shropshire ; great saving of property effected, 2486. 2493, 2494——Insufficiency of the borough police of Shrewsbury ; they do not work so well as the county police, 2494-2498——The borough police do not readily co-operate with the county police ; cordial co-operation between the police of the counties of Shropshire and Montgomeryshire, 2497-2501——It is very desirable to establish a uniform system of police throughout the country, 2502, 2503——Appointment and removal of the police of Shropshire by the chief constable, 2504-2506.

 Assistance given by the Shropshire police in the suppression of vagrancy ; decrease therein since their establishment, 2507. 2510-2518——The certainty of detection of crime is much greater now than it was before the establishment of the police in the county, 2508, 2509——Parish constables are perfectly useless for the purpose of detecting crime, 2519-2522——Although the expense of the police is larger than that of the parish constables, there have been no complaints by the ratepayers, as the advantage of the system is so much greater, 2523-2527——Amount of the pay of the chief constable and superintendent of police in Shropshire, 2528, 2529——It is desirable to employ the police in everything ; if they were employed to keep the courts of justice a great saving would be effected, 2530, 2531.

Lewes. The bonfire riot at Lewes, two or three years ago, when the metropolitan police were sent down might have been prevented, if the Brighton and County Constabulary had been under one head ; had those two forces co-operated on the occasion, they had a sufficient force to suppress the disturbance, *Martin* 3785-3793.

Lincoln. General meeting held at Lincoln to discuss the propriety of adopting the provisions of the Rural Police Act of 1839, when it was agreed by the magistracy that there was no necessity for it, *Sir R. Sheffield* 576-578.

 See also *Caistor.* *Kesteven.* *Lindsey.* *Quarter Sessions.* *Rate,* 2. *Superintending Constables,* 1.

Lindsey. Return from the parts of Lindsey, Lincoln, in which superintendent constables have been appointed, stating whether as superintendents of lock-ups solely, or as superintendents of parish constables, or as acting in both capacities, with the pay and allowances, the area of the petty sessional division, with the total expense incurred, for the year ending January 1853, *Sir R. Sheffield* 578.

 See also *County Rate.* *Lock-up Houses.* *Superintending Constables,* 2.

List, Alfred John. (Analysis of his Evidence.)—Superintendent of the county police in Mid-Lothian, 3875. 3876——Particulars as to the police force in Edinburgh ; annual expense thereof ; insufficiency of the force ; there are no police in the small towns, 3877-3888—— Remarks relative to the police assessment ; the assessment being entirely upon the landed property in Scotland is one cause why the police have not been originally appointed in other counties in Scotland, 3889-3899. 3934-3936——Increased number of men required for the police force of Mid-Lothian, on account of the vicinity of the district to the town of Edinburgh, 3899-3908——Police force of Edinburgh town ; they have a local Act, and a board of commissioners of police, 3909-3917—— It is very desirable that the police of Edinburgh should be amalgamated with the county force, 3918-3920——Inconvenience of the control of the police of Edinburgh being in the hands of a board of commissioners, 3920-3924.

 Great inconvenience arising from the counties adjoining Edinburgh which have not adopted the police force ; instance of this in the Upper Ward of Lanark, 3925-3933—— A system of patrols is not necessary in the rural parts of Scotland, 3937——Increase in the value of property in Edinburgh since the establishment of the police, 3938, 3939 ——In those districts of Scotland where there are no rural police, parish constables are appointed

List, Alfred John. (Analysis of his Evidence)—*continued.*

appointed ; they are not of any use whatever in the prevention of crime or in the detection of offenders, 3940-3949——Return of the police in the counties of Scotland, with their expenses, delivered in, 3950-3953——Number of counties in Scotland which have adopted the rural police force, and the counties that have partially adopted it, 3954-3958——It would be desirable to make the Rural Police Act imperative instead of permissive, for the sake of uniformity of action, 3959.

A uniform system of amalgamated police force would be a great improvement in Scotland ; suggested plan for the establishment of such a force, 3960-3981——If there were a uniform system well organised, with central management, it might be more efficiently and cheaply managed than by each county maintaining its own police force, as is at present the case, 3964-3974——The management of the police in Scotland should be vested in paid commissioners under the Crown, as in the metropolitan police, and answerable to the Lord Advocate, 3967-3981——Remarks relative to the local management of the police by the commissioners of supply ; there is no difficulty in their continuing to manage police affairs, provided they did not interfere with them in the execution of their duty, 3970-3981——The prevention of crime is only one of the duties of the police ; varied nature of the duties performed by the metropolitan police, 3982-3986.

The police force is very much more efficient for the purpose of quelling a riot than the military ; the military should only be employed in extreme cases, 3987-4001——It is very advantageous to move the police from one station to another, 4003, 4004——Importance of the inspection of the lodging-houses in Scotland by the police, 4005——By a uniform system of police vagrancy might be greatly checked, and a great deal of crime prevented, 4005——It might be advantageous to have a superannuation fund connected with the police, as it would induce men to join the force, 4006, 4007.

Liverpool. Remarks relative to the efficiency of the police force of Liverpool, *Redin* 1458-1463——Evidence as to the police force of Liverpool ; the force is under the management of the watch committee ; the magistrates being possessed of the power of dismissal of the men, *Redin* 1465-1490 ; *Wybergh* 1793-1805——The whole of the north docks of Liverpool are under the charge of the police ; the dock police were amalgamated with the town force in 1836 with good effect, *Redin* 1492-1500.

    See also *Borough Police,* 6.

Local Constables. No additional protection to the public arises from the existence of common constables, still retained in some counties, *M'Hardy* 800-802——Uselessness of the local constables in cases of disturbance ; they could not be depended on for investigating cases without rewards, *Parker* 898-902——Return showing the number of persons selected to act as local constables in the county of Essex, for the years 1841 and 1842, *Rep.* ii. *App.* 134——Letter from Captain M'Hardy to the magistrates and clergy of the county of Essex, dated 22 October 1840, relative to persons willing to serve as local constables, *ib.* 139——Return of persons qualified and willing to serve as local constables, *ib.* 140.——*See* also *Parish Constables. Superintending Constables.*

Local Control. The duties of the local police committees should be similar to those exercised by the visiting justices to the county gaols, *Oakley* 3361-3365——The police should be under the control of some local body, but this should not be an annually elected body, *Murray* 4144-4162.——*See* also *Borough Police,* 3.   *National Force.*

Lock-up Houses. Observations as to the erection of lock-ups, and the appointment of paid constables in the parts of Lindsey ; amount expended on these lock-ups, *Sir R. Sheffield* 579. 667-673——Observations relative to the lock-ups in Bucks, *Swabey* 852, 853 ; *Hamilton* 1079-1091. 1103-1105 ; *Carrington* 3217-3222——Considerable number of lock-ups in Lancashire ; these are a species of barracks, and comprise good lodging rooms for the constables and superintendents, *Woodford* 1662-1668——Recommendations of Captain Black, the chief constable of Norfolk, for the erection of lock-ups and stations ; great saving contemplated by carrying out these arrangements, *Holmes* 1732-1754——Suggestions by witness for the erection of lock-ups and stations in Wilts ; proposed cost thereof ; nature of the existing lock-ups in the county, *Meredith* 2447-2461——The system of lock-ups in Stafford is nearly complete ; expense attending their erection, *Hon. A. Talbot* 2652-2659——The lock-up houses in Essex may be considered as a valuable investment for the county ; should the police be at any time disbanded, they are admirably suited for private dwellings, *M'Hardy* 3394——The question of lock-up houses has reference to either system, the rural police or the superintending constables, *Clifford* 3823——Remarks on the state of lock-up houses in different parts of Essex, *Rep.* ii., *App.* 148.——*See* also *Station Houses. Superintending Constables,* 1.

Lodging Houses. Inspection of the lodging-houses in Andover by the police ; to a great extent tramping has ceased in the town, *Thompson* 489-497——The lodging-houses in Carlisle are placed under the Lodging House Act ; return from the police officers of the number of persons in the lodging-houses from 23 November 1851 to 20 November 1852, *Redin*

Lodging Houses—continued.

Redin 1428-1433——The low lodging-houses are unquestionably receptacles for stolen goods, *ib.* 1431——The vigilance of the police has lessened the number of the lodging-houses that were frequented by thieves and beggars in Calne, *Wayte* 1925——Advantage derived from the adoption of the Lodging House Act in the borough of Carlisle : constant examination of the lodging-houses by the police, *Fawcett* 3000-3003. 3015——Inspection of the lodging-houses in the Derwent division by the police, and beneficial effect thereof in the decrease of vagrancy, *Brown* 3067-3072.

Great benefit would result from the inspection of lodging-houses by the police officers, *Mathews* 3531-3537——Importance of the inspection of the lodging-houses in Scotland by the police, *List* 4005.——Inspection of lodging-houses by the Glasgow police, and various other duties performed by the force in the city, *Smart* 4074-4076. 4101-4103 ——The well-being of a community depends very much upon the proper regulation of the lodging-houses, and the suppression of vagrancy, *Murray* 4153——Inspection of the tramps' lodging-houses in Dumfries by the police, *Jones* 4279-4282.

See also *Superintending Constables*, 2.

Lymington. The borough of Lymington has lately joined the county ; statement of facts illustrating the benefits of the arrangement, *Harris* 41.

M

M'Hardy, Captain John B. B., R.N. (Analysis of his Evidence.)—Chief constable of the county of Essex, 676, 677——Number of the constabulary force in Essex ; it is calculated to insure the greatest amount of efficiency practicable under existing arrangements, 678, 679——Want of great union of action, not only between the boroughs, but between the counties themselves, 680-685——The adoption of an efficient constabulary in Essex obliged the adjoining counties, with the exception of Kent, to follow the example, 686, 687. 713-716——Causes which led to the adoption of the police in Cambridgeshire, 687. 717-719——Great decrease of vagrancy in Essex since the police of the county were appointed assisting relieving officers for casual poor; this diminution is entirely attributable to the police regulations, 687-712——Sending police from the metropolis into the counties where they have no local knowledge is very little benefit, 720.

Great want of a satisfactory system of mutual co-operation between the police in different counties and boroughs ; if the spirit of the Act of Parliament were carried out, it would be effected, 721-726——As a remedy for the want of union between the counties, witness proposes that England be divided into four districts; that there should be a general constabulary and a chief constable of each district, 726-729——Witness is not favourable to a centralization of the police in London ; for numerous reasons it would be anything but advisable, 730——Impossibility of thoroughly training recruits before entrusting them with the responsibility of their duties, from the constant demand for constables in Essex, 733, 734——Popularity of the police force with the ratepayers in Essex, 735. 816——The separation of the police force leads to unnecessary expense, from requiring a greater number of staff officers, 736, 737.

Remarks as to the station-houses and strong rooms built in every division of the county ; cost thereof; statement proving that they produce a greater interest than the capital invested and paid for by the county, 738-748——Number of boroughs in Essex having separate police forces ; appointment of the police by the watch committee; objection to consolidating with the county, as they would lose these appointments, 749-752——General inefficiency of the borough police, 752——Number of police in the borough of Colchester; number witness would consider necessary if the borough were consolidated with the county, 753-755——The ends of justice are frustrated by the existence of separate jurisdictions, from the want of co-operation, 756, 757——Instance of the county constabulary being required to act within the borough of Colchester at the time of the election, 758-762.

The system of giving rewards to the police for the detection of crime is very objectionable, as it is an encouragement to the men to have an interest in crime, 763-765. 792-794——When any disturbance is anticipated in the boroughs, the system adopted is to swear in special constables ; witness considers special constables are useless upon such occasions, 766, 767——Remarks relative to the system of parochial constables under superintending constables; want of some central or head authority under that system, 768——The boroughs which do not adopt the county police rely upon the military in cases of disturbance ; this is a very dangerous practice, 770——The police in Essex are not trained to arms; some of them are armed to assist the coast-guard in the prevention of smuggling, 771, 772——The experiment of local constables under superintendents was fairly tried in Essex, and failed, 773-776.

Nature of the supplementary duties performed by the police in Essex beyond the maintenance of the peace; additional duties which they might perform, 777-783——Necessity for a night patrol for the prevention of crime, 784, 785——How far the police
of

Reports, 1852–53—*continued.*

M'Hardy, Captain John B. B., R. N. (Analysis of his Evidence)—*continued.*

of Essex are indirectly employed in the preservation of game, 786, 787——The escape of criminals is facilitated by the uncertainty of detection; a general and efficient system of police would tend to shorten the criminal career of offenders, 788, 789——Inconvenience and delay arising from the necessity of backing magistrates' warrants, 790——The establishment of a national constabulary, on a more uniform system, would be one of the greatest blessings that could be conferred upon the country, 791.

Great defect in the criminal code from there being no public prosecutor, 794–809—— Diminution in the number of cases of ordinary violence and petty assaults since the establishment of a permanent and perfect police force in Essex, 795——Principles upon which the county police system could be adapted to wild districts of counties thinly inhabited, such for instance as Northumberland, 796–799——A horse patrol is most inefficient for the detection of crime; witness would never recommend its introduction except for supervision, 796——Witness has never seen an instance of special constables being of any avail, 800——No additional protection to the public arises from the existence of common constables still retained in some counties, 800–802——Objections to the appointment of the constables resting with the local authorities in boroughs, 803–805.

Decrease of fires in Essex since the establishment of the police, 806–808——Total expense of the police in Essex in 1852, and amount of the set-off from allowances from Government and other sources, 810–812——From the irregularities of the Essex coast a large coast-guard force is necessary, 813, 814——The establishment of electric telegraphs would tend to the efficiency of the police force, 815——The police might be employed as surveyors of roads, 817——Reference to the Maldon election, as showing the want of peace officers in the borough, 818, 819.

[Second Examination.]—Statement of the savings and earnings effected by the Essex county constabulary as compared with the expense of the system of parochial constables, 3389–3396——The lock-up houses in Essex may be considered as a valuable investment for the county; should the police be at any time disbanded, they are admirably suited for private dwellings, 3394.

[Third Examination.]—Owing to the inefficiency of the Harwich constables an application has been made for the assistance of some of the Essex police to keep the peace during the election for the borough, 3809——Steps taken in Essex on the police receiving information of a felony having been committed, 3810, 3811——The difficulty, from the want of unity of action between the counties, greatly facilitates the escape of offenders, 3811——It would be a great advantage, on the establishment of a uniform police force throughout England, that the officers should have the power to act indiscriminately in all counties; disadvantage arising from the delay in getting warrants backed, 3811–3814—— Great advantage would result if all the officers employed by the Customs afloat were made special constables, and required to co-operate with the police in the apprehension of offenders who are about to leave the sea-ports of the country, 3811, 3812.

Mackay, Captain Henry Fowler. (Analysis of his Evidence.)—Chief constable of East Sussex, 1883——Strength of the police force of East Sussex; insufficiency of the force; indisposition shown to increase the number on account of the expense, 1884–1903. 1919 ——Statement as to the police force of Brighton; by whom managed, 1904–1908—— Difficulty arising from the police of Brighton not readily co-operating with the county constabulary, 1909——Instance in which the county constabulary has had to apply to the metropolitan police for assistance; those disturbances would not have taken place had there been a sufficient force in the county, 1912–1920——The decrease of crime resulting from the establishment of the police has led to the increase of the value of property, 1921.

Macleod, Robert Bruce. (Analysis of his Evidence.)—Proprietor of a large estate in Ross, 4181——State of the county of Ross with regard to police; sufficiency of the force for the general wants of the county, though not in case of any extraordinary emergency, 4182–4187——It is very desirable to establish a uniform police force generally all over Scotland, 4188–4199——Remarks relative to the extent of sheep-stealing in the Highlands; proposed formation of a police for the prevention of this crime, 4200–4203—— Application made for the assistance of the Inverness police at the time of the Free Church riots in Ross, 4204–4206.

Magistrates. Witness never heard of the rural police having met with undue interference on the part of the county magistrates, *Redin* 1507–1510.——See also *Appointments.*

Magistrates' Warrants. Inconvenience and delay arising from the necessity of backing magistrates' warrants, *M'Hardy* 790.——See also *Jurisdiction.*

Maldon. Reference to the Maldon election, as showing the want of peace officers in the borough, *M'Hardy* 818, 819.

Reports, 1852-53—*continued.*

Mallalieu, Francis Mayall. (Analysis of his Evidence.)—Connected with the P. division of the metropolitan police force; witness's division of the metropolitan force is stationed in Kent; extent of the district, 2798-2806——Amount of the rate paid by the portion of Kent under the superintendence of the metropolitan force; witness is not aware of any dissatisfaction being felt by the farmers as to the high rate, 2801-2812——Marked difference in the amount of crime in the metropolitan district and immediately beyond it, 2813-2817——Great saving resulting from the prisoners being conveyed to Maidstone gaol by the metropolitan police instead of by the county, 2818-2827——Advantage of a police force in times of popular commotion; the military have never been called out since the establishment of the police, 2828-2835——Incomplete system of police at Bristol; a high state of police efficiency cannot be obtained whilst the control of the force rests with the watch committee, 2835-2841——The head of the police in any district, county or place should have the sole appointment of his subordinate officers, 2841.

It is indispensably necessary that the rural districts should be united with the towns in order to procure the highest state of proficiency in the police, 2842-2850——The system of rural police generally might be made as efficient as the metropolitan police under good management, 2851——The suggestion of Mr. Talbot for urban, suburban and rural districts is very valuable, and might be adopted with advantage, 2852-2857 ——If a general system of police were adopted the men might be employed in other duties beyond those of police duty, such as inspectors of weights and measures, service of summonses, &c., 2859-2867——Length of time necessary to make a man an efficient policeman; the discipline of the metropolitan force is rapidly improving, 2868-2875—— The increase of buildings in the metropolitan district will necessarily lead to the increase of the police force; proportion which the police ought to bear to the population, 2877-2887.

Manchester. Particulars as to the police force in Manchester; proposed increase of the number; expense of the force, *Willis* 2890-2898.——*See* also *Borough Police,* 6.

Marris, George. (Analysis of his Evidence.)—Solicitor at Caistor, Lincolnshire, 1114, 1115——Clerk and treasurer of an association for the prosecution of felons, 1116—— Frequent depredations committed in Caistor and its neighbourhood, from their being no police for the protection of property, 1117-1204——Representation made to the magistrates of the want of protection; memorials presented; refusal of the assistance applied for, 1120-1138. 1162-1182——Impossibility of the superintending constables protecting the large districts to which appointed with the assistance of parochial constables; inefficiency of the parochial constables, 1139-1161——Association formed at Caistor for the prevention of crime and punishment of offenders, 1146-1152. 1183-1202——The payment of a county rate of 2¼ d. in the pound for the police would not be deemed a heavy burden in witness's district, looking at the losses which people now sustain, 1203.

Martin, George. (Analysis of his Evidence.)—Superintendent of the G. Division of the metropolitan police in Clerkenwell, 3727——Particulars relative to witness being sent with some men into Wales at the time of the Rebecca riots; disorderly state of the country; witness received no assistance from the local constables upon that occasion, 3728-3736—— Statement as to witness being sent down to Huddersfield in 1837, with some of his men, upon the occasion of a serious disturbance in opposition to the poor-laws, 3737-3741 ——Evidence showing the perfect uselessness of special constables in cases of disturbances; they are fearful of making themselves obnoxious by interfering, 3738-3755——Opinion that the police are much more efficient for the suppression of riots and the dispersion of a mob than the military, 3756-3785——Remarks relative to a serious Chartists' riot in Birmingham in 1839, when witness and some of his men were sent down; had there been a good police in the town things would not have got to the head they did there, 3775-3782.——The bonfire riot at Lewes two or three years ago, when the metropolitan police were sent down, might have been prevented if the Brighton and county constabulary had been under one head; had those two forces co-operated on the occasion, they had a sufficient force to quell the disturbance, 3785-3793.

Mathews, Henry. (Analysis of his Evidence.)—Was formerly in the metropolitan police, 3517——Evidence relative to witness being sent down from the metropolitan police force for the detection of crime at Caistor, in North Lincolnshire, in consequence of the frequent depredations, 3518, 3519——Alarmed state of the district from the numerous crimes committed at the time of witness's arrival; great diminution of crime whilst witness remained in the district, 3520-3530. 3538-3555——Witness did not receive any assistance from the parochial constables or the superintending constable whilst on duty at Caistor, 3524-3529——Great benefit would result from the inspection of lodging-houses by the police officers, 3531-3537.

Meredith, Captain Samuel. (Analysis of his Evidence.)—Chief constable of Wiltshire, 2338——Statement as to the police force of the county, and the cost thereof; sufficiency of the force, 2339-2342——Out of five boroughs in Wilts four are consolidated with the county police; advantage would result from the amalgamation of all the borough and

                                                                  county

Report, 1852-53—*continued.*

Meredith, Captain Samuel. (Analysis of his Evidence)—*continued.*

county forces, 2343-2355——System of police in Salisbury; saving that would be effected by consolidating this force with the county constabulary, 2345-2355——Difficulties from the want of co-operation of the borough police with the county police, 2356, 2357——Diminution of crime which would result if a system of consolidation were carried out throughout the counties of England; decrease of crime in Wilts since the establishment of the police, 2358-2362——Saving of expense from the borough police being amalgamated with the county force, 2363, 2364——The county police stationed in the boroughs are occasionally shifted, 2365-2372.

Reduction of the number of vagrants in Wilts since the appointment of the police as assistant relieving officers, 2373-2378. 2422——Inspection of weights and measures by the police; great saving effected thereby, 2381-2384——Arrangement of the police in the different parishes of the county; great advantages of this system, 2385-2398——Amount of the police rate in Wilts; satisfaction expressed by the ratepayers with the present force, 2399-2408——Payment of the police; allowances made for extra duties performed, 2409-2415——Course pursued by the police who have been appointed assistant relieving officers, with reference to the treatment of vagrants, 2414-2422——Calculation with respect to the expenses of police constables and parish constables, showing that the parish constable making his own charges in his own county is a much more costly person than a police constable, 2422-2431.

Frequency of private persons tendering rewards to the police; circumstances under which they are allowed to accept such rewards, 2432-2442——The Wilts police have a superannuation fund; amount of that fund invested, 2443-2446——Recommendations made by witness for the erection of lock-ups and stations in Wilts; proposed cost thereof; nature of the existing lock-ups in the county, 2447-2461——The police of Wilts are sufficient for other services than those they have to perform as policemen; they have recruited three-fourths of the militia, 2462-2465——The police should be employed in recruiting for the army, 2462——Importance of the police being clothed in uniform; crime would not be more efficiently detected by men in private clothes, 2466-2469.

Metropolitan Police. Sending police from the metropolis into the counties where they have no local knowledge is very little benefit, *M'Hardy* 720——Instance in which the county constabulary has had to apply to the metropolitan police for assistance; those disturbances would not have taken place had there been a sufficient force in the county, *Mackay* 1912-1920——Marked difference in the amount of crime in the metropolitan district and immediately beyond it, *Mallalieu* 2813-2817——The increase of buildings in the metropolitan district will necessarily lead to the increase of the police force; proportion which the police ought to bear to the population, *ib.* 2877-2887——Reason why an extension of the system of the metropolitan police would not prove effectual or satisfactory in the rural districts, *Oakley* 3293——Although witness does not consider that the system of metropolitan police would be beneficial to the rural districts, still it would not be desirable to cut off all intercommunication between the county police and the metropolitan police, *ib.* 3354-3356——List of the parishes in Essex within the metropolitan police district, showing the sum contributed by each in the year 1849 towards the support of the police, which costs an 8*d.* rate, three-fourths being borne by the parishes, and one-fourth by the Government, *Rep.* ii., *App.* 153.

    See also *Detection of Crime.*   *Discipline.*   *Rural Police.*   *Staff Officers.*

Mid-Lothian. Nature and extent of the police force in Mid-Lothian; management of the force by the head of the police, subject to the control of the police committee, *Gordon* 2135-2144. 2176-2186——Increased number of men required for the police force of Mid-Lothian on account of the vicinity of the district to the town of Edinburgh, *List* 3899-3908.——See also *Decrease of Crime.*   *Lanarkshire.*

Military. The boroughs which do not adopt the county police rely upon the military in cases of disturbance; this is a very dangerous practice, *M'Hardy* 770——Opinion that the police are more effective than the military in the suppression of riots, *White* 1873-1882; *Mallalieu* 2828-2835; *Willis* 2919-2925; *Martin* 3756-3785; *List* 3987-4001.——It has not been found necessary to call in the aid of the military since the establishment of the police in the county of Stafford, *Hon. A. Talbot* 2673——The military should only be employed in extreme cases, *List* 3987-4001——Suppression of riots in the city of Glasgow without the assistance of the military, *Smart* 4062-4067.

Mining Districts. Possibility of establishing the rural police in the mining districts of Cumberland; the mining occupation is no bar to the establishment of police, *Redin* 1501-1506; *Fawcett* 3018-3023——The habits of miners interfere with the efficiency of the police; the difficulty of detection is increased in the mining districts, *White* 1856-1862.

Montgomeryshire. Statement as to the number of the police force in Montgomeryshire, *Sir B. Leighton* 2480.

Murray, David. (Analysis of his Evidence.)—Has been provost of the borough of Paisley, and chief magistrate from 1844 to 1850; 4112——The rural police was adopted in Renfrewshire for about two years, when it was discontinued; the result of the abandonment of the police system is that the county is without protection, 4113-4120——It is very desirable to make the Police Act compulsory on all counties, 4118-4121——A uniform system of police throughout Scotland is very desirable; this should be under local management, 4122-4126—— Impracticability of amalgamating the borough and county forces; no advantage would result from such consolidation 4127-4142——Advantage of placing the management of the police under the commissioners of supply, 4143——Defective state of the Paisley police, 4144——The police should be under the control of some local body, but this should not be an annually elected body, 4144-4162——The well-being of a community depends very much upon the proper regulation of lodging-houses, and the suppression of vagrancy, 4153——There are some constables in Renfrewshire supported by voluntary subscriptions, 4163, 4164.

N.

National Force. If there were a national police there would be no jealousy whatever; want of co-operation between the borough and county police from the jealousy which exists, *Harris* 233-236——Opinion in favour of a national police; the compulsory enforcement of a system of police upon all counties would be beneficial, *Stanley* 297-304; *M'Hardy* 791; *Fawcett* 3008, 3009; *Irving* 4175-4178——The Government having done what they have done, ought to appoint a rural police over the whole kingdom, and make the expense of the police a national charge instead of a parochial charge, *Denison* 2963-2969 ——In forming a national police it should be formed in districts, with distinct centres; how many distinct centres would be a matter of arrangement, *Chadwick* 3645——If the local management were entirely set aside and a general police system were adopted, under the control of the Crown, it would not be received with satisfaction by the people, *Smart* 408c——Scheme for an efficient constabulary and defensive force throughout England and Wales, co-operating with the coast-guard, affording increased protection to the public revenue, improving the present system of recruiting for the army, obviating necessity of enrolling the militia, supplying crews for the advanced ships, an efficient sea fencible, and checking the rapid increase of vagrancy, *Rep.* ii., *App.* 153-154.

　　See also *Districts.*　　*Government Control.*　　*Private Watchmen.*　　*Prosecutions.*
　　Railway Termini.　　*Rate.*　　*Uniformity of System.*

Newcastle. See *Tynemouth, &c.*

Night Patrol. Necessity for a night patrol for the prevention of crime, *M'Hardy* 784, 785; *White* 1827; *Brown* 3074-3077; *Oakley* 3261——Explanation of the check in Gloucestershire by which it is ascertained that the police are upon night patrol, *Blathwayt* 2098, 2099——How far the superintending constables have authority to order a night watch, *Carrington* 3242-3244——The police of Essex are an efficient night patrol, *Burnardiston* 3617.

Norfolk. Existence of a police force in Norfolk since 1840, *Holmes* 1722-1724——Statement of the police force of Norfolk; contemplated increase thereof, *Holmes* 1731; *Postle* 2548-2556——There is no doubt that the establishment of the police has been of great advantage to the county, *Holmes* 1762, 1765—— Great advantage has resulted from the establishment of the police, *Dover* 1766-1781—— Special meetings of magistrates held in conjunction with the police committee for the drawing up of rules and regulations for the police force, *Postle* 2535, 2536.

　　See also *Expenses of the Force,* II. 3.　　*High Constables.*　　*Lock-up Houses.*
　　Rate, 2.　　*Sheep Stealing.*　　*Voluntary System.*

Northumberland. Evidence relative to the county police of Northumberland; number of men of which the force consists; efficiency of the force; decrease of crime since the establishment of the force from offences being more frequently detected, *Fennick* 526-571——The magistrates of Northumberland have occasionally applied to the police authorities at Newcastle for assistance; instance of this at the election last year at Hexham, *ib.* 571 ——A very good and efficient police might be established in the county at almost the same cost as the parish constables, *Hughes* 1311-1313.

Norwich. Observations on the inefficiency of the system of police at Norwich, although various alterations and improvements have been made therein, *Dunne* 1939-1946——The police rate of Norwich is 2 *d.* in the pound, *ib.* 1947, 1948——Inconvenience resulting from both the watch committee and magistrates having jurisdiction over the police force, *ib.* 1991-1993. 2042——How far there would be any opposition on the part of the city to their police being amalgamated with the rural police, *ib.* 2038.

　　See also *Appointments,* 1.　　*Public Houses.*

O.

Oakley, William. (Analysis of his Evidence.)—Governor of the county gaol of Somerset, at Taunton, 3249——Has served in the Essex county constabulary, and has been chief of the police in Bath, 3250–3254——The system of police in Somerset is that of parish constables in the rural districts, and in some of the towns local police forces, 3255–3258 ——Beneficial operation of a county rural police, as instanced in Essex, 3259, 3260—— Necessity for a night patrol being established, 3261——The system of rural police is capable of improvement; the staff is too great, and therefore too expensive, 3262–3269 ——It is very desirable that a uniform system of police should be established throughout the country, 3263, 3264——The remuneration of constables by fees and allowances tends to frustrate the ends of justice; the objection to the payment of constables by fees applies particularly to the detection of offences committed upon the poorer classes, 3270–3276——It is quite impossible that the description of persons who are usually appointed as parochial constables are capable of efficiently performing their duty, 3273.

Remarks relative to the cases of sheep-stealing in Somerset, 3277–3282——So far from the appointment of superintending constables improving the system of parochial constables, it increases the evils, 3283–3286——The existing want of uniformity amongst police forces in counties and towns prevents mutual co-operation, and thus frustrates the ends of justice, 3287–3290——The restrictions of the powers of constables within certain limits is very prejudicial, 3291——The establishment of a uniform system of police throughout the kingdom is practicable, and would be in the highest degree beneficial, 3292–3358——Reason why an extension of the system of the metropolitan police would not prove effectual or satisfactory in the rural districts, 3293——Great advantage of employing the police upon all public occasions, such as meetings and elections, 3294.

Efforts which have been made in the Bath division to obtain the county constabulary, but without success, 3295 *et seq.*——Adoption of the Superintending Constables Act in the Bath division, 3295–3300——Statement showing the comparative expense of superintending constables and parish constables as compared with the rural police; examination thereon as to the data on which witness calculates the saving of the police force, 3295–3338——There should be police stations wherever there is a police force; saving that would be thus effected in the conveyance and lodging of prisoners, 3306, 3307—— The swearing in of parish constables where there is a rural police force is an unnecessary expenditure both of time and money, 3311–3313——Proposed employment of the police as inspectors of weights and measures; amount paid to the inspectors; if the police did the duty the whole amount would go to the county, 3326–3337.

Recommendation that the inspectors of police should be appointed assistant relieving officers for vagrants, as it would tend to diminish the number, 3338–3341——The suggestion that there should be three separate rates for urban, suburban and rural districts, might be carried out with advantage, 3342, 3343——The expense of a uniform system of police would not be more than what is now actually paid to parish and local constables, 3343. 3358——Objections to the chief constable having the undivided control of the police force; he should have the appointment of the police, 3344–3348. 3370– 3374. 3382–3388——If an efficient rural police were established in every county it would be possible to dispense with the coroner's court, 3349–3353——Although witness does not consider that the system of metropolitan police would be beneficial to the rural districts, still it would not be desirable to cut off all intercommunication between the county police and the metropolitan police, 3354–3356.

The application of the electric telegraph to the police stations throughout the county would be advantageous, 3357, 3358——Evils arising from the payment of parish constables by fees, 3359——It would be a great advantage if the police were drilled in the performance of their ordinary duties; they should not be entrusted with anything beyond a truncheon or cutlass, 3360——The duties of the local police committees should be similar to those exercised by the visiting justices to the county gaols, 3361–3365—— The watch committee is a very improper body to control the police, 3366–3369—— Necessity for the active co-operation of the county forces with the metropolitan force, 3375–3379——Instance of information being given to offenders by the parish constables to enable them to elude the police in pursuit of them, 3377——The Essex police force is the most efficient in England, 3380, 3381.

[Second Examination.]—Explanation as to the basis on which witness founds his statement of the expense of a police force for the county of Somerset, showing that there would be a saving of 6,000l. a year between the expense of superintending constables and an efficient police force, 3794–3803——The amount of police force required in Somerset is not anything like that in Essex, in proportion to the population, 3804–3806——The Taunton constabulary are under no control, and recognise no authority, 3808.

Occupation of Land. Witness would prefer renting and occupying land in a county where there is a police to where there is no police; this is the general feeling amongst farmers, *Beadel* 2771-2784.——*See also Protecton of Property.*

Officers. See *Staff Officers.*

Oxfordshire. Particulars relative to the system of police in Oxfordshire, which is that of superintending constables, over the parochial constables; expense of the force; inefficiency of the parish constables, *Smith* 3665-3689.

P.

Paid Constables. See *Rural Police.*

Paisley. Remarks as to the defective state of the Paisley police, *Murray* 4144.

Parish Constables. Opinion of the Committee, that any system of police mainly dependent on the aid of parochial constables must prove ineffectual for the protection of property, the maintenance of order and other duties of a police force for which their necessary avocations and local connexions entirely disqualify them, *Rep.* ii., *p.* iii.——Inefficiency of the parish constables for the proper discharge of their duties, *Sir W. Heathcote,* 248-252; *Stanley* 281-284; *Fenwick* 546; *Swabey* 833-837; *Hamilton* 1044-1149. 1101, 1102; *Hughes* 1293-1295; *Redin* 1441-1449; *Blathwayt* 2063-2071; *Sir B. Leighton* 2519-2522; *Postle* 2582-2589; *Hon. A. Talbot* 2677-2688; *Brown* 3043-3052. 3070; *Claydon* 3116-3118; *Oakley* 3273. 3311-3313; *List* 3940-3949——Existence of parish constables in all the parishes in the parts of Lindsey; these are entirely distinct from the system of superintendent constables adopted by the county, *Sir R. Sheffield* 647-650——Remarks relative to the system of parochial constables under superintending constables; want of some central or head authority under that system, *Sir R. Sheffield* 653-664; *M‘Hardy* 768——Frequency of the parish constables allowing motives of private interest to interfere with the performance of their duty, *Hamilton* 1092, 1093—— Witness knows of no plan by which the parish constables can be made effective under the present law, *ib.* 1100.

Under a perfect organisation of the rural police force it would be possible entirely to dispense with parish constables; their duties might be discharged by the police, *Redin* 1511-1521——In those counties in Scotland where the police have not been introduced, parish constables are employed, *Gordon* 2221-2223——Remarks relative to the payment of parochial constables in cases of the pursuit of prisoners where no apprehension takes place; there is no uniform practice as to payment in those cases, *Carrington* 3245-3248 ——Instance of information being given to offenders by the parish constables to enable them to elude the police in pursuit of them, *Oakley* 3377——Opinion that parish constables could, by a proper selection and by proper remuneration, be made as effective a police force as the requirements of a rural district would demand, *Healy* 3424-3427. 3479-3488——The parish constables are very badly paid; with better pay they might be made a more efficient body, *ib.* 3447-3451. 3480——The parish constables in Kesteven division are not constantly employed in the detection and prevention of crime; they follow their several occupations; the duties of the constables are almost a sinecure, *ib.* 3493-3502——Although the appointment of superintending constables may improve the parochial constabulary, they can never be rendered an efficient force, *Smith* 3691-3714.

See also *Bath.   Buckinghamshire.   Capture of Offenders.   Chief Constables. Detection of Crime.   Expenses of the Force,* 1. *Fees and Allowances.   Kesteven.   Local Constables.   Poorer Classes.   Prosecutions.   Pursuit of Offenders.   Rural Police.   Somersetshire.   Superintending Constables.*

Parker, James. (Analysis of his Evidence.)—Solicitor residing at Great Baddow, Essex, 868——Clerk of the peace for the county up to 1847; has held the office of clerk of indictments, 869-872——Great assistance rendered by the police in the preparation of indictments, by the collection of evidence; this has been the means of saving expense to the county, 873-877. 911-919——Advantage resulting from the employment of the police as inspectors of weights and measures, which is an important office; saving effected by this arrangement, 878-880. 932-935——Greater certainty of detection of offences by the police as compared with the parochial constables, 881-884——Advantage which has resulted from the police being appointed as relieving officers for vagrants, 885, 886—— Decrease of crime in Essex since the establishment of the police, 887-888. 903-907 ——Increase of the value of property since the establishment of the police in Essex, 889-891——Public expression of opinion on the part of the magistrates as to the Essex constabulary being highly valuable and essentially necessary, 892-897——Uselessness of the local constables in cases of disturbance; they could not be depended on for investigating cases without rewards, 898-902——The county expenditure for the expenses of the police has not been lessened under the present system, but their services are more than equivalent for the expenses incurred, 899-901. 936-950——Advantage of establishing
a uniform

Parker, James. (Analysis of his Evidence)—*continued.*

a uniform system of police in the different counties of England generally, 908–910—— The police have not the slightest interest in prosecutions; objections to any system which would give the police an interest in crime, 920–927.

Parochial Constables. See *Parish Constables.*

Pay of the Police. Particulars as to the pay of the police of Bath; manner in which the officers are paid for pursuing offenders in the county, *Hughes* 1239-1248——Rates of pay of the different grades in the Lancashire police force; duties of the several officers, *Woodford* 1651–1660——Particulars relative to the payment of the police in Wilts; allowances made for extra duties performed, *Meredith* 2409-2415——Amount of the pay of the chief constable and superintendent of police in Shropshire, *Sir B. Leighton* 2528, 2529——Amount of the pay of the superintendents and chief constable of the Stafford county police, *Hon. A. Talbot* 2700–2708——Rate of pay to the constabulary of Scotland, as approved of by the sub-committee, *Rep. ii., App.* 165.

    See also *Bath.*   *Fees and Allowances.*   *Parish Constables.*   *Scotland.*

Petty Offences. Diminution of petty offences since the establishment of the police in Hampshire, *Sir W. Heathcote* 256, 257.——See also *Assaults.*

Police Commission, Scotland. The police commission is a body very little calculated to manage the police department with efficiency, and should be abolished; their power should be vested in the town council, *Gordon* 2197–2208.

Poorer Classes. It is very desirable for the poorer classes of society that there should be a rural police; there are several aspects in which it is so, *Sir W. Heathcote,* 253, 254. 268, 269——The want of a police force is felt more by the poorer classes of society than any other; the parish constables will not move in pursuit of offenders until they are paid, *Blathwayt* 2081–2085; *Healey* 3473-3478.

Popularity of the Force. Popularity of the police force in the county of Hants, *Harris* 209-211; *Stanley* 288——Popularity of the force with the ratepayers in Essex, *M‘Hardy* 735–816——Popularity of the police in Lancashire, *Woodford* 1644–1647——Popularity of the force in Durham, *White* 1828, 1829.

Postle, Rev. Edward. (Analysis of his Evidence.)—Magistrate for Norfolk, 2532, 2534 ——Special meetings of magistrates, held in conjunction with the police committee, for the drawing up of rules and regulations for the police force, 2535, 2536——Appointment of a committee in 1852 to take into consideration a report of the chief constable, Captain Black, with respect to building station-houses in the county and other matters in reference to a different system of police; this committee have determined to report in favour of the recommendations of Captain Black, 2536–2540——Manner in which the county accounts are audited and published by the finance committee of Norfolk, 2541–2544——Every ratepayer may ascertain exactly what he pays to the county rate and to the police rate, 2543. 2546, 2547. 2565——Statement of the police force of Norfolk; contemplated increase thereof, 2548–2556——The police does not cost the county of Norfolk more than 1½ d. in the pound; under the increased system the rate will be 2 d., 2548, 2549. 2562–2564.

Suggestion that the police should perform the duties of inspectors of weights and measures, 2557. 2566, 2567——Great advantage would result from employing the police in the relief of vagrants, 2557, 2568–2571——Number of station-houses in Norfolk; proposed erection of new buildings, 2558–2563——It is desirable to establish a more uniform system of police throughout the kingdom, 2576——Existence of high constables in Norfolk; nature of their duties; these duties might be performed by the police, 2577–2581. 2594–2597——Uselessness of the parish constables, 2582–2589.

The parochial constables, even under superintending constables, cannot be made an efficient force, 2590–2593——The advantage derived from the police force is more than equal to the expense; the value of property saved is more than the rate, 2598–2602—— There were districts in Norfolk in which a police force was voluntarily paid for previously to the establishment of the rural police, 2603, 2604——Decrease of sheep-stealing since the establishment of the police, 2605, 2607——Remarks as to the superannuation fund of the Norfolk police, by which means a pension is provided for every member of the force but the chief constable; opinion that the magistrates should have the power of granting a pension to the chief constable, 2608.

Private Watchmen. In the western division of Sussex, the ratepayers are so convinced of the advantage of a police force that they have established a private watchman; this is a faulty system, and they would willingly see the man displaced by a general police force for the county, *King* 346-366 376-381. 403-405.——See also *Rate,* 2.

Reports, 1852-53—*continued.*

Procurators Fiscal. Witness sees no objection to the police being under the same control as the procurator fiscal is in Scotland, *Smart* 4068-4073——Recommendation that the superintendents of police should be procurators fiscal, *Jones* 4246-4255.

Prosecutions. Remarks of the Committe with regard to the reduction in the cost of prosecutions consequent upon the adoption of the rural police, *Rep.* ii., *p.* iv.——Statement with regard to the amount that might be saved in the cost of prosecutions by the establishment of a consolidated police, *Harris* 228 ; *Chadwick* 3648-3652——Comparative expense of prosecutions under the rural police, and under the old system of parish constables, showing the saving under the former system, *Redin* 1522-1525——Improved mode of conducting prosecutions since the establishment of the police in Norfolk ; saving of time and expense from unnecessary witnesses not being brought up, *Dover* 1782, 1783—— Average expenses of prosecutions in Essex ; from information witness has received he finds that the average expense of the prosecution of a city prisoner is double that of a county prisoner, *Dunne* 2042-2044——Opinion that the money which is now spent by the Government and the county of Stafford, if properly economised, might very nearly give an efficient police all over the kingdom, *Hon. A. Talbot* 2689.

    See also *Assizes.*   *Public Prosecutor.*   *Rewards.*   *Witnesses Expenses.*

Protection of Property. Remarks of the Committee, that the effectual protection afforded to property by the establishment of the rural police has, in the opinion of owners and holders of land, rendered its occupation more desirable, *Rep.* ii., *p.* iii.——Great benefit witness has derived from the establishment of the police in the county of Hants, in the better protection of his property, *King* 337-343——Remarks relative to the expenditure on the police force in Norfolk ; the expense is more than repaid by the great security of property, *Holmes* 1755-1764——Advantage derived by the landholders of Essex from the police ; the gain by the saving of property is equal to the amount of the police rate, *Beadel* 2767-2770——The police is a preventive force, and saves property immensely, *Burnardiston* 3609-3616—— Property is much more efficiently protected in Essex than in Oxfordshire, *Smith* 3711.——*See* also *Parish Constables.*   *Value of Property.*

Protection of the Revenue. See *Coast Guard.*   *Government Aid.*   *Illicit Distillation.*

Public Houses. Improved condition of witness's parish in Hampshire since the existence of the police ; the public-houses and beershops are better regulated, *King* 400-402—— Improved regulation of the public-houses and beershops in Andover since the establishment of the police, *Thompson* 487, 488——Defective state of the police in the boroughs of Lancashire not under the county constabulary ; the beershops and public-houses are not under proper supervision, *Woodford* 1636-1640——Large number of public-houses and beershops in Norwich ; in many of the low public-houses crime is fostered, *Dunne* 1994. 1997-2002. 2024-2026. 2039——Inspection of public-houses and beershops under the system of superintending constables in Herefordshire, and general efficiency thereof, *Clifford* 3850, 3851——The superintendence of public-houses is one of the most important duties performed by the police, *Smart* 4074.

    See also *Superintending Constables,* 2.

Public Meetings. Great advantage of employing the police upon all public occasions, such as meetings and elections, *Oakley* 3294.

Public Prosecutor. Great defect in the criminal code from there being no public prosecutor, *M'Hardy* 794-809.

Pursuit of Offenders. Observations of the Committee on the inefficiency of parish constables for the prompt detection and pursuit of offenders, *Rep.* ii., *p.* iii.——Evidence as to the efficiency of the county constabulary over the superintending constables in following in pursuit of criminals, *Harris* 674, 675——Under the old system of parochial constables, pursuit could only be made after offenders by persons capable of paying them, *Dover* 1776-1778—— Inconvenience experienced in the pursuit of criminals from the want of a uniform system in the adjoining counties, *White* 1830, 1831.

    See also *Parish Constables.*   *Poorer Classes.*

Q.

Quarter Sessions (Lincoln). Statement as to the mode in which the business of the court of quarter sessions is conducted in the parts of Lindsey, Lincoln, *Sir R. Sheffield* 576.

    See also *Audit of Accounts.*

Reports, 1852-53—*continued.*

R.

Railway Police. There would be no difficulty in amalgamating the railway police with the rural police, *Woodford* 1633-1635——Advantage would result from the railway police being placed under the control of the head of the county police, *Jones* 4256-4268.

Railway Termini. In the event of a general police being established, great benefit would result from having a detective constable at the terminus of every railway, *Harris* 241.

RATE:

    1. *Remarks as to the injustice of the present Assessment; suggestions for its improvement.*

    2. *Particulars relative to the Rate in various places.*

    1. *Remarks as to the injustice of the present Assessment; suggestions for its improvement:*

Opinion of the Committee that where the population of separate districts within the same county differs in amount and in the character of its employments, and consequently in its requirements for a police force, an equitable adjustment of the police rate to meet those cases should be provided for by enactment, and that such an arrangement would tend to remove the objections now partially entertained against the adoption of the Rural Police Act, *Rep.* ii., *p.* iv.——The assessments in Scotland are laid upon the old valuation; the chief burden of the assessment falls upon the land, and not upon trades and houses; this is one cause why the most important counties have not adopted the police system, *Gordon* 2159-2167. 2189-2192; *List* 3889-3899. 3934-3936; *Irving* 4178-4180; *Jones* 4235-4237——The Rural Police Act would have been fully carried into effect in the West Riding of York but for the inequality of the application of the rate, *Denison* 2983——Supposing there were a general system of police all over the country, provided it is done by a general rate, there should be an urban or suburban and a rural rate, *Hon. A. Talbot* 2637-2643; *Mallalieu* 2852-2857; *Oakley* 3342, 3343——By a general county rate a greater proportion of rates is thrown upon the agricultural districts than upon the manufacturing districts; this is the ground of witness's objection to a county rate, *Denison* 2985——Proposal that the rates for the support of the police should be levied in districts, a distinction being made between rural and manufacturing districts, *Chadwick* 3657-3660 ——Suggestion that all houses and property in Scotland, except houses under 10 *l.*, should be assessed to the police rate, *Jones* 4238-4241.

    2. *Particulars relative to the Rate in various places:*

Witness pays double the amount for bad watching by a private watchman in Sussex to what he pays for good watching in Hampshire under the system of police, *King* 418-420 ——Amount of the rate for the support of the police in the borough of Andover, *Thompson* 468-472. 499, 500——Opinion that the payment of a county rate of 2½ *d.* in the pound for the police would not be deemed a heavy burden in Caistor, Lincoln, looking at the losses which people now sustain, *Marris* 1203——Remarks as to the rate in Bath; amount of the rate in the pound, *Hughes* 1287, 1288; *Kitson* 2293-2295——Amount of the rate for the support of the police in Liverpool, *Redin* 1491——Amount of the police rate in Durham, *White* 1867——Statement of the cost of the police force in Cheshire; amount of the rate in the pound, *Corbett* 2270-2275.

Amount of the police rate in Wilts; satisfaction expressed by the ratepayers with the present force, *Meredith* 2399-2408——The police does not cost the county of Norfolk more than 1½ *d.* in the pound; under the increased system the rate will be 2*d.*, *Postle* 2548, 2549. 2562-2564——The advantage derived from the police force in Norfolk is more than equal to the expense; the value of property saved is more than the rate, *ib.* 2598-2602——Amount of the rate paid by the portion of Kent under the superintendence of the metropolitan force; witness is not aware of any dissatisfaction being felt by the farmers as to the high rate, *Mallalieu* 2801-2812——Amount of rate which is levied for county purposes in the parts of Kesteven, *Healy* 3438-3442——Opinion that farmers paying 100 *l.* a year rent in Kesteven division do not pay near 17 *s.* for the services performed by the constables, *ib.* 3452-3455——Return referring to that part of the county of Essex subject to police rate, *Rep.* ii., *App.* 138.

    See also *County Rate.   Edinburgh.   Expenses of the Force.   Metropolitan Police. Norwich.   Scotland.*

Rebecca Riots. Particulars relative to witness being sent with some men into Wales at the time of the Rebecca riots; disorderly state of the country; witness received no assistance from the local constables upon that occasion, *Martin* 3728-3736.

Recruiting the Army. How far it would be possible to recruit for the army through the means of the police; the police of Lancashire were actively engaged in inducing volunteers to join the militia, *Woodford* 1702. 1706-1716——The police of Wilts are

Reports, 1852–53—*continued.*

Recruiting the Army—continued.

sufficient for other services than those they have to perform as policemen; they have recruited three-fourths of the militia, *Meredith* 2462-2465——Suggestion that the police should be employed in recruiting for the army, *ib.* 2462.—— *See also National Force.*

Redin, Thomas Heagren. (Analysis of his Evidence.)—Governor of the county gaol at Carlisle, 1373, 1374——Has served in the Essex county constabulary and the Liverpool borough police force, 1375-1378——Beneficial working of the county constabulary in Essex, 1380-1382——The Lancashire county police has also worked very well since its establishment, 1380-1383——Want of co-operation between the Liverpool police force and the Lancashire county constabulary; this might be remedied by combining the two forces, 1383-1388——Suggestion for the amalgamation of two or three adjoining counties, including the boroughs, under one system of police and one superintendence; there would be no difficulty in working the force on a more extended scale in the country, 1383-1405. 1453-1457——The establishment of county police forces has been attended with very beneficial results, 1406, 1407——Particulars relative to the constabulary in Cumberland; there is no rural police, but a system of superintending constables; these are efficient as far as they go, but the districts are too wide, 1409-1416.

The eastern parts of Cumberland are infested with vagrants; these are principally itinerant thieves, 1416. 1423, 1424——State of crime in the county of Cumberland; in the average of the seven years ending 1852, the convictions are slight, 1417-1422——The police force in the city of Carlisle is established under the Municipal Corporation Act; number of police; the force is well managed, 1425-1427——The lodging-houses in Carlisle are placed under the Lodging House Act; return from the police officers of the number of persons in the lodging-houses from 23 November 1851 to 20 November 1852; 1428-1433——The low lodging-houses are unquestionably receptacles for stolen goods, 1431——Daily average of prisoners in Carlisle gaol for the years 1851, 1852, and part of 1853; 1434-1436——Large number of vagrants continually in Carlisle passing to and from England and Scotland; inefficiency of the parochial constables for remedying this evil, 1437-1441.

Inefficiency of the parochial constables, from their local connexion, 1441-1449——Considering the question of efficiency, the expense of a well organised police force is not greater than that of the parish constables, 1449-1451——Parochial constables cannot be rendered an efficient force by the appointment of superintending constables, 1452—— Remarks relative to the efficiency of the police force of Liverpool, 1458-1463——Beneficial results of transferring local duties to the county constabulary, as experienced in Essex, 1464——The police of the borough of Liverpool are entirely under the control of the watch committee; great inconvenience resulting from the committee possessing this power, 1465-1490——Amount of the rate for the support of the police in Liverpool, 1491.

The whole of the north docks of Liverpool are under the charge of the police; the dock police were amalgamated with the town force in 1836 with good effect, 1492-1500—— Objection to a system of rewards for the detection of crime; they have a demoralising effect upon the police, 1492-1496——Possibility of establishing the rural police in the mining districts of Cumberland; the mining occupation is no bar to the establishment of police, 1501-1506——Witness never heard of the rural police having met with undue interference on the part of the county magistrates, 1507-1510——Under a perfect organisation of the rural police force, it would be possible entirely to dispense with parish constables, 1511-1521.

[Second Examination.]--Comparative expense of prosecutions under the rural police, and under the old system of parish constables, showing the saving under the former system, 1522-1525——Opinion that the management of the police should be concentrated as far as possible in the hands of the head of the police, instead of being under the watch committees, 1526-1528.

Relieving Officers. Advantage arising from the constables being appointed assistant relieving officers; check given to vagrancy by this means, *Swabey* 838, 839; *Parker* 885, 886; *White* 1865, 1866; *Postle* 2557. 2568-2571; *Oakley* 3338-3341; *Smith* 3715-3726 ——Course pursued by the police in Wilts who have been appointed assistant relieving officers, with reference to the treatment of vagrants, *Meredith* 2414-2422.
     See also Vagrancy.

Removals. Importance of the constabulary being constantly shifted; impossibility of any man doing his duty if locally connected, *Harris* 78-80. 91-93; *Hughes* 1299-1304; *List* 4003, 4004——Great attention paid by the police at Andover to their duties; one of the points in the effectiveness of the police is that they are constantly changed, *Thompson* 474, 475——The county police stationed in the boroughs are occasionally shifted, *Meredith* 2365-2372.

Renfrewshire.

Reports, 1852–53—*continued.*

Renfrewshire. There is no police in Renfrewshire; this is a great inconvenience, *Smart* 4044, 4045——The rural police was adopted in Renfrewshire for about two years, when it was discontinued; the result of the abandonment of the police system is that the county is without protection, *Murray* 4113-4120.——*See* also *Voluntary System.*

Rewards. The system of giving rewards to the police for the detection of crime is very objectionable, as it is an encouragement to the men to have an interest in crime, *M‘Hardy* 763-665. 792-794; *Parker* 920-927; *Redin* 1492-1496; *Woodford* 1717-1719——The police have not the slightest interest in prosecutions in Essex, *Parker* 920-927—— Remarks relative to the fees or rewards paid to the police of Bath for special services, *Hughes* 1213-1215——Frequency of private persons tendering rewards to the police of Wilts; circumstances under which they are allowed to accept such rewards, *Meredith* 2432-2442.——*See* also *Local Constables. Parish Constables.*

Romsey. Remarks relative to the state of crime in the borough of Romsey; this borough is not consolidated with the county, *Harris* 42-44——Return of the number of felonies affecting property that have been committed in the Romsey division, the first amount of loss, the amount recovered, the number of persons committed for trial, and the number of undetected cases, between 1 January and 31 December 1850, *ib.* 44——Return of the number of offences against property that have come to the knowledge of the Hants constabulary as having been committed within the borough of Romsey during the year 1850, *ib.*——Unsatisfactory condition of the police of Romsey for the purposes of the prevention and detection of crime; for all useful purposes the borough is totally devoid of police, *Stanley*, 271-279. 285-287; *Beddome* 504-516——Exertions used by witness to induce the town council to amalgamate the borough police force with the county; memorials presented from the ratepayers; opposition which the proposal met with in council, and rejection thereof, *ib.* 504-511——The additional expenses of the police of Romsey, if amalgamated with the county, would be more than compensated for by the saving of property, *ib.* 518-522.——*See* also *Vagrancy,* 3.

Ross. State of the county of Ross with regard to police; sufficiency of the force for the general wants of the county, though not in case of any extraordinary emergency, *Macleod* 4182-4187——Application made for the assistance of the Inverness police at the time of the Free Church riots in Ross, *ib.* 4204-4206.

Rural Districts. See *Metropolitan Police.*

Rural Police. Resolution of the Committee that the Acts for the appointment of district constables have failed to provide such a general and uniform constabulary force as is essential for the prevention of crime and security of property, *Rep.* ii., *p.* iii.——Observations on the beneficial effects which have resulted from the adoption of the Rural Police Act in those districts where it has been carried out, *ib.*—— Return of the several counties that have adopted the provisions of the Constabulary Act for the whole county, and for parts only, as also the counties which continue the system of parochial constables, *Harris* 3-9——General feeling among the farmers in Western Sussex in favour of a rural police; opposition of the lord-lieutenant to its establishment, otherwise it would have been carried out before now, *King* 385-399——The adoption of the rural police was proposed in Bucks, but was rejected on account of the expense, *Swabey* 840, 841——Witness is desirous that the Rural Police Act should be introduced in its entire force in the county of Bucks, *ib.* 864-867.

The rural police system, as it is established in Surrey and Essex, is as perfect as the limited cost will permit, *Hughes* 1305——The system of rural police generally might be made as efficient as the metropolitan police under good management, *Mallalieu* 2851—— Objections to the establishment of a paid constabulary under the Rural Police Act in the county of Buckingham, *Carrington* 3150-3155. 3226, 3227. 3230-3232——The working of the Rural Police Act, considering the measure has been only partially carried out, has been more satisfactory than was anticipated, *Chadwick* 3639-3642——The introduction of the rural police force into Herefordshire would be an unnecessary expense to the county, *Clifford* 3872-3874——Statement of the number of counties in Scotland which have adopted the rural police force, and the counties that have partially adopted it, *List* 3954-3958.

See also *Borough Police. Cambridgeshire. Coast Guard. Commission of* 1839. *County Constabulary. Decrease of Crime. Districts. Duties of the Police. Ely. Essex. Expenses of the Force. Government Aid. Hampshire. Lock-up Houses. Magistrates. National Force. Parish Constables. Poorer Classes. Prosecutions. Protection of Property. Railway Police. Rate. Vagrancy,* 2. *Workhouse Riots.*

Reports, 1852–53—*continued.*

S.

Saffron Walden. Inefficient state of the police in Saffron Walden; the expense is paid out of the corporate funds, *Claydon* 3087–3099. 3105–3115. 3122–3134.

See also *Borough Police,* 4.

Salisbury. Remarks as to the system of police in Salisbury; saving that would be effected by consolidating this force with the county constabulary, *Meredith* 2345–2355.

Scotland. Statement as to the system of police generally in Scotland; the system is different in the cities and the counties, *Gordon* 2130——Act passed in 1839 which permitted but did not enjoin the counties to levy assessments for maintaining a constabulary force; some counties have adopted the Act, *ib.* 2130–2134——The county police in Scotland are much superior men to the city police; jealousy existing between the forces, *ib.* 2151–2153——Return of the police in the counties of Scotland, with their expenses, delivered in, *List* 3950–3953——The police might be managed in Scotland upon the same principle as in England, the only difference being in the pay of the men, *Smart* 4085–4088——Statistical return of Scotch counties, with population, rental, area, police, rate of pay, rate of assessment, cost of constabulary, &c. &c., *Rep.* ii., *App.* 167.

See also *Borough Police,* 4.   *Commissioners of Police.   Commissioners of Supply. Compulsory Act.   Criminal Officer.   Lodging Houses.   Parish Constables. Pay of the Police.   Procurators Fiscal.   Rate.   Rural Police.   Sheep Stealing.   Uniformity of System.   Vagrancy.*

Self-supporting Force. Opinion that the police may to a certain degree be made a self-supporting force, *Beadel* 2793–2795.

Service of Processes. A great saving is effected by the employment of the police of Andover in the service of all processes and summonses, as also the notices on coroners, &c., *Thompson* 476–486. 498——Employment of the police of Northumberland in the service of all warrants and summonses, *Fennick* 553–561——Employment of the superintending constables of Lindsey, Lincoln, in the service of summonses, &c.; extra payments allowed for this service, *Sir R. Sheffield* 618–627——The Gloucester county police serve all summonses; the parish constables give notice to the coroner, *Blathwayt* 2121.

See also *Coroners.*   *Duties of the Police.*   *Inspectors of Weights and Measures.*

Sheep Stealing. Remarks relative to sheep-stealing in Sussex, *King* 373–375——Observations as to the crime of sheep-stealing in Essex; diminution of this offence since the establishment of the police, *Baker* 990–996; *Burnardiston* 3616–3623——The proportion of undetected crime is much greater in Somersetshire than in Gloucestershire; reference to the cases of sheep-stealing, *Blathwayt* 2074–2080——Decrease of sheep-stealing in Norfolk since the establishment of the police, *Postle* 2605–2607——Remarks relative to the cases of sheep-stealing in Somerset, *Oakley* 3277–3282——Extent of sheep-stealing in the Highlands; proposed formation of a police for the prevention of this crime, *Macleod* 4200–4203.

Return of the number of sheep and the value of property which came to the knowledge of the Essex constabulary, either by report or inquiry, as having been stolen during the year 1841, *Rep.* ii., *App.* 136——Return of the number of sheep stolen during the year 1839 in the North Hinckford and Epping divisions, *ib.*——Return of the number of cases of sheep-stealing that have occurred in the county of Hants between the years 1847 and 1852, both years inclusive, *ib.* 158.

See also *Agricultural Property.*   *Decrease of Crime.*

Sheffield, Sir Robert, Bart. (Analysis of his Evidence.)—Chairman of the court of quarter sessions of the parts of Lindsey-in-Kirton, Lincoln, 572–575——Mode in which the business of the court of quarter sessions is conducted in the parts of Lindsey, 576—— General meeting held at Lincoln to discuss the propriety of adopting the provisions of the Rural Police Act of 1839, when it was agreed by the magistracy that there was no necessity for it, 576–578——Remarks relative to the appointment of superintendent constables for the management of certain districts of Lincoln; duties and salaries of the superintendents, 578——Return from the parts of Lindsey, in which superintendent constables have been appointed, stating whether as superintendents of lock-ups solely or as superintendents of parish constables, or as acting in both capacities, with the pay and allowances, the area of the petty sessional division, with the total expense incurred for the year ending January 1853; 578——The expense of the system of superintendent constables is not above one-fourth of the expense of the rural police, 579.

Observations as to the erection of lock-ups and the appointment of paid constables in the parts of Lindsey; amount expended on these lock-ups, 579. 667–673——Account of the charges and expenses of lock-up houses and superintendent constables in the parts of
Lindsey

Sheffield, Sir Robert, Bart. (Analysis of his Evidence)—*continued.*

Lindsey for the year ending January 1853; explanation of that account, 579-593——Improved condition of the parts of Lindsey since the adoption of the system of superintendent constables; the beerhouses and vagrants' lodging-houses are better looked after and more orderly kept, 593. 644——Saving that has been effected by doing away with the old system of chief constables, and adopting the system of superintendent constables, 594-601——Satisfactory working of the system of superintendent constables in the parts of Lindsey; the feeling of the neighbourhood is in favour of the system, 602-612.

Remarks relative to the conveyance of prisoners to gaol; when the superintending constables are on duty, they are conveyed to gaol by the parochial constables, 613-617——Employment of the superintending constables in the service of summonses and warrants; extra payments allowed for this service, 618-627——Attendance of the superintendent constables at assizes and sessions; allowance made them for such attendance; this is included in the expenses of the prosecution, 620-634——Statement of the amount of the county rate for the parts of Lindsey for the 20 years, 1833 to 1853; if the Rural Police Act were put in operation it would more than double the county rate, 637-640 ——The appointment of superintendent constables has had the effect of reducing the number of vagrants in the parts of Lindsey, 641-644——Existence of parish constables in all the parishes in the parts of Lindsey; these are entirely distinct from the system of superintendent constables adopted by the county, 647-650——Remarks relative to the appointment of parochial constables; class of persons holding the office; want of a chief constable to superintend this force, 653-664.

Shields. See *Tynemouth, &c.*

Shrewsbury. Insufficiency of the borough police of Shrewsbury; they do not work so well as the county police, *Sir B. Leighton* 2494-2498——Circumstances under which the Shrewsbury authorities severed themselves from the rural police and established a police of their own, *Hon. A. Talbot* 2661-2671.

Shropshire. Statement as to the number of the police force in Shropshire; expense of the force; sufficiency thereof, *Sir B. Leighton* 2473-2479. 2481-2483. 2487-2492.

    See also *Appointments*, 2.   *Decrease of Crime.*   *Expenses of the Force,* II. 4.   *Pay of the Police.*

Smart, James. (Analysis of his Evidence.)—Superintendent of the Glasgow police, 4008-4010——Particulars as to the police force of the city of Glasgow; extent of the force and its sufficiency; rate of assessment, 4011-4021. 4035-4039——It is only in certain portions of the county that the police has been adopted; reason why the whole of the districts have not adopted the Police Act, 4022-4029——It would be a great improvement if the Rural Police Act were made compulsory on all the counties in Scotland, 4030-4032——The fear of expense, which has prevented certain districts from adopting the police, has been a very unwise economy, 4034——Whatever uniform system of police is adopted, it would be desirable, for the purpose of co-operation and diminishing the expense, to reduce the staff, by having as many districts as possible under one head, 4040-4043——There is no police in Renfrewshire; this is a great inconvenience, 4044, 4045——A uniform system of amalgamated police force for Scotland generally would be an improvement, 4046——The control of the Glasgow city police is vested in a committee of the town council, 4047-4055.

It is indispensably necessary that the chief constable should have the appointment and dismissal of the officers under him, 4056-4061. 4081-4083——Suppression of riots in the city of Glasgow without the assistance of the military, 4062-4067——Witness sees no objection to the police being under the same control as the procurator fiscal is in Scotland, 4068-4073——The superintendence of public-houses is one of the most important duties performed by the police, 4074——Inspection of lodging-houses by the Glasgow police, and various other duties performed by the force in the city, 4074-4076. 4101-4103——If the local management were entirely set aside, and a general police system were adopted, under the control of the Crown, it would not be received with satisfaction by the people, 4080——The police might be managed in Scotland upon the same principle as in England, the only difference being in the pay of the men, 4085-4088——A superannuation fund is indispensable to a good system of police, 4089-4098. 4103——Statement of the cost of the police of Glasgow; rate of pay of the men and salaries of the officers, 4087, 4088. 4099, 4100. 4105-4111.

Smith, David. (Analysis of his Evidence.)—Superintending constable in Oxfordshire, 3663, 3664——System of police in Oxfordshire, which is that of superintending constables over the parochial constables; expense of the force; inefficiency of the parish constables, 3665-3689——Considering the efficiency of the rural police, as compared with the inefficiency of the parochial constables, the former system is the cheapest of the two, 3690——Although the appointment of superintending constables may improve the parochial constabulary, they can never be rendered an efficient force, 3691-3714——Property is much
  715—I.   E 3

Smith, David. (Analysis of his Evidence)—*continued.*

more efficiently protected in Essex than in Oxfordshire, 3711——The employment of the police as assistant relieving officers acts as a great check upon vagrancy, 3715-3726—— Vagrancy is one of the great sources of crime, 3722.

Smuggling. See *Coast Guard.*   *Excise Officers.*

Somersetshire. Existence of a great deal of crime in the county of Somerset, *Hughes* 1274- 1276——The only system of police in Somerset is that of the constables appointed under the Parish Constables Act; inefficiency of the force, *Warry* 1327-1331; *Blathwayt* 2053. 2123-2125; *Oakley* 3255-3258——Desirableness of introducing a better system of police into the county, *Warry* 1332. 1362-1370——Steps taken by witness with a view of improving the constabulary by the introduction of the superintending constables, but the county would not adopt it, *ib.* 1333-1337——Explanation as to the basis on which witness founds his statement of the expense of a police force for the county of Somerset, showing that there would be a saving of 6,000 *l.* a year, between the expense of superin- tending constables and an efficient police force, *Oakley* 3794-3803——Opinion that the amount of police force required in Somerset is not anything like that in Essex, in proportion to the population, *ib.* 3804-3806——Paper delivered by Mr. W. Oakley, relative to the establishment of the system of superintending constables in Somerset, *Rep. i., App.* 158-164——Statement of the estimated comparative expense of superin- tending and parish constables, under 5 & 6 Vict., c. 109, and 13 & 14 Vict., c. 20, and a police under 2 & 3 Vict., c. 93, and 3 & 4 Vict., c. 88, for Somerset, *ib.* 163, 164.

　　See also *Sheep Stealing.   Vagrancy,* 3.

Southampton. Extent of the police force in Southampton; insufficiency of the force, *Harris* 75, 76.

Special Constables. When any disturbance is anticipated in the boroughs the system adopted is to swear in special constables, *M'Hardy* 766, 767——Evidence showing the perfect uselessness of special constables in cases of disturbances, *M'Hardy* 766, 767. 800; *Hamilton* 1095-1099; *White* 1838, 1839; *Dunne* 2037; *Blathwayt* 2053-2059; *Martin* 3738-3755——Occasionally special constables have been sworn in in Manchester, but they have never been called upon to act, *Willis* 2929-2933.

　　See also *Customs Officers.*

Staff Officers. The separation of the police force leads to unnecessary expense from requiring a greater number of staff officers, *M'Hardy* 736, 737; *Oakley* 3262-3269—— With respect to the metropolitan force, it would be improved if there were more men of education as superior officers, *Chadwick* 3662——Whatever uniform system of police is adopted, it would be desirable, for the purpose of co-operation and diminishing the expense, to reduce the staff by having as many districts as possible under one head, *Smart* 4040-4043.

Stafford. Statement as to the system of police in the county of Stafford; insufficiency of the number employed; expense of the force, *Hon. A. Talbot* 2612-2631. 2634, 2635. 2639-2658——Increased force necessary to render the police efficient, *ib.* 2659.

　　See also *Borough Police,* 2.   *Lock-up Houses.*   *Pay of the Police.*

Stanley, William Hans Sloane. (Analysis of his Evidence.)—Magistrate for Hampshire, 270——Inefficiency of the police in the borough of Romsey, under the control of the watch committee of the corporation; if the police were placed under the control of the chief constable of the county, the position of the borough would be very different, 271- 279. 285-287——Inconvenience arising from the want of co-operation between the county and borough police, 278, 279——Improved condition of the borough of Andover since they have joined the county police, 280——Decrease of crime since the establish- ment of the police in Hampshire, 281-283——Inefficiency of the parish constables for the proper discharge of their duties, 281-284——Popularity of the police with the rate- payers of Hampshire, 288——Great saving which has resulted from the establishment of the police in Hampshire, 288-296——Opinion in favour of a national police; the com- pulsory enforcement of a system of police upon all counties would be beneficial, 297-304.

　　Readiness of the police to assist in every possible way, both in the detection and pre- vention of crime; how far they interfere in the apprehension of poachers and the preser- vation of game, 305-311——The appointment of the police by the chief constable has worked very satisfactorily; the appointments should not be transferred to Government unless the expense of the force is defrayed out of the consolidated fund, 316-320——The present system of police in Hampshire is very satisfactory; anxiety of the population to get employment in the police; rate of pay, 321-330. 334——The expenditure of the police is regularly brought before the court of quarter sessions, and the accounts are audited by the finance committee, 331-333.

Reports, 1852-53—*continued.*

Station Houses. Manner in which the police force are lodged; divisional stations erected in Hampshire for the accommodation of the police, *Harris* 94-107——Remarks as to the station houses and strong rooms built in every division of the county of Essex; cost thereof; statement proving that they produce a greater interest than the capital invested and paid for by the county, *M‘Hardy* 738-748——Large number of police stations in Durham; they serve as barracks, *White* 1868-1872——Appointment of a committee in 1852 to take into consideration a report of the chief constable, Captain Black, with respect to building station houses in Norfolk and other matters in reference to a different system of police; this committee have determined to report in favour of the recommendations of Captain Black, *Postle* 2536-2540——Number of station houses in Norfolk; proposed erection of new buildings, *ib.* 2558-2563——There should be police stations wherever there is a police force; saving that would be thus effected in the conveyance and lodging of prisoners, *Oakley* 3306, 3307——Return of monies borrowed for the erection of police stations in Essex, *Rep.* ii., *App.* 149——Return showing the revenue and savings produced by the police stations in Essex; also the annual interest and instalments paid on money borrowed to erect them, in the years 1845, 1846, 1847, 1848 and 1849, *ib.*——See also *Lock-up Houses.*

Stockton-upon-Tees. List of boroughs in Durham which have a separate police; incorporation of Stockton-upon-Tees with the county force with great satisfaction to the borough, *White* 1832-1837.

Stowe Green Fair. Remarks relative to Stowe Green Fair; steps taken to organise the parochial constables so as to repress crime at that assemblage, *Healy* 3412-3423. 3428-3430. 3497.

Summonses. See *Service of Processes.*

Superannuations. Amount of stoppage per head for the superannuation fund of the Hants police; age at which the men are entitled to superannuation, *Harris* 73, 74——Remarks relative to the superannuation fund of the police in Lancashire; deduction made from the pay of the force for the fund, *Woodford* 1659-1661——The Wilts police have a superannuation fund; amount of that fund invested, *Meredith* 2443-2446——Remarks as to the superannuation fund of the Norfolk police; opinion that the magistrates should have the power of granting a pension to the chief constable, *Postle* 2608——Remarks as to the superannuation fund of the Stafford police, *Hon. A. Talbot* 2674——It might be advantageous to have a superannuation fund connected with the police of Scotland, as it would induce men to join the force, *List* 4006, 4007——A superannuation fund is indispensable to a good system of police, *Smart* 4089-4098. 4103——Want of a superannuation fund for the Dumfries police force, *Jones* 4269-4271.

SUPERINTENDING CONSTABLES:

     1. *Generally.*
     2. *Approval of the system of Superintending Constables.*
     3. *Remarks as to the inefficiency of the system.*

1. *Generally:*

Remarks of the Committee that the superintending constables appointed under the 5 & 6 Vict., c. 109, have proved useful as police officers to the extent of their individual exertions within their respective divisions, *Rep.* ii., *p.* iii.——Remarks relative to the appointment of superintendent constables for the management of certain districts of Lincoln; duties and salaries of the superintendents, *Sir R. Sheffield* 578——The expense of the system of superintendent constables is not above one-fourth of the expense of the rural police, *ib.* 579——Account of the charges and expenses of lock-up houses and superintendent constables in the parts of Lindsey for the year ending January 1853; explanation of that account, *ib.* 579-593——With regard to the superintending constable system in the Dewsbury division in Yorkshire, there is a population of 80,000, and only a superintending constable, with parish constables, in substitution of the police establishment, *Dunne* 2044——How far the superintending constable has any means of punishing the parish constables, *Carrington* 3228, 3229——Each of the superintending constables acts independently of the others; they have printed rules for their guidance, *ib.* 3233-3236.

2. *Approval of the system of Superintending Constables:*

Improved condition of the parts of Lindsey since the adoption of the system of superintendent constables; the beerhouses and vagrants' lodging-houses are better looked after and more orderly kept, *Sir R. Sheffield* 593. 602-612. 644——Saving that has been effected by doing away with the old system of chief constables, and adopting the system of superintendent constables, *ib.* 594-601——Opinion in favour of the system of superintending

SUPERINTENDING CONSTABLES—continued.

2. *Approval of the system of Superintending Constables*—continued.

intending constables, *Carrington* 3188; *Clifford* 3817——The superintending constables would be much more efficient if they had more means of giving remuneration to parochial constables when they are out watching at night, *Carrington* 3196–3200——When the arrangement of superintending constables has got thoroughly into operation in Buckinghamshire, it will be sufficient for the preservation of the peace and the protection of property, *ib.* 3223–3225——Witness in conjunction with Mr. Deedes brought a Bill into Parliament this session for the amendment of the Act for Superintending Constables, *Clifford* 3816——List of boroughs in Herefordshire having a police separate from the county; the superintending constables work well with the town police, *ib.* 3820–3822. 3869.

3. *Remarks as to the inefficiency of the system :*

Opinion that the appointment of a superintending constable in each petty sessional division provides no remedy for the inefficiency of parochial constables, *Rep.* ii., p. iii.; *Swabey* 842–850; *Hamilton* 1028–1032. 1064–1078; *Marris* 1139–1161; *Hughes* 1254–1266. 1286; *Redin* 1452; *Postle* 2590–2593; *Oakley* 3283–3286——The experiment of local constables under superintendents was fairly tried in Essex, and failed, *M‘Hardy* 773–776; *Burnardiston* 3587—— Inefficiency of the system of superintending constables, *Hamilton* 1008–1015; *Dunne* 1951–1953. 1967–1986.

See also Assizes.   Bath.   Buckinghamshire.   Chief Constables.   Conveyance of Prisoners.   Cumberland.   Expenses of the Force, I.   Herefordshire. Lindsey.   Lock-up Houses.   Night Patrol.   Oxfordshire.   Parish Constables.   Public Houses.   Pursuit of Offenders.   Relieving Officers. Somersetshire.   Vagrancy, 1, 2.   Yorkshire.

Surrey. See Rural Police.

Surveyors of Roads. Opinion that the police might be employed as surveyors of roads, *M‘Hardy* 817; *Fawcett* 3010, 3011.

Sussex. Strength of the police force of East Sussex; insufficiency of the force, indisposition shown to increase the number on account of the expense, *Mackay* 1884–1903. 1919.——See also *Private Watchmen.*   Rural Police.   Sheep Stealing.

Swabey, Maurice. (Analysis of his Evidence.)—Magistrate for Buckinghamshire, Surrey and Middlesex, residing at Langley Marsh, Bucks, 820–823——The system of police adopted in Buckinghamshire is that of superintending constables, 824–832——The parochial constables are entirely under the direction of the superintending constables; these constables are not of the slightest use, 833–837——Advantage arising from the superintending constables being appointed assistant relieving officers in Bucks; check given to vagrancy, 838, 839——The adoption of the rural police was proposed in Bucks, but was rejected on account of the expense, 840, 841——It is desirable to have a more general system of police in Bucks; the system of superintending constables does not render the parochial constables efficient, 842–850——Vagrancy is a great source of crime, 844, 845——Want of a chief constable amongst the superintending constables, 851——Remarks relative to the lock-ups in Bucks; it is proposed to have one in each division, 852, 853——The ratepayers of Bucks are satisfied with the present protection of property, and would be opposed to any alteration in the system of police, 853–859——The counties where there is a police drive the vagrants into the surrounding districts which have no police, 860–863——Witness is desirous that the Rural Police Act should be introduced in its entire force in the county of Bucks, 864–867.

T.

Talbot, Hon. and Rev. Arthur. (Analysis of his Evidence.)—Magistrate for the county of Stafford; has been chairman of the police committee, 2609–2611——Statement as to the system of police in the county of Stafford; insufficiency of the number employed; expense of the force, 2612–2631. 2639–2658 ——Boroughs in Stafford that have a police of their own; the borough police does not work so well as the county police, and is more expensive, 2616–2630——Advantage of the borough police being incorporated with the county force, 2618. 2630–2633. 2636. 2671——System of police in the borough of Stafford; this force gives no assistance to the county force, 2634, 2635——It is very desirable that a uniform system of police should be established throughout the country, 2637——Supposing there were a general system of police all over the country, provided it is done by a general rate, there should be an urban or suburban and a rural rate; this is the system adopted in Stafford, 2637–2643.

The

Talbot, Hon. and Rev. Arthur. (Analysis of his Evidence)—*continued.*

The system of lock-ups in Stafford is nearly complete ; expense attending their erection, 2652-2659——Increased force necessary to render the county police efficient, 2659——Circumstances under which the Shrewsbury authorities severed themselves from the rural police and established a police of their own, 2661-2671——It has not been found necessary to call in the aid of the military since the establishment of the police in the county, 2673——Remarks as to the superannuation fund of the Stafford police, 2674——General inefficiency of the system of parochial constables, 2677-2688 The money which is now spent by the Government and the county of Stafford, if properly economised, might very nearly give an efficient police all over the kingdom, 2689.

The police force of Stafford has been very useful to the inland revenue in the detection of illicit stills, 2689-2693——It would be better that the police should do nothing but the duty of policemen, 2694-2698——It is very desirable that the police should wear uniform, 2699, 2700——Amount of the pay of the superintendents and chief constable of the Stafford county police, 2700-2708——The expenditure would be much less if there were a general force under the control of Government ; one chief constable would be sufficient to superintend three counties instead of one, 2700——Decrease in the cost of conveyance of prisoners to gaol in Stafford ; this is partly owing to the extension of railways and partly to the police, 2708, 2709.

Taunton. The Taunton constabulary are under no control and recognise no authority, *Oakley* 3808.

Thompson, Henry. (Analysis of his Evidence.)—Mayor of Andover, 421-424——Consolidation of the police of Andover with the county in 1846 ; 425-427——Bad state of the town of Andover as to crime previously to the establishment of the police, 428-434 ——The expense of the police to the borough is greater now than it was before the consolidation with the county, but the benefits are more than equal to the additional expense, 435-448——Number of cases convicted before the magistrates in petty sessions at Andover, and of committals for trial in each year, 1843 to 1852 inclusive ; causes of the great decrease of crime, 449-460——Return of the cost of crime at Andover from 1841 to 1852, showing the expenses of sessions, prosecutions, maintenance of prisoners, &c.; since the establishment of the police the expenses have rapidly decreased, 460-463.

Decrease of depredations on agricultural property since the establishment of the police, 466, 467. 473——Amount of the rate for the support of the police in the borough of Andover, 468-472. 499, 500——Great attention paid by the police at Andover to their duties ; one of the points in the effectiveness of the police is that they are constantly changed, 474, 475——A great saving is effected by the employment of the police in the service of all processes and summonses, as also the notices on coroners, &c., 476-486. 498——Improved regulation of the public-houses and beershops in Andover since the establishment of the police, 487, 488——Inspection of the lodging-houses in Andover by the police, 489-497.

Townley, Reverend William Gale. (Analysis of his Evidence.)—Chairman of the quarter sessions in the Isle of Ely, 2711, 2712——Establishment of the rural police in the Isle of Ely ; increase of the force in 1853 ; expense of maintaining the force, 2713-2723—— The borough of Wisbeach has a separate police, 2717, 2718——The Isle of Ely is divided into three districts; no advantage arises from that division; circumstances under which the division took place, 2715-2717. 2724. 2729——Inconvenience to the Isle of Ely as to vagrancy from the adjoining county of Lincoln not having a police, 2731-2742——A more uniform system of police is very desirable, 2741—— Decrease of crime in the Isle of Ely since the establishment of the police, 2742-2748 ——Establishment of the rural police force in Cambridgeshire ; opinion that the police of the Isle of Ely and Cambridgeshire might be united, and placed under one chief constable, 2749-2754. 2759, 2760——Advantage would result from the borough police being amalgamated with the county force, 2755-2758

Tramps. See *Lodging Houses.*   *Vagrancy.*

Turnpike Keepers. It would be attended with considerable advantage if every turnpike-gate keeper was a police constable, *Woodford* 1703-1705.

Tynemouth, &c. With reference to Tynemouth, Shields and Newcastle, the police force is very inefficient, *Hughes* 1314-1316.

Reports, 1852–53—*continued.*

U.

Uniformity of System. Opinion of the Committee, that it is most desirable that legislative measures should be introduced without delay by Government, rendering the adoption of an efficient police force, on a uniform principle, imperative throughout Great Britain, *Rep.* ii., *p.* iv.—— Great advantage would arise from the establishment of a uniform system of police in the different counties of England generally, *Sir W. Heathcote* 255; *Parker* 908-910; *Hughes* 1306-1308; *White* 1843, 1863, 1864; *Blathwayt* 2086-2088. 2118-2120; *Sir B. Leighton* 2502, 2503; *Postle* 2576; *Hon. A. Talbot* 2637; *Townley* 2741; *Oakley* 3263, 3264. 3292. 3358; *Chadwick* 3642-3644; *Jones* 4244——Impossibility of the different systems of police in force in adjoining counties working well, *Hamilton* 1094——The expense of a uniform system of police would not be more than what is now actually paid to parish and local constables, *Oakley* 3343, 3358; *Chadwick* 3642-3644——Conclusions set forth in the report of the Constabulary Commissioners, showing that the adoption of a uniform system of police throughout the country would be a great advantage, both in an economical and in a moral point of view, *Chadwick* 3654-3656.

A uniform system of amalgamated police force would be a great improvement in Scotland; suggested plan for the establishment of such a force, *Gordon* 2193, 2194. 2210-2214. 2224-2227; *List* 3960-3981; *Smart* 4046; *Murray* 4122-4126; *McLeod* 4188-4199; *Jones* 4244——A general system would be much more economical as well as more efficient than the present system; the advantages of a general system would more than counterbalance any extra charge upon the counties, *Gordon* 2215-2220——If there were a uniform police system, well organised, with central management, it might be more efficiently and cheaply managed than by each county maintaining its own police force, as is at present the case, *List* 3964-3974——Copy of report laid before the Commissioners of supply and justices of peace of county of Edinburgh, on the subject of an uniform police throughout Scotland, *Rep.* ii., *App.* 165, 166.

See also *Compulsory Act.   Escape of Criminals.   Expenses of the Force.   Jurisdiction.   National Force.   Parish Constables.   Pursuit of Offenders. Rural Police.   Staff Officers.   Vagrancy,* 2.

Uniforms. Importance of the police being clothed in uniform; crime would not be more efficiently detected by men in private clothes, *Meredith* 2466-2469; *Hon. A. Talbot* 2699, 2700.

Union of Forces. See *Borough Police.   County Constabulary.   National Force.*

Upper Ward of Lanark. See *Lanarkshire.*

V.

VAGRANCY:

1. *Generally.*
2. *Opinion that Vagrancy might be suppressed by an efficient system of Police.*
3. *Remarks as to the existence of Vagrancy in certain places.*
4. *Papers laid before the Committee.*

1. *Generally:*

Vagrancy is a great source of crime, *Swabey* 844, 845; *Dover* 1775; *Fawcett* 3004-3007; *Smith* 3722——Generally speaking, the counties where there is a police drive the vagrants into the surrounding districts which have no police, *Swabey* 860-863——Impossibility of suppressing vagrancy under a system of superintending constables, *Dunne* 2034-2027——Remarks as to the minute of the Poor Law Board issued by Mr. Buller, respecting the rapid increase of vagrancy, and suggesting certain modes of proceeding by the rural police for its suppression, *Sir J. Walsham* 3560-3571.

2. *Opinion that Vagrancy might be suppressed by an efficient system of Police:*

Statement that vagrancy has greatly decreased in those districts where the Rural Police Act has been adopted, *Rep.* ii., *p.* iii.; *Harris* 183-186. 205-208; *King* 367-372. 415-417; *M'Hardy* 687-712; *Dunne* 2032, 2033; *Meredith* 2373-2378. 2422; *Sir B. Leighton* 2507. 2510-2518; *Beadel* 2787-2791; *Sir J. Walsham* 3559 *et seq.*——The appointment of superintendent constables has had the effect of reducing the number of vagrants, *Sir R. Sheffield* 641-644; *Carrington* 3213-3216——Opinion that with the aid of the constabulary force this kingdom might be freed from vagrants; recommendation that all destitute persons should be passed to their parishes, *Wayte* 1928——Vagrancy would be entirely destroyed by the establishment of a uniform system of police throughout the country, *Sir J. Walsham* 3575-3579; *Chadwick* 3653; *List* 4005——The present law of Scotland applicable to vagrancy is defective; were the police empowered to deal with vagrants crime would diminish at least one-half, *Jones* 4276-4286.

3. *Remarks*

Reports, 1852–1853—*continued.*

VAGRANCY—continued.

3. *Remarks as to the existence of Vagrancy in certain places:*

Arrangement under which the constables take charge of the vagrants who apply to the union workhouses in Hants, *Harris* 194-208——Great extent to which Romsey is infested with vagrants, *Beddome* 523——Necessity for the establishment of an efficient police force for the suppression of vagrancy and tramping in the county of Somerset, *Warry* 1345-1361——The eastern parts of Cumberland are infested with vagrants; these are principally itinerant thieves, *Redin* 1416. 1423, 1424——Large number of vagrants continually in Carlisle, passing to and from England and Scotland, when they steal where they can; inefficiency of the parochial constables for remedying this evil, *ib.* 1437-1441 ——Witness has for many years past been engaged in the suppression of vagrancy at Calne; assistance rendered by the police, *Wayte* 1922*-1927——Inconvenience to the Isle of Ely as to vagrancy, from the adjoining county of Lincoln not having a police, *Townley* 2731-2742.

Great extent to which vagrancy exists in Cumberland, *Fawcett* 3004-3007——The establishment of a police force all over the county would have the effect of materially checking vagrancy, *ib.* 4024-3029——Remarks relative to vagrancy in the parts of Kesteven, *Healy* 3490-3492——Comparative statement, showing the total number of vagrants admitted into the vagrant wards of certain unions of Kent and Essex during the four years ended 25 March 1851; explanation upon the subject of that statement, *Sir J. Walsham* 3567-3574——Causes to which witness ascribes the difference in the per centage of decrease of vagrancy between Essex and Kent, *ib.* 3573——Queries addressed by witness to the guardians of certain unions in the county of Essex with respect to vagrants, and answers returned thereto, *ib.* 3574——Similar queries and answers for certain unions in the county of Kent, *ib.*——Existence of vagrancy in Dumfries, though it has somewhat diminished, *Jones* 4275-4278.

4. *Papers laid before the Committee:*

Return of in-door vagrants in the county of Essex in the years 1848 and 1849, *Rep.* ii., *App.* 151——Return of out-door vagrants, *ib.*——Commitments of vagrants to the several prisons in Essex during the half-years ended Michaelmas 1848 and Michaelmas 1849, *ib.* 152——Return of the number of vagrants received in the unions of the county of Hants during the years 1848 and 1852, the year 1848 being the last year previous to the constabulary undertaking the duties of assistant relieving officers for vagrants, *ib.* 158.

     See also *Chippenden Union.*   *Lodging Houses.*   *National Force.*   *Relieving Officers.*

Value of Property. The appointment of the police is a great advantage, as the value of property is greatly increased by an efficient force, *Sir W. Heathcote* 246, 247; *Parker* 889-891; *Baker* 964, 965. 1063; *Warry* 1364; *Doeer* 1781; *Mackey* 1921; *Blathwayt* 2118-2120; *Gordon* 2194; *Beadel* 2792, 2793; *List* 3938, 3939.

     See also *Occupation of Land.*   *Protection of Property.*   *Rate,* 2.

Voluntary System. There were districts in Norfolk in which a police force was voluntarily paid for previously to the establishment of the rural police, *Postle* 2603, 2604——There are some constables in Renfrewshire supported by voluntary subscriptions, *Murray* 4163, 4164.——See also *Lanarkshire.*

Voting at Elections. The police at Norwich vote generally at all Parliamentary and municipal elections; witness's objection was overruled by the watch committee, *Dunne* 2028-2030——Evils resulting from the police of Bath being allowed to retain their right of voting at municipal and Parliamentary elections, *Blathwayt* 2127.

W.

Wakefield House of Correction. See *Detection of Crime.*

Walsham, Sir John, Bart. (Analysis of his Evidence.)—Poor-law inspector in Kent; counties of which witness's district consists, 3559-3568——Decrease of vagrancy in Essex from the efficiency of the police and the appointment of police officers as assistant relieving officers, 3559 *et seq.*——Remarks as to the minute of the Poor-law Board issued by Mr. Buller, respecting the rapid increase of vagrancy, and suggesting certain modes of proceeding by the rural police for its suppression, 3560-3571——Comparative statement showing the total number of vagrants admitted into the vagrant wards of certain unions of Kent and Essex during the four years ended 25 March 1851; explanation upon the subject of that statement, 3567-3574——Causes to which witness ascribes the difference in the per centage of decrease of vagrancy between Essex and Kent, 3573——Queries addressed by witness to the guardians of certain unions in the county of Essex with respect to vagrants, and answers returned thereto, 3574——Similar queries and answers

Reports, 1852-53—*continued.*

Walsham, Sir John, Bart. (Analysis of his Evidence)—*continued.*

for certain unions in the county of Kent, 3574——Vagrancy would be entirely destroyed by the establishment of a uniform system of police throughout the country, 3575-3579 ——Valuable and prompt assistance afforded by the rural police in cases of disturbances in workhouses in Essex ; without such assistance the disturbances would have been very disastrous, 3579.

Warry, George. (Analysis of his Evidence.)—Magistrate for Somerset, 1325, 1326 ——The only system of police in Somerset is that of the constables appointed under the Parish Constables' Act; inefficiency of the force, 1327-1331——Advisability of introducing a better system of police into the county, 1332——Steps taken by witness with a view of improving the constabulary by the introduction of the superintending constables, but the county would not adopt it, 1333-1337——Great difficulty in the detection and capture of offenders under the system of parochial constables, 1335. 1338-1341. 1371, 1372—— Statement as to the expenses of the parish constables for the Bridgewater division of Somerset, 1342-1344——Necessity for the establishment of an efficient police force for the suppression of vagrancy and tramping in the county, 1345-1361——Advisability of incurring the expense of police in Somerset ; the advantages would be quite commensurate, 1362-1370——The value of land in the county would be increased by the establishment of a well-regulated police, 1364.

Watch Committee. Opinion that the watch committee is a very improper body to control the police ; the power of control should be vested in the head constable, *Redin* 1526-1528 ; *Woodford* 1610-1612. 1631, 1632; *Wybergh* 1806-1813 ; *Oakley* 3366-3369——The police of the city of Bath is entirely under the control of the watch committee ; very little inconvenience arises from this arrangement, *Kitson* 2282. 2284, 2285. 2304-2314—— Number of members of the watch committee ; the committee is indiscriminately selected from the town council ; there is no publican or brewer on the committee, and but one wine merchant, *ib.* 2315-2330.

     See also *Appointments,* 2.   *Bath.*   *Carlisle.*   *Liverpool.*   *Norwich.*

Wayte, John. (Analysis of his Evidence.)—Resides at Calne, in Wiltshire, 1922——Has for many years past been engaged in the suppression of vagrancy at Calne ; assistance rendered by the police, 1922*-1927——The vigilance of the police has lessened the number of the lodging-houses that were frequented by thieves and beggars in Calne, 1925——Reduction in the number of vagrants relieved in Chippenden Union from the exertions of the police, 1926, 1927——With the aid of the constabulary force the kingdom might be freed from vagrants ; recommendation that all destitute persons should be passed to their parishes, 1928.

West Riding of York. See *Yorkshire.*

White, Major George F. (Analysis of his Evidence.)—Chief constable of Durham, 1820 ——Strength of the Durham police force ; insufficiency of the force, 1821-1827 —— The establishment of a night patrol in the county is very desirable, 1827——Popularity of the police force, 1828, 1829——Inconvenience experienced in the pursuit of criminals, from the want of a uniform system in the adjoining counties, 1830, 1831——List of boroughs in Durham which have a separate police ; incorporation of Stockton-on-Tees with the county force with great satisfaction to the borough, 1832-1837——Special constables are of very little use in cases of disturbance, 1838, 1839——A uniform system of police would be as beneficial to the boroughs as to the counties, 1843. 1863, 1864——It would be useful if the electric telegraph were established in the different divisions of the county, 1846-1851——Difficulties arising from the want of co-operation between the borough and county police, 1852-1855——The habits of miners interferes with the efficiency of the police ; the difficulty of detection is increased in the mining districts, 1856-1862—— Decrease of vagrancy since the police have been employed as assistants to the relieving officers, 1865, 1866——Amount of the police rate in Durham, 1867——Large number of police stations in the county ; they serve as barracks, 1868-1872——The police are more effective than the military in the suppression of riots ; the police of Durham are armed with cutlasses, but they have never had occasion to use them, 1873-1882.

Willis, Captain Edward. (Analysis of his Evidence.)—Head of the police of the borough of Manchester, 2888, 2889——Particulars as to the police force in Manchester ; proposed increase of the number ; expense of the force, 2890-2898——In the event of the amalgamation of the borough and county forces, Manchester should not be included in the county, but taken as a separate district, 2899-2914——Great advantage would result from the borough and county police being placed under one head ; want of co-operation under the present system, 2901-2918——It is much more desirable to employ the police in the suppression of disturbances than the military, 2919-2925——Occasionally special constables have been sworn in in Manchester, but they have never been called upon to act, 2929-2933.

Reports, 1852–53—*continued.*

Wiltshire. Statement as to the present police force of the county, and the cost thereof; sufficiency of the force, *Meredith* 2339–2342——Arrangement of the police of Wilts in the different parishes of the county; great advantages of this system, *ib.* 2385–2398.

    See also *Decrease of Crime.*   *Lock-up Houses.*   *Pay of the Police.*   *Rate,* 2.

Wisbeach. The borough of Wisbeach has a separate police, *Townley* 2717, 2718.

Witnesses Expenses. Return of the payments made to prosecutors and witnesses in the county of Essex, in the years 1839, 1840 and 1841, *Rep.* ii., *App.* 141.

    See also *Prosecutions.*

Woodford, Captain John. (Analysis of his Evidence.)—Chief Constable of Lancashire, residing at Preston, 1529, 1530——Number of the police force for the county of Lancashire, and its classification, 1531, 1532——Division of the county into districts, each of which pays its police expenses separately, 1532–1537——The police force are completely under witness's direction, 1538–1540 —— The boroughs in Lancashire have a police of their own separate from the county; inadequacy of the borough police in the event of a disturbance; applications made to witness for assistance by several boroughs at the time of the elections, 1541–1589. 1605——In the event of the amalgamation of the boroughs with the county police of Lancashire, Liverpool and Manchester should not be included, but each of those boroughs should be left as districts by themselves, 1590–1604.

Disinclination of the borough police to co-operate with the county police in the detection of offenders, 1606——Growing feeling in some of the boroughs in favour of amalgamation with the county constabulary, 1607–1609——No more prejudicial system to the working of a good establishment of police can exist than for the management of the men to be vested in a fluctuating body, such as watch committees or town councils; the power should be vested in the head constable, 1610–1612. 1631, 1632 —— The arrangement of Lancashire into petty sessional divisions has answered very well, 1613–1618——The amalgamation of the boroughs and the county would not necessitate an additional expense, 1619, 1620.——The boroughs as they are now managed are the nurseries of crime, 1620—— Different systems of police existing in the division of Ashton-under-Lyne; under such different systems it is impossible they can act with effect or cordiality, 1622–1629. 1648–1650.

The objection entertained on the part of the boroughs to join in the county constabulary is the fear of losing their patronage in the police appointments, 1630–1632——There would be no difficulty in amalgamating the railway police with the rural police, 1633–1635——Defective state of the police in the boroughs of Lancashire not under the county constabulary; the beershops and public-houses are not under proper supervision, 1636–1640——Popularity of the police in Lancashire, 1644–1647—— Decrease of crime in Lancashire since the establishment of the police, 1646, 1647—— Rates of pay of the different grades in the Lancashire police force; duties of the several officers, 1651–1660 ——Remarks relative to the superannuation fund of the police in Lancashire, 1659. 1661——Considerable number of lock-ups in Lancashire; these are a species of barracks, and comprise good lodging-rooms for the constables and superintendents, 1662–1668 ——The police should be drilled like soldiers; desirability of the police in Lancashire being armed, 1669–1674——Nature of the supplemental duties performed by the police; saving effected by this arrangement, 1674–1689.

Advantage of the duties of inspectors of weights and measures being performed by the police, 1674–1680——Circumstances under which the police of Lancashire have occasionally gone into Yorkshire to suppress disorders; complaints made upon the subject, and discontinuance of the practice, 1690–1700——The system of police in force in Yorkshire is that of parish constables under superintending constables, 1697–1701——How far it would be possible to recruit for the army through the means of the police; the police of Lancashire were actively engaged in inducing volunteers to join the militia, 1702. 1706–1716——It would be attended with considerable advantage if every turnpike-gate keeper was a police constable, 1703–1705——Objections to the police being allowed to receive rewards indiscriminately, 1717–1719——The expense of the constabulary in Lancashire is rather under than over 2½ *d.* in the pound, 1720.

Workhouse Riots. Valuable and prompt assistance afforded by the rural police in cases of disturbances in workhouses in Essex; without such assistance, the disturbances would have been very disastrous, *Sir J. Walsham* 3579.

Writtle, Essex. The improvement of the condition of the parish of Writtle is not entirely owing to the system of police, though that may be considered as the main instrument, *Baker* 965–977. 997–1000.

Wybergh, John, Jun. (Analysis of his Evidence.)—Clerk to the magistrates at Liverpool, 1792——Evidence as to the police force of Liverpool; it is under the management of the watch committee, the magistrates being possessed of the power of dismissal of the men, 715—I.

Wybergh, John, Jun. (Analysis of his Evidence)—*continued.*

1793–1805——Great inconvenience resulting from the police of the borough being under two jurisdictions, 1806- 1813——Suggestion that Liverpool should remain a separate police district, 1814, 1815——Witness is not cognisant of the existence of a want of co-operation between the borough police of Liverpool and the Lancashire county police, 1816–1819.

Y.

Yorkshire. Circumstances under which the police of Lancashire have occasionally gone into Yorkshire to suppress disorders; complaints made upon the subject, and discontinuance of the practice, *Woodford* 1690–1700——The system of police in force in Yorkshire is that of parish constables under superintending constables, *Woodford* 1697–1701 ; *Denison* 2936–2940——The subject of the rural police has been more than once discussed in the West Riding of Yorkshire, but its establishment has never been determined on in consequence of the expense, *Denison* 2940–2969.

See also *Expenses of the Force*, II., 5.

POLICE IN AMERICA

An Arno Press/New York Times Collection

The American Institute of Law and Criminology.
Journal of the American Institute of Law and Criminology:
Selected Articles. Chicago, 1910–1929.

The Boston Police Strike: Two Reports. Boston, 1919–1920.

Boston Police Debates: Selected Arguments. Boston,
1863–1869.

Chamber of Commerce of the State of New York.
**Papers and Proceedings of Committee on the Police Problem,
City of New York.** New York, 1905.

Chicago Police Investigations: Three Reports. Illinois,
1898–1912.

Control of the Baltimore Police: Collected Reports.
Baltimore, 1860–1866.

Crime and Law Enforcement in the District of Columbia:
Report and Hearings. Washington, D. C., 1952.

Crime in the District of Columbia: Reports and Hearings.
Washington, D. C., 1935.

Flinn, John J. and John E. Wilkie.
History of the Chicago Police. Chicago, 1887.

Hamilton, Mary E.
The Policewoman. New York, 1924.

Harrison, Leonard Vance.
Police Administration in Boston. Cambridge, Mass., 1934.

International Association of Chiefs of Police.
Police Unions. Washington, D. C., 1944.

The Joint Special Committee.
**Reports of the Special Committee Appointed to Investigate
the Official Conduct of the Members of the Board of Police
Commissioners.** Boston, 1882.

Justice in Jackson, Mississippi: U.S. Civil Rights
Commission Hearings. Washington, D. C., 1965.

McAdoo, William.
Guarding a Great City. New York, 1906.

Mayo, Katherine.
Justice to All. New York, 1917.

Missouri Joint Committee of the General Assembly.
Report of the Joint Committee of the General Assembly Appointed to Investigate the Police Department of the City of St. Louis. St. Louis, Missouri, 1868.

National Commission on Law Observance and Enforcement.
Report on the Police. Washington, D. C., 1931.

National Prison Association.
Proceedings of the Annual Congress of the National Prison Association of the United States: Selected Articles. 1874–1902.

New York City Common Council.
Report of the Special Committee of the New York City Board of Aldermen on the New York City Police Department. New York, 1844.

National Police Convention.
Official Proceedings of the National Prison Convention. St. Louis, 1871.

Pennsylvania Federation of Labor.
The American Cossack. Washington, D. C., 1915.

Police and the Blacks: U.S. Civil Rights Commission Hearings. 1960–1966.

Police in New York City: An Investigation. New York, 1912–1931.

The President's Commission on Law Enforcement and Administration of Justice.
Task Force Report: The Police. Washington, D. C., 1967.

Sellin, Thorsten, editor.
The Police and the Crime Problem. Philadelphia, 1929.

Smith, Bruce, editor.
New Goals in Police Management. Philadelphia, 1954.

Sprogle, Howard O.
The Philadelphia Police, Past and Present. Philadelphia, 1887.

U.S. Committee on Education and Labor.
The Chicago Memorial Day Incident: Hearings and Report. Washington, D. C., 1937.

U.S. Committee on Education and Labor.
Documents Relating to Intelligence Bureau or Red Squad of Los Angeles Police Department. Washington, D. C., 1940.

U.S. Committee on Education and Labor.
Private Police Systems. Washington, D. C., 1939.

Urban Police: Selected Surveys. 1926–1946.

Women's Suffrage and the Police: Three Senate Documents. Washington, D. C., 1913.

Woods, Arthur.
Crime Prevention. Princeton, New Jersey, 1918.

Woods, Arthur.
Policeman and Public. New Haven, Conn., 1919.

AMERICAN POLICE SUPPLEMENT

International Association of Chiefs of Police.
Proceedings of the Annual Conventions of the International Association of Chiefs of Police. 1893–1930. 5 vols.

New York State Senate.
Report and Proceedings of the Senate Committee Appointed to Investigate the Police Department of the City of New York. (Lexow Committee Report). New York, 1895. 6 vols.

THE POLICE IN GREAT BRITAIN

Committee on Police Conditions of Service.
Report of the Committee on Police Conditions of Service. London, 1949.

Committee on the Police Service.
Minutes of Evidence and Report: England, Wales, Scotland. London, 1919–1920.

Royal Commission on Police Powers and Procedures.
Report of the Royal Commission on Police Powers and Procedure. London, 1929.

Select Committee on Police.
Report of Select Committee on Police with the Minutes of Evidence. London, 1853.

Royal Commission Upon the Duties of the Metropolitan Police.
Minutes of Evidence Taken Before the Royal Commission Upon the Duties of the Metropolitan Police Together With Appendices and Index. London, 1908.

Committee on Police.
Report from the Select Committee on Police of the Metropolis. London, 1828.